A History of Mysticism

A History of Mysticism

RICHARD H. JONES

SUNY
PRESS

Published by State University of New York Press, Albany

For information, contact State University of New York Press, Albany, NY
www.sunypress.edu

Library of Congress Cataloging-in-Publication Data

Name: Jones, Richard H., 1951– author.
Title: A history of mysticism / Richard H. Jones.
Description: Albany : State University of New York Press, [2024] | Includes
    bibliographical references and index.
Identifiers: LCCN 2023029856 | ISBN 9781438497150 (hardcover : alk. paper) |
    ISBN 9781438497167 (ebook) | ISBN 9781438497143 (pbk. : alk. paper)
Subjects: LCSH: Mysticism—History.
Classification: LCC BL625 .J639 2024 | DDC 204/.2209—dc23/eng/20231026
LC record available at https://lccn.loc.gov/2023029856

10 9 8 7 6 5 4 3 2 1

Contents

Abbreviations

AN	*Anguttara Nikaya*
APP	*Ashtasahasrika Prajnaparamita* (*The Perfection of Wisdom in 8,000 Lines*)
ASC	Altered states of consciousness
BG	*Bhagavad Gita*
BGR	Ramanuja's commentary on the *Bhagavad Gita*
BS	*Brahma Sutras* of Badaranyana
BSR	Ramanuja's commentary on the *Brahma Sutras*
BSS	Shankara's commentary on the *Brahma Sutras*
BU	*Brihadaranyaka Upanishad*
BUB	Shankara's commentary on the *Brihadaranyaka Upanishad*
CU	*Chandogya Upanishad*
D	*Dao De Jing*
DN	*Digha Nikaya*
Enn.	Plotinus's *Enneads*
GK	*Gaudapada-karikas*
GKS	Shankara's commentary on the *Gaudapada-karikas*
IU	*Isha Upanishad*
KaU	*Katha Upanishad*

KeU	*Kena Upanishad*
KeUB	Shankara's commentary on the *Kena Upanishad*
KsU	*Kaushitaki Upanishad*
MaiU	*Maitri Upanishad*
ManU	*Mandukya Upanishad*
MK	Nagarjuna's *Mula-madhyamaka-karikas*
MN	*Majjhima Nikaya*
MunU	*Mundaka Upanishad*
Q	Quran
RV	*Rig Veda*
SN	*Samyutta Nikaya*
SU	*Shvetashvatara Upanishad*
TU	*Taittiriya Upanishad*
TUB	Shankara's commentary on the *Taittiriya Upanishad*
YS	*Yoga Sutra*
Z	*Zhuangzi*

Preface

Writing a history of all the major mystical traditions of the world is certainly a daunting undertaking. But the narrow definitions of mysticism and mystical experience employed in this book make the task more manageable. Individual chapters each present an overview of one tradition through the teachings of its most prominent mystics. However, certain methodological concerns about doing any history of mysticism must be addressed first.

The Problem of Understanding Mystics

A history of mysticism is not directly or primarily a study of mystical experiences but a study of the related phenomena of mystical traditions. Nevertheless, one basic concern is whether students of mysticism need to have had the types of experiences and altered states of consciousness that will be considered here as central to mysticism in order to understand mystical phenomena and in particular to understand what mystics say and teach.[1] We cannot present anyone's inner mental states for public inspection by others, nor can anyone enter into another person's consciousness for any type of experience—the only experiential states to which we can have direct access are our own. However, can those who have not had any mystical experiences understand mystical teachings at all? Indeed, wouldn't non-mystics who never experience nondualism and have only their dualizing mind necessarily distort mystical phenomena by reducing them to something they are not? Overall, how can we study non-dualistic phenomena from a dualistic point of view?

However, non-mystics arguably can substantially understand mystics' claims. Understanding the meaning of what someone says does not require getting inside their mind. Mystics themselves only speak and write while in a mystical or non-mystical state of consciousness that permits the use of language. In such a state, mystics must look at their experience and at what they supposedly experienced as an object, which is how non-mystics also look at them.[2] Words are public terms that others can understand, and their meaning is independent of the mystics' inner life. Thus, we may be able to get at the intended meaning of mystics' claims even if we cannot see the full significance that these claims have for mystics themselves or why they were chosen. The role that non-ordinary experiences play in developing doctrines increases the difficulty of understanding those claims, but it does not rule out the possibility of understanding, and thus of studying, mystical doctrines by non-mystics. Most mystical writings are, after all, intended for the unenlightened, so mystics must believe something valuable, meaningful, and understandable is being conveyed by their teachings to their readers.[3] Thus, historians can safely assume that mystical writings can reflect mystics' intents even if they are produced in a state of consciousness that may not reflect the mystics' experiences.

It is also not necessary to practice within a given mystic's tradition to understand their claims; outsiders can view mystical claims in terms of the meaning that a mystic gives a doctrine, especially if we have a sufficient amount of their writings and also other texts from that culture and era to give them context. If such understanding is not possible, we are trapped within our current worldview and cannot understand anyone else's beliefs, nor can we ever change our worldview or create new ones. No history of one's own culture or any study of anything in other cultures would be possible. Moreover, conversion is not needed to understand a tradition, and some initial understanding does seem possible to outsiders. Indeed, a person would need some understanding of the tradition's claims before conversion in order to accept what they would be converting to, even if their understanding may change afterward. This is also so with esoteric groups: some teachings may be given only to the initiates (as in Mark 4:11–12), but this does not mean that the uninitiated cannot understand the teachings taught to the initiates.

This is so even though mystics notoriously have a problem with language and resort to using metaphors and analogies. The unenlightened can follow many of the analogies without much difficulty, even if our understanding remains dualistic: for example, Advaitins treating the world as a dream of a transcendent dreamer (Brahman) or comparing our misperception of the world to misperceiving a coiled rope as a snake. We can also understand that a transcendent reality is not part of the natural world even though we do not know what that reality is like; we set it off as merely another object in another realm. So too can we understand mystics' general denial of the applicability of language designed for negotiating the phenomenal world to the reality that they allegedly experience. Paradoxes present barriers for understanding, but we can accept that we need mystical experiences to understand why paradoxes are employed in mysticism and how they actually apply. All attempts to understand or explain mystical experiences arise from a dualistic state of consciousness, but this does not mean that we cannot understand that altered states of consciousness are involved or force us to reduce those experiences to our commonplace dualistic ones.

Still, must students at least be mystically minded to understand mystical claims? Or is the threshold for understanding mystical claims low? Can students be mystically "unmusical," as Max Weber claimed to be concerning religion, and yet still understand mystical texts? Being empathetic in such circumstances may help in initially understanding mystics' claims, but even those without such empathy can understand something of what mystics state. Thus, we can conclude that being a non-mystic is not an insurmountable barrier to studying mysticism. However, even if a mystical experience is not required to understand mystical doctrines, a student who has had no mystical experiences is in the position of a blind art historian studying Renaissance paintings.

The Danger in Having a Mystical Experience

Ironically, having had a mystical experience may be a danger for studying mysticism. Having a mystical experience may give someone the general sense that there is more to reality than they previously believed, but it may also lead to believing that they have now had the same experience that all mystics have had and now know what all mystics know. Thus, we do not have to study the teachings of mystics to know what they really mean. However, having a mystical experience does not by itself lead to understanding. In the case of understanding the Medieval Christian Meister Eckhart's doctrines of the Godhead and the "birth of the son," even if we could say "Now I know what Eckhart was talking about," we still could not say "Now I understand Eckhart's Neoplatonist metaphysics" without actually studying Eckhart's works. In addition, how can we know that our experience is, in fact, the same type of mystical experience that underlies

Eckhart's teachings? In sum, we cannot conclude that simply because we had a profound experience that Eckhart, the Buddha, and so forth must all have had the same experience, but having our own mystical experience may lead to the error of assuming that all mystical experiences are of one type and that all mystics have the same understanding of what is involved in the experience that we have.

There is also the danger of confirmation bias: we may take our experiences as confirming the doctrines of our own religious tradition or whatever beliefs we hold. This may lead us to impose our understanding of our experience on all mystical doctrines; the sense of profundity and certainty given in a mystical experience may lead the experiencer to believe that all mystics must hold the same beliefs that we hold since we now know what all mystics know. But this can lead to distorting mystics' teachings, including those within one's own religious tradition. Consider the nature-mystical experience that bestselling author Mark Waldman had in which the trees, fence, and weeds outside his office window all seemed "perfect" and in which he felt a "pure bliss." The first thing he remembered thinking was "Oh! This is what those Buddhists and Hindus were writing about when they described enlightenment" (Newberg and Waldman 2016, 190). Actually, that is *not* what the Buddhists and Hindus traditionally claim. The Buddhist enlightenment experience is about seeing the impermanence and conditionality of all phenomena, not their perfection, and Hindu ideas of enlightenment involve both something interior to one's being and something transcending the natural world, not something observed in the natural realm. In addition, Waldman's beliefs suddenly and radically changed at the moment of his experience: he *knew* that there was no heaven or hell or a god and that when he died that would be his end (190). This, of course, is not what Buddhists and Hindus conclude in their mysticisms. After several months, Waldman's feeling subsided and feelings of doubt arose. One day, a small voice whispered to him: "Mark, you don't know a damned thing about religion" (190–91). He then started to study the works of mystics.

Postmodern Concerns

Postmodernists also raise some basic issues for any project like this one: Can we even speak of a history of mysticism? Is the very term *mysticism* legitimate? Although the term *mystical* has roots going back more than two thousand years, the nouns *mysticism* and *mystic* are modern Western inventions. These terms do not have exact counterparts in other cultures and languages. This has led postmodernists to question whether the term *mysticism* can be used to classify phenomena from any other culture or era. To them, it is inherently anachronistic and Eurocentric to impose a modern concept on any non-modern or non-Western culture. If so, there can be no history of mysticism beyond modern Western culture.

However, even though the term *mysticism* is a modern Western invention, it does not follow that phenomena that existed earlier in the West or in other cultures cannot be labeled mystical in the modern sense, nor must the use be inherently linked to modern Christian theological concerns. (If we restrict the term *mysticism* solely to the study of the tradition in which it arose—Christianity—we would still have to invent a new term to cover similar phenomena in other traditions, and postmodernists would again object.) All claims are made from particular perspectives that are set up by culturally dependent conceptualizations and beliefs—there is no universal "view from nowhere"—but this does not mean that culturally dependent points of view cannot capture something significant about reality.

This is true for any term: inventing a concept does not invent the phenomena in the world that the concept covers. The natural historian Richard Owen invented the term *dinosaur* in the 1830s to classify certain fossils that he was studying, but to make the startling claim that "dinosaurs did not exist before 1830" would at best only be a confusing way of stating the obvious fact that classifying fossils this way was not possible before the concept was devised—if dinosaurs existed, they existed many millions of years earlier, and their existence did not depend in any way on our concepts, whenever and wherever they were devised. Terms establish what phenomena are included in or excluded from a study and reorder the phenomena by creating a new perspective from which to study them, but in no way do the terms create the phenomena. To modify a postmodern image, a map does not create the territory that is mapped.

The same applies to terms for human phenomena. Even if there are no equivalents for *mysticism, mystics,* and *mystical experiences* or a comprehensive term for all types of *meditation* in Arabic, Hebrew, Sanskrit, Chinese, or any other language, scholars may find phenomena in other cultures to which the Western terms apply, and Western concepts may illuminate something significant about those phenomena. The absence of similar umbrella terms in other cultures is irrelevant,[4] as is the fact that mystical experience became a topic of interest in Indian, Chinese, and other cultures only in the modern period after their encounters with the West. But the Western term *mysticism* becomes more abstract once it is expanded to encompass traditions other than Christianity, including non-theistic ones. (*Theistic* will be used in this book rather than *monotheistic*.) Nor does employing a Western umbrella term for cross-cultural purposes mean that we do not need to study phenomena from other cultures in detail in their own terms—the mystics and mystical phenomena of a culture still need to be understood in their cultural context.

However, using umbrella terms such as *mystical experience* and *enlightenment* as translations for different culturally embedded terms may obscure ideas specific to a culture. It would be an anachronism to claim that premodern cultures had those umbrella concepts. Changes in meaning over time presents a similar problem. For example, the meaning of *God* in the West has changed over the centuries, and we may well read our contemporary understanding into all Western and Eastern theists' use of the term.[5] Likewise, claiming that some concepts from different cultures fall into the general category of *transcendent realities* does not mean that different cultural terms all mean the same thing, that all terms refer to one reality, or that all terms can be translated as "God." Using umbrella terms is not an endorsement of perennialism. However, for these reasons some key terms are left untranslated (e.g., *Nous, Brahman, Atman*, and *Dao*), and each chapter's exposition explains the relevant culturally specific meanings when umbrella terms are utilized as translations. The total configurations of terms in a specific culture's discourse show their meaning in a translation. The abstract terms should not be taken as Eurocentric or necessarily loaded with modern meanings but as placeholders for particular local concepts.

Likewise, classifying something from, say, India as mystical in the modern sense does not make it Western or modern any more than classifying Sanskrit as a language makes it into an English phenomenon or leads to mashing all languages into one. Few scholars would advocate expunging the word *language* from English or deny that the cross-cultural study of languages may reveal something of the nature of all languages. Few would deny that linguists can legitimately study the history of language in a culture or study languages cross-culturally without distorting the languages, but many scholars treat the term *mysticism* differently.

Historians create a narrative through what historical events they choose to include and how they choose to characterize what is included. A history is mediated by theory in that way. Non-postmodernists do not believe that utilizing modern umbrella categories for cross-cultural purposes changes the character of the phenomena of any particular culture, but postmodern historicism rules out the possibility for engaging in meaningful study with cultures and eras other than one's own and the possibility of finding common elements therein. Nevertheless, the fact that Westerners can produce accounts of other cultures and translations of texts that are accepted by informed members of those cultures severely damages the postmodernist position. Even if the new terminology surprises the subjects under study (and they may reject all abstract classifications), they may accept that it does not distort their tradition once it is understood.

Thus, the general category mysticism can be accepted as a filter for selecting certain aspects of human phenomena for attention. The term *mysticism* does not need to suggest that mystical phenomena are autonomous and independent of other phenomena, nor does it need to suggest that mystical phenomena have no non-mystical dimensions. Mysticism itself has many dimensions: internal and external, individual and social, neurological and cultural. Thus, mystical phenomena must be approached through many different academic disciplines (Jones 2021a), and all facets of a mystical phenomenon should be studied for a comprehensive understanding. Scholars should become increasingly aware of studies in disciplines other than their own. Mystical experiences themselves (as opposed to the doctrines and phenomena of the mysticisms surrounding them) can be studied indirectly through neuroscience, and Frits Staal (1975) is not alone in advocating for the direct study of mystical experiences through students of mysticism themselves having the experiences. Historians must focus on the cultural context of a mystic to understand their writings, but they still may see elements that are common to mystics from other cultures. Only postmodern historicism would rule out the possibility of meaningfully studying other cultures and eras and the possibility of finding common elements.

Classifications and Essences

A related postmodern attack is that use of the term *mysticism* suggests some unchanging and identical transhistorical essence present in all mystical phenomena from different cultures and eras. No one is confused by the term *language* into thinking different languages are all really the same, but people do tend to think all mystics are alike. Likewise, the fact that mystical experience is usually referred to in the singular—*the* mystical experience, *the* mystical consciousness—leads people to falsely believe that all mystical experiences are the same. With the singular term *mysticism*, people are easily misled into thinking that all mystical doctrines and ways of life are really the same, despite the appearance of diversity, and that one mysticism transcends all religions and cultures. That is, rather than there being a pluralism of genuinely different mystical experiences, doctrines, and ways of life, mysticism is singular and all mystics really teach the same thing. Perennial philosophers maintain that universal, "esoteric" doctrines are merely expressed differently in different cultural idioms (Jones 2021b). But, as discussed in the next section, to maintain that there is only one set of transcultural mystical doctrines underlying all mystical traditions is the perennialists' theoretical overlay and is not derived from actually studying the history of mystical teachings. History does not reveal one common, generic mysticism but differing and even conflicting mystical teachings in different traditions and subtraditions. History does not reveal an essentialism in which all mystical experiences are the same in type.

However, we can use abstract concepts to classify certain phenomena without assuming they designate some unchanging core to those phenomena; umbrella terms do not imply a changeless essence of any type, only that an aspect of the phenomena is the focus of attention. Indeed, by postmodernists' reasoning, no classificatory terms of any kind could ever be used. There would be, to continue the same example, no such thing as language. No one speaks *language* in the abstract, but only concrete *languages*—English, Japanese, etc.—so by this reasoning, there can be no history of language or anything to say about the nature of all phenomena classified as linguistic. In fact, *English* is as much an umbrella term as *language* and must be denied since essences do not evolve, while languages do. Even if there are some words and rules of grammar common to all English-speaking eras and countries, the English of today is not the same as Shakespeare's English, as anyone who has tried to read his plays in the original Elizabethan knows. Even the English of the Victorian period differs from today's English, and this is not to mention Middle and Old English. Thus, there is no unchanging "essence" to English to be discerned, and no timeless entity called *English* actually exists. But for non-postmodernists, using *language* as an umbrella category does not entail that there is an unchanging essence to all languages or that languages do not evolve or that all languages are really one. A term can indicate general defining characteristics for phenomena to qualify being covered by that term, and yet the phenomena can still be constantly changing.

The same applies to the classificatory terms of mysticism: there is no unchanging mysticism in any religious tradition, only individual mystics and evolving subtraditions. Labeling someone today as a *Christian mystic* does not mean that they believe Christian doctrines or practices the same way as early Christian desert hermits. Even if the essence of Christianity is to accept that there is a loving, creator god and that Jesus of Nazareth held a unique relation to him, this essence is an abstraction: particular conceptions of God and the role of Jesus have changed over time, and the total web of beliefs of any given Christian mystic incorporates that essence differently. Christian mysticism is not stagnant. The same can be said of Buddhist or Hindu mysticism, even though *Buddhism* and *Hinduism* are foreign labels (labels that Buddhists and Hindus nevertheless have generally adopted).[6] This is the case for mysticism in all cultures, hence the need for a history of each tradition.

In sum, there are different expressions of key themes but no timeless essence or abstract core to any tradition, let alone all mysticisms. Additionally, there may not be hard and fast boundaries between mysticism and other cultural phenomena, like art and music. Abstract terms may only work in terms of Wittgensteinian "family resemblances," but this does not mean that they are not useful for classifying some phenomena or that the classification may not lead to seeing something interesting about the nature of such phenomena.

Doing Cross-Cultural History

The abstract category *mysticism* may lead to insights about diverse phenomena. If so, the cross-cultural study of mysticisms may lead to learning something of the nature of all mysticisms beyond what earns the phenomena the label *mystical*. So too, studying mysticism in other cultures may reveal something about mysticism in one's own culture and era, showing what is distinctive about it. Thus, a cross-cultural approach can also help members of a particular religion to understand their own religion's mysticism better. The nineteenth-century German Indologist Max Müller famously said that a person who knows only one religion knows none. One does not understand what makes a religion a religion without studying other religions. The same applies to mysticism: a Christian who knows no other mysticisms does not know what makes Christian mysticism mysticism, what is unique about it, and what is not. Furthermore, only with a cross-cultural perspective can one come up with insightful theories about the nature of mysticism. To understand language, linguists must study languages from different language groups—Arabic, Swahili, Chinese, and others—not just English and the Romance languages. To gain a sense of mysticism, scholars cannot confine their study to the Abrahamic traditions.

Thus, there is value in taking a comprehensive view that is lost to specialists who confine themselves to one mystical tradition. Indeed, approaching a general topic from the limited point of view of only one tradition may lead to distorting even that tradition through a provincial understanding of mysticism. And if specialists utilize terms such as *mysticism* that apply cross-culturally, they need to study of the work of scholars of other traditions to gain a cross-cultural perspective. But the methodological concern here is that any general history of mysticism necessarily involves studying multiple foreign cultures and multiple historical eras. The scope is so vast that no one person could possibly gain a thorough knowledge of the complete history of mysticism, or indeed even of only one tradition. The languages alone are too numerous to master. One must rely on the work of others, both for translations and histories, for all traditions, including those in one's own area of specialization. Thus, all historians covering more than a very limited scope must also be second-hand historians.

Moreover, no attempt will be made here to present an exhaustive account of all the world's mystics, even ignoring the fact that most mystics are no doubt unknown to the historical record. Bernard McGinn does not claim that his monumental history of the Western branch of Christian mysticism (which includes nine volumes to date, each longer than this book) includes all known Christian mystics; it is comprehensive in covering all eras and major mystics but not exhaustive. In this book, the attempt is to give an overview of each tradition's major mystics and their beliefs, but this broad sweep limits the depth of detail that can be presented for each tradition.

In addition, presenting the world traditions individually is not to deny that there have been interactions between the different traditions and cultures. Some interactions have been noted. In fact, the cross-fertilization is sometimes quite great. Indeed, perhaps a better way to write the history of Indian mysticism would have been to treat the various Indian schools as different responses in continuing debates on certain topics rather than as separate Hindu, Buddhist, Jaina, Muslim, and Sikh traditions (Potter 1963).

Historians can present mystical doctrines as the traditions present them and accept them for that purpose without endorsing, rejecting, or criticizing them. No commitment to the existence (or nonexistence) of any transcendent realities is needed—a historian merely has to accept that mystics are logically committed to the existence of whatever realities their beliefs and practices entail. Thus, the word *alleged* is not added before every claim of knowledge, insight, or existence; what the mystics write is accepted on their own terms. This is also the case for visions and paranormal powers. Each tradition's history is also presented with few references to causes external to the culture's own religious and philosophical beliefs as explanations of the beliefs and values. In sum, the framework for understanding those beliefs is the culture and tradition of each given mystic. Imposing a theoretical explanatory scheme from the outside can lead to distorting an alien tradition, as I have argued occurred with Carl Jung's understanding of Asian traditions (Jones 1993a).

However, we can approach any subject only from our own background, and a basic problem today for anyone who has been influenced by science is that we see the world through the lens of modern science. This led Joseph Needham to distort the nature of Daoism (Jones 1993b) and today has led many New Age advocates to distort mysticism (see Jones 2010, 2019b). Modern science may have made it impossible for us today to see the world the way that premoderns saw it: a world where everything bears the imprint of the sacred or is not truly real. We simply are not capable of experiencing the sacred world of the medieval Christians, let alone experiencing the world as early Hindus or Daoists experienced it. We can imagine, say, an animistic world without difficulty, but we do not truly believe it and so cannot truly see the world that way. We cannot, for example, encounter any reference to the moon without implicitly thinking in terms of its nature in light of modern astronomy and physics. We can easily *understand* the claim that the moon is the manifestation of a goddess, but we cannot truly *see* the moon that way. Sympathetic imagination cannot get us into the inner life of any premodern person from any society. Participating in the meditations or rituals of other cultures cannot change that. We can follow the reasoning of Plotinus or Shankara and even produce new arguments along their lines, but genuinely to think within their cultural frameworks is another matter. So, too, the modern Western emphasis on individualism affects our ability to enter into another culture's world of meaning. Even if one has had the same unconstructed mystical experience as some others have had, one's understanding of the experience afterward will reflect one's own worldview.

Thus, the possibility that we may inadvertently make other people into mirror images of ourselves cannot be ignored. Postmodernists object that no history can be presented objectively; a historian's selection of data is always controlled by social forces, and we need to study the historian as much as the narrative they present. But, as discussed, this does not mean that we cannot genuinely understand the meanings of others' claims or that we always unconsciously make others' claims into our own claims. We can grasp the basic outlook of premoderns by studying their writings and practices without major distortion, although accomplishing this may require extensive study of those cultures. Nevertheless, we can understand what others are saying without experiencing the world as they do. That is, historians cannot place us within the mind of a traditional mystic and thereby convey what it is actually like to *be* a medieval Tibetan mystic or an early Daoist mystic, but with some effort we can understand their claims from their point of view even if we cannot walk in their shoes and see the world as they did. Even if historians cannot convey the full mysticisms of those eras, they can make it possible for us to understand mystical teachings. That is enough of an insider's perspective for creating a history. Historians can then present their accounts and see how others inside and outside that tradition judge their efforts.[7]

This is also the case with translating mystical works; translators can never be certain that they are conveying what authors truly meant.[8] When we have a very limited number of texts from a specific mystic or cultural era, this problem is at its greatest. This issue is intensified by the possibility of authors being influenced by altered state of consciousness experiences, but this problem is mitigated if we can look at a large amount of a given mystic's work with ample works from the context of their tradition and culture. Simply reading brief snippets in translation out of context from secondary sources such as William James or Walter Stace cannot be the sum of one's research—one's general theory of mysticism would then control one's understanding of mysticism rather than letting mystics' works build one's understanding. Western theistic beliefs of a personal being external to the natural universe distort our view of the Neoplatonist One, Brahman, *Dao*, and Indian theisms. A prime example today involves the Buddhist Nagarjuna on emptiness (*shunyata*): Western theologians and philosophers who have not studied the Prajnaparamita and Madhyamaka works routinely go directly against what Nagarjuna actually taught (i.e., emptiness as only denoting the lack of anything that would make a worldly phenomenon self-existent) and reify emptiness into an analog of God or Brahman as a transcendent source of the phenomenal world, labeling the entity Emptiness with a capital *E* or the Void.

The Contextual Approach versus Perennial Philosophy

As previously discussed, the approach in this book is to convey the believers' own perspective. Any accounts are in terms that informed participants themselves are willing to accept, even if outsider umbrella terminology is employed. The cross-cultural history presented here goes one step into the realm of theory in one regard: a typology of categories of mystical experiences is utilized in descriptions. A typology is a theoretical framework used to catalog phenomena in more abstract terms than the concepts of a particular mystical tradition and, thus, goes one step beyond mere description.[9]

This approach is contextual; the meanings of mystical claims come from understanding the claims within the setting of a given mystic's culture and era, not from some imposed philosophical or theological perspective. Thus, mystics are not detached from their biographies. Even if some mystical experiences are not affected by any cultural elements, mystical claims cannot be detached from their religious and cultural settings. Such a contextual approach is not a matter of valuing the exoteric shells of different traditions over an esoteric doctrinal core, as perennialists assert, but a matter of examining what mystics actually believe and practice rather than employing the matrix of an alien framework of beliefs, such as perennialists do, or giving a Christian or other theological reading to all mystical works. Mystics live by employing the externals of their religion, however much their private mystical experiences may have affected their understanding. Classical mystics did not think of themselves as mystics but as Christians, or Muslims, or Vaishnavas, and so forth. They followed their religion; they did not practice mysticism. Thus, it is necessary to understand the exoteric religious framework to understand what mystics actually taught and how they actually lived.

Under the contextual approach, the study of all historical mystical traditions must occur before any generalizations about mysticism can be made. One cannot claim, "A true mystic must . . ." by filling in the blank with the beliefs and values of only one's own religious tradition, even if one's own mystical experience provokes a deep conviction in one's beliefs. Likewise, if there is in fact more than one type of mystical experience, one cannot assume that all mystics have had the same experiences one has had. (Since mystics may intentionally hide their own experiences behind the accepted lexicon of a tradition's basic texts, the problem of determining what types of experiences a given mystic had—or even if he or she had one—is exacerbated.) Values are a special concern here. The Christian context of a loving life is so ingrained in our sense of what a religious person should be that many today naturally deem a transformation of character and the fruit of moral action to be necessary criteria for claiming to have had a "genuine," "authentic," or "true" mystical experience. However, we cannot decree that unless a person fulfills our own expectations they did not have a genuine mystical experience or is not a real mystic. In particular, the relation of mysticism to morality cannot be answered merely by decreeing that someone must be transformed into a moral saint or must exude love to be a true mystic. Rather, all major mystical traditions must first be examined on the issue of values and actions before any conclusions can be drawn (Jones 2004). In addition, it must be considered that, based on the phenomenological descriptions of their experiences, some people today have had mystical experiences without any subsequent changes to their personal traits at all.

In the alternative to the contextualist approach, perennialists treat mysticism in the singular; *mysticism* is not an umbrella term covering various mystical ways of life but one belief system independent of any religion that is expressed opaquely in different religious traditions. All mystics have the same experience or state of consciousness, described variously as "union with God" or "being one with Brahman," and all mystical claims are really the same but cloaked in the disposable covering of different cultures. There is no need to understand the cultural settings of mystical claims since the true understanding is the alleged esoteric core supplied by perennialists. No history of mysticism is really needed—it would only be a history of the dispensable cultural expressions of the same esoteric truth. All that is needed is to show how various mystics in different cultures and eras manifested perennial philosophy. Swami Abhyananda (2012) has written such a history. He often had to disregard what mystics actually wrote, instead telling us what the mystics really meant. His overlay on mysticism penetrated down to creating very misleading translations of key terms in order to make all mystical ideas seem the same. By imposing a metaphysics of beliefs that he thinks all true mystics hold, he badly distorted the doctrines of the different religions of the world.

Instead, the position I take here is that the point of traditional mysticism is to align oneself with the way reality truly is, and this depends on how each mystic sees the world in terms of a tradition's exoteric beliefs, not in terms of an alleged transcultural doctrine. To modify one of George Santayana's remarks, no one practices mysticism in the abstract any more than one speaks language in the abstract. Classical mystics typically believe that they experience something discussed in their own tradition (even if the doctrines are reinterpreted), not something negating the tradition's teachings, and that their tradition has the best understanding of what is real. Thus, there is not one universal mysticism but various genuinely different mysticisms in different religions and cultures, each with its own history.

The Scope of This Book

If private mystical experiences were all there is to mysticism, there would be no history of mysticism but only scientific and philosophical examinations of mystical experiences and people undergoing mystical experiences. However, mysticism involves more than just mystical experiences and their cultivation—traditional mysticism involves total *ways of life* by which one can arrange one's life in accord with what is deemed a fundamental reality. Making certain personal experiences the unique element of mysticism does not privatize mysticism in the sense of making it an exclusively internal phenomenon; mysticism still contains observable and social phenomena. Further, each tradition's ways of life are developed collectively. Mysticism can be seen as a personal matter of cultivating certain states of mind without concluding that traditional mystics are all isolated from their communities or unconcerned with public matters. Most mystics known to history were, of course, not living totally outside of society—even the wandering ascetics of Hinduism played a role in their society (by giving the laity a means to gain merit for a better rebirth). Likewise, the central role of the master/ student relationship in all major mystical traditions cannot be ignored.

The central subject of the history presented here is one element of mysticism: the doctrines of the world's diverse mystical ways of life, that is, the expressions of the basic beliefs and values that inform the tradition's accounts of how to align one's life through mystical experiences with "reality as it truly is" (however that is defined in a given tradition).[10] Most important is a tradition's view of the nature of the world and any transcendent realities, the nature of human beings, its diagnosis of the human condition and its remedy, and its values for individuals and society as a whole. The history of mystical doctrines is the history of how mystics interpret their mystical experiences and how they incorporate those interpretations into the framework of the way of life expressed in their doctrines. Focusing on certain experiences and states of consciousness as central to mysticism in addition to a religion's meditative, contemplative, or otherwise mystical traditions keeps a history of mysticism from simply being a general history of religion. Many aspects of religion will be omitted, but this does not reduce any religion to a form of mysticism. Studying the full religious framework is necessary to understand the mystics. So too, presenting only a slice of each mystical tradition need not distort any tradition since examining more of a mystical tradition is necessary to present that slice properly. One still needs to understand that tradition as fully as possible by studying more than the chosen aspect.

In particular, the intent here is to present each mystical tradition's basic beliefs concerning what is fundamentally real and valuable. This shows how particular mystics saw the world and why they asked the questions they asked and accepted the answers they accepted. Often, basic beliefs are not explicitly defended or even articulated, but such doctrines form the philosophical presuppositions of a tradition's practices: they express how the world and a person must be for a way of life to make sense. What is needed for this is not merely *thin* listings of bare beliefs or ethical precepts. Muslim, Jewish, Christian, and Hindu theistic mystics may believe in a creator god, but they talk about that god in different ways and hold differing beliefs. Rather, to understand what mystical claims and values meant in the mystic's own framework requires a degree of *thick* depictions of the context and background of claims—the intellectual horizon within which a mystic assesses their options and makes choices. However, the breadth of the overview in each chapter limits the depth of context that can be given.

Thus, this book could be entitled *A History of the Basic Beliefs in Mystical Traditions*. Focusing on beliefs and their articulation in doctrines may seem odd in the case of mysticism since mystics are constantly telling us that doctrines are inadequate and that concepts cannot apply to what is experienced. Additionally, not all traditions are as fastidious as Christianity in doctrinal matters. Focusing on beliefs and doctrines does not reduce a mystical way of life to those beliefs, nor does studying those beliefs disembody them from experiences and full ways of life. This focus does not distort the mysticisms of different traditions as they are practiced or mysticism's role in an encompassing religion, but if the purpose of mysticism is to align one's life with reality, then understanding a tradition's doctrines of fundamental realities and values is central to any understanding of mysticism.

However, the focus here presents only one slice of mystical traditions. Other aspects of a culture will only be touched upon as they pertain to understanding mystical ontological, epistemological, and ethical doctrines. Scholars interested in other aspects of mysticism (e.g., rituals, art, meditative techniques, gender, social dimensions) would write different histories. For example, Carl Ernst's (2011) history of Sufism has relatively little on doctrine but gives an overview of some other aspects, especially poetry and music. Or, rather than presenting a history as I do here, one could present mystical traditions more abstractly around recurring themes without any historical development as James Miller (2003) presents Daoism. Some may question my preferences—too much on Meister Eckhart and not enough on Augustine, too much on Plotinus and early Daoism, too much on drugs, reducing Jainism and Sikhism virtually to footnotes. Each scholar will have their own mix on such matters depending on their interests, but a philosophical spine grounds the full body of each way of life, and understanding each tradition's beliefs is vital to understanding that mystical way of life.

After a chapter on the nature of mystical experiences and mysticism and a chapter on the prehistory of mysticism, each chapter attempts to give an overview of the history of mysticism within a particular religion or culture.[11] The key themes of each tradition are summarized at the end of each chapter. Again, this is not to suggest that any tradition is static or ahistorical but only that there are recurring topics and positions that are treated differently in the tradition in different eras and cultures. The book concludes with a chapter looking at mysticism today and its possible future and an appendix highlighting some significant contemporary misunderstandings of mysticism.

Chapter 1

Mysticism and Mystical Experiences

The first issue in writing any history of mysticism is getting a handle on what phenomena will be covered. The adjective *mystical* (from *mystikos*, meaning hidden or secret) arose in connection to Greek Mystery cults to describe certain types of knowledge (*gnosis*) and rituals that were kept from the uninitiated. Christians adopted it to refer to theological mysteries, such as how Christ's body is present in the Eucharist or how the church is the "mystical body of Christ." It also came to refer to hidden meanings within the Bible, in addition to the text's literal meanings, in which theologians saw how scriptures point to Christ. Those were the principal uses of the term *mystical* in the history of Christianity. The nouns *mystic* and *mysticism* were invented in the seventeenth and eighteenth centuries when spirituality was becoming separated from general theology in Western Christendom. (The terms were first used to disparage overly "enthusiastic" worshipers in France and England.) Only later did the term *mysticism* come to refer primarily to certain types of private experiences involving "infused contemplation"—as opposed to ordinary grace—in which God, although transcendent, dwells within a person.

But this does not mean that there were no mystics, in the modern experiential sense, earlier in Christianity. The first use of *mystical* as a way of knowing God directly is from Origen of Alexandria in the third century (Bouyer 1980, 50). Such experiences informed Christian thought before the fifth century when a Neoplatonist, Pseudo-Dionysius the Areopagite, first wrote of mystical theology. By the twelfth century, when Bernard of Clairvaux first referred to the "book of experience," the "mystical" allegorical meanings of biblical passages that Christian contemplatives expounded were

1

ultimately based on direct experiences of God: in Bonaventure's words, "the mind's journey into God." That is, *mystical theology* then meant the "direct awareness of God," not the academic discipline of theology in the current sense. It is direct in the sense that one's awareness is not mediated by the presence of a second reality (as with a vision) or through the mental conceptual apparatus that normally structures our experiences. It is an awareness that overcomes the sense of separation.

Today, the term *mystical experience* has been separated from the singular context of Christianity, but it has also become notoriously vague. Among the general public, astrology, magic, spiritualism, and paranormal occurrences have all been lumped together under the banner of mysticism. Academics often use the term interchangeably with *religious experience*, but there is no common scholarly definition. In such circumstances, all one can do is stipulate a definition and defend it. In this book the term *mystical experiences* denotes short-term episodes that involve a direct awareness of fundamental realities (that is, realities deemed "more real" than everyday realities); loosen the conceptual divisions that normally structure the mind; and, most importantly, free the person experiencing the event of a sense of a discrete phenomenal ego or self.[1] The term *mystical states* denotes similar but more enduring states of such consciousness. Such experiences and states are other than the ordinary, ego-centered waking state of sensing and thinking and, thus, occur in altered states of consciousness (ASCs).[2] *Mysticism* refers to the phenomena—teachings, texts, practices, social institutions, and so forth—surrounding one's interior quest to turn off their sense of self and to stop the conceptualizing mind from controlling their experience in order to bring oneself into alignment with what is ultimately real (as defined by a mystic's tradition). Thus, mysticism is more encompassing than simply having mystical experiences. For someone on a quest for such experiences, it involves not merely a web of cultural phenomena but also a comprehensive, total way of life having practices, codes of conduct, rituals, and a specific goal with doctrines about the nature of what is deemed real as their philosophical spine.[3] Other non-ordinary phenomena, such as paranormal powers and visions, may or may not occur in such ways of life. But *mysticism* as used here is not merely a matter of holding certain metaphysical beliefs or propositions but is related to ASCs and their experiences.

Mystical experiences are private, and the goal of mysticism is individualistic: a personal inner transformation of how one experiences and lives. However, much of mysticism involves observable social and cultural phenomena. Mystical experiences may occur outside of mystical ways of life, but mysticism relates to transforming a person by means of mystical practices, experiences, and states of consciousness. The quest of traditional mysticism is not to attain mystical experiences for their own sake; mystical experiences are not themselves the goal but a necessary *means* to seeing reality correctly in order to inaugurate a new state of being, a life aligned with reality. Thus, mystical experiences play an essential role in mystical ways of life but are not all that matters in the study of mysticism.

Thus, *mysticism* as used in this book is not simply the name for the inner religious life of all intensely pious or scrupulously observant followers of any strand of religiosity, nor is it for anyone who performs supererogatory practices or who dedicates themselves utterly to God. Mysticism is also not the essence or core of all religions; mystics have been a shaping force in all major religions, but there are other ways of being religious and other types of religious experiences, and other factors may be deemed more central. Likewise, not all ASC experiences are mystical. Nevertheless, what distinguishes mysticism is its experiences: it is the central role of certain types of ASCs and their experiences that separates mysticism from other forms of religiosity and from metaphysical speculation. Neuroscientists today are coming to accept that mystical experiences are based in distinctive configurations of neurological events. That these are neurologically "genuine" experiences does not mean that introvertive mystical experiences necessarily involve transcendent realities: nonspatial and nontemporal realities that transcend not just appearances but the entire natural realm and, thus, are not open to scientific study. This does not mean that mystical experiences necessarily provide knowledge. It only means that these experiences are not more ordinary experiences that have simply been interpreted mystically.

It is also important to note that not all people today who have mystical experiences are *religious*. For some people, these experiences have no religious significance. That nonreligious people can have mystical experiences and yet remain secular and naturalistic in their metaphysics presents problems for most definitions of mystical experience. Any sense of transcendence is understood in terms of social and natural realities. It shows that mystical experiences need not be given any transcendent explanation but can be given a naturalistic explanation in terms of unusual but perfectly normal brain activity without resorting to the claim that the brain is malfunctioning. They are then seen as having no cognitive significance.[4] This tempers the emotional impact. Spontaneous mystical experiences (ones that occur unexpectedly without any prior cultivation through meditation or other practices) are often taken today to have no ontological implications; no matter how intense a mystical experience may be, it will affect how one sees reality and oneself only if it is taken not to be a hallucination. In particular, experiences enabled by drugs are often seen as overwhelming at the time and as giving some profound cognitive insight (such as the interconnectedness of all phenomena) only to be dismissed the next day as merely subjective, brain-generated events. In short, one can have mystical experiences without the experiences having existential significance or a lasting effect.

Other Altered State of Consciousness Experiences

The definition of *mystical experience* employed here reflects recent scientific interest in certain ASCs, but no definition of *mystical experience* is dictated by science; unless all ASCs have the same neurological states underlying them, which currently appears not to be the case, scholars still have to decide what range of ASCs to include as mystical and what range to exclude. The definition used in this book takes a middle path between including all ASCs as mystical and restricting mystical experiences to only introvertive "pure consciousness" experiences in which the mind is totally empty of all differentiated content. The segment of the spectrum of ASCs deemed mystical covers those experiences and states of consciousness in which the mind is partially or completely empty of differentiated content—in particular, a sense of self—and has switched to another mode of cognition, as indirectly indicated by changes in the brain's configuration of activity. This is not arbitrary since states of consciousness resulting from such emptying are central to all classical mystical quests to align one's life with reality as it truly is, while experiences from other ASCs are more peripheral to the quest.

Classical mystics may show little interest in non-mystical ASCs, including visions. For example, the Upanishads and Shankara recognize only four states of consciousness: waking, dreaming, dreamless sleep (in which one is one with Brahman), and the fourth state (*turiya*) in which one realizes Brahman while awake (ManU 3–7, BSS 3.2.10). But mystics may also have visions, locutions, a paranormal sense of sweet fragrance, pleasant touches, other religious experiences, or paranormal abilities. Many traditions utilize visualization exercises in mediation. Mystics may also have "somatic" experiences in which an energy flow akin to an electric charge is felt through the presence of the Holy Spirit, a touch of a guru, or the unblocking of the *kundalini* or *qi* power present in the body (see Cattoi and McDaniel 2011). But all of these experiences involve a duality of experience and what is experienced—a sense of separation in which experiencers see beings or symbols and may receive verbal information.[5] When duality is involved, experiences are not *mystical* as it is defined here, although one experience may fade into the other.

However, many scholars treat all paranormal experiences as mystical. Jess Byron Hollenback believes that paranormal phenomena are not peripheral to mysticism (1996, 276–300) and so includes the psychic D. D. Home as a mystic but excludes Buddhists' realization of *nirvana* as mystical. I stipulate that the center of mysticism is an inner quest to still the whirling conceptual and emotional apparatuses of the mind, subduing one's sense of a self as a distinct reality within the phenomenal world in order to sense reality without one's personal mental constrictions. Visions and other paranormal phenomena are mentioned as part of the content of some mystical ways of life, but such experiences do not become mystical experiences in the sense employed here simply because some mystics have them. Likewise, most mysticisms involve quelling desires, not fulfilling them through paranormal powers. Paranormal powers and experiences such as levitation may occur in mystical practices, but they are disparaged as distractions to mystical realizations and sources of attachment. Moreover, many theistic mystics point out the dangers of accepting visions and voices as cognitive even when they did not come from Satan. According to John of the Cross, we should renounce all external things including supernaturally given external visions (*Ascent of Mount Carmel* 2.17.9). Contemplative experiences were more reliable. In Zen Buddhism, visions, sounds, and sensations occurring during meditation are dismissed as hallucinatory demon states (*mayko*).

All normal human cognitive experiences and thoughts involve a duality between someone experiencing or thinking *of* something. Thus, the only terminology that mystics can adopt from general culture to give the sense of experiencing a reality is dualistic: to contact, encounter, perceive, touch, pierce, hear, unite *x* and *y*. However, mystical experiences do not involve the subject/object duality of a reality set off from the experiencer, as with other types of religious and nonreligious experiences. Mystics may say that an introvertive mystical experience is "seen" or "heard" internally and not through the eyes or ears—for example, "heard in the soul"—but the reality is not presented to them as something separate from themselves. Many cultures see the mind as having an "inner eye" that makes seeing mental content the same as a sensory perception. Thus, when mystics adopt a culture's language of visions, they may not be referring to a dualistic experience. For example, Teresa of Avila had inner "intellectual visions" (*Interior Castle* 6.9.4) in which she did not see or hear as with her "external visions" (6.8.6). She said that although she used the word *vision* in this way, the soul does not see anything (6.10.2). Non-dualistic terminology was simply not available to her.

Mysticism also should not be equated with asceticism. One can be an ascetic without having the experiences that distinguish mystics. The term *asceticism* comes from the Greek word *askesis*, referring to an athlete's training, and meant a spiritual preparation and training of the body that purified or guarded the mind, as through spiritual exercises. But in the modern usage, it means something more specific: depriving the body of anything that brings pleasure, to the extent of even depriving what it needs. Ascetics see their renunciation of all material things or physical mortification (such as self-flagellation) as ends in themselves to show repentance, to please God, or to stop actions rather than a means for emptying the mind of a sense of self. Ascetics may also become attached to the practices themselves and may not have mystical experiences. Mysticism instead involves an inner asceticism with a different intention: to eliminate all self-will and renounce personal desires. Asceticism to purify the body and mind can lead to mystical receptivity, and some ascetics have had mystical experiences. Likewise, some classical mystics practiced primarily ascetic deprivations. Some meditative techniques involve working the body, not just the mind. Mysticisms also typically embrace simplifying one's life (often including celibacy) and lessening desires, but the Buddha was not alone in ultimately rejecting extreme ascetic practices as a way to enlightenment. Sufism is a tradition that first embraced asceticism but became less ascetic later.

Mystical Paths

Classical contemplatives and monastics are exemplars of mysticism as understood here. Today, many people who meditate do so only for health benefits, but the traditional objective of meditation is to still the mind in order to attain the knowledge of what is fundamentally real in order to overcome misalignment with reality. However, mysticism involves a total way of life, not merely meditation, and it leads to enlightenment: enduring states of consciousness in which any sense of a phenomenal self is eradicated and one's life is in sync with reality. Through a mystical quest, a mystic comes to see the reality present when their sense of self and the background structuring of their normal awareness are removed from their mind, either experiencing in extrovertive states the world independent of their conceptualizations and manipulations or, in introvertive states, their normally concealed real self or the ontological source of the entire natural realm.

Cultivating nonconceptualized awareness is central to mystical ways of life, but classical mystics actually discuss mystical experiences very little, either their own or more generally.[6] People who have visions discuss their experiences more, but the style of mystical literature in classical cultures was not to report one's own spiritual accomplishments, even in autobiographies.[7] There are classical mystical texts like Teresa of Avila's *Interior Castle*, in which she discusses different types of experiences. (There, she refers to her own experiences in the third person, following the example of Paul in the New Testament: "I know a person who . . ." [2 Cor. 12:1–4].) Mystical texts sometimes discuss states of consciousness, including mystical ones, and sometimes analyze the general nature of experience (with mystical experiences not being a distinct category), but how one should lead one's life, the path to enlightenment, meditative techniques, knowledge, and experienced realities are more common topics. Since mystics' traditional goal is to achieve a continuous new existence aligned with the nature of a fundamental reality, the reality experienced remains more central than any transient experience or a state of mind. Likewise, early meditation texts are more interested in the doctrines behind meditation (such as the metaphysical presuppositions of yoga) and the states of mind it can produce than the practices (Eifring 2016, xiii).

To treat all mystical texts as works about the psychology of various states of consciousness is to misread many texts in light of modern thought. Works like Plotinus's *Enneads* are not only performative texts designed to induce mystical experiences when read out loud. The effect of hearing or speaking some texts may have mind-altering effects, but philosophical texts also have discussions explaining what is ultimately real and make other aspects of a mystical way of life intelligible. Even when discussing mental states, mystics refer more to a transformation of character or an enduring state of alignment with reality than to mystical experiences, including any transitional enlightenment experiences in which a sense of self is finally dissolved. This does not mean that cultivating mystical experiences and states is not the defining characteristic of mysticism or that enlightened states are not altered states of consciousness. It only means that traditional mystics value most the reality experienced, the knowledge attained, and the long-lasting transformed state of a person. Even if mystics value the experience of a transcendent reality over all doctrines, the resulting transformed state of a person to live an enlightened way of life is still valued more, and doctrines are still deemed necessary to see how to live.

Western theisms accept the reality of the world and individuals apart from God, and thus Western mystics do not typically deny the existence of a soul, although a sense of self may be in abeyance during mystical experiences. But in many of the world's mysticisms, the sense of a separate self within the natural world is only an illusion generated by our baseline state of waking consciousness. We normally think that we are an independent, self-contained entity, but in fact, self-consciousness is just another function of the analytic mind. By identifying with what is experienced in self-consciousness, we reify a separate entity—the *self*—and set it off against the rest of reality in a dualism. Our sense of a self, then, controls our life.[8] However, as the Buddha emphasized, there is no such separate self-existing entity within the field of everyday experience but only an ever-changing web of mental and physical processes, and thus we should not identify with any contents of our consciousness, even self-awareness. Our error is not merely an absence of correct knowledge but an active error inhibiting seeing reality as it is. More generally, the error is that our attention is constricted by the conceptualizations that our analytic mind constantly generates. Mystical experiences break the hold of that dualistic state of consciousness and enable us to see reality free of the felt sense of self and the other distinct entities set up by our conceptualizing mind.

The inner quest necessary for overcoming this fragmentation involves a process characterized in different traditions as "forgetting" or "fasting of the mind"—emptying the mind of all conceptualized content (especially the sense of self and its accompanying self-will) and, in the case of the depth-mystical experience, eliminating all sensory input and all introvertive differentiated mental content. The Christian Meister Eckhart spoke of an "inner poverty": a state free of any created will, of wanting anything, of knowing any image, and of having anything. Such a state leads to a sense of the identity with what has always been present—the being, (*esse*) emanating from the Godhead beyond God, that is of the natural world and also of God. Anything that can be put into words except being encloses God, and we need to strip away everything in this way of knowing and become one with the beingness (Eckhart 2009, 253–55). It is a process of disentangling one's mind from all things phenomenal, an "unknowing" of all mental content, including all prior knowledge. Yet, throughout the process, one remains awake and fully aware. The result is a clear awareness where all sensory, emotional, dispositional, and conceptual apparatuses are in abeyance to one degree or another (including a state of complete absence).

Meditation, like mysticism, is a Western term with no exact counterpart in most languages. In its broadest scope, it is any attention-based technique for inner transformation (Eifring 2016, 1).[9] Livia Kohn characterizes it as "the inward focus of attention in a state of mind where ego-related concerns and critical evaluations are suspended in favor of perceiving a deeper, subtler, and possibly divine flow of consciousness" (2008, 4). Meditation involves an attempt to calm the mind by eliminating conceptualizations, dispositions, and emotions by either sustaining one's focus of attention on an object or opening up one's awareness. This disrupts our normal state of consciousness and removes our collective dimension. There are many meditative techniques (see Shear 2006). In no tradition is meditation restricted simply to breathing exercises while sitting.

Overall, meditation has two different tracks. In Buddhism, the distinction is between concentration (*shamatha*) and open monitoring mindfulness (*smriti*, *vipassana*). In the former track, attention is focused on a sensory or mental object—for example, a flame, a crystal, a tradition's doctrine, a textual passage, or a visualized God. The person meditating gently brings their attention back to the object when their mind wanders. Thus, the mind is not empty of objects at the beginning of these practices, but one progressively withdraws attention from any meditative object. Focusing the mind in this way calms and stabilizes consciousness and culminates in one-pointed attention (complete *samadhi*). It leads to tranquil states of feeling absorbed in the object of meditation, although mindfulness may also do the same. The second track is not about emptying the mind of content but about observing that content objectively; one simply passively notes whatever floats into the mind. Mindfulness frees up experience by removing conceptual encrustation in perception, ending ultimately in a dynamic pure awareness or effortless attention that mirrors the flow of what is real as it is presented to the mind unmediated by conceptualizations or a sense of self. Both tracks can empty the mind of the sense of self and all conceptual divisions, leading to a non-dualistic awareness that abolishes the distinctions of subject, object, and action. With the loss of a sense of a self-contained experiencer, consciousness is altered; without boundaries separating the self from anything, consciousness may seem to expand to encompass the entire universe. Practitioners can engage in both tracks and shift from one to the other since mindfulness requires a degree of concentration and vice versa.

Since Origen, the mystical path in Christianity has traditionally been divided into three phases: purgation, illumination, and union. Other traditions divide the quest differently. Some, such as Sufism and Buddhism, have many stages or levels of development and attainment, but progress is not steady, nor are all experiences positive. A mystical quest may be unpleasant and strenuous—it is likened to climbing a mountain. The stress of a mystical way of life can make one physically and psychologically ill. There is also the distress and anxiety in periods in which there appears to be no progress—arid "dark nights of the soul," as John of the Cross called them, in which one feels the pain that God is absent (although John asserted that God is actually working away, clearing the meditator's mind). Theists may feel a sense of abandonment. They may have periods of pain even when they feel that God is present and purifying them. Nontheists report this less often than theists, but they too discuss distress and other problems of the path. One may also become satisfied with a blissful state on the path—what Zen calls the "cave of Mara"—and remain there without attaining a selfless enlightenment. The Christian *Theologia Germanica* also warns against leaving images too soon and thereby never being able to understand the truth aright, as did John of the Cross (*Ascent* 2.13–14). We should not quit "discursive meditation" before God brings the soul to objectless contemplation (2.17.7). There may also be visions and paranormal powers, and after an introvertive mystical experience, the wandering analytic mind usually returns quickly.

Mystics, in general, do not claim that the transcendent reality that is experienced is to be feared, as occurs often with other types of religious experiences. There is no "trembling in the presence of God" as with many revelations. Transcendent realities are usually seen as benevolent or neutral. For Meister Eckhart, there is nothing in God to be feared but only loved, and God is a source of joy (2009, 522). But introvertive experiences can lead to confusion, fear (especially with ego-loss), panic attacks, and paranoia if meditators cannot handle the experiences. In emptying the mind of other content, meditation may also open the mind up to "demonic" phenomena— that is, negative states that are usually attributed to demons or to the meditator's own subconscious and are not projected onto a fundamental reality. Thus, William James rightly refers to "diabolical mysticism" (1958, 326).

Such possible negative effects on a mystical path should not be overlooked. Psychedelics and meditation destabilize one's sense of a self and may exacerbate the conditions of people with mental disorders. Indeed, mystical experiences may open the same subconscious territory trod by schizophrenics and psychotics. A large percentage of serious meditators report at least mild adverse effects. Some negative effects are strong enough to cause people to stop meditating or require hospitalization. In one psychedelic drug study, 44 percent of the volunteers reported delusions or paranoid thinking (Griffiths et al. 2011). A quarter of the subjects reported that a significant portion of their session was characterized by anxiety, paranoia, and negative moods; 31 percent experienced significant fear. Few reported completely positive experiences without significant psychological struggles such as paranoia or the fear that they were going insane or dying. The researchers suspected that difficult moments are significantly under reported. In one study of intensive *vipassana* mindfulness meditation, 63 percent of meditators reported at least some adverse effects, and 7.4 percent reported negative effects strong enough to stop meditating, and one had to be hospitalized for psychosis (Lindahl et al. 2017, 5). In one survey, 73 percent of respondents indicated moderate to severe impairment in at least one mental domain, with 17 percent reporting thoughts of suicide, and 17 percent requiring inpatient hospitalization (21). Some psychological preparation and a framework of beliefs that would prepare meditators or drug users to handle what is experienced, as provided in traditional teacher/student meditative training, may be essential before any serious mystical training is undertaken to avoid such negative reactions. Otherwise, detachment from the sense of self can lead to depression or worse. Even extrovertive mystical experiences may seem bewildering and lead to confusion and distress if they occur outside a religious framework that gives them meaning (Byrd, Lear, and Schwenka 2000, 267–68).

Mystical Knowledge

As noted in the last section, for classical mystics, knowing how reality truly is and living accordingly is what is important, not the experiences that induce the knowledge. Mystics do not claim to discover new truths but only to find the knowledge already expressed in the sacred texts of their traditions.[10] Nor did classical mystics take their experiences as empirical verification or proof of their tradition's doctrines or as authority for those doctrines; for them, those doctrines do not need any experiential verification. Such concerns about verification arise from modern empirical science. In fact, for classical mystics, the reverse is true: scriptures are taken as validating their mystical experiences.[11] The writings of mystics only help to recover knowledge that already exists in foundational scriptures. Thus, if the criteria for being a mystic include the discussion of one's experiences and reliance on those experiences as authority, one would be hard pressed to find any mystics before the modern era.

While mystical experiences typically have a great emotional impact, mystics also claim that they realize a reality that is present when all the personal and conceptualized content of the mind is removed. A hidden reality is distinguished from appearances. Like all experiences, mystical experiences are internal, but to mystics, they are not subjective in the negative sense of being merely brain-generated events. Mystics claim to have direct awareness of the bare being-in-itself—the "is-ness" of the natural realm apart from the conceptual divisions that we impose—or of a transcendent reality. Even the consciousness they experience does not seem personal or to belong to the experiencer but seems impersonal and objective. Mystical experiences may not even feel like one's own if they seem to come from a transcendent reality, wiping out any sense of individual existence.

Thereby, mystics gain knowledge of a reality. Their experiences are considered a liberating breakthrough to a fundamental reality. It is not a matter of knowing that some proposition is true or even of knowledge by acquaintance with a reality distinct from the experiencer, nor is it an intuition in the sense of intellectually jumping from a line of reasoning to a new conclusion—such intuitions remain a matter of dualistic content. Rather, if valid, mystical awareness is another type of experiential knowledge—knowledge by participation or knowledge by identity—one *becomes* or *is* the reality that is realized. Unlike ordinary knowledge by acquaintance, here, distinctions between the subject, object, and act of knowing collapse. Knowing we are aware, even though this occurs in an ordinary dualistic state of consciousness, is like this: We never know our awareness as a separate object, only as a subjectivity that we participate in. But mystical knowledge does not rely upon normal modes of apprehension; it transcends normal cognitive faculties and strips away all human effort. No reflection is involved, just being.

To emphasize the difference between attained mystical knowledge and knowledge attained through sense experiences and reasoning, mystics often use terms such as *gnosis*, *nonknowledge* (to distinguish this knowledge from everyday knowledge), *intellect* (to distinguish the mental function involved in mystical experiences from sense experience and reasoning), or *nonconscious* (to denote a state of consciousness utterly unlike normal ones). If one accepts a metaphysics in which God or Brahman is our being or in which one has always had a Buddha-nature, then paradoxically, one has not achieved anything in one's mystical quest, no matter how strenuous. One merely realizes what has always been the case.

Mystical experiences may be ego-shattering implosions of reality, but the actual insight that mystical experiences are taken to provide does not occur when the mind is in an introvertive mystical state of consciousness. That is, the insight occurs *outside* introvertive mystical experiences; it is an insight into the nature of reality that can occur only when thought has returned. Thus, Advaitins disconnect the depth-mystical experience from the insight that Brahman alone is real. This insight occurs only in our baseline dualistic state of consciousness or in an extrovertive mystical state after the introvertive mystical experiences are over. In those states of consciousness, the mind makes what was experienced into a mental object of reflection for the mystic. And in those states, a mystic's beliefs, shaped by their religious way of life and culture, determine how the insight is understood. The diversity of mystical doctrines shows that mystical experiences alone do not determine knowledge claims in any simple empiricist fashion (see Jones 2016, 80–81). That is, mystical experiences do not carry their own interpretations, even for mystics themselves. Thus, the actual knowledge that is gained in a mystical experience involves elements of the mystic's specific religious and cultural beliefs. Thus, there is no one universal mystical knowledge, and there could not be even if all mystical experiences were the same. This also means that *insight* can be understood in two senses in mystical discussions: it may refer to the mystical experience itself or to the doctrinal knowledge claims adopted after the experience is over from the mixture of input from the experience and cultural beliefs.

The Diversity of Mystical Experiences

Many scholars implicitly assume that all mystical experiences are the same in nature. They refer to "*the* mystical experience" and characterize all the experiences as a "union with God." However, while mystical experiences share common elements that permit them to be classified as mystical, there are different types of mystical experiences and, thus, should not be treated as the same in all regards. Neuroscientists have found that the neurological states for concentrative meditators differ from those of mindfulness meditators (Hood 2001, 32–47; Dunn, Hartigan, and Mikulas 1999; Milliere 2018). Neuroscientists also have detected that the effects of a temporary loss of a sense of self differ from the traits of enduring selfless states (Milliere 2018, 19). This strongly suggests that there is not one mystical state of consciousness or mystical awareness but several. This leads to rejecting any essentialism in which all mystical experiences are of one type.

There are two general classes of mystical experiences in the sense specified here, and there are different types of mystical experiences within each class. The distinction is between *extrovertive* and *introvertive* experiences, to use the terminology set by Walter Stace (1960a)—that is, between experiences oriented outwardly and those oriented inwardly. Additionally, a mystic's ascent gradually intensifies to a sense of selflessness: a state of consciousness without even an implicit self of ownership.[12] Many mystical experiences may not involve the complete elimination of a sense of self. Mystics may have both extrovertive and introvertive mystical experiences, and they both may occur on the path to enlightenment. Extrovertive mystical experiences can also transition to introvertive ones, but the neural state of the experiencers then changes. Different types of non-mystical ASC experiences such as visions may also occur. A mystical experience may not be a singular event but may involve different phases or a series of episodes. Visions and theistic mystical elements may occur during the transitional states of consciousness to and from an empty depth-mystical experience to the baseline ego-state or to an extrovertive state of consciousness. In addition, different or more thoroughly emptied mystical experiences may occur after one loses a sense of self or attains enlightenment.

William Wainwright offers a typology of extrovertive and introvertive experiences that captures the phenomenological evidence from different cultures and eras reflected in recurring, low-ramified descriptions of the mystical experiences (1981, 33–40).[13] With a slight modification of his terminology and categories, the types are:

EXTROVERTIVE EXPERIENCES

- Experiencing being connected or united to the rest of the natural realm with a loss of a sense of real boundaries between the experiencer and the world or borders within nature

- Experiencing a lack of separate, self-existing entities with no emphasis on a connected whole (mindful states)

- Experiencing a sense of an undivided interconnected whole

- Experiencing a vibrant luminous glow to nature

- Experiencing the presence of a personal or nonpersonal transcendent reality that exists outside of time and space but is also immanent in the world (cosmic consciousness)

INTROVERTIVE EXPERIENCES

- Experiences with differentiated content—e.g., an inner bright white light or being enveloped in a golden light

- Experiences of a connection in love or identity with a personal god (theistic)

- Experiences empty of all differentiated content (including any sense of a self) leaving a pure consciousness (depth-mystical)

There are different experiences within each category, with the exception of the depth-mystical experience. The differentiated content in introvertive experiences depends, at least in part, upon one's mind-set and their physical and social setting. In either class, mystical experiences can occur spontaneously without any prior practices. Indeed, spontaneous mystical experiences may be much more common than those cultivated through meditation or other practices. Even when the experiences occur after a long period of mystical cultivation, they are instantaneous, although *sudden* and *abrupt* are most often ascribed to introvertive experiences and non-mindfulness extrovertive experiences. Meditation may lead to different types of mystical experiences within either group. Not all mystical experiences are transient—they may last only a few minutes or last for years and be permanent states of consciousness. So, too, there are different degrees of intensity.

For traditional mystics, both introvertive and extrovertive experiences involve an awareness of a fundamental component of reality that people whose awareness is confined to the natural order of phenomenal objects and mental conceptions have not had. In extrovertive experiences, the beingness of the natural universe shines forth through phenomena free of any cultural coverings. The sense of a transcendent reality that is also immanent may be present. In introvertive experiences, a transcendent reality is directly realized. These realities may include a self or consciousness existing independently of the body, a creator god, or a nonpersonal source of the natural world, but for mystics, such a reality is also immanent to the natural realm in the consciousness of a person or in the ground of being in the phenomenal realm. Being immanent, that reality is experienceable in mystical experiences even though it is not experienceable as an object and hence is not a phenomenon.

All mystical experiences of both classes share some phenomenological features in one degree or another: the weakening or total elimination of the sense of a separate self within the natural world; the seeming deathlessness of the true transcendent self or consciousness; a sense of timelessness; a heightened awareness, including sense perceptions in extrovertive mysticism; a sense that both the experience and what is experienced cannot be adequately expressed in words or symbols (ineffability); and a resultant feeling of bliss or peace (although a mystical experience may involve a feeling of ecstasy). Often, people who have mystical experiences have positive emotions toward other people and the natural realm and an absence of negative emotions like anger and hatred. Traditionally, there is also a common cognitive quality—a sense that one has directly touched some ultimate reality and attained an insight into the fundamental nature of oneself or all reality—with an accompanying sense of absolute certainty and objectivity. One can attain a sense of pure existence or boundless existence either introvertively as consciousness or extrovertively as nature free of being cut up into distinct entities. But again, classical mysticism was never about attaining isolated mystical experiences, including enlightenment experiences; its objective was to become aligned with realty in an abiding state of consciousness through the knowledge revealed in mystical experiences.

With the analytic mind at rest, the mind in both classes of experience is more passive and receptive, even while one actively focuses their attention on an item. The experiences feel like they are happening *to* the experiencers, not initiated by them. One may do things to cultivate such experiences, but in the end, one cannot force the change in consciousness involved in a mystical experience. Thus, theistic mystics speak of "grace," "surrendering one's will to God," and "other-power" as sources of the experiences. Meditators cannot force or manipulate the mind to become still by following any technique or series of steps and thus cannot compel a mystical experience. The experiences seem uncaused and spontaneous. Mystical training techniques and studying doctrines can lessen a sense of self, remove mental obstacles, and calm a distracted mind, thus increasing the occurrence of mystical experiences, but they cannot guarantee a complete end to the activity of the conceptualizing mind. Meditators can clear the ground in the mind, but what happens next is not up to them. And as long as meditators are trying to "get enlightened," they are still in an acquisitive state of mind and cannot succeed in becoming selfless. One begins the quest with an active desire and utilizes the analytic mind along the way, but no act of self-will can force mystical experiences to occur, nor can any preparatory activity (including artificial triggers such as psychedelics). One must surrender— simply let go and not try to control or manipulate reality. Even the desire to become enlightened must be given up. But once meditators end their ego-centric striving and become receptive by letting go of any attempt to control what happens, the mind becomes free of grasping, fear, and anger and stills itself. Mystical experiences then occur on their own.

Extrovertive Mystical Experiences

Extrovertive mystical experiences involve a greater receptivity to what is presented to the mind in sense experiences. Once the mind is free of conceptual, dispositional, and emotional apparatuses, the diffuse phenomena presented to it are no longer seen as a dualistic collection of a self and multiple ontologically distinct entities. This may lead to a sense of a connectedness or unity with the flux of impermanent phenomena in the world. Unlike in visions, only the phenomenal world presented to the senses is seen. Thus, mystical experiences and states with differentiated content have something for the mind to organize with the concepts from a mystic's culture.[14] But one extrovertive state of consciousness may be free of all conceptual structures: a dynamic, pure mindfulness involving sensory phenomena unmediated by any conceptualizations or associations—that is, sensations not mentally structured into perceptions. Such an extreme state cannot last long since we cannot survive in the world without distinguishing, say, water from poison.

Thus, not all mystical experiences are non-sensory and otherworldly. Not all mystical experiences involve delving into a changeless transcendent reality but can involve an experience of the beingness of the phenomena of the natural world as it is prior to any cultural prism. All extrovertive experiences but mindfulness are types of nature mysticism. The experiencer's metaphysics may remain confined to the natural realm. Even if there is a sense of a transcendent source immanent in the natural realm, the natural world is still the focus of the experience. What is retained from all extrovertive mystical experiences is a sense of fundamental immutable beingness and a lack of discrete realities. Thus, ASC experiences reveal aspects of the phenomenal world that are not in focus in an ordinary state of consciousness.

Indeed, revealing an aspect of reality not otherwise known is so significant to mystics that, to them, it is almost as if another sense in addition to our normal five is involved.

If we assume that there is only one type of mystical experience, it is natural to consider extrovertive experiences to be low-level, failed, or partial cases of introvertive depth-mystical experiences, as Stace did (1960a, 132). But, as previously noted, neuroscience suggests that extrovertive and introvertive are distinct types of experiences. In addition, Buddhism and Daoism are traditions in which extrovertive experiences are considered more central than introvertive experiences for aligning one's life with reality. Thus, from a historical perspective, extrovertive experiences are not a failure—it is not as if mystics were really shooting for introvertive experiences and missed.

Nature mysticism and cosmic consciousness do not often occur in mystical training (or at least, they are not often reported) but occur more spontaneously in the general populace. Since this book is on mysticism, such isolated experiences will not be mentioned as often as other types of mystical experiences. However, the experiences of such people as William Wordsworth and Walt Whitman are no less mystical for being so. Not all cases of being enthralled by nature are mystical; a sense of self must be lost partially or completely. In different types of nature mysticism, ending our conceptual barriers and sense of self makes us feel connected or identical to what is experienced in the world. Feeling tranquility, ecstasy, or awe is common. Things feel in harmony. Differentiated phenomena are present but without the reification of the content of consciousness into discrete entities. Nature becomes more vivid and may seem to be alive. Objects seem to have an inside, not just an outside. The being of the world may appear luminous; the sensory realm may take on a glow, feeling of being alive, made of vibrant light, or appear translucent and crystal-like. The sense of self may expand to include nature, like how Thomas Traherne felt that the entire universe was inside him. To William Blake, it was "To see a World in a Grain of Sand / And a Heaven in a Wild Flower, / Hold Infinity in the palm of your hand / And Eternity in an Hour." When one feels the worldly presence of a God or other reality that transcends time and grounds the universe, the experience shifts from nature mysticism to cosmic consciousness—a sense of a timeless, transcendent reality of light or love that is immanent to the natural world and present in everyday life.[15] However, the transcendent element to God remains, so cosmic consciousness is not a form of pantheism. Indeed, no classical form of mystical metaphysics equate fundamental reality with the phenomenal world.[16]

Yet, all extrovertive experiences have in one degree or another a lessening of a sense of a phenomenal self and of any boundaries set up by our analytic mind between the experiencer and nature. Likewise, borders within nature are lessened, leading to a sense of connectedness. All things share the same beingness, and one participates in that shared beingness in a timeless now: the experience seems outside the eternal temporal sequencing of events.[17] The natural world may become seen as an interconnected whole or partless unity (oneness) of oneself with all of nature. Both nature mystical experiences and cosmic consciousness come in various degrees of intensity, but there is always a profound sense of knowledge, being connected to the natural world, and making contact with something fundamentally real. The event may be a brief experience or a longer lasting state of consciousness.

Mindfulness

With mindfulness, as exemplified in Buddhism, complete focus is on whatever is being presented to the mind in the present moment. (Mindfulness in Buddhism does apply an interpretation to what is presented to the senses in terms of impermanence and conditionality.) This produces a clarity of awareness. Mindfulness is extrovertive when sensory input is involved, but it may also involve monitoring internal mental activity. To mindfulness mystics, the analytic mind alienates us from what is real, and language is its most effective tool: conceptualizations fixed by language distort what is actually there. Mindfulness loosens the grip that the concepts we create have on our sense experiences and inner experiences; thereby, the images of the world and ourselves that the mind creates are shattered. The sense of a discrete self within the phenomenal realm vanishes.

Mindfulness results in seeing the flow of sensory input and the inner activity of the mind as it is presented to consciousness free of memories, anticipations, judgments, and emotional reactions. Likewise, the flow of sensory input is free of the normal process of editing and reifying the input into distinct objects based on conceptualizations. With some or all of the background structuring normally associated with such content deactivated, observation is sharpened: the world is seen as in constant flux without independently existing objects (or experiencers), an objectless sensory stream. Because ego-driven consciousness is ended, states of mindfulness are necessarily different from ordinary states of consciousness. Such mindfulness may be a transient experience, but it also may become an enduring stable state of transformed consciousness and, thus, an enduring character trait.

In mindfulness meditations, one focuses attention on, for example, breathing without trying to control or manipulate the breath, simply observing what is happening. The input coming into the mind does not change, but there is a change in the meditator's relation to that content. The content is perceived without a conceptual apparatus. There is a "bare attention" to what is presented to the senses without attention to anything in particular and without any accompanying expectations or habitual reactions.

This relates to the notion of *illusion* in extrovertive mysticism. We normally conceptualize independent entities apart from the flow of events and react to our own conceptions. We need to rend the conceptual veil to what is really there, but the discrete objects of sense experience and introspection are unreal only in this limited sense; the beingness behind conceptual differentiations remains real, and appearances are not differentiated into parts. To convey a sense of what is real and what is illusory, *Chandogya Upanishad* (6.1.3–4) gives the analogy of a clay pot: the clay represents what is real (the permanent substance lasting before and after whatever temporary shape it currently is in), and the form of the pot, or pot-ness, represents what is illusory (the impermanent form the clay is in at one moment).[18] If we smash the pot, its thingness is destroyed, but what is real in the pot (the clay) continues unaffected. Mindfulness mystics focus on the clay and see the pot as only temporary and contingent and, in that way, incidental and illusory. They do not dismiss the world as unreal or illusory in any stronger sense unless their beliefs dictate otherwise for nonexperiential reasons.

Thus, mindfulness involves a realism, in the broadest sense, about the experienced realm: something exists independently of our conceptions. But this realism is not grounded in an awareness of sensed differentiations based in linguistic distinctions—there can be something objectively real even if there are no objective entities (objects). Since language refers to the differentiations in the natural realm and is itself a matter of differentiations, extrovertive mystics have trouble applying language to undifferentiated beingness. True phenomenal reality cannot be mirrored in any conceptualizations. Words denote distinct entities, and what is real is not constructed out of ontologically discrete parts.

Through mindfulness, ultimately, there is a Gestalt-like switch, not from one figure to another (for example, from a duck to a rabbit in the Köhler drawing) but from any figure to bare patches of colors. In pure mindfulness, the being of the patches is not seen *as* anything; even the labels *patches*, *white*, and *black* would only arise after the purely mindful state is over. Awareness becomes focused on the beingness of the natural realm rather than the things that we normally conceptualize out of it. In the ocean of phenomena, mindfulness mystics focus on the common water and not the distinctions of the constantly changing waves. There is an open receptivity not previously present in the mystic's mind that permits a greater richness to the sensory input once it is freed from being routinely reduced to objects by preformed characterizations. The experiences may not have the intensity or vibrance of nature mystical experiences, but perception is refreshed by the removal of conceptual restrictions, and one type of mystical experience may slide into another.

In the enduring state of mindfulness, the mindful live fully absorbed in the present moment, free of temporal structuring, witnessing whatever arises in their consciousness without judgment and without a sense of possession and responding spontaneously. The mind becomes tranquil and lucid. To mindfulness mystics, as long as we have a dualizing mind, we are blocking direct access to reality as it really is. With a mindful mind, we no longer identify with our thoughts and emotions but simply observe and accept whatever is presented to the senses, living fully in the moment without a sense of a self. In sensory mindfulness, one can be aware that there is content in your mind without dropping out of the experience, unlike in most mystical experiences. If an extrovertive experience involves a sense of the presence of a transcendent reality or the "mind of the world" in nature, mindfulness is still possible.

The field of perception is no longer fragmented into discrete enti-ties—in Buddhist terms, the mind no longer "abides" anywhere or "grasps" anything. Only now can we see it as it really is, free of conceptualizations setting up dualities. The mind mirrors only what is there without adding or distorting what is presented. Thus, mindfulness sustains attention without the customary habituation of our perceptions. However, some conceptual structuring will remain present in all but a state of pure mindfulness. While on the path to enlightenment, a mindfulness mystic still sees individual objects, but it is their beingness that is the focus of attention. Once enlight-ened, any self-contained individuality within the experienced world or in the experiencer is seen as illusory. What the unenlightened conceptually separate out as entities, the enlightened see to be only impermanent and conditioned eddies in a constantly flowing and integrated field of events.

Mindfulness is thus not about attaining a state of consciousness unconnected to observing the mundane world or seeing anything more (or less) profound than seeing the flow of phenomena as it is free of the constraints of our conceptualizations and emotions.

Introvertive Mystical Experiences

Introvertive mystical experiences occur spontaneously or in the concentrative track of meditation when there is no sensory input. There is an inner awareness of one's own transcendent self or of another transcendent reality. An important distinction is between introvertive experiences with differentiable content and those without. Both theistic and nontheistic experiences occur in extrovertive states of consciousness. Extrovertive states may be long lasting or even permanent, but introvertive experiences are more transient, being disrupted by life in the phenomenal world. The experience is not a catatonic trance-like state of frozen consciousness or a state of unconsciousness: the conceptualizing mind is shut down, but one remains fully awake and alert even if one appears to be dead to others and is unresponsive to being touched.

Differentiated introvertive experiences are not merely post-experience interpretations of the depth-mystical experience. The experiences themselves involve differentiated content. They can be seen as the presence of a reality that is personal in nature, and theists typically understand these experiences as instances of communion with and being fully and unconditionally loved by a limitless, benevolent god. The sense of the divine is especially strong when a sense of bliss is part of the experience, but nontheists dismiss the sense of being loved as a mere misreading of the peace that comes when the analytic mind is turned off while one is still aware. The sense of love is a product of enculturation in a theistic society or the result of the theist's specific mystical training, not from the presence of a transcendent reality.

Because theistic introvertive experiences are differentiated, it is possible that there may be a unique flavor to these experiences in each tradition due to cultural influences. For example, Christian theistic mystical experiences in general may differ in form from Hindu Bhakti theistic mystical experiences, and so on. In any case, differentiated introvertive mystical experiences are not all the same.

Depth-Mystical Experiences

Inwardly focusing one's attention begins with an object of concentration, but attention can be withdrawn from all objects. This leads to complete inner stillness in the last category of introvertive experiences: the depth-mystical experience. This experience is not a matter of replacing normal mental content with an image of nothingness (that is, a big, black, silent, unmoving, empty space). If you are aware of sensing a void, or silence, or any other thing, you are not having a depth-mystical experience. Rather, a depth-mystical experience requires completely eliminating all distinguishable content from the mind. It is without conceptual content, structuring, or other conceptual associations. Even in the Abrahamic traditions, there are mystics who affirm a "Godhead beyond God" free of all features. Some theistic mystics such as Jan van Ruusbroec report both differentiated introvertive theistic mystical experiences and depth-mystical experiences. According to Meister Eckhart, by means of a mental faculty that is distinct from reasoning and sense experience—the intellect (*Nous*)—one can breakthrough to the ground (the being supplied by the Godhead) that is free of self-will, God's will, all creatures and images, and even God himself. The normal workings of the mind—including the sense of self—are stilled and inner silence results.

In the depth-experience proper, the mind is free of all differentiated content, yet the experiencer is still awake. In this state, language cannot operate (since nothing with distinctions is in the mind), so one in the empty state cannot say something about it. One can either be aware in the depth-experience or say something about it, but one cannot do both at the same time. The mind is free of all dualities and conceptualizations. If you think, "I am having a depth-mystical experience," you are not having one. The experience cannot even be called *self-awareness* since the experiencer is not aware of a subject experiencing anything. One is not even aware of being aware: if one were aware of being aware or observing, a duality is set up. So, too, there is no sense of personally possessing this awareness or any sense of *I* since the depth-mystical experience is devoid of all personal psychological characteristics. Indeed, the awareness does not seem to be an individual's consciousness at all but something that transcends all phenomenal subjects.

However, mystics do not black out and go unconscious, nor do they suffer from amnesia for the period they undergo a depth-mystical experience. Rather, the mystics remain conscious, and a sense of something real is retained after the experience is over: stillness, silence, simplicity, naturalness, calm, relaxation, rest, bliss, joy, sense of knowing, freedom, wholeness, security, unity, depth, and profundity (Woods, Windt, and Carter 2022, 41).[19] That is, the experience feels free of all content at the time of its occurrence—empty of all thoughts, images, concepts, perceptions, and feelings (37, 42)—but looking back at the experience after it is over, something is perceived as having been present in the silent state. Thus, the event is an experience or awareness. If the experience were truly empty, mystics could label it after it is over, but they could not know anything about it. Thus, they could not form any beliefs or values about what they experienced based on the experience or reject any competing understandings of it, nor could the experience leave any emotional impact on the experiencer. But mystics claim that some profound reality is experienced with at least some abstract characteristics: oneness, consciousness, immutability, and fundamentality.

This consciousness is what remains when all differentiated content is removed from the mind and one remains aware. The active mind of sensing and thinking ends, and pure consciousness—a core consciousness present when all phenomenal content is absent—reigns.[20] It is like a beam of light that illuminates but cannot reflect back upon itself and so is never an object within awareness. Normally, we see only objects and not light, but in a depth-mystical experience, there are no objects; a light without objects to illuminate is all there is. This light is the content of the depth-mystical experience even though mystics are unaware of this content while the experience is occurring.

Thus, in the depth-mystical experience, the mind is not truly empty even though it is often characterized that way. There is a positive content that fully occupies the mind: consciousness free of any differentiated content. However, the ultimate nature of that consciousness is a matter of interpretation. Its minimal ontological characterization holds that in such experiences, depth-mystics are aware of their own consciousness or of the beingness of the natural realm. However, mystics may also conclude that when the mind is completely emptied and stilled, a reality greater than consciousness or the being of the natural realm bursts forth, an unmediated implosion of a more fundamental reality that transcends the natural realm. Theists can interpret the depth-mystical experience as an experience of the bare beingness of God but not of any of God's personal aspects since theists cannot be said to experience anything personal or loving if what they experience is devoid of all subject/object duality and all differentiated content. In the words of John of the Cross, the mind is "cleansed and emptied" of all "distinct ideas and images." That is, theists do not experience personal properties in depth-mystical experiences as they seem to in differentiated theistic introvertive experiences. Rather, after the experience, theists transfer their previous beliefs to the sense of reality and finality witnessed in the experience.

As the experiencer's consciousness shifts from this mystical state of consciousness back to an ordinary waking consciousness or an extrovertive mystical state, memory returns and what was experienced becomes an object of reflection. There is no space available during the experience itself to make labeling or interpreting the content possible, but looking back on the experience in another state of consciousness retains an image of it. Plotinus made clear that seeing an image of the One differs from being "one'd" with it (Enn. VI.9.11). Seeing the image involves duality; the analytic mind makes the One into an object that cannot reflect the One accurately but necessarily alters its nature. In the transitional states back from the depth-mystical experience, dualistic phenomena may also flood back into the mind. This phase of the event is not part of the depth-mystical experience itself, but after the whole experience is over, theists may well mistake content from the transitional states for experiences in the depth-mystical phase. If the transition involves subconscious processes, that content may not seem to come from the experiencer but to be infused with reality.

From a phenomenological point of view, the unified state of consciousness in a depth-mystical experience may be only consciousness itself, but what is present in the mind at the time of the event has been open to four types of ontological understanding:

- Only the natural mind is present; it is either a pure consciousness state of the mind, an inward awareness of the being of the natural world, or a feedback effect occurring when the mind is empty of differentiated content to work with but still active.

- A transcendent consciousness distinct from the body is present; this consciousness may be an individual's (as in the Samkhya and Jaina metaphysics) or shared by all sentient beings.

- A transcendent nonpersonal ground of being underlying all subjective and objective natural phenomena is present; such a ground may be conscious in nature.

- A transcendent creator/sustainer god who is personal in nature is present (or the mind is already participating in the god's being), but only the god's nonpersonal being is experienced.

Naturalists deny the existence of transcendent realities, but they can accept that experiences empty of differentiated content do occur, resulting in a sense of unity; they simply give this sense the first explanation. However, if consciousness is a fundamental property of matter (panpsychism) or the substance of the natural world (cosmopsychism), naturalists can accept that the depth-mystical experience is an experience of something fundamentally real in the natural realm. On the other hand, theists can give that experience a theistic interpretation, but this does not make the experience a differentiated theistic introvertive experience. As discussed, theists may also have extrovertive experiences that are felt to be the presence of God in creation (cosmic consciousness) and introvertive experiences with differentiated content that are taken to be communing with God. Thus, to theists, three types of mystical experiences can be theistic.

Mystical Enlightenment as a State of Consciousness

Mystical enlightenment is a matter of aligning oneself with the fundamental nature of reality once one is totally free of a sense of self.[21] Thus, one must "die" to any sense of self. This is not simply a matter of proper belief but of reshaping one's inner life. A sense of a self is so ingrained in our baseline state of consciousness that ending this sense and becoming selfless necessarily takes a person out of their normal way of experiencing into an altered state of consciousness. But no mystical experiences, not even repeated depth-mystical ones, necessarily transform consciousness into a continuing ASC. No action or event can force it; no individual effort can cause the state of selflessness any more than it can cause mystical experiences.

    After a mystical experience, one's sense of self usually returns. Thus, one would then see the world dualistically in the normal baseline state of consciousness. The experience may dramatically affect one's beliefs, general outlook, or attitude toward life or inspire one to undertake a new way of life without producing a lasting ASC. Instead, one's consciousness will return to an ordinary, ego-driven state. That is, one may attribute great religious significance to what they think they experienced yet view the experience, themselves, and the world only with ordinary, self-driven, dualistic consciousness without their awareness transforming into a selfless state. Isolated experiences occurring spontaneously or enabled by psychedelics are less likely to have lasting effects on consciousness than those occurring to people who actively cultivate them within a religious tradition. An experience may inspire forming such beliefs as "all is one" or "there is no self," but the mere intellectual acceptance of a proposition that there is no phenomenal self is not enlightenment. Indeed, we do not need a mystical experience to follow philosophers' arguments against a distinct center to mental activity (the self as a fiction of the analytic mind) or to accept that we are all tiny specks of the refuse of an earlier star in one interconnected natural whole free of any ontologically distinct entities. Likewise, we do not need any psychological preparation or clearing of the mind to understand or accept, say, that a transcendent source sustaining the universe is experienced. Simply adopting such a belief need not transform a person's state of consciousness.

Any effects of a mystical experience on consciousness may be short-lived and fade away, especially if one decides that the experience is delusory. In fact, mystical experiences can reinforce the ego, as seen with some New Age gurus (discussed in chapter 10). Mystical experiences may have a lasting impact on a person without terminating their sense of self; simply having a mystical experience does not make one enlightened. Such experiencers may have tasted the awakening knowledge (as defined by their religious tradition) in a transient experience, and the memory of the mystical state may greatly affect them. This may change their character, beliefs, and actions, but they still see that knowledge, the world, and themselves from a dualistic state of consciousness.

Enlightenment, on the other hand, is a long lasting or even permanent ASC free of any sense of self. That is, the enlightened have entered an enduring selfless state of consciousness in which the non-dual knowledge gained in a mystical experience has become fixed in one's consciousness. One may have the sense that experiences are happening "here," in oneself, but there no sense of a discrete entity doing the experiencing. Enlightenment experiences thus initiate a new way of being in the world. It is when mystical experiences occur in religious settings and one is seeking a mystical goal through how one lives that such a transformation of the person is most likely. That is, actively practicing a form of mysticism most likely provides the mental set to make its experiences transformative. A mystical insight internalizing one's religious and philosophical ideas becomes an enduring part of one's cognitive and dispositional framework, thereby transforming how one sees the world and how one reacts, but transformation is only mystical enlightenment when it involves completely ending any sense of a phenomenal self in the world. (Theists still typically affirm the existence of a transcendent soul that is at least partially distinct from God.) The entire inner life of a person—perception, cognition, desires, emotions, motivations, dispositions—is reorganized. Their consciousness is permanently altered into an extrovertive mystical state: mindfulness, a nature mystical state, or cosmic consciousness.

This new, enduring, stable, selfless state of consciousness is the goal of classical mysticism, not any isolated experience or retaining mystical knowledge in ordinary consciousness. Enlightenment integrates mystical insight into one's way of being. True reality is allegedly revealed. The depth-mystical experience may be the accepted paradigm of mystical experiences, but the enlightened extrovertive mystical state of consciousness is more enduring and, thus, more difficult to achieve and maintain. The effect of meditation on altering the sense of self is greater than the temporary effect of experiences enabled by psychedelics (Milliere 2018, 19). The mystic's metaphysics may include a transcendent self or soul, but one acts free of a sense of a phenomenal self.

A sense of self may be our most deeply rooted feeling, but this does not mean that it is impossible to end permanently. Meditation works on the consciousness and, in the case of classical mysticism, it is also part of more encompassing ways of life. All that may remain of an individual personality is what is compatible with unimpeded consciousness. However, if one thinks, "I am enlightened," one may have fallen back into a dualistic state unless one realizes that this is only a conventional but inaccurate way of stating things and there is, in fact, no self.

In addition, the enlightened state can be lost as the effect of the experiences or meditation recedes. But falling out of enlightenment involves not simply forgetting some knowledge claims, it involves a change in one's state of consciousness. If losing enlightenment involved only forgetting an analytical proposition, it could be regained merely by being reminded of the claim. Thus, the enlightened in Hinduism and Buddhism continue to meditate after enlightenment.

This stringent requirement for mystical enlightenment means that it is rare. An enlightened state of consciousness is an ASC, and this is much harder to attain and maintain than having a temporary isolated mystical experience. When prominent traditional Buddhist meditation masters are asked how many enlightened Buddhists they know, they inevitably say none or, at most, very few. For example, when asked by Winston King, the German-born Theravadin Nyanaponika Thera (1901–1994) said he knew of no enlightened monks. In Tibet, with a population of between three and four million people, 20 percent of whom were ordained monks or nuns, it is claimed that only about thirty people in the twentieth century attained enlightenment (Revel and Ricard 1999, 51). Few mystics attain enlightenment since the ties to ordinary mental life and to the world in general are very strong. Indeed, many Indian traditions deny that "enlightenment in this life" (*jiva-mukti*) is possible at all.

The Enlightened State

It is important to reiterate that classical mystics are not interested in isolated mystical experiences but in the longer lasting states of an inner transformation of selflessness. Mystical experiences illuminate what is real behind appearances and artificial fabrications, but classical mysticism is not about merely cultivating episodic experiences for their own sake. It is about transforming a person in a way that aligns them with reality (as defined by their tradition) by dissolving any sense of a phenomenal self and its accompanying drives. What classical mystics believe they experienced figures more in their writings than do their own experiences. Deeper mystical experiences may be sought after enlightenment, but accumulating isolated mystical experiences is not a goal: experiences are valued only for the alleged knowledge of reality that they convey, and once a mystic has gained the necessary knowledge, they need not undertake to collect more of such experiences. Maintaining the selfless enlightened state of consciousness becomes their concern.

Enlightenment involves knowing the fundamental nature of reality as defined by the mystic's tradition and living accordingly, normally by following the values and ethics of the mystic's tradition and emulating its exemplars. The mystic's will is now corrected since an individual's will is based on the groundless sense of an independent self within the everyday world, but the enlightened no longer see things from a personal point of view. Now free of a sense of self and, thus, all self-will, mystics can live effortlessly aligned with how they see the nature of reality. The full beliefs and values of a way of life are not given in a mystical experience, so enlightened mystics in different traditions have different doctrines and see their experiences in light of those beliefs and values. Since beliefs and values from a mystic's tradition figure in their enlightened way of life, there is no one abstract state of enlightenment but different enlightened states. Indeed, enlightenment differs from person to person: the beliefs and values that each mystic brings to enlightenment will differently structure their awareness and how they live, but all such states involve ending a sense of a real phenomenal self in light of the nature of reality.

In introvertive mysticisms, our everyday sense of a distinct, socially constructed self is replaced by a continuous inflow of what is deemed the ground of either the true self or all of reality. The result is a continuous, selfless, extrovertive mystical awareness, but it is one in contact with a transcendent reality. It is state of consciousness with an immovable inner calm, even while the person is engaged in thought and activity; one remains centered in a transcendent reality while remaining fully conscious of thoughts and sensations and still acting in the world.[22] Depth wisdom can coexist in the enlightened person's consciousness once it has been awakened and is, in fact, always present in their consciousness (Johnston 2000, xvi). Thus, two levels of consciousness become active in one integrated state: the surface and the silent depth.

The initial cracking of the sense of self does not exhaust the depth of reality open to a mystic. The enlightened state is open-ended: more introvertive and extrovertive mystical experiences may occur, and the enlightened state may be further deepened by these experiences or by mystical exercises. In fact, mystics often attach little significance to an event inaugurating the enlightened state since it is the latter state and its further development that matters. For theists, becoming enlightened may be treated only as a stage in the continuing long-term development of one's relation to God. In Zen Buddhism, after an initial *satori/kensho*, one continues to practice meditation as before, without thought of a goal. Even if the process of further awakening continues, with the last residues of a sense of a separately existing self completely uprooted from one's consciousness and subconsciousness in a stabilized state, a new stage of life has begun.[23]

One's knowledge changes in light of what they now accept as real. One has gone from thinking "I am walking" to "I am the walking" to "There is walking" or, for theists, "God is walking through me." But as long as we ask "Who does the walking?" we look at the situation in a dualistic way. Even if beliefs and values are thoroughly internalized in the enlightened state from the religious tradition in which the enlightened trained, mystics now know them to be true in a way they did not before; they no longer interpret the metaphysical claims within a dualistic framework but see reality differently. Their knowledge is participatory. In a Buddhist analogy, it is the difference between intellectually accepting the claim that water will quench thirst based on the authority of others and actually drinking water (SN 2.115). Drinking the water does not reveal any new propositions, and the claim "Water quenches thirst" remains the same, but one now knows that it is true in a way that one did not when only relying on the testimony of others. They experience the reality; they do not merely accept a proposition formed by the dualizing mind. The knowledge is no longer theoretical but part of one's being. Naturalists may accept the metaphysical propositions that everything is made of one common substance and that there are no selves, but only by drinking the water do mystics integrate the proper non-dualist understanding of these claims into their very being and how they live.

In fact, many mystical claims about reality are unexceptional as a matter of metaphysics, but a mystic's understanding of the claims may be very different from those who see the world in dualistic terms. Mystical knowledge may change mystics' understandings of the doctrines of their traditions. Mystical experiences may reinforce mystics' beliefs, but they also may alter those beliefs, leading to new interpretations of scriptural claims, though they may express new ideas in the tradition's old terms. Mystics are typically conservative about orthodox religious doctrines, but their teachings can also be innovative, renewing a tradition or leading to its evolution. In some cases, they may even be heretical.

Emotions driven by a false sense of a self—such as fear, envy, anger, greed, anxiety, and even self-centered joy—melt away as one realizes the true state of things and accepts them for what they are. Mystics enjoy the peace resulting from no longer constantly striving to manipulate reality to fit their artificial images and ego-driven emotions and desires. The emotional center shifts toward detachment, harmonious affections, and acceptance. They may or may not have an accompanying sense of awe, beauty, wonder, or amazement at the very existence of the world.

The serenity accompanying mystical illumination is not the happiness of fulfilling personal desires. Rather, it is a sense of peace and contentment at whatever is prevails, hence the common term *bliss*. Contemplative bliss is distinguished from ecstatic joy (BSS 3.3.14). Such joy may be central in the religious way of life for both the enlightened and unenlightened—as with Hasidic Jews and Hindu Bhaktas—or exuberant joy may be entirely absent. It is the inner calm or coolness of not being troubled by the vicissitudes of life that is the principal emotion connected to living a mystical life aligned with reality as it truly is. This gives mystical bliss an otherworldly air. Temporary joys and sorrows may still occur, but they are greeted with a detached, even-minded acceptance and can no longer dominate the inner life. The Daoist Zhuangzi saw his own grieving over the death of his wife as improper and countered by celebrating her transformation (Z 18). In the end, however, mystics neither grieve nor celebrate; they respond with an inner serenity to the events swirling around them. Physical pains and suffering may still occur to the enlightened even as the soul is at rest; in fact, the entire body may ache (*Interior Castle* 7.2.9–11). For Christians, the closer to God, the more the suffering. This is part of the imitation of Jesus's life that God grants (7.4.4–5). With this internal calm, external calm is desired less; one can deal with suffering and labor (7.4.10).

Much of the enlightened life of one who was on a mystical quest may seem quite ordinary to an observer; the enlightened enjoy all of life and typically follow a tradition's ethics, so their actions may not look all that different than those of an ordinary believer, although the actions may be performed more spontaneously and effortlessly. With the self seen as just another mental construct, this state has abiding traits induced by experiences that involve no sense of self. The enlightened's character traits may have only subtle changes if they were advanced on a mystical path before enlightenment.

However, when they act, enlightened introvertive mystics remain in touch with the transcendent reality that they have experienced, and they engage the world with mental clarity and calmness. Enlightened extrovertive mystics also have an inner stillness. The enlightened live in the world in a state of freedom from the attachments and concerns generated by a false sense of an individual phenomenal self, but their inner stillness is integrated in their extrovertive experiences. There is an openness to whatever occurs. The enlightened live with all attention focused on the present, free from imposing products of the background framework produced by the dichotomizing mind. With no predetermined expectations, they act without deliberation toward what is presented to them as their way of life and values dictate, indifferent to success or failure. In Zen, the action is called *non-dual* because there is no sense of duality between an independently real actor and an action.

Since the enlightened do not impose their will on things, they often react like many dying people who have accepted their impending death. With no self-image to maintain, they are free of any preoccupations or attachments; they accept things as they are and let go of personal desires. They feel that they have nothing to lose and no needs to fulfill; there are no future goals to achieve or any futures to plan for; they take joy in simple matters. Their values may change from self-centeredness and materialism toward concern for others; they no longer fear death, for being is eternal, and they may not care if they continue individually after death. (Of course, accepting one's impending death may crack one's sense of self and initiate a mystical selfless ASC.) They have more appreciation for being alive; life seems purposeful and meaningful even if no exact "meaning of life" is given. All is well with the world as it is, and there is no need to institute social changes; everything is an end in itself; things appear more beautiful. The enlightened become less judgmental and more accepting of others; they are more flexible and less competitive; they often feel an all-encompassing love and a tremendous sensitivity to other people's feelings and sufferings.

Enlightenment, Conceptualizations, and Language

The enlightened, despite their awareness and the inner stillness at the core of their being, are still aware of a world of distinctions. Thus, an enlightened state still involves differentiations—sense experiences, emotions, thoughts—even if the content is not configured into discrete objects. The enlightened are not in an unconscious trance, evidenced by the fact that enlightened mystics taught and left writings. Speaking involves words, and any language necessarily makes distinctions. While the ability to use language may be in abeyance during certain mystical experiences, the ability of a mystic to use language in the enlightened state shows that the enlightened do, in fact, make and understand distinctions. (The only alternative explanation is that the enlightened parrot back words mindlessly.) Thus, enlightenment is not a nonconceptual animal state. However, unlike the unenlightened, the enlightened do not project language's distinctions onto reality. Thereby, they avoid the creation of a false world of multiple discrete objects.

Thus, in the enlightened state there still is conceptual structuring, not a pure mindfulness, and the enlightened can still draw linguistic distinctions concerning the flux of phenomena without seeing the phenomena cut up into separate fixed entities. A famous Chan/Zen saying from Qingyuan Weixin (ninth century CE) goes: "Before my training, there were mountains and rivers; in the middle, there were no mountains and rivers; after completion, there were mountains and rivers again." That is, the unenlightened think that a mountain or a river is an entity independent of its surroundings; with extrovertive mystical experiences, it is evident that there are, in reality, no distinct objects for the terms *mountains* and *rivers* to apply to, only undifferentiated beingness; finally, in the enlightened state, the enlightened integrate the analytic mind into their life, seeing what is really there without thinking in terms of a set of independent entities corresponding to concepts. Once again, some phenomena can be referred to as *mountains* and *rivers* even if they are not unconnected to the rest of reality or permanent. Language then refers only to constantly changing eddies in the stream of phenomena. Thereby, the enlightened need not abandon language but can use it to navigate the world of diverse phenomena and to lead others toward enlightenment. Similarly, Zen Buddhists continue to think in the state they call *non-thinking*—they simply do not make discriminated phenomena into reified objects. Consciousness is purified and the mind is non-dual only in not setting up divisions among phenomena or between consciousness and what is perceived.

In sum, an enlightened mystic's experience of the world is still mediated by conceptual structuring, but that structuring is not taken as representing an objectified, pluralistic world of isolated items ontologically cut off from each other.

Mystical Metaphysics

If all that mattered to mystics was inducing experiences of selflessness or detachment or easing existential suffering, then mystical doctrines could be dismissed as only aids. However, classical mystics were not interested in the experiences themselves but in living aligned with reality. To do that, mystics need to understand what they have experienced in order to incorporate the reality into their life. In fact, some philosophically minded mystics have advanced elaborate theories.[24] Metaphysics in mystical traditions typically arises not from reflecting on mystical experiences alone but from a mixture of mystical and non-mystical ideas concerning reality and other considerations in a given religious and cultural framework. Some doctrines are more closely tied to interpreting mystical experiences than others. For example, in Buddhism the no-self doctrine is closer to direct experiences than the Abhidharmists' theories, which advanced to explain the continuity of rebirths and karmic effects that are distant in time. Likewise, mystical doctrines within a religious tradition may be developed by non-mystics without any continuing mystical experiential input.

Mystical experiences involve a sense of having experienced something irreducible and, thus, ultimate,[25] but not all mystical metaphysics are the same. The experiences do not give specific doctrines, and both mystics and non-mystics require some speculation to fit what is allegedly experienced in ASCs into their way of life. But mystical theories are not products of detached philosophical speculation: mysticism is a matter of experiences, practices, and usually religious considerations, not mere intellectual acceptance of some metaphysical ideas. It is a way of life, not a belief system. Conversely, adopting a metaphysical system that mystics also utilize does not make a person a mystic in the sense employed here.

On the level of the world, a mystic may focus on the common substance of phenomena or, as in Buddhism, on the perpetual change of phenomenal forms; that is, one can focus on the unchanging *being* or on the perpetually changing *becoming*. In the depth-mystical experience, one's consciousness is unified in a non-dual state, and the experiencer feels an objectivity and certainty to the experience, but as noted earlier with regard to consciousness, there are different understandings of the nature of what is experienced:

- Non-Dualisms: Only one reality exists (Brahman, Godhead); the phenomenal world is an emanation of this reality or is an unreal "dream."

- Dualistic Theisms: God supplies all being, but creation (the natural world) and persons remain realities distinct from God even though they are dependent upon God for their existence and, thus, are not independently real.

- Pluralisms: There are multiple transcendent selves, each existing independently.

- Naturalism: Only the self or the natural realm exists, and its being is experienced; no transcendent realities are involved.

A theistic mystic may take God to be ever-present in everything as both the ground of the phenomenal realm and the active ground of love in some or all people. Emanation figures prominently in many mystical traditions, but it is a matter of ontological dependence rather than a temporal outpouring of creation. (As noted earlier, pantheism is not espoused by any classical mystics.) The emanated reality still has a transcendent source in some sense—it supplies a being or essence. If a transcendent reality is taken to be the source of a person or all the phenomenal world, that reality is taken to be ineffable both in the sense that it encompasses more than can be expressed/conceived and in that terms for the phenomenal do not literally apply (including being personal in nature).

The Mystical Traditions of the World

There is no disembodied, universal mystical tradition present in all the world. Moreover, no religion's mystical tradition is monolithic: there is no one homogenous Christian mysticism but different Christian forms of mysticism even within the same era and culture. Not all of Hinduism can be reduced to Advaita or to Vaishnava theism, let alone all Asian traditions to one abstract Oriental mysticism. Some subtraditions within the same religion are more devotional, while some are more wisdom oriented.[26] Conceptions of transcendent realities, rewards and punishments, ethical norms, and practices within these subtraditions may also evolve. There are many variations and exceptions in every religious tradition and antinomians in all theistic traditions. Different mystical groups within the same religion often disagree over doctrines and practices. (Buddhism first split over monastic rules, not doctrines.) Some doctrines may be common enough to most schools to be called "official" for an entire tradition. Nevertheless, the understandings of the doctrines in each school lead to significant differences and disputes. So, too, there are non-mystical influences: in all the world religions, mystical experiences interact with non-mystical elements of practices, values, beliefs, and soteriological goals. Cross-fertilization from other mystical traditions occurs in all traditions.

Likewise, all religions have mystical traditions; people having mystical experiences have, no doubt, been present from the beginning of each world religion, and all traditions have accommodated mystics to one degree or another. The influence of mystics on religious doctrines is especially great in Asian religions, but even with a mainstream view of the absolute otherness of God, the Abrahamic traditions all have had vibrant mystical traditions in the past. In fact, a scholar of Judaism, Brian Lancaster, has said: "There is effectively no such thing as 'non-mystical Judaism'" (2005, 14). In the Abrahamic traditions, salvation is not achieved by mystical enlightenment, unlike in most Buddhist and Hindu traditions, but many Christians see mystics as living the Christian life to the fullest. Most mystics remain orthodox. In Christianity, 10 percent of medieval saints were mystics (Kroll and Bachrach 2005, 203). Indeed, a strong case can be made that many Christian beliefs are merely mystical doctrines formulated dogmatically (Louth 1981, xi), but many mystics were also in tension with the established traditions of their time. Some reacted to the apparent worldliness of the faithful; some, including women, presented a challenge to the power of those in charge.

Some of Meister Eckhart's teachings were declared to be tainted with the "stain of heresy." The Christian Marguerite Porete (1250–1310) was burned at the stake for heresy, and the Muslim Husayn al-Hallaj (d. 922) was executed for exclaiming "I am the Real!"

Chapter 2

The Prehistory of Mysticism

Mysticism as a complex way of life dedicated to cultivating a mystical alignment with reality may have arisen only with rise of developed societies, but there is no reason to believe that mystical experiences did. Nothing at present suggests that the neurology that permits mystical experiences developed only within recorded history. And it is safe to say that once psychedelic plants and animals were discovered, some mystical experiences occurred. Experiences resulting from emptying the mind of conceptual control do not require any form of cultural or social organization and so can predate the rise of complex societies.[1] The long presence of an oral tradition in Hinduism for basic religious texts even after writing was invented shows that written texts are not necessary to mysticism. But mysticism does require societies where there is a separation of labor so that religious specialists can teach mysticism.

Thus, we should look to see if there are experiences or practices suggesting mysticism in preliterate tribal societies. This brings up the connection of shamans' practices and experiences with psychedelic plants and animals. Sources for this section include anthropological studies of the current practices of tribal societies, oral traditions, and archeological information of preliterate societies.

Shamanism

Beginning in the Stone Age, shamans were the religious specialists of nomadic and seminomadic foraging hunter-gatherer societies.[2] Anthropologists find shamans in almost all tribal societies, not merely those of Central Asia and Siberia from which the term *shaman* comes.[3] Shamans appear to be a universal in these societies, thriving in much the same form in cultures with unconnected languages and no social contact, rather than the result of diffusion from one early society. Evidence from graves, rock carvings, and cave paintings suggests that shamanic practices existed well over ten thousand years ago and even into the Paleolithic period (Clottes and Lewis-Williams 1998, Lewis-Williams and Pearce 2005), although extrapolations from hunter-gatherer societies are controversial.[4] Shang kings in early China (ca. 1700 BCE) may have been shamans. Among American Indians of the Northern Plains and Southwest, shamanic experiences played an important role into the nineteenth century (for example, in the Ghost Dance). Shamans exist today in societies in Siberia, Mongolia, the Himalayas, Africa, Australia, Oceania, and the Americas.

In hunter-gatherer and pastoral tribe societies, shamans help maintain their society—for example, by divining the location of game or determining when to plant—and help the society to live in overall harmony with nature. They gain paranormal powers, such as making it rain and otherwise affecting the weather. Shamans also help individuals. They have visions and locutions pertinent to an individual's needs as well as the group's. They are healers who enter ASCs and travel to spirit realms to retrieve the souls of the sick and speak to the dead, guiding the dead to the realm of the spirits.[5] They placate angry spirits, perform exorcisms, and fight evil spirits or the actions of other shamans. They may be telepathic or clairvoyant. They may be oracles, fortune tellers, sorcerers, or mediums in contact with ancestors. As charismatic leaders of a society, they oversee rituals that maintain social order like individuals' rites of passage. Their tasks in some societies include maintaining the oral history and secret lore of the community and mediating disputes. In some societies, shamans, through their inner power, kill those who have offended them. Many are experts on psychedelic and healing plants. They have a special connection with animals and know the secret languages of the animals, documented in cave paintings being found today. That many of these paintings were created on the walls of caves away from residences and hidden in darkness suggests secrecy.[6]

Shamanism is not one religion or set of beliefs but a matter of techniques and purposes within different societies. Not all societies with shamans have the same worldview or ethos. However, some generalizations can be made about the neolithic worldviews of hunter-gatherer societies. First, they had a three-tiered cosmos (with various sublevels) consisting of the world we occupy and two realms of spirits: a positive, tent-like realm above the world and a negative underworld below. (The two spirit realms should not to be confused with Western notions of the paradise of heaven and the realm of suffering of hell; we arise from the lower world.) The shaman's society was located at the center of the visible world with the *axis mundi*—a world tree or a pillar connecting the three tiers—and they were the "holy people" or, indeed, the only people. The neolithic worldview was animistic and anthropomorphic: invisible spirits occupied humans, plants, animals, and the inanimate natural world (Winkelman 2021, 50–51). The world was seen as sacred in that it was inhabited by spirits and pervaded by a universal vital force. This force connected everything, and shamans could tap into it in a trance. Deities were the ancestors of the group. These communities accepted an all-powerful creator god, but it typically played no role in the daily communal life of the group.

The shaman's world is performance-oriented: vital matters are expressed visually in symbols and art, and their powers are activated in rituals in which the shamans enter an altered state of consciousness and become a spirit or fly to the spirit realms. There are rituals for everything from healing individuals to meeting the communal needs of the tribe. There are rituals for creating all things of significance to the tribe, through which shamans in the present actively participate in and reactualize major acts of creation from the past; they do not merely reenact or commemorate them. The ethos of shamanic practices is oriented toward this world: shamans' focus is on helping people in this world, not on the afterlife. To communicate with the spirit world and to accomplish their tasks, shamans need the help of spirit guides and guardian spirits in their dreams, visions, and bodiless journeys. They also become connected to the spirits in animals by wearing their skins, which allow shamans to transform and become the animal spirit. Likewise, they become connected to cosmic powers by utilizing symbols. For these societies, symbols do not merely represent or point to some reality; symbols participate in the reality they symbolize, and shamans can participate in the reality through them.

Shamanic Altered States of Consciousness

What set shamans apart from other religious specialists are their ASC journeys to the higher and lower spirit realms. Shamans enter states of ecstasy (apparently at will) to perform many of their tasks by attaining power or knowledge through contact with the hidden realities of the spirit worlds. As Mircea Eliade said, the shaman is the "great master of ecstasy" (1972, 4). By leaving their bodies in a trance, shamans can travel freely between this world and the spirit realms by flight or by climbing a pillar (the *axis mundi*) or traveling through portals or tunnels connecting the upper and lower worlds with this world.

Shamanism may have developed as a socially positive way of utilizing the ASCs occurring from indigenous plants and other triggers. Paleolithic communal nighttime campfire rituals that focused attention (which other hominids did not practice) may have affected parts of the brain as meditation does and played a role in the origin of modern human cognition (Rossano 2007, 2009). The early communal rituals organized around shamanic inducement of ASCs also reenforced in-group social bonding. One study of forty-seven societies spanning 1750 BCE (the Babylonians) to the present found that they all used ASCs for religious and healing practices (Harner 1973, ix). We routinely dismiss experiences in states of consciousness altered from our baseline state of consciousness as being, by definition, delusional since we consider the most common ASCs (dreaming, some illnesses, and being drunk) to produce only delusions. Only the ordinary sober state of consciousness is deemed cognitive. But in societies valuing shamans, ASCs are valued as cognitively equal or superior to the baseline state of consciousness; the shaman's dreams and other experiences are at least as real as perceptions occurring in an ordinary state of consciousness.

The basic shamanic ritual takes place community-wide and at night. Shamans prepare for their rituals through austerities such as fasting, dehydration, exposure to extreme temperatures, and sleep deprivation. In a typical shamanic nighttime session, first an appeal is made to spirit helpers, allies, and guardians (typically animals or birds) and a dialog with them in a secret language ensues. Next, drumming, chanting, and dancing prepare for the shaman's "soul journey."[7] The shaman collapses in an ASC state, during which the shaman's soul leaves their body or is transformed into an animal and enters the spirit worlds. (Out-of-body flights are not part of North American Indian shamanism.) Such shape-shifting is depicted in art on cave walls—for example, man into lion—from the last Ice Age.[8]

Others in the society may also enter ASCs, but only the shaman voluntarily enters this state and controls it, unlike the involuntary and passive spirit possession mediums experience. Being able to enter and leave these

ASCs (sometimes with the aid of other shamans or assistants) without losing consciousness is crucial to being a shaman. They are "masters of the spirits" (Pharo 2011, 41). They retain their personalities and control the spirits, not vice versa (48), and they are the only ones to undertake a voluntary journey to the supernatural realms (46). Attaining this ecstasy is necessary since only in that state can a shaman leave the body and fly to the higher spirit realm or descend into the underworld to fulfill their mission of curing illness or shepherding souls.

The path to becoming a shaman begins in childhood with youths who show signs of mental instability—this means that the youth's soul is able to be carried away by spirits—but only those youths who are able to control negative and dangerous alternations proceed onward to become shamans. Most, but not all, shamans are men. Their arduous training typically includes a vision quest, usually undergone alone. The initiatory ritual often involves the ASC triggers noted in the next paragraph, as well as preparation such as fasting, social isolation, or abstaining from sex. The ritual is one of death and rebirth: the candidate seems to die, ascend and descend to the spirit realms, and then return to this world. Visions of being chopped up and reassembled by spirits, torn apart and devoured by animals, or having their bones cleaned or their eyes plucked from their sockets are common.

Once practicing, a shaman utilizes many different techniques to activate the spirit powers in ASCs. These ASCs are usually called *trances* by Westerners, but shamans remain conscious during these experiences—they are in states of awareness although the body is not moving. In moderately altered states, shamans remain aware of their physical surroundings; in deep states, shamans appear rigid and dead to observers but remain acutely aware of higher or lower realms. Their experiences often are so intense that the experiencers take them as undoubtably real. Shamans also lose awareness of the everyday world (die) when they journey (fly, ride, ascend) to the spirit realms. Shamans' experiences in the other realms are described as visions and dreams. The content of their experiences most likely differs from culture to culture due to differences in beliefs and practices, even if the experiences are based in common neural features of the brain.[9] It is likely that at least part of the content of shamanic visions is culturally dependent, as Christian visionaries typically do not see Krishna and Hindu visionaries typically do not see Mary. A Shipibo shaman of the Amazon would not see the Oglala Sioux Great Father of Black Elk's vision. Likewise, how shamans react to their visions and act afterward depends on their culture's values and practices.

Psychedelic Drugs in Religious History

Some triggers of shamanic and mystical altered states of consciousness were mentioned earlier. These and other triggers include: ritualized chanting (constantly repeating short phrases); ritualized rhythmic drumming (drums and rattles being the shaman's principal tools, acting as the "boats" that transport shamans to the spirit worlds); rhythmic rocking and dancing; sensory deprivation in darkness (like in caves); overstimulation through music and singing (although people creating a general dissonant noise does not usually work to achieve sensory overload); strenuous physical exertion leading to exhaustion; mental techniques to still the rational activities of the mind by depriving the mind of new input (such as endlessly working on a riddle); isolation; enduring extreme pain; physical and verbal punishment; stress (especially among the young); long vigils and sleep deprivation; near-death experiences; hyperventilation.[10]

One traditional trigger deserves special attention because of its widespread use, both inside and outside of shamanic traditions, and its resurrection in research on mystical experiences in neuroscience today: psychedelic drugs.[11] Drugs that touch off a sense of the divine in a large percentage of users are called, in a term invented in 1979, *entheogens*: "generating God within." Their effects usually arise much faster than with the other triggers. Over a hundred natural psychedelic plants, fungi, and animals have been identified (for example, the Colorado River toad's poison contains DMT and Bufotenin). The most familiar ones today are peyote cactus (mescaline), certain mushrooms (psilocybin), cannabis, coca, opium poppies, and the ayahuasca brew (DMT) from the Amazon and Orinoco rainforests.[12] Psychedelic mushrooms were especially important and were common throughout temperate regions in prehistoric times (Winkelman 2019). Plants with DMT were also once common throughout the Mediterranean region. They were used as medicine or in carefully crafted rituals. Their mind-altering effects were probably discovered by accident early in human evolution (as, no doubt, were these effects on the mind from hunger, fatigue, and so forth). All of these "flesh of the gods" or "sacred medicines" are found wild and do not require cultivation, but they apparently became more popular in agricultural societies of the Paleolithic era than in roaming hunter-gather societies. In fact, there is evidence that psychedelics were among the first plants that human beings domesticated—indeed, perhaps the first—rather than foodstuffs (Rudgley 1993, 140–41).

Experiences from psychedelic drugs may not have been merely an incidental byproduct but may have had adaptive genetic advantages for humans' early evolution (see Winkelman 2014).[13] Terence McKenna (1992) argues that psychedelic plants played an important role in stimulating the evolution of the modern human brain through mutations caused by the drugs, thereby altering our consciousness. To have that wide of an effect, such plants would have to have been consumed by more than only a few shamans in each tribe. Use of psychedelics may account for some of the divergence between human and chimpanzee neurology (Winkelman 2010). Some scholars argue that drug-enabled brain states were catalysts for the development of our general cognitive abilities related to linguistic thinking, abstract thinking (as indicated by the use of symbols), and reasoning as well as imagination and integrating nonverbal corporeal, visual, and auditory information in visions (Weil 1986; Wasson et al. 1986; Winkelman 2013, 2017). Others argue that such drug-enabled visions explain why human beings have an ability to think symbolically that other primates do not have and that, from their use in the context of shamanic practices, such drugs were the source of art and poetry (see, for example, Lewis-Williams and Pearce 2005). Some scholars see psychedelic experiences as a cause of philosophy and, in fact, of all culture in Greece and India.

Neo-animists in anthropology see drug-related shamanic practices as the origin of religion, not social or material needs. Ecstasy-based shamanism was the ur-religion from which all historical religions evolved (see Forte 1997, Roberts 2001). Others have also claimed that mystical experiences or drug-enabled ASCs are the origin of religion (Stace 1960a; Newberg, d'Aquili, and Rause 2002, 133–40). However, today most anthropologists studying early and preliterate societies tend to see the origin of religion without appeal to such experiences; religion, including belief in anthropomorphized supernatural agents who are like us but more powerful, is seen as a natural evolutionary byproduct of social interactions. More must have been involved in producing all the complex cultural phenomena of religion since religion is much more than cultivating ASC experiences. Thus, advocates of psychedelics may want to revise their historical claim to emphasize that profound drug-enabled shamanic ASC experiences were either the source of or a major reinforcement of the ideas of a soul independent of the body, life after death, spirits, heaven and hell, grace, and forces behind nature. The social role of such ASC experiences does suggest that these religious beliefs were formed in conjunction with them. In addition, some supportive beliefs may have preceded, or co-existed with, the religious significance and meaning of these experiences in early religion. But at a minimum, shamanic practices constitute one of the oldest surviving forms of religiosity, and shamanic ASC experiences reenforced the idea of transcendent realities.

In any case, drug-enabled ASC experiences appear to have been part of religion since its early days (Winkelman 1999). The discovery of psychedelic plants no doubt predates written history. Various statues and rock carvings strongly suggest their use. For example, cave paintings in northern Algeria from around 5000 BCE show human beings with mushrooms (Richards 2016, 7). Evidence is found in early Mesoamerica, sub-Saharan and northern Africa (including Egypt), Anatolia, Greece, and Crete and even from the Paleolithic era in territories from Europe to China. Some Neanderthal graves also contain psychedelic plants. The fly-agaric mushroom was apparently used by shamans in Siberia as well as in the Baltics and Scandinavia. Germanic tribes apparently used opium poppies in rituals.

In mythology, there are vestiges of shamanic practices including evidence of psychedelic drug use (Wasson et al. 1986). Greeks may have imported the role of shamanic ASCs from Central Asia through Scythia to the northeast, Asia Minor, or even India, or it may have been indigenous. Robert Graves suggested that the ambrosia of pre-Hellenic tribes that gave the Gods their immortality was the fly-agaric mushroom. The lotus of the Lotus-Eaters in the *Odyssey* has yet to be identified, but it is also described as having a psychedelic effect. In the second-millennium BCE, the Maenads worshiped the god of wine, Dionysus, and utilized wine and other drugs in their rituals. (Fermented honey, mead, predates this and was utilized in the Greek world and Western Europe.) Initiates in the Eleusinian Mysteries fasted and then drank a brew (*kykeon*) in a darkened temple of Demeter whose central component may have been a fungus ergot parasite in barley or rye that had psychedelic properties similar to LSD's.[14] This produced visions of a goddess. Apollo's Pythia oracles at Delphi may have uttered their prophecies under the influence of psychedelic ethylene vapors emanating from fissures in the earth.

As societies became more complex, drug-enabled shamanic states and some shamanic practices were dropped from the mainstream in various world religions in favor of more sedate practices. But references to their continued use have survived in early texts. In India, almost 12 percent of the hymns in the late second millennium BCE *Rig Veda*—including all of one of its ten books—are devoted to *soma* (Old Persian, *haoma*), a psychedelic concoction used in rituals, and it is referred to in many other hymns (see Jones 2014a, 22–29, 170–71). Indeed, *soma* permeates the *Rig Veda*, and its ritual was the original central ritual of the Vedic religion. It is the only plant deified in Indian texts. The god Soma was the power in the drug. It gave Indra his strength and fury in his struggle with the dragon Vritra. It stimulated poets and warriors. It induced ecstasy. It had healing powers and bestowed immortality. What exactly the plant or plants were is no longer known—by the time the Aryans settled in northwest India, *soma* rituals were still performed but with non-mind-altering substitutes[15]—but Vedic hymns still reveal the ecstasy from drinking the brew that gives immortality.

The *Rig Veda* presents a stage of cultural development where priests had taken over some of the functions of shamans. Separating one's soul from the body and soul flights are not prominent themes, but one Vedic hymn is devoted to a long-haired ascetic flying through the sky (RV 10.136; Jones 2014a, 27–28). This hymn sticks out as strange in the Vedic corpus; it may have been included in the *Rig Veda* because its compilers felt compelled to acknowledge that ecstatic experiences were continuing in society below the level of the high Vedic ritual culture, perhaps from indigenous sources. After Vedism, only informal references to psychedelic drug use are recorded in later Hinduism. For example, the god Shiva, the "lord of herbs," is often portrayed with the psychedelic datura flower in his hand. He is also portrayed as blue-throated, perhaps a reference to the stem of certain psychoactive mushrooms; his early temples are also mushroomed-shaped. Buddhism condemned getting intoxicated as interfering with a mindful state, but there is evidence of psychedelic use in its Indian history. (Psychedelics may not have been seen as clouding the mind but giving clarity.) Later Hindu and Buddhist Tantrics retained the use of psychedelic drugs (including cannabis). Tantric traditions are the last traditions within the world religions where psychedelic experiences are considered useful.

In the West, psychedelic drugs appear to have been part of the Greco-Roman Mystery cults whose popularity peaked early in the Common Era, but non-mystical forms of religion won out in Judaism, Christianity, and Islam. There is archeological evidence of shamanism in the Galilee region predating the rise of Judaism, and some events in the Bible can be interpreted as shamanic: Jonah being swallowed by a lower-world spirit ally (a whale); Elijah rising to the upper world by a chariot; Jacob's ladder connecting the earth and upper world; and hearing the voice of God. (Ladder symbolism is common in mystics' accounts of their ascent to the transcendent.[16]) The story of the forbidden fruit of the tree of knowledge of good and evil in the Garden of Eden may have evolved from tales of psychedelic herbs that were forbidden to the general population. Additionally, Moses's encounter on Mount Sinai with a voice coming from a burning bush that was not consumed but which made his face shine brightly may have been drug-enabled (for example, Shanon 2008). Some biblical passages suggest spirit possession (for example, 1 Samuel 18:10).

Dan Merkur (2001) has proposed that the manna that the Israelites received from heaven in Exodus was a psychedelic and became the "hidden manna" in medieval Christianity that is usually interpreted as a symbol for contemplation. Some scholars suggest that the frankincense or myrrh given by the wise men (*magi*) to honor the birth of Jesus contained one or more psychedelics. Some also theorize that the original Eucharist was a psychedelic sacrament. John Allegro (2009) went so far as to deny that Jesus actually existed, claiming instead that he was only a literary device to spread the knowledge of the sacred mushroom. There is also some evidence that psychedelics played a role in the religious life of early Middle Eastern Christians and that some medieval European Christians were initiated into a secret tradition, as perhaps occurred also in Islam (Ruck 2006, Shanon 2008, Muraresku 2020). Christianity in the Greek world may have been influenced by the mysteries of the Eleusinian Mystery cult that lasted until 392 CE when the Christian emperor Theodosius banned it. Medieval Kabbalah medical texts refer to the hidden powers of some psychedelics such as mandrake. (Such theories are, of course, controversial; most Jews, Christians, and Muslims are not willing even to consider the possibility that hearing the voice of God and so forth might be merely drug-enabled hallucinations.) In modern America, psychedelics may have played a role in the founding of the Church of Jesus Christ of Latter-Day Saints (Mormonism) (Beckstead et al. 2017). Today, a few Christian churches make psychedelics part of their ceremonies (for example, the Santo Daime churches in Brazil), and some advocates of psychedelics are trying to make them part of mainstream religious ceremonies (for example, Roberts 2012, Richards 2016).

Shamanism and Mystical Experiences

Scholars routinely call shamanic practices the "earliest form of mysticism" and shamans the "first mystics" (for example, Walsh 1990, 215), but shamanism does not fit narrow definitions of mysticism, including the one utilized in this book. The important shamanic ASC experiences are not central to mysticism, and shamans did not seek mysticism's selfless experiences free of differentiated content. Shamans' important experiences remain visions and out-of-body flights. Their ASC states are not fundamentally the same as those of mystics, although mystics do occasionally mention the flight of the soul from the body (for example, Enn. VI.7.34, VI.9.11; *Interior Castle* 133–37). The community's role in inducing shamans' experiences is not central to mysticism, although there are some group meditative practices. Over the course of time, some mystics did become leaders and healers, but the central role that shamans play in the life of these societies is not replicated by most mysticisms. Shamans enter ASCs for the benefit of others or the community, not to gain knowledge themselves, as in mysticism.

Cultivating ASCs to transcend the baseline state of consciousness may be a cultural universal; there seems to be an innate human desire to alter our consciousness (Walsh 1990, 14). If so, mystics are not necessarily drawing on earlier shamanic practices simply because they too alter their normal waking consciousness. Scholars of shamanic traditions tend to assume that shamanic and mystical ASC experiences are the same, claiming the experiences differ in the degree that they alter the mind but not in type. However, not all ecstatic experiences are of the same type, nor can we assume that all shamanic ASCs are the same, nor can all ASC experiences simply be labeled *shamanic*. Mystics tend to devalue precisely the types of experiences that shamans undergo, valuing as cognitive only those ASC experiences that are devoid of images and voices. That shamanic visions do not involve a transcendent source of a person or the phenomenal world's being also distinguishes these experiences from introvertive mystical experiences. Shamanic visions do not involve seeing the world as a manifestation of consciousness or a transcendent spirit, and shamanic experiences are not experiences of consciousness alone. Likewise, extrovertive mystical experiences do not involve visions; they involve loosening the boundaries that the conceptual mind sets up in human perceptions, but they are not experiences of a reality set apart from an experiencer and nature as in a vision. Extrovertive mystics do not journey to a realm of spirits or otherwise gain access to spirits but see the natural world differently when conceptual barriers are lowered. Nothing suggests that shamans, after their visions, are in an enlightened extrovertive state of consciousness. Shamans cultivate emotional states; they do not attempt to quell them with even-mindedness and detachment.

Jess Byron Hollenback points out two reasons why Lakota shamans do not seek "formless" mystical states: visions are sought to obtain useful information from spirit beings, and thus there is no reason to cultivate states in which forms and images are altogether absent; preliterate tribal religions also assume that the divine becomes manifested through the phenomena of the natural world. The notion of divine realities that utterly transcend the natural world and cannot be represented by any image or metaphor derived from nature has not yet made their way into these tribes' religious imaginations (1996, 613–14, 354–55). Their worldviews and values simply have no place for the realities experienced in introvertive mystical experiences or for cultivating an "empty" awareness.

Psychedelic drugs do not change the picture. They more typically enable visions—of various types of spirits and shape-shifting beings (Davis et al. 2020)—than mystical experiences empty of all conceptualized content, but these drugs can enable mystical experiences: drugs can break the hold on us that the dualizing mind driven by the sense of a self has by altering the blood flow of the brain in relevant areas. This can permit extrovertive and introvertive mystical experiences as well as other ASC experiences, but what fills the mind after our baseline consciousness is disrupted depends on factors outside the drug effects (see Jones 2019). Shamanic experiences fit better in the *visions* category even if no transcendent source is involved.

The techniques that shamans utilize to induce their ASCs may open the mind to mystical experiences, but as Roger Walsh notes, shamans traditionally aim for experiences of soul travel in spirit realms, and few have explored mystical experiences (1990, 241). Conversely, mystical practices may open mystics' minds to other experiences, such as visions or paranormal powers, but these remain experiences that are not ultimately valued by most traditional mystics. There may be common elements to both types of experiences—like loss of a sense of time—but the experiences overall remain distinct. Ninian Smart noted that studies of contemporary nonliterate societies of his time did "not reveal the presence of much of any mysticism proper"; for example, in the Nuer tribe in Sudan, only prophecy and other shamanic experiences occur (1967, 420). In 1990, Walsh had found no references to "mystical union" in any study of shamans (1990, 239), nor has anyone reported any since. Walsh also detailed the differences between shamans' experiences, Yoga's concentrative-type mystical experiences, and Buddhism's mindfulness-type mystical experiences (as well as the differences between shamanic states and schizophrenia) (223–32), though he considers all three mystical.

Shamanism is not Primitive Mysticism

In sum, both shamanic and mystical ways of life incorporate an inner turn that cultivates ASCs, but different types of experiences are considered central and their ways of life have different objectives. Thus, even if shamans do have some mystical experiences, it is difficult to see shamans as prototypes of meditators, yogins, and other mystics or to claim that mysticism—ways of life oriented toward aligning one's life with reality through mystical experiences—began in shamanic practices. Thus, although mystical experiences no doubt occurred in early societies, shamanism is not primitive mysticism: shamanism is a set of practices and techniques oriented around other goals and experiences. The role of shamans in their societies differs from mystics' place in theirs, and mystical experiences were not incorporated into their social practice. At most, shamanism is a precursor to mysticism or proto-mystical only in the weak sense of enabling societies to take ASC experiences to be socially valuable.

Mysticisms as ways of life more likely only appeared after the development of specialized religious professionals in the Axial Age (ca. 800–200 BCE) that replaced any all-encompassing shamanism. When cities arose, societies became more complex and stratified, and cultures became more differentiated, with different specialists taking over different functions of the shamans (for example, as priests, healers, and mediums). It is also reasonable to suppose that mysticism developed in the worldviews of the Axial Age with their ideas of a transcendent source of the natural world that is directly open to experience, unlike the earlier Neolithic worldviews in which shamanisms thrived. Mystical experiences apparently acquired importance at this stage of cultural evolution as validating eternal, unchanging realities and providing stability in a world of change (Ellwood 2012, 58–59). Thus, mysticisms as ways of life cultivating these experiences most likely developed at that stage. Shamanism's social role began to be given less significance at that time, so the paradigmatic shamanic ASC experiences did not play a central role in more complex societies, perhaps being suppressed by priests or others. Mystics prioritized different ASC experiences and personal goals that led to emphasizing meditative practices to alter the human state of consciousness.

But again, even if shamanism is not a form of mysticism, it did institutionalize ASCs and psychedelic drugs as having positive roles in society. It may also have led to widespread beliefs about transcendent realities. Some shamanic techniques for altering consciousness were adopted in early ascetic and yogic practices and so survived into later mystical traditions such as the whirling dervishes of Islam and the Tantric use of drugs in India. Some are natural cultural universals and cannot be attributed to shamanism alone as the source. Aspects of early tribal worldviews were adapted into later worldviews (for example, the *axis mundi* became Mount Meru in Indic mythology). The idea of a power pervading all the natural world, breaking down the division between transcendent and nature, also occurs in mysticism (including Daoism and cosmic consciousness experiences). Mystics, too, may have visions and out-of-body experiences, evinced by Daoist masters riding in chariots drawn by dragons to the heavens. However, the centrality of different types of experiences and goals precludes shamanism from being a type of mysticism.

Chapter 3

Mysticism in Classical Greek Philosophy

After the pastoral and agricultural stages of social evolution came early urbanization, expanding industry and trade between cultures. With this came what Karl Jaspers labeled the pivotal Axial Age, touched upon in the last chapter. This age lasted from around 800 to 200 BCE. For reasons currently unknown, religious thought in Greece, West Asia, India, and China in this period all took a turn toward realities that transcend this world and took interest in an individual's fate after death. A society's gods began to merge into one god or a transcendent nonpersonal principle. All of today's world religions became rooted in this period. Now supported by the invention of writing, thinkers engaged in critical reflection on their earlier cultures, especially in Greece and India. People were also more aware of other peoples, and this may have prompted a more universal outlook on humanity and the cosmos and a search for what is ultimately real, although each civilization responded differently in this new intellectual environment. The distinction between reality and its manifestation (appearance) entered human thought, and the distinction between subject and object became clearer. In a new development to consciousness, self-awareness may also have first arisen then.[1] Middle Eastern texts began to appear in or just before the Axial period. The earliest surviving Indo-European texts from this period—the Vedas, Brahmanas, and Aranyakas from India and the *Avesta* from Iran—were composed at the end of the pre-Axial period and beginning of the Axial period (ca. 1200–700 BCE). These texts show only hints of mysticism. Rituals remained prominent in religious activity, but an inward turn also took place for some thinkers. By 500 BCE, texts indicate developing mysticisms, most obviously in India and China.

Greek philosophers in this period had a more secularized concern for the world's natural order. A concern for society also was important. They reinterpreted earlier mythologies and criticized anthropomorphism in religion. Greek philosophers in the Axial Age sought a single nonpersonal principle, beyond the gods, that was responsible for the existence of things, a deep unity of which the many divine powers were but manifestations (Kenney 1997, 324). This took a naturalistic turn, replacing *mythos* with a rational nonpersonal underlying order within the universe (*logos*). Philosophers' interest in rational explanations of the fundamental nature of the phenomenal universe and its contents led to seeking law-governed causes within nature—rather than the will of the gods or supernatural beings inhabiting nature—enabling explanations of the workings of nature in natural terms. This eventually made knowledge a matter of observation and reasoning, not ASC experiences, leading to an interest in medicine, science, and mathematics that turned away from possible transcendent matters. For example, Democritus (b. ca. 460 BCE) explained ecstatic trance states as abnormal physiological states characterized by the rapid motion of atoms.

Nothing in the historical records suggests that mysticism was a factor in the rise of the new naturalist outlook, but it was in this cultural setting that mysticism, with its inward focus, entered Greek history.

Was There Mysticism in Early Greek Philosophy?

Friedrich Nietzsche believed that all Greek philosophers, from the pre-Socratics to the Neoplatonists, were mystics. Indeed, the objective of all philosophy for him is an *intuitio mystica*. Some more recent scholars, such as Pierre Hadot, agree (see Stròżyński 2008, 25–31). However, most scholars today claim that there was no mysticism in early Greek culture. At that time, the word *mystical* referred only to the esoteric mysteries of the Mystery cults. What role these cults may have played in the transition of Greek thought from mythology to philosophy is a matter of debate. These cults showed some shamanic elements, but whether they had an interest in mysticism proper or in philosophy is not clear.

Today, philosophers treat Heraclitus, Parmenides, and Plato as non-mystical philosophers whose thought was based solely on reason and ordinary experiences. Heraclitus's claim that "all is in flux" would be agreeable to extrovertive mystics, but non-mystical naturalists can also readily accept that. So too, Parmenides's ideas that "all reality is one" and "time and change are unreal" could be mystical in origin—introvertive mystics may well agree—or only the result of reasoning about what could be real. One can espouse mystical-sounding metaphysical doctrines without having had mystical ASCs. For example, a century ago the Cambridge philosopher J. M. E. McTaggart argued that time is unreal for reasons completely unconnected to ASC experiences.[2] More generally, scientists and philosophers can argue for unities without a mystical state of consciousness ever being involved. Naturalists' doctrines will differ since they view phenomena in terms of interacting entities, but mystical and non-mystical doctrines will use the same language of oneness. However, mystics can also reason in mindful or ordinary states of consciousness once thought returns: ecstatic mystical experiences do not render someone incapable of rational thought in all states of consciousness (see Jones 2016, 233–60). In short, one can be both a mystic and a philosopher—it is not an either/or proposition. Mystics simply have a different set of allegedly cognitive experiences from which they work, expanding their views of reality and what is fundamentally real.

There is also evidence to suggest that some Greek philosophers came up with their ideas based on experiences in mystical ASCs. First, the influence of shamanic phenomena on Greek culture must be noted (see Dodds 2004) even if they are not directly mystical.[3] As noted in the last chapter, shamanic influence may have come from the North, from Anatolia, or elsewhere—there is currently no evidence of indigenous Greek shamanic traditions—and, as discussed in the last chapter, shamanic practices open up the mind to ASCs. Visions and voices were central in shamanism, but there may also have been mystical experiences. Ecstasy (*ekstasis*)—literally, "standing outside of oneself"—and being possessed by a god (*enthousiasmos*) were valued in early Greece. As Plotinus put it, this involves a "kind of seeing when one is out of oneself" (Enn. VI.9.11). Songs and poetry, unlike prose, were seen as coming from divine inspiration. Apollo, himself a shamanic figure connected with flight, was seen as a source of poetic inspiration. Seers and oracles also may have had ASC experiences. Mystery cults dating from at least 1500 BCE probably included psychedelics or ASC practices in their initiation ceremonies and rituals in caves. These were labeled *mystery* (*mysterion*) because members kept their rituals and knowledge (*gnosis*) secret from the general public, reserving them for only the initiates who vowed silence concerning the secrets—the *mystai*, from the root *muo* meaning "to close the eyes and mouth." *Mystes* were those initiated into the mysteries. Thus, the mysteries were esoteric, but this does not mean that the mysteries were inexpressible. They were expressible but were to be kept secret, not least to protect the public itself from misunderstanding and misusing the powers of the secret knowledge. Contact with the divine by visions and "becoming a god" was apparently central to these cults. Stories of individuals spending long isolated sojourns in dark caves—the sensory-deprivation tanks of the day—followed by ecstatic illumination and paranormal powers are also common (see also Ustinova 2009).[4] There may also have been Persian and Indian influences on the cults' practices and beliefs.

ASC experiences may have led to the belief that the soul is not merely the life of the body (as Aristotle espoused) but exists apart from the body and can travel outside of it. In early Greece, such experiences may also have led to one key theme: distrusting human reason as the ultimate source of knowledge. True knowledge requires certainty, and this can come only after death or from experiences that are considered divine in origin, not from faulty human efforts of reasoning. Sense perception was also considered unreliable or imperfect for showing what is truly real. Thus, only by leaving the body and entering the realm of the gods could true knowledge be attained. The flight of the soul placed an experiential ASC element squarely at the heart of early Greek philosophy.

The Pre-Socratics

Consider one of the legendary Seven Sages, Epimenides of Crete (fl. seventh or sixth century BCE).[5] He is described as long-haired and tattooed, both signs of Central Asian shamans. (In early Greece, tattooing was regarded as degrading and reserved only for slaves.) He was an exorcist, a seer (*mantis*), a poet, and a root cutter (a gatherer of herbs for healing). He was also a philosopher, famous today for being credited with the Liar's Paradox "Cretans always lie." If the statement is true, then it must be a lie when uttered by a Cretan and, thus, also false. Epimenides was also considered a master of ecstatic wisdom. He fasted and slept for fifty-seven years isolated in the cave of Zeus in Crete, and when he awoke, he was revered as a man "most beloved by the gods." He claimed that his teacher was "a long sleep with dreams" and that he talked with the gods and met Truth (*aletheia*) and Justice (*dike*) in his stay in the cave. Like shamans, he claimed to have often died and been reborn—that is, his soul left his body and he appeared to others to be dead until his soul returned. (These stories may combine legends of two persons, an earlier healing shaman and a later wise man, although this theory may only be an attempt to keep philosophy separate from ASCs.) While we cannot tell if any of these ASC experiences were mystical rather than shamanic, the story of Epimenides does show a veering away from shamanic visions toward more philosophical thinking, and mystical ASC experiences may have figured in this process.

Other pre-Socratic philosophers also have stories connected to them that suggest mystical ASCs. First, Pythagoras of Samos (ca. 570–480 BCE).[6] He is most famous for the Pythagorean theorem, which he probably got from Persian or Indian mathematicians who devised it earlier. Legends have him studying in Egypt and Babylon. That he was said to wear trousers suggests he had a foreign origin—perhaps Persia or Scythia—since it was not the custom in Greece. The late Neoplatonist Iamblichus said of him: "Of rational beings, one sort is divine, one is human, and another such as Pythagoras." He is also famous for a metaphysics of an invisible mathematical order structuring the visible world: "All is number." Pythagoreans believed that the vibrations of the universe formed a perfect harmony of all of its parts, the "music of the spheres" vibrating on different levels.[7] Pythagoras himself was portrayed by Plato and Aristotle as a charismatic teacher and a founder of an ascetic contemplative school—which included women students—related to the Orphic rituals and the Mystery cult of Dionysus that integrated various philosophical and religious ideas.[8] He was also portrayed as a shaman-like figure—a tattooed wonder-worker who magically controlled storms, healed the sick, predicted natural disasters, spent time in dark caves, and descended into Hades to attain true knowledge. He could recall his previous incarnations. (His belief in repeated rebirths may have come from cultural contacts with Indian teachings.[9]) The initiations and practices of the Mystery cults played a prominent role in his school. Later Pythagoreans kept most of their teachings highly secret, although their belief in immortality and reincarnation (*metempsychosis*) became widely known.[10] They practiced breath control and other means of altering consciousness and engaged in long periods of silence (Ustinova 2009, 188).[11]

Heraclitus (ca. 540–475 BCE) is famous for claiming everything is in a perpetual state of becoming: nothing is permanent or unchanging. Rather, "all things are in flux." "No man steps into the same river twice." However, he also said: "There is one reason [*logos*] for everything throughout the one cosmos." This immanent order is an eternal underlying reality guiding all things in the phenomenal world. It guides all changes and all dualities of good and evil, light and darkness, birth and death. (His emphasis on dualities and some of his other ideas may have come from Zoroastrian influences when his homeland of Ephesus was under Persian control.) The idea of such an underlying nonpersonal but intelligent reality could have come from reflecting on introvertive experiences, and the idea that all is impermanent may have come from reflecting on extrovertive ones, but we have little of his life story, so we cannot tell if any of his ideas were based on ASCs or simply from observation and reasoning.[12]

Parmenides (ca. 515–450 BCE), from the Greek colony of Elea in Italy, held the opposite of Heraclitus's view: all change and differentiation is an *illusion*; only what is permanent and immutable can be *real*. In fact, the only thing real is the one motionless and unchanging Being (*eon*). There are no real entities but only undifferentiated Being, and we know nothing but it. Being exists either absolutely or not at all. It cannot arise from non-being since it is impossible to imagine that not-being is any type of reality, nor is there anything that could have stirred Being into activity, nor is Being revealed in sense experience. Sense experiences that suggest change and multiplicity are unreliable sources of knowledge. This belief may not have been the result of a philosophical argument alone. Being is one, without parts, and motionless: "Being is without beginning and indestructible; it is universal, existing alone, immovable and without end; nor was it ever not, nor will it ever not be since it now is all together, one, and continuous" (Parmenides *On Nature*, fragments 60–65). All possibilities of change must rely upon "what does not exist," but that—by definition—does not exist, and there is nothing outside of "what exists."

It is significant that Parmenides wrote his philosophy as a poetic work, since poetry was considered divinely inspired. The poetics of the prologue to his poem parallel magical texts of his time and correlate with known examples of incantatory poetry that aimed to produce ASCs. The motions of the prologue's language were intended to lead to an experience of the motionlessness that is precisely the nature of Being depicted in the poem (Decker and Mayock 2016, 35). The poem begins by recounting Parmenides's chariot flight as a youth over "all the cities" of the world and follows his descent into the underworld. (These experiences may have been the results of an initiation into a Mystery cult.) At the end of his descent, he meets the Goddess (*thea*) beyond the gates of night and day who reveals the "unshakable heart of the rounded truth."

Thus, Parmenides may have relied on divine revelation rather than defective human opinion (*doxa*) and belief (*pistis*). His radical monism could have come from reasoning alone, but in light of how he presented his ideas in a setting of experiences in a poem, the revelation of the oneness of being most likely came from an ASC. The experiences may have been dualistic revelations or introvertive mystical experiences of oneness empty of visions and voices but expressed later as revelations. (He also had a vision of the universe as a series of rotating burning light and dark rings.) The Goddess went on to instruct Parmenides to "estimate by reason the hard-hitting refutation [of change and differentiation] uttered by me"—that is, to use reasoning to confirm the divine truth. He is also considered the founder of a lineage of healers who served Apollo and who employed a method of stillness (*heychia*); one manifestation of this stillness was the practice of incubation, which entailed lying down in total stillness for extended periods of time to await contact from the divine in caves and other quiet places (Decker and Mayock 2016, 36). He may have learned this practice of stillness from Ameinias, a Pythagorean. It is hard to see such stillness as not related to dreaming and other ASCs.

Thus, mystical experience and philosophy may well have converged in Parmenides. His student Empedocles (ca. 495–435 BCE) is remembered today for his naturalistic "physics" of four elements—earth, water, fire, and air—governed by Hereclitus-like dual principles of love and strife. Like his teacher, he thought that to be real something must be permanent and everlasting, but he accepted sense experience as cognitive and the four elements as real. In his day, he was renowned as a sorcerer (*goes*) who entered Hades and retrieved deceased souls, as a wonder-worker who controlled the winds and rain, and as a healer who made herbal remedies that were defenses against old age and death. (Lucian connected him with the Persian Magi, whose practices may have been derived from North Asian shamanism.) He believed that he was a being from a higher realm exiled to the physical realm. He followed Pythagorean and Orphic ideas of reincarnation, believing that a final release from the world of the senses is possible only through asceticism. He may also have taught other Pythagorean and Orphic practices and secrets. In his poem *Purifications*, he presented himself as an immortal god. He had a vision, in what may well have been an ASC, of the universe arising as a vortex. This cosmogonic vision cannot be related in any simple way to his physics, but Empedocles once again is someone who had ecstatic trances and yet practiced philosophy. (One passage in his writings suggests breathing exercises, but whether they were yogic in nature cannot be determined.)

We probably will never get a clear picture of what role mystical or other ASC experiences played in the philosophies of the pre-Socratics or the role Mystery cults may have played in the lives of philosophers. Today, philosophers tend to view mysticism as only a matter of the beliefs one holds and often do not look for evidence in these texts suggesting ASC experiences. Historians and philosophers since Plato have produced a narrative of philosophy as replacing mythology, so the writings of Pythagoras, Parmenides, and others that would be most illuminating on the question of mysticism were not preserved *in toto*. Major features of their works were pushed aside, while others were disproportionately emphasized to accommodate the view that early Greek thinkers were trying to accomplish the same ends as later Greeks (Decker and Mayock 2016, 26–27). However, enough fragments have been preserved in other Greek writings to suggest strongly that mystical experiences or other ASCs may lay at the very foundations of Western philosophy. In particular, the extant fragments show that Parmenides and Empedocles were, in the words of Jessica Decker and Matthew Mayock, "prophets of a mystical tradition endowed with a unique set of practices transmitted esoterically" (27).

Socrates

The pre-Socratics might be taken as mere vestiges of an earlier shamanic time, but they show—most clearly in the case of Parmenides—that mystical experiences and philosophy can coexist. One role of ASC experiences is clearly suggested even with the founder of critical philosophy and hero of rationality, Socrates (ca. 470–399 BCE).

Modern philosophers attach no significance to Plato having Socrates say in *Phaedrus* (244a–b) the one dialogue that takes place out in the country: "Our greatest blessings come to by way of madness (*mania*), provided it is a gift given to us by the divine (*daimonion*)."[13] However, this is important for understanding his response to the Delphic oracle's claim that no man was wiser than Socrates; his reply was that he had no wisdom (*sophia*), great or small. For Socrates, as for the ancient Greeks in general, true knowledge only came from the gods, not from human reason (*Apology* 23a). Thus, pure knowledge is not possible while we are embodied. His elenchus exchanges with others concerning definitions and discursive knowledge were only a way to purify the soul (*Sophist* 230c–d) for higher wisdom (Bussanich 2016, 96–97), like exercises in mystical training. He claimed that all worldly knowledge is faulty and true knowledge of reality comes only from the divine; he was wisest of men only because he knew that. One could leave the body temporarily in this world through an out-of-body experience in a trance or permanently at death, which may explain why Socrates greeted his impending death so calmly or even cheerfully.[14] (He appears to have accepted beliefs in a cycle of rebirths [*Gorgias*, 493a] and immortality [Bussanich 2016, 101].)

Many of Plato's dialogues—including the *Symposium*, *Phaedo*, and *Republic*—portray Socrates as leading an ascetic life, and the passages on keeping still, quiet, calm, and controlled (including *Republic* 604b–e, 571d–572b; *Phaedo* 107e, 117e) were later cited in the Eastern Orthodox Church for the practice of quietude (*hesuchia*). There are accounts of Socrates going into trances for hours, trances from which others could not rouse him. Socrates remained motionless on a porch for twenty-four hours from sunrise to sunrise (*Symposium* 220d), and he remained impervious to extremes of heat and cold (219b–220b). He exhibited detachment from pleasure and pain and was said to have exhibited radical detachment and calm even in battle (220d–221b) and at his approaching death.

According to John Bussanich, Plato presents Socrates as a master of dialectic argument but also as a yogic figure (2016, 102). Any ecstasy Socrates may have experienced would be of the quiet or inward-turning kind mentioned in the *Symposium*, the meditative states alluded to in the *Phaedo*, or the quieting described in the *Republic* (Bussanich 2013, 299). Xenophon portrayed him as self-sufficient and free from desire, asserting that self-control (*enkrateia*) was the foundation of virtue and necessary for achieving wisdom (300).

Socrates also refers to hearing since his childhood an inner guiding voice in his dreams that he considered a gift of the gods: his *daimonion* (*Apology* 31c–d).[15] He also received divine signs from Apollo (*Apology* 401c), and in the *Phaedo* (65c) he remarked, "The soul can best reflect when it is free of all distractions such as hearing or sight or pain or pleasure of any kind—i.e., when it ignores the body and becomes as far as possible independent, avoiding all physical contacts and associations as much as it can, in its search for reality." Thus, one should remove oneself so far as possible from the eyes, ears, and entire body (66a). (Socrates may have gotten the idea that the soul is an immortal entity capable of acting independently from the body from contacts with shaman-like teachers in Greece; he may also have gotten techniques from them for detaching consciousness from the physical world [Bussanich 2013, 296].) According to Xenophon, Socrates counseled his associates to concern themselves with divination "if any of them wanted to prosper beyond the limits of human wisdom" (Bussanich 1999, 39–40).

These passages suggest ASCs, not merely utilizing reasoning such as mathematics to abstract a reality that is independent of the senses.[16] However, modern philosophers take these references as referring to a pathology or as simply irrelevant to Socrates's thought. Or, they may take these passages only to indicate that rationalism is needed to get to the real essence of a thing, that only pure reasoning in the baseline state of consciousness without the distractions of the world or the body is needed. To them, these passages no more refer to ASCs than when Socrates said in *Theaetetus* (184e) that finding what things have in common is not a matter of sight or hearing but of reflection (i.e., reasoning). That is, Socrates emphasized keeping the mind uncontaminated by the body: in the present life, the nearest approach to pure knowledge that we can make is "when we have the least possible intercourse or communion with the body, and are not surfeited with the bodily nature, but keep ourselves pure until the hour when the god himself is pleased to release us" (*Phaedo* 67a). However, this passage may be taken literally: the soul reasons best when it withdraws from the senses and their objects and leaves the body in an ASC. This is a matter of actually "taking leave of the body and as far as possible having no contact or association with it in its search for reality" (65c). In this understanding, pure knowledge is possible only by escaping from the body; this occurs at death, but it is also "the preoccupation of philosophers to separate the soul from the body" (67e). True knowledge comes from the "eye of the soul" alone, and we are nearest such knowledge in this life only when we avoid the body. If Socrates was entranced for long periods of time and could not be roused, it is hard to conclude that he was simply lost in thought.

Thus, it is possible that Socrates had ASC experiences. His rationality suggests that he relied on his own experiences rather than myths, and he seemed at times possessed by gods such as Apollo, whom he claimed to serve (*Apology* 20e–23c). Only divine experiences could give certainty. Some of these experiences may have been mystical in nature, but we cannot tell from Plato's dialogues. However, a strong argument can be made for Socrates being a mystical philosopher who experienced a *daimonion* (also connected to Apollo) in dreams and perhaps in meditative states of absorption, in contrast to the speculation of Plato (Bussanich 1999, 49). He, then, was a midwife who assisted others in gaining wisdom (*Theaeteus* 150cd). In any case, Socrates apparently placed ASC-based knowing at the center of any true knowledge of reality that we can attain.

Plato

The picture is also not clear regarding the epistemology and metaphysics of the Forms (*eidos*) of Socrates's student Plato (ca. 428–348 BCE). Plato employed language of visions, but the experiences he described seem more mystical. Gregory Vlastos sees Plato as a mystic and his metaphysics as grounded in mystical experiences, although his mysticism is not confined to sporadic episodes of ecstatic awareness (1981, 56, 54). R. T. Wallis (1986, 463) argues that Plato did not envision a mystical experience like Plotinus's contemplation of the One from within the Nous but that he saw philosophical insight (*noesis*) as involving moral and intellectual purification, "turning the whole soul toward the light" and aiming at a "likeness to God as far as possible" (*Theaetetus* 176b). Bussanich (2016, 96–103) discusses evidence of mystical practices in Plato's works, especially the later dialogues. David Yount points out that most Platonic scholars classify Plato as a mystic (2017, 10)—although they may have different definitions of *mystic*—and he goes on to make the case that however Plotinus is classified as a mystic, we must classify Plato the same way because they have essentially the same views on philosophical matters and rely on the same type of experiences. Thus, Plato is not saying that true knowledge of the Good is merely theoretically possible, but that he actually has attained that knowledge in experiences (50).

Plato may have been influenced by the Pythagoreans on stillness and silence (Bussanich 2016, 97) and by the Orphic Mystery cult, although he did not think that philosophy was to be reserved only for initiates or otherwise esoteric. Some dialogs such the *Phaedo* mix metaphysics and Orphic mysticism (Kingsley 1999, 79–132). He used the language of secret visions from these cults in discussing the contemplation of the Forms and Beauty (*kallos*) (*Symposium* 210a, *Phaedrus* 250a). He stated that he and others who were initiated into the "most blessed of Mysteries" and who followed the "train of Zeus" and other gods had visions when pure and free of the body in which they are imprisoned of "perfect, simple, calm, and happy apparitions" in the "pure light" of the "state of perfection" (*Phaedrus* 250b–c). He believed that the "final and highest mystery" was beyond our reach (*Symposium* 210a), and he used the term *mystical* in regard to a sudden experience of Beauty (210e–212c).

Plato distinguished the eternal, uncreated soul from the worldly body (*Phaedrus* 245c–246a). For him, the body was a tomb for the soul. He thought that the soul reflects the macrocosm, and we can reach and participate in the eternal and unchanging Forms through contemplation. We need to contemplate the Forms with the "eye of the soul" (*Symposium* 254a–b; *Republic* 519b, 533d; *Sophist* 254a–b) because they could be perceived only by the intellect (*nous*). Unlike discursive thought and reasoning (*dianoia*), the intellect is a divine faculty existing in our soul (*Timaeus* 90b–c). Today, philosophers take any reference to the intellect as merely insights of the rational mind into the Forms rather than another function of the mind, but Plato indicated something more experiential and mystical.

Philosophical contemplation (*theoria*) is "the activation of the soul's natural divinity, a supreme realization" through purification (*askesis*) (McGinn 1994, 34, 25). It is a matter of ascent to the highest form, the Good (Wallis 1986, 462). Divine (*theion*) contemplation is contemplation of essence and the brightest region of being by the "eye of the soul" (*Republic* 517d, 518c). The Forms constituted an intelligible order of archetypes above our material world; they are not human inventions or mere universalizations but transcendent realities that things participate in. For Plato, the Forms participate in an underlying unity just as sense objects participate in a single Form, but the Forms—including Beauty—transcend all description and knowledge (*Symposium* 210e). However, contemplation can result in a sudden vision of the Supreme Good. (The suddenness [*exaiphnes*] of the vision is a theme in Plato's and Plotinus's works.) The process begins with observing beauty in an object. Gradually, the object is left behind, and the intellect realizes the Form of Beauty itself (210–11). The nonconceptual experience of the Forms transcends discursive knowledge (*Republic* 532c). This process is not initiated by the supreme, but at the end, the supreme reveals itself to the intellect. The experience is blissful and like a rest at the end of a journey (519c, 532e).

According to Plato, what we experience in sense experience is not true reality but only shadows. What is real has no "becoming," and what has "becoming" is not real (*Timaeus* 27d–281). His famous parable of the cave (*Republic* 514a–518b) treats the phenomenal world as a realm of mere shadows with the bright light of the sun as illuminating the true reality behind the realm of appearances. We are like prisoners who only see shadows on the wall and not the reality that casts the shadows. One day, a prisoner is dragged out of the cave into the sunlight and is able to look directly at the light itself and thus see the actual reality. As an allegory, this suggests that the realm of the Forms can be experienced in this life in an introvertive mystical experience (and that a teacher must drag a student there). Only then, by a divine light, we can see true reality. We must ascend gradually out of the cave through difficult purification to the realm of light to gain knowledge of reality. (Plato notes that experiencing this light may be painful. Gaining a bright light in darkness is part of initiation into the Mystery cults.) He believed that we are innately endowed with knowledge of the Forms that can be remembered in this world through a life of philosophy.

Plato deemed all human reasoning as ultimately flawed or incomplete, and immediate experience is necessary to realize the Forms in this world. The prisoner who saw reality pitied what his fellow prisoners considered knowledge, but they considered his eyesight ruined by the blinding vision; they laughed at him and would kill anyone who tried to free them (517a). Still, Plato has Socrates add that the point of education is not to convey facts but to open students' eyes to vaster worlds that they did not know existed.

Plato also spoke of the madness (*mania*) of the intoxicating passion (*eros*) that is manifested when one sees beauty here on earth and is transported with the recollection of true Beauty as it is in the realm of Forms (*Phaedrus* 249d–e). That may refer to an introvertive mystical experience or the enlightened state after such an experience. Some scholars suggest that Plato was initiated into the Eleusinian Mysteries, whose initiation lasted weeks and culminated in drinking psychedelic *kykeon*.[17] One prepared for the drink by fasting. He wrote that many carry the wand of the Mysteries, but the true worshipers of Dionysus are few—"only those [who] have practiced in the right way"—and that he left nothing undone in his life in order to be counted among the true worshipers as far as humanly possible (*Phaedo* 69c–d). Those "who have pursued philosophy in the right way" have treated the soul as separated at death from the body (80e–84b). In a letter to the friends of Dionysus (*Letter* no. 7), Plato wrote (if the letter is genuine) that the knowledge with which he was concerned was not something that could be put into words, but after a long-continued discussion between teacher and pupil in joint pursuit of the subject, suddenly, like light flashing forth when a fire is lit, knowledge was born in the soul and straightway nourished itself (Yount 2017, 14); a "spark of illumination" passes from one soul to another. His goal, like that of his predecessors, appears to be to provide guidance toward an ultimate experience of the truth: the reality of the Good (16). Plato also said that there are sudden moments of experiencing the Form of Beauty in a state that neither comes nor goes, neither waxes nor wanes, and one should lead one's life there (*Symposium* 210e).

However, very few people are able to reach Beauty and experience it (*Republic* 476b) or come to know things as they really are (*Phaedrus* 250b). This would be so if the realizations were not only a matter of reason but also of ASCs. To know the Forms, Plato insisted that we should not attach ourselves to bodily pleasures (*Republic* 519a). Rather, we should purify the soul for such knowledge: separate the soul from the body, gather the soul together from every part of the body, and have it dwell by itself (*Phaedo* 67c). This sounds like meditation or asceticism (see 82b). So, too, one best grasps truth in a dream state in which self-consciousness is clear, pure, and not disturbed by passion or emotion (*Republic* 571d–572b). When the soul investigates itself, it passes into the realm of what is eternal, immortal, and unchanging and is akin to that; it ceases to stray and remains in the same state while it touches things of the same kind; and its experience (*pathema*) then is called a *practical wisdom* (*phronesis*) (*Phaedo* 79d). Thus, the highest knowledge is experiential, not conceptual or propositional, unlike in modern philosophy.

Again, we cannot dismiss the possibility that Plato had mystical experiences or advocated a mystical way of life simply because we know he was a philosopher; one can be both. We can speculate why Plato may have been reluctant to speak explicitly of mystical experiences: his teacher, Socrates, was put to death for unconventional religious ideas and perhaps because of his private religious experiences (Bussanich 1999, 32), and, as the parable of the cave states, others may consider those claiming to have ASC experiences mad and think they should be killed. We cannot tell if the way of life that Plato required of his students—one of virtue, courage, honesty, and so forth—was a mysticism leading to cultivating mystical experiences. (He was familiar with the Pythagoreans' way of life and Pythagorean practices continued in his academy for some time, but his school was less connected to the Mystery cults' rituals.) Some scholars see evidence of breathing exercises and meditatively withdrawing the senses and concentration in the *Phaedo* (see Bussanich 2013, 297). His disapproval of poetry and other products of the Muses as arousing emotions and thus interfering with the intellect also suggests trying to keep the mind clear for mystical insights.

After Plato

By the time of Socrates, shamanic flights had dropped out of the picture, although the metaphor of ascent continued. After Plato, any suggestions of ASCs among philosophers became rare, starting with the decidedly unmystical Aristotle. Regarding his statement in the *Metaphysics* that reasoning is the highest activity and that reason realizes the essential characteristic of absolute thought through the unity of subjective thought with objective thought, nothing suggests a mystical or other ASC experience, only a way of thinking.[18] He contrasted study (*mathon*) with the ecstatic experience (*pathon*) of the Eleusinian Mysteries and valued only the former.

But philosophy as a contemplative way of life, rather than simply an intellectual search for understanding, did continue. Various transcendentalist movements occurred in this era (Wallis 1986, 465). Pythagoreanism continued in one form or another into the Common Era. Plato's Academy continued for a few hundred more years. The most famous of the eclectic Middle Platonists was the Jewish Hellenistic philosopher Philo Judaeus of Alexandria. His school took elements from Aristotelianism (such as an unmoved mover), religious Neopythagoreanism, and especially Stoicism and its idea of an ordering principle (*logos*). He fused Plato's conception of the Forms with Aristotle's intellect (*nous*), making the Forms into thoughts in the mind of God, and adopting the Stoic idea of inner serenity by giving up self-will and conforming to the divine will. This fusion influenced the founder of Neoplatonism, Plotinus.

Philosophy students practiced various types of meditation as part of their training. The skeptic Pyrrho of Elis (ca. 360–270 BCE) believed that we should suspend all judgments since we do not know the reality behind experienced phenomena and that this suspension (*epoche*) leads to inner tranquility (*ataraxia*). The Greek philosophical sense of detachment from desire (*apatheia*) that is usually associated with the Skeptics and the later Stoicism of Epictetus and Marcus Aurelius also should be noted. Inner tranquility was deemed the only shield against fear and suffering. For Stoics, everything was seen as the expression of divine will or fate, and thus, we should greet all events, including death, with an even-minded detachment. There should be no attachment to anything external since anything material can be lost at any moment. Such detachment can lead to an ASC of a mystical nature, but it can also be developed without any ASCs. Although Epicureans posited pleasure as the ultimate good, they practiced asceticism, subsisting on the simplest food and shelter and abstaining from sex, believing only natural and necessary desires should be fulfilled since peace of mind and the absence of negative feelings is the only pleasure worth having. They, like the Stoics, practiced an inward examination of their passions to cleanse their souls. In addition, Greek philosophers of the time in general attached great importance to removing the fear of death and living in the present moment without concern for the past or worrying about the uncertainties of the future (Hadot 1995, 268). Living in the moment became central because the present is the only reality that truly belongs to us: it is the only time that we are actually alive and can control things. All of this suggests mystical practices and mystical ways of life, but the attitudes could also be practiced without necessarily living a mystical way of life. There are no written records of mystical experiences by these philosophers.

The Greco-Roman Mystery cults must be noted again since at least some philosophers belonged to them. They lasted well into the Common

Era, only to be replaced by Christianity. From the early Eleusinian Mysteries to the Roman Mithraic Mysteries, these cults held their meetings in darkened chambers and had initiations, rituals, and trainings that apparently involved mind-altering drugs and practices. Some advanced members were said to have been ascetics who engaged in practices to purify the body. Their goal was to free the immortal soul from the material body, and in the Dionysiac and Orphic Mysteries, the goal was to escape reincarnation and to unite with the god Dionysus/Bacchus. Mystical experiences were not the type of ASC experiences that were valued most. However, did mystical experiences also occur? The highest and most sacred experiences in these cults were kept secret, so we will probably never know. Some mystical experiences may well have occurred, but the sense given in mystical experiences of an unchanging oneness may have presented a problem for the cults' beliefs, so such experiences may have been suppressed.

Plotinus

This brings us to the Greco-Roman mystic whose metaphysics has been the all-time most influential in Western mysticism: Plotinus (ca. 204–270 CE). He may have been born in Upper Egypt. He studied with several teachers in Alexandria, but in his late twenties he began to study exclusively with Ammonius Saccas, who also taught the Christian Origen. We do not know anything directly of Ammonius's teachings. Later Neoplatonists said that he wanted to harmonize Plato and Aristotle and that he believed that all reality derived from God. However, Alexandria was a crossroad of Eastern and Western cultural ideas, and the fact that after studying with Ammonius for eleven years Plotinus left with the intention to study in Persia to get acquainted with Persian and Indian philosophy—an expedition that never came to fruition—suggests that Ammonius's teachings may have involved Eastern knowledge.[19] Plotinus then settled in Rome, where he taught for the rest of his life. Porphyry mentioned that Christians were among his students (*Life of Plotinus* 16).

Plotinus is the paradigm of a mystical philosopher, exhibiting both reason and its transcendence. All of the Greek philosophical traditions influenced him. He gravitated to the more mystical Plato and the Pythagoreans, but he incorporated some of Aristotle's ideas, such as a knower must become like the object to be known (*De Anima* 429a), following earlier claims by Anaxagoras and Empedocles that only things of like nature can be known

(Enn. V.3.6).* (Aristotle had a greater impact on later Neoplatonists.) He rejected the Stoics' materialism but incorporated some of their ideas on a rational order (the *logos*) to nature, cosmology, and the soul. He also continued the Greek philosophical search for a changeless first principle.

Plotinus's metaphysics is an emanationism centered around a single transcendent reality that, for convenience, he labeled simply *the One* (*to hen*). This combination affirms both the pre-Socratic principle of unity (Enn. V.1.9) and the Pythagorean negation of multiplicity (V.5.6). Indeed, the One is beyond all dualities (V.5.4–6). There is ultimately an ontic simplicity to things: one underlying order and one ontic element constituting reality from which everything emanates. The One is not a Platonic Form but is formless; it is beyond the Forms, including the Good and Beauty (VI.7.32–33, VI.9.6). The Forms are only "traces" of it (VI.7.33). Plotinus was not a theist, even if he used some personal terminology (as did Plato). The One is not personal in nature; it is not a creator (a demiurge fashioned the world in light of the Platonic Forms); it does not love human beings and is, in fact, unaware of them; it is not affected by prayers or rituals, nor is it worshiped, nor does realization of the One involve grace.[20] Plotinus's sole prayer was only for orienting the mind inwardly toward the One (V.1.6). He did call the One "the Good," but by this, he meant only that it is the true value that we seek; it is not a description of the One in itself but only indicates what is valuable to us—what is *good* for us. Conversely, matter is "evil" only in that it is the opposite of the Good that we seek (II.9.13). That is, desiring anything material is "evil" only in that it directs us away from the Good. But the world is not evil in itself or in a separate reality, as it was for the Gnostics, whom Plotinus severely criticized. The world is only a distraction to our quest to have our soul realize the One. Evil is the absence of being, nonexistence (I.8.3). It is a privation because it has no Form (I.8.11, V.9.10). Human evil for Plotinus results from self-assertion (*tolma*) (V.1.1).

The One is the first of three cosmic principles (*hypostases*). Following Greek philosophy, the One must be simple if it is to explain all complexity, and it must be self-caused and not contingent to be the cause of everything that follows. The One is immanent in all its emanations—and thus, its emanations are real and not illusions—but it also transcends all of them— the root and the emanations are never one. It is alone, single, simple, and

---

pure: the source upon which things, life, mind, and the Being (*ousia*) of the emanations depend (Enn. I.6.7, V.5.10, VI.7.15). It is beyond Being (I.7.1, II.4.16, II.9.9, V.3.14, V.4.1, V.5.5–6, V.5.13, VI.7.40, VI.8.19, VI.9.3–4), as it is for Plato (*Symposium* 509b). Thus, the One is not Being; Being is merely a trace (*ixvos*) of the One (Enn. VI.9.5). The One is a radiant luminosity (as in VI.7.15). It is not conscious and has no knowledge or awareness of its emanations (VI.7.37). It does not think (VI.8.12–17) and so is free of thoughts (VI.7.40). It is self-sufficient, independent of everything, self-determined, and self-caused (VI.9.6, VI.8.7, VI.8.14, VI.8.16). Through its own passionate longing (*eros*) it brings itself about (VI.8.15); it is simultaneously the subject, object, and activity of *eros* (VI.8.16). However, the One does not literally originate, so it only appears to cause itself (VI.8.13). It exists through self-will (VI.8.9) and is, in fact, all will (VI.8.21). It is an awakening without an awakener (VI.8.16). The One is paradoxically both everything and not anything: the One is other than anything because all things emanate from it, and yet it is also everything because it supplies the being of all things (V.2.1–2, V.2.24, V.7.32). It is not a thing and, thus, cannot be compared to anything or described in such terms (V.3.14, V.4.1–2, V.5.6, VI.7.38). It is unlimited (*aperion*) (VI.9.6). It is ever present with the Nous but other than it (V.1.6).

Since the One is ontologically distinct from Being (Enn. III.8.8–9) and yet is Being's source, Plotinus's metaphysics is not a pantheism that equates the One with the phenomenal realm. In fact, he said we are to *despise* the delights of the world (VI.7.34–35, I.6.7), which would not be the case if all the things of the world were the One. He explicitly denies that the One is "the all" (V.5.12) and affirms that what has been emanated is outside the One (VI.8.19). The One is the cause of things, not a material substrate within the world (V.3.11). But we are never "cut off" from the One (VI.9.9). In short, the One is not the being of all things but the ontic power behind things giving them real being (for example, V.1.7, V.3.15, V.4.2).

All things emanate (*proodos*, meaning to flow forth or overflowing) from the stillness of the One like multiple rivers flowing from a never-emptying, still spring boiling over with life (Enn. III.8.10, VI.7.12). Or, emanation is like the diffusion of light from a source (I.7.1, V.1.6, V.3.12).[21] The One is the unmoving center from which all circles radiate (IV.4.16). All things that emanate are real since the One is giving them being. The emanations that it flings out are part of its act of will to exist (Rist 1967, 78, 83, 87).

The first emanation is the second cosmic principle: the Nous. It is eternally united with the One (Enn. VI.7.35). The One is simple, but multiplicity enters the picture with the Nous since the Nous constitutes the Platonic Forms (V.9.8). It is a reflection of the One, but it also contains the archetypes of all things.[22] The Nous is both being and a perpetual divine consciousness (the intellect) in everything. Thus, it is both Being and how we can know being. We can participate in that Being through contemplation (*theoria*) (III.8.6). It is not equivalent to our analytic consciousness, which is lower (I.1.7–8).[23] The Nous "turns back" and contemplates the One, and through this, it attains the One (III.8.11). Since the One is above the Nous, it has none of its activity and no contemplative object (VI.7.40). The One does not contemplate or desire (III.8.11). Moreover, the Nous and its activity (*noesis*) are one (V.3.6); in turning toward the One, the Nous sees the One, and this seeing is itself the Nous (V.1.7). Thus, there are two movements: an overflowing from the One (*proodos*) and a turning back (*epistrophe*) toward the One (VI.9.9). The Nous creates through contemplation and contemplates both what is above and what is below it. In fact, the Nous's only activity is contemplation. However, the human soul has lost the ability to contemplate the higher reality within oneself and must regain it.

From the Nous emanates the last cosmic principle: the World Soul (*psyche*). The One is pure light, the Nous is sunlight, and the World Soul is reflected moonlight (Enn. V.6.4). The higher part of the World Soul turns back and contemplates what is above it (the Nous), and the lower part produces the material objects below it. Individual souls and the eternal natural order (*physis*) underlying the material world are levels of the World Soul. The material world is *not* an emanation, but it too results from the World Soul's contemplation. The higher World Soul orders the material universe through an immanent principle (*logos*) that enables it to govern the material realm providentially, and the lower World Soul pervades all of the material realm. These underlying principles weave the world together harmoniously (IV.3.15). Matter (*hule*) both participates in and does not participate in the intelligible order of the Nous (VI.4.8); it is contemplated thought, as it were. The material world is a reflection of the Platonic Forms emanating from the Nous in the World Soul. Thereby, it is an image (*eikon*) in what is itself an image of the One (III.6.7). The Nous itself is beautiful, situated in the light and radiance of the One, and our world is but a shadow and an image of that beauty (III.8.3).

The true realm of Being is within the Nous, not the material world. Matter has no Form or Being, but matter is not unreal in the sense that it does not exist at all.[24] Matter has no light but reflects the Forms; the Forms are seals that stamp the formless matter (Enn. V.8.7). The sensed world is a reflection that is fading away into darkness (I.8.13, II.4.10). The greater part of reality is the divine (III.2.8), and the material world is a phantom (II.5.5). Material objects are like ephemeral and insubstantial phantoms in a mirror—phantoms within a phantom (III.6.7). Thus, matter barely exists. It is the least substantive element of reality. Its existence ultimately depends on the One since that is the only source of any reality (see I.8.7). Matter's nonbeing is not nonexistence, but it is still something other than Being (I.8.3). The Form in each thing is only an image of Being (V.9.5). People who think sense experience reveals reality are like people who are dreaming (III.6.6) and take what is in the dream to be real. Each thing in the material world participates in the entirety of the Nous since the intelligible Nous (the All) cannot be cut up (VI.4.2). Thus, each bit of the material world reflects all of the Nous to the extent that this is possible (VI.4.2).[25] The Nous has all things, and each thing is the whole; yet, paradoxically, the things are not confused but separate (I.8.2). All things are transparent and not dark or opaque; all things are clear to the inner most part of everything since light is transparent to light; each thing has everything in itself and sees the being of all things in each thing since each thing has all of being. Thus, each thing manifests all things because each thing is both part and also the whole of Being at once (V.8.4). However, one who is aware of having become one with the Nous is still also aware of themselves (IV.4.2).

Individual souls are emitted from the lower World Soul (Enn. IV.3.8) like rays of light radiating from the sun (VI.4.3). Thus, there is a multiplicity of souls in the World Soul but not in the Being of the Nous. Souls are rooted in the World Soul (IV.3.12, IV.8.8, VI.4.14) and can return to it. Each soul is eternal: each is real and distinct within the World Soul, though all have the same being from the One (IV.3.5). Souls are like multiple overlapping circles that share one center: the World Soul (VI.5.5). By our souls, we are connected to everything in the region of spirits and what is beyond (IV.4.45). Souls are not in our material bodies (IV.3.20). Each soul is not in the realm of time, for time—which is co-existent with the world (III.7.12)—is posterior to the emanation of souls (IV.4.15). But the entire Nous is present and active in each soul, just as all of a sound is heard by each distinct listener (VI.4.12) even though each listener hears it differently.

Our higher (rational) soul never descends into the material realm. It has no individual personality or memory but remains tranquil, constantly contemplating what is above it.[26] The higher soul is always within the Nous (Enn. I.4.9). It lives in the *logos* (IV.3.10). In fact, all of Being resides in each (higher) soul (VI.4.2). The higher soul is the Nous, and only the lower soul touches matter (VI.2.22). The World Soul and individual souls make our material bodies.[27] Our lower (nonrational) soul then becomes embodied and thereby gains material defilements. (Porphyry begins his *Life of Plotinus* by stating that Plotinus "seemed ashamed of being in a body."[28]) All that is distinctive about each person's personality is part of the lower soul that is lost when one returns to the Nous; the higher soul in the Nous is pure contemplation. We forget what we truly are and misidentify ourselves with the lower soul; thus, our minds fall out of the Nous. However, our true eternal soul is not the small embodied self. Rather, we are amphibious by nature (IV.8.4), living in both the transcendent realm and the material world. Our error, and the beginning of evil, is our lower soul's wish to belong only to itself—its audacity and desire to be self-centered (V.1.1).

The total otherness of the One from phenomena makes the *via neg-ativa* central to Plotinus's thought (see also Plato's *Parmenides*). No words apply to the One (Enn. VI.8.13). Any property is a characteristic of Being, not the One, so all properties must be denied (VI.9.3). In a remark echoed by Augustine and Thomas Aquinas concerning God, Plotinus said that we can only state what the One is not, not what it is (V.3.14). All predicates must be denied: even *the One* does not apply to what transcends Being since *one* is a number among numbers and thus may suggest some multiplicity. Silence is ultimately the only proper response (V.3.12–14, V.5.6, VI.7.38, VI.9.5). Only the "sheer dread of holding to nothingness" forces mystics back to the everyday realm of language (IV.7.38), but "whoever has seen knows what I am saying" (Enn. VI.9.9; see also Eckhart 2009, 180).

Stripping away concepts applied to the One is an integral part of the path. Indeed, the mystical path is a matter of stripping away everything but the light of the One (Enn. V.3.17). We must strip off what we put on in our descent from the One (I.6.7). All doctrines and thinking must be left behind (VI.7.36). In fact, the One cannot be communicated; it is indescribable because whatever one says about it makes it a *something* (Enn. V.3.13; see also Plato *Parmenides* 142c)—that is, some *thing*. It is beyond discursive thought and reasoning (*dianoia*) as well as the Forms (Enn. V.3.12–17; VI.7.17, 38; VI.9.11). It is beyond intellect, has no knowledge (*gnosis*), and cannot be grasped by thought (V.3.12, VI.7.40). If we speak of it, it is only to point out the direction, the road for one desirous of seeing it (VI.9.4). We cannot denote the One as a cause or anything else. Any property is a characteristic of the world, not the One, so all properties must be denied, as must causation and creation (III.8.9, VI.9.3–4). We can denote the One as a source, cause, Good, Father, or God, but each only denotes the One in relation to us, not the nature of the One in itself (VI.9.6). We cannot properly even call it *one*: that word does not denote its nature but merely denotes simplicity—that it is not many and is without otherness (*heterotes*). The word merely directs the mind away from the realm of multiplicity; thus, *one* also must be negated (V.5.6, VI.7.36, VI.9.4–5). Ultimately, no name suits it (VI.9.5). Indeed, we cannot even say *it* or *is* or *exists* in connection to the One (VI.8.8, VI.9.3) since those terms apply to phenomena in this world. We must add "so to speak" or "as it were" (*hoion, hosper*) whenever we speak of the One (VI.8.11, VI.8.13) because all language makes what is transcendent into a phenomenal object. Thus, anything said of the One will be a mixture of positive attribution and negation.

The objective of Plotinus's philosophy is not to present a systematic metaphysical picture of reality but to induce an ascent of the soul to the One: to fill one's individual psyche with as much of the cosmic psyche as possible. We are to turn our awareness inward and hold it there (Enn. V.1.12). The objective is to realize, through direct experience, that the One is both transcendent and also immanent in us. Plotinus was the first Greek philosopher to make this identity (Majercik 1995, 48). The One and its emanations are mirrored in our souls (Enn. VI.5.12, VI.8.18), so we can realize it within ourselves. An individual begins the ascent through reasoning, but the One cannot be known through philosophical knowledge. It can be realized, but only through an ASC mystical experience beyond reasoning and discursive knowledge (see IV.8.1, V.3.6, VI.5.7, VI.9.10–11). The One is a presence beyond all discursive knowledge, including knowledge of the Nous (VI.9.4).[29] The activity of the Nous (*noesis*) is not discursive knowledge (IV.8.1): we need a knowledge (*gnosis*) (V.1.1) that transcends discursive, scientific knowledge (*episteme*) because the One is beyond such knowledge (VI.9.4). The One itself does not have *gnosis* (V.3.12) any more than the Being it emanates, but infallible knowledge of the One is possible because the higher soul is immaterial and always within the Nous.

Thus, the ascent to realizing the One requires turning inward (Enn. V.8.10). One must withdraw into oneself and observe, letting all but the One go (I.6.9). It is a process of abstraction (*aphairesis*) that negates everything but the One. The mental effort needed for realizing the One requires surrendering (*epidosis*) the soul in a stillness (VI.9.11). Plotinus saw this path as a matter of purifying the mind through an inward turn away from all things (including the lower soul) (VI.9.7) and all mental and ethical disciplines (VI.7.34, VI.9.3). Asceticism is recommended for purifying the lower embodied soul (I.4.14, V.8.11), preparing the way for contemplation (*theoria*).[30] (Plotinus also adopted vegetarianism, as did the Pythagoreans.) The soul abandons external things and ignores even itself (VI.9.7).

In the flight in solitude to the solitary, the soul takes no pleasure in earthly things (Enn. VI.9.11). The higher soul remains contemplating in the Nous. Everything could be destroyed and a sage would not care (VI.7.34, I.4.7). The World Soul is not troubled by anything in the world, and so neither is the sage (II.9.18). No pleasures or pains penetrate the inner soul (I.4.8). Wealth is irrelevant to the well-being of the wise (I.4.15). Even the deaths of friends or relatives do not cause the sage grief (I.4.4), but Plotinus did not totally withdraw from society: he was a teacher and spiritual advisor on directing one's awareness toward the One, a caretaker for many orphans, the educator of young boys and girls, and an arbitrator of disputes. He also had many friends (*Life of Plotinus* 7, 9). He planned a city of philosophers (Platonopolis) ruled by Plato's laws that most likely would have been monastic in nature.

Nevertheless, Plotinus paid no attention to his turbulent times and ignored Plato's social and political teachings. Social concerns were irrelevant to his mystical interests. The sage need not return to Plato's cave to help his fellow prisoners. Morality is only a matter of the lower soul's activity in the material realm and can, in fact, bind the soul more firmly to this realm (Enn. V.9.5). Virtue was a necessary base for the mystical path (II.9.15), but the focus of one's virtuous acts is one's own sake, not a concern for others.[31] Virtue, to Plotinus, was a matter of cleansing one's inner disposition. Love or concern for one's neighbor for their own sake is absent in the *Enneads*. Plotinus said, "The sage would like all men to prosper and no one to suffer evil, but if this does not happen, he is still happy" (I.4.11). His ethics were even more self-centered and otherworldly than most Greek classical ethical thought (Dillon 1996, 319–20; see also Rist 1976).

However, those who are enlightened and also wish to communicate the Good may do so by teaching (Enn. VI.9.7), proposing laws that reflect the image of the Good, or being models of wisdom and virtue (I.2.6), but he discouraged political involvement (*Life of Plotinus* 7). His objective was to live with detachment (*apatheia*)—an emotional isolation of the higher soul from the body. Only in cases of extreme social distress—war, famine, extreme injustice—should a sage engage in any actions other than contemplation (see Enn. VI.8.5). Such detachment is a higher virtue that cannot be attained without mastering the lower virtues (I.2.1–6). With detachment, nothing of the material realm can affect us, and the higher soul that dwells in the World Soul is able to ascend within the realm of the higher World

Soul to unite to the Nous and contemplate the One (I.6.7–9). (Beginning with Porphyry, Neoplatonism added more extensive worldly concerns.)

With being morally virtuous as a base (Enn. I.2.2, II.3.9, II.9.15), the first step of the ascent is to have faith that there is an immaterial reality (I.3.3) and that intellectual purification—mastering philosophy, especially dialectic reasoning (*dainoia*), in order to know the truth (I.3.4–6)—is possible.[32] For Plotinus, no rituals, magic, grace, or religious prayers are involved. Reason is necessary at the foundation of the quest, but Plotinus believed it must be surpassed since all human knowledge is imperfect. This purification (*katharsis*) is not a matter of purifying the soul, which is part of the Nous and thus always pure (III.6.5), but purifying the mind. Such purification remains active in the baseline ego-driven state of consciousness. So too, the *via negativa* remains a matter of rational reflection on the One (V.3.13, V.5.10, VI.7.38, VI.8.11, VI.9.5). As well as requiring the advanced virtues of purification (I.2.7), the quest requires practicing the civic virtues of Plato's *Republic* but with a mystical cathartic twist: courage (especially in the face of death), moderation (abstaining from the pleasures of the flesh), prudence (turning away from earthly matters), and justice (fairness in our actions toward others) (Enn. I.2.1–2; Majercik 1995, 49). By these means, an individual can return their soul fully to the Nous. The goal is "to be a god" (Enn. I.2.6): a divine being existing within the Nous. Virtues help to produce the necessary inner stillness necessary for this process.

The second movement toward the One is driven by the passion (*eros*) of the soul within the Nous that longs for its Good, going from contemplating the Forms in the Nous to being intoxicated with the divine nectar and the passion (although emotionally detached) that leads to contemplating the One (Enn. VI.7.34–35; see also I.6.7, III.5.1–2, V.3.17, V.9.2, VI.7.22, VI.9.4). The soul passionately longs to be with the One (VI.6.9). The soul puts aside all learning (VI.7.36) and discards all Forms (VI.7.34; VI.9.7, 11), detaching itself from all things (VI.7.34; VI.9.7, 15, 20). The soul shuts its eyes and awakens to another way of seeing (I.6.8, III.6.5). It is an "inward awakening" (see I.6.8, IV.4.8.1, VI.9.4).

Thus, the ascent has stages: first through the higher soul in oneself to the World Soul within oneself and then to the Nous. We start with first contemplating nature—even though Plotinus speaks of the world as distraction and something to be escaped—then contemplating the higher soul, and then the Nous (Enn. III.8.8). Plotinus interpreted Plato's allegory of the cave to mean that we must break the fetters of the body, rise out of the body, and ascend to the Nous (IV.8.1). The isolated soul is no longer aware of being in a body (VI.7.34) but remains aware in the Nous. Within the Nous, the higher soul contemplates the Forms in themselves. Beauty is seen to be the essence and being of all the Forms and plays an important role in the ascent (II.9.16–17). It is derived from the One (VI.9.4). Here, the soul realizes through participatory knowledge the Forms of Beauty and Being. The Nous, not contemplating anything particular, draws itself inward and sees a light that is neither within nor without (V.5.7).

By stripping away everything that is not the One, the soul comes to rest in the Nous (see Enn. IV.8.1, VI.9.3) in a "perfect stillness" filled with the One (VI.9.11). The body becomes quiet (V.1.2). The mystic sheds the other *hypostases* and imitates the stillness or quietude (*hesuchia*) of the One (VI.7.35, III.7.1). Being calmed, the soul does not turn to anything, even within itself (VI.9.11). Finally, the soul passes beyond contemplating the Nous and realizes the dazzling light of the One (V.5.8, VI.7.36). The higher part of the soul returns to the One in this experience: the "flight of the alone to the Alone" (VI.7.34, VI.9.11; see also I.6.7, V.1.6). The soul does not see or distinguish; it is then joined with the One, center to center, but there is duality when the soul is separated (VI.9.10). At the moment of touching the One, there is no power whatsoever to make any affirmation, but after this experience, the soul can again reason about the One and knows that it had a sudden vision of the light from the Supreme (V.3.17). However, after the separation, what the soul sees is not the One but an object of the analytic mind.

The higher soul is "one'd" with the One in its direct contemplative experience of it from within the Nous (Enn. IV.8.1; V.3.17; VI.9.3, 9, 10, 11), but the soul does not merge with the One even though the One supplies its being. The soul can be said to emerge from the World Soul and merge into the Nous; thereby, it loses its identity and becomes the Nous of all things. However, even the Nous never merges with the One but only contemplates it, and so does the individual soul. Once the soul has experienced the Good, the One remains in the soul's company, even during torture (I.4.13). One becomes like a god (I.6.9, III.2.8, VI.1–3). But eventually, the soul regains awareness of its lower identity and returns from the Nous to the body and the harshness of this world, although Plotinus does not tell how this is possible (IV.8.1) for the body cannot be escaped. (Suicide is condemned [I.9].) The individual's mind again has discursive reasoning (IV.8.1), but it is now informed by the Nous.

When Plotinus alludes to personal experience (*pathema*), he employs a phrase commonly used in the Mystery cults: "Whoever has seen, knows what

I am saying" (Kenney 1997, 333n36). In fact, he frequently employs the language of the Mystery cults—including references to the ascent and descent of the soul, purification, and sanctuary (328). He uses the language of vision (e.g., Enn. I.6.7–9, VI.9.10), touching (*synaphe*) (e.g., VI.9.7–11), penetration (V.5.10), embracing (VI.9.8), lovers (VI.9.9), and presence (*parousia*) (e.g., I.6.7, V.8.11, VI.9.4) in his realizations, but the One is without any Form (VI.7.32) and so cannot be literally seen or touched. Plotinus seems to have preferred the language of touch and penetration since the language of vision implies a duality of a seer and the seen (III.8.11) while touch implies immediate contact. The experience does not involve a dualistic presence set off from the experiencer; one no longer sees a sight but mingles one's seeing with what is contemplated and becomes that reality (VI.7.35). All one sees is the light that illuminates (VI.7.36). The Nous sees nothing of what is perceived by the senses or of anything mortal. Illuminated by the Good, it sees only eternal things (IV.7.10).

The One is always within the soul, and realizing this is an inward turn to the reality that has constituted us all along (Enn. V.9.7–8). Plotinus also uses the language of union (*henosis*, oneness) (e.g., VI.7.34) to refer to the unity of the soul or unity with the Nous. It is not a dualistic vision of another reality but an apprehended unity (VI.9.11). One has "grasped" the reality in oneself that is the same reality constituting everything (V.3.14). We can grasp the One both because we resemble the Nous in our power to know and contemplate and because there is a trace of the One in us since it is the source of our being (III.8.9). However, the One is utterly unknowable as an object (VI.9.4). The lower soul and its way of knowing are jettisoned during this experience (see V.3.4), but this is not a matter of uniting one reality with a second, separate reality; it is a matter of realizing the oneness of Being emanating from the One. Plotinus uses a variety of words for *unity* (for example, *henothenai*), but none suggest absorption or absolute identity. Rather, they mean "to be brought into unity," "to be joined to," "to be united to," or "to be associated with" (Kenney 1997, 332n35). He used *ekstasis* only once in connection to mystical experiences (Enn. VI.9.11).

Moreover, any talk of "union with the One" must, like all talk of the One, be qualified with "as it were" (*hoion*); the soul never gets past the Nous (Enn. V.3.17, VI.9.11). One remains within the Nous, contemplating the One. So too, the experience of being one'd with the One is only "as it were." The lower soul that gives us personality completely falls away (VI.9.10), but the higher soul is never annihilated and remains a distinct entity within the Nous. Plotinus never said "I am the One" (Rist 1967, 227; 1989, 184). The soul is not the One (Enn. VI.9.1). Nothing changes in one's ontic nature, only one's knowledge and awareness change. The One is the source of our existence, and we are never cut off from it, but we also never become the One, remaining other (VI.9.1, VI.9.9). During a mystical experience, the soul is glorified and filled with light. Thus, the seer does not see and does not distinguish and so does not imagine a duality (VI.9.1, VI.9.9).

Thus, even though the One is the only being of anything, each soul remains distinct within the Nous and is never obliterated or absorbed.[33] The soul is always connected to its source, but it also always retains its identity. Plotinus used the metaphor of coinciding circles: being one'd with the One is like two different circles having the same center (Enn. I.7.1, III.8.8, VI.5.5, VI.8.18, VI.9.8, VI.9.10). The One is never separate from us—though, when one'd, the soul and the One seem indistinguishable—but the difference between the soul and the One becomes clear when the soul moves apart.[34] The soul does not lose its individual existence in contemplating the One, and after the experience in the Nous, the soul returns to the body. Thus, each soul always remains a distinct drop in the ocean of Being.

In a mental reverse of the emanation process, consciousness moves as it travels through the hierarchical levels of reality, but the two distinct realities are not united. In fact, the One is ever-present and the souls in the Nous dance around the One (VI.9.8–9, VI.7.31). Thus, there is nothing, actually, to search for since the One is always present. We only have to *realize* our true situation properly. As part of the ascent, the individual can become aware of the oneness of their higher soul with the Nous (IV.8.1, 4; VI.7.12). Because of the analytical mind, this new state can be painful. The mind reaches for the formless but finds it cannot grasp it; it becomes distressed from "the sheer dread of holding to nothingness" (VI.9.3) and slips back into the realm of diversity.

In such an experience, the individual realizes what has always been within them. The Nous is both Being and the intellect of the higher soul; the Nous, the act of realizing it, and the realization are all one (Enn. III.7.3, V.3.6). The experience is participatory in nature: the experiencer *becomes* the formless (VI.7.34, VI.9.7). To see the divine as something external is to be outside of it (V.8.11). Thus, to see the Nous as an object ends the experience (V.8.31) since a dualizing state of consciousness has returned. During contemplation of the One, the soul is incapable of thinking that it possesses what it sought because it is not other than what it knows—the One—during the experience (VI.9.3). Here the knower, the known, and the knowledge are all the same and all together (VI.6.15) in contemplating the

One. The higher soul was always in the realm of the Nous and always contemplating (III.3.5). It is never unenlightened or material. The awakening comes suddenly (III.9.19–22; V.3.4; VI.7.34, 36). Likewise, it is transitory and ends abruptly (V.5.7; VI.7.34, 36; VI.9.9). It cannot be caused by any preparation or action. Thus, one cannot chase it but must wait quietly until it appears, like waiting for the sun to rise above the horizon. It occurs only when all intellectual activity has ceased (V.5.8; see also VI.7.23).

According to Porphyry, Plotinus's "end and goal" was to be one'd (*henothenai*) with the One—to contemplate the One from within the Nous—and he had this introvertive mystical experience four times during the six years late in his life when Porphyry knew him (*Life of Plotinus* 23). Porphyry also claimed to have had one such mystical experience himself. Plotinus stated that he had "many times" been "lifted out of his body" to become identical with his divine higher soul in the Nous, later returning to the realm of discursive reasoning (Enn. IV.8.1–11; see also V.3.6, VI.5.7). But the soul in the phenomenal world cannot constantly be in that state, and that Plotinus was one'd with the One only rarely does not mean that his was a failed mystical way of life. The purpose of being one'd is attaining a resulting continuous, enlightened state of consciousness in the Nous while in the body (see V.8.11). Being one'd through direct experience is necessary to gain the requisite knowledge; only through experience can one achieve a permanent, stabilized state of consciousness of the One established in the Nous. Attaining as many brief experiences of ecstasy as possible is not the goal. The goal is to attain the knowledge (*gnosis*) that enables one to participate in the world as it truly is, not to repeatedly experience that knowledge, and one fails only if they do not gain the knowledge (I.6.7).

Thus, Plotinus valued the lasting, transformed, nousified state (*nootheisa*) (Enn. VI.7.35) over transient ecstatic experiences of the One from the Nous. The introvertive state in which the soul is lifted up to the Nous (V.8.4, VI.7.12) becomes "the seat of the best life." The soul is now set firmly in the Nous (IV.8.1). In fact, the soul *becomes* the Nous (VI.7.15) since the Nous cannot be divided. The soul is no longer subject to the illusion that it is only a small embodied self. The soul has a stabilized, constant state of consciousness within the Nous even while it is in a sensory state. Thus, the nousified mind is both within the Nous and having experiences of the Nous. Plotinus claimed to have lived this "best life" (IV.8.1). Porphyry states that Plotinus "never relaxed his intense concentration upon the Nous" and continuously turned in contemplation to the Nous, except in sleep. Even while engaged in conversation, he kept his mind fixed without break on the Nous (*Life of Plotinus* 8, 9; see also Enn. VI.9.9), although speech is absent in the Nous itself (IV.3.32, IV.4.1).

Despite the mind's return to awareness of diversified phenomena, it maintains a mystical state: a nousified state in which the Nous takes over one's outward awareness even while one remains embodied. The individual is detached from the needs of the body and the phenomenal world in general, leading to a kind of depersonalization—a transcendence from personal memories and feelings (Bussanich 1997a, 359). The individual with a nousified mind leading such a contemplative life is in an ASC involving sense experiences. They are in a continuous, extrovertive mystical enlightened state: they no longer sense a self that exists independently of their transcendent source. The individual's awareness remains pure, although objects still appear in it without causing an effect (Stróżyński 2008, 65–69). They experience a life of wisdom (*sophia*) that is not acquired by reasoning but that is always present to the higher soul (Enn. V.8.4). The perfected philosopher who has achieved such wisdom, tranquility, and well-being (*eudaimonia*) is a different person, untouched by evil and without fear (I.4.15). This well-being is not a matter of ecstatic joy but of good feelings (*eupatheia*). Their depth-awareness of Being is harmonized with their everyday perception, and thus, they can remain constantly in contemplation, perhaps even in sleep (I.4.9).

Consequently, Plotinus refers to three types of mystical experiences: the depth-mystical experience of being one'd with the One through contemplation of the One from within the Nous; other introvertive experiences within the Nous; and an extrovertive, enlightened, nousified state in which the individual has sensory input once they have returned to the body. Ecstatic contemplative experiences of the One in which nousified awareness is absent may still occur in the enlightened state but only as transient moments within the long-lasting enlightened state of peaceful repose with a nousified mind. While Plotinus's reports of union with the One have analogs in Plato and Hellenistic writers, his mystical experiences of the reality of the Nous apparently have no precedent or parallel (Bussanich 1997a, 347n27, 349). In the nousified state, the individual is aware of differences in phenomena, but they are also constantly aware of the oneness of Being.

Plotinus believed in reincarnation (Enn. III.4, IV.3.8, IV.7.14). Human beings may be reborn as animals (III.3–4, III.6.6, IV.3.13–15) or perhaps even plants (III.4.2), being embodied according to their disposition (IV.3.12). They may also be able to remember former lives (IV.3.27), but the soul is not freed from the cycle of rebirth by uniting the higher part of the soul with the One. (In contrast, Porphyry believed it was a release from rebirth.) For Plotinus, souls exist eternally. The lower soul continues to exist in this life and is unchanged by the higher soul being one'd with the One (VI.8.18). The most that an individual can hope for is to become free of the lower soul in another life, reincarnated as a god within the Nous who contemplates the One continuously. However, since the soul and the world are real, releasing the lower soul from rebirth was not a crucial issue for Plotinus. All that matters is that the higher soul is in a permanent state of deliverance (Majercik 1995, 54).

Later Neoplatonism

Plotinus, like most mystics, did not see himself as an innovator or as establishing new doctrines or a new tradition. (The term *Neoplatonism* was not invented until the nineteenth century.) He thought that he was only an expounder of Plato's doctrines (Enn. V.1.8). But his innovations go well beyond Plato's ideas, and Neoplatonism evolved beyond Plotinus's ideas after his death. The One "beyond Being" was retained, but even his student Porphyry (ca. 232–304 CE) did not usually name it as such when speaking of "a non-Being above Being." Porphyry also brought the esoteric Chaldean Oracles, with its gods and theurgy, into Neoplationism.[35] Trying to reconcile these texts with Plato and Plotinus became a major theme in the school.

More philosophy and conventional Greek religiosity also took over Neoplationism starting with Porphyry, who saw the One as the true substance of the phenomenal world. Iamblicus of Syria (ca. 245–325 CE) took the Aristotelian position on the soul and rejected the idea of a soul separate from the body, as did his student Proclus (ca. 412–485 CE). To them, the soul was not itself divine and so needed divine action to be saved. Hence, theurgy was needed, and religious and magical theurgical rituals to invoke the presence of God replaced contemplation. This became the standard position in Neoplatonism. Iamblicus also distinguished the One as the material substance of the world from the One as the transcendent source. He also spoke of an ineffable (*arreton*) principle above the One. Damascius (458–538 CE) postulated the ineffable principle above the One because unity entails a relation to plurality and thus cannot be the Ultimate (Wallis 1986, 477). The logical ineffability of a "wholly other" reality became stressed while mystical experiences were not, although the last head of the Athenian school, Isidorus (ca. 560–636 CE), was said to have approached the gods within himself "in the hidden depths of unknowing."

By the time of the Neoplatonist Christian Pseudo-Dionysius the Aero-pagite in the sixth century, Neoplatonism was essentially non-mystical and its metaphysics had been significantly altered from Plotinus's, although his doctrine of the One being transcendent, beyond knowledge, and beyond expression and his type of emanationism remained important. The Pseu-do-Dionysius's teacher, Proclus, presented a synthesis of Greek ideas on cosmology with Plotinus's doctrine of the nonpersonal transcendent One and emanationism.

These synthesized post-Plotinian forms of Platonism, based on Plotinus's framework, would go on to be fundamental in all Abrahamic mystical traditions for a thousand years until Thomas Aquinas and the rise of Aristotelianism in Christianity in the thirteenth century. As Bernard McGinn says, Greek philosophy (primarily the Platonic tradition) accounts for the remarkable similarities among the Abrahamic mystical traditions more than their real, but limited, cultural contacts (2013, 160). (He adds that more interesting are the differences that evolved in each mystical tradition.) Neoplatonism also returned to influence esotericism in the Renaissance and continues to influence Eastern Orthodox Christianity today.[36]

Philosophical Texts as Spiritual Exercises

Lloyd Gerson is the most prominent advocate today of the position common to philosophers and Christian theologians that Plotinus's philosophy is essentially non-mystical and mystical references can be cut from it without harm (1994, 218–24).[37] However, this misses the entire point of why Plotinus taught and his teachings. His experiences were not a "sort of accidental feature of his philosophy" (219). That the ascent of the soul to the Nous "is directed not to producing occasional visions or states, but rather to more enduring states of contemplation" (219) does not mean that his philosophy is not mystical but only that, like all classical mystics, he valued an enlightened mystical way of living in the world—here, a life permanently tied to the awareness of the Nous—over isolated ecstatic experiences. Gerson's position also overlooks the fundamental role of other mystical experiences in attaining an enlightened nousified state. The fact that Plotinus was able to teach and reason after having had introvertive depth-mystical experiences does not mean he is not a mystic (219–20). It only means that the nousified state of consciousness that is in constant contact with the Nous is an extrovertive mystical sensory state.

Gerson appears to equate *mystical* with *irrational,* but the *Enneads* is a prime example of a text that is both mystical and rational. Of course, Plotinus's metaphysics can be presented without reference to the mystical ascent, but that would not present his actual philosophy; the mystical quest is central to his philosophy and cannot be severed or seen as merely auxiliary. In fact, treating his philosophy outside of a mystical framework may lead to misinterpreting his metaphysics through a dualistic prism—for example, taking his metaphors literally and making the One an object of some sort that exists distinct from the natural world, or reducing the Nous to the mind in our modern sense or to ordinary thinking. From this perspective, we can only see normal philosophical reflection and speculation when, in fact, mystical experiences are being interpreted or even described. Equally importantly, this perspective misses the principal objective of his works: Plotinus was not merely conveying philosophical speculations but urging students toward an experience (Enn. VI.9.4). It is an attempt to transform students, to get them to have ASC experiences of the One and to achieve a nousified mind. In short, the *Enneads* are fundamentally mystical in nature. One cannot cut away this aspect of Plotinus's philosophy without deforming all of it.

As Pierre Hadot has presented well, classical Greek philosophy, in general, was not simply an intellectual matter but a way to transform a person's life into a life of well-being (*eudaimonia*): philosophy was a spiritual exercise. Works were "written not so much to inform the reader of a doctrinal content but to form him" (Hadot 1995, 264). Philosophy was not merely a matter of thought but one's whole way of being (270). "Love of wisdom" (*philo-sophia*) was not about accepting some beliefs but a "radical conversion and transformation of the individual's way of being" (265). It turns one's life upside down to achieve the most authentic human state (83). *Contemplation* (*theoria*) in Greek philosophy is broader than mystical meditation, but it ends in using a meditative practice to participate in what is known, thereby unveiling the structure of things through insights that are beyond the rational mind. This participation (*methexis*) in the supreme reality becomes central. Moreover, it encompasses all of how one lives.[38] Even Neoplatonists used the word *mystical* sparingly, but philosophers adopted the idea of an inward experiential vision as the summit of philosophical contemplation from use of the word in Mystery cults (Hadot 1986, 239).

In sum, we misconstrue Greek philosophy if we view it as only a matter of doctrines. Doctrines can be abstracted out of a total way of life, and getting the correct picture of reality was a necessary foundation for Greek philosophy. As such, doctrines were presented and defended in its philosophical discussions, but they were never the end. "Being philosophical" did not describe one's way of thinking but one's way of being in the world. It was an art in how to live. Wisdom (*sophia*) required training in both how one sees the world and how one lives. This gave philosophy an inward orientation, with examining one's inner life and self-mastery being vital. The goal was to achieve inner serenity, free of passions and indifferent to the troubles and evils of the world. Skeptics attained this by suspending all judgments. The study of nature (especially the heavens) was for realizing that humans are part of the infinite cosmos, consequentially devaluing oneself and leading to living in harmony with nature (Hadot 1995, 266). As noted previously, living in the present without concern for the past or future was important for inner tranquility (268). Inner peace led to the most effective actions, but the actions alone were not the objective; living contentedly in the world in the face of adversities and without fear of death was.

All of this shows continuity with mysticism as a way of life: adopting new doctrines, changing one's actions, or inducing isolated ASC experiences was not the primary objective in Greek philosophy; inducing a new way of being always was. Medieval Christianity adopted this view of philosophy as spiritual exercise. Indeed, Christianity presented itself as the true philosophy since the *logos* was revealed in the Christ. Christian monasticism resulted from the idea of philosophy as a way of life. (That Greek philosophy was always practiced in groups or at least in discussions is also worth noting.) However, with some major exceptions, by the late Middle Ages theology had become a scholastic exercise, and in the modern era philosophy was reduced to an academic interest alone. Living in conformity to how reality truly is was reduced to only intellectually accepting correct ideas about the surface appearances of reality. Some philosophers (including René Descartes and Benedict Spinoza) and mystics bucked the trend.

In fact, inducing ASC mystical experiences may also have been an objective in many cases of Greek philosophy, not just for Plotinus. Hadot makes a strong case that we misread classical Greek philosophical texts when we treat them like modern written works in nature (see also Rappe 2000; Stróżyński 2008, chaps. 2 and 5). Philosophical teachings were meant to be delivered orally in order to induce a transformation in the listener's consciousness. (Even Aristotle's works might be included here.) This may partially explain why some pre-Socratics wrote poems. It also suggests a reason to explain why Plotinus was so reluctant to write any treatises.[39]

In Plato's *Symposium* (216a–d), Alcibiades spoke of his own experience: Socrates's speech induced a trance similar to ones the Corybantes induced by playing flutes. He compared Socrates's voice to the seductive voices of the Sirens (Dodds 2004, 77–79).[40] Treating the texts simply as delivering positions on philosophical issues misses the effect the sounds and rhythms of the words had in potentially transforming the consciousness of the student.[41] The written texts were meant to be read out loud for the same effect as oral teaching. (Reading silently to oneself apparently did not take hold until well into the second millennium CE.) The texts are not meditation manuals or full accounts of a teacher's spiritual exercises, but they are devices to help transform the listener's consciousness.[42] One way that the theories presented in a text may induce ASC experiences is if the listener contemplates the theories and lives in accordance with them. But reading texts only to study their philosophical content misses the texts' primary purpose as well as this acoustic dimension. Such a truncated reading reduces the texts to something they were not intended to be.

Certainly in the case of Plotinus, the purpose of teaching appears to be not to convince students to adopt some new metaphysical doctrine through rational arguments but to inspire them to abandon all dualistic thinking, contemplate the One in a mystical ASC, and achieve an enlightened ASC state by having one's consciousness nousified. Discursive thinking plays a central role on the path, but it is to be surpassed; one is to be transformed experientially in a nondiscursive wisdom. His is a way of life, not a modern philosophical discussion. The treatises of the *Enneads* do not constitute a systematic presentation of a metaphysical theory. They are answers, sometimes contradictory, to queries from his inner circle and presume prior knowledge of Plotinus's ideas.[43]

Key Themes

Even though Greek culture may well have had mystical influences from its very beginnings (either indigenously or through trade and other cultural connections with Egypt, Babylon, Persia, and India), inducing mystical states of consciousness and mysticism in general were not major themes in classical Greek culture. It turned in a different direction in the Axial Age. But as with all cultures, mystics were no doubt present, and there are some characteristics within Greek philosophy that are common in Greek mysticism.

- With the Axial Age, interest in the *self* arose, and with at least Pythagoras and Heraclitus, there was an inward turn toward attaining true knowledge.

- Knowledge of the truth was central to Greek thought, but knowledge did not end with rational thinking and sense experience. Distrusting human opinion and sense experience and valuing divine knowledge were common themes in both mystical and non-mystical philosophy. For mystical philosophers, reality is eternal and unchanging, knowledge is a matter of certainty, and knowledge of reality is not attained by devising rational truths but is revealed in divine experiences. It is a matter of recovering something we have forgotten rather than discovering something new about reality. Philosophical reasoning forms a preliminary step for inducing such experiences, but genuine knowledge involves participation in the reality to be known. This knowledge is possible after death, when one has left the body, and in this way, a philosophical way of life prepares for death by attempting to separate the soul from the living body (*Phaedo* 64a, 67d–e, 81a). Mystics believed that at least a taste of divine knowledge was attainable here by turning away from the world and looking inward, leading to an ecstatic mystical experience. In a vestige from the shamanic past, the quest for divine knowledge was seen as a journey of the soul—an ascent from the darkness of the shadow realm to the light—but the objective of philosophy was to transform the entire person and to live a contemplative life in this world, not to have isolated ecstatic experiences.

- The only clearly identifiable, full-blown mystical way of life came late in this period with Plotinus. His is an otherworldly mysticism showing little social concern or, indeed, little interest for life in this world. He made no instruction manuals for meditative exercises, but there are allusions to such inner activities, so it appears that such exercises were well-known and part of the daily life of the philosophical schools (Hadot 1995, 83). Other philosophical ways of life also attempted to transform persons, but whether ASCs were involved is not as clear.

- Plotinus's emanationist mysticism is introvertive and nontheistic.[44] Introvertive mystical experiences and the resulting extrovertive, enlightened, nousified life are central, and his metaphysics focuses on a transcendent framework with a unified, unchanging, and nonpersonal ultimate source. The One's nature in itself is unknown and unspecifiable. Plato and Parmenides can also be included here. The soul is never treated as extinguishable. There may have been more types of mystical experiences in the Mystery cults, but we cannot know.

• Plotinus did not speak of overcoming desires as most mystics do. Rather, desire (*pothos*) is to be redirected from worldly objects to being fulfilled by the One, our ultimate Good (Enn. I.6.7). This can involve a longing passion (*eros*) in mystical matters. So too, he said nothing about overcoming the self since the soul is real and eternal. There is also much less about consciousness than in most nontheistic introvertive mysticisms since the One is beyond even that worldly attribute. Beauty plays a far larger role here. Plotinus also does not tell anything about a personal relation with the One, as in theism, since it is not a separate reality with which to have a personal relation, nor would it reciprocate our concern. Even later Neo-platonists who viewed the One as generally benevolent toward all creation saw no personal relationships.

• In philosophy, the Greek turn in the Axial Age led to there being one final ontological source or explanatory reality and multiple souls. In Plotinus's mysticism, a cosmic source sets the natural order of things in this world (*logos*), but none of the three transcendent principles are otherwise active in worldly events. The One is transcendent to the world and is utterly unlike anything phenomenal, but it is also experienceable inwardly. The world is ultimately deceptive or something that is not to be valued at all, but it has no eternal Being.

• The immortal and nonmaterial soul is distinct from the material body. The soul is not part of the material world, and human beings are essentially spiritual beings. This permits participation in the realm of eternal truth, and after death we can know pure truth. Reincarnation was accepted by some traditions, but escaping a cycle of rebirths might have been a concern only in the mystery cults.

Chapter 4

Jewish Mysticism

Greek thought fed the mystical traditions in all three Abrahamic religions that arose in the Western regions of Asia. First, the Jewish tradition. Mysticism in Judaism arose out of its earlier visionary traditions and the study of the esoteric meanings of the letters and words of the Hebrew Bible. Its history is more a series of disconnected phases with different foci than one connected, unfolding historical phenomenon; both Christian and Muslim mysticisms show more continuity.

The revelations and prophetic experiences of the Hebrew Bible are vital to all branches of Jewish mysticism, although there is no expression of contemplative experiences in that text (Smart 1967, 423). Later Kabbalists claimed that a secret (*sod*) oral tradition going back to Moses on Mount Sinai was codified in the Bible. They believed that the texts had to be written in code to hide their true intent from most readers and had to be decoded to reveal certain profound mysteries. In addition, a strong case can be made that there were esoteric initiation practices for the priests of the First Temple period concealed in the Bible that had mystical elements (Kohav 2013).

Philo Judaeus of Alexandria

The first Jewish thinker to write of the possibility of mystical experiences was the philosopher Philo Judaeus of Alexandria (ca. 25 BCE–50 CE). Philo lived in the ascetic and spiritual Hellenistic environment of Alexandria, where Stoicized Middle Platonism—which stressed the transcendence of the First Principle—flourished and where Plotinus would later study (see Louth 1981, 18–35). He mentions a monastic community of contemplatives near Alexandria, and mysticism may also have been part of the Essene way of life (Smart 1967, 423). However, whether Philo himself had mystical experiences or was only a theorist inspired by the teachings of mystics is not clear. His ASC experiences appear limited to an inner voice in his soul filling him with ideas (Winston 2001, 169), but he may have practiced a mystical way of life since he wrote of the need to cleanse the mental faculties, feelings, and will to bring them in line with the "Eternal Will" (Winston 1996, 77).

Philo was the first to fuse Greek philosophical contemplation with theism and to develop the idea of "union with God." He made Plato a disciple of Moses and Moses the supreme teacher of Middle Platonism. Indeed, he claimed that all Greek philosophy that he deemed valid came from Moses. For Philo, creation is nothingness (*oudeneia*) compared to the one true reality, God. God alone has true being. Things after him have no real being but are only believed to exist in our imagination. To see God, we need to discard the sense that an independently real individual self exists within the phenomenal world. The soul ascends through inward contemplation in solitude and darkness, culminating in a direct vision of the Uncreated. Philo also spoke of *deification* as "an unbroken union with God in love," but the highest union was of the mind with the intermediate *logos*, not with God himself. God is totally transcendent.

Philo utilized a method that already existed among Jewish scholars of reading scripture allegorically to get at its hidden esoteric meanings. In commenting on the biblical passage of standing next to God (Deut. 5:31), he was the first to give a mystical interpretation of the notion of *cleaving to God* (*devekut*) (Deut. 4:4, 10:20, 11:22, 13:4, 30:20) that became prominent in the Middle Ages. Rabbinic theologians emphasized the community, and *cleaving* had previously been a matter of the people of Israel as a whole, but for Philo it was about an individual's experience—an intimate communion with God that overcomes the gap between God and an individual (see Gen. 2:24). He wrote of seeing "God's light" by God's own light (rather than via the *logos*). In addition, he wrote of the need for asceticism to attain a vision of God, the "sober intoxication" of the divinized state that produces tranquility and stability, and forgetting the self (Winston 1996, 79–80).[1] These topics suggest mystical experiences, but he makes no mention of ecstasy. He did mention a "purified mind" capable of seeing God through God himself (Winston 2001, 159). This appears to be an inner intuitive intellectual illumination resulting from a rational, analytical process of (159). The direct vision of God results from intuitive reason and does not bypass our rational faculties (162). Philo compared the final ecstasy to the state of the Old Testament prophets, and this does not appear to be a case of hiding mystical experiences with orthodox language.

Philo may have been the first Platonist to bring up the matter of unity (*henosis*) with God in any form. His ideas on the One, the *logos*, and mystical oneness were part of the environment that influenced Plotinus. He introduced the Greek sense of an unknowable transcendent creator and negative theology into Judaism, and his is the first recorded reference to the idea of the literal *ineffability* of God—no phenomenal attributes or even a name apply to God.

However, due to his influence by Greek thought, Philo was outside the mainstream of Jewish thought and piety at the time (Smart 1967, 423). Due to the destruction of the Jewish community in Alexandria, Philo had no direct influence on medieval Jewish mysticism. Indeed, there is no evidence that Jews even heard of him in the Middle Ages. (Christians did read his available works.) The idea of mystical union was reintroduced into Judaism from Muslim and Latin sources in the tenth century.

The Hekhalot Visionary Texts

In the Hebrew Bible, people often saw God (e.g., Gen. 32:30, Exod. 24:9–11, Job 42:5). Prophets saw him (e.g., Isa. 6:1). Famous Biblical encounters with the divine include Moses's experience with the burning bush on Mount Sinai, Jacob's dream of ascending a ladder to heaven, and Jacob wrestling with God.[2] Ezekiel's vision of a heavenly chariot or throne (*merkavah*) (Ezek. 1:10; also see Gen. 5:21–24) became of particular importance: he had seen God's home. From the seventh to eleventh centuries CE a class of esoteric literature, hymns, and magical "seals" for safe journeys developed from meditating on Ezekiel's vision of the diverse "heavenly palace" (*hekhalot*) texts. With the temple of Solomon destroyed, the presence of God was now only in a heavenly temple, but the pious could go to that temple, stand before the throne of God, and see and hear him directly by means of prayer.[3] The heavens are rooms of the heavenly temple. These secret teachings were kept only for the elite, not intended for the general Jewish population. At some point, this went from being esoteric theological speculation to advocating an experiential ascent; an individual could actually be in the presence of the transcendent and remote God seated on his throne in order to praise him. (Some scholars reverse the order: visionary experiences preceded or underlay the earliest speculation.) This meant that revelations did not end with the Torah (the law or the first five books of the Hebrew Bible) as rabbinic theologians asserted: God continued to reveal himself to human beings, and they could initiate the process. They could storm heaven and force direct access to God (Schäfer 1992, 161).

This individualized eschatology. One could personally experience the presence of God (or at least his throne) in this lifetime and not have to wait until the end-times. These authors rebelled against the notion that divine truth could only be reached by oral tradition or exegesis; they demanded a direct experience of God (Dan 2002, 19). The esoteric teachings of the Hekhalot texts showed how this journey was possible. There was also an interest in magic—for example, incantations to make the Prince of Torah appear. The especially pious could become "chariot (*merkavah*) riders," ascend to the unseen realm, and return with new knowledge. There were seven courtyards or chambers guarded by angels leading to the throne of God. Seals on seven rings had to be shown to each angel. (This may be code for different types of meditation or states of consciousness.) Enthronement was not union with God but still a type of quasi-deification; to see God required becoming like God (Wolfson 1995, 137). Likewise, the pious could have other visual and auditory experiences and may be granted paranormal powers.

The central experiences of communion with God remained visionary rather than mystical, but there is evidence that some early Talmudic rabbis practiced asceticism and self-purification for their ascent to heaven (Smart 1967, 423). The texts contain techniques ranging from magical to contemplative for attaining the ASC states that mystics use (Arbel 2016, 64). Ritualized chanting of songs or the names of God and praying were the most common techniques. In a story in the Jerusalem and Babylonian Talmud and Tosefta texts from the second century CE, four famous rabbis glimpsed the garden (*pardes*) of God; one died, one went mad, one became a heretic, and the fourth "entered in peace and came out in peace" (Dan 2007, 13). "Entering the garden" may be code for meditative states, and this example may be evidence of early visionary practices (see Scholem 1961, 52–54). This is a matter of dispute, but two rabbis of the early Talmudic period do refer to personal experiences: "I saw," "I heard," "I envisioned" (Dan 2007, 14). But even if visions were the important ASC experiences, at least the Hekhalot literature valued ASC experiences and gave a warrant for experiences of God in later Jewish mysticism. The literature also showed that individuals could take the initiative in the process.

Cosmogonic Speculation

Merkavah/hekhalot mysticism declined by the seventh century, but its revival in the ninth and tenth centuries may have influenced medieval German Hasidism (Dupré 2005, 6352). However, Rabbinic speculation on the letters of the Bible in the Babylonian Talmud spread to Europe definitely influenced later Jewish mysticism. (Such speculation is often labeled *language mysticism*.) This speculation did not arise from mysticism but from reflection on the hidden meaning of the creation story in Genesis, for God hides himself (Isa. 45:15). Speculation was influenced by earlier Hellenistic Jewish thinkers such as Philo and later by Neoplatonists. According to the cosmogony of the short and enigmatic *Book of Creation* (*Sefer Yetzirah*), God sitting on his throne created both the manifest universe and human beings through thirty-two "wondrous paths of wisdom": the twenty-two letters of the Hebrew alphabet and the ten creative forces (*sefirot*) which appeared through emanation (*atzilut*) from God. That is, God did not merely speak to create the universe; the letters were the actual material or energy through which God created. The shortest version of this book may be from the second century CE, but it, like the Hekhalot texts, did not have much impact on the Judaism of the time.

This cosmogony develops the ancient Jewish ideas that Hebrew is a sacred language and that God utilized its letters to create the world. It also presents a harmony of the universe that could be utilized to present human beings as universal microcosms. The first emanation was the spirit of the living God (*ruach*), and the twenty-two letters and air emanated from this spirit; water emanated from air, fire from water, and then came the eight directions of the cosmos (north, south, east, west, up, down, beginning, and end) and also good and evil. The emanations are the forms into which all things are created, as set forth in the beginning of the book of Genesis. Water formed the earth, fire the heavens, and spirit the region in between. The Hebrew letters are the creative force that caused this process. For example, the seven double Hebrew letters produced the seven planets; when pronounced hard, the planets approach the earth, when pronounced soft, they recede.

Such an emanationism makes God not only transcendent, but his being is also immanent to the natural world. Thus, the natural world is not set off, distinct from God. The *Book of Creation* began to be given an esoteric meaning in the second half of the twelfth century in Europe, often suggesting ASCs if not mystical experiences.

Early German Pietists

In the Rhineland during the twelfth and thirteen centuries, where Christian mysticism was also flourishing, the pious (Hasidei Ashkenaz) wrote on the mystery of the unity of God. All anthropomorphic depictions of God in the Bible were interpreted as referring only to God's glory (*kavod*), formed of divine fire, not to God himself. This glory was either a created light extrinsic to God, an emanation from God (and thus attached to him), or only an image in the mind of a mystic or prophet (Wolfson 1995, 141). The elite were to focus on God's glory, while others were to focus on God's transcendence as the creator.

One can attain a vision of this glory through a life of piety cultivated by a life of charity or contemplation beyond merely following Jewish law (*halakhah*). While the Godhead remains eternally perfect, the created world is severely flawed, and thus the pious must reject all worldly temptations. This led to an austere ascetic life—within the duties of a married life—of constant repentance. Humility before God and even-mindedness (*hishtavut*) were important virtues: the egoless pious were unmoved by praise, insult, reward, or punishment (Horwitz 2016, 82, 356). It also led to accepting persecution and even martyrdom at the hands of Christians. But the pious exhibited a deep love of God. Through this, they attained an experiential vision of the presence of God in the world: God's glory permeating all things. They also gained magical powers.

Prayers were likened to Jacob's ladder extending from earth, a means for the pious to ascend to heaven. The pious also engaged in a numerical meditation (*gematria*) regarding these prayers; the number of words in a prayer and the numerical value of their letters were correlated with biblical passages and the names of God. The creation account in Genesis expresses the letters, words, and numbers God utilized to create.[4] The pious also utilized female and sexual imagery, perhaps preserving an ancient esoteric reading of the Song of Songs (Wolfson 1995, 144–46). Whether this figured in meditation, as in Kabbalah, is not clear, nor is how much of this was driven by experiences rather than esoteric speculation.

Early Kabbalah

At the same time this was occurring in the Rhineland, in Provence—in southern France—the Kabbalah tradition was emerging. *Kabbalah* means "handed down." Kabbalists did not see themselves as innovators but as exposing the true meaning of traditional texts and conveying a knowledge preserved through a line of teachers going back to Moses, Abraham, and Adam, although historical antecedents for all of the Kabbalist ideas have not been identified.

Kabbalists reinterpreted Jewish practices in a meditative direction. The school's earliest text, the *Book of Light* (*Bahir*), was probably composed around 1185. It presents a Neoplatonist reinterpretation of the doctrine of emanations first elaborated in the Hekhalot texts and the *Book of Creation*. In their interpretation, the unity of God allowed for the emanation of powers (Dan 2002, 26). Isaac the Blind (ca. 1160–1235) conceived the emanations as emitting from a hidden dimension of the Godhead: the silent Infinite (*Ein Sof*, meaning boundless, without end). The Infinite first emanated divine thought, and from these thoughts, the other emanations came forth. The powers of evil are depicted as the fingers of God's left hand, but there is no duality of good and evil as in later Kabbalah. One was to ascend the ladder of emanations and ultimately unite with the divine thought, but unity with the Infinite was considered impossible. In Girona in Catalonia, Kabbalists substituted divine will for divine thought. These Kabbalists also helped Kabbalah gain legitimacy in Jewish communities by writing commentaries on the Torah. Other Spanish esoteric schools at the time were influenced by Sufism in Egypt and the philosopher Moses Maimonides (ca. 1135–1204). Maimonides was not a mystic, and his writings do not suggest that a human being could become one with God in any sense. Rather, he emphasized finding God through reason. However, he validated the idea that revelations could occur in the present day. He also applied the Aristotelian adage that "to know something one must become like that thing" to knowing God.

Kabbalah around Girona remained an esoteric tradition. How much of their work is a matter of theological speculation alone rather than being experience-inspired is not clear. Doctrines were taught in small circles to a select few. The Kabbalists constantly expressed fear that this knowledge, if obtained by the unlettered without the guidance of a teacher, could lead to antinomianism and heresy (Katz 2013, 13). Some Kabbalists deliberately wrote obscurely, using only hints and opaque references that could not be understood by the public (Dan 2007, 37). They adopted the mainstream rationalism of the time resulting from Greek thought: God was conceived as being without limit (*ein sof*), perfect, and unchanging rather than anthropomorphically as in the Hebrew Bible. In their study of the *Book of Light*, they incorporated Gnostic-like dualities.

The result of their speculation was the Kabbalists' principal composition—the *Book of Splendor* (*Zohar*). It was finalized by Moses de Leon (1240–1305) in the 1280s in Castile. He presented four types of interpretation of the Torah: literal, analogical, homiletical, and expounding the secret sense. Most of the *Zohar* is about the secrets in the Torah, which is itself also considered divine. It is also theosophical; it investigates the inner life of God through the rungs of creation (*sefirot*). It was written in Aramaic and set in the second century and attributed to a famous early rabbi. It presumes knowledge of the Bible, the Talmud, and Kabbalist doctrines and is written in a code of complex symbols for revealing the true meaning of the Torah. The ASC experiences in it are mainly visionary. Through it, the enlightened (*maskilim*) contemplate secrets that are not disclosed to the public (Wolfson 1995, 154–55). Through an "impulse" from below, an impulse from above is awakened; and through that impulse, an even higher impulse is awakened from below, until that impulse reaches the place where a lamp is to be lit; the lamp is lit, sending a blessing to all the world (*Zohar* 1.244).

According to this Kabbalah school, the divine energy of the luminous emanations of the Infinite emerged from the fog of the Infinite like flames. There is a hierarchy of ten interpenetrating rungs of emanation, as with earlier speculation, but these rungs are different. From the Infinite's power, or will, first emerged the supreme crown (*keter*); from that emerged wisdom (*hokhmah*), then understanding (or knowledge), greatness (or mercy), judgment, beauty, eternalness, glory (or majesty), foundation (or the righteous ones), and lastly, the material world (kingdom, or sovereignty). Thus, the material world is the farthest removed from God's perfection. These are the spheres of existence for all finite objects, and different Kabbalists understood the same terms to mean different things; one Kabbalist might understand the spheres to be a Neoplatonist series of divine emanations, while another might understand them to be symbolic reifications of ethical principles. The spheres manifest the inner life of God—the emanations are not out of the Infinite but within it—while the hidden depths of the Infinite are never revealed but remain forever beyond all human comprehension. Kabbalists depicted the process of emanation as an upside-down tree spreading downward from its roots in the Infinite above. They also depicted the process as a primordial human spreading downward from the head, each *sefirah* as an energy center along the spine, with the right side of the body identified as male and the left side as female. Another image depicted ten concentric circles or spheres. In this way, the one undivided Godhead produces a multiplicity, and all things in the natural realm continuously exist within its divine emanations. The idea of a Neoplatonist return—the absorption of later emanations into the first by being drawn into the source of the flame of creation—is a minor theme in Kabbalah.

Although women are almost totally absent in classical Kabbala, Kabbalists gave the divine world a female side: God's "dwelling place" or "presence" (*shekhinah*). In the *Zohar*, the *shekhinah* is depicted as the moon. She is the lowest power of the divine realm and, thus, the closest to the created world and human beings. The presence of female power in the divine world is one of the most important ways that Kabbalah is distinguished from other Jewish worldviews (Dan 2007, 45). This female element was introduced to the divine perhaps under the influence of Christians' glorification of the Madonna that peaked in the twelfth century (48). Dualities in this world—day and night, sun and moon, sky and earth—become understood in terms of gender duality in the divine world (44).

Creation is self-initiated from the divine nothingness (*ayin*) of the Infinite (Matt 1995, 65–72). *Nothingness* is not literal nonexistence; it is a transcendent reality that is devoid of anything phenomenal and out of which things arise. As one Kabbalist put it, "Nothingness is more existent than all the being of the world." From nothingness, there is a transition to something (*yesh*): the phenomenal world. Thus, the existence of everything depends exclusively on the transcendent, unchanging Nothingness. It is unknowable; hence, the scriptures do not refer to it. Some Kabbalists have argued that creation cannot occur within the divine Godhead, but under the common understanding, God is both transcendent and immanent to the cosmos. Emanation has occurred since the distant past (starting with a small shining point), but it continues today. (Emanation states an ontological relation, not a temporal process.)

Evil and suffering presented problems, as they do for any panentheistic emanationism. Some Kabbalists took the Neoplatonist position, denying that evil had any actual reality. Others incorporated a Gnostic-like dualism, claiming that emanation contained evil as a sort of overflowing waste product of the growth of judgment, like the shell that surrounds the heart of a nut. The *Zohar* depicts this "other side" as being its own emanation. The powers of evil came to be seen as impious emanations of the "left side," paralleling the holy emanations of the right side. But others suggested that evil arose through human action: the Tree of Life and the Tree of the Knowl-edge of Good and Evil were bound together until the fall of Adam split the presence of God (*shekhinah*) in the world from the Infinite (*Ein Sof*).

Human beings are made in the "image of God" (Gen. 1:26) and, thus, are a microcosm reflecting the ten emanations. In fact, the human mind is isomorphic with God's: in seeing the depths of oneself, one sees God and vice versa. While embodied in the natural world, however, the transcendent soul's heavenly knowledge is lost. The soul consists of three parts: the "gross" component responsible for actions and desires, the moral component, and the rational component (*neshamah*) that studies the Torah and apprehends the divine. But the soul is only a created image of the *logos* and, thus, is absolute nothingness in itself. In order for the rational component to attain a perfect state, the soul reincarnates in a wheel of souls (*gilgul neshamot*) until it is perfect.[5] Once a soul is perfected, it returns to heaven to become united to its divine source. While embodied, one can achieve a state of ecstasy in which one experiences God's love. The *Zohar* explains that this self-perfection can come through service: "Whoever serves God out of love comes into union with the holiness of the heavenly world to come."

People can not only perfect themselves but can repair (*tikkun*) the disharmony of the world that resulted from Adam's sin and restore the connection of the presence of God (*shekhinah*) with the Infinite by keep-ing the Torah's 613 commandments (*mitzvot*), praying, and studying the Torah. Sinful acts increase the disharmony in the cosmos. Thus, the com-mandments' primary purpose was cosmic, not merely social, and there is no other reason for them but God's purpose. Each person has part of the material rung of the emanations in them and can therefore literally repair the cosmos. The actions of Jews have a cosmic impact and thereby take on a cosmic significance.

The means to ascend to the heavenly realms in this life were reciting prayers and blessings and performing rituals with the proper devotional intent (*kavvanah*) by eliminating all attachment to one's will and align-ing one's will with God's intention. This became a form of meditation to "purify" the consciousness.[6] Meditating in this way involved focusing on the Kabbalist understanding of the esoteric content of orthodox prayers. The Hebrew alphabet and the names of God were also utilized as objects of a type of concentrative meditation that aimed to empty the mind of all worldly matters.

The highest form of intimacy is a mystical cleaving to God (*devekut*). Beginning with early Kabbalists in Provence, this has remained the goal of the Kabbalist way of life. All sense of oneself or the world as separate and independent of God or autonomous must be banished as idolatrous; nothing emanated has an independent existence or is truly separated from God. To Isaac the Blind, cleaving to God is achieved by contemplating the names of God. According to Moses ben Nahman of Cirona (Nahmanides, 1194–1270), this cleaving is a state in which one constantly remembers God and his love while performing mundane activities, even to the point that when one speaks with others, one's heart is not with them but is still before God. In the highest rapture, divine reality is disclosed. For most Kabbalists, cleaving was not seen as a way to eliminate the soul or unite the soul with the transcendent Infinite but only to unify the person with their base in the emanation process. A state of ecstatic rapture—being enflamed (*hitlahavat*)—is their goal. (Sufis, Neoplatonist Muslims, and Christians all had influences here.)

Classical Kabbalah

By the fourteenth century, Kabbalah had spread throughout Western Europe, the Middle East, and North Africa. By the sixteenth century, Jews were expelled from Spain, Portugal, and much of Western Europe. Jews, now dispirited, fled to greater Poland and the Middle East. The town of Safed in Galilee became a major center of Kabbalist activity that emphasized meditation, ASC experiences, and paranormal powers. Messianic hopes also were revived in light of Jews' suffering and persecution at that time. Ascetic practices were common. Asceticism and concentrated devote intent (*kavvanah*) in all acts purified the soul (Smart 1967, 424). Moses Cordovero (1522–1570) refined Zoharic emanationism, emphasizing that the Godhead itself is manifested in the finite world through its emanations, which were vessels in which the light of the Infinite is contained and through which the light is reflected in different forms.

The most important doctrines came from Isaac Luria (1534–1572), known as "the Lion." He was born in Jerusalem and spent seven years on an island in the Nile River contemplating the *Zohar*. He was charismatic, worked magical wonders, and forecasted fates. His meditation techniques included combining divine names. He believed in reincarnation, claiming it gave people fresh chances at a living pure life and provided punishment for those who transgressed (Smart 1967, 424). He wrote no books and kept his teachings within a small circle, but his disciples spread his ideas, which rapidly became absorbed into mainstream Kabbalah. According to

Luria, creation involved a contraction (*tzimtzum*) of the Infinite in order to establish an empty space for finite beings to occupy apart from God. God and his light were initially absent from this empty space, but a shaft of light was emitted from the Infinite into the empty space. The first emanation arose in the form of the primordial man, Adam.

Thus, creation was seen as an emanation from God himself but still also within him. However, after the fall of Adam the emanations could not contain the intense energy of the light, and the vessels shattered (*shevirat ha-keilim*), bringing disaster to the remaining emanations and enabling evil to exist as a separate entity. The divine presence (*shekhinah*) was separated from the *Ein Sof* and no longer pervaded the whole world (Smart 1967, 424). Space was divided into two parts: the lower part had splinters of the divine light, and the higher had the light of God that escaped in its purity. Thus, the cosmos was divided into a kingdom of evil (which nevertheless contains some sparks of divine light) and a kingdom of light. Adam failed to defeat evil, and God chose the people of Israel to complete the task of removing evil by raising up the sparks of light that are currently in the kingdom of evil and returning them to one of the root forces (*sefirot*) of the emanation process. (For Luria, the *sefirot* bring order to the constant interplay of events in the cosmos; nothing happens by chance or is meaning-less.) God entered into a contract (covenant) with the Israelites, protecting them in exchange for their work recovering the light. Thus, both sides had obligations, but evil was renewed when the Israelites built a golden calf during the exodus from Egypt. Since then, Jews have tried to collect the scattered sparks of light by keeping God's commandments. Each prayer and moral deed by a Jew contains a spark that is redeemed, and each sin by a Jew returns a spark to the kingdom of evil. As a result, one who seeks perfection cannot withdraw from the world and history to try to unite with the eternal unity of God (Dan 2002, 33).

There is a dynamic ebb and flow in the world, not just of good and evil but also of the divine power sustaining existence. Restoring the world's harmony also completes the divine, and God assigned Jews this role. Indeed, according to Luria, achieving this goal would create the first state of perfection since before creation, when the potential for evil was present in the Godhead (Dan 2002, 33). Thus, God needs human action, and human beings can affect the divine. This idea was exemplified in Genesis (18:17–32), where Abraham "softens God's heart." This theurgic power is not central in the mystical traditions of any other world religions. The Neoplatonist Iamblicus (d. ca. 330 CE) approached mystical union through magical acts and rituals; likewise, individual actions have cosmic effects in Hinduism. However, as Joseph Dan says, it is very difficult to find a parallel to Kabbalah's radical conception of interdependence between human beings and divine powers (2007, 56).

Luria emphasized the coming of the Messiah that would indicate that the Jews' task had been completed and that the world would soon be restored. Messianism thereafter became an important part of Kabbalah, and by the seventeenth century, Jews were looking for the Messiah.[7] Enter Sabbatai Zevi (1626–1676) from Smyrna—in what is now Turkey. He became a Kabbalist in Cairo, and in 1665 the healer Nathan Benjamin Levi of Gaza proclaimed him to be the Messiah. Sabbatai was rejected by many local Jews, and he and Nathan traveled to Constantinople in 1666. There, he was imprisoned by the Islamic authorities. However, this only enhanced his reputation among the Jews, and many flocked to Constantinople to visit him and to perform ascetic practices in anticipation of the imminent dawning of the messianic age. The authorities saw this and gave Sabbatai a choice: convert to Islam or be executed. He converted, but he claimed that God commanded him to do so. Nathan argued that it was, in fact, necessary for the final redemption of the world that the Messiah be humiliated and declared a traitor by his own people so that he could descend into the kingdom of evil to retrieve the final sparks of light of the Infinite. Many followers accepted this and retained their belief in his messiahship even after he died in 1676. A small number of followers still exist today.

The connection of Sabbatai to Kabbalah hurt its standing in the Jewish community. The orthodox restricted its study to those over the age of forty who had great knowledge of the Talmud. Some of Sabbatai's followers also evolved into antinomian groups indulging in practices that violated Jewish sexual laws.[8] (Prior to his conversion, Sabbatai was also known to violate the commandments deliberately upon occasion.) However, his followers argued that the commandments were obsolete for anyone (including the Messiah himself) in the new messianic age since the divine order had been restored to the world's harmony, so the purpose of the commandments had been fulfilled.[9] Moreover, they argued, the underlying dimension of reality had no distinction of good and evil; these only appeared with the emanations. Most scholars attribute this antinomianism to the dynamics of messianic belief rather than to mysticism. No Kabbalists connect this movement to cleaving to God. For them, fulfilling the commandments retained its cosmic function of restoring the cosmos since the messianic age had not arrived. This had the conservative effect of strongly reinforcing strict orthopraxy in prayers and rituals, observing the Sabbath, helping the poor, and performing one's daily activities. Indeed, later Kabbalists remained very conservative in their observance of Jewish law—Eliot Wolfson (2006) characterizes Kabbalists as *hypernomian*—while also emphasizing contemplative prayer.

Not all of Kabbalah is mystical—much is more magical in nature—and not all Jewish mysticism can be labeled *Kabbalah*, but Kabbalah drastically spiritualized Jewish religious culture (Day 2007, 59). It created a new type of mystical religiosity within Judaism, and some Kabbalists argued that Judaism without Kabbalah was an empty shell. However, with its Neoplatonist and Gnostic-like speculations and its messianic expectations, classical Kabbalah veered farther away from some orthodox doctrines, while still maintaining orthopraxy, than the other classical theistic mystical traditions of the world religions.[10]

Hasidism

By the middle of the eighteenth century, Kabbalah was known and accepted by all Jewish communities. Its doctrines and rituals were integrated into mainstream Judaism. At that time, Jewish communities were persecuted throughout Europe, and Jews were disillusioned by the Sabbatai episode. Many also rejected the rationalism of then-current rabbinic theology. In greater Poland, many Jews turned to the earlier practices of the pious (*Hasidim*) in the Rhineland. (Pietism was also developing among German Lutherans at this time.) Contemplation gained more traction among the pious from Kabbalah beginning in the eighteenth century (Smart 1967, 423).

The charismatic magical healer and wonder-worker Israel ben Eleazer (ca. 1700–1760) from Carpathia is credited as the founder of Hasidism. He is known as the Baal Shem Tov—"the master of using the name of God" for spiritual and magical purposes—or *the Besht* for short. Most scholars believe that he introduced a new form of mystical religiosity that integrated simple prayers and pious acts into Judaism, but some believe that he merely exposed an esoteric mysticism that had existed for centuries within small circles. Either way, he spread Kabbalist ideas and his religiosity to the general Jewish populace of the region. After a visionary "ascent of the soul" experience in 1746 induced by incantation, he began chanting Hebrew phrases and sentences in the meditation room of his house to focus his attention, combining Hebrew letters in his mind to form various permutations of the names of God. His soul was then released from his body and traveled to the heavens, eventually arriving at the palace of the Messiah (Ariel 2006, 203–205). After spending some time in the Carpathian Mountains, he traveled in Russia with his wife, performing miracles and instructing followers in Kabbalah.

After the Besht's death, Hasidism grew rapidly, especially through the efforts of the Besht's principal successor, his energetic disciple Dov Baer of Mezeritch (ca. 1705–1772), known as the Great Maggid (the Preacher). Hasidism spread from southern Poland to Lithuania and brought many esoteric Kabbalist ideas to the attention of the general populace. Rabbinic leaders were hostile to its rejection of rabbinic authority and its emphasis on the individual, but the movement flourished. Many of the Hasidim's opponents were themselves ardent Kabbalists who wanted to retain the tradition's esoteric nature and restrict its doctrines to the elite. Some were miracle workers and trance-mediums, but they did not want another Sabbatai incident. Eventually, a relatively civil truce between the factions was reached (Hoffman 2010, xxxi–xxxii).

Classical Kabbalists had adopted earlier medieval pietism and engaged in ascetic practices, but the Hasidim made cleaving to God in everyday activities through prayer a goal for all Jews, not just for an esoteric elite. The Hasidim were not as intellectual as the Kabbalists. Hasidism was more a spiritual awakening movement than a theological one, but the movement did involve general study. Some schools emphasized study of the Talmud; others emphasized Kabbalistic speculation. Dov Baer gave a philosophical basis to the Besht's new teachings: because of the immanence of God, all activity is divine activity. Think of yourself as nothing. "Whatever one does, God is doing it." Thus, God is performing his own commandments. To perceive oneself or the world as existing independently of God is an illusion or a lie; that the fundamental somethingness (*yesh*) must be annihilated into nothingness (*ayin*) is the foundation of the Torah. Attachment to one's will is incompatible with the divine nothingness. One should think of oneself as nothing (*ayin*) and forget oneself totally. Thus, any pride or anger is idolatrous. One should dissolve into the nothingness and reemerge transformed into a new selfless being.

The Hasidim accepted the Kabbalist framework of the transcendent Infinite, its immanent presence (*shekhinah*), and God's manifestations as the ten forces of emanation, although their theosophic interest in the inner workings of God's mind was absent; seeing the world and the self as dependent creations was more central. They emphasized the omnipresence of God. For them, no space is empty of God. However, they did not adopt messianism or all of Luria's metaphysics. Messianic expectations became individual-ized and internalized. The mystic became one who aimed to perceive God behind the veil of appearances (Sherwin 2006, 97). Indeed, according to the Besht, "Nothing other than God exists in all the universe." The contraction of God to allow a phenomenal universe was apparent, but the Hasidim were more interested in the individual: they emphasized the nothingness (*ayin*) of the individual over the transcendent Nothingness that is the source of the phenomenal realm, prioritizing annihilating thought and forgetting the self. They also emphasized humility to counter any megalomania connected to breaking through to the Nothingness.

The Hasidim accepted the doctrines of the shattered emanations, the scattering of divine light, and the mission of retrieving the fallen sparks of that light; but for them, divine light is everywhere. Since God is everywhere, this includes in every human being, even when they sin and when they suf-fer. "The whole world is full of God's glory" (Isa. 6:3). This comprehensive divine presence rendered the phenomenal world relative: all is divine, and all worlds are merely imaginary—illusions—when they are not apprehended in relation to the ever-sustaining divine light that preconditions their material manifestation (Elior 2006, 209).

Hasidic masters such as Schneur Zalman (d. 1813) of Liadi in Belarus, the founder of Chabad Hasidism, were influenced by a non-mystical Tal-mudic scholar, Judah Loew ben Bezalel (ca. 1520–1609). He was not a Kabbalist but popularized their doctrines.[11] Some Hasidim also adopted his interpretation of "There is none beside him [God]" (Deut. 4:35) to mean not that Yahweh was the only god but that there is nothing other than God: "God is all that exists." Loew saw opposites combining into a synthesis. For example, the soul is spiritual but, in fulfilling God's commandments, it combines with physical actions; the spiritual and the physical coalesce. He saw human love for God as actually the love of God for himself since God is everything. Through our love for God, the human soul returns to its source and is reunited with it. This return goes beyond the sexual analogy of one person cleaving to another person. It was not a union; Talmudic rabbis rejected that possibility. The soul cannot become identical to all of God. Rather, the soul is a spark from the divine flame, so the experience is a reunion of a part with the rest of the whole. As the Besht put it, "There is nothing to us but the soul within us, which is part of God above." (By the sixteenth century, mystics had interpreted the phrase from Job 31:2, "a part of God from above," to mean that the human soul is a part of God above.) We are already part of God, so there is no gap to bridge between us and Him. All that is needed is for us to realize what we are. Yet, a person's individuality is not lost in the return, even if their being a drop in an infinite ocean is only an illusion. Thus, mystical cleaving did not bridge the insurmountable gap between the Infinite and the finite. Nevertheless, the essence of the soul and God is the same. For Loew, no mystical experiences were needed. Studying the Torah, observing its commandments, and cultivating moral virtues achieved this realization (Sherwin 2006, 88–94). However, for the Hasidim, personal experiences—including those mystical in nature—were necessary.

To some Hasidim, cleaving to God means that nothing separates God and the person. According to the Besht, God and the person are "glued" together with no space in between (Horwitz 2016, 361). The mainstream doctrine maintains that, by cleaving to God in prayer, the shell of one's selfhood in the natural world is shattered, and the transcendent soul ascends to the divine light. Personal requests in prayer are considered only a distraction. Selfless cleaving to God is to be maintained in all daily affairs, including work. Thus, all ordinary activities in everyday life become expressions of devotion if performed with the proper attitude. Indeed, since God is immanent to creation, all activities are interactions with God. This means that cleaving to God is attainable by all Jews, not just an elite as in Kabbalah. The daily practice of the path of purity (*derekh hasidut*) entails withdrawal from this world, solitude, asceticism, dedication to holiness, and an equanimity achieved by ignoring the world of the senses (Elior 2006, 211). Such even-mindedness (*hishtavut*) to all events requires an ascetic state in which all values and concepts related to concrete existence are regarded as meaningless (212). The Besht disseminated meditative techniques, but since there is nothing other than God, many Hasidim believe that there is no need for complex meditations and prayers and little need for self-mortification (Horwitz 2016, 355). For example, one need not fast but only meditate on the divine sparks in the food one eats.

Like Kabbalists, the Hasidim formed their own groups within larger Jewish communities, and, like Kabbalist masters, Hasidic masters are often leaders within their communities, but Kabbalists have a greater esoteric side. The Hasidim do not typically withdraw from society into isolated communities. However, the Hasidim's preference for interior personal relationships with the divine rather than public worship led the Hasidim to segregate themselves from traditional Jewish congregations (Elior 2006, 209). They are also more emotive: joy plays a greater role among the Hasidim than among the Kabbalists. Rejoicing and celebration are justified by various Psalms. The Besht said, "No child was born except through pleasure and joy, and by the same token if one wishes his prayers to bear fruit, he must offer them with pleasure and joy" (Hoffman 2010, xxxi). Celebrating, humility, gratitude, and spontaneous dancing are central to Hasidic worship. In fact, personal bliss is considered a higher objective than repairing the world. Many scholars see this element of exuberant joy as the defining characteristic of Hasidism.

More important to the Hasidim than rabbinic authority is the authority of charismatic righteous individuals (*tzaddikim*), although they too are considered rabbis. (Neither the Besht nor Dov Baer ever proclaimed themselves a *tzaddik*.) They were chosen by God because they achieved the highest level of cleaving to God. They are divine mediators between God and humanity who can ascend to the heavens in this life and draw down divine abundance from the Infinite into the finite world for their followers. They perform such beneficial acts as healing, but their principal duty is to aid their followers to attain the divine light. This includes counseling followers on daily worldly matters but also pleading to God for them. Different righteous individuals developed their own doctrines, customs, and music. Some lived lavishly and established family dynasties. None have claimed to be prophets. Most Hasidic literature is the testimony and accounts of famous righteous individuals' teachings and miraculous deeds, starting with the *Book of the Pious*.

The Hasidim revitalized the mystical elements of Kabbalah and made it accessible to many. Bringing mysticism into the everyday life of many people was the reason for the initial success and spread of Hasidism, but it may have succeeded in the long run because it transitioned from being concerned solely with the religious renaissance of individuals to being a model of religious and social organization with mystical foundations (Elior 2006, 10). As with Philo, biblical communal concepts were given individualistic mystical readings, but over time, Kabbalist concepts that originally applied to mystical relationships between individual people and God (unification, devotion, love, and annihilation of the self) came to be applied to new social relations between community members (brotherly love, selfless devotion, devotion to comrades, unification with comrades, devotion to their charismatic leader, and unification with their leader) (9). In modern times, the Hasidim came to see repairing the world (*tikkun*) as a matter of social justice, not a cosmic matter of returning sparks of divine light to God (Ariel 2006, 207).

Modern Era

There were non-mystical aspects of Kabbalah, and not all Kabbalists or Hasidim were engaged in mystical ways of life. Many Kabbalist ideas became part of modern mainstream rabbinic theology, and Kabbalah became the principal form of Jewish spirituality until the Holocaust. Nevertheless, the Jewish Enlightenment (*Haskalah*)—which began in Germany with Moshe Mendelsohn (1729–1786)—had a devastating effect on Kabbalists and the Hasidim. Western intellectuals saw mysticism as a medieval form of religiosity that should be cut away. Mysticism survived only in areas untouched by the Enlightenment: for Hasidism, in Eastern Europe and the Middle East and for Kabbalah, in North Africa and the Middle East.

By the nineteenth century, Kabbalah in North Africa had degenerated into matters of magic, to help in worldly affairs, and saint veneration. Some interest survived into the early twentieth century. (Even into the twentieth century, Jewish mysticism remained mostly an esoteric matter, passed orally from teacher to student and not disclosed to the public at large. Likewise, its books were kept limited.) A Kabbalist from Poland, Rabbi Yehuda Ashalag (1885–1954), immigrated to Palestine in the 1920s and combined Kabbalah with socialist ideas. He also tried to introduce Kabbalist ideas to the general public. Rabbi Isaac Kook (1865–1935) emigrated from Latvia to Palestine in 1904 and combined Kabbalist ideas with Sufism and yoga. His universalist vision included even secular Jews as serving God's purpose. Occult forms of Christian Kabbalah also arose—to prove Jesus was the Christ—and Madame Blavatsky (1831–1891) treated Kabbalah as expressing a universal theosophy.

But by the 1940s, mysticism had become a peripheral phenomenon. The Holocaust wiped out most Hasidic lines, and among the survivors, the Kabbalist prayer and meditative techniques that the Besht had taught became all but extinct (Hoffman 2010, xxxii). The study of Kabbalah also virtually disappeared from liberal Orthodox, Reform, and Conservative forms of religious Judaism, as well as secular Judaism and Zionism. Hasidism remained the main representative of Kabbalah and mysticism, but there was a decline in Jewish mystical creativity (Dan 2002, 41–42).

However, three scholars—Martin Buber (1878–1965), Gershom Scholem (1897–1982), and Abraham Joshua Heschel (1907–1972)—who were not practicing Kabbalists or Hasidim did generate academic interest in Jewish mysticism. In the 1980s, interest in mystical and magical practices within Judaism was renewed. In North Africa, some Kabbalist leaders are now seen as having supernatural powers for healing and other matters, and many people, both Jewish and non-Jewish, turn to them for advice and blessings. Neo-Hasidic groups have arisen in Israel, Europe, and America. In Brooklyn, the Chabad Lubavitch movement thrives. The Lubavitch Hasidim developed "the most intense and radical worldview in modern Judaism," claiming all phenomenal existence is an illusion and reality itself can be achieved only by completely rejecting sensual and intellectual perceptions and withdrawing into the realm of nothingness (*ayin*), which is true being (Dan 2002, 41). This requires severing all contact with the world and negates all historical activity (41). In the 1990s their leader, Rabbi Menachem Mendel Schneerson (1902–1994), was identified as the Messiah; he did not clearly disclaim the title, and many of his followers await his return. (Other Jewish groups, including Kabbalist ones, objected to the quasi-messianic pretensions of this group.) His teachings retained a greater nondualism than mainstream Hasidic teachings.

There are also New Age forms of Kabbalah in the United States and Europe, but New Age Kabbalah has stripped traditional Kabbalah of its inherent Jewish ritual framework. It is more a New Age spirituality for individuals, both Jewish and non-Jewish, involving an eclectic syncretism of ideas and practices from different Western and Eastern religious traditions, utilizing magic largely unconnected to traditional Jewish life. Thus, these New Age interpretations of Kabbalah bear little or no relation to actual Kabbalah (Ariel 2006, xix; Dan 2002, 43, 45, 48). Similarly, some American Jews now attend Buddhist, Hindu, and Sufi meditation groups. The embrace of Buddhism by some Jews has led to the phenomenon of *Jubus*. Secular Jews who are interested in Kabbalah often substitute the idea of the Being of the natural world for God and proceed with the mystical practices.

The Question of Unitive Mystical Experiences

The nature of Jewish esoteric writing makes it difficult to determine who were mystics trying to understand reality in light of their experiences and who were theorists influenced by mystics. It is also difficult to determine what types of experiences may have stimulated the creation of such texts. These texts are usually presented as commentaries on the Torah and Talmud that reveal their true meanings; they are not typically presented as treatises on experiences and their role in a mystical way of life. In the Axial Age in Israel, the theistic conception of a universal god emerged, replacing earlier ideas of multiple tribal and nature gods. Instead, one god created the phenomenal universe and imposed ethical laws. In the Hebrew Bible, Axial Age consciousness was expressed by individual responsibility, and prophets, not mystics, were the exemplars of devotion. Revelations and visions given to those whom God chose were the central ASC experiences, not mystical ones. Likewise, early *merkavah/hekhalot* spirituality appears to have been a matter of visions.

ASC experiences were not emphasized by all early pietists. The Kabbalists' Neoplatonist-influenced speculations on God and creation may have been simply that, and ASC experiences may not have inspired the new direction in Jewish thought. The authors may have adopted metaphysics from mystics or mystically inclined theorists without being mystics themselves or advocating attaining mystical experiences since their enterprise was primarily an intellectual one that did not arise from reflecting on input from altered states of consciousness. Or, underlying the metaphysical speculation may be a "deeply spiritual component" (Wolfson 1995, 152; see also Scholem 1961, 121–22). In either case, the number of actual mystics who relied on ASC experiences among the Kabbalists may be small. According to Joseph Dan, Kabbalists were "first and foremost exegetes, preachers, theologians, and traditionalists," and the number of those who could be labeled *mystics* may be "exceedingly small" (2007, 10).

Orthodox Jewish beliefs also shaped historians' views of mysticism within Judaism. Gershom Scholem argued on theological grounds that there was no mystical union or unification (*yihud*) in Judaism. Jewish theology forbade closing the gap between creator and created (1965, 8–11). Early on, only Philo used the word *ecstasy* (122–23). Not only could human beings not become one with God, such a union would eliminate the two-person relational intimacy or communion with God that is central to Judaism. It may also lead to the heresy of pantheism. Only more recently has the possibility of mystical union been accepted in the history of Judaism (Idel 1988a, 1988b). In fact, today Adam Afterman goes so far as to claim that Judaism is a religion of union (or at least communion), and the desire for union with God is a natural development of a monotheism with ideals of love and cleaving (2016).

There is also evidence that some mystical techniques for inducing altered states of consciousness by drawing down (*meshikhah*) divine energy were employed. These techniques arose first in Babylonia and included asceticism, chanting, meditation on the sacred Hebrew letters, mantra-like recitations of letters and divine names, visualization exercises—such as imagining being bathed in light or visualizing the letters *YHWH* or the *sefirot* occupying the mind—concentrative prayer, pondering existential questions, dance, controlling speech and thought, limiting pleasures, and breathing exercises (see Idel 1988, 74–111; 2013, 101–106; Besserman 1997, 28–52, 124–38; Ariel 2006, 211–15; Horwitz 2016, 256–68). Swaying (shuckling) during ritual prayer occurs more broadly than in just mysticism, but the Hasidim also practice it, and such repetitive motions can lead to ASCs. Sensory deprivation was not widely practiced. Passivity as a mystical technique got some Hasidic masters into trouble when the orthodox concluded that this entailed ethical antinomianism. However, for some Hasidim, it seems that radically transforming oneself into a constant extrovertive state was the objective (Ariel 2006, 209). Their goal was a life of continuously cleaving to God without a sense of an independently existing self, not isolated experiences of rapture. That is, being glued to God was a matter of a continuing an enlightened extrovertive mystical state of consciousness, not episodes of introvertive union with God. This can also lead to extrovertive "cosmic consciousness" mystical experiences.

But how much introvertive mysticism in a narrow sense occurred in the popularist Hasidic movement is not clear. Part of the problem is that the desire to conform to orthodoxy may well have caused mystics to conceal their experiences in coded terminology. When Kabbalah was a new spiritual phenomenon, it was expressed in traditional literary forms (Dan 2007, 37–38). Direct contact with the divine realm was not an acceptable part of Jewish culture after the biblical period. Such experiences were regarded as characteristic only of the ancient past, when prophets and others selected by God were allowed to experience divine revelation (38). There was no tradition in mainstream rabbinic Judaism of mystically returning to God in this life, nor would mainstream rabbis place abrogating discursive thought over the study of the Torah. Humility of one's place before God was a central virtue, but this did not lead to the total denial of the individual's existence.

Some passages clearly indicate visionary experiences (Dan 2007, 39), but is there evidence of introvertive theistic or nontheistic unitive experiences? The *Zohar* rarely refers to unitive expressions and, when it does, only collectively about the "assembly of Israel" being united to the Godhead on the Sabbath. One can cleave with a *sefirah* force, thus producing an indirect union: when all the *sefirot* are united, God's grace flows down and benefits the mystics (Ariel 2006, 208–209). But Jews could have experiences that other traditions would have seen as direct contact with God. Some Kabbalist and Hasidic texts clearly suggest mystical experiences (see Idel 1988, 59–73; 1996, 27–57; Wolfson 2005, 160–210). For example, Isaac of Acre spoke of *cleaving* as the soul's ascent to union with the Godhead (*Ein Sof*) (Idel 1988, 48). He and other Kabbalists and Hasidim used the image of a drop of water merging into the ocean but also warned of the dangers of sinking and losing one's identity—dangers that are inherent in unitive experiences (67–70). They also used the image of God "swallowing" the mystic, leaving the possibility of complete assimilation of the person to God (70–73). Ezra of Girona (1160–ca. 1235) spoke of the soul of a prophet ascending and being united to the Neoplatonist World Soul (but not to God) in a "complete union" (42).

Indeed, some mystics reached the same extremes of discourse that some Sufis did. Rabbi Nahman of Braslav (1772–1810) stated that one can be integrated into the Infinite itself, claiming: "If I knew [God], I would be him"; "He who knows and attains a divine understanding is really there [in God]"; and "The greater his knowing, the more he is integrated in his root, in God" (Ariel 2006, 209). All of these statements suggest participatory mystical knowledge. Much earlier, Abraham Abulafia (1240–1295), a student of Sufism and yoga, claimed to have had a mystical experience at age thirty-one. He prophesied, but he also produced manuals for meditative practices (breathing exercises, postures, meditations involving the Hebrew letters, and solitary contemplation) to untie the knots binding the soul to the body and the world. He spoke more extremely of the union of the soul with the Godhead. In the final state of ascent, "now he is no longer separated from his Master, and behold he is his Master and his Master is he; for he is so intimately adhering [*devekut*] with Him, that he cannot by any means be separated from Him, for he is He" (Idel 2013, 115). As Abulafia summarized succinctly: "He is I and I am He" (Wolfson 1995, 156).

Expressions of union were more common among the Hasidim, who were more concerned with personal experiences, than the Kabbalists, who cared more about repairing the world. Their goal was the annihilation of the self (*bittul ha-yesh*): absorbing the human *I* into God's *I* (Sherwin 2006, 91–92). In this way, God is no longer *you* and the mystic is no longer *I*. There is only the *I* of the infinite God (*ayin*) (91–92). Nahman of Braslav stated that one can climb the ladder beyond the *sefirot* in order to be integrated into the Infinite (*Ein Sof*). Schneur Zalman spoke of the annihilation of the soul in its absorption into God: in true cleaving, "he becomes one substance with God in whom he was swallowed, without being separate from him to be considered as a distinct entity at all" (Idel and McGinn 1996, 43). Expressions of a passionate love of God that depicted an erotic union were not unheard of. Some examples included joining to the female dwelling place of God (*shekhinah*) as the mystic's bride or Moses as the husband and *shekinah* as the wife (Ariel 2006, 210; see also Wolfson 2005).

Yet, expressions of union are still rare since, for most classical Hasidim, God is the only reality and the soul is already not apart from God; there is no separate reality in which to unite to God. Most classical Hasidim expressed this idea in terms of annihilating one's sense of self-will and one's sense of the individual as a separate entity as the soul ascends and is integrated into the emanations: to think of oneself as nothing and to forget oneself totally (Ariel 2006, 210). In this way, the Hasidim connected cleaving to God with the extinction of a sense of self (210–11).

Nevertheless, Kabbalist and Hasidic orthodoxy tended to control understandings of what was experienced, and they affirmed that the soul is in some sense separate from God. Consider the case of Martin Buber. He had an "unforgettable experience" in which he knew "well that there is a state in which the bonds of, the personal nature of life seem to have fallen away from us and we experience an undivided unity" (Buber 1947, 24). However, he continues:

> But I do not know—what the soul willingly imagines and indeed is bound to imagine (mine too once did it)—that in this I had attained to a union with the primal being or the godhead. That is an exaggeration no longer permitted to the responsible under-standing. Responsibly—that is, as a man holding his ground before reality—I can elicit from those experiences only that in them I reached an undifferentiated unity of myself without form or content. . . . In the honest and sober account of the responsible understanding this unity is nothing but the unity of this soul of mine, whose "ground" I have reached . . . (24–25).

This "responsible understanding" was dictated by his Jewish doctrinal frame-work, in which the gulf between God and creature is unbridgeable. His understanding, however, only came into play after the experience. It did not penetrate the experience itself, and it did not change his experiential sense of an "undivided unity" that he initially interpreted to be union with the Godhead. His religious beliefs controlled his understanding but not the actual felt content of the experience itself. The pull of orthodoxy may also have controlled the understandings of earlier Kabbalists and Hasidim, but different types of mystical experiences may have been concealed in their writings. As Joseph Dan puts it, the price that Kabbalists had to pay for blending in with traditional Jewish culture was a suppression of expressions of individual spiritual and mystical experiences (2007, 38).

Overall, the orthodox position was that cleaving to God maintained a distinction between God and the human being. There is no absorption of the individual into the Godhead or annihilation of the true transcendent soul, only a loving intimacy that maintains the mystery of God. (However, there is less *love mysticism* and God as love in Judaism than in the mystical traditions of the other two Abrahamic religions.) In light of some of these expressions, unitive mystical experiences no doubt occurred and were one source of Kabbalist and Hasidic spiritualities, but such experiences were not emphasized in traditional texts. To fit in with the orthodox, they had to be camouflaged in writings or totally omitted.

Key Themes

• Mysticism appears more peripheral within Judaism than in the other two Abrahamic traditions, but it did influence mainstream Judaism. Jewish mysticism is also more isolated than the other mystical traditions of the world. It absorbed some influences from other traditions, including Neoplatonism and Sufism, but it did not have much influence on the mysticisms of other traditions. At least part of the reason for this is that, until relatively recently, Jewish mysticism has been more esoteric than the mysticisms of other world religions. Its elaborate emanationist metaphysics interested some non-mystics but not the other mystics of the world.

• Mysticism in Judaism is seen as a way to love God with all of one's heart, soul, and strength (Deut. 6:5) and a way to develop one's ability to follow God's will. The basic Jewish requirement of conduct is summarized in the Bible in Micah 6:8: "What does the Lord require of you? To act justly, to love mercy, and to walk humbly with your God." Humility, in a mystical sense, is a central value. (That is, *humility* in theistic mysticism generally does not mean being modest about one's accomplishments but realizing that we have no reality without God: we do not exist without God. The context is our ontological dependence on God.) In Jewish mysticism, this humility led to ecstatic ASC experiences ranging from visions of being in the presence of God to direct contact with God. Human effort here led to God choosing certain persons as righteous. Practical effects such as magical powers were also important.

• The framework of the various branches of Jewish mysticism is a panentheism with an emanationism from the one forever hidden transcendent source. This framework overcame the inherent tension between a transcendent god who creates *ex nihilo* and introvertive mystical experiences. For most theists, God is wholly transcendent and limitless, and creation is good but set off from God (Gen. 1:31). God is also unknowable: all we can know of God comes from the revelations recorded in scripture. Despite the biblical suspicion of all images of God, the mixture of mystics and non-mystical authorities in Judaism did not lead to a fully developed negative theology (the philosopher Maimonides being the notable exception).[12] Overall, Jewish mystics focus on a nonpersonal aspect of God rather than on the full features of a personal theistic god. On the other hand, many Kabbalists and Hasidim claim, as do many Sufis in Islam, that not only is there only one god but there is also nothing but God. The idea that individuals and the phenomenal world exist independently from God is an illusion. Each person is a part of God from above but remains a distinct soul.

• Orthodox Jews view that the Torah was revealed, but "secret things" still belong to God (Deut. 29:29). Jewish mystics affirm an unknowable mystery as central to the divine. We can never know one aspect of God: the qualityless Infinite (*Ein Sof*) or the Nothingness (*ayin*). But most Jewish mysticism can also be labeled *theosophy*.[13] That is, mystics speculated on the inner workings of God himself. The Godhead is separated from the process of creation, but in their cosmogonies, Jewish scholars elaborated an emanationist metaphysics of how God created. Christian and Islamic mystics as a rule did not engage in this. To many non-mystical Jewish scholars, the emanationist system of ten forces (*sefirot*) compromised the unity of the Godhead even more than the Christian doctrine of a trinity since the forces are not separate from the Infinite.

• Giving the divine a *female* side is unique in the history of Western mysticism. In the Hebrew Bible, wisdom (*hokhmah*, Gk. *sophia*) was female (as in Prov. 8) and was utilized by Christian mystics, but it was not part of God.

• The Jewish mystical tradition also has a type of practice shared with later Neoplatonism but not with any other theism: *theurgy*. That is, human actions have the power to affect the divine by modifying the inner life of the Godhead. Beginning with the Hekhalot literature, knowledge of the names revealed by God gave human beings power to affect not only the world but also God.[14] Human action is seen as necessary for restoring both harmony in the world and divine perfection. The ten emanations are the framework for both mystical and theurgical actions. There is a dynamic ebb and flow of the light of God in the world, and human actions are needed for capturing the light currently in the evil realm and repairing the world (*tikkun*).[15] This role is reserved for Jews and involves Jews obeying the biblical commandments as elaborated in the Talmud.

• The possible restoration of perfection led to messianic expectations in esoteric circles. Even without messianism, Kabbalists and Hasidim are not as world-affirming as Judaism overall. God is an abiding presence in the world, but their focus is on the source of the emanations; the material world is ultimately to be rejected.

• The importance of the study of scripture had a wider application in Judaism than in other religious traditions, but most branches of Jewish mysticism remained esoteric in their practices and knowledge, open only to an inner circle of disciples.

• Direct individual experiences of God became important. Early on, visions were the principal experiences. The soul could ascend to heaven and bring down divine power. Judaism stresses a gap between creator and creation more than the other two Abrahamic religions, but mystical experiences still became a part of the experiential picture. The otherness of God from creation is overcome in introvertive mystical experiences.

• "Cleaving to God" (*devekut*) means different things to different Kabbalists and Hasidim, but most generally it means a total devotion to the extent of renouncing the material world and transcending one's own self to achieve spiritual communion, but not union, with God (Elior 2006, 211). The worldly self is cracked, and the transcendent soul in a person returns to its original disembodied state. Earlier mystics spoke of a return to the Neoplatonist World Soul, but later, some expressions of introvertive unitive experiences with God or the Godhead did occur.

• The soul's reality is not denied. During a mystical experience, one has annihilated any sense of it (and so is unaware of it), but it is never abolished within the divine reality. However, its existence remains dependent upon God. In their return to a worldly state, the enlightened are transformed, but in the mainstream understanding, their true transcendent souls are not changed from what they originally were. Hasidism emphasizes this extrovertive mystical state of consciousness.

• Jewish mystics take its language to be a creative power: the Hebrew letters were part of what God used to create the natural world. Hebrew is not a human invention but a divine creation or even an aspect of God.

Letters have a cosmic rather than merely linguistic significance. The sacred alphabet is the key to creation and can also be used as a meditation device and a means to reveal the hidden meaning of the Torah (as disclosed in Kabbalist doctrines). Meditative practices that focused on the names of God and the Hebrew alphabet were prominent.

• Kabbalists and the Hasidim are orthodox and conservative in their ritual practices, but traditional Jewish doctrines did not stop an experiential sense of unity in some introvertive experiences. Rather, the orthodox held that these experiences were only personal communion with God—what Martin Buber called an *I-Thou* experience (1970)—not union.[16] But mystics were able to adapt to traditional theistic terminology and doctrines to express even introvertive experiences free of differentiated content.

Chapter 5

Christian Mysticism

At its origin, Christianity appears to have been a mystical religion or at least to have had a mystical element (McGinn 1994, 65) Even some passages in the New Testament suggest mystical experiences rather than visions. Christian mysticism was shaped early on by Philo's Middle Platonism and the visionary Jewish religiosity of the time, but by the end of its first century, Christianity had features that were uniquely its own.[1] From then on, it owed more to its Hellenistic environment. For example, Christians got the concept of an inner soul from the Greeks, not the Bible. Terminology from the Greek Mystery cults was imported, and more importantly, so were Greek philosophical ideas. (Whether the Greek adaptations distorted the basic nature of Christianity is a matter of debate.) There is also more continuity in the history of Christian mysticism than in Jewish mysticism: the early period laid the foundation for more than a thousand years.

The New Testament

Like mystics in the other Abrahamic traditions, Christian mystics see their mysticism as based in the foundational scriptures of their tradition. The earliest writings in the New Testament are the letters of Paul (ca. 5–67 CE), a Pharisaic Jew from Tarsus in what is now Turkey. He had an overwhelming visionary experience, reflecting the Jewish apocryphal literature of the time, on the road to Damascus of a "light from the heavens" and a voice that caused him to go from persecuting followers of Jesus to becoming one (Acts 9:1–9, 22:6–21, 26:12–18; see also 1 Cor. 9:1, 15:8). This experience is portrayed as of a being distinct from Paul, not a mystical experience within him (Rom. 7:22, 2 Cor. 4:16, 1 Cor. 14:19). He took this to be a revelation of Jesus (ca. 6 BCE–30 CE) (1 Cor. 15:8, Gal. 1:12–16).[2]

Paul emphasized the sacrifice and resurrection of Jesus, not his teachings and worldly actions. What was important was the salvific role of the crucified Christ and the mystery of God.[3] God's "hidden wisdom" and "secret purpose" (1 Cor. 2:7) according to Paul is "Christ in you" (Col. 1:27).[4] Who has the "mind of Christ" can see "even the depths of God" that the ear and eye have not heard or seen (1 Cor. 2: 9–10, 16). Through faith, one may know the fullness of Christ's love, though it is beyond knowledge (gnosis), and attain "the fullness of being, the fullness of God himself" (Eph. 3:18–19). Paul also spoke of a man (probably himself) who, as with Jewish heavenly chariot/throne experiences, was "caught up" in two other experiences and ascended to the third heaven and to paradise where he heard secret words; whether these occurred in his body or out of it, he did not know (2 Cor. 12:1–4). Either way, he ended up with the mystical sense that he did not live but that Christ lived in him: "I have been crucified with Christ: the life I now live is not my life, but the life which Christ lives in me" (Gal. 2:19–20).[5] He was transformed by Christ from a "life of the flesh" to a "life of the spirit of God." When one is united to Christ, there is a new act of creation (2 Cor. 5:17; see also 1 Cor. 15:44–49, Rom. 8:9–11) and a new life "hidden with Christ in God" (Col. 3:3). For Paul, in God "we live and move, in him we exist" (Acts 17:28). The synoptic Gospels refer to the disciples being "with" (Gk., *meta*) Christ, but for Paul Christ is "in" (*en*) him.

The Gospel of John and his letters support Paul's idea of a sonship in Christ, conceived as a new beginning from above (McGinn 1994, 78–79). This Gospel, probably written a few decades after Paul's letters, appears to have been composed in a mystical environment.[6] It stresses the unity of Jesus and God. Indeed, John begins by proclaiming that the Christ was the *logos* that existed before creation (John 1:1; see also 8:58, 17:5).[7] But while Paul focused on the Christ half of the equation of Jesus and God, John focused on the God half. Jesus proclaims, "My Father and I are one" (10:30). No one has seen God, but his son makes God known (1:18): "Seeing me, he sees who sent me" (12:45); "I am not the source of the words I speak to you: it is the Father who dwells in me doing his own work" (14:10); "I am in the Father, and the Father in me" (14:11); "I am not alone, because the Father is with me" (16:32); and "If you knew me, you would know my Father as well" (8:19; also 14:7). Sometimes the mutual indwelling is between Christ and God (14:10), but other times it is between Christ and the believer (6:56, 15:4): "I am in you, and you are in me" (14:20). Jesus also prays that his followers may be one as God is in Jesus and Jesus is in God so that all are in God (17:21); that they may be one as God and Jesus are one through the "glory" that God gave Jesus and Jesus gave his followers (17:22); and that they may be perfectly one, Jesus in them and God in him (17:23). (In early Christianity, God's "glory" became identified with Jesus.) There are no mystical or ecstatic experiences or heavenly journeys mentioned in the Gospel for believers. In fact, it states that no one has ascended into heaven except the one who has descended—the "Son of Man," whose home is in heaven (3:13)—but that someone could be paradoxically both fully human and fully God led to grounding mystical senses of oneness as being connected to God himself. The light imagery used in this Gospel also became important through the Middle Ages.

Denying oneself and imitating Jesus is considered the only way to God (John 14:6, 10:9). To keep Jesus's commandment is to "love one another, as I have loved you" (15:12). God will love those who keep what he says, and "we will come to them and make our dwelling with them" (John 14:23; see also 1 Cor. 13). Thus, Christians are to exhibit this love because this is the active love that God has in creating and sustaining his creation. Love for one's neighbor (*agape/caritas*) thereby became central in Christian mysticism: God is love, and whoever abides in love abides in God, and God abides in him (1 John 4:16). In an enlightened mystical way of life, this can lead to treating all people alike with absolute impartiality, for the rain falls on the just and unjust completely alike (Matt. 5:45, 20:1–16).[8]

Paul and John may not have been mystics, but their writings are certainly susceptible to mystical readings (McGinn 1994, 66). How particular mystics understood these texts rather than the original meaning is what is important. Christian mystics imitate Jesus in a life of unconditional love. That love makes Jesus the archetype of what a human being should be. It is God's actions embodied. Once Jesus was gone, the Holy Spirit (breath)—the "go between" dimension of God—was the action of God on earth.

Desert Monastics

By the first generation after the apostles, a divide formed between a mystical Christianity bent on the reception of the Holy Spirit and a non-mystical

Christianity based on institutional authority, with the latter winning out and controlling orthodoxy. The idea of being able to unite with God in any sense became heterodox at best, and in the first centuries after the initial generation of Christians, there appears to have been few mystics, with the possible exceptions of some Gnostics.[9] But in what E. R. Dodds called the "Age of Anxiety" in the Roman Empire, by the fourth century, ascetics were turning to experiences in the desert as the way to follow the life of Jesus and to find certainty through experiences. It was a way to become "perfect" as God is perfect (Matt. 5:48) and for the "pure in heart" to see God (Matt. 5:8). Jesus withdrew into the desert to pray (as in Luke 5:16), and his forty days in the desert (Mark 1:12–13, Matt. 4:1–11, Luke 4:1–13) became the model for withdrawing from the world in pursuit of holiness through a life of self-denial. His temptation by the Devil also became the model of visions. Jesus's escape from the world first took place in Egypt—where asceticism was part of the training in Alexandria that also produced Plotinus—and later in the Syrian, Turkish, and Palestinian deserts.

The ascetic life of self-denial—fasting, celibacy, and poverty—was considered a way of inwardly "taking up the cross" and following Jesus (Matt. 8:34–35, 16:24; Luke 9:23).[10] The demanding ascetic lifestyle cut down all physical pleasures and needs as thoroughly as possible. It also entailed sexual abstinence; celibacy played a greater role in Christian mysticism than in Jewish or Islamic mysticism. More austere practices included extended fasts and sleep deprivation. The New Testament belief that the end-times were at hand made its world-renouncing ethical teachings—giving up all of one's possessions (Luke 14:33; see also 1 John 2:15), renouncing one's family (Matt. 10:37), and treating marriage as only a concession (1 Cor. 7:1–5)—appropriate. It also justified ascetic renunciation when the world did not end. But poverty was also given a mystical interpretation in terms of *inner detachment* from whatever possessions one had in order to receive the Holy Spirit (for example, *Ascent of Mount Carmel* 1.5.2).

After Christianity became the official religion of the Roman Empire in the fourth century, martyrdom was no longer an option, and flight from the world into the desert by both men and women for a life of constant prayer, meditation, and ascetic penitence became the highest ideal. Their experiences were seen as foretastes of a beatific vision in the afterlife. Ascetics wanted to fulfill the biblical command to "pray without ceasing" (1 Thess. 5:17).[11] They lived simple lives of humility and poverty sustained by begging. They either lived as solitary hermits—the term *hermit* comes from the

Greek term for "of the desert"—or in loosely organized communities—even though the term *monastic* comes from the Greek word for "one." The point of monasticism was individual personal spiritual development, and classical Christian monasteries and convents were very much collections of solitary individuals, each working on their own spiritual development under the guidance of masters. The institutions were noted for their general silence (except during collective prayers and chanting) and lack of social interaction among members, even during work and meals.

The desert monastics are known not for innovative doctrines but for their ascetic practices of a life of "purity of the heart," leading to a freedom from passion (*apatheia*). According to Athanasius of Alexandria (ca. 297–373), the deification (*theosis*) of humanity was achieved through the incarnation of the Word (*logos*): "The Word [*logos*] of God became man so that we might become God." This enabled people to draw close to God through ascetic practices. (Deification came to mean being "God-like," but not literally being God.[12]) It was a matter of training the will, not new knowledge. The monastics' life of asceticism and prayer had physical effects: they were known for having faces that shone like lightning and radiant white bodies (cf. Mark 9:2–8). However, they did not have a Gnostic hatred of the body. Rather, their asceticism was an attempt to purify the body and return it to a pre-fallen state, enabling it to become a dwelling place for God.

Prayer and contemplation (*theoria* and *contemplatio*) were central as the monastics strove to imitate Jesus and the apostolic life. Their monastic practices—including communal prayer and reciting and reading scripture—greatly influenced monastics both in the West in the Middle Ages and at Mount Athos in Greece. Their writings, like those of most mystics, were not about personal experiences but about what was experienced (God) and the practice of a new life. Writings and stories about such monastics as Antony of Egypt (d. 356), Simeon Stylites of Syria (d. 459), and Evagrius Ponticus (d. 399) of Egypt show an emphasis on silence and the constant awareness of God in all activities. For Evagrius, contemplative prayer was not about leaving oneself (*ekstasis*) but coming to one's true state (*katastasis*). "Pure prayer" involves no images. At least some of these men and women no doubt had mystical experiences and not just visions or other paranormal experiences,[13] but all experiences were considered the result of God's grace—gifts of the Holy Spirit. And these monastics were not reluctant to display these gifts by performing miracles or telling of their battles with demons. Their terse writings remind many of the *koan*-related encounters between masters and disciples in Zen Buddhism (see Harmless 2004, 471).

John Cassian (ca. 360–435) modified Ponticus's practices and established the first Egyptian-style ascetic monasteries in Western Europe in southern France. He believed that human effort could begin the quest that ended in receiving the gifts of grace. In a life of perpetual "prayer of fire," a person's soul is consumed by God. Like many monastics, he stressed the absolute necessity of a perpetual awareness of God. He longed for the state "when that unity which the Father now has with the Son and which the Son has with the Father is carried over into our understanding and our minds, so that, just as he loves us with a sincere and perpetual and inseparable love, whatever we breathe, whatever we understand, whatever we speak may be God" (*Collationes* 10.7). Like many mystics, he did not see his innovations as innovations but argued that monastics simply led the life of the apostles to the fullest. His writings became required reading for monastics living under the sixth-century Rule of St. Benedict (480–543).

Mystical experiences came to be seen as the key for understanding the secret meanings of scripture; the literal meaning of the Bible was its body, but these hidden meanings constituted its soul. Beginning with Origen (ca.185–254), who argued that the Bible used the same terms to denote different things, biblical passages were given mystical readings that exposed the text's "spiritual sense." That practice continued through the Middle Ages. Moses ascending Mount Sinai to receive the Ten Commandments and Moses approaching the darkness where God was (Exod. 20:21) were understood to represent the soul's ascent to God. Mary and Martha (Luke 10:38–42) became symbols of the "contemplative life" and the "active life" in the world, with preference given to the former.[14] (Pope Gregory I made this distinction in the sixth century.) Giving up one's possessions (Luke 14:33) expanded to include emptying one's mind of all "possessions" (ideas, emotions, and so forth). But the most popular image was from the Song of Songs: marriage. The idea of an enduring "spiritual marriage" became the central allegory for mystical union. Everything in the Bible became an interior matter of the individual soul. Meister Eckhart gave mystical readings to whatever passages were the subjects of his sermons; for example, Jesus cleansing the temple of money changers (Matt. 21:12–13) became an allegory for clearing the soul of all images so that Christ could enter. His Latin commentaries often contained more than one mystical interpretation of a verse.

The Christian Path

The path to enlightenment was seen as an ascent, and the desert monastics developed a threefold division of the path—the *ladder of perfection*—that became the traditional classification for Christian mystics: purgation, illumination, and union. In the first stage, mystics actively purify their bodies and minds through discipline—prayer, various types of renunciation, ascetic practices, and acts of mercy toward the poor—within an all-encompassing concept of humility: knowing one's place before God through self-knowledge. Purification is an inner cleansing of the soul that strips away all self-interest and self-will. Some mystics such as Francis of Assisi stressed material poverty, but all mystics stressed an inner poverty of the spirit, removing all matters related to self-interest or self-will. This led to more detailed contemplative practices. The warrant for this comes from Paul: our "lower nature" has no claim upon us and we are not obliged to live on that level, so we must "die," but "if by the Holy Spirit you put to death all the base pursuits of the body, then you will live" (Rom. 8:12–13). There will be a spiritual death and resurrection in Christ.

Purification only prepares the way. The second stage (illumination) does not refer to visions but to drawing nearer to God by meditating on passages from the Bible and religious teachings, leading to flashes of God's self-disclosure. The third stage (union) was typically seen in terms of a union of the wills, not of substances. As Teresa of Avila put it, one's impulses come from the center of the soul that is in contact with God, not from one's mind or memory; actions do not come from anything suggesting that the soul did something on its own (*Interior Castle* 7.3.8).[15] That is, Christian mystics eliminate all self-will and self-interest and align themselves with God's will, but the substance or nature of the mystic does not change from being created, instead remaining in some sense distinct from God.

Thus, the culmination of the path is not an isolated mystical experience but the continuing, mystical, unitive life in which all sense of individual self-will is destroyed. The ideal was this resulting enlightened state, not any heights of temporary ecstasy caused by abstention from the bodily senses or rapture (or ravishment) with effects on the body (such as levitation, tears, or fragrant odors). There is an inner transformation of the total person, not just of their actions or beliefs but also of their intentions, emotions, and dispositions. Mystics who emphasized knowledge over love spoke more of emptying the mind of all mundane knowledge—an *unknowing* or *for-*

getting—so that God's presence could enter. Mystics who emphasized love focused on the change in a person's wills. But for all of these mystics, a permanent transformation of one's character into God's love is the ultimate goal. Love permeates the participatory knowledge of the enlightened state. Love and knowledge of God are one, as Gregory of Nyssa (ca. 335–395) wrote.

In the enlightened state of consciousness, there is a continuous infusion of God's love that the mystic cannot control. Emptied of oneself, one is "resting in God." One abides continually in the unmediated divine ground of reality. There is a fusion—a permanent marriage of wills and spirits but not of substances.

Greek Influence

The ascetic practices of Greek Neoplatonist, Neopythagorean, and Stoic philosophers for restraining passions and cultivating virtues greatly influenced Christian spirituality (McGinn 1994, 30). Christians also adapted Plato and Plotinus's idea of a passionate longing (*eros*) into a drive to know God: a power of yearning desire implanted in the soul by God (125).[16] It is, in Origen's words, a "seething with passionless passion." Greek philosophy, especially later Neoplatonism, also influenced all Abrahamic mystical traditions from their earliest stages, although by the fourth century, Christianity was modifying the Neoplatonist framework. As with Neoplatonism, humanity was considered to be made to contemplate God, but Christ showed that God and humans could be united. Christians adopted the word *mystical* from the Greeks—it has no equivalent in the Bible or the Quran—to refer to the hidden "mystical meaning" of biblical passages and, as with the Mystery cults, to refer to the power behind rituals. Early on, it also came to mean the knowledge (*gnosis*) of God or the mystery of Christ granted by God in mystical contemplation (*theoria mystike*) after inner purification (*askesis*).

Greek influence on Christian mysticism began probably with the ascetic Origen. He was a student of Ammonius Saccas in Alexandria, as was Plotinus (although there is no evidence that the two students ever met). He was the first to use *mystical* to mean directly perceiving or experiencing God (Bouyer 1980, 47). The language of contemplation dominated his descriptions of the goal of the mystical itinerary, as it did for Clement of Alexandria (McGinn 1994, 128). He also developed themes that continued in Eastern and Western Christian mysticism, such as the mystical ascent, allegorical readings of the Bible that disclosed its hidden spiritual meaning, the importance of asceticism for imitating Jesus, knowing through inner "spiritual senses," and the importance in spiritual training of combining contemplation and moral action. For him, mystical oneness (*henosis*) is a union of the hearts and minds of lovers, not literal identity (McGinn 1994, 129). This understanding is grounded in 1 Corinthians: "He who links himself with Christ is one with him, spiritually" (6:17). Additionally, for Origen, the world is a set of symbols pointing to a Platonic-like realm. He believed in reincarnation—human beings had to pass through all types of human existence before reaching heaven[17]—and he did not believe that anyone was condemned eternally to hell.

Bishop Gregory of Nyssa (ca. 335–395) brought some of Philo's ideas, later Neoplatonic ideas, and the *via negativa* into Christian mysticism. He also introduced the idea of a "darkness of unknowing" that went beyond contemplation since, by means of love, the soul penetrates more deeply into the incomprehensibility of God than the knowing mind could (Louth 1981, 85, 88, 97). For him, God the Father—the One beyond the Being of the natural realm—was unknowable and, thus, incapable of being grasped by any term, idea, or other device of human apprehension. He considered God to be beyond even the intellects of angels or other transcendent beings and, thus, utterly unthinkable and above all expressions in words.[18]

Augustine of Hippo (354–430), a city on the coast of Algeria, may not have had any mystical experiences himself—only visions are related in his *Confessions*—but he shaped subsequent mysticism in Western Christendom through his incorporation of Neoplatonism into a theistic framework. He made love of others (*agape/caritas*) more central than the intellect (*nous/intellectus*); stressed the difference between a free creator and his creation; and adopted the need for grace, revelation, and the incarnation of God in this world.[19] He did not follow the Neoplatonist doctrine of the unknowability of God, although he stressed that God's nature is inexpressible and not understandable by human beings. For him, there was an ascent of a triune soul (intellect, memory, will) to the triune God. He considered God "more inward than my most inward part and higher than the highest element within me" (*Confessions* 3.6.11). His idea of humility before God and his conception of self-transcendence became central to Western Christian mysticism. For him, there are three ways of knowing: seeing through the eyes of the body; visions through the eyes of the soul via images; and interior visions by the Neoplatonist intellect (*nous*), in which the soul strips away all sense experiences through reason to discover necessary truths without images and in which the soul transcends itself to encounter something beyond the soul "in the flash of a trembling glance."[20] This is a matter of the heart, not reason. He quoted Paul: "Now we only see puzzling reflections in a mirror; after death, we shall see God face to face" (1 Cor. 13:12).[21]

Around 500 CE, a Syrian monk wrote under the name of one of Paul's early converts (Acts 17:34), Dionysius the Areopagite. Through the Middle Ages, he was seen as a disciple of Paul, so his work held great authority and had a seminal influence on both Eastern and Western Christianity. He was important for solidifying Neoplatonism in Christianity in order to understand Christian scriptures, including the cosmology of emanation and return. His influence was more of the Aristotelian/Stoic Neoplatonism of his non-Christian teacher, Proclus of Athens, than of the earlier Plotinian type; although, Plotinus's doctrine of the One, emanationism, and ineffability remained important. The Nous, as a cosmic level, dropped out of the picture. This mystical theorist also appears to be the first to use the phrase *mystical theology* to refer to a direct contact with God. With him, theology first became explicitly mystical (McGinn 1994, 182).[22] However, by *theologia* he meant "the word of God," not "theology" in the modern academic sense. Also, *mystical* still retained connotations of the dark mysteries of the Mystery cults.

The Pseudo-Dionysius wrote of a union with God beyond the intellect (*nous*) and its knowledge. Through unknowing, a union is achieved that is far beyond the mind since the mind has turned away from all things (including itself) and is made one with the dazzling yet dark rays from God (*Divine Names* 872B). He used *ecstasy* to refer to the role of passion (*eros*) in the process of return to the One (Wear and Dillon 2007, 128–29). In stressing God's utter transcendence of all human categories, he also emphasized the *via negativa* of the apophatic way of mystical practice and theology that had already existed in Christian mysticism: the unknowing (*agnosia*) of all worldly matters and even images of God. (The Pseudo-Dionysius actually used the term *apophasis* [unsaying] very little. He instead employed the term *denial* [*aphairesis*] to remove the idea that God has any phenomenal features and to affirm something greater about him than anything phenomenal.) One must leave behind all that one perceives and understands, all that is perceptible and understandable, and all that is and is not and strive for union with he who is beyond all being and knowledge

(*Mystical Theology* 997B). This is an inner turning away from all things, thus allowing a "ray of darkness" to enter that is beyond all Being (*ousia*), hidden in the silence beyond any assertion (1000A). In the "truly mysterious darkness of unknowing," one is neither oneself nor something else by nature but supremely united by a complete unknowing of all knowledge, knowing beyond the mind by knowing no object (1001A). However, for the Pseudo-Dionysius there is a positive reality beyond the negations and assertions that can be known (experienced) through unknowing all mental conceptions (1000B). It is something above all mind-generated cognitive powers, and thus all of our understanding must be eliminated. It is God who initiates contact with us.

However, although God "surpasses all discourse and knowledge," the Pseudo-Dionysius in the *Divine Names* stated that "the Source told us about itself in the holy words of scripture" (589B). There are positive attributes in the Bible, and thus the Pseudo-Dionysius wrote works in the affirmative *via positiva* (the kataphatic way) on religious symbolism and the names of God while still stressing that God cannot be fully captured by any name. God is the "pre-existent" beyond Being from which all things derive their being (*Divine Names* 820A). He was aware of the contradiction between the positive and negative ways but reconciled them by claiming that all the language in scripture is metaphoric and symbolic. God still surpasses all literal denotation.

Moreover, for him the *via negativa* was a stage beyond all positive ascriptions, negating all such claims. One begins one's ascent at the level of discourse with the divine names but unknows all knowledge to reach God himself; hence, the images of shadow and "divine darkness" both blind and illuminate. Even denials and negative ascriptions must be transcended.[23] To Augustine, "If you understand it, it is not God." Gregory of Nyssa adds: "Every concept formed in order to reach and encompass the divine nature succeeds only in fashioning an idol of God and not at all in making him known." The final stage is a way of darkness (*gnophos*) in which one does not see God but feels the presence of the Word (*logos*). For the Pseudo-Dionysius, we attribute an absence of reason and perfection to God because he is beyond or above (*hyper*) reason and above and before all perfections, not because he lacks them. Thus, neither affirmation nor negation applies to God. God is beyond every affirmation and also every denial, and thus, is hidden from reason.

In this way, as with subsequent theologians in Christianity and Islam, ineffability is combined with the revealed word of God: we can know from scripture that God exists, is the creator, is at least personal and loving in nature, and acts in the world, but he is still utterly different in nature from anything phenomenal.

Early Middle Ages

Until the twelfth century, the cultivation of the immediate consciousness of God took place within the exercises of reading, meditating, preaching, and teaching the Bible. The context was often liturgical or quasi-liturgical (McGinn 1994, 64). Exegesis discussing the hidden mystical content of the Bible was the primary form of mystical writing for a thousand years. The mystical writings that have survived from the early Middle Ages are those of monastics such as the Cistercians and Victorines. These may in fact have been most, or perhaps all, of the mystical writings since monastics were the primary literate class.

Monasticism under the Rule of St. Benedict governed Western Christian mysticism into the thirteenth century, emphasizing poverty, celibacy, and obedience to one's abbot.[24] The Rule was on the practical side of mysticism—manual labor, study, prayer every day—rather than the doctrinal. Reading biblical passages, along with meditating and praying on them to absorb their meanings, led ultimately to silent contemplation.[25] For these contemplatives, apprehending God was not an object set off from them. Rather, God became active in the ground of the soul (McGinn 2008, 52). In medieval Christian terminology, there is a radical *recollecting* of the senses and a *purging* of the mind of all cognitive and dispositional content, especially self-assertion. This involves a stilling of mental activity, a *withdrawal* of all powers of the mind from all objects.

In Paris, the Neoplatonist Johannes Scotus Eriugena (ca. 800–877) from Ireland translated the Pseudo-Dionysius's works into Latin, introducing the *via negativa* to Western Europe. For Eriugena, God is the ineffable One, incomprehensible and inaccessible to the intellect of any being: the "God beyond God." Even God cannot know God because God is not an object; God is not a *what* or limited. Eriugena called God *nothing* (*nihil*), and this terminology occurs occasionally afterward in Christian (and Jewish and Islamic) mysticism. However, Eriugena meant only that God is not a phenomenal thing and his being is not phenomenal being, so as a simple matter of logic, God—in terms of phenomenal attributes—is nothing. This is part of the logic of ineffability even independent of mystical experiences.

But by this, he did not mean that God has no reality. God or the Godhead beyond God is still the transcendent superabundant abyss out of which things come.[26]

This knowledge approach of primarily utilizing the intellect had dominated Christian mysticism since the desert monastics, who followed Greek Neoplatonism. It focused more on God the Father, or the Trinity as a whole, than on God the Son, and introvertive mystical experiences empty of differentiated content were most important. However, Augustine began a mysticism of love tradition, and by the twelfth century it had gained traction in Western Christendom, possibly due to a growing cult of courtly love. God was seen less as the Old Testament angry god threatening eternal damnation and more as a god revealing his love in the sacrifice of his son. In mysticism, personal love of Christ came to dominate over the more intellectual knowledge path. (The Sufi mysticism of love occurred prior to the Christian variety and influenced Christianity when Muslims were still in Spain.)

Unlike Neoplatonic mysticism, love mysticism involved a spiritual love, often expressed with erotic imagery. Cistercians Bernard of Clairvaux (1090–1153) and William of St. Thierry (ca. 1080–1148) were prominent early advocates, and Francis of Assisi (1181/2–1226) and Bonaventure were later ones (ca. 1217–1274). (William was one of the few classical mystics after Augustine who made the trinitarian nature of the Christian conception of God central.) The love mystic Catherine of Siena (1347–1380) was active in social work—caring for victims of the plague—as part of her ascetic self-discipline. She was also active in ecclesiastical matters and advised the pope. She became one of only four women "doctors" of the Catholic Church along with Teresa of Avila, Therese of Lisieux, and Hildegard of Bingen, all of whom were mystics or visionaries. For her, spiritual senses gave experiential knowledge of God: the *affectus* (emotions and spiritual senses of sound, touch, smell, and taste) superseded the *intellectus*. Franciscans and Dominicans debated whether the will or the intellect was the higher power of the soul and, thus, whether love or knowledge was primary. However, both knowledge mystics and love mystics of this period considered both powers necessary and leading to God, who is love, and thus to a life of love.

All classical Christian mystics employed the language of sense experience in their ecstatic knowing of mystical experiences: touching (kissing, embracing), seeing God face-to-face, hearing, tasting, and even smelling.

John of the Cross wrote of the "wound" or "burn" of the "flame of love." Like Jewish mystics, Christians spoke of "cleaving" to God (see Eckhart 1999, 489–90). Some wrote about physical effects on the body: being impervious to pain, the face shining brightly, or the body emitting a fragrant or sweet aroma. Richard Rolle, Bernard of Clairvaux, and Jan van Ruusbroec wrote of a sense of warmth and fire. During a vision of a crucified angel, Francis of Assisi was the first to receive the stigmata. Teresa of Avila, Catherine of Siena, and Henry Suso all wrote of levitation. Many spoke of uncontrollable weeping. Many also reported miracles.

The ecstatic type of mystical experience is the *rapture*. These are short events of being snatched away and standing outside oneself or one's mind. One could be raptured while feeling within the body or outside it. Neither are visions but involve a passive sense of being overpowered by a divine presence. However, many mystics downplayed such episodes in favor of a continuing participatory knowledge of God. Starting with Gregory, the orthodox position was that there is no ecstasy when a soul transcends its created nature and passes into uncreated God. There were images of dying, ascending, breaking through, crossing, penetrating, and coming to rest, but the substance of the mystic does not become the substance of God. An inner transformation was involved, but union was a matter of one's will converging with God's. Common images of this union included an iron being heated in fire, air penetrated or transformed by sunshine, burning wood, and the spiritual marriage (often with erotic imagery) of a person as a bride and Christ as the bridegroom, yet these occurred without the soul ever losing its identity or nature.[27]

Bernard of Clairvaux (1090–1153) made personal experience (checked by scripture) almost an equivalent authority to the Bible, proclaiming that "today we are reading in the book of experience" (McGinn 2013, 158–59). Bernard claimed to have experienced the presence of God "many times," but he saw his administrative work in reforming monasticism and his involvement with papal politics as making him less than a model of the contemplative. Late in life, Bernard said of his "monstrous life" and "bitter conscience," "I have kept the habit of a monk, but I have long ago abandoned the life" (Harmless 2008, 47).

In *On Loving God*, Bernard advanced four degrees of love: love of oneself for our own sake; love of God for our own sake; unselfish love of God for God's sake; and a love of oneself only for God's sake, in which one's will is fully in accord with God's. (Bernard wrote that it is proper to love oneself for God's sake since God loves us.) However, he was not certain that anyone on earth could in fact attain this highest degree of love in which all self-love completely fades away and only God's will remains. For him, mystical union was a union of wills, and thereby, one who cleaves to God is one spirit with him (1 Cor. 6:17). To describe this union of wills, Bernard used such images as a drop of water seeming to disappear in a vat of wine but added: "No doubt, the substance [of the soul] remains though under another form, another glory, another power" (McGinn 2006a, 436). Only the will is melted with God's (436). Thus, he did not believe that individuals lost their identities in this union and used the Song of Songs and its marriage imagery to describe the relation of the soul to God in mystical experiences. The "glue of love" joins two substances (God and the soul) tightly into an "indivisible unity." Bernard is much noted for his view on loving one's neighbor, but he did not extend his circle of love to include heretics or anyone he considered enemies of God. He also advocated for the Second Crusade. He began the process of driving a wedge between heart and head in Christian theology (Louth 1981, 180).

Richard of St. Victor (d. 1173), an Augustinian abbey near Paris, advanced a doctrine of four degrees of violent love (*caritas*) that transform the mystic: wounding love, binding love, love that makes one ill, and dying love. This love is described as *violent* because of the passion and madness involved, as with *eros* in the Neoplatonist tradition. All four sound negative, but they are about an inner effect: the soul dies and is conformed to divine splendor in the highest state. The soul is resurrected with Christ and leads a life conformed to Christian humility. With Richard, the symbolic use of the eroticism in the Song of Songs began to be replaced by more personal statements.

Many monks adopted a vow of poverty in reaction to the corruption within the church at the time and the perceived hypocrisy of the priests and bishops. However, even without that incentive, many wanted to live the apostolic life, and inner devotion and renunciation were central to that. Francis of Assisi epitomized this renunciation and the vow of poverty. He cut all ties to worldly things in order to become bound to God, but his asceticism was also a protest against the wealth of the church, the growing commercialization of the society of his day, and the laity's growing greed. In a case of cosmic consciousness, he also saw God immanent in all of creation. "Heaven and Earth are full of [God's] glory" (Ps. 72:19). Thus, he claimed that nature is sacred and should be an object of our love. He wrote of Brother Sun and Sister Moon. His compassion extended beyond human beings to all life. The harmony of God, nature, and humanity was central to his *Canticle to the Sun*. In an image also applied to the Japanese Buddhist Basho and the Buddha, Francis was said to walk effortlessly in his master's footsteps precisely because he did not try, in contrast to the clumsy and faulty efforts of the learned.

For Francis's Neoplatonism-trained follower Bonaventure, the "mind's journey into [Lat. *in*] God" begins with meditating on traces of God within the natural world and then contemplating God within oneself through reason (purgation). Next, the intellect is lifted up to contemplate the divine light (illumination). Finally, the soul finds lasting repose in God through "burning love" for the crucified Christ (union). In the last stage, one must leave behind one's "senses and mental activities, sensible and invisible things, all nonbeing and being." In this state of unknowing, one is restored to the extent possible for any creature to "the unity with him who is above all essences and knowledge." For him, "God is a sphere whose center is everywhere and whose circumference is nowhere."[28]

Eastern Orthodoxy

Fewer Eastern Orthodox mystics have been identified in history than in Western Christianity, not because there are fewer of them but because there is greater emphasis on not bringing attention to oneself or one's own achievements. Additionally, mysticism is the standard for monastics and theologians, not the exception, so fewer mystics have stood out. Indeed, most Eastern Orthodox theologians have been mystics. Even today, mysticism and theology have not separated. A group of monasteries formed on Mount Athos in northern Greece, and by the tenth century, it had become the most important center in the Eastern Orthodox tradition for monastic groups and has remained so since then. The ascetic Rule of Basil the Great (ca. 330–379), following the knowledge approach to mysticism, became the basis for all Eastern Orthodox monasteries. Following Gregorius Palamas (1296–1359), this tradition distinguishes God's *essence* (*ousia*), which remains an unexperienceable and unknowable mystery forever beyond our comprehension, from his emanated but uncreated *energies* (*energeia*), through which God can be known at least in relation to the universe. (Opponents think that the idea of such energies introduced polytheism.)

Eastern Orthodox theologians assert that the goal of every Christian is an inner transformation through conquering the passions of *deification* or *divinization* (*theosis*). The term was first used by the theologian Clement of Alexandria (ca. 150–215). For him, Christian perfection was to "become like God." This was to "share in the very being of God" (2 Peter 1:4; see also Luke 20:36). As the second century Greek theologian Irenaeus said in *Against Heresies*, "God made himself what we are in order to make us what he is." (In Western Christendom, Augustine picked up the idea.) The incarnation of God in Jesus accomplished this possibility by uniting the divine with human nature. The image of God within us has been lost but can be recovered.

Light and the illumination of the soul figure prominently in deification. Through asceticism, Symeon the New Theologian (949–1022) inwardly experienced the death and resurrection of Jesus. (Eastern Orthodoxy emphasizes the suffering of Christ less than in the West.) He identified our inner light with the glory emanating from God, as with the transfigured Christ at Mount Tabor (Matt. 17:1–9, Mark 9:2–10, Luke 9:28–36, 2 Peter 1:16–18): our mind is pure and simple, so if we strip away everything alien to it, it becomes still and unthinking, and it enters and rests in the sweetness of the pure and simple divine light. One does not literally become God but God-like. No actual union with God himself is possible, nor does our nature change. Rather, deification is the illumination of the soul by God's light.

The central Eastern Orthodox training to raise the inner divine light is the *hesychasm* (from the Greek, stillness or silence). It originated with the desert monastics' practice of inner silence and constant prayer. Breath control and fixing one's gaze were practiced but died out by the eighteenth century. Ultimately, one attains repose in the uncreated emanated light of God. By the time of Palamas, the practice of hesychasm became a standardized meditative technique closely identified with the *prayer of the heart* (the Jesus Prayer): "Lord Jesus, son of God, have mercy on me, a sinner." It is used in mantra-like repetitions and can enable ASCs. While these monastics focused more on the incarnation, icons, and liturgical prayer than did their Western counterparts. Icons, in the words of Basil the Great, communicate silently by representing what words communicate by sound. (Medieval mystics in the West were not especially iconoclastic; they drew heavily on sacred Christian images.) Eastern Orthodox theologians also stressed paradoxical language when it comes to God and the *via negativa* more than in Western Christendom. Aristotelian philosophy had very little influence.

Late Middle Ages

The monastic ideal of holiness established by the desert monastics lasted almost a thousand years. Asceticism remained a strong form of spirituality. Western and Eastern Christianity did not have strong meditative traditions prior to the eleventh century, but extreme, injurious forms of asceticism to induce ASCs were condemned (Kroll and Bachrach 2005, 2).[29] By the year 1200, the old order of Benedictine monasteries isolated from towns began to give way to the new Franciscan and Dominican *mendicant* (begging) orders of friars and to lay groups of men and women, opening up the possibility of attaining mystical perfection in the secular world. The mendicants followed the apostolic life of wandering and preaching without "purse or wallet or sandals" (Luke 10:1–12), a life of poverty in which one gave away one's property (Luke 18:21–22). (In 1323, the pope responded by decreeing that it was a heresy to claim that Jesus or his disciples did not possess property.) They lived in their own communities, begging or performing manual labor for food, and led lives of chastity. Preaching, penitence, and poverty became their hallmarks. The phrase *unio mystica* was generally replaced by talk of sharing the being (*esse*) of God or being one in being. The Pseudo-Dionysius used the phrase *mystical oneness* or *union* (*henosis mustike*) in the *Divine Names* (2.9), but its Latin equivalent (*unio mystica*) was rarely used before modern times (McGinn 2001, 132; Harmless 2008, 252–54). The *via negativa* also flourished in all three Abrahamic traditions for a century at this time.

Works for the laity written in vernacular languages began to supplement those in Latin since many did not have access to educational institutions. The works become internationally available when translated into Latin. Devotions outside of the church's liturgical practices also grew, as the laity requested greater prayer and meditative practices. (The division of the papacy in 1378 hurt the credibility of church authority in the eyes of many in Western Christendom.) Mystical training and practices were no longer confined to monastics. All of this opened up the possibility for the church to accept the laity's ability to directly experience mystical awareness of God. One no longer had to flee the world to attain mystical knowledge. The growth of accounts of visionary experiences in the thirteenth century hinted at a visionary explosion in the later Middle Ages, especially among women (McGinn 2013, 158). Autobiographical accounts of mystics' and visionaries' experiences began to appear and take precedence over commentaries on scripture, again, especially among women. This optimism about lay mystical experiences and the universal message that mystical encounters with God were accessible to all lasted until the sixteenth century (159).

Bernard McGinn (1998) calls this period the "new mysticism" of Christianity and the high point of Western Christian mysticism. With the common monastic and Latin core disappearing in Western Europe, regionalism began to grow in the fourteenth century. The English mystics of this period were less concerned with theology and instead wrote on practical ways of developing the inner life. These mystics included the layman Richard Rolle (ca. 1290–1349). Walter Hilton (ca. 1340–1396), after three or four years of purgation, had the ecstasy of being "intoxicated, ravished, and annihilated," one-ing to Jesus through feeling his presence. An anonymous monk wrote the *Cloud of Unknowing* (ca. 1375) within a Neoplatonist framework, as interpreted by the Frenchman Thomas Gallus (ca. 1200–1246). The author advanced two *clouds*: the cloud of forgetting all created things, and the cloud of unknowing that permanently lies between us and God. Passing through the first cloud involves our preparatory effort in prayer: a naked intent on knowing God. He suggested that short prayer be used, a short word or even just one syllable—*God* or *sin*—for objects of contemplation. Thereby, one strips away all awareness of oneself to see only one's naked being that has always existed in God. God always remains beyond the second cloud and is never clearly perceived. Only through desire and love, not knowledge, can one be prepared to receive by grace the ecstasy of God's rays of dazzling darkness coming from beyond the second cloud. Thereby, one experiences some of God's ineffable mysteries. We must "leave aside this everywhere and everything in exchange for this nowhere and nothing." This author (and Hilton) placed the contemplative life above the active one (chap. 17), but he included action as part of the contemplative life (chaps. 24–25). It is only an active life without contemplation that is rejected.[30]

Three influential figures from the Rhineland and Flanders were Johannes Tauler (d. 1361), Henry Suso (ca. 1295–1366), and Jan van Ruusbroec (1293–1381). All were heavily indebted to Meister Eckhart. For Tauler, one can become divinized in the deepest ground of humility and the annihilation of all sense of self since everything that constitutes oneself is, in fact, God, and everything that one does is God's action in them. When one un-becomes through self-annihilation, the personally created abyss (*abgrunt*) in us compels the uncreated abyss of the Godhead to take over, and the two become one pure being. One's spirit becomes lost in God's spirit, drowned in a bottomless sea.

Tauler denied that he had had this highest mystical experience, but he was a popular mystical theorist and master of living. For him, when one is engulfed in the oneness of God, one is in an abyss in which all differences are lost: one knows nothing, neither God nor oneself. However, he clarified that it is only the sense of distinction that is lost. The difference between God and the created soul does not actually disappear. The enlightened become God-hued and God-like, attaining by grace what God is by nature, but there is no union: God still remains far beyond what we can see or understand in his unfathomable abyss.

For Suso, God is a "creative Nothing." (Suso practiced extreme asceticism for twenty years before Gold told him that it was not necessary.) The soul is also nothing, but it remains a real creature and cannot experience the hidden Godhead. After the inner experiences, when one is able to reflect, one realizes that the ontological distinction remains even if one loses awareness of the soul during a mystical experience. In addition, he believed that the Godhead was trinitarian and that we need to break through Christ's suffering to get to it.

For Ruusbroec, with an "imageless naked understanding," one goes beyond all works, all practices, and all things to the summit of one's spirit. He also was explicit about the soul remaining a distinct substance or nature: the iron is in the fire and the fire is in the iron, but the fire and the iron are not the same. According to him, never does a creature become so holy that it loses its status as a created being and becomes God, even if one loses awareness of the soul during mystical experiences. Nevertheless, the ultimate stage for him occurs beyond a oneness of spirit (*unitas spiritus*): a union without difference or intermediary beyond the Trinity. For him, the "God-seeing life" is the "unitive life" of contemplation informing action.

The laywomen in Northern Europe, known as the Beguines, and the laymen, known as the Beghards, were anti-scholastic and anti-intellectual. They embraced a life of poverty, chastity, and prayer. They also often cared for the sick and dying. Some lived in communities, and some of these communities became convents under the supervision of Dominican friars. They stressed contemplative prayer and visionary experiences, not mystical experiences. Well-known Beguines include Mechthild of Magdeburg (ca. 1212–1297) and Hadewijch of Antwerp (fl. thirteenth century), who was banished from her Beguine community for her elitist attitude. For them, the "annihilated soul's" rest in God is not disturbed by works. For Mechthild, "the overflow of Divine Love is never still but ever ceaselessly and tirelessly pours itself, so that our little vessel is filled to the brim and overflows."

However, they believed that none of the deeds of the enlightened could violate Christian ethics. The enlightened were beyond any concern with virtues because the virtues had become ingrained in their souls; the only difference was that it was now God, not the soul, who worked through the person and carried out good deeds that ministered to a neighbor's needs. Thus, they held no general antinomian repudiation of Christian ethics. Nevertheless, they were in constant tension with the church authorities.

Jean Gerson (1363–1429) conveyed the sense of mysticism in this period: "Mystical theology is experiential knowledge of God realized through an embrace (*complexum*) of unitive love" (*De Mystica Theologia* I.28). The philosopher and theologian Thomas Aquinas (1225–1274) wrote in his *Summa Theologia* that there are two ways to know God's will: speculative thought and a direct and immediate contact with God (Ps. 34:9), knowing God through experience of him (*cognito dei experimentalis*).[31] For Aquinas, by the "affective and experimental knowledge of divine beauty," one "experiences within oneself the taste of God's gentleness and the kindness of his will." He also applied the Aristotelian adage to knowing God: to know something, one must become like that thing.

However, the new mysticism also challenged Christian orthodoxy more than did earlier mystical writings. The traditional monastic view of mystical union was a loving union of the mystic's will with God's; this kept the individuality of the two subjects intact (McGinn 2013, 159). It was a union of spirit, not an identity of two distinct realities, substances, or natures. But beginning with some women mystics and visionaries in the thirteenth century, union with God became a matter of identity in a bottomless abyss of absolute mutuality and equality (159). In this union, the mystic loses any individual existence in God. Such teachings were regarded as heretical, but their proponents defended them with scripture. Jesus prayed that his followers may be one as God is in Jesus and Jesus is in God, so that all would be in God (John 17:21). Needless to say, the idea that one could be absorbed into God bypassed the need for priests as religious intermediates or, indeed, for the church to be the vehicle of salvation, thus opening these mystics to the charge that they believed they were no longer bound by the church's rituals and authority. Some (especially women) based their claims on the authority of their own experiences of God. By the fourteenth century, men in positions of authority in the church began to exert control. This led to condemnations, persecutions, and executions for the next four and a half centuries (McGinn 2013, 160).

Bernard McGinn distinguishes mystical and visionary experiences, and he notes that much of the new mysticism involved visions, not mystical experiences (1994, 325–28).[32] Many of the women labelled *mystics* were actually *visionaries* (McGinn 2013, 158). In the literature, women most often reported visionary experiences. Hildegard of Bingen (1098–1179) wrote of being "bathed in a bright light of glowing fire" and hearing a voice from heaven. In her *Showings*, the English Julian of Norwich (1342–ca. 1416) related her very graphic visions of Jesus being crucified. She stated that Jesus's suffering was shown to her "without any intermediary." The differences between her earlier short accounts of her experiences and later more elaborate ones show how mystics may change their view of their experiences over time. She also had a mystical experience of feeling one'd or fastened to God—"alike in kind and substance"—but upon later reflection, she concluded that "God is God, and our substance is a creature in God." She also wrote that "God is as truly our Mother as our Father." She became an anchoress devoted to ascetic practices. Many of the women reflected an anticlerical sentiment that was a harbinger of things to come. Their objections were not so much to doctrine but to the laxness they saw in the observance of religious practices by clergy and laity alike.

In the mystics' uncompromising attempt to live the simple apostolic life, Christian virtues—including humility and, above all, love—became internalized on the path. Mystics "took up the cross" inwardly by surrendering the self. Many, such as the Brethren of the Common Life in the Netherlands, did not feel called to the monastic life. The famous *Imitation of Christ* by Thomas of Kempis (ca. 1380–1471) advanced emulating Jesus—being like Christ in thought, word, and deed—as the way to become one with God. One is "to learn perfect self-surrender, and to accept [God's] will without argument or complaint." This leads to a life of renunciation and poverty but also to a life of love toward the poor and needy. One no longer lives one's life as one's own but as God's. One no longer seeks one's own good but God's. Some Christians may be "hirelings," working for a reward of heaven or out of fear of hell, but the enlightened are the "friends" or even "sons" and "daughters" of God (Gal. 4:4–5), detached from all personal concerns of reward or punishment.

The fifteenth century produced a notable mystical theorist: the Neo-platonism-influenced German Nicholas of Cusa (1401–1464). He was a mathematician and a Cardinal. Some consider him the first modern thinker. For him, *learned ignorance* is the recognition of the limits of all theological thinking. The highest learning that we can attain is to realize that we are ignorant of God. (This insight may have come to him in an experience in 1437 as a gift from the Father of Lights, but by his own admission, he was a failed mystic.) God in himself cannot be known by us, even after death, and all attempts at positive characterizations must be rejected. God is an ineffable mystery beyond the reach of the human intellect, transcending both the *via negativa* and *via positiva*, but we can know that God is one and being itself, in which all opposites coincide. God is the undifferentiated, absolute maximum that precedes all differentiations and unites all opposites as their cause. God is not *wholly other* but is, in fact, *not-other* due to his immanence in creation (although he is not phenomenal). To explain this coincidence of opposites to some German monks, Nicholas sent an icon (probably of Jesus) that was painted in such a way that its eyes appeared to be looking right at the viewer no matter where they stood. This was symbolic in two ways: when we look at God, he is also always looking at us, no matter where we are; and no matter how many viewers there are, God is always looking at each person individually. God in relation to us (rather than God-in-himself) also has some positive attributes that are known based on scripture: God is love and has the other attributes set forth in the Bible. But there is no proportionality between creator and creatures, so metaphors ultimately fail.

Meister Eckhart

The great German Dominican preacher and theologian Meister Eckhart (ca. 1260–1327/8) from Hochheim deserves special attention for his radical statements. These statements got him in trouble with the church. Papers to excommunicate him were allegedly on their way from Rome when he died, and after his death a papal bull declared some of his teachings to be tainted by the "stain of heresy" and others to be "evil sounding and very rash and suspect of heresy" (Eckhart 2009, 26–28).*

Mysticism and medieval scholasticism may collide since the schoolmen rely on reason alone to resolve or expand issues of faith, but Eckhart combined both. He held a Neoplatonist-influenced emanationist metaphysics, reinterpreted in theistic terms, in which the ground of the soul and God's

---

*All page references in this section are to Eckhart 2009 unless otherwise indicated.

ground are the same: the Godhead beyond God the creator (109). McGinn calls Eckhart's metaphysics a "mysticism of the ground (*grunt*)" and points out that it is something new to Christianity (2005, 83). There is only one ground to all that is real, so all creatures and God himself have the same one being (*esse/ens*). Paradoxically, all creatures are also simultaneously "pure nothing" since they have no being of their own (Eckhart 2009, 226).[33] This is not to deny that we exist but only to emphasize that we have no existence apart from our source; without the Godhead, we are nothing.[34]

Central to his metaphysics is the distinction between God (*Gott*) and the Godhead (*Gottheit*) (293–94). The former is the personal god of theism that creates, acts, and has attributes, but the latter is the "God beyond God": the still, inactive abyss or ground that is the source of our being.[35] God may be "omni-nameable," but the Godhead is nameless (Harmless 2008, 118). The Godhead has no action in it (218–23). It is a silent desert where no distinction ever peeped (311). All of existence emanates from it and returns to it. God, the first reality emanated, boils up (*bullitio*) and the Trinity is created. Then, everything else is emitted (boils over, *ebullitio*) from God. God has the same being from the Godhead as all that is created, for everything grows out of the "not God" (461). God unbecomes in the ground and the fount of the Godhead (294), but God is also beyond all images and above understanding. To say that God is good, or wise, or a being is not true; when we are chattering about God, we are lying and committing a sin (463).

The being that the Godhead provides is absolutely identical in all of reality, but God created all things. Thus, the being of the universe is the same as God's being. To combine ideas from Eckhart's scholastic Latin works with his more provocative German sermons: God is the being of the natural realm, and the Godhead is the source of that being and, thus, is beyond being; creatures qua creatures are nothing. Nothing can exist apart from God. God is immanent in every creature as its being. If God were not in all things, nature would cease operation and not strive for anything (Eckhart 2009, 235). However, God also transcends the natural realm since God is its creator and is completely unlike any creature. Ultimately, God as transcendent is not goodness, or truth or even being, nor is he in any other way phenomenal: he is pure nothing. If you think of anything, he is not that (287).[36]

However, Eckhart did not deny our creaturehood or a dualism of creator and created. God is not a creature, and we remain created since the soul has a created nature in addition to its uncreated nature (the same being from the Godhead as God has). Yet, the sense of self is idle or forgotten during a mystical experience while God works in the inner, silent, uncreated part of the soul giving birth to the Son (*Gottesgeburt*) in the ground of the soul. With this birth, one is transformed in God (Eckhart 2009, 541), but the soul is not annihilated. Eckhart sometimes equated God with being and thus claimed that we are already God, but individuals do not lose their individuality or their createdness. God dwells only in the soul's innermost part. God the creator never absorbs the spark, or castle, or uncreated light in each creature in a mystical union, nor is one creature identical to another. In our being, we are unborn and eternal (424). The being of God and creatures is one, so the soul is not united to God (392). When Eckhart spoke of being fully "united" to God (509), he explained that it is a matter of oneness with God's will (522), not a oneness of natures or identity. There is no other reality for us to be united to in a mystical experience; there is only the being that we already are and its source (the Godhead) where everything is already one (294). Eckhart said that you should sink away from your *you-ness* and dissolve into God's *his-ness*, becoming completely one *mine* in his uncreated self-identity (*isticheit*), sinking from our nothingness into God's nameless nothingness (*nihtheit*) (463, 465). Through the intellect, one comes to know God without images or means, but to do this, one must become God and God must become them. That is, the individual must become one *is* (being) and one *here and now* (464). But again, we still must understand our created identity and the nameless nothingness that is the source of our being (463). Thus, for Eckhart our soul and creaturehood are both real.

In a mysticism centered on the Godhead beyond a personal god, the means to get us to the core is the intellect (*intellectus*); knowledge, not love, reveals bare being (Eckhart 2009, 207–208).[37] Love is a major theme in Eckhart's Latin and German works, but the intellect is above the will and, hence, above love (344). The intellect is uncreated, like the soul that it knows. Realizing the source requires unknowing (*unwizzen*), emptying the mind of all content to become receptive to the action of God and to come to a transformed knowledge (34–36, 42–43). The soul draws back into itself all the powers it granted the senses and becomes free of the senses, entranced (33, 571). It draws into God and becomes nothing (573). Memory, understanding, the senses, and the powers governing the body no longer function (33). One forgets all things and their images, and in the silence, one lets God work and speak (33). Completely unknowing and forgetting the self and creatures is required; there is a blinding light in the darkness that can be seen only by knowing nothing of all creatures (460). To know God immediately or directly without means, the mind must be emptied of all ideas and images (*bilde*)—including all sense of self—and must be detached from all emotions.[38] One must unknow oneself and all things and know only God. One then knows God as God knows us (530–31). Then, one is transformed in God's will and become "one-willed with God" so that one wills nothing but what God wills, in the way that God wills (531). It is the radical transformation of a person who realizes the "nothingness" of anything created (including their own created existence).

Three things keep us from becoming a begotten son or daughter of God: multiplicity, temporality, and corporeality (Eckhart 2009, 295, 337, 347). One must strip away all distinctions and properties. One must become estranged from all multiplicity—including anything that permits a hint or shadow of difference, including goodness and truth (541)—for the mind is unmoving (569). To be full of creatures is to be empty of God, and to be full of God is to be empty of all creatures (569). If one knows any thing, one does not know God (342). And, like the contemplating Nous in Plotinus's system, God the Father knows nothing but the Son (408). God is above being, time, and place (341–42). God is nothing (*niht*), not in the sense that he lacks existence but in the sense that he is "neither this nor that" thing (342, 408). God is not a being and worked before creation had being (342). To attain oneness, one must turn away from one's self and all created things (310). One must renounce oneself and all things, not discriminate between this or that good, and strip God naked of all attributes but being (318–19), or even being (344).

In short, the soul must be stripped naked of all multiplicity. This freedom from all creatures and images signals an introvertive depth-mysticism, not an extrovertive experience of the natural realm. Freed from images, we achieve a radical inner simplicity and stillness—an inner desert or inner poverty—beyond all conceptual categories and desires. The inner desert is not attained by fleeing into a physical desert away from all outward things but by becoming emotionally totally free of all things and finding only emptiness in them. Only then can one break through and seize God so that God's presence shines forth without effort (Eckhart 2009, 492). Through such poverty, the poor in spirit has, knows, wants, wills, and desires nothing (420–25). They have nothing of the human spirit and go naked to God (542). They do not even have a will to fulfill God's will (423), for a desire to conform to God's will would mean that one still has a personal will. On the contrary, one does not long for anything but instead is empty. Only when the mind is empty of all things, including images of God, can it get to the uncreated being beyond all mental images. To be aware of knowing God is to know about God and the soul—to still have images—not to be directly experiencing the being of God (562). We need to learn to penetrate the shell of all things (images) and find the kernel of being at its core that is beyond the reach of understanding. In that darkness, God shines. In this central silence, no idea may enter, and the soul neither thinks nor acts. Once one is empty of anything pertaining to a self, one passes into the naked being of God; there, nothing is hidden in God that is not revealed (74). Nothing is in a son of God but God—no image of God but only God, alone, naked, and pure (525). Only then has the soul also broken through all images to love God as he is—as a non-god, non-spirit, non-person, and non-image, as simply the pure One detached from all duality (465). God is not goodness, being, truth, or one (287).

There are degrees of perfection (Eckhart 2009, 541), but once we are completely passive, detached, and receptive, God is compelled to act (160, 566). Since God and the soul are one in being, the soul is God's natural place. There is then the birth of the Son in the soul like a bolt of lightning. This birth occurs continuously in the single eternal now, in which God acts outside the continuum of time (58, 79, 178, 281, 338, 341). Thus, the birth of the Son did not occur only once in the past with Jesus but also occurs continuously in mystical experiences. (It is the birth of the same *Son* over and over in the same *now*.) God must perform this continuous, repeated birth out of necessity, and he is ever at work in the eternal now begetting his son (394–95). (The idea that God is compelled to act was one point that got Eckhart in trouble with the church. Eckhart did not deny the need for grace [see 347, 401], but he interpreted it to mean the "indwelling and cohabiting of the soul in God" [396].)

Thus, we all can become begotten sons and daughters of God. The purpose of the incarnation was that humans can gain by grace what Christ was by nature (Eckhart 2009, 566). But, in his defense to charges of heresy, Eckhart stated that no one ever becomes Jesus and that no one is saved by anyone but Jesus, the first begotten. Nothing ontologically changes with this birth in our soul—substantively, we are the same being and nature that we have always been—but our awareness is transformed. The final stage is the rest and blessedness of becoming free of all images, attaining complete oblivion of our transient life, being transformed into the image of God and thus becoming God's child (559). One is at peace only to the extent one is in God (521–22). We then have a direct awareness of God unmediated by any image.

Eckhart is not always clear whether he is discussing being or God—God is more than simply being since he is a creator—but he is clear that our goal is to transcend God with a type of mystical experience other than the birth of the son: a break through even God into the Godhead (*durchbrechen*) (2009, 294). That is, the goal for creatures is not the creator but the source of God. Eckhart prayed that we may be free of God to gain the truth (421–22), to be free of creator and creatures and to stand in the first cause (the Godhead). This is not a denial of God—Eckhart is, after all, praying to God—but his objective was to get beyond the creator. One wills to be without God for God's sake (531). Likewise, he did not mean that God cannot be characterized. Eckhart said God is love (see 62, 388–90, 464), but he pushed further. The soul must break through even the soul's own image into the source of being that is the Godhead beyond God. It is a return to our state of existence before we were created by God as creatures. There, one perceives where God, the experiencer, and all else have one common ground.

As with most classical mystics, Eckhart valued this permanent state of a person above any transient ecstatic raptures. In this state, the constant awareness of God permeates one's dispositions and intentions. One lives a life in God without God (that is, without the concept *God* interfering). One lives a life in God himself (Eckhart 2009, 531). Thus, the best and loftiest life is to be silent, without interposing any ideas, and to let God speak and act through us. God is then acting in us. In this state, one lives without a *why* (*sunder warumbe*): without a personal purpose or goal and without planning (110, 239, 332, 363–64). Thus, one is like God, who also acts without a *why*. God is not moved to perform any deed by anything but his own goodness (508, 542–43). If someone asks why you live, the only possible reply is "I live because I live" (110). No other motive—which would have to be personal—is involved. You live only to live and do not know why (180). God's love acts through the mystic, and self-giving love has no *why* (129). There is no further goal but living from one's nature. Just as one loves God only for the sake of loving God, so too one does all of one's work without calculation and as an end in itself: self-giving love is automatic. Those who seek something in their works or who work because of a *why* are hirelings, not the just man (*iustus*) who has God working in him (305). One conforms to Jesus inwardly in all things (507).

In sum, Eckhart asserts that the enlightened perform acts of love out of the ground of being with no other motive. If we cling to God, God and all virtues cling to us (Eckhart 2009, 489–90). It is a selfless life of purely disinterested action for others. One should seek only God's will, not knowledge, understanding, inwardness, piety, or repose (289). To the author of the *Theologia Germanica*, living without a *why* means living for no personal ends and for no other reason except to fulfill God's eternal will. The inner man is immovable and has no independent will; the outer man moves and fulfills the duties and obligations ordained by God. As Ruusbroec put it, this is a "wayless state." However, the actions are not truly purposeless or aimless; only personal motivation is absent. Christian beliefs and values will no doubt inform actions in the enlightened Christian way of life.

Eckhart emphasized detachment (*abegescheidenheit*) from all worldly things. Detachment is the state in which the mind stands unmoved by all accidents of joy, sorrow, honor, shame, and disgrace as a mountain of lead stands unmoved by the wind (Eckhart 2009, 568–69). It is the mystical application of giving up all things to follow Christ (Matt. 19:21). All of one's works are consigned to God, for all of one's works are wrought by God, and he who causes the works is more genuinely and truly their owner than the one who performs them (Eckhart 2009, 490). By "naughting and shrinking" the self, our inward and outward activity cooperates with God (517). Unmoving detachment is the unmoving hinge on which the door of actions moves (571). Thus, the inner person is unmoved while the outer person works, just as God's detachment is unmoved by creation. All works are undertaken with the same disinterested frame of mind. Nothing is done for hope of heaven, fear of hell, or any other personal desire. Those who love God because of what they can get for it treat God as they would a cow (117). One takes all things, including suffering, as if one had wished and prayed for them (530). Indeed, the detached soul cannot pray since prayer is to ask for something and the soul has no will but God's. At most, they can pray only to uniform with God's will. The detached are still alive, but Christ is living in them (568). They take all things great and small equally since God is equally in them all (588–89). Detachment is both necessary to attain enlightenment and an integral part of the enlightened life of abandoning oneself to God.

The completely dispassionate heart is the most receptive state for the inflowing of God. It is beyond humility, knowledge, and love. It is above love because love is possessive and because God must give himself over to the disinterested. It is detachment from all things and concepts; those who are detached want nothing, have nothing, will nothing, and know nothing. They are free of all personal will and self-interest. Eckhart can say, "If the pope had been slain by my hand, and if it had not occurred by my will, I would go up to the alter and say Mass as usual" (2009, 94). To be detached is to be inwardly unmoved by anything. One is even-minded in the face of all the joy and sorrow caused by the passing things of this world, totally disinterested in oneself and others, not loving oneself or one's family more than other people or one's own happiness more than that of others (503–504). One is empty of all things created. All sorrow comes from partiality in one's loving and from holding something dear that is perishable (529). By abandoning oneself to God, one can accept any kind of suffering with joy and gratitude (506). Thus, detachment overcomes sorrow. The detached receive all things alike from God. They are dead to the world; nothing created can move them. They love God and could as easily give up the whole world as give up an egg. They have penetrated all images and reached their being. One is detached from all creatures and loves God alone, for his own sake alone (see 542). But one is never totally selfless—there is always more to leave (489).

Eckhart claimed that detachment brings us closest to God since God always acts disinterestedly toward everything within creation. Such detachment involves desiring nothing, neither loving nor hating the world or people. It is the equanimity (*gelazenheit*) of letting all things be without clutching or self-assertion. It remains an inner attitude—relinquishing all senses of ownership and attachment (*eigenschaft*), even of one's own acts— and does not entail the external renunciation of anything or resignation concerning the effects of actions on other people. With this inner calm of being interested in "neither this nor that," the outer man works while the inner man remains unmoved by whatever occurs. One accepts things free of all emotional response. In short, one lets God be God in them.

Moral action results: the fruit of contemplation is loving action toward others. The enlightened soul is no longer a virgin but a wife that bears the fruit of moral action. He whom Eckhart called the "just man" (*iustus*)—or the good, noble, humble, inner, or poor man—does not seek or desire anything. His claim that we are all "aristocrats" might have influenced Anabaptists or other reformers, but Eckhart made it clear that he meant that all people are equally noble by their own inner nature (Eckhart 2009, 108). His was a claim about one's inner life, not about any external social status. He advocated neither an endorsement of the status quo nor a call for social change. Each person's nobility exists inwardly and remains intact regardless of what happens in their outward circumstances. Nothing external can affect it. The just have no self-will and are even-minded (328–32, 339). Like God, one is just because one gives each person their due.

While accepting external monastic poverty, Eckhart's emphasis here is on being internally empty of possessions (including all images of things and God), not external poverty (2009, 374). Eckhart was concerned with giving up a sense of self through detachment rather than giving up material possessions. External poverty without detachment leads nowhere, and the latter does not need the former. He preferred inner penitence to exterior acts such as fasting and going barefoot (503). He rejected extreme asceticism, mortification, or any prescribed path (52): whoever seeks God in a special way gets the way and misses God (110). He prescribes a "pathless path," a "wayless way, free and yet bound, raised, rapt away well-nigh past self and all things, without will and without images, even though not yet in essential being" (86).[39]

Antinomianism

Most Christian mystics in the Middle Ages were theologically orthodox and also accepted the need for the church and its sacraments for salvation. Both love mystics and knowledge mystics emphasized the distinction between God and the created soul: the individual only becomes one "in spirit" with God. But some mystics rejected church authority and orthodox doctrines. In Northern Europe in the late thirteenth and early fourteenth centuries, the language of indistinct union with God spread among the Beguines. (Some of Eckhart's remarks may well have influenced them and their remarks him.) This led to the possibility of antinomianism.

The basic idea of antinomianism is that the elect are free of any legal, social, moral, or religious authority or duty. The inner spirituality of the elect places them above the law in every sense. In the enlightened state, one no longer has any self-will, and thus, in Augustine's phrase, one can "love and do what you will." A form of antinomianism apparently existed even in the early Christian community: some intentionally continued to sin so that the grace they received would be that much greater (Rom. 6:1). The orthodox, starting with Paul, condemned this understanding of freedom from sin as heresy, and by 1300 the church was concerned about mystical heresy more generally. Orthodox enlightened Christian mystics may believe that they are beyond good and evil in the sense of no longer needing to consult a list of rules on what to do and not do since their will is now fully aligned with God's. However, antinomians go further. They do not merely occasionally or inadvertently break one rule or another; they repudiate all social or religious rules as not being binding or even applicable in their enlightened way of life. No act is rejected as sinful. Whatever actions the elect perform are, by definition, pure and free of sin. This does not mean that antinomians constantly engage in immoral acts, but they do ignore social norms, and the orthodox believe they act against the norms intentionally.

Christian antinomians could cite many New Testament passages for support: "If you are led by the Spirit, you are not under law" (Gal. 5:18); "To the pure, all things are pure" (Titus 1:15); "Nothing is impure in itself" (Rom. 14:14; see also 8:2–3); "Sin has no dominion over you, and you are no longer under the law" (Rom. 6:14); "Where the Spirit of the Lord is, there is liberty" (2 Cor. 3:17); "Whoever is born of God does not sin . . . [and] cannot be a sinner" (1 John 3:9); "No one who dwells in Christ is a sinner" (1 John 3:6); and of course, "It is no longer I who lives but Christ who lives in me" (Gal. 2:20).

Not all antinomians were mystics, but many were enthusiasts who placed all importance on experiences for their own sake and denied the need for any outward actions or Christian rituals. They were routinely accused of holding the belief that only God is real and, thus, nothing in the world matters, so humans can do whatever they want. Indeed, classical theistic metaphysics can easily lead to an antinomian conclusion: everything is from God, thus all things are good and nothing is bad. If everything is the product of God, nothing we can possibly do is wrong. Or, if God is the only real agent, nothing that happens is not his will. Thus, whatever happens, including whatever the enlightened do, is God's will.

Prominent among the mystical antinomians were the ascetic Brothers and Sisters of the Free Spirit of northern France and Germany. This was not an organized sect but, rather, a broad movement of individual mendicants and informal groups (Lerner 1972, 178). They believed that God and human beings share the same substance, and the enlightened become divine and need not follow the commandments; and since God is sinless, so are they, whatever they do. Some Beguines and Beghards crossed the line of orthodoxy in their more extreme expressions—if not in their conduct, in conflating identity with God through the annihilation of the soul; rejecting the need for sacraments, church authority, or even Christ; and being morally indifferent to other people.

For the Free Spirit Marguerite Porete of Hainault (1250–1310), the created will is annihilated by humility and, thus, the illuminated soul is nothing. She mistrusted visions and momentary ecstasies since they may be misleading. Only freedom from the will and detachment from external and internal works was necessary in the permanent enlightened selfless state. In her *Mirror of Simple Souls*, she stated that the annihilated soul can grant to nature whatever it desires, but the soul is so well-ordered by prior training that "nature does not demand anything prohibited." (Her book may have influenced Eckhart.) For her, the sacraments of the church no longer order the enlightened soul; the soul is free of all self-will, personal desire, and even reason, so a person no longer needs spiritual practices. Any will would reveal a sense of self, so desire itself must be annihilated. One must no longer will even to do anything for God. This leads to the abyss beyond the soul. One no longer desires or despises poverty or tribulation. Reason is dead since the task of reason is taken over by divine love. Her claims led to her arrest, and during her imprisonment and trial, she refused to speak. She was burned at the stake, along with all but a few copies of her book.

These antinomians asserted the possibility of literal deification in this life. Since God is the substance of human beings, we can become God. Through breaking self-will and meditation (including sitting still and becoming emptied of images), the soul can become permanently indistinguishable from God. Everything the enlightened then do is attributed to God. Saying "I can do anything I want" would have no meaning since there is no *I*. One no longer acts at all, but God alone acts through the person (see Matt. 10:20, Gal. 2:20). Prior to enlightenment, the gross soul must conform to social and religious rules, but upon deification, the Free Spirit has no such restrictions. Commandments and ethics in general no longer apply. Purged of self-will and personal desires, one is then incapable of sinning. One attains a state of sinlessness beyond grace and beyond need for the church's rituals, priests, scriptures, or Christ. Thus, the Free Spirits saw no obligation to keep any external rules. They had no remorse in whatever they did. Hell does not exist—God is all there is, and we return to him at death—so there is no punishment to be feared.

The enlightened felt so in tune with God's will that they could grant their body whatever was pleasing to it. That is, once they became divine, they could no longer sin and could "let the body do whatever it wants." To them, the highest holiness is following one's own nature without restraint, living in a state of emptiness satisfying every inclination of spirit and body. Whatever nature requires comes from God, so whatever the body requires, they may simply let it happen. However, the claim that a "perfected" Free Spirit is incapable of sinning left the general impression among church leaders that the Free Spirits were constantly indulging their senses in a scandalous libertinism. Whether they treated their proclamations merely as theory or actually practiced them is not clear. After years of austere mystical training, could a selfless person lead a life of genuine license—a life driven by hedonistic impulses? How indulgent could an enlightened person's natural impulses be after years of discipline? Robert Lerner is doubtful that such license was their standard practice (1972, 179–80), and there are no records of any of them having been arrested for a secular crime. Most of their writings suggest that they were poor and highly ascetic in their pursuit of perfection; they renounced property and spent most of their time working on their inner life in self-emptying contemplation (239–40). But an active life helping others was no longer necessary, hence the charge of passivity and moral quietism. Indeed, their greatest sin may have been one of moral indifference and inaction.

Eckhart, Tauler, Ruusbroec, and the Friend of God who wrote the *Theologia Germanica* all attacked the antinomianism of their time as a "false illumination," "false freedom of the spirit," "false passivity," or "false emptiness." To Eckhart, it is impossible for a person who is in God's will to do something against virtue (2009, 125). To the author of the *Theologia Germanica*, the Free Spirits' case was one of "spiritual pride": thinking they were free of a sense of self when, in fact, they were not. To Ruusbroec, the Free Spirits had emptied themselves of everything including self-will but had not been infused with the grace of God, nor had they filled that new void with works of virtue. Later, he went further, claiming the Free Spirits had not yet completely emptied themselves of any sense of *I*. They had turned inward and felt nothing but the bareness and simplicity of their own being, which they mistook for God. He was willing to see antinomians burned at the stake to save the Christian community. Later, John of the Cross also condemned mystical antinomians who believed they had reached a state where they no longer had a need for the Christian sacraments or performing good works.

There may be relatively few antinomians in any tradition, but the fact remains that Christian antinomians cited scripture for all their points and considered themselves good Christians. As Eleanor McLaughlin concludes, antinomianism was not a perversion of medieval Christian mysticism, but it is a "latent possibility" within the mystical search for Christian perfection (1973, 51). However, antinomianism is not a product of mysticism per se since other mystics condemn it and non-mystics accepted it. To say that they misunderstood the Bible or the writings of Eckhart cannot explain it all; their ideas and values still had to come from somewhere. Indeed, the Christian mystical antinomian practices appear to be as logical a conclusion from the doctrine that all that happens is God's will as advocating moral action. Moreover, since God could not sin, the actions of the enlightened only expressed God within them. Thus, whatever they did was sinless. In England after 1650, another group—the libertine Ranters—worked out the logic of the doctrine of predestination in an antinomian manner. Whether a person is among the elect or the damned is fixed at the beginning of time, so nothing they can do in this life can alter their destiny. Thus, none of their actions in this life matter, so they might as well enjoy themselves.

The Reformation Period

Eckhart shows that mystics can also be scholastics, but the creation of a separate theological class in medieval schools led to a separation of *spirituality* from *theology* and of contemplatives from academics in Western Christendom. By the fourteenth century, the growing rift between scholastic theology and mystical piety increased mystics' suspicion of, and opposition to, the theology of the schools and vice versa (McGinn 2005, 248). The rise of new mysticism and the growing prominence of women may have been results of this separation, leading to less theological control of mystics. By the sixteenth century, this separation had created a true gulf between the two enterprises. Mystical experiences had always been interpreted theologically, but subsequent interpretations were controlled by the theological enterprise separate from valuing such experiences as significant. Mystics thereafter had less of an impact on institutional churches and doctrines.

The new mysticism of the late Middle Ages was one factor in people turning away from institutional authority. One might think that mysticism would have been important to the Protestant reformers who stressed a personal relationship to God, but they considered mysticism merely another unbiblical Catholic practice. They stressed the conversion of being "born again" and the certitude of salvation, not imageless rapture (Smart 1967, 427). Any immediate awareness of God would bypass grace, the role of Christ, and rely solely on the biblical word of God. Reformers downplayed miracles, and mystical experiences were just small, individual miracles. Likewise, reformers did not approve of allegorical rather than literal readings of scripture since they believed there were no hidden meanings in the Bible to expose. Some more radical reformers adopted the language of mystical identity and marriage of medieval mystics; for example, Thomas Muntzer cited mystics to justify violence and warfare.

Mysticism did indirectly influence Martin Luther, who had been a monk in an Augustinian order, and he thought highly of Johannes Tauler's notion of human passivity before God. He also published the *Theologia Germanica*, a mystical text that he considered the most important work after the Bible and Augustine's writings for teaching about God and Christ. However, later in life he turned against mysticism. His doctrine of justification by faith alone led him to seeing mystical experiences as attempts at "sinful self-salvation." Mysticism was self-centered, relied on individuals' efforts rather than grace, and was generally unbiblical. He included mystics in his condemnation of overly emotional enthusiasts. After his death, most Lutheran theologians adopted a non-mystical scholasticism (John Arndt being an exception). John Calvin did use the word *mystical* occasionally and the phrase *sense of the divine* (*sensus divinitatis*), but he appears not to have meant anything involving ASC experiences. Like Luther, he meant only that, in a life of faith, Christ dwells within us and the Holy Spirit "engrafts" a Christian into the body of Christ (the church) in a spiritual union. Also like Luther, he attacked the Pseudo-Dionysius's *Mystical Theology* as more Platonist than Christian: believers should "flee like the plague all those who try to infect you with such excrement" (Tamburello 2013, 416). He associated the contemplation taking place in the monasteries of the time with idleness (418). More generally, since mystical experiences do not involve a dialogue with God, they cannot be experiences of God.

In any case, the Protestant countries did not produce any major mystics during the Reformation. The idea of experiencing God without the mediation of priests and the church would seem to make mysticism anathema to Catholics, then more than ever, but some important mystics did emerge in Catholic countries. These mystics aided in a spiritual renewal during the Counter Reformation. In Spain, three important mystics appeared, the first of which was Ignatius Loyola (1491–1556). His manuscript *Spiritual Exercises* was designed to open people, through spiritual direction, to a receptive mode of consciousness in which they could experience God. Besides meditative practices such as visualization, his treatise included teachings on how the mind connects to the will and how to withstand experiences of spiritual desolation.

Teresa of Avila (1515–1582) was the granddaughter of a Jew who was forced to convert to Christianity but who apparently continued to practice Judaism in secret. She joined the Carmelites mendicant order and ended up its head. She reformed the order and established small hermitages for women and men dedicated to lives of inner prayer, not vocal recitation. They practiced poverty, fasting, and silence. On her spiritual advisor's and confessors' directive, she wrote about her life of prayer. She used the allegory of the soul as a castle with many rooms to explain how the stages of meditation lead to union with God in the center (the bridal chamber). Her autobiography contains accounts of her paranormal events—including levitations, which she found annoying—but her *Interior Castle* downplays the significance of such events. One empties oneself of all that is creaturely and detaches oneself from it (7.2.7). The way to union with God is love, and the union is a matter of a "marriage": the spirit of the soul is united to God and cannot be separated. The end is "a loving union with divine love." The spiritual "betrothal" is beyond ecstatic raptures. Inner "intellectual visions" (rather than external ones) occur, but the marriage is a permanent union of wills (7.2.5). Thus, two substances become one in spirit and love, as with two candles joined so that their light is one or two streams flowing into one sea even though the two entities can be separated (7.2.4). Two wills become one, and that one is God's will (*Ascent of Mount Carmel* 1.11.3).

In one of her external visions, Teresa felt an angel plunge a spear tipped with fire into her heart. John of the Cross (1542–1591), who joined Teresa's Carmelite order of friars, used the same image. Unlike some theologians, he wanted "to know creatures through God, not God through creatures" because "God in his own being is all these things" (*Living Flame of Love* 3.9).[40] For John, the soul knows effects (creatures) through knowing their cause (God), not vice versa (4.4; John 1:3–4; Acts 17:28). God dwells in the heart of each soul, and we can experience his presence there (*Living Flame* 4.14). The "thread of love" binds God and the soul and makes a mystic one with God in love, although they still differ in substance (*Spiritual Canticle* 31.1). God's substance and the soul's substance "touch," and there is a "taste" of eternal life, but life in this world precludes more (*Living Flame* 2.21). Two natures are one in spirit and love, like the union of the light of a candle and the sun (*Canticle* 22.3). However, there is no union of "essences" or "nature." The union is a matter of wills that results in being imbued God's love; the soul is not destroyed (38.3). Union with God, insofar as it is possible in this life, is achieved through love, not knowledge (*Ascent* 2.8.5). However impressive may be our knowledge or feelings of God, that knowledge and those feelings have no resemblance to God and amount to very little (2.4.4). Only the Holy Spirit awakens knowledge of the Godhead (*Living Flame* 4.17). In the spiritual marriage that culminates in the union of love, the soul is totally transformed. Through mystical participation, the soul becomes divine; that is, it becomes God to the extent that is it possible in this life (*Canticle* 22.3). It is a permanent union of spirits, not only temporary moments of the union of spirits. Through that participation, we become the "shadow" of God (*Living Flame* 3.78). The soul no longer acts. Rather, the Holy Spirit makes one act (1.9, 1.29).[41]

The bridegroom (Christ) is actively seeking the bride (the soul). Our role in the spiritual quest is to lessen our worldly desires and to unknow all worldly wisdom (*Ascent* 1.4.6; *Canticle* 39.12). The light of God's knowledge is always in the soul, and we must empty ourselves of all forms and images that cover it (*Ascent* 2.15.4). All worldly knowledge is ignorance, so the soul must become ignorant of such knowledge to be clean, pure, and empty of all forms of figures (*Canticle* 26.13). One can arrive at perfection only by eliminating all desires (appetites), no matter how much virtue one practices (*Ascent* 1.5.6). The soul must, through its own efforts, empty its affections and wills of all earthly and heavenly things insofar as it is possible, including understanding and imagining (2.4.2, 2.5.8). It must pass beyond everything into the unknowing of all natural things (2.2.4). Renunciation of every affection cleanses the soul and leads to a "nakedness and emptiness" (2.5.8–2.6; *Canticle* 39.12). John interpreted biblical passages in terms of eliminating these appetites (*Ascent* 1.5). A "flight from the body" is best for communicating with the Holy Spirit because receiving God in the body causes considerable suffering (*Canticle* 13).

John revised the traditional three stages of the mystical path after the manner of bridal mysticism and included two dark nights in the ascent: a dark night of the senses and a dark night of the soul, in which the senses and soul are purged of all worldly appetites through the Holy Spirit by God's fire of love. They are *dark nights* because they do not contain the light of the senses or intellect. The former is more common—the latter occurs only to proficient meditators—but both nights may occur at the same time. In the nights, the person seems not to be making progress in meditation and feels the pain and despair of apparently being deserted by God, but God is at work.[42] In the night of the senses, periods of dryness alternate with periods of serene and loving contemplation (Kavanaugh 1987, 195n17; *Ascent* 2.13–15). Both God and the mystic are active in the first night, but only God is active while the soul remains passive in the second night (*Ascent* 1.13.1). The mystic is purged of memory, will, and intellect (2.2–2.3). First, "voluntary appetites" are eliminated since "natural" desires (such as for food) are little or no hindrance to attaining perfection; however, in the end, all desires must be purged to align with God's will (1.11, 3.16.3). The first night is described as "bitter and terrible" to the senses and the second as "horrible and awful" to the spirit (*Dark Night* 1.8.2).[43] The mystic suffers while God is purifying the meditator's senses and the spirit. The soul is, in Kieran Kavanaugh's words, "being conducted by God along a sublime path of dark contemplation and aridity" (1987, 59). The internal life of the mystic is being transformed into God's love. In the dark nights, God's flame of love purges the soul like fire dries out a log, and then the living flame of love engulfs the purged soul. The fruit of the fire in the depths of one's very being is loving actions toward others.

John also cautioned against desiring visions, voices, and alleged messages from heaven since there was nothing to be revealed that was not already revealed by the Bible and Jesus (*Ascent* 2.22.4, 7). "The Devil causes many to believe visions and false prophecies" (*Dark Night* 2.2.3). They lead only to temptation and error. Even visions from God are not to be desired (*Ascent* 2.17.2). In short, visions are not the way to union (2.11.12). One cannot see God face-to-face in this life. Acts of charity are more important than visions (2.22.19). Teresa concurred (*Interior Castle* 9.6). Indeed, both visions from the Devil and visions that are not stand in the way of the fruits of faith (*Ascent* 2.11.8).

Both Teresa and John got in trouble with the Catholic Church for their writings.[44] They defended inner prayer when the king of Spain condemned it. The Spanish Inquisition investigated Teresa five times. A papal nuncio wrote that she was a "restless female" who "under the semblance of piety . . . thinks up false doctrines . . . [and] lectures like a professor of theology." Pope Gregory XIII called her "a filthy and immoral nun." John also appeared before the Inquisition. He was imprisoned and tortured and accepted banishment to Mexico but died before the trip materialized. Yet, both ended up Catholic saints. Indeed, both were named Doctors of the Church, and he the *doctor mysticus*.

Modern Era

Protestant theologians in general, following Luther and Calvin, have continued to oppose mysticism. They reject the very idea that God can be experienced directly or united with in any way; that there is a spark of the divine in human beings; or that God can ever be immanent in nature. God remains transcendent and wholly other.[45] Conversion experiences of the presence of God are not seen in mystical terms. There is an unbridgeable gap between God and humans, and thus he is not open to any experience. When the only choices available are between a transcendent God and pantheism—rather than the alternatives of emanationism and panentheism—theologians emphasize the gap. Mysticism also seems to bypass reliance upon grace and the role of the Christ; it suggests that the problem with human existence is being overcome by oneself from within oneself, not from a transcendent god. Many see mysticism as tainted by the heresy of Gnosticism: an alien incursion by pagan Greek philosophy into Christianity; an overemphasis on the nonrational and the inner life; pantheistic, self-denying, antinomian, not sufficiently prophetic, and escapist rather than being socially engaged. As the nineteenth-century theologian Albrecht Ritschl presented it, mysticism necessarily involves individualism, quietism, and a divisive elitism that portrays mystics as better Christians than the ordinary faithful (Tamburello 2013, 412). Likewise, in the eyes of many Protestants, that mystical experiences are common among theists and nontheists alike points to them being only internal, subjective, brain-generated events; none could be experiences of God. In sum, many Protestants today see all mysticism as inherently anti-Christian. In most Christian traditions, there also are no monasteries or convents to cultivate mysticism or established rules and paths to encourage mysticism or advocacy of withdrawal from the world or conventions of masters counseling students.

Bernard McGinn (2013, 160) calls the seventeenth century the "Era of Crisis" for Western Christian mysticism: the Enlightenment's criticism of all traditional forms of Christian belief and practice undercut the worldview upon which Christian mysticism had been based. Contemplation was also no longer seen as the culmination of Christian prayer but, rather, as unsuitable for Christians. Mysticism in Western Christendom began to ebb, although it continued in Eastern Orthodox countries. In Russia, mysticism remained a vital force until the Russian Revolution. In Western Europe, the corrosive effects of the secular Enlightenment brought about disdain for the mystical element in Christianity and led to a serious decline in mysticism during the eighteenth and nineteenth centuries (McGinn 2012, xi).

Mystical experiences no doubt continued to occur, perhaps in connection with prayer, but mysticism lost its impact on culture. Jakob Boehme (1575–1624), a German shoemaker from Poland, was a mystic and visionary who developed an elaborate and controversial evolutionary metaphysical system in which all of creation was in harmony. His first insight into the being of all things and the abyss from which they arose occurred after he saw a flash of light reflected off a pewter dish. For him, God was the ground of all the universe yet fully present in each part. In his negative theology, he refers to this ground as the *unground* (*Ungrund*) and *nothing* (*Nitchts*). His esoteric theosophy is difficult to understand but helped shape perceptions of mysticism in this period. His followers flourished in England. Isaac Newton and William Blake read his work.

English mystics and mystical theorists included the Anglicans John Donne (1573–1631), Thomas Browne (1605–1682), Thomas Traherne (ca. 1636–1674); the ascetic William Law (1686–1761, for whom the spirit of the world, not the devil, is the enemy); the Puritans Richard Baxter (1615–1691) and John Bunyan (1628–1688, author of *The Pilgrim's Progress*); the first Methodist, John Wesley (1703–1791, whose brother Charles wrote mystically themed hymns); and the Catholic Augustine Baker (1575–1641). Also in England, the Family of Love took an inner experience of God as an authority to supersede the scriptures, and—according to their opponents, who labeled them *Seekers* and *Ranters*—also morality. (The rise of millenarianism in Europe also gave rise to concerns about any group seen to reject morality.) In this period too, George Fox (1624–1691) founded the Society of Friends (Quakers) with its doctrine of inner light, where God spoke directly to people inwardly. This led to less emphasis on uniformity of doctrines among Quakers.

In Germany, there were a few mystics, including Johann Arndt (1555–1621). French mystics included Francois de Sales (1567–1622). The mathematician and philosopher Blaise Pascal (1623–1662) had an intense experience lasting two hours in 1654 that he described with the word *fire*; the experience gave him tears of joy and absolute certitude concerning Jesus and the "God of Abraham, God of Isaac, God of Jacob, not of philosophers and scholars." He wrote down a brief memorandum of the experience and sewed it into the lining of his coat, where it was found after his death.

These mystics were not so much innovators in doctrines as they were aides in different revivals of pietism and in bringing writings influenced by earlier mystics to the people. The charge of antinomianism also arose in the seventeenth century with the Quietists in Spain, France, and Italy. Like other theistic mystics, they aimed for a state in which all self-will is replaced by a total receptivity to an infusion by God. For these love mystics, the highest state is one containing a pure love for God and nothing else and the total absence of personal will. Thus, one wills nothing but attains a "holy indifference" to one's own salvation and to everything that is not God. However, inwardly this included being empty even of virtues. Thus, they emphasized quiet contemplation and passivity over not only more active forms of meditation but also outward actions and Christian rituals. Once one attained the enlightened state, one could perform neither immoral nor moral acts on one's own initiative since they lacked any self-will. God controlled all that is done. In a state of perfect resignation, the perfected were, in effect, no more than passive puppets through whose bodies God performed actions. God acted alone, and thus, the Quietists let whatever happened happen. Orthodox mystics could defend the quietistic state as one in which the soul does nothing while God works through the mystic in a totally disinterested charity toward others; inwardly they possessed a tranquil state, but outwardly they were still morally active. However, for Quietists this meant that whatever the body did came directly from God, so they could follow any bodily desires because these did not come from themselves. In a state of pure disinterested love, one is indifferent to sin, salvation, virtues, or ecclesiastical authority.

The first Quietist, Miguel de Molinos (1628–1696), was brought before the Inquisition in 1681. He said that "natural activity is the enemy of Divine grace." However, he drew the wrath of church leaders when he led a life of sexual excess with his women followers. In 1687, he made a public profession of his errors. He explained that his errors resulted from acts by the Devil that he did not try to resist since they did not affect his inner tranquility but only deepened that quiet. Thus, the errors were not sins but, in fact, purifications of the truly inward Christian. He was sentenced to prison for life and died there. The clumsy writings of Jeanne-Marie Guyon (1648–1717) also did not help convince other authorities of the Quietists' position. She spent seven years in the Bastille. However, Archbishop Francois de Fenelon (1651–1715) defended his Quietism against the charge of inaction and was, in fact, an active and effective church administrator. However, Catholics remained suspicious of all mysticism for two centuries, and the church offered mysticism little support.

Few mystical writings were produced in the eighteenth and nineteenth centuries, and there were few recorded mystics in Catholic or Protestant countries. Some of the writings of English and German Romantic poets such as William Blake (1757–1827) suggest nature mystical experiences. They reacted against the Enlightenment's anti-mystical thrust, as did such American Transcendentalists as the mystical theorist Ralph Waldo Emerson (1803–1882), who had Hindu and Buddhist influences. (Whether mysticism figured in the various American Protestant awakenings is a matter of debate.) Therese of Lisieux (1873–1897)—in the midst of a French tradition that emphasized the Christian values of prayer, sacrifice, and suffering—stands out in the anti-mystical age.

Around the turn of the twentieth century, interest in mysticism revived slightly as some scholars looked for an empirical method modeled on natural science to confirm the tenets of Christian faith. But theologians remained anti-mystical. Western Christianity became more concerned with social issues, and mysticism seemed too individualistic (Johnston 2000, 161). Nevertheless, some important mystics lived during the twentieth century including the economist and diplomat Dag Hammarskjold (1905–1961), if the journal found after his death is any indication. For him, the "road to holiness" passed through the world of action, but there is "the point of rest at the center of our being." Simone Weil (1909–1943) experienced a sense of infinity, within the ordinary expanses of perception, filled with a silence that was not merely absent of sound but filled with a presence more positive than sound; she also intensely experienced the presence of Christ within her (McGinn 2006a, 249). For her, we must offer up our ego in order to experience God (being). She studied Hinduism and learned Sanskrit. Her physical suffering, as also with Therese of Lisieux, made suffering a central point of interest.

More recently, some Christians also have been drawn to the teachings of Asian religions. The French Benedictine mystic Henri Le Saux (1910–1973) went to India and started an ashram. He was initiated by a guru as a renouncer (*sannyasin*) of Christianity. He struggled all his life to reconcile his experiences of non-duality with his Christian faith in a trinity and a god of love with whom we can have a personal relationship. He hoped mysticism would renew Christianity. His disciple Father Alan (Bede) Griffiths (1906–1993), a former Oxford don who moved to India and headed an ashram, is better known through his writings on Christianity and Hinduism. Both looked to synthesize Advaita Vedanta into a truly Indian form of Christianity without it being absorbed into Hinduism.

But the most influential twentieth-century Christian mystic was the Trappist monk Thomas Merton (1915–1968), who complained about the spiritual laxity of most monastics. (In practice, most monastics around in the world today, and most likely in most time periods, are apparently not seriously practicing a mystical way of life. Complaints about spiritual masters are common in all monastic traditions.) Acting on his love of others and out of concern for the world was central to his way of life. His was a mysticism of waiting in silence: emptying oneself of all personal desires, finding detachment to free oneself from worldly cares, practicing ascetic discipline, and living in solitude without losing concern for others on both personal and social scales. His goal was to have God living within him "so that there is nothing left of any significance but God living in God" (2007, 284). He studied Sufi, Hindu, and Buddhist mysticism, found some commonality between traditions, and became interested in how dialog with other religions could deepen one's own faith. In 1968, he had a deep religious experience while meditating in front of statues of the Buddha in Sri Lanka. Through all this, he never gave up his Catholicism.

Modern Protestant theologians followed Friedrich Schleiermacher's continuation of the idea that mysticism is an attempt at self-salvation. In the twentieth-century, most theologians opposed mystical experiences as attempts to attain God through human effort. German Protestant theologians thought that the idea of union with God was world-negating and solipsistic, but English theologians saw mysticism as affirming the goodness of the world and the continuity between nature and spirit, viewing the mystical life as finding one's true expression in an active love of one's neighbors

(McGinn 1994, 275). French theologians also paid attention to mysticism (280). The consensus among at least Catholic theologians was that mysticism was not a special, higher, or elite form of Christian perfection (290). The premiere Protestant theologian of the first half of the twentieth century, Karl Barth, saw mysticism as a form of esoteric atheism. Emil Brunner saw it as a form of human religiosity that opposed the revealed Word of God. Paul Tillich saw mystical experiences as pointing to the abyss of the ground of being but still as opposed to revelation. Albert Schweitzer, however, did see the mystical experience of oneness as grounded in the unity of being and interpreted believers being in Christ in terms of mystical union. Ernst Troelsch thought mysticism might reinvigorate Protestant spirituality.

Interest in mysticism, particularly in Protestant circles, has shown recent signs of life, beginning with the "Centering Prayer" of the 1970s. This interest may be a reaction to New Age activity both inside and outside of Christianity. However, theologians remain suspicious; mysticism seems to threaten a religion's claim to exclusive ownership of absolute truth. In 1989, the Vatican released a letter comparing the "impersonal techniques" of Zen, yoga, and Transcendental Meditation, concluding that "getting closer to God" cannot be based on any "technique" and that techniques "can create a kind of rut, imprisoning the person praying in a spiritual privatism which is incapable of a free openness to the transcendental God." Additionally, "God is not one to be manipulated as one can manipulate a machine or appliance." It derided the "direct influence of foreign religions" leading to "a pantheistic understanding of reality" and the reduction of "pure grace" to an experience. Nevertheless, many Catholics have adopted forms of meditation from other religions, and since 1990, the Vatican's negative views of Asian religions (especially Buddhism) have been softening (Johnston 2000, 45–53). Today a new mysticism may be emerging in Christianity: one that remains traditional but is influenced by Asian mysticisms, with Asian metaphysics perhaps replacing Greek ones (57).

Key Themes

• Christian mysticism is "a search for and experience of immediacy with God" (Louth 1981, xv). At its origin, its objective was to lead all believers to an experience of God: to escape the corrupt world and "share in the very being of God" (2 Peter 1:4). There is less in mystical writings on God's historical incarnation in the world in the past than on God's action in the soul in the present. Mysticism has ebbed and flowed in various branches of Christianity ever since. For most of its history, mystical practice was limited to monastics. Mysticism is more influential in Eastern Orthodoxy, but mysticism did also influence classical Western Christian theology.

• Orthodox mystics did not rely upon their mystical experiences as a source of authority: scripture validated the experiences, not vice versa. The Bible is accepted as the only source of knowledge of God available to fallen humanity. However, as with Jewish mysticism, biblical passages are seen as hiding a mystical meaning. Thus, the Bible is accepted as authoritative but is understood in light of mystical beliefs. In this circularity, a mystic's beliefs end up controlling their understanding of the Bible. This exemplifies how mystics can go beyond the control of doctrine and develop new ideas while under the guise of being orthodox.

• Classical Christian mystics showed a disdain for all things worldly. Even for the non-ascetics, overcoming the body's appetites was essential. The world was not deemed an illusion or unreal but a genuine creation of God's love and the place of the incarnation of God's son. However, mystics were more world-rejecting than non-mystics in Christianity. Despite this dispassion, at least orthodox Christians showed a moral concern for the suffering of others in this world.

• Christian mystics tend to stress proper belief (orthodoxy) as it is defined by a mystic's particular subtradition more than do Jews and Muslims, and most have been theologically conservative and accepted the need for the institution of the church (for example, Eckhart insisted on the role of the sacraments). Some mystics have advocated doctrines and practices that got them into trouble and would cause controversy even today. For example, Julian of Norwich and William Law saw no hell and believed that all people will be saved, including non-Christians. The institutional church no doubt silenced and marginalized some mystics by insisting that they use the right words and subscribe to the right formulas or be excommunicated or burned at the stake (Johnston 2000, 138). Esoteric traditions played a far lesser role here than in Judaism or Islam.

• Abrahamic monotheism was modified by the doctrine of the Trinity. The mystery of Christ may be what separates Christians from other theists, but not all Christian mystics have been Christocentric (focusing on the life or sacrifice of Jesus); many have instead focused on God the Father. The roles of the incarnated Christ and the Holy Spirit mean that God the creator is not only the ground of being but also active in the phenomenal world. The embodiment of God in creation is alien to Greek, Jewish, and

Islamic thought and should make mysticism more congenial to Christianity than the other two Abrahamic traditions. That God became incarnate was taken to mean it is possible for human beings to become united in some sense with God; by grace, we all can become what Jesus was by nature and become sons or daughters of God (*Ascent of Mount Carmel* 2.5.5). However, Christian mystics consider God's grace—a gift we cannot earn—essential for any experience of God.

• The otherness of the Godhead remains for orthodox mystics; the being supplied by the Godhead is already present in our soul, but literal deification is not possible. Accepting both God and the Godhead also helps to reconcile the experienced changeless and still being in the depth-mystical experience with the active, living, theistic God that is personal in nature. God remains a creator, and the world is not God, but God is immanent to the natural universe as the source and sustainer of its very being. Thus, classical Christian mysticism was never pantheistic; it always maintained the transcendent dimension of God or the Godhead. At most, Christian Neoplatonist emanationism is a panentheism in which the world is part of God or at least within him. This enables theists to see God in all things and to see all things in God while still distinguishing God from his creation.

• For over a millennium, late Platonism provided the philosophical framework for the Christian world-picture (Louth 1981, xiii). Only when Aristotelianism replaced Neoplatonism in the twelfth and thirteenth centuries was emanationism rejected and the creator placed outside of creation. But Christian mysticism broke earlier from Greek mysticism: God is a personal loving reality, not the nonpersonal One of Neoplatonism, and the soul is not in part divine. Not only are mystics searching for God, but the loving God is active in drawing them in. The idea of an incarnation of the *logos* of the universe is also foreign to Greek thought. In addition, Christian mystics asserted that grace, not merely human effort, was required to experience God, while Neoplatonists asserted the divine soul's innate capacity to achieve transcendence and that the One was not conscious and could not initiate a mystical experience or aid in a mystic's quest.

• The mind cannot totally comprehend God. However, despite the role of the apophatic *via negativa* in mystical trainings and understandings of God, the kataphatic *via positiva* has always remained prominent in Christian mysticism due to the existence of what is considered the revealed word of God (the Bible) and the son of God. There is a divine mystery that is beyond all human understanding, yet God can be understood as a creator and as love, revealed in the Bible (1 John 4:9). Thus, all negative and paradoxical accounts of the abyss of the ground are not the final word even if mystics deny anything positive can be said about the mystery.

• Human souls have a created nature; they are not divine by nature and do not participate in the divine nature, even though human beings were created in the "image of God" (Gen. 1:26–27), are dependent on God for their existence, and may even share the same being as God supplied by the nonpersonal Godhead. There is also a unity of body and soul in Judaism and Christianity—flesh and spirit (2 Cor. 4:16)—that is not derived from Greek thought, where the divine soul is separate from the body that ascends to the divine. This created nature cannot be overcome in any experience, nor is a mystical experience a return to a prior divine state.

• So too, the centrality of loving others did not arise from Greek influence. For the Greeks, ethical actions toward others had a purificatory role only; for Christian mystics, they had both that role and were a blossoming fruit of their experiences. Mystical experiences are not the "flight of the alone to the Alone" but more like Moses ascending Mount Sinai on behalf of his people (Louth 1981, 201).

• In sum, Christians used language drawn from Plato and Plotinus to express very different ideas (Louth 1981, 71, 198). That Christians adopted any of the Neoplatonist framework at all points to the adaptability of both Christianity and mysticism. Some mystics studied other religions to convert others. For example, the Spanish mystic Ramon Llull (ca. 1232–1315) studied Islam in order to convert Muslims. However, over the millennia, Christian mysticism has absorbed influences from Judaism (both early on and later from Kabbalah), other world religions, and also local cultures.

• As Bernard McGinn points out, medieval mystics placed far less value on episodic mystical experiences than do many modern theories of mysticism (1998, 29). An ASC enlightened life of moral action resulting from an inner mystical transformation of character is what is central to Christian mysticism. The goal of the mystical quest was to be like God or Jesus, not to have isolated ecstatic experiences; a "God-intoxicated" mystical life aligned with God's will, having annihilated all sense of the self. A mystical experience is neither necessary for salvation nor essential to the Christian message but is a way to perfect the Christian life of love.

• The term *mystical union* (*unio mystica*) was rarely used by classical Christian mystics, and when it was used, it usually meant *communion* with a personal god, not *identity*. The soul was not denied as ontologically real, even though it dependent upon a source (God or the Godhead). The ontological distinction between God and the soul is affirmed even if one's awareness of the distinction is absent during some experiences. Introvertive mystical experiences were seen as a matter of a personal relation between the lover and the beloved. The permanent marriage of two persons is a common image of the new state. With a mystical experience, there is no change in a mystic's ontological relation to the ground of reality, only a change in knowledge, dispositions, and will.

• The most important indication of enlightenment in this tradition is the absence of any self-will: the "poor in spirit" have reduced their sense of self to nothingness and do not claim anything in a proprietary sense: not life, being, power, knowledge, goodness, or deeds. The proprietary urge vanishes, and one wills, desires, loves, and intends nothing but the eternal goodness that God wills. For the enlightened, "it is no longer I who lives but Christ who lives in me" (Gal. 2:20). Sin is reduced to asserting self-will, to desiring other than what God desires. As William Blake said: "There can be no Good Will. Will is always Evil." For Teresa of Avila, "nothing burns in hell but self-will." Prayers are not prayers of petition for a particular benefit for oneself or others but simply that "thy will be done on Earth as in Heaven" (Matt. 6:10). For Eckhart, the "just" have no will at all; whatever God wills, it is all one to them, however great the hardship (2009, 329). For monks and nuns, obedience to the rules of their order freed them from making decisions and from any personal will. Ultimately, one's character becomes thoroughly infused with God's self-emptying love. One is then totally aligned with what is taken to be God's will, so self-will does not enter the picture. However, one's sense of having no self-will can also lead to antinomian actions.

• Love mystics focus more on Christ, while knowledge mystics focus more on God the Father or the Godhead. Francis of Assisi can be contrasted with Eckhart here. However, Christianity's ethos of self-giving love grounded in God shapes both of these mystical ways of life: there is no loving God without loving one's neighbor. As Eckhart put it, if a person were in such a rapturous state as Paul once entered (2 Cor. 12:1–6) and he knew of a sick man who wanted a cup of soup, it would be far better to withdraw from the rapture for love's sake and serve him who is in need (2009, 496). God's love was expressed in Jesus's worldly actions, and—except perhaps for antinomians—God's love guides all Christian mystical enlightened ways of life.

• Thus, even if mystics gave the Bible allegorical interpretations that interiorized its stories, their claims were solidly Christian: an all-loving God is the source of Christian reality, souls are real and remain distinct from God and each other, and self-emptying love of others reflects ultimate reality, even though knowledge mystics focus on the nonpersonal being of God. Christian mystics may ground the loving god in a nonpersonal Godhead, but a loving god remains the creator of this real realm. In this way, both personal and nonpersonal mystical experiences were accommodated in Christianity, but love was firmly grounded in the fabric of reality. The force at the center of this reality was a selfless love for others.

• Thus, mysticism became a way to fulfill the commandments to love God and to love one's neighbor as oneself (Mark 12:30–31) by participating in God's love. With mysticism, love of one's neighbor becomes an expression of one's whole character, not merely a matter of rule-following or gaining a reward. Prior to enlightenment, Christian mystics may need to be commanded to love, but after enlightenment, loving one's neighbor flows naturally. The enlightened live the Christian ethics of their day from the deepest level of their being. The life of Jesus as a humble servant serving other was the model of how to live (Johnston 2000, 237). Action infused with inward quiet spontaneously pours out from the awareness of divine love they have experienced. They imitate Jesus's love for others, and they experience his death and resurrection by dying to self-will and being filled with God's love. They also interiorize the eschatological teachings and, thus, live the life commanded in the New Testament to the fullest in the present. It is no coincidence that most known Christian mystics have been canonized (Dupré 1981, 56).

• Early mystics, following the Greek philosophers, valued the contemplative life over action toward others, but the Christian ethos of an active life of love for others prevailed. The common position by the late Middle Ages was that the two lives should be integrated. In Ignatius of Loyola's expression, one can be "active in the midst of contemplation." That is, awareness of God can be maintained during daily activities; thus, loving action toward others is possible for the contemplative. John of the Cross also warned that those who act without first going through a contemplative stage will accomplish little good or may even do harm. Eckhart similarly warned that action without contemplation in God is meaningless. Ruusbroec argued for the integration of action and contemplation—activity and receptivity—in the comprehensive life and attacked anyone who would devote themselves to contemplation while ignoring action. There may be periods of contemplation without outward activity, but outside those periods, mystics act with the constant awareness of God's love. What is gained in Christian-informed contemplation guides the active life. Thus, the interior way of knowing does not end exterior action—the result is the mystics' extrovertive enlightened state of "contemplation in an active life." Thus, Catherine of Siena said that the more contemplative she became, the more active she became. In sum, in the Christian comprehensive enlightened state, there is the inner stillness of habitually "resting" inwardly in God (and thus being neutral to all that happens), but one can simultaneously engage in work for others outwardly. "Resting in God's love" becomes the wellspring of loving action. Love of God and love of others are two phases of the same thing.

Chapter 6

Islamic Mysticism

In the eighth century, the label *Sufi* became employed for Sunni mystics and has stuck as the term covering all branches of Islamic mysticism throughout Islam's history; it later also included some non-mystics.[1] The term was first applied by outsiders to Muslim ascetics. Its origin is probably from the Arabic *suf*—meaning coarse, undyed wool—and refers to the rough woolen garments some early ascetics wore as a symbol of their rejection of all worldly things. Classical mystics did not refer to themselves as *Sufis* but as *the poor* (Arabic, *faqir*; Persian, *darwish*): wandering begging mendicants traveling on the path to God (Q 35:15). However, opinions on Sufism have run from praising it as the most intense expression of Islamic faith to criticizing it as idolatrous, antinomian, excessively emotional, and not Islamic at all. Even the wearing of wool was condemned as imitating Jesus and Christian monastics, since Muhammad wore cotton.[2] Mainstream Muslim theologians and jurists rejected the claim that Sufis had a source of knowledge beyond sense experience and reason that was not available to others, let alone that God could be experienced by anyone at all.

The Quran

Early Islam was not especially conducive to mysticism since its main spirit was that of the prophetic dynamism of Muhammad's numinous experiences, but the general structure of Islamic faith was adapted to the service of the inner life (Smart 1967, 427). In fact, Islam more easily adopted mysticism than the other two Abrahamic traditions; Sufis simply extended the initial inward bent. Additionally, Sufis were able to ground their ways of life in the Quran.[3]

Like mystics in other traditions, mystics did not see themselves as innovators but as living the life set forth in their tradition's basic scripture. The Quran (meaning *recitations*) is the collection of revelations given to the prophet Muhammad (d. 632 CE) by the angel Gabriel in a cave on Mount Hira near Mecca over a twenty-three-year period beginning around 609.[4] These recitations are considered the eternal word of God and co-eternal with him.[5] The Quran may seem to be incompatible with mysticism since it stresses the utter transcendence of God (Allah) and is a matter of revelations coming down from him.[6] Moreover, because the word of God is revealed in the Quran, negative theology (adopted from Neoplatonism) and claims by Sufis that God is ineffable were attacked by the orthodox since something of God's nature has been revealed. God is the all-powerful and all-knowing creator, law-giver, and stern—but also merciful and compassionate—judge, and people are his servants. Traditionally, his seven leading attributes are life, knowledge, will, power, speech, generosity, and justice. Only human beings can manifest all of these since we are created in the image of God—"upon his form," as Muhammad put it. All physical representations of him are avoided by Sufis and non-Sufis alike; the cardinal sin of idolatry (*shirk*) is to associate God with anything phenomenal or otherwise finite.

Sufis saw themselves as fulfilling Islam's basic requirements of submitting one's will to God (*islam*), faith (*imam*), and doing the beautiful (*ihsan*).[7] However, mysticism also generated hostility from the majority of Muslims as not being a product of Islam but the product of contact with Christians, Hindus, and Buddhists. Zoroastrianism, Kabbalah, and Greek thought were other non-Islamic sources of influence on Sufi doctrines and practices (and on Islam more generally). There may also have been shamanistic influences from Central Asia (Eliade 1972, 402–403, 489). Neoplatonism was encountered in Syria and Alexandria and was especially influential. It became the philosophical framework for most schools of Sufism.[8] Sufis also seemed to many to flout the Islamic religious/civil law (*sharia*) that is the "cord of God" (Q 3:103). Islam is more a religiosity of orthopraxy than orthodoxy, but as noted throughout this chapter, some Sufi teachings were problematic.

However, despite absorbing non-Muslim influences into their ways of life, the Quran was vitally important to Sufis. The Sufi Muhammad Ibn al-Arabi (d. 1240) represents the majority of Sufis in agreeing with mainstream theologians and jurists that the Quran contains all knowledge of God. The Persian poet Abd al-Rahman Jami (d. 1492) said, "A Sufi who does not know the Quran by heart is like a lemon without scent." Sufis always looked to the Quran and were able to cite passages for support. God is one, and he does not beget and is not begotten (Q 111:1–3). Sufis took this to mean that God is the only reality.[9] Of particular importance to Sufis, God is the transcendent creator but is also immanent in all the natural realm: "Wherever we turn, there is God's face" (2:145). Sufis took this to mean that God is omnipresent and omniscient. God is unseen (11:31, 11:123, 13:9, 16:77, 53:18, 53:35), yet one can seek God's face in prayer (6:52, 13:22, 18:28). Also, God is always with us wherever we are (57:4). In fact, God is closer to us than our own jugular vein (50:16). The Quran also relates the original covenant God made with human beings before the creation of the universe: God asked, "Am I not your Lord?" and the people responded, "Yes, indeed, we bear witness" (7:171–72). The goal of the mystical path is to reclaim that moment of intimacy when nothing separated human souls from God (Awn 2013, 248): "Be truly pious, and I will teach you" (2:282). Love of God also had a warrant: "He loves them, and they love him" (5:54).

The Quran states, "Remember me and I will remember you" (2:152). This is also the root of the Sufi ritual practice of remembering or recalling God (*dhikr*) (33:41), either individually or in group by chanting phrases containing one or more of the ninety-nine names of God in a mantra-like manner in order to clear their minds of all other thoughts. However, Sufi masters stressed that the meditator must understand the meaning of what they chanted—blind repetition of the words achieved the opposite of remembering. By recollecting God, the heart becomes pure (13:28).

Esoteric exegesis (*tawil*) of Quranic passages also began very early on (Q 3:5–7), carrying the accompanying claim that inner spiritual development was needed for one to see the mystical meanings. However, proponents of mainstream theology (*kalam*) disputed Sufis' claim that God unveiled (*tajalli*) himself to them in a direct vision (*mushahada*) so that some human beings experience the direct presence of Truth/Reality (*haqiqa*). For them, God's only self-disclosure was to the prophets. Other than that, God remains utterly transcendent to the world and not experienceable by human beings. Any vision (*ruya*) of God is reserved for those in paradise.

Muhammad

In sixth-century Arabia, there were ascetics and contemplatives—Hanifs— who held firmly to the monotheism of Abraham. They often kept all-night vigils. Muhammad (d. 632) was influenced by them and may have been one (but few of his companions were ascetics). He is considered a purely human being but one who had visions and auditory experiences (Q 17:1, 53:1–12, 51:13–18; 81:19–25). Muslims considered him the last in the line of prophets of God that began with Adam. He is the "seal" of God's message to humanity (Q 33:40) in the sense that the revelations given to him complete the revelations given to earlier prophets and correct the corruptions of previous revelations. Thus, Muhammad is also the last of the prophets. Jesus was the last prophet prior to Muhammad, and Sufis consider him the ideal ascetic and pure lover of God (Schimmel 2011, 34). However, Muhammad is the exemplar of a life of poverty and purity.

Sufis see themselves as aligning their lives with the Prophet's teachings and routinely quote from the collection of Muhammad's sayings and actions (hadith), even though some of these are no doubt later inventions. For example, the Prophet said, "He who knows himself knows his Lord." Sufis cite God saying, "I was a hidden treasure, and I longed to be known, so I created creatures that I might be known." Or, God tells Muhammad, "I am present when my servant thinks of me." One hadith of special importance is God saying, "My servant does not stop drawing close to me by extra acts of devotion until I love him. Then when I love him I am his hearing by which he hears, his sight by which he sees, his hand by which he grasps, and his foot by which he walks" (Knysh 2000, 28). This defines sincere (ikhlis) acts. Sufis also cite Muhammad saying, "Poverty is my pride" as a warrant for their ways of life. Overall, like Christian mystics with Jesus, Sufis saw their goal as emulating the Prophet's life.

Early Asceticism and the Rise of Sufism

By the eighth century CE, asceticism (zuhd, meaning abstinence or renunciation) had taken hold among some Muslims in Egypt, Iraq, and Persia, perhaps influenced by Christian ascetics in the region—some of whom converted to Islam—and their severe practices and sayings. Hasan al-Basri (d. 728) and others objected to the great wealth and political power of the leaders of the Islamic community following the Islamic conquest of the region. But Basri did not join in political action against the rulers. Early Sufis did the same; concern for politics seemed to treat the world as too important. For example, Junayd advised his disciples not to challenge the political and religious authorities of his time; he viewed political and social activism as a sign of spiritual and intellectual immaturity and as an attempt to rebel against the divine order (Knysh 2000, 56). Total renunciation of the world would go against the Quran, and seeking wealth is not prohibited (Q 2:198), but ascetics saw such worldliness as conflicting with the values of the Quran and as showing interest in what is only transient. Nevertheless, Sufism did eventually become of part of the religious establishment and the political order in the Middle Ages.

Basri spent a long period as a wandering ascetic in the Syrian desert. (His teacher was from India and may have introduced him to yogic practices.) He defined *asceticism* as "contempt for the world and all things worldly." He believed that "a grain of piety (*wara*) is worth a thousand weight of fasting and prayer." His feeling of brotherly love (*ukhuwwa*) toward others and his altruism (*ithar*, preferring others to oneself) were adopted by later Sufis as attitudes conducive to their mystical goal (Knysh 2000, 12).

Ibrahim ibn Adham (d. ca. 782) made the first classification of the stages of asceticism: renouncing all worldly things, renouncing the happy feeling of having renounced worldliness, and regarding the world as so unimportant that one no longer looks at it at all (Schimmel 2011, 37).[10] Later Sufi texts attacked greed as much as they advocated asceticism. They believe there are different elements of the self, and their task is to look into oneself and exercise restraint over the carnal self (*nafs*) that we share with animals, thereby doing away with the sense of a worldly self and all the impulses emanating from it (Knysh 2000, 10; see also Q 12:53, 89:27).

The ascetics were hermits and naked wanderers. Some became prestigious holy men. Withdrawal into the desert and mountains was warranted by Muhammad's temporary withdrawals into the mountains for solitude and prayer. Ascetics could also point to the Prophet's fasting and general way of life. Isolation in a solitary place (*khalwa*) for contemplating God—surrendering everything to be in the presence of God—was important, but ascetics did not typically withdraw from society to the desert for life or even for long periods. Such withdrawal was practiced only intermittently by even early ascetics, not permanently as with Christian ascetics. Early manuals such as Shaqiq al-Balkhi's (d. 810) focused on fasting and asceticism, fear of God's judgment, longing for paradise, utter indifference to worldly things, and love of God.

Early Sufi Ways of Life

Although mysticism took root in Islam in this ascetic atmosphere, mysticism is not a product of asceticism, and Sufism in the ninth century mostly replaced the purely ascetic approach in what are today Iraq and Iran. It did not completely reject asceticism but made inner detachment more important than outward physical mortifications and deprivations. Some early Sufis did advocate long withdrawals from society—including the Egyptian Dhu al-Nun al-Misri (d. 859) and Abu Bakr al-Shibli of Baghdad (d. 945)—but such seclusion was condemned as not following the model of Muhammad, who was married and lived in the social world. Over time, forty days became the standard period of a spiritual retreat, probably based on the forty days of Jesus—the ideal ascetic—in the desert. Life within a community was seen as more beneficial since each individual's behavior could be controlled by others (Knysh 2000, 315). By the thirteenth century, Abu Hafs al-Suhrawardi (d. 1234) noted that communal life was what distinguished Sufis from ascetics (315). Still, solitude within that context was valued; institutionalized solitude was occasionally described as the spiritual greater *jihad* (struggle) against the egoistic self (316).[11] Sufis' cells were cave-like: they were typically a dark room with little or no light, and their purpose was to shutter the external senses and open the internal senses (316). Thus, one could be secluded in spirit even while living within society at large (317). Likewise, Sufis rejected celibacy early on, and many Sufis were married with children and had all the practical responsibilities and encumbrances that accompany that state.

The guidance of a spiritual master or elder (Arabic, *shaykh/murshid*; Persian, *pir*) was also considered vitally important. By the ninth century, the practices of disciples and masters had become firmly established. According to Bistami, "One who has no master has Satan for a leader." A master was considered essential along the path for passing along oral teachings and counseling disciples. Masters shape their disciple's character (*khuluq*) so that it conforms to the model of the Prophet (Chittick 2000, 28–29). Their image is also used for meditative visualizations. Disciples could also see how a Sufi should behave by observing their master's example. Absolute obedience to a master was also required to overcome one's sense of ego and self-will since decisions were made by the master. Thus, a disciple must have complete trust in their master. Masters also began to write manuals on the stages of the mystical path, temporary states of mystical consciousness (*ahwal*), and training programs. Issues discussed in these manuals throughout the history of Sufism include the nature of meditative experiences, the role of music and dance rituals in the life of a Sufi, the pros and cons of celibacy, the proper interpretation of physiological and spiritual experiences, and the overall structure of the path (Awn 2013, 250).

Sufis commonly see the path to God as a matter of the purification of the soul (*tazkiyat an-nafs*, see Q 97:7–10). A wayfarer early on the Sufi path prefers others to themselves (*ithar*), but in the unitive state (*hal*), the difference between *mine* and *yours* becomes subsumed in the divine oneness (Schimmel 2011, 99). Their goal is to see God or Reality (*haqq*): to enter a state where one feels to be in the direct and unmediated presence of God and thus can serve him "as if one sees him" (Knysh 2000, 301). Spiritual conditions or states of consciousness (*ahwal*) are transient, unlike enduring stable stations (*maqamat*) from which it is possible observe the nature of things from different perspectives. Spiritual states are bestowed by God, but attaining the stations requires effort (304, 305). Thus, spiritual states such as ecstasy/spiritual intoxication, joy in mystical experiences, or negative dark nights are beyond the control of mystics themselves. Religious and mystical practices may prepare the way for them, but these experiences are matters of God's grace, not human effort. Like mystics in other traditions, Sufis also warn against becoming attached to such temporary states as the goal. They are not the end; a permanent transformation of the person is.

The traditional stations on the path that must be mastered are repentance, trust in God, poverty (*faqr*)—which may lead to contentment—and different degrees of love (*mahabba*) or direct mystical knowledge (*marifa*) of God, depending on the mental predilection of the wayfarer (Schimmel 2011, 100). The highest station occurs when the mystic has annihilated the sense of self and become one with God. To Ibn Arabi, this human perfection is the "station of no station" because it represents the full realization of all the divine attributes and character traits (Chittick 2016, 94). Truthfulness (*sidq*) and sincerity (*ikhlis*) are the two cardinal virtues.[12] Sincerity is "a complete agreement of one's inner conviction with one's outward acts," and for mystics, any good deed is futile unless it springs from a sincere and disinterested desire to obtain God's pleasure (Knysh 2000, 307). Thus, intention as well as the act itself matters. Acting with the utmost degree of sincerity and truthfulness signifies that the wayfarer has reached the stage of "perfect servanthood" (309). Early on, all Sufis also performed the five pillars required of all Muslims: the declaration of faith (the *Shahada*) that "there is no god but God and Muhammad is his messenger," five daily ritual prayers (*salat*), giving alms, fasting during the month of Ramadan, and the pilgrimage to Mecca. Various types of meditation (*muraqaba*) are matters of vigilance in watching over various mental states (see Ernst 2011, 106–11).

Sufis stress inwardness over external actions, contemplation over action, spiritual development over legalism, and cultivation of the soul over social interaction (Chittick 2000, 23). Islam is more a matter of orthopraxy than orthodoxy, and, as with Jewish and Christian mystics, most classical Sufis were orthopraxic. In fact, they intensified Islamic ritual life by paying careful attention to the details of the religious law and focusing on remembering God (*dhikr*) in every moment (26). Such remembrance keeps the heart tranquil and is a sign of love of God (Q 13:28). The practice went from originally being individualized to having a fully ritualized and choreographed structure. Practicing remembrance of God under the guidance of a master, who showed how it should be done on different stages of the path, became *the* central meditative technique in Sufism (Chittick 1983, 150–51). Indeed, more than anything else, the practice of constant *dhikr* came to differentiate Sufis from other Muslims; it was a basic method for achieving one-pointed concentration on God (Chittick 2000, 64). Perseverance in remembering God also led to attention to posture and breathing (64). Dhu al-Nun al-Misri (d. 859) said that the ritual music and dance is the rapture of God that incites hearts toward God (Ernest 2011, 185). Ritual chanting and dance, performed either individually or collectively, could lead to an ecstatic experience (*wajd*). It was not uncommon for people to collapse into a trance-like state from emotional overload (Awn 2013, 254–55). Drugs, too, have sometimes become connected to this practice (Schimmel 2011, 179). For example, hashish and opium were employed in some Persian orders beginning in the twelfth century and probably used earlier.

Later, Sufis regularly claimed that their rigorous program internalized all the ritual requirements of Islam, so they did not need to follow them in external actions. Why should they bother with, for example, the daily ritual prayers when they were always praying? Why go on a pilgrimage to Mecca when one's whole life is a spiritual pilgrimage to God? Antinomians argued that the rules of proper conduct (*abab*) under the religious law only applied to ordinary Muslims and Sufis on the path to enlightenment, but the enlightened have no sense of self, so the rules do not apply. There is nothing but God who acts through them, and since God is pure love, nothing but pure love emanates from them (see Aminrazavi 1995). Their knowledge of God (*marifa*) placed them beyond the demands of religious actions. For example, the Persian poet Abu Said ibn Abul Khayr (d. 1049) practiced severe asceticism while on the path that reduced him to skin and bones. He was also said to have hung upside down in a pit at night reciting the Quran. However, once he attained enlightening knowledge, his attitude to the physical world changed, and he immersed himself in the sensual delights of human life, claiming that the true saint does this while never forgetting God for a single moment (Awn 1995, 370). He added that mystical knowledge so transforms mystics that they are no longer subject to the power of the world (370).[13] In the ninth and tenth centuries, the Malamatis (meaning "those who draw blame") deliberately tried to provoke the contempt of the world by committing unseemly unlawful and even immoral acts while claiming that inwardly they preserved perfect purity of heart and loved God without a second thought (Schimmel 2011, 86). They claimed the contempt only proved their worship was authentic. They also performed good deeds in private and thereby avoided any spiritual pride in their outward appearances and actions. Qalandar Sufis in India and Pakistan also deliberately flouted social and religious conventions (Ernst 2011, 129–30). However, Sufi masters routinely criticized those who flouted Muslim precepts, considering them false Sufis.

Rabiah and Love Mysticism

In a reverse of the history of Christian mysticism, love mysticism arose first and knowledge mysticism followed.[14] Early Sufi ascetics feared judgment day and Hell (as Basri stressed) and hoped for paradise in the next life, but the Sufi ascetic Rabiah al-Adawiyyah (d. 801) of Basra was among the first to make "selfless love of the Beloved" an end in itself (Abrahamov 2003, 27). She shaped early Islam, and her idea of loving God for no personal gain became central to later mysticism in Islam. This was perhaps adopted from pre-Islamic Arabic love poetry. Intense longing and yearning for the Beloved has remained a dominant theme in Sufism even if the final realization of God has not always been a loving communion of two distinct realities. The lovers of God devote themselves totally to the Beloved.[15]

For Rabiah, Heaven and Hell were only veils (*hijabs*) separating us from God.[16] She argued that only by asceticism could Sufis detach themselves from the world in order to achieve the soul's loving communion with God. She claimed that contemplation of the creator occupied her so much that she did not care even to go outdoors and look upon his creation. The love of God should be pure with no other motives. She said: "Oh God, if I worship you out of fear of Hell, burn me in Hell, and if I worship you in hope of attaining paradise, forbid it to me. But if I worship you for you, do not withhold from me the everlasting beauty!" She said that her love of God so filled her heart that she could not hate the Devil because there was no room left in her heart to love or hate anyone else but God. Likewise, there was no room for devotion to Muhammad, but her writings on love for God remained comparatively sober compared to Rumi's.

For Shaqiq al-Balkhi (d. 810), love of God was the highest station of the mystical life. Later mystics enumerated various stages of love. They also utilized Neoplatonist categories, including a return of everything to the One, which aided in the development of the idea that everything is one reality. Love for God was like the Neoplatonist passion (*eros*) driving the quest for the One. Ghazali defined love for God as an "intense longing" (*shiddat al-shawq*) for him (Abrahamov 2003, 29). Dhu al-Nun al-Misri connected love for God with beauty (29). For him, love of God meant obedience (30). Generally speaking, Sufis—along with Muslims in general—place a higher value on knowledge than Christian and Jewish mystics, but from the thirteenth century onward, few themes play as important a role in Sufi teachings as love (Chittick 2000, 74).

The Persian poet, philosopher, and mathematician Ayn al-Quzat Hamadani (d. 1131) represented a more extreme brand of love mysticism. For him, not only are human beings the lover and God the Beloved, but simultaneously, God also is the lover and human beings the Beloved. The burning fire of love totally consumes the mystic into a nothingness in which God is most fully revealed, but this fire is all consuming, leaving the Beloved consumed.

Knowledge and the Annihilation of the Self

The importance of mystical knowledge is connected to the idea that we are veiled from seeing God, a major point in Islam. This went beyond the need to have the correct knowledge of God's will in order to align one's will with God's. God's face is covered by many veils, including the natural universe itself. Anything that blocks the path to seeing God is a veil. Even our ignorance of God in this world is a veil. Other veils include reason, worldly knowledge, the will, sense perceptions, and the ego—the greatest veil. The conceptualizing mind cannot comprehend God, just as a bat's eyes are blinded by the sun. Thus, Sufis must empty themselves of the will and anything else connected to the phenomenal ego. Unknowing our worldly knowledge removes veils. However, it is God himself who actually tears away the veils, not the mystic. Ibn Arabi stated that everything is a veil and that any vision of God occurs, inescapably, through a veil: "The veils remain forever hung down." Thus, unveiling (*kashf*) is never complete. We never perceive God through the senses except through a veil, and even unveiling the heart is never final until death. Paradoxically, since God alone is real, all the veils are themselves also God: God is simultaneously both different and identical to the veils. We may only ever see the forms and names of things and not their realities, but they are also God (Chittick 2000, 178–200). Thus, we never see God, as he is free of the coverings that are also God and are manifested to us.

In the ninth century, Dhu al-Nun al-Misri introduced to Islam the idea of a direct knowledge of God (*marifa*) that transcends all rational knowledge—a light sent by God in which a mystic becomes lost.[17] The idea that one's sense of an individual self should be annihilated (*fana*) and replaced by the continuing presence of God (*baqa*, abiding in God) also entered Sufism early. In short, when what is exclusively human passes away, only the divine presence remains (Q 55:26–27). Since God created and sustains us, he is always present in us and is what remains when one's sense of an individual self is annihilated. To Ibn Arabi, Sufism is simply "assuming the character traits of God." Junayd defined the Sufi way of life (*tasawwuf*) as God causing one to die in oneself and then live in him. The standard position is that one can completely forget all sense of self during a mystical experience; the space created by forgetting oneself is then filled by the presence of God. Thus, when one returns to a sense of self, one's attributes are transformed; the self is still there, but it is transformed. An awareness of God's continuing presence in the self results in the enlightened state.

This perception of God's presence establishes a renewed consciousness of the differentiated multiplicity of the created world (see Knysh 2000, 310). One now sees that there is nothing else but God; there is no independent reality. However, the world is not an illusion, nor is each self. Rather, both the world and each self are mirrors reflecting God and thus are themselves separate and real. The self is a created entity and is distinct from the creator who sustains its existence. Hence, the standard Sufi goal is a loving communion of two distinct realities: God and the soul. Thus, unlike Buddhist *nirvana*, the loss of a sense of self in a mystical experience does not indicate that there is no self but only that one loses awareness of it in the blinding light of God's presence. One well-known aphorism to this point resonates with Buddhist thought. Since Sufis live in the constant awareness that their selves are nothing but what they are in the present moment, "the Sufi is a child of the moment" (Chittick 2000, 55–56).

For many Sufis, there is ecstasy (*wajd*) in being found by God. These experiences are distinguished from both longer lasting conscious states in the stations of the path and the state of enlightenment filled with God's presence. In ecstatic states, the Sufi can become absolutely senseless and apparently lose consciousness, even for years (Schimmel 2011, 179). Some extravagant utterances (*shatahat*) about the ecstatic experience of being "drawn in" by God crossed the boundaries of orthodoxy and got Sufis in trouble; Sufis seemed to claim that they had become God. Abu Yazid al-Bistami (d. 874) exclaimed, "Glory be to me! How great is my majesty!" He wrote of the annihilation of the soul (*fana*) as well as the "annihilation of the annihilation": the annihilation of the soul is itself annihilated by God's presence in a person (*baqa*). This doctrine may have come from his teacher Abu Ali al-Sindi, an Indian Sufi. He took Muhammad's journey to Heaven (Q 17:1) as a model for mystical experiences. He also had a dream of a journey in which he ascended through all the heavens and received a vision of God's throne, in which he "melted away like lead" into an ineffable fusion. He threw himself on God's throne and looked around for God but found nothing but himself.

In Baghdad, al-Harith al-Muhasibi (d. 857) taught the importance of self-examination (*muhasaba*) and the willingness to bear all hardships—even death—for God, the "First Beloved." His student, the Persian Shaykh Abul Qasim al-Junayd (d. 910), who also taught in Baghdad, brought a less ecstatic and more intellectual approach to Sufism. He also stressed the need to follow Islamic rituals law, but he applied a Neoplatonist emanationism to Islamic concepts: God creates by emanating realities. Each preexisting soul is annihilated before each person is created, so each person is created from nothing. We must return to our prior state in which we saw God (see Q 7:171–72). He emphasized that those who experience the passing away of the soul (*fana*) do not remain in a state of absorption in God but God returns them to the world of the senses, where they find that the experience of selflessness has transformed them. Thus, *passing away* does not mean that individuality, a gift from God, is destroyed. Rather, the soul is transformed and perfected by God while in God (*baqa*). With the annihilation of the ego, the soul is returned to the state it had prior to entering a physical body, but in this state a Sufi's attributes are replaced by God, and it is God's attributes that now carry out the Sufi's actions. In its reacquired state, the soul remains distinct from God. Goodness is the inherent disposition (*fitra*) in this state, created in the image of God. In a state of sensed separation from God, God remains veiled, and this leads to yearning for the "divine Beloved" (Knysh 2000, 55). Junayd also gave the classic Sufi definition of mystical oneness (*tawhid*): "the isolation (*ifrad*) of the Eternal from what originated in time." (Note that the oneness of being still involves a duality: what is created remains other than God.) He seems to have written for those who had already had the experience about which he wrote; the writings evoked the experience once again.

Bistami, like the Persian poets, preferred the state of mystical intoxication (*suhr*) attained in the presence of God because Godly adoration obliterates human attributes, thereby taking one out of oneself. (Classical Sufis follow the Muslim ban on alcohol, but they still utilize language of intoxication along with language of madness and sexual ecstasy.) Any consciousness of a self disappears and is replaced by divine light (or darkness). Joy results. Sufis express fear of God less than many Muslims. However, Junayd preferred a state of sobriety (*sahw*) or, to be more exact, a "second sobriety" after the ecstatic intoxication. One then becomes aware of oneself but in the new "life of God," in which all attributes have been transformed, spiritualized, and returned to the experiencer (Schimmel 2011, 58–59). Reason dominated over intoxication. Many who expressed themselves in the daring poetry of union also wrote in prose about separation and servanthood; they were inwardly drunk with God and outwardly sober with the world (Chittick 2000, 34, 45).[18] So too, to keep their prose sober, Junayd and others began to write in code (*isharat*, subtle allusions) with only the initiated knowing the true meaning. This style of writing disguised his teachings from those who might consider them heterodox or heretical. Lists of the esoteric meaning of virtually every word developed over time.

Junayd considered an interest in miracles, along with too much attention to works of obedience and hope for a heavenly reward, veils that cover the hearts of the unenlightened (Schimmel 2011, 211). He valued the revealed knowledge (*ilm*) that every Muslim should possess in order to carry out their religious duties over mystical participatory knowledge (*marifa*). In contrast, some other Sufis advocated rejecting all such ordinary religious knowledge as well as all scholarly knowledge, "breaking the ink pots and tearing the books" (17–19). The Persian Sufi Abu al-Husayn al-Nuri (d. 907) similarly eschewed all speculation on the nature of mystical experiences. For him, "the intellect is weak, and that which is weak only guides to what is weak like itself" (Knysh 2000, 60).

The wandering preacher Husayn ibn al-Hallaj (d. 922) was a disciple of Junayd, but he was expelled from Junayd's circle for his extreme speeches. According to his son, after his third pilgrimage to Mecca, he was completely transformed. He spoke of union with God as a temporary state, not permanent deification, but he went so far as to exclaim in ecstasy, "I am the Truth/

Reality (*al-haqq*)!" (*Al-haqq* is one of the ninety-nine traditional names of God.) He probably only meant that he had attained a state of awareness of God or became an instrument of God; other Sufis had used the same phrase. Overall, he seems to have been a love mystic who considered love to be the essence of God. He appears to have retained a duality between God and the soul; when united, he believed there were two spirits dwelling in one body. He used the common theistic analogy of an iron so heated by fire that it seems to be fire, but he always affirmed God's transcendence. However, he also was involved in politics in Baghdad, and he said the wrong thing in the wrong place at the wrong time and was arrested for violating ritual practice. He was imprisoned for eight years and finally convicted of blasphemy (*kufr*) and claiming to be an incarnation of God. He was also considered a cunning sorcerer. He was executed following Quran 5:32 (whipped, mutilated, crucified, his tongue cut out, and decapitated); his body was burned, and his ashes were thrown in the Tigris. His last words were "It is enough for the lover that he should make the One single": that is, his individual existence should be cleared away from the path of love (Schimmel 2011, 69). His followers considered him a martyr.

Later Sufis defended Hallaj's claims by differentiating the bewildering utterances that are exclaimed in a state of intoxication in the throes of mystical love from those claims that can be legitimately maintained in the state of sober consciousness. The former were deemed beyond reason. Thereby, both the mystery (*sirr*) of God and the madness of union with him could be maintained. Rumi asserted that Hallaj saying "I am the Real" was like a piece of iron in a furnace saying "I am the fire." More extremely, Hallaj also claimed that there was nothing other than God, so with his ego annihilated, the words he uttered were those of God. That is, Hallaj had annihilated himself and only the Real remained. Thus, "I am the Real" were words spoken by God, and the claim was true since nothing else exists but God (Chittick 2000, 21). Sufis defended the claim of being one with God more generally by interpreting the first half of the Islamic basic declaration of faith: "There is no god but God [*la ilaha illa Allah*]." This was taken to mean not simply that there is only one God but that there is no reality other than God to mistake for him. (This claim also arose later in Hasidism.) Thus, in claiming "I am the Real," Hallaj was not claiming any special state or status for himself alone but only that there was never any other reality present in him or in anyone or anything else. Nevertheless, after Hallaj, Sufis were careful not to speak of union (*ittihad*) when speaking of God's unity (*tawhid*).

Sufi Theorists

For the great Sufi teachers, Sufism is essentially the "living heart" of Islam (Chittick 2000, 28). However, Sunni traditionalists objected that Sufism was un-Quranic and seemed to suggest that experience was an alternative source of religious authority and emphasize the interior life over performing external rituals and duties. Conservative Muslim theologians also opposed Sufism. Islamic theology (*kalam*) stresses the complete transcendence of God and his stern judgment.[19] In contrast, Sufis emphasize God's immanence within the universe and within human beings and his love (12–13, 29–30). In theology, Sufis speak of God's mercy, gentleness, and beauty far more than they discuss his wrath, severity, and majesty (23). Theologians assert that God is utterly incomparable to anything in the universe, while Sufis assert that all things are similar (*tashbih*) to him since they derive their reality from him (31). Some classical Sufis asserted God's omnipresent and immanent oneness and the possibility of a union with him, while others sided with theologians and stressed his transcendence and creatures' duties of servanthood (32). Sufism in this regard influenced the general population's attitude toward God more than did theologians' abstract theorizing (141).

Two Sufi theologians deserve special mention for their impact on both Sufism and Islam as a whole. First, the Persian Abu Hamid Muhammad ibn Muhammad al-Ghazali (d. 1111) was one of the most important Islamic thinkers of the medieval period and arguably Islam's greatest theologian. He began his career as a scholar in theology and religious law, but in 1095 doubt, skepticism, and even unbelief caused a physical and psychological breakdown that left him almost catatonic. He believed that we are saved by our actions, not our intentions or theological beliefs; he also believed that a virtuous life is not compatible with serving rulers. His doubts about the efficacy of the intellectual life and religious rituals were so great that he could no longer teach, and he abandoned academia to undertake Sufi training in the hope that he might come to "taste" the Truth that he had previously only embraced intellectually (Awn 2013, 251). Just as the word *wine* cannot cause intoxication, intellectual understanding without experiences and actions is worthless. He believed that Sufi adepts were of the best character and conduct and that their path was the straightest to God. He ended up spending eleven years as a wandering Sufi.

The results of this endeavor were books integrating spiritual training with learning and ritual observance. Reason alone, Ghazali believed, leads only to universal doubt, intellectual bankruptcy, and moral and social collapse. He was probably the first Sufi to master the Greek philosophy that Islam had previously absorbed, and he raised important objections to aspects of it. For example, if the One is utterly simple, how could it emanate something complex? That is, how does endorsing the simplicity of the One solve the problem of the One and the many? That creation was a matter of God's free will was a mainstay of his philosophy, and Ghazali believed that inquiring into the manner in which the world of multiplicity proceeded from God's will was in vain, simply idle speculation, and God condemns those who learn useless knowledge (Q 2:96).

Ghazali's most important works for reforming mainstream Islam were *The Revivification of Religious Sciences* (on proper Muslim conduct) and *The Incoherence of the Philosophers*. These dealt a severe blow to non-mystical, purely rational philosophy (*falsafa*) within Islam. Sufis prefer his *Niche for Lights*, a commentary on Quran 24:35 in which God is declared to be the light of the heavens and the Earth; God is the sole being, agent, and light of the universe. He identified God with the light, whose radiance is creation itself, which illuminates the intellect of prophets and mystics. There is nothing in being or existence (*wujud*) but God. Worldly phenomena are said to exist only as it were since God alone is real. Thus, all entities have no reality of their own and are pure nothing in themselves, including the human soul.[20] Some Kabbalists and Christian mystics a few centuries later stated similar claims, but like the Kabbalists and Christians, Ghazali did not mean that the soul is unreal but only that it has no existence apart from God. Everything perishes save for the face of God, who is eternal (Q 28:88, 55:26–27). True beauty applies to God alone; thus, he is the highest object of love. Human beings are the highpoint of creation since they are created in God's image.

Ghazali showed how Sufism could be reconciled with orthodox Muslim theology. According to him, prophets and Sufi masters (friends of God, *awliya allah*) have a knowledge that is not available through reasoning. Seers (*wasilun*, those who have arrived) are able to "see" God by a power above sense experience and reason. Mystical knowledge (*kashf*) is a light that, by grace, God casts into the heart and grants the experiencer certainty about God's existence. Unlike most Sufis, for Ghazali seeing God was not limited to introvertive experiences: one can be aware of the unity of things through observing the world of external phenomena.[21] The visible world is a reflection (*mithal*, similitude) of the world of dominion. Following the model of the Prophet's ascent to Heaven, there are four levels to seeing God's oneness (*tawhid*): uttering "there is no god but God" without understanding its meaning, understanding and affirming it, witnessing its truth through the unveilings that bring humans close to God, and seeing nothing in being but the One (*wujud*). The last level is annihilation in God's oneness. However, we can only perceive God through a veil of light that conceals his true nature, and thus, we see only glimmers of truth. In the state of the extinction of the soul (*fana*)—the extinction in unity or extinction in extinction—mystics are so absorbed by the light that they are no longer aware of themselves and have no recollection of their state afterwards. However, creatures always remain creatures, and mystics retain a soul even though God is One. Sufis see this once they return from being blinded by the light. Nothing in Ghazali's writings justified identifying the creator with his creations, rejecting the reality of the world, disobeying Islamic religious law, ignoring ritual observances, or permanently abandoning society. His *Niche for Lights* also makes the distinction paralleled in Jewish and Christian mysticisms between scripture's plain meaning (*zahir*) and concealed meaning (*batin*), but the need for an allegorical exegesis to discern scripture's concealed meaning led to the charge of esotericism.

After eleven years of training as a Sufi, he returned briefly to teaching in a university but then retired to a Sufi community. Overall, Ghazali made Sufism more respectable to political leaders and elite. He gave Sufism a high profile in the official religious establishment (Chittick 2016, 85).

The most intellectually rigorous Sufi theorist, the Neoplatonist Abu Bakr Muhammad ibn al-Arabi (d. 1240), was also important in this regard. Ibn Arabi was considered even by mainstream Muslims as the revivifier of religion. He was born in Spain and had visions since he was young. Two of his Sufi masters were women. After traveling, he settled in Damascus. He concluded that mystical knowledge was the highest form and only certain source of knowledge. While he agreed that some philosophical doctrines are correct, he admonished philosophers for relying upon reason alone. He stated that philosophers and theologians were barred from attaining the highest forms of mystical experiences. He even suggested, like Eckhart, that beliefs about God stood in the way of gaining mystical knowledge.

However, Ibn Arabi's major impact was on Sufis' ideas of the nature of reality. He took a belief held by many Muslims that God alone is real and gave it a twist, claiming that God in himself is utterly simple and one—the pure light or pure good—but since he is both the creator and creation (*khalq*), he is also multiple as the totality of created things. All the universe is only a manifestation of the preexistent nonpersonal Neoplatonist One. Human beings mirror God's essence (*dhat*). We can experience God's presence through the unveiling of God, but this unveiling is never complete. Unveiling may reveal the form of knowledge, but Ibn Arabi insisted that reason provides an indispensable check on experience, without which we could not differentiate the divine from demonic inrushes into the soul (Chittick 2000, 30).

Ibn Arabi stressed the absolute oneness of (the transcendent and immanent) being (*wahdat al-wujud*), although he did not use that phrase. He went from making the central Islamic declaration that God is one (*tawhid*) to claiming there is nothing but God—God is the only reality and essence—to finally claiming that all reality is one, unknowable, unchanging, and nonpersonal. Mainstream theologians accused him of espousing pantheism and unbelief since he claimed that God and the universe could not be distinguished. However, his claim was not a pantheistic one since God also transcends the world. God is immanent to creation, but the two are not the same. His claim was a Neoplatonist, emanationist panentheism. (Ayn al-Quzat Hamadani [d. 1131] was executed for asserting the actual identity of God and his creation.) The world is just the forum within which God's names become manifest. Phenomena are God's self-disclosures (*tajalli*) and, thus, are metaphors (*majaz*) pointing to God. Creation did not occur by a personal god speaking the creative word "Be!" (Q 2:117, 36:82) but by emanation: a "breathing out" from the One. Human beings are the reason for creation and are created in God's form. The intellect's power (imagination) is how Platonic Forms become embodied in creation. We are God's vice-regents (*khalifa*) in the world. All prophets had as their essence the *logos* (*kalima*) that is also the creative expression of the divine reality. Ibn Arabi believed that, through mystical knowledge, a Sufi could attain a level of perfection similar to that of Muhammad, who is the archetype of human perfection. The perfect man is a visible manifestation of the divine since he is created in God's image and mediates the human and the divine essences.

For Ibn Arabi, the One is a hidden treasure that created the universe out of a desire to be known (as stated in one of Muhammad's hadith). God is the Reality of realities. However, the One not only breathes forth the content of the universe but also breathes it back in. For him, "There is nothing to existence but God." There is no being but Being. Though we all exist, our existence is only through God: "One who exists through something other than himself is in fact nonexistent." Each soul is a separate, created substance distinct from the body, but like everything else, it is only a drop of water that will eventually return to the ocean from which it emerged (Q 2:210, 3:109). Thus, God's immanence in the phenomenal world cannot be cut off from his transcendent essence, which remains unmanifested. There is both unity and multiplicity. Nothing is God—since he is transcendent and is not, in any sense, created things—yet everything is God—since the being of all of creation is God. This paradox leads to another: God is both the seeker and the sought. No one loves God but God. There is no lover and no beloved but God. Likewise, God is necessary to us since he provides our being, but we are necessary to him since we allow him to manifest himself. Ibn Arabi also pointed to a theological problem for all theists concerning the attributes of God: What do the avenger, terrible in punishment, and overpowering have in common with the compassionate, forgiving, and gentle?

The goal of mysticism for Ibn Arabi is not an intimate loving relation between an individual and God but the discovery that there is no such thing as an independently existing individual. We can attain an experiential state (*dhawq*) through the annihilation of the sense of self, in which we are able to experience the oneness of God, creation, and all created things. This annihilated state is a station beyond the traditional stations of the path. Love plays a role on the path, but it is superseded by this enlightening knowledge (*marifa*), an insight into how things really are that transforms the Sufi (Awn 2013, 253). Nevertheless, Ibn Arabi wrote love poetry about God and used sexual union as a symbol of mystical union. (His poetry may have influenced the Christian John of the Cross.) But in the end, there is no loving communion because the soul has returned to the One, and there is no dualism; it is a oneness (*jam*) of the being of all reality that has existed since before the emanation, not a union (*ittihad*) of multiple realties or essences. The mystic must overcome the state of delusion and realize that diversity is an illusion. All reality is, in fact, identical to the One. The individual's higher spirit (*ruh*) is to be separated from their animal self (*nafs*), but in his Neoplatonism, being is not just supplied by the One but identical to the One's being that existed before creation.

Thus, there is a oneness of all being. Yet, Ibn Arabi never rejected the Islamic view of humanity's dependence on God. The One and the many both remain, even if all things exist only in the imagination (*khayal*) of God. Like reflections in a mirror, all things are what they appear to be, but they are also something else; they are images that are both real being and nothingness (Chittick 2016, 88). His use of the word *imagination* should not be confused with modern ideas of imagining or being imaginary. It has nothing to do with the rational mind but is a separate mental activity. It is the cognitive activity of our inner eye, like the intellection of the Nous in Greek Neoplatonism. Only the intelligible realm, not the visible sensory realm, is open to it. To keep the true balance of transcendence and immanence, we must see with both the rational eye and the imaginal eye that are both in the heart (88). Human beings too are only reflections in a mirror. Thus, we mediate the created and the uncreated; we are like an isthmus between the seen and unseen (Q 23:99–100). The idea that human beings are a microcosm and the universe a macrocosm also appears in Sufi thought.

Ibn Arabi's metaphysics of a nonpersonal ultimate reality became the standard position for Sufis. However, many Sufis did retain the personal nature for God as ultimate and objected that his metaphysics was not Quranic but, rather, reflected Advaita Vedantic and Buddhist influences. The Indian Sufi Ahmad Sirhindi (d. 1625) argued that the experience of the unity of being was only cognitively penultimate. The experience of the oneness of God and creation is only an illusion to the individual who has annihilated their sense of a soul (*fana*) but who has not yet reached the ultimate truth that the One is personal in nature, not a nonpersonal cosmic principle. A sense of the presence of God's personal nature does not yet fill the person's mind.

Love symbolism never left Sufism even for those who emphasized knowledge, as exemplified by Ibn Arabi. The difference in the approaches was only a matter of emphasis. Both love and knowledge were accepted as necessary by all Sufis: knowledge mystics accepted that love is either part of the path or the resulting enlightened state; love mystics stated that it is necessary to discern what is Real from what is unreal in order to love God properly. As Rumi put it, we must be able to discern true gold from gold-plate in order truly to love the gold.

The Persian Poets

Not all Sufi works are theological treatises or training manuals. Sufi literature also includes fables and poetry. One class of poetry that uses rhyming couplets is called *mathnawi*. These contain basic spiritual teachings, tales told by wise fools, stories about historical figures illustrating the teachings, hagiographic tales of earlier Sufis, proverbs, quotations from the Quran, and the sayings and actions of Muhammad, some of which were made up by Sufis.

Sufism plays a more important role in Persian literature than Arabic literature (Chittick 2000, ix).[22] The second most renowned mathnawi author is the Persian Farid ad-Din Attar (d. ca. 1221). His most famous work is *The Conference of the Birds* (*Mantiq ut-Tayr*). This book is ostensibly about a group of birds searching for their king, the Phoenix, of whom they have only vague recollections. However, the story is, in fact, a lengthy allegory of the Sufis' journey and the troubles that they face striving for their goal. The different birds represent different personality types, each with their strengths and weaknesses. Those that survive the journey through seven valleys of hope, love, knowledge, independence, unity, bewilderment, and annihilation have their attachments and individuality stripped in the Valley of Annihilation and become one with their king as a moth becomes one with a flame.

The most famous of the mathnawi authors and Persian poets is Jalal al-din Rumi (d. 1273), who is currently the best-selling poet in the United States. Born in what is now Afghanistan, he and his family fled the invading Mongols when he was young and eventually settled in Turkey.[23] He attacked rationalistic philosophers who had no mystical experiences, saying their "legs are made of wood, and legs of wood are infirm indeed." Besides his poetry, he is famous for his dancing and spinning. He did not only dance for joy; Rumi claimed he did his best praying and thinking while skipping or spinning, saying it lifts the soul out of the body into another world. After his death, his work also inspired the order of the Mawlawiyya (Turkish, Mevlevi)—the whirling dervishes (*darwish*)—with their ritualized dancing in circles with a head jerk. This order still flourishes today, mainly in Turkey. They use dance and music as aids in concentration—spinning and dancing also are ways to induce ASCs in other traditions—but overall, dance plays a minor role in Sufism, including in this order (Chittick 2000, 91).

Rumi's poetry, sometimes erotic and rather crude, expressed his intense love for God. It appeared in a book after the disappearance—and perhaps murder—of his mentor, a Sufi named Shams al-Din from whom he was inseparable. His *Rhyming Couplets of Profound Spiritual Meaning* (*Masnavi*) is an encyclopedic collection of stories in verse derived from the Quran, events in Muhammad's life, Muhammad's sayings, and other sources that illustrate aspects of Rumi's Sufi way of life. His work addressed topics including the lower bodily self (*nafs*), reason, knowledge, and the need to reject earthly existence to understand God's existence. (He may have attended lectures by Ibn Arabi in Damascus.) He produced thousands of verses on the interplay of separation and union, hope and fear, sobriety and drunkenness, annihilation and subsistence, and the pain of separation from God and joy (Chittick 2000, 86).

Rumi was tolerant of different Abrahamic paths, stating, "Every prophet, every saint has his path, but as they return to God, all are one." "The lamps are many, but the light is one." "I am neither Christian nor Jew nor Zoroastrian nor Muslim. I am neither of the East or of the West." "I have put aside duality and have seen that the two worlds are one. I seek the One, I know the One, I see the One, I invoke the One." "For those who seek unity, there are many ways to pray, and when I pray there is neither belief nor unbelief."[24]

For Rumi, the One is first and last, the external and internal reality, the creator and creation. The world is the surface foam of an ocean, and God's attributes are the ocean itself: "The foam veils you from the Ocean's purity." God alone is the Real. He supplies existence to all things, and everything in the manifest world is a veil that both hides God and reveals him. God was a hidden treasure, so he created the cosmos to make himself manifest, but God's motive was also pure love: "If not for pure love, why would I give existence to the spheres?" Love is a divine attribute, and our love for anything is actually love for God, even though we do not realize it. "Love is the astrolabe of all we seek."

The mother of all idols, according to Rumi, is the ego. His image for the annihilation of the self in the light of God is that of a moth that spirals into a candle and burns itself up. In the *Masnavi* he says that he was once a mineral; when he died as a mineral, he became a plant; when he died as a plant, he became an animal; when he died as an animal, he became a man. Why, then, should he fear death? For he never became less by dying. Next he will soar with the angels, and lastly, he will return to the One and become nonexistent.

After Rumi, the Persian poet Abd al-Rahman Jami (d. 1492) also utilized the language of erotic union mixed with a monistic reality, claiming "all is he." For Jami, pure love reveals itself in God when he is experienced. For him, Sufis, who are not concerned with only their own salvation, return from that experience to lead others on the path to God.

Sufi Orders

The Quran condemns Christian-style monasteries and convents (57:26–28; but see 5:82–85), and in a hadith Muhammad claimed, "There is no monasticism in Islam." However, in the twelfth century, Sufis began to form monasteries, convents, and communities called *brotherhoods* or *orders* (*tariqahs*, meaning paths or ways) in which Sufis worked or lived together under the guidance of a master. (The different orders should not be seen as rival sects.) Isolation from the Muslim community was not common. Sufis spent most of their time inside towns and cities. There had already been master/disciple relationships, but during this time period, permanent institutions that continued past the death of the first master were established and became the norm. Some had family dynasties. Shrines built around the graves of the founders became sites of pilgrimage and alleged miracles (*karama*). Some masters predicted the future and cured the sick. The Sufi doctrines were considered the secret teachings of Muhammad, and unbroken chains of teachers extending back to famous earlier Sufis and companions of Muhammad were set forth to establish the authenticity and accuracy of the teachings. In the initiation, the master's spiritual force or blessing (*baraka*) was passed to the student and to their descendants. These blessings were seen as possessing the gift of divine grace.

Some orders advocated rejection of the world; others advocated engagement with everyday life; some were highly intellectual; others appealed to the less educated (Awn 2013, 254). Some were pacifist; others were incorporated into regiments of the Ottoman army.[25] Some were bands of roaming mendicants; others were merchant guilds. Some were somber, but on the other extreme were the Rifaiyya, the howling dervishes. Some were highly orthodox in their beliefs and practices; others diverged greatly, such as the Muridiyya in Senegal. A few left towns for isolation in the wilderness. Some orders became authoritarian. Some lodges were not teaching institutions but simply retreats for Sufis. The diversity of available practices permitted pious devotion for many who had no interest in theology or philosophy as well as more intense practices for the few who followed a strict mystical path toward enlightenment.

Sufi orders were the main reason people converted to Islam in Central Asia, India, and Southeast Asia. Sufis also adopted new practices from these contacts with other cultures; for example, Indian Sufis became vegetarians and incorporated yogic practices. Indeed, some orders in India were Indianized, such as focusing on God as fire after the Agni rituals or adopting the Hindu caste in defiance of Islam's emphasis on equality of all persons. Abul-Fath Jalal ad-din Muhammad Akbar (d. 1605), the third ruler of the Mughal Empire in India, began a movement aimed at uniting Hindu and Islamic thought (Schimmel 2011, 359–63).

There was little originality in doctrines among Sufis after the orders became well-established, but the orders transformed Sufism from a way of life for the few to a spirituality for the many. They also helped to broaden Sufism from being mainly a lower-class phenomenon. They also assimilated some esoteric Sufi teachings about interiority into the most popular forms of religiosity (Chittick 2016, 91). Sufi orders also popularized rituals including repeating the divine names (*dhikr*) and ritual music (*sama*) and dance to wider groups of Muslims (Schimmel 2011, 167–86).

In principle, one entered an order to learn doctrines passed down by masters, the remembrance of God's names, and meditation (*muraqaba*); but over time the orders took on worldly roles for many Muslims. Not all members were even tangentially engaged in mystical ways of life. By the modern era, the orders had become involved in the type of worldliness condemned by earlier Sufis. Some orders acquired great wealth through donations. Many passed along not only teachings but also their wealth and the power of blessing (*baraka*) through their family lineages. As a result, some lodges became opulent, prompting criticism of the hypocritical "poor fakirs" living in luxury. Claims of detachment and inner poverty did not placate critics, nor did claims that Sufis who were married with children kept an inner celibacy through detachment. Political and economic power often outweighed traditional Sufi interests, and many orders did attain political power. Many people affiliated themselves with an order for social and political reasons even though they had no interest in mysticism. However, today the orders have assumed a smaller political role.

Influence, Decline, and Revival

Sufism began as a protest against worldly power and wealth, but once mysticism became accepted within the structure of Islam, Sufism became an integral part of every Muslim regime until the modern era. Sufism also influenced most Muslims up to the beginning of the twentieth century. Sufi holy men and healers remained the principal agents for converting people to Islam in border regions, Central Asia, and the West. In the nineteenth and early twentieth centuries, Sufi orders led the jihads against European advances into Muslim countries. Moreover, after Ghazali and Ibn Arabi, all major Muslim intellectuals until the middle of the nineteenth century were either Sufis or deeply influenced by them.

However, the charge that Sufism is not Islamic goes back to its early days and continues today. Sufism's influence on the populace upset both secular and religious authorities. It was and is seen as heretical, idolatrous, corrupt, superstitious, impious, and a distortion of the teachings of the Quran, particularly for hinting at pantheism and alleging that a creature could contact the creator. It also gave a greater role to women than most Islamic traditions. Sufism's antinomian rejection of the requirement of five daily prayers—since Sufis constantly pray to God—upset all Muslims. Sufism also has become more and more associated with claims of miracles and magic, not mysticism. Since its early days, ascetics and Sufis have often been considered local holy men; the community goes to them to arbitrate social disputes and perform miracles (such as healings) and intercessory prayers. Some Sufis are considered saints (*walaya*), and visitors show great devotion to tombs of deceased Sufis that have become shrines in hopes of sharing in the holy person's *baraka*. Towns have grown up around some saints' tombs. This veneration of saints and relics strikes many Muslims as at least approaching idolatry or polytheism. Whirling dervishes also now tour the West to entertain secular audiences. Writings that were kept secret within certain groups for centuries are now widely published and read without a master's oral commentary.

Since the rise of conservative Wahhabism in what is now Saudi Arabia in the early nineteenth century and the later rise of a strict Islamic fundamentalism, Sufism has been in decline in the Arabic-speaking world. Fundamentalists today, including ISIS, have destroyed Sufi shrines and mosques.[26] Because Sufism was the main way Islam was presented to the West, many saw Sufis as collaborators with the Europeans who occupied Muslim countries. Muslims educated in the West also tended to reject mysticism as medieval and backward or, at best, escapist and an impediment to spiritual reform within Islam. In the early twentieth century, many Muslims completely disavowed Sufism, claiming that it has nothing to do with true Islam.[27] Conversely, some advocates of Sufism tried to disassociate it completely from Islam, seeing its relation to Islam as purely incidental.[28]

By the 1950s, Sufism in its mystical and non-mystical forms was practically dead. However, since the 1960s, there has been a resurgence of interest in Sufism within Islam and without. Idries Shah's rather unorthodox interpretations of Sufism helped to popularize it. There are also eclectic Neo-Sufi groups in the West that attempt to synthesize Sufism with Western thought and separate Sufism from Islamic thought and practice. In 1922, Hazrat Inayat Khan (1882–1927) founded the Universal Sufi Movement in London, and his son Pir Vilayat Inayat Khan (1916–2004) carried on his work, spreading Neo-Sufism throughout Western Europe, Russia, the United States, Canada, and Australia. The guru Bawa Muhaiyaddeen (d. 1986) attempted to synthesize Sufism with various Hindu teachings.

Today, Sufism is found in all parts of the Islamic world except in and around Saudi Arabi, and it has retained a vigorous form of spirituality in some parts of the Islamic world, including South Asia and Africa. Overall, Sufism has affected Islam as a whole, attacking worldliness and presenting Muslims with one way to conduct an intense and profound religious life.

Key Themes

• Sufis try to align their lives with God's will—live in the presence of God—by following the path laid out in the Quran and exemplified in the life of the seal of the prophets, Muhammad. The Islamic creed "there is no god but God, and Muhammad is his messenger" remains true for Sufis.[29] Islam exhibits a radical monotheism—the oneness of the divine— but classical Sufis typically go further. God is not only one but is the only reality: there is nothing real but the Real. That is how Sufis interpret the declaration of faith "there is no god but God" and the hadith "God was, and nothing was with him." God is transcendent, but he also continues to supply being to the world. Thus, he is immanent to the natural realm and to human beings, and, in fact, God constitutes the only actual reality of any phenomenon. There are different views on the relation of God to the world, but no form of pantheism is affirmed by most Sufis. Because of his transcendence, God is never reduced to the natural world. Rather, Sufis distinguish the eternal from the temporal, the real from the unreal in this world. Prior to existence, things (including human beings) were latent images in God's mind. Sufis do not deny the contingent reality of the world, but they do attack preoccupations with worldly wealth, secular knowledge, and social or political power as being in conflict with the Quran.

• Sufis attempt to focus upon God at all times. Forms of prayer and meditation are central to all types of Sufism. Meditation is often connected to the constant remembrance (*dhikr*) of God by chanting his names or phrases from the Quran. Over time, such meditation superseded discursive meditation (*fikr*). Saying the basic declaration of faith became a form of meditation. As Ibn Ata Allah (d. 1310) put it, "No one says 'No god but God' correctly unless he negates everything other than God from his soul and heart" (Chittick 2000, 70). The experiences may be personal, but group prayers, chanting, and dancing are common in Sufism.

• Mainstream Sufism rejects the idea of a mystical experience being a literal union (*ittihad*) of two distinct realities. Becoming one with God's oneness (*tawhid*) is a matter of realizing that we already are one with God's being and have always been so since God is the only reality. Things in the phenomenal world are treated as having no reality apart from God, so some Sufis treat them as unreal. Thus, God supplies the being to everything created, but the creations are not identical to God. That is, our being is from God, but we are still distinct realities in some sense. Additionally, no new ontological is state achieved through a mystical experience.

• The oneness of being may be realized in ecstatic introvertive mystical experiences (*hal*, *wajd*), including differentiated introvertive experiences in which a loving communion with God is achieved. The void created by extinguishing one's sense of self (*fana*) is filled with the presence of God (*baqa*), and the Sufi filled with the awareness of God continues in an enduring extrovertive enlightened state. Through such experiences, the submission of one's will to God becomes complete.

• Mystical knowledge (*kashf, marifa*) is usually given preference over basic revealed knowledge (*ilm*) and becomes the basis for mystical interpretations of Quranic passages. Such knowledge is a direct, unmediated light that God throws into the hearts of those whom he chooses (Knysh 2000, 311). Sober claims of the status of a lover and the beloved were generally preferred over the intoxicated claims of union. Sufis may lose a sense of a self or soul when blinded by the blazing light of God during a mystical experience, but after the experience, they know that the soul is a separate entity created and sustained by God. That is, God is indeed experienced, but afterward one sees that even though God is the only reality in any phenomenon, God is still the creator, and created phenomena are in some way differentiated from him, acting as a veil. Neoplatonist emanationism was usually adopted to explain these differences between creator and creation. In the end, the personal god won out over the nonpersonal Neoplatonist One for many Sufis.

• Sufis typically use the language of both love and mystical knowledge. Different Sufis emphasized one or the other, but the two are not absolutely separated as approaches to realizing God; both are necessary. However, the enlightened state is typically depicted as a state of loving adoration of the essential Reality since God is always the target of limitless attraction.

• The role of spiritual masters in conveying esoteric knowledge was always very important. Later, the masters' spiritual force (*baraka*) was also considered important, and popular practices developed around it.

Chapter 7

Hindu Mysticism

Trying to summarize Hindu mysticism is virtually impossible since each guru has their own variation on doctrines, but some generalizations can be made. The place to begin is with the arrival of the nomadic Aryans (the "honored" or "respected" ones) in northwest India and Pakistan in the late Bronze Age from the steppes of Central Asia or the Middle East. They likely arrived around 1700 to 1500 BCE or, perhaps, through a slower migration and gradual assimilation over the previous hundreds or thousands of years; there is no evidence of a swift invasion or war. The role indigenous groups from the Indian subcontinent had in the resulting mix is a matter of debate. However, the culture that emerged in this period in northwest India spread throughout the subcontinent, and the Aryans' Indo-European language (Sanskrit) became the vehicle for the dominant Indian culture.

The Vedic Background

The liturgy for the Aryans' most important sacrifices to the gods was finalized in their current form by 800 BCE and collected into four books: the Vedas. The name *Veda* comes from a Sanskrit root for *knowledge* (*vid*). The orthodox position holds that the Vedas are eternal and authorless; seers (*rishis*) merely hear them when a god repeats them at the beginning of each world-cycle. Each Veda consists of a large section of hymns supplemented by Brahmanas, Aranyakas, and Upanishads. The Brahmanas and Aranyakas include instructions on how to carry out sacrifices and explanations of the rituals. They were probably composed from 800 to 600 BCE. The Aranyakas were probably composed by priests (Brahmins), not ascetics who separated themselves from general society, but they are texts on rituals that were kept from the public and repeated and studied only outside of the cities, hence the title *forest books*. They also contain teachings about the symbolic meanings of the Vedic rituals. This knowledge had to be kept secret because its power was dangerous if misunderstood or applied improperly. Consequently, it was required to study the texts with teachers (*gurus*).

Sacrifices permitted people to participate in the creative act of preserving the cosmos by feeding the gods who maintained the cosmic order (*rita*). Thus, the sacrifices held the world together and renewed it. Over time, Vedic sages began to express agnosticism toward the gods. No god was present at the initial appearance of the universe, leading thinkers to ask where the universe came from and postulate different hypotheses (for example, RV 10.90) or admit our inability to know (RV 10.129). Thinkers began looking for something more fundamental than the gods of various natural phenomena. By the time of the Brahmanas, ritual sacrifice itself became more important than the gods for sustaining the universe. The rituals were seen as maintaining the entire cosmos through hidden connections (*bandus*). Thus, human beings properly performing the rituals was essential to maintaining the cosmos. This led to downplaying the gods' power in favor of the nonpersonal power behind the ritual utterances (*brahman*).[1] In the Brahmanas, connections between cosmic phenomena and the human body—such as the eye and the sun—were identified.

In the Brahmanas and the Atharva Veda, the sacred speech of rituals was seen as the supreme cosmic essence underlying all the universe, both what exists (*sat*) and what does not yet exist (*asat*) (see Jones 2014b, 188–90). The reasoning was straightforward: the process of connecting different phenomena through hidden connections led to the idea that all phenomena are connected and, thus, that ultimately only one power is behind them all. When this idea was combined with the centrality of sacred speech in world-sustaining ritual sacrifices, the conclusion naturally followed that the power behind the ritual speech (Brahman) was the real power behind all phenomena.[2] In a kind of metaphysical Grand Unified Theory, everything became manifestations of this power. Brahman became not a god but the one all-pervading nonpersonal ontological essence (*atman*) of all phenomena.

This formed the belief matrix for most Indian mysticism. Moreover, new doctrines appeared in the Brahmanas and Aranyakas that led to dramatic changes in the interests and ethos of the Upanishads. Hope for a

permanent life in a heaven became the idea of dying there (re-death), resulting in a perpetual cycle of deaths and rebirths (*samsara*); a world-affirming ethos became a world-renouncing one, where seeking worldly comfort
became seeking escape from all worldly and heavenly existences (*moksha,
murti, nirvana*); views of priests as supreme became respect for ascetics and
mystics; *karman* as ritual action became *karman* as all desire-driven actions
based on a beginningless root nescience (*avidya*) that saw diverse realities
when there was only one; the addition of an interest in mysticism became
the interest in magic that is present in the Brahmanas and Aranyakas (and
which also has remained present throughout Indian history); a social focus
on maintaining the world through communal rituals became an individualized focus on liberation from rebirth based on knowledge and personal
experiences of Brahman. This new sense of *karman*, belief in rebirths, and
hope for escape from rebirth remained virtually universal in Indian religiosity. However, there were materialists in India from ancient times—including
the Ajivakas and the Charvakas—who denied the existence of a self or life
after death. Some led ascetic lives.

These new doctrines did not develop gradually from Vedic ideas but
appeared fully formed in the Upanishads. Likewise, they are not defended
there but simply assumed. This is also the case in Buddhist and Jaina works.
This suggests that these doctrines had already been accepted in certain circles. India shared a search for a permanent transcendent principle with
other Axial Age cultures, but these interests and ideas were absent in the
other great civilizations of the Axial Age. What were their sources? Why
was there a nonpersonal principle and not a god? Historians debate two
obvious candidates: (1) the resurgence or continuation of interest in ascetic
practices and drug experiences among the Aryans and (2) the indigenous
Indian cultures that the Aryans encountered as they spread through India.

A potion drank during the rituals made of the psychedelic plant *soma*,
and perhaps others, played an important role for the early Aryans. It was
rooted in an earlier Indo-European heritage and probably came from the
mountains northwest of India. Karel Werner (1989) goes so far as to argue
that Vedism was originally a mysticism-inspired religion of nature and magic
that was later suppressed by the priests who valued the rituals that they
controlled. Unlike hymns to other gods, the hymns to Soma concentrate
on an immediate experience. However, by the time some Aryans had split
off and entered India, the *soma* plant had been lost. The Upanishads make
only token references to it. The Vedas also include one hymn to naked

long-haired ascetics (*keshins*) taking drug-enabled, shaman-like flights (RV 10.136), perhaps to acknowledge that such experiences were occurring in the indigenous society.[3]

The Upanishads

Vedism emphasized external ritual actions, but the Upanishads turned inward. The traditional etymology of *Upanishad* is from Sanskrit roots meaning "to sit near," thus indicating that the texts involve secrets that were only to be communicated by a teacher to a few. In the Upanishads themselves, the term refers to a secret doctrine—in particular, rebirth—or a secret meaning or hidden connection between phenomena. The earliest Upanishads are merely a philosophical portion of the Aranyakas. In effect, they are long anthologies of teachings taken from different teachers. The principal independent Upanishads were composed between 500 and 200 BCE on the subject of metaphysical issues. Upanishadic thinkers accepted that rituals maintained the world but rejected the rituals' value for ultimate personal salvation. The Upanishads' doctrines are not uniform. In fact, teachings within the same Upanishad sometimes conflict.

It is significant that the early Upanishads were probably composed only after the Vedic people had pushed eastward into the lower Ganges River plain of central and northeastern India. That the Upanishads were composed in the same area that produced Jainism and Buddhism is no doubt no coincidence. There, the Vedic people encountered a new urban setting and various ascetic recluses (*shramanas*), wanderers (*vratyas*), silent ones (*munis*), and renouncers (*samnyasins*) whose practices and traditions were most likely pre-Vedic. Some of these practitioners emphasized magic, some transcendence and meditation, and some bodily purity. Many were ascetics, and asceticism continued to flourish throughout Indian history.

The groups that the Vedic people encountered in the Indian subcontinent may well be a source of their inward turn. At the least, renouncers rejected the Vedic religion as authoritative. (It is worth noting that the Upanishads are the only basic religious texts in the world that proclaim their earlier revealed texts, the Vedic hymns, are only a matter of lower knowledge [*apara-vidya*] [MunU 1.1.4–6; see also CU 7.1.4]). They were experience-oriented and asked questions about the nature of a human being. Members of the warrior/ruling class (*kshatriyas*) taught Brahmins something new: rebirth (BU 6.2.8) and *karman* (CU 5.3.7). This suggests that input came from another source than Aryan society, in which priests held the doctrines, and that it must have been startling. Likewise, that women were among the questioners would have been unusual for Aryans. Indeed, one woman (Gargi Vachaknavi) pushed the great teacher of the Brihadaranyaka Upanishad (Yajnavalkya) further than men did on the nature of Brahman—all the way to a philosophical question he deemed unanswerable (BU 3.6.1).[4] The idea of non-injury (*ahimsa*), which is barely mentioned in the Upanishads, also probably came from ascetic movements such as Jainism since it conflicts with the Vedic ethos.

Knowledge in the Upanishads

The Upanishads' common purpose is to lead practitioners from the unreal to the real (*sat, satya*), from darkness to light, and from death to the deathless (BU 1.3.28) to gain something permanent beyond the unsatisfying changes of this life. The means to attaining this is knowledge of Brahman (*vidya*). Knowledge was considered important for its power. The formula common in the early Brihadaranayaka is: "Who knows thus [*ya evam veda*] . . . becomes [*bhavati*] . . . ." The magical power of knowledge over things of value (wealth and so forth) was present in the Upanishads, but most important was the idea that one could escape rebirth and, thus, gain true immortality by knowing the underlying cosmic essence (BU 1.2.7, 3.3.2, 6.2). By knowing Brahman, one becomes Brahman (BU 4.4.9, MunU 3.2.9). Thus, like Brahman, one becomes immortal (for example, BU 5.14.8, KaU 6.14). One becomes the ontic essence (*atman*) of all beings (BU 1.5.21). All of one's desires are thereby fulfilled or extinguished. Thus, we should strive to perceive that from which we are born, live upon, and return to at death (TU 3.1).

It may seem that knowledge in the Upanishads is not mystical—Brahman can be grasped only by saying, "It is!" (KaU 6.12–13), so no ASC experience is needed.[5] It may seem that all we have to do is follow an argument to its logical conclusion. The process of correlating and connecting all different phenomena leads to the conclusion that only one hidden principle connects everything; this world, the world beyond, and all beings are strung together on one thread (BU 3.7.1). Even the central idea that we must come to know the "unknowable knower of knowing" (BU 2.4.14, 4.5.15, 3.7.18–23, 3.8.11) is no more than accepting the logical point that the knower we are aware of through ordinary self-awareness must be different from any knowable object, including other mental phenomena. It is experienced subjectively and never known as an object. There is no further esoteric doctrine involving exotic experiences. All new knowledge has been revealed in the texts. The public debates in the Brihadaranyaka and Chandogya are only a matter of arguments based on reason, analogies, and examples, with no references to mystical experiences. When Uddalaka teaches "you are that" to his son Shvetaketu (CU 6), there is no indication of a need for further practices or ASC mystical experiences. The son learned the secret doctrine, and that was that. It came down simply to understanding the doctrine and believing Uddalaka. Indeed, the doctrine of Brahman as the sole ontic essence (*atman*) of everything is a relatively simple and straightforward metaphysical claim. We can readily understand the arguments for it and may find plausible the claim that "my being is constituted by a transcendent reality that constitutes the same being of everything in the universe."

However, the Upanishads also claim that the ontic essence cannot be known by simply hearing about it (KaU 2.7) or attained by instruction or learning (KaU 2.23, MunU 3.2.3). Even the earliest Upanishads indicate that more is required than mere intellectual conviction concerning a metaphysical claim. Yajnavalkya states: "He who knows thus and has become tranquil, controlled, quiet, patient, and collected sees the essence [*atman*] in himself alone and sees that the essence is everything. . . . He has become a knower of Brahman, free from evil, free from stain, and free from doubt" (BU 4.4.23).

This strongly suggests that ASC mystical experiences informed even the earliest Upanishadic teachings on knowledge. *Vidya* (knowledge of Brahman) contrasts with *jnana* (the act of knowing or cognition) or what is gained through *vijnana* (understanding or perceiving) (BU 4.3.21). *Vidya* involves a direct, nonreflective type of experience: one becomes what one knows. (Over time, the meanings of *vidya* and *jnana* became mixed.) There is a merging with the knowledge itself, so the mental distance required for examining and understanding something distinct from oneself is obliterated (BU 2.4.12, 2.4.14). It is beyond the mediated dualistic situations of sensing another (BU 2.4.14, 3.7.18–23, 3.8.11, 4.5.15). Thus, discovering Brahman requires direct experiential knowledge obtained by participation, not simply by adopting a new metaphysical belief with the dualistic mind. This reality is our ontic essence, but it is also the ontic essence of everything else and thus transcends us. Any experience of it will replace the dualistic state of mind that divides subject and object and will, therefore, be an ASC.

Moreover, "the imperishable" is in everything, including subjective phenomena—in particular, the unseen seer and unknown knower (BU 3.8.10–11). That is, we must know what is common not only to the world's external phenomena but also to the internal mind. However, we can directly find this universal reality in all things only within us, and this requires an introvertive mystical experience of our essence, not any experience of the external world. Through knowing Brahman, this entire world (*loka*)—the totality of everything that is not Brahman—is known (MunU 1.1.3). We cannot know what is unique in every possible phenomenon that emanates from Brahman, nor can we know all factual information about the world— the enlightened are not omniscient in that sense—but we can know the reality constituting the essence of all things. In that sense, whoever knows "I am Brahman" becomes all this world (BU 1.4.10, 4.4.9; MunU 3.2.9). When we experience the reality within ourselves, we participate in the one reality that is in everything else. However, in the Upanishads' emanationism, we remain our particular emanation of Brahman and do not become a tree or a rock or any other emanation of Brahman. Phenomenal reality is not one in that sense.

The otherness of the ontic essence from anything phenomenal makes Brahman inconceivable, indescribable, and unknowable as an object. It is invisible and ungraspable but present everywhere (MunU 1.1.6). Brahman is beyond understanding (*vijnana*) even by the gods (Mun 2.2.1). Nor can it be reasoned about (MaiU 6.17). Words and the mind turn back, never reaching it (TU 2.9). Only where there is duality of knower and what is known can one see or know another (BU 4.5.15): "Where understanding is not of a dual nature—without action, cause, or object—it is without speech, incomparable, and indescribable. What is it? It is impossible to say" (MaiU 6.7). Conceptualizing (*samkalpa*) is related to seeing diversity; a separate mental function (*buddhi*, the intellect) realizes Brahman (KaU 3.10). The transcendent Brahman is not an object for the mind to conceive. Thus, "the eye, language, and the mind do not go there. We do not know or perceive how one can point it out. It is other than what is known, and it is also above the unknown" (KeU 1.3–4). It is unknown since it cannot be perceived as an object distinct from us or grasped by the dualizing mind as an internal object. It cannot be experienced even indirectly through sensing external phenomena, but the same reality that is in everything is within us and can be experienced directly inwardly (KaU 4.1). Thus, it is "above the unknown" because it can be directly realized in a mystical experience. "That which cannot be thought by the mind but by which the mind thinks" is other than what is known because it is not an object of the senses or the conceptualizing mind (KeU 1.5). One who conceives it (*mata*) does not know it (*veda*) (KeU 2.3), but it can be conceived by one who awakens to it (KeU 2.4). Likewise, it is inconceivable and cannot be grasped by reasoning, but it can be taught by another to one who holds fast to reality/truth (*satya*) by at least pointing us away from all worldly phenomena (KaU 2.9).

Yoga in the Upanishads

Actions cannot achieve this knowledge because actions are a matter of duality: a person achieving something. Desires and conceptuality involve duality with something other than the actor. No amount of action or merit (*punya*) accruing from actions for a better rebirth can force mystical insight. Likewise, rituals were seen as leading only to a heaven, not to knowledge. Ordinary knowledge also involves duality: knowing something distinct from the knowing. Only participatory knowledge is nondual in nature, so only it can attain Brahman.

The Upanishads are not always clear or consistent on the means to achieving the necessary knowledge, including whether Brahman can be known by ascetic austerity, but the most common position is that one must withdraw their senses from external objects and unknow what the learned know (CU 7.1.3; see also IU 9–12). There is a forgetting, an absence of the awareness of this or that. The quest to find the reality underlying phenomena can begin externally—as with contemplating the clay common to all pots—but it ultimately requires introvertive mysticism since the reality can be realized without mediation only internally. The Upanishads also speak about ways of cultivating knowledge of Brahman and preparing the mind by means of yoga. The term *yoga* appears even in the early Upanishads (see TU 2.4). In this period, it meant any technique or application for stilling the mind. Words from the root for *dhyana* relate to thinking or perceiving and occur in the early Upanishads (e.g., BU 4.4.21); only later did *yoga* denote a direct experience of Brahman rather than mere mental reflection on it (see SU 1.2).[6]

The Brihadaranyaka lists virtues that renouncers desiring to know Brahman must have: tranquility (*shanta*), self-control (*danta*), emotional detachment (*uparata*), patience (*titikshu*), and a concentrated mind (*samahita*, becoming collected) (4.4.23). The Katha has several passages about stilling speech, stilling the mind, yoga, banishing desires, and disciplining or controlling the five senses, the mind, and the intellect (*buddhi*) (2.12, 2.20, 3.5, 3.15, 6.9–14, 6.18). The highest state occurs when the five senses, together with the mind, are stilled and even the intellect does not stir (6.10). The Mundaka has several passages related to disciplining the mind (2.2.4, 2.2.6, 3.1.8, 3.2.4). The later Shvetashvatara has the longest passage discussing yogic practice (2.8–15). It states that the "supreme mystery" of the end of the Veda should not be discussed to one who is not tranquil (6.22). "Those who have practiced the discipline of meditation have seen the power of God's essence [*atman*] that is hidden by his own qualities" (1.3; see also 1.14). The last classical Upanishad, the Maitri, summarizes the method by which one who knows attains oneness with the One: the sixfold yoga of control of breathing (*pranayama*), withdrawal of the senses from sense objects (*pratyahara*), meditation (*dhyana*), holding an object in the mind (*dharana*), rational investigation (*tarka*), and the culmination of meditative concentration (*samadhi*) (6.18).[7] It also has other verses on yoga (6.10, 6.19–20, 6.24–25, 6.28–29). It states that one who knows withdraws the mind from external objects and continues without conceptualizations (6.19, 7.11). Twenty-one Upanishads devoted solely to yogic practice and theory were composed later in the early medieval period.

The celibate life of a Vedic student (*brahmachariya*) is a traditional prerequisite. Ethics are given a token amount of attention. The Upanishads also usually consider thought and reflection part of the path, but they are not sufficient means of release from rebirths. Asceticism is also an aid. It is often paired with confidence or trust (*shradda*) in the texts. However, asceticism is not the same as yoga: it is a matter of renouncing the world and austerity (*tapas*) connected to the body, not necessarily yogic control of the senses and mind. The Upanishads' general position is that asceticism does not lead to release (for example, MunU 3.1.8; but see also MunU 3.1.5). After all, asceticism is a matter of actions. At best, it purifies the body, preparing the way for the mystical experience, but knowledge is still needed (MunU 3.2.6).

Becoming desireless is sometimes presented in the Upanishads as being the product of knowledge of Brahman, not a necessary prerequisite to it. This is also the case with tranquility. This is important since in the Upanishads desire (*kama*) arising from the error of seeing a multiplicity of independent real entities (for example, KaU 4.11) causes rebirth (BU 4.4.19). Desire, like conceptualizing, comes from the part of the mind that must be stilled (BU 1.5.3). With *vidya*, this changes: one no longer has the misleading illusion of an ontic diversity of phenomena that generates desires and thereby keeps one being reborn. As long as we desire something, we are propelled on to more rebirths, but knowers of Brahman are not reborn (BU 4.4.8, KeU 2.15). Once we see that we are not ontologically self-contained entities whose interests can be enhanced or favored but only Brahman, we become free of desires. In short, knowledge of Brahman ends desires, thereby ending the cycle of rebirths.

The delineation of different states of consciousness also has relevance to the nature of the knowledge of Brahman. The Mandukya lists four: waking, dream sleep, dreamless sleep, and a fourth state (*turiya*) that is neither cognitive or noncognitive. (Note that visions and ASC experiences other than dreams and the fourth state are not mentioned.) Dreamless sleep is considered cognitive, but in the last state there is a loss of a sense of a separate *I* set apart from what is real. Thus, one cannot be cognitive of a separate reality. The fourth state "is unseen, not open to interaction, ungraspable, without a defining mark, inconceivable, indescribable, the cessation of mentally proliferating objects [*prapancha*], tranquil, auspicious, and without a second [reality, *advaita*] . . . That is the essence [*atman*]. That is to be known" (ManU 7). Earlier Upanishads held that there were only the first three states, claiming that we are automatically reabsorbed into Brahman or Brahman's world in dreamless sleep and at death without being aware of it (BU 2.1.17–19; CU 4.4.3, 6.8.1, 6.8.6, 8.6.3, 8.11.1). Either way, the purpose of yoga is to attain a state beyond cognition of any object while still remaining conscious, thereby losing a sense of individuality and merging with Brahman.

Renunciation

The path to attaining this mystical knowledge is difficult—as hard as walking the edge of a sharp razor (KaU 3.14). It starts with renunciation. However renunciation entered the Aryans' way of life, it was later given a formal spot in the Hindu way of life in stages of life—after the stage of household life—first as a forest-dwelling hermit who still participates in religious rituals and may have a family and, in the final stage, as a homeless renouncer (*samnyasin*) who wanders alone, living only on offerings. A renouncer has fulfilled all of their social obligations and no longer performs rituals. Cultivating the inner heat of austerity (*tapas*) replaces the ritual fires. According to the standards set forth in the *Laws of Manu* and exemplified in the epic *Mahabharata*, the renouncer's actions reflect the universal social and religious duties (*sadharana-dharma*): truthfulness, patience, and non-injury (*ahimsa*).[8] The hermits in the *Ramayana*, however, do not come close to fulfilling those standards; among other things, they leave before completing the householder duties, have children, eat meat, and use their power to curse to kill.

In the Upanishads, renouncers abandoned their property and all the social *dharma* (class and stage-of-life duties and virtues) in favor of the quest for release from the cycle of rebirths. Their observance of prescribed duties only accumulated the merit that leads to a heaven and did not produce the final escape from rebirth. Thus, renouncers have a different goal and some different values from those of householders. They adopt practices to gain the necessary knowledge. The enlightened are freed from *dharma* and its sanction, *karman*. Free of desires, they are tranquil, content, and indifferent to everything, including life and death.

The idea of an inner renunciation of things, even of the sense of ownership of one's own actions, later became more central, as in the *Bhagavad Gita's karma-yoga*. One need not abandon one's home or duties or enter a monastery for this.

Brahman/Atman

What is to be known in the Upanishads is what is deemed real: what is eternal, permanent, unchanging, and unaffectable.[9] To be common to all outer and inner phenomena in this world, this reality must also be totally different in character from any particular worldly property (including mental states). Otherwise, it would have the characteristics of only some particular phenomena and not what is common to all. Thus, reality must be "not this, not that" (*neti neti*, literally no so, not so) (BU 2.3.6, 3.9.26, 4.2.4, 4.4.22, 4.5.15; see also 3.8.8). Reality does not belong to any entity but only to the underlying source. Names and forms (*nama-rupas*) of objects pass away, but the underlying reality remains.

Thus, the Upanishads' focus is on identifying the unchanging ontological reality (*sat*) underlying all transient external and internal phenomena. However, the Upanishads are not entirely consistent on the nature of that reality, and their metaphysical doctrines sometimes conflict. They also differ in tone. The Brihadaranyaka is more negative—with its great saying of "not this, not that," focus on becoming desireless, and emphasis on Brahman as the hidden source transcending the phenomenal realm—while the Chandogya is more positive and realist about phenomena—with its great saying of "you are that reality," focus on fulfilling desires, and emphasis on Brahman as immanent in worldly phenomena.

According to the Brihadaranyaka, the secret doctrine is that cosmic essence is "the Real of the real" (*satyasya satya*) (BU 2.1.20, 2.3.6; see also BU 4.4.18, KeU 1.2). That is, Brahman supplies being to a fully real world. Being (*sat*) is the ontic essence (*atman*) of anything, and it is the only attribute that matters in the final analysis. The world, the gods, and all beings are emanations from that essence like sparks from a fire (BU 2.1.20, MunU 2.1.1), web from a spider (MunU 1.1.7, SU 6.10), rays from the sun (MaiU 6.26), or branches from roots (KaU 6.1). For example, in one list, Brahman is the essence (*atman*) from which space arose; from space, air arose; from air, fire; from fire, water; from water, earth; from earth, plants; from plants, food; and from food, human beings and other earthly beings (TU 2.1). The analogies make the world parts of Brahman, and Brahman is sometimes portrayed as the world (CU 7.25.1).

Thus, the worlds, gods, and beings are real (*satya*), and the transcendent ontic essence (*atman*) is the reality (*sat*) in them (BU 2.1.20). Our world is not merely an appearance or illusion. However, the emanated world hides the source of its reality. There is an apparent proliferation (*prapancha*) of diverse entities from the source, and, due to our nescience (*avidya*), we mistakenly take the entities to be independently real (MunU 1.1.7, SU 6.6). In fact, there is no diversity of real entities (BU 4.4.19, KaU 3.10). One source supplies the only reality; thus, there is one common reality pervading all things. The ontic essence is in everything but also distinct from any phenomenon (e.g., KaU 5.9–10). Thus, no Upanishadic metaphysics is pantheistic. All worlds rest on Brahman (KaU 6.1); the world is "woven" on Brahman (BU 3.6.1). Thus, the "Real of the real" also transcends the phenomenal world.

In a holdover from earlier times, Brahman is sometimes called the *universal person* (*purusha*), although it is usually portrayed as nonpersonal. And as discussed later, there is also a theistic strand to some Upanishads. In phenomena, this power is called *atman*: its essence (*animan*) or taste (*rasa*). The Upanishads do not express any uncertainty, nor do they express the puzzlement of Rig Veda 10.129 about the existence of such a reality since it is open to direct inward experience. Because Brahman is the reality behind all phenomena, its main descriptions emphasize its permanence; it is eternal, unchanging, uncreated, constant, and imperishable. It is real in the final analysis since it is not dependent on any other reality, and asking for any further reality will only make one's head split (BU 3.6.1). It is self-born (*svayam-bhu*): self-become, self-created, or its own cause (BU 2.6.3, KaU 4.1, IU 8). It is bliss (*ananda*) or joy (*sukha*) and other than the painful and unsatisfying temporary phenomena of this world. It is pure (*shuddhi*) and must also be limitless (*ananta*) since it is the reality of all possible phenomena. Brahman's nature is beyond our senses and reasoning and can be described abstractly as reality/truth (*satya*), cognition (*jnana*), or the limitless (TU 2.1.1). Beyond that, its nature cannot be identified.

In the Upanishadic emanationism, each phenomenon has an ontic essence (*atman*). Since Brahman supplies the only reality (*sat*) to phenomena, Upanishadic thinkers can say both that the world arises from Brahman (CU 7.25.2) and that Brahman is the whole world (CU 3.14, 7.26.2). Nevertheless, Brahman can be identified with any individual phenomenon since it supplies all being. The Upanishads often identify Brahman with phenomena such as space (BU 5.1, CU 3.12.7) or the sun (CU 3.19.1), but these phenomena are not seen as the essence of all other phenomena. Likewise, one can meditate on "Brahman is the ear," "Brahman is food" (TU 3.10.6), "Brahman is space," or "I am Brahman," but this does not mean that these phenomena are more fundamental than others. The same applies to calling Brahman *sentience* or *consciousness* (*chitta*), the unknown "seer of seeing," or the "knower of knowing" (BU 3.7.23, 3.8.11). Brahman is the reality immanent in everything, so it is as much the reality of known phenomena as it is the knower. (Advaita gives another view.) Additionally, Brahman is not a "knower" in the sense of an agent that has changing acts of knowledge; that understanding objectifies Brahman as much as it being the object of an act of knowing.

The ontic essence of any object, as well as the entire phenomenal world, can be said to be its *atman*. The word *person* (*purusha*) is also used interchangeably with *atman* for a human being (see MunU 1.2.11). Thus, the same things are said about the Atman as are said about Brahman (for example, CU 3.14.2). As Yajnavalkya said: "Your Atman is the Atman within all things" (BU 3.4.1). Thus, *Brahman* and *Atman* are simply two different names for the same thing. The difference is in the point of view. *Brahman* is the name of the reality when looking at all things collectively, and *Atman* is the name of the same reality when looking at the ontic essence of a particular thing (the "breath" animating that thing) (BU 4.4.5).[10] The term *Brahman* accents the universality of the ontic principle, and each Atman is identified with it.

Since Brahman is the reality in everything, it is the Atman of everything. Phenomena do not each have their own unique ontic essence—there is only one essence. It is not as if there are multiple individual atmans that merge into the cosmic Brahman. There is only one Atman: Brahman. Brahman is not made up of a collection of essences. Brahman is the only "Real of the real," so it is the reality that we refer to when we refer to our essence (*atman*). Thus, that Brahman is Atman is not a union of two different entities—a combination of a transcendent reality and our individual transcendent soul. Likewise, claiming "I am Brahman" is not solipsistic when each phenomenal person (*jiva*) can claim the same. Enlightenment is realizing that one's ontic core is the same as everything else's.

In Advaita Vedanta metaphysics Brahman is uniquely identified with consciousness, but this is not the position of all Upanishads. In these texts, consciousness (*chitta*) is distinguished from the mind (*manas*), which is treated as merely another sense organ with concepts as its sense objects. (Thus, both mind and body are rejected as ultimately real.) Brahman is attributeless, inconceivable, and indescribable since it is not open to any phenomenal categories. Even *consciousness* does not apply to Brahman from the ultimate point of view but only refers to limiting adjuncts (KeUB 2.1). In a person, the Atman is identified most commonly with the life breath (*prana*) and elsewhere with fire, among other things. Consciousness is not essence. There are passages that note the person is made of mind (BU 3.8, 5.6; CU 3.14.2; TU 1.6.1), but life breath and even food are sometimes considered higher essences than mind (see CU 7.9). So too, the Chandogya states that the mind merges into the life breath and then into fire before merging into Brahman (6.8.6). That is, life breath was seen as a person's true essence, not mind. Mind is only another phenomenon with a higher essence. Additionally, consciousness is not something that plants or inanimate objects have, but they still have Brahman as their Atman. When Uddalaka taught Shvetaketu about the essence of a banyan tree, there was no suggestion of consciousness as its Atman or that consciousness is the essence of the human body (CU 6.12). Focusing on one's consciousness in a mystical experience is how one knows Brahman in them directly, but Brahman is no more uniquely consciousness or subjective than anything external in the world. No phenomenon, including the mind, is privileged. Brahman is what all phenomena—subjective and objective—have in common.

This leads to the most famous phrase in Asian mysticism: "You are that [*tat tvam asi*]." The phrase's line reads: "That finest essence [*animan*] is the Atman of all of this world. That is [what is] real [*satya*]. It is the Atman. You exist in that way" (CU 6.8.7). Neither Brahman nor consciousness are mentioned anywhere in the passage. Rather, a father is teaching his son that he exists in the same way all living things do—by the same essence that, like salt dissolved in water, pervades everything and can be experienced but cannot be seen (CU 6.1.1–3). In short, the phrase means that we have the same ontic essence as every other thing: Atman which alone is real (*satya*).

Nowhere in the Upanishads is the identity of Brahman and Atman in a human being proclaimed as the secret doctrine, nor do the Upanishads ever use *nonduality* (*advaita*) to refer to the relationship of Atman and Brahman. *Nonduality* is instead used to indicate that there is only one reality (Brahman) (ManU 7, 12); there is no second reality or a plurality of realities. That Brahman is nondual means there is only one ontic essence to all the phenomena of the world. Everything shares one unchanging reality (*sat, satya*)—the "Real of the real"—whether it is labeled *Brahman* or *Atman*.

Thus, even though we can only know Brahman internally, there is a danger in translating *atman* as "self." Indeed, Brahman is not the self of a person in the sense that an individual can be substantiated as an independent reality. Moreover, when we see a self as our essence, we naturally extend the term *personal self* to refer to the essence of any phenomenon. But this extension tends to psychologize the ontic essence and anthropomorphize Brahman. Atman is not a matter of the human psyche, individual subjects, or personal souls,[11] nor is knowledge of the Self psychological self-knowledge of an individual (*jiva*). Likewise, Brahman is absolutely distinctionless: it is not a person or personal in nature. In addition, the mind (*manas*) dualizes and is not the Atman but is to be ended. The Upanishads speak of a hierarchy of Atmans within a person and of the "highest Atman" (TU 2). Essences can be ranked with quintessence deemed the highest, but it makes no sense of speak of multiple selves within a person.

Theism in the Upanishads

The dominant metaphysical position in the Upanishads involves a nonpersonal principle (Brahman). It is the ontic essence and is referred to as the Lord (*Ishvara*) in the context of it being the efficient cause creating the world. However, there is also a more theistic thread, mainly in the Katha and Shvetashvatara, in which a personal god underlies Brahman. This gives a theistic reading of Brahman, but Brahman is not personified in these texts. Traditional Western theistic attributes of omniscience and omnipotence—but not omnibenevolence—are occasionally scattered in lists of attributes, but a full-blooded theism never developed. In particular, Brahman is said to be beyond human moral distinctions (Jones 2014a, 214–17). The term *lord* (*isha*, a ruler, master, or owner) is often used, but it is not clear how theistic the intent is. Brahman and Atman are often called "the lord of all beings" (BU 2.5.15) without ascribing to it anything personal in nature. The Isha refers to the One as the Lord and names no god (IU 1).

The closest to a clearly theistic claim in the early Upanishads is that Brahman within us (Atman) is attained only by those whom it "chooses" or "favors" (*prasada*) (KaU 2.20, 2.23; MunU 3.2.3–4; SU 1.6, 3.20, 6.10). This is the theistic understanding of the fact that both mystical experiences and the awaking to the resulting knowledge cannot be forced by any action but seem uncaused and spontaneous. However, knowledge of the transcendent reality is needed even in theistic passages (SU 3.8). Likewise, it claims the practice of yoga can increase the chances that the transcendent reality will favor a person with the insight.

The Shvetashvatara is the first truly theistic Upanishad. It is also the most numinous Upanishad, expressing worship, fear, and awe. It has the only reference to devotion (*bhakti*) in the classic Upanishads (6.23), although this may be a later insertion. It became a key text for Shaivism. The Lord (Shiva) is a transcendent magic-maker (*mayin*) who creates and sustains the world and is immanent in it (1.11). God is the Lord of all and hidden in all things (4.15). The text expounds yogic practices, but it disclaims that we cannot become the Lord. It attempts to subordinate the Samkhya dualism of a self and matter to Atman as a creator god in a framework incorporating Brahman. The result offers no consistent view of Brahman, but the text states that God is the source of Brahman (5.6) and made this world from Brahman (4.9).

Samkhya

The Upanishads form the foundation for most of the subsequent history of Hindu mysticism, but an early school, Samkhya, rejected the fundamental Upanishadic assumption that one reality underlies all external and internal phenomena. For this school, there is an eternal dualism of matter and consciousness: reality consists of nonconscious, inert matter (*prakriti*, *pradhana*) and multiple transcendent, eternal conscious persons (*purushas*). There is no one common reality (Brahman) constituting the reality of everything or underlying everything. Instead, the universe contains multiple real selves, each totally distinct from each other and independent of nonconscious mat-ter. Samkhyans identify eternal self-contained entities of pure consciousness as our true selves and distinguish them completely from the equally real and eternal world of matter. This metaphysics became the framework for most theistic traditions until various Vedantas replaced it, but its influence (and that of the Yoga school) returned in the sixteenth century CE.

However, the mind in this dualism is quite different from how it is viewed in the modern West. Pure consciousness (*chitta*) is separated from all mental activities—sense perceptions, memory, will, emotions, a sense of *I*, and so forth—and the latter activities are taken to be material. Only matter moves. The consciousness that constitutes each person is an unchanging, inactive, nonintentional, eternally observing awareness. The other activities that we consider mental are actually different modes of nonconscious mat-ter. As with the Upanishads, a *purusha* is not the thinking mind (*manas*): the mind is a sixth sense, with the heart as its sense organ and ideas as its sense objects. Each *purusha* silently witnesses or illuminates the thoughts and other material content of the mind. A *purusha* exists independently of such content and continues to be aware even in the absence of any content. It is like a searchlight that is on even when no objects are being illuminated. Thus, each true self is free of all dualistic content.

Everything other than consciousness consists of different groupings of three strands of matter (*gunas*): the lucid (*sattva*), the active (*rajas*), and the inert (*tamas*). Consciousness itself is unmoving, yet it affects matter like—to use the Samkhya simile—a magnet controlling iron filings. This effect upsets the balance of the three strands. Matter then emanates into different categories, including the mind and senses in addition to the observ-able material elements. The process begins with a basic awareness (*buddhi*), from which emerges the sense of self (*ahamkara*, the *I* maker); unseen (subtle) and visible (gross) material elements emerge out of the mind. The *Samkhya-karikas* (ca. 400 CE) attributed to Ishvarakrishna give an ontology of how matter evolves.[12]

Enlightenment in Samkhya involves metaphysical knowledge; *sam-khya* means "enumeration" or, perhaps generally, "reflection." It discrimi-nates consciousness from matter, in short distinguishing the self (*purusha*) from the non-self (*prakriti*) (*Samkhya-karikas* 64–65). This discernment ends future embodiments. Upon death, the enlightened person is not reborn and their *purusha* remains in its transcendent state free from matter. Thus, each *purusha* is not united to anything but is isolated from matter in the state of *kaivalya* (aloneness). (Jainas hold a similar doctrine.) This entity is conscious but stripped of anything unique or personal in nature since everything personal is material.

Yoga

Is there a need for preparing or purifying the mind for this discernment? Is the insight of the basic duality of self and matter experienced in a mystical experience? Or is the conscious self? The *Samkhya-karikas* do not suggest that, but the Yoga school is traditionally seen as providing the practice needed to attain this knowledge. The term *yoga* may come from a Sanskrit root meaning "control" or "striving," taking on the yoke of meditative discipline. In general, it refers to any mental or bodily meditative praxis for escaping the cycle of rebirths or attaining powers, not only the system of the *Yoga Sutra* attributed to Patanjali (somewhere between 100 BCE and 400 CE). Yogic cultivation (*bhavana*) became accepted in some form by all Indian traditions. Some yogic practices among the wanderers and renouncers were probably indigenous to India prior to the arrival of the Aryans. The wanderers encountered in eastern India probably contributed to the yogic practices in the Upanishads noted previously. In western India, the early Indus Valley script has not yet been deciphered, but some artifacts may indicate yogic practice. One image may depict a meditating three-horned Lord of the animals with a trident, later deemed to be Shiva (who is considered the exemplar of yogins), and the city Harappa's name may be derived from *Hara*, a name for Shiva.

The *Yoga Sutra* adopted the post-Vedic valuation of the world: all is suffering (YS 2.15). Thus, the discriminating person withdraws from the world. The text systematized already existing yogic practices for stilling the mind, both asceticism (*tapas*) and meditation. It does not have an explicit metaphysics, but all early commentators state that the framework is Samkhya. In addition to the Samkhya metaphysics, there is traditionally also a physiology of the body for meditation that became prominent in Tantric circles: a serpent energy (*kundalini*, meaning coiled) that flows as a life force (*prana*) in the subtle body, which can be seen only in ASCs, through a system of knots (*chakras*) and channels (*nadis*) running from the crown of the head to the base of the spine (see CU 8.6.6). Through the yoga of force (*hatha yoga*), one works the body and comes to dominate the *kundalini* energy. When the energy rises up through the body—activating each knot—and finally pierces the crown of the head, one is united with Shiva, who resides there.

According to the Yoga school, because of a beginningless nescience (*avidya*), we mistakenly connect the pure consciousness of a person (*purusha*) with insentient matter. There is no creator god nor one underlying reality such as Brahman. The *Samkhya-karikas* do not include a god in their inventory of what is real, although early commentators did. In the Yoga school, the Lord Ishvara is an undefiled *purusha* who was never entangled with matter but is eternally free; he is not a creator of the universe but only an exemplar for yogins. At most, he may be able to aid other selves or act as an object for meditative focus (YS 1.24). Nothing in the text suggests that the world is unreal or that matter is not eternal, and its goal is isolation (*kaivalya*) of the self from matter. There is no object to unite with, and enlightenment does not conform actions with the will of God.

For the Yoga school, *raja yoga* is a process of turning inward to eliminate sensory experiences. It results in "stilling [*nirodha*] the fluctuations [*vrittis*] of the mind [*chitta*]" (YS 1.2). Thereby, one's attention is focused and undisturbed. (Buddhism influenced the *Yoga Sutra*, and Hindu yogic practices in turn influenced Buddhism.) When ordinary awareness has ceased, a yogi abides in their true nature as a *purusha* (YS 1.3). This involves restraining the mind and senses and transcending the sense of a phenomenal ego resulting from the *ahamkara* (*I* maker). Mental disturbances (*antarayas*) are calmed through one-pointedness of the mind (YS 1.30–32). Thereby, one's state of consciousness is transformed. External perceptions are purified, free of afflictions (*kleshas*) in an ASC extrovertive mystical state. The important point for the Yoga school is that the mind cannot see the *purusha*. Even if the mind is in a pure sattvic *guna* state, one cannot know the knower of knowing dualistically. One must realize one's *purusha* directly. At best, the mind reflects the *purusha* in a dualistic image.

The text sets forth an eight-limbed practice (YS 2.29). (1) Restraints (*yama*): non-injury, truthfulness, non-stealing, celibacy, and freedom from avarice. (2) Disciplines (*niyama*): cleanliness, serenity, asceticism, study of Yoga doctrines, and effort to make God the purpose of all actions. (3) Bodily postures (*asanas*): cultivating stability and removing fluctuations from the body by reducing physical effort to a minimum while fixing the body in a single position. (4) Rhythmic breathing (*pranayama*). (5) Withdrawing sense perceptions (*pratyahara*): removing oneself from the outer world, like a turtle withdrawing its limbs into its shell, and focusing the mind on the essence (*tattva*, that-ness) of an inner meditative object. (6) Greater fixation (*dharana*): focusing attention on a single object—such as the tip of nose, an idea, or God—to the exclusion of everything else (YS 3.1), leading to a one-pointed focus (*ekagrata*). (7) Meditation (*dhyana*): maintaining one's focused attention for longer periods (YS 3.2). (8) Union (*samadhi*): completely stilling of mental fluctuations in concentrated attention (YS 3.3). The last three stages are called *discipline* (YS 3.4) and lead to insight (*prajna*) (YS 3.5).

The final experience is usually called *ecstasy*, but Mircea Eliade (1970, 79–80) coined the word *enstasis* to depict it since one realizes the deeper reality within oneself. After the first steps, one's consciousness is altered, and the text delineates several types of experiences. Effort (*abhyasa*) toward enlightenment is required along the path. Detachment (*vairagya*) is the enlightened attitude. One also can attain various paranormal powers (*siddhis*) (YS 3), but in the Yoga school the yogin uses them for help on the path to enlightenment, not to gain power over the world, which would be only a distraction from the goal of liberation.[13]

A yogin goes through a progression of states of consciousness. The early stages involve beginning to focus attention (*dharana*), and later stages expand awareness (*dhyana*). These are dualistic states of consciousness: one is aware of being in a blissful state, a sense of self, or a meditative object. One identifies with the object of meditation. All of these mental absorptions involve conceptual construction (*vikalpa*). Next comes absorptions without any conceptualizations operating in the mind (*nirvitarka samapatti*). The material mind is stilled; the mind does not reflect, and the object of meditation shines forth. There are stages of concentrated attention (*samadhi*). The first four have objects as supports (*alambanas*) for meditative focus (YS 1.17): the mind becomes absorbed into the observable gross object (*vitarka*) of meditation; then the subtle object (*vichara*) that transcends space and time (the *tanmatra* element); then bliss (*ananda*); and finally, the sense of *I* (*asmita*, I-am-ness). There is no sense of awareness, only as sense of being (*satta-matra*). Awareness here is free of mental structuring.

However, these stages are not realizations of the *purusha* because the mind can only see stages of matter, not the other (YS 1.18; ManU 7, 12)—that is, the eternal consciousness that is the *purusha*. There is a danger here of mistaking the temporary bliss and absorption into the *I* as attaining the final goal of yoga. The sense of *I* is merely a material covering of the *purusha*. *Samadhi* culminates with a state of concentration that does not require the support of any object for focusing awareness (*asamprajna-*

ta-samadhi): a depth-mystical state of consciousness empty of objects and self-awareness. Being free of even the subtle object, the lucidity of the inner *purusha* shines through (YS 1.47). This step is a direct realization of the *purusha*, although this state is not considered an experience but a change in knowledge since experiences are modes of matter, not consciousness (YS 3.35). It is a permanent change of consciousness. The samadhic experience is deemed enlightenment, but one is not aware of being enlightened while in the highest *samadhi* state. Only after the experience does one realize what one has always truly been: a conscious entity distinct from matter. Realizing this distinction is the "reality/truth-bearing insight" (*ritam-bhara prajna*) (YS 1.48). Theistic yogins adapted this to be an experience of the Lord.

The enlightening experience does not immediately disentangle the *purusha* from the material body. One returns to a state of nonseparation (*avibhaga*) of the *purusha* and matter until death. Nevertheless, after the awareness of the phenomenal world returns, one has internalized the enlightened point of view, so one is liberated in life (a *jivan-mukta*). All the enlightened's karmic residue from past actions and all their subconscious mental impressions (*samskaras*) are destroyed (YS 1.50). The actions of the enlightened are non-karmic since they are free of desire for anything connected to matter (YS 1.16). One's embodied mind (*manas*) consists entirely of lucid matter (*sattva*), with no passion or dullness (YS 3.3). In a meditative state, the fluctuations of the mind have ended, and the mind mirrors what it sees without the interference of the conceptualizing mind. The Yogic practice, which is primarily introvertive and concentrative in nature, has the effects of the enlightened state of Buddhist mindfulness meditation: with one's mindfulness (*smriti*) made pure, the mind appears empty of its own form (*svarupa-shunya*), and only the object (*artha*) is illuminated (YS 1.43). The mind is clear as a crystal and shapes itself to any perceived object of sense perception or inner perception (YS 1.41).[14] In this pure mental state, one is in a state of bliss.

Advaita Vedanta

The word *Vedanta* means "the end of the Vedas" and initially referred to the last sections of the Vedic texts (the Upanishads), but subsequent attempts to understand and systematize the Upanishads spawned various schools labeled *Vedanta*. The earliest surviving Vedantic text is the *Brahma Sutra* (*Aphorisms on Brahman*) attributed to Badarayana and finalized around 200 to 450 CE. It is a book of study-aid aphorisms (*sutras*), whose meanings are to be explained by a teacher.

Schools of Vedanta differ on nature of the individual (*jiva-atman*), the phenomenal world (*jagat*), the reality transcending the phenomenal universe (Brahman/God), the nature of the liberated state, and spiritual practices (*sadhanas*). The earliest Vedanta tradition espoused the doctrine of "difference and non-difference" (*bheda-abheda*): the phenomenal individual is both different from the one reality underlying the world (Brahman) and yet not different from it. That is, any person is substantively nothing but Brahman and, thus, is not different from it; however, a person is not identical to it either since there is more to Brahman than just one person, and each have some properties that the other does not (for example, Brahman is changeless). There is a relation of a whole and its parts. This is the case for the entire phenomenal world. This involves an emanationism: the phenomenal world is emanated from Brahman as its radiance like rays of light emitted from the sun.[15] Bhartriprapancha (sixth century CE) and Bhaskara (eighth or ninth century CE) advocated this view, and the tradition continued with Chaitanya after the three better known branches of Vedanta—nondualist, qualified nondualist, and dualist—arose.

The *Brahma Sutra* also espouses such an emanationism. Nothing real exists separately from Brahman. Brahman is the world's only cause and substance, but Brahman still transcends the phenomenal world. When this world disappears at the end of each world-cycle, Brahman remains and is unaffected. Whether the world is considered a real transformation (*parinama*) of Brahman or only the illusion of a change (*vivarta*) became a central point of dispute. The emanationism of the *Brahma Sutra* and the Bheda-Abheda traditions has a form of realism that concerns the world and individuals: Brahman becomes an objective, extended reality that is both one and many. The many are real parts of Brahman. This may have been the prevailing Vedantic view at the time of the text's composition.

The school espousing nonduality (*advaita, advaya*) rejects the difference prong of the Bheda-Abheda formula and advances an absolute oneness of reality. Only Brahman is real; the phenomenal persons and world are not parts of Brahman.[16] The term *advaita* refers to this denial of any other reality than Brahman: no second reality (*a-dvaita*). It does not refer to a union of an individual essence (*atman*) with Brahman since there is only one essence, not many.

The earliest surviving Advaita text, the *Gaudapada-karikas*, still accepts a realist emanationism. Parts of this work probably date from the sixth or seventh century CE. The work is ascribed to Gaudapada, who is said to be the teacher of Shankara's teacher. He was influenced by Buddhism. The text defends Advaita ideas philosophically, not merely theologically relying solely on the authority of the Vedas, and it makes no appeal to mystical experiences as evidence. In Gaudapada's ontology, there is only one reality: Brahman (or its preferred term, the Atman). This goes beyond the Upanishads. Brahman is not the source of a real emanated world—the "Real of the real"—but is the only reality. Nothing else is "real" to be dependent upon it. Any sense of a multiplicity of subjects and distinct entities (as with the Bheda-Abheda doctrine) is a result of our root-nescience (*avidya*) and the cause of our misguided desires and, hence, suffering.

For Gaudapada, Brahman, and thus all of reality, is actually only consciousness (*chitta, chaitanya*).[17] The dreaming and waking states are modifications of that one eternal, unborn, formless, unchanging, ever-present, immutable, contentless, and self-illuminating consciousness. The phenomenal realm is an emanation of this consciousness and thus part of Brahman, but the appearance of a duality of a subject and multiple objects within this realm is an illusion. The mind (*manas*), through nescience, causes consciousness to appear to "vibrate," thereby giving the appearance of a subject and objects (*spandita*, vibration, pulsation, or shimmering). But since there is only one consciousness, the world is nondual. Nothing real is created or changes. Just as light appears to create a straight line, crooked line, or circle when a burning stick is waved—even though the fire remains unchanged—so the vibrating consciousness appears to be a perceiver and something perceived even though it is free of all appearances when it is not in motion (GK 4.47–51). The light's appearances do not come from somewhere when the firebrand is in motion and do not go anywhere when the firebrand is not moving, nor do the appearances emerge from the firebrand; the appearances simply do not exist. Likewise, when the mind causes consciousness to vibrate in waking or dream states, the appearances do not come from somewhere else, and when consciousness is not vibrating, the appearances do not go somewhere. Nor do they emerge from or enter into consciousness itself. Stilling the vibration caused by the mind simply stops the illusion of discrete subject and objects. Only the real emanation remains.

The Advaita criterion for what is real comes from the Upanishads; what is real is permanent, eternal, unborn, and unchanging. Gaudapada emphasized Brahman being unborn (*ajati*). Brahman is the entire being (*sat*) of the universe. The phenomenal realm is not the appearance of an underlying reality but is the reality itself and thus is real. If you dream that you are being attacked by a tiger, the tiger and the event are not real, but the dream consciousness itself is real. So too, with Brahman. The phenomenal world is real even though the characters and other contents we create are not. The content of waking consciousness is constantly changing, but the state of consciousness remains the same unchanging reality. Believing that the differentiated content of our dream realm is real and has reality independently of Brahman is the illusion to be overcome, not the reality of the phenomenal realm itself. The realm of Brahman's magical work (*maya*) is real and thus eternal because it is Brahman's radiance and not an illusion (GK 3.17–18, 4.4–5).[18] But like a magician's trick, the phenomenal realm is dependent upon the magician—here it *is* the magician's own radiance— and its ontic nature is easily misperceived. No real creation or birth occurs in the eternal, changeless, nondual reality. Since Brahman is inconceivable (*achintya*, unthinkable) and inexplicable in any worldly terms, so too is *maya* since it is Brahman (GK 4.41, 4.52).

Each phenomenal person is a character in the mayic realm. Each person is the narrative self created by *avidya*, not the ontic essence (*atman*) of them. Thus, there is no solipsism here. Any character within the "dream" is not the substance or cause of the dream itself. In fact, Advaita metaphysics is the opposite of solipsism since no individual actually exists—only the one undifferentiated consciousness does.[19] The consciousness constituting Brahman is the consciousness in a dream character, but Brahman has no connotations of a person. Instead, the only reality is a nonpersonal consciousness with no real objects of consciousness. The activity of the *jivas* is no more real than the empty activity of characters in a dream. There never was any real *jiva* in any real chain of rebirths nor any real liberation from it (GK 2.32, 3.48).

Root nescience (*avidya*) is not merely a lack of knowledge but a positive error made by the discursive mind (*manas*) that affects perception and understanding. The classic Advaita example is mistaking a rope at dusk for a snake; there is something real there (the rope), but it is misperceived. No snake was ever there (it is totally nonexistent). This is the same for our situation in the phenomenal realm. The phenomenal realm is in fact real—Brahman's radiance projected through *maya*—but we misperceive it through our *avidya* as an independent world of discrete and independent objects. *Avidya* is the source of the illusion, not *maya*. The illusion has no reality whatsoever. Nothing real is imposed on a substratum, like the rope; we merely misperceive what is really there. In this way, Gaudapada answers the question "Who has *avidya*?" by stating that Brahman deludes itself through its own *maya* (GK 2.12, 2.19). Once we see the world correctly, the world does not disappear; *maya* as a mode of Brahman is real and hence remains for the enlightened.

Enlightenment for Gaudapada is simply a matter of knowing and seeing reality correctly. The illusion that the phenomenal realm is other than Brahman and populated with multiple distinct perceivers and entities has ended. The enlightened are aware of the mayic realm but do not have the dualities set up in the mind during *avidya*-driven awareness. They see this world of apparent multiplicity and at the same time know it to be nothing but the nondual Brahman. There is no ontic change in one's state since one was Brahman all along. All that changes is that one realizes they and all the world are non-different from the unborn Brahman. The enlightened are free of desire, fear, and anger and produce no new karmic effects from their actions because they have no desires for things that they now see are illusions (GK 2.35). The enlightened see through the mayic dream and are at peace with whatever happens to the *jiva*. How can one care about what happens in a dream? Thus, one is no longer attached to what occurs. One moves in the world with apathy (*jadavat*, lifeless) (GK 2.36). One also has a state of no-mind (*a-manasta*) since the dualizing mind (*manas*) that grasped objects no longer functions (GK 3.31–32). The enlightened are "without mind" in that sense (MunU 2.1.2).

This enlightening knowledge is not simply a matter of studying the Upanishads and understanding the claim that "all is Brahman" and accept- ing it. Rather, the mind must be brought under control "with unrelenting diligence" by always remembering that everything is the unborn Brahman (GK 3.41–43). This requires practice (GK 3.43–44). Only when one is enlightened, experiencing the world as an illusory realm, and seeing that there are no other realities is the claim self-established (*svatah-siddha*) and not in need of any further proof. Merely accepting a new factual claim that the world is consciousness and free of dual realities remains a matter of the dualistic imagination.

Hence, yogic training of the mind (*manas*) is needed. It is a yoga of no-contact (*yoga-asparsha*) since there are no objects for the mind to contact (GK 3.39–43). Gaudapada stated nothing about how to practice this disci- pline, but the mind must be controlled in order to perceive that there are no sense objects or internal objects to contact. The result is a state of pure mind and concentration (*samadhi*) having sensory input in which one sees the world free of any sense of duality. However, the depth-mystical experience free of all content that is cultivated in the Yoga school is neither necessary nor sufficient for Advaita enlightenment (GK 3.39–40). That experience may even be a hindrance if one thinks it is the end state to attain, concludes that consciousness is separate from matter, or becomes attached to the bliss resulting from emptying the mind of all dualistic content. Rather, Advaita enlightenment requires direct insight into the true nature of the phenomenal realm, and that can only occur outside the depth-mystical experience.

Shankara

The Advaita position was dying when Shankara came along (fl. early eighth century CE). He took a less realistic view of the phenomenal world than Gaudapada, but his was still a more realistic view than is usually ascribed in popular books on Hinduism. In treating the phenomenal world as an illusion, he was not an ontological nihilist. He said that we can deny the existence of something only in favor of something else being real, and that reality is Brahman (BSS 3.2.22).

Like Gaudapada, Shankara affirmed that all that exists is a nonpersonal, nonintentional, featureless consciousness (Brahman). However, he rejected Gaudapada's emanationism that made the phenomenal universe a mode of Brahman. For Shankara, such an emanationism introduced diversity into Brahman. It also made the world a sort of transformation (*parinama*) of Brahman itself, but Shankara transitioned later to the view that the world only has the appearance of change (*vivarta*). From a dualistic point of view, this consciousness is the witnessing consciousness (*sakshin*) in one's mental life—Brahman is the "inner light" within us (BUB 4.3.7)—but since there is only one reality, there is nothing separate to observe and, therefore, no observer. The phenomenal world is not real (*sat*) and, thus, is not a manifestation of Brahman or an extended part of Brahman any more than the snake is part of the rope. Even thinking of Brahman as the Lord Ishvara is a misconception by the unenlightened since Brahman has no will or other personal attributes and is not a creator since nothing is created.

Thus, Shankara poses a more radical nondualism than Gaudapada: the phenomenal world is not an ontological level of Brahman. Yet, Shankara did not claim that the world is totally nonexistent. The world is not real (*sat*) since it is not the eternal and unchanging Brahman, but it also is not totally unreal (*asat*)—like the son of a barren woman or the horns of a rabbit—since we experience it (BSS 2.1.18, 2.2.26). Later, Advaitins gave the phenomenal world a degree of reality but considered it indefinable or indescribable (*anirvachaniya*). They and Westerners prefer to see Shankara's ontology as two-tiered: ultimate reality and an indeterminate reality that is neither ultimately real (*sat*) nor nonexistent (*asat*). Such an ontology is simpler and easier to visualize, but Shankara rejected the claim that the phenomenal world can be neither real (*sat*) nor unreal (*asat*) as a contradiction (BSS 2.2.33). At best, only from the unenlightened point of view can we speak of the world being both real and unreal.

A better way to look at Shankara's philosophy is not as advancing a two-tiered reality (since there is only one reality and a baseless illusion), but as advancing two perspectives: the enlightened and unenlightened points of view. He may have gotten the idea of these two points of view from Buddhism. Shankara stringently rejected any ontological dualism but had to advance an epistemic dualism to deal with what we see. For him, there are no "degrees of reality" nor is Brahman "more real" than the world; there is only Brahman. However, an epistemic or experiential dualism is possible even if there is only one reality and no ontological dualism. We can see reality from either an enlightened (*brahma-vidya*) or deluded (*avidya*) point of view—not that he had any explanation for why that dualism can exist.

Much of his most important work—his commentary on the *Brahma Sutra*—is about the individual person, Ishvara, and presents rituals from a dualistic point of view, but he denies all dualism through his non-dualistic metaphysics. From a dualistic point of view, the phenomenal world is the play (*lila*) of Brahman seen as the creator god Ishvara. This does not mean that the world is frivolous but that the world has no goal and does not fulfill any necessity or desire. He gives no further explanation, reason, or purpose for why the world appears (BSS 2.1.33); manifesting the world is just what Brahman does naturally and spontaneously without an act of will, like breathing is for us. For Shankara, the phenomenal world is not a creation or emanation in any sense of the unchanging and inactive consciousness that is Brahman. However, from a faulty, nescience-driven, dualistic point of view, we see the phenomenal world as the creation (*srishti*, emission, letting loose) of Ishvara. In the final analysis, even calling the universe the play of Brahman is wrong since seeing any sort of creation or cause and effect is the product of nescience, so there is no ultimately correct explanation for why the phenomenal world is there.

Yet, Shankara adamantly rejected the claim—which he ascribed to the Buddhist Yogacharins—that the external world does not exist (BSS 2.2.28–31). Ishvara's creation survives any individual person's enlightenment; the diverse world does not disappear for the enlightened, just as a person with an eye disease still sees two moons even though they know there is really only one (BSS 4.1.15, GKS 3.19).[20] Thus, the enlightened do not see the undifferentiated Brahman in a cosmic consciousness (as with Gaudapada, nondualist Kashmiri Shaivism, and Tantrism) but still see the illusory phenomenal realm. Thus, the enlightened are having a lucid dream: the dream still occurs as before, but the enlightened now know they are dreaming. Later Advaitins explained their continued experience of the phenomenal realm in one of three ways: enlightenment in life (*jivan-mukti*) is impossible; the enlightened overcome the perception of duality and realize Brahman only during transient periods of depth-mystical, one-pointed concentration without content (*nirvikalpa samadhi*); or the enlightened still have a trace (*lesha*) of nescience in their enlightened state.[21] Shankara may have held the second position, indicated by his claim that after enlightenment one still sees two moons in the ordinary state of consciousness; in this understanding, only one's knowledge has changed.

For Shankara, the entire illusory projection (*maya*) is only an effect of nescience—identifying the ontic essence (*atman*) with what is not real (*sat*) (GKS 1.6). All the limiting adjuncts (*upadhis*) of the conventional realm are imagined; everything is a pure, featureless consciousness. (The Bheda-Abheda traditions take the adjuncts to be real.) We only superimpose unreal ideas onto what is real (Brahman) based on memories, like superimposing the idea of a snake onto the misperceived rope.[22] That superimposition (*adhyasa*) is our basic nescience (BSS intro.).[23] The rope does not underlie or support the snake in any sense. There is no contact between what is real (*sat*) and what lacks reality.

For Shankara, the illusion arises solely from speech, which is a product of nescience (BSS 2.1.27). The very process of naming produces the idea of separate realities and diversity.[24] For Advaita, names are the domain of the mind (*manas*) and thus do not apply to Brahman. Even the words *Atman* and *Brahman* are only superimpositions on what is real (BUB 2.3.6). From the highest point of view, Brahman's true nature or form (*svarupa*) is a reality without form (*arupa*) (BSS 1.1.20, 1.3.19, 3.2.14; TUB 2.7). Nevertheless, the unenlightened need guidance toward enlightenment, so from our point of view within the realm of root nescience, we can conceive of Brahman in two forms to guide us toward realizing it(BSS 1.1.11): Brahman with attributes (*saguna*) as the god Ishvara (the highest Lord) and Brahman denying all attributes (*nirguna*). From our unenlightened dualistic point of view, we think of Brahman as a creator god, the world as a creation, superimposition as a substratum, and realization as a union with Brahman, or we think of their opposite. However, all must be rejected from the ultimate point of view. Any term can be applied to what is actually real (Brahman) only figuratively and must be qualified using "so to speak" or "as it were" (*iti*) because all terms introduce dualisms. Even the word *self* (*atman*) is qualified by "as it were" to indicate that the word does not actually apply (BUB 1.4.7). "Brahman with attributes" is not a creator god emitted from "Brahman without attributes" but a misperceiving of "Brahman without attributes" (BSS 4.3.14). Even calling that reality "Brahman without attributes" is a product of nescience—a mental image devised in contrast to "Brahman with attributes" that still makes Brahman into an object of dualistic thought.[25] Neither form of Brahman is an object of the senses (BSS 1.1.1). What is real is beyond all concepts. Thus, Advaita's standard characterizations of Brahman as reality (*sat*), consciousness (*chitta*), and bliss (*ananda*) too must be rejected in the final analysis. Even terms such as *eternal, one, unborn,* and *exist* do not apply to the nondual consciousness (GKS 3.37, 4.60–62, 4.74). Brahman is simply unspeakable (*avachya*) and inexpressible (*anirukta*) (TUB 2.7.1).

For Shankara, the revealed Vedas are the only "means to correct knowledge" (*pramana*) of Brahman, not personal experiences or reasoning (BSS 1.1.1–2). No mental act provides the liberating knowledge. No temporary experience, ritual, merit, meditation, visualization exercise, or any other action can produce knowledge (*vidya*) or knowing (*jnana*). Likewise, Shankara did not ground his doctrine of nondualism in mystical experiences. Any experiences are based on our previous experiences and ideas, so they are not reliable means to correct knowledge. Nevertheless, for him knowledge of Brahman does culminate in an experience (*anubhava*) of formless Brahman-in-itself (BSS 1.1.2).[26] Shankara said that the appeal to revealed authority (*shruti*) is necessary for correct understanding since philosophers constantly contradict each other (BSS 2.1.11). In this passage, Shankara acknowledged the objection that this is itself an instance of reasoning, but he still asserted that the Vedas, being eternal, provide the necessary true knowledge on ultimate matters. However, the Vedas are authoritative only for the unenlightened (BSS 4.1.3). The enlightened do not need any authority; all the means to correct knowledge, including the Vedas, apply only in the dream realm.

The standard of knowledge for Shankara is certainty, and certainty is only provided by the revealed texts. But Shankara realized that not all passages in the Upanishads support nonduality, and he insisted that even the Vedas needed interpretation when the literal meanings of passages did not conform to his nondualism.[27] He attempted to get around passages that clearly suggest emanated entities or other dualities by distinguishing passages of indirect meaning, which reflect the conventional dualistic point of view, from passages of direct meaning, which express nonduality (GKS 3.14). However, even passages of direct meaning must be negated in the end since nothing literal can be said of Brahman.

It is not possible to attain union or identity with Brahman. For Shankara, enlightenment is merely coming to realize what has always been the case: that there is only one reality and no separate essences (*atmans*) or independent objects.[28] Enlightenment, thus, is a matter of discriminating the real from the unreal and negating the unreal objects of nescience. Enlightening insight occurs outside the depth-mystical state of consciousness—when there is content in one's mind. One once again sees the dream realm but realizes that there is only one reality; everything is, in fact, only an undefinable dream, not real or unreal. Thus, seeing the phenomenal world is not the same as dropping out of the enlightened state of consciousness. The dream continues, but the enlightened, with their concentrated and enlightened minds in an enduring extrovertive ASC, are not deceived into thinking it is real. They see its true nature.

As for Gaudapada, knowledge of Brahman for Shankara is seeing reality non-dualistically. One may understand and accept the proposition "all is Brahman," but logical understanding is just another product of the unenlightened dualizing mind. It is not the same as realizing the actual truth of nondualism through an experiential participatory knowledge. If nescience were only a matter of a philosophical error, then we would simply have to change our beliefs. But nescience is an active cognitive error about reality ingrained in the consciousness, and removing it requires a change in consciousness. By realizing that only the dreamer exists and we are not independent characters in the dream, nothing new is gained; *avidya* and wrong knowledge (*ajnana*) are merely overcome. The illusion of multiple realities is not "removed" since it was never real and, therefore, never really there. Any yoga outside of hearing, studying, and concentrating upon (*nididhyasana*) sayings such as "You are that" (CU 6.7.8) is only of indirect value (BU 2.4.5; BSS 1.4.19). Meditation, at best, helps prepare the mind for gaining enlightening knowledge, but it remains an action. Ascetic renunciation and the path of action (*karma-yoga*) may also aid in this, but they are still actions, and actions cannot produce enlightening knowledge.

Shankara was silent on many basic issues. For example, how did diversity ever enter the pure consciousness of Brahman? How can there be even the appearance of a world? Who has *avidya*? Ramanuja pointed out that what is real (Brahman) cannot have what is not real (*avidya*) within it; pure nondual consciousness cannot be obscured by what is not real, nor can individuals (*jivas*) have it since they are a product of it.[29] So what is the locus of *avidya*? And what is its object? It cannot be what is real (Brahman) since it has no diversity, nor can it be what does not exist. Shankara gives an ambiguous answer to the question of who has *avidya*: "It belongs to you who are asking!" (BSS 4.1.3). He was content to dismiss such questions as senseless (BGS 13.2) and to stress the basic point that there is only one reality. His writings defend only that basic claim against schools that rejected it.

Perhaps Shankara thought that answering other philosophical issues would only distract students from the quest for enlightenment or present obstacles to attaining liberating knowledge by increasing the conceptual mind's activity. As Karl Potter states, Shankara, like the Buddha, apparently was more interested in teaching his pupils how to overcome nescience than discovering the proper account of the relation between Brahman, the self or selves, and the phenomenal world; he philosophizes not so much by propounding a satisfactory theory of his own as by criticizing what he saw as the inadequate theories of other schools (1963, 165). However, Shankara's two points of view lead to problems. He used arguments based on a dualistic point of view against other schools and then turned around to reject all dualistic ideas. However, using dualistic arguments gave the illusory world a reality that he never accepted. In the end, he did not overcome the dualism of Brahman and the illusory world.

Advaita after Shankara

Shankara's influence was not immediate. Until the tenth century, he was overshadowed by his older contemporary, Mandana Mishra, whose theory of *avidya* became the most accepted in Advaita. According to Mandana, the locus of nescience is the individual *jiva*, not Brahman, but Brahman is its object. Likewise, there are multiple phenomenal essences (*atmans*)— each a reflection of Brahman (BUB 4.3.7, CUB 6.3.2). But according to Shankara's students Padmapada and Sureshvara, Brahman is the only reality, so nescience must reside in it. These two competing positions became the basis for the later Bhamati and Vivarana branches of Advaita. For the former, each individual had their own *avidya*. Also, according to Mandana, gaining enlightening knowledge requires a direct experiential realization of Brahman that can only be attained through meditation; simply hearing and reflecting on the Upanishads produces only mediated knowledge within the dream, not actual knowledge of Brahman. However, according to Sureshvara, knowledge alone is directly liberating, and meditation is, at best, only a useful aid in preparing the mind for reflecting on the meaning of the Upanishads by removing obstacles. Shankara espoused the latter position. Vachaspati Mishra (ninth or tenth century CE) required yogic concentration (*samadhi*) to make Advaita knowledge immediate (*paroksha-vidya*) and, thus, enlightening. This became the standard position in Advaita.

A sixteenth-century Advaitin, Prakashananda held an even starker nondualism than Shankara's: there is only Brahman, and to call it the essence (*atman*) of any phenomenon is only a faulty, dualistic way of speaking derived from *avidya* because there are no phenomena to have essences. The world is not an indefinable (*anirvachaniya*) realm that is neither real nor unreal. The phenomenal realm has no reality, even as an illusion. It is completely nonexistent. When we wake, the dream disappears, as does the phenomenal realm. When all (nonexistent) individuals are enlightened, the illusion will disappear—unlike for Gaudapada, who saw the realm as an eternal mode of Brahman (BSS 2.2.41). He saw this as the logical consequence of the doctrine that the world only has the appearance of a transformation of Brahman (*vivarta*), but most Advaitins affirm that if nescience resides in Brahman, then the phenomenal world exists in some sense, even if only as an impermanent appearance.

This shows how far Advaita had evolved from Gaudapada's acceptance of the phenomenal realm as a part of Brahman and, thus, ultimately real. Nevertheless, most Advaitins have given the phenomenal world some reality, even if saying it is neither truly real (*sat*) nor totally unreal (*asat*) shows their difficulty in handling the world.

But before anyone overgeneralizes from Advaita to all Hindu traditions, it should be noted that—contrary to most Western opinion—Advaita was never the most popular school of philosophy or even the most popular school of Vedanta in India prior to its modern incarnation in Western-influenced forms of Neo-Vedanta. Its starkness never resonated with most Indians; its oneness of Brahman was not a problem, but its treatment of the phenomenal world and individuals was. The dualism of Samkhya thought and the Vedantic theisms of Ramanuja and the dualist Madhva were more popular. Advaita did reshape the philosophical landscape of India. After Shankara, most thinkers directly or indirectly responded to Advaita's positions, and many incorporated some Advaita ideas.

The *Bhagavad Gita*

In fact, the majority of Hindus from the classical period to today have been theists. The various deities are taken to be manifestations of the one God (usually Vishnu/Krishna or Shiva), who has the attributes of all the gods: "God is one but called different names." Likewise, they have not been followers of the philosophical schools but have instead followed less rigorous traditions and texts—in particular, the *Bhagavad Gita* (Song of the Beloved). The Gita (finalized ca. 200 CE) is the first full text of the emerging Bhagavata tradition of loving devotion to God (*bhakti*). In it, the god Krishna exhorts the disheartened warrior Arjuna to take part in an upcoming battle in which Arjuna is sure many of his relatives and teachers will be killed. He also had conflicting claims of duty (*dharma*): duties to his family versus to society at large and non-injury (*ahimsa*) versus his warrior duties.

The Gita has always been popular because it brings together many different strands of philosophical thought and grounds them in a theism. Unfortunately, in finding a place for many competing ideas, the text is not always clear or consistent on its basic ideas.[30] From the Vedic tradition, it adopted a life-affirming ethos and the need to fulfill one's duties under religious and social law (*dharma*) in order to maintain society and the world. From the Upanishads, it adopted Brahman, the idea that desire-driven action (*karman*) propels rebirth, and the idea of release from rebirths. From Samkhya, it adopted the dualism of self (*purusha*) and matter and various ontic categories. From the yogic tradition, it adopted meditative practices. All of this was placed in a theistic framework from the Bhakti tradition. Krishna is a theistic god: he is the one ultimate source of the world—and, paradoxically, the one being incarnated within it—and he remains concerned with our welfare. Whether he is ultimately personal or nonpersonal is not clear (see XIV.27 and VIII.21). Some passages suggest an indwelling panentheistic god (for example, VII.7).

One possible reconstruction of the Gita's metaphysics is that Krishna is the "highest person" (*purushottama*) who underlies Brahman (X.15, XI.4, XIII.12, XIV.3, XIV.27, XV.17–18), and out of Brahman emerge both matter (*prakriti* and its evolutes) and individual selves (*purushas*). Thus, God both transcends and sustains the world (XV.17). The liberated are united with Krishna at death, but whether there is a final plurality of individual selves or they dissolve into Krishna is not clear. However, the religious goal is a return to Krishna so that one is not reborn (IV.9–10, VI.15, VII.19, VIII.15–16, X.3). One who knows the true nature of God or the self and matter, one who is free of any desires or personal attachments, is released from the cycle of rebirths (IV.23, XIV.2, XIV.20, XV.4) and attains eternal peace in a sorrowless state (II.71).

Part of the Gita's synthesis is to affirm four paths (*margas*) or disciplines (*yogas*) leading to enlightenment: the way of knowledge (*jnana-yoga*), the way of devotion (*bhakti-yoga*), the way of actions (*karma-yoga*), and the way of meditation (*dhyana*). The way of knowledge involves the Samkhya discrimination of one's *purusha* from matter—that "I" am not the actor in "my" actions (V.8). The way of devotion involves fixing one's mind on Krishna and making offerings to him—in particular, offering all of one's actions as sacrifices (III.9, IV.23, IX.27). Lower classes and women can attain liberation this way (IX.33). The way of actions involves a renunciation, not of actions themselves but of the fruit of one's actions for oneself (II.47–53). Desire-driven action (*karman*) leads to rebirth, and detachment from personal concerns in one's actions ends desire, thereby permitting performing actions without karmic consequences. We cannot gain liberation by not acting or by renouncing actions (III.4); we should see our actions as belonging to Krishna alone. One should perform one's *dharma*-prescribed actions and rituals—for Arjuna, fighting in the war—with no personal investment in the outcome of the actions and with an even-minded detachment to good and bad personal repercussions, pleasure and pain, and without love or hate (II.56–66, VI.1). Then, one's insight (*prajna*) is firm (II.55). Those who know (*vidya*) see a Brahmin and a dog as the same (V.18). Abandoning attachment to the fruit of one's actions is Krishna's highest doctrine (XVIII.6), and performing actions with detachment is compatible with liberation. One then acts for the maintenance of the world (*loka-samgraha*). The way of meditation involves withdrawing the senses from objects and generally calming and concentrating the mind to one-pointedness (II.44, II.58, VI.10–32, VIII.12, XIII.24–25).

All paths lead to Krishna, and one should choose whichever path fits one's nature (III.3). However, the Gita does not always distinguish the different paths neatly (for example, XVIII.51–63) since all four paths involve knowledge—either of Krishna or of discrimination of the self and non-self—

and desirelessness. In addition, meditation is best when the meditative object is Krishna (VI.46–47, VII.1, XII.2), and meditation prepares the mind for knowledge. Knowledge, in turn, is necessary for the even-mindedness of the way of actions. The way of actions is a form of devotion—one's actions are dedicated to Krishna—and devotion involves concentration and proper knowledge. Nevertheless, all paths lead to the supreme secret or secret wisdom that Krishna is the supreme reality (IV.3, IX.1–3, X.1, XIV.1, XIV.19, XVIII.63–64), and he draws to himself those who know this (XVIII.65).

Bhaktism

There is a theistic strand in the Upanishads, but the idea of a fully theistic god arose only later with the Bhagavata movement. This tradition may have been responsible for the final version of the Shvetashvatara Upanishad, but it began to blossom more fully only in the seventh century CE. Here, there is a personal god or goddess who is transcendent and also immanent to the universe.

For Bhaktas, one who takes refuge in God (*sharanagati*) is liberated through unmerited grace (*prasada*). God is an all-knowing, all-powerful, and all-pervading creator and ruler who sustains the phenomenal realm and is a loving bestower of grace. They deemed Brahman with attributes (*saguna*) the ultimate reality and, early on, denied the very idea that Brahman could be without attributes (*nirguna*). God or Brahman is the substance of the phenomenal realm and individual selves; he is the inner controller (*antaryamin*) of those selves and, thus, Lord of all. Only through *bhakti* devotion or the simple, sincere act of total surrender (*prapatti*) can one make oneself worthy of grace. Grace is preceded by one's resolve to conform totally to God's will (*anukulyasya sankalpa*), one's rejection of everything that is contrary to God's purpose, and one's acceptance that they are literally nothing—have no being at all—without God.

However, Bhaktism's emphasis is on personal devotion and experiences, not theological doctrines. Experiences of a longing fervent devotion (*bhakti*) and emotional love (*prema*) are valued most, and it is safe to assume that such devotion in this framework led some to have theistic introvertive and extrovertive mystical experiences. The term *bhakti* comes from a root meaning "to serve" or "to give a part of." It carries a connotation of participating in God, and its objective is a single-minded relation (*eka-antika*) with God. (Bhaktism influenced Pure Land Buddhism and also how Christianity and Islam are practiced in India.) To Bhaktas, *bhakti* devotion is seen as the easiest—indeed, the only—path to God in this dark age (the *kali-yuga*) at the end of this world-cycle where our cognitive capacities have dimmed. Extreme devotion leads to continuously calling to mind God's attributes and experiencing the love of the deity. It can be so intense that devotees feel unable to live without the presence of God. Most Bhaktas also express hatred toward those who do not love God. Even the *Bhagavad Gita* condemns those who do not love Krishna as evil-doers (VIII.15). But some Bhaktas stressed that love of God meant treating everyone with friendship. As with other forms of Indian religiosity, teachers are vitally important here. Gurus are often seen as incarnations of a Bhakta's deity, and shrines are frequently built around their tombs. This carried over into Tantrism.

By the second century BCE, Bhagavatas were worshiping either Vasudeva or Vishnu's incarnation as Krishna as a genuinely theistic god. The sources of this theism are not fully known. There was theism in late Vedic culture, but the renouncer traditions and indigenous local cults of spirits, gods, and goddesses probably were also factors. This may also indicate a religious revolt by lower classes against oppression by Brahmins and against the renouncer traditions of Buddhism and Jainism. (Bhaktism did more to eliminate Buddhism in South India than the philosophical schools.) The *Bhagavad Gita* became the Bhaktas' principal text, but Vaishnavas also treat the Bhagavata Purana from South India as authoritative.[31] The Gita was from the north, but most early devotional literature came from the south and was composed in South Indian Tamil languages. By 200 CE, devotional vernacular poetry and hymns by Tamil poets known as Alvars praised the local god Murukan, Sanskritized as Shiva. Hymns to Vishnu and the Pancharatra texts followed. Nayanars composed hymns to Shiva.

Singing, chanting the names of the Lord, praising him, and dancing can induce a state of constant absorption in the deity. Music was important for the traveling Bhakti minstrels of Bengal: the Bauls. The Bauls, like the Sants before them, believed that God lies in our hearts and that religious institutions are obstacles, not aids, to realizing this. Sufism influenced them. They, like Tantrikas, intentionally violated rules of purity and caste. At their peak in the nineteenth century, they influenced the Bengali poet Rabindranath Tagore (1861–1941), who believed that the universe is a manifestation of God and that "true knowledge is that which perceives the unity of all things in God." The Bauls concentrated on God dwelling within the body.

In orthodox Hindu rituals of worship (*puja*), an image of God is offered fruit and flowers. (Images of the god in a temple are considered the living presence of God, not mere symbols.[32]) However, the central *bhakti* practice of fervent devotion to the one god or goddess, under any given name, is more emotional than mainline Hindu worship. Bhaktas also developed a strong sense of dependence on God and God's control of their lives. This led to intense emotional states and ecstatic experiences (*bhavas*). They also made ecstasy more central than it is in the *Bhagavad Gita*. They sought a loving participation in God and vice versa, considering it supreme blessedness. Some traditions view devotees as God's lovers, while others view them as God's servants. Liberation from rebirth is still the goal, but the resulting state is seen as one in which any sense of self is lost in an experience of self-transcending love, thereby attaining an abiding intimate communion with God as his lover or servant. Communion with the Lord ranges from visions to entering the Lord's body (*sayujya*). Marriage symbolism is common. There are brief moments of union but also moments of anguished separation (*vishlesha, viraha*). Views of the state of the permanent union with God after death differ, but the Bhakta's individuality is not usually seen as lost.

A Bhakta's life has three stages: a passionate longing with all of one's heart for the presence or awareness of God; experiences of ecstasy; and, finally, a life of service to God as his servant or lover. Renouncers founded most sects, and some Bhakti traditions have ascetic practices, but most Bhaktas are not ascetics, nor do they live apart from society. Indeed, *bhakti* devotion ended up contrasting with the renouncer traditions. First, Bhaktas value the body since the Lord is in it. They do not treat it as a prison as many renouncers do. Second, they exploit emotions and passions rather than eliminating them, resulting in supreme joy (BG 9.2). Thus, attachment to God replaces even-minded detachment, and affective experiences are valued over yogic knowledge. They do not employ experiences of empty *samadhi*. Third, God is treated as personal and present in the world, not subordinate to a nonpersonal transcendent reality. The Lord is the *bhagavad*—the "beloved" or "adored."[33] Fourth, some traditions accept that no act is necessary for liberation other than acknowledging our helplessness and need for God—a total surrender to God (*prapatti*). However, many Indians see *bhakti* as "cheap grace" and ask why God does not save everyone but only those who humbly seek refuge in him.

After the classical period (400 BCE–1000 CE), this devotional mysticism became dominant throughout India. Vaishnavas worship one of his two most important incarnations: Krishna or Rama. Shaivas worship Shiva and the goddess Shakti, either as the spouse of Shiva or as a goddess in her own right. Shiva is seen as not inactive but as the creator, sustainer, and destroyer of phenomenal realm.[34] Shaivism is generally more yogic, less emotional, and less orthopraxic than Vaishnavism. It also accepts more paradoxes; for example, Shiva is the lord of both sexual abundance and sexual abstinence, both the god of fertility and the great yogin—an ash-covered ascetic with matted hair who carries a human skull as a begging bowl. Shaivism may have arisen from wandering renouncers who lived in cremation grounds or in the forests. Siddhanta Shaiva ascetics in southern India accept a pluralistic metaphysics in which the Lord, selves, and the world are all real. Their goal is to escape the cycle of rebirths and to realize the self's likeness to Shiva (*sivatulya*), but no identity with him is possible. The third Bhakti branch is Shaktism, in which local goddesses become manifestations of the cosmic mother (*devi*). It emphasizes her cosmic power (*shakti*) for creating, maintaining, and destroying the universe. The Goddess is erotic, ferocious, and a loving mother.

Ramanuja

Yamuna from southern India (fl. tenth century CE) began incorporating elements of bhakti devotion into Vedanta, but the principal philosopher/theologian of the Bhakti movement was the Vedantin Ramanuja (fl. eleventh century CE), a high orthodox Vaishnava official from South India. He presented a theistic Vedanta and made Bhaktism acceptable to orthodox Hindus. In his initiation to a Bhakta group, his teacher whispered to him the secret of the Bhakti salvation and told him to keep it a secret or he would go to hell. Ramanuja immediately climbed to the top of one of the temple's towers and shouted the secret. When confronted by his teacher, he responded: "Certainly I know that I will go to hell, but I alone will suffer, while those who heard me now share your secret and will be saved." By this act of compassion, the teacher realized that Ramanuja was the rightful leader of the community.

Much of Ramanuja's work constitutes an attack on Shankara's claim that Brahman is undifferentiated, formless, and without attributes. He argued against this claim as "resting on a fictitious foundation of altogether hollow and vicious arguments," "incapable of being stated in definite logical alternatives," not grounded in the Vedas, incompatible with religious duties, and devised by those who are not chosen by the Supreme but whose intellects are "darkened by the impressions of beginningless sin [*papa*]" and who do not know the real import of the Upanishads or how to argue soundly (BSR intro.). Shankara's notion of nescience (*avidya*) comes under special attack (intro.); its locus can be neither Brahman, since the real cannot support the unreal, nor the individual (*jiva*), which Shankara claims is a product of *avidya*, so it cannot exist. Likewise, nescience cannot obscure the real and cannot be removed by knowledge alone. We also could not know a reality having no attributes. According to Ramanuja, all scripture proclaims Brahman to be a personal reality and the ontic essence (*atman*) of the phenomenal universe and all finite beings, so passages suggesting a qualityless Brahman must be interpreted to fit. Thus, scriptural passages on Brahman without qualities are interpreted to mean only that defiling qualities are denied for Brahman, not all qualities (BSR 1.1.32). Further, if everything in the world is an illusion, then the Vedas are also illusionary, which contradicts Shankara's claim that the Vedas validate truth. So, too, all distinctions drawn in language are illusory. Indeed, Shankara's appeal to argument, sense experience, or inference proves that differentiations are real. Thus, scripture accepts distinctions within Brahman—in particular between Brahman and individuals.

In giving a theological foundation to Bhaktism, Ramanuja amended nondualism. He adopted the Upanishads' dominant emanationism. Being a Vedantin, he affirmed Brahman as the source and substance of all reality—the Real of the real—but unlike Shankara, in adapting Bhakti devotionalism to nondualism, Ramanuja affirmed God, the world, and individuals as all fully real. Thus, he had to qualify nondualism: Brahman with attributes (God) is real, and selves and matter are its equally real emanations. Followers later labeled his position *vishishta advaita Vedanta*: "nondualism of the differentiated."[35] That is, the one Brahman exists in multiple forms: God, selves, and matter. Both the unchanging one and the changing many are real, and the Upanishads should be interpreted to give weight to each. Thus, unlike in Advaita, there are three realities: the inner controller Lord Vishnu (the highest person or Lord of lords) who is distinct from other persons, multiple finite conscious individuals (*chit*), and insentient matter (*achit*) (BSR 1.1.1, 2.3.18). All three are eternal and without cause, although material objects—including human bodies—arise and decay. Vishnu is Brahman-in-itself. God is an infinite and supreme self (*atman*), all-powerful and all-pervasive. He may become embodied in this world in pure matter to help people. Each individual self (*purusha*) is another real mode of Brahman that is equal to

God. After the enlightened die, they attain a purity equal to Brahman's (BSR 4.4.4); but in a *bheda-abheda*–type way, each self remains a distinct reality even though it is inseparable from God as God's emanation. Thus, the individuality and identity of the person is never lost in the enlightened's communion with God. "You are that" means only that Brahman underlies all selves. That is, all *atmans* are emitted from Brahman-in-itself (BSR 1.1.1). Likewise, the world is not an illusion like the snake in the rope/snake analogy but a mode of Brahman and, thus, real. *Karman* also is eternal and causes nescience and our repeated rebirths.

God is personal in form, unchanging, and both transcendent and immanent to the world. The material world and finite selves are modes of God's existence. They are the body (*sharira*) of God and dependent on God for their nature (*svarupa*), existence (*sthiti*), and activity (*pravritti*) (BGR 7.19; see also BU 3.7.7). By *body*, Ramanuja means any substance that a conscious being is capable of completely supporting and controlling for its own purposes (BSR 2.1.9). God is not embodied in the sense of being enclosed by the universe. God and the selves have a "body/inner-controller" relationship (*sharira-shariri-bhava*): the finite self is to God as the material body is to the finite self. Yet, selves remain responsible for their karmic actions.[36] In the dissolution of the universe, each being retains a subtle form while still not distinct from God's being. At the emergence of a new universe, the Lord declares, "May I be many!" and the various beings with specific names and forms emerge and constitute his body (BSR 2.3.18). Ramanuja interpreted the claim "there is no reality but Brahman" to mean only that there is no reality equal to Brahman as a source of other realities, not that there were no distinct beings or forms of matter that remain dependent on God. He interpreted scriptural passages on nonduality to mean only that everything shares one common source of being; everything other than God is a "spilling from the plenitude of his being" (*shesha*). Ramanuja also drew a distinction between God's unknowable essence (*svarupa*), which includes reality (*satya*) and knowledge (*jnana*), and his knowable powers (*vibhuti*), such as parental love (*vatsalya*), mercy, and generosity.

Unlike in Advaita, the ritual portion of the Vedas is as important for Ramanuja as the knowledge portion since the enlightened continue to worship. Actions are also necessary for becoming enlightened, not merely knowledge. Enlightened knowledge is not, as in Advaita, seeing that there is only one ontic essence to all things but seeing that individuals are dependent upon—but not identical to—God, and the world—even with all its defilements—manifests God's glory (*vibhuti*). Additionally, the consciousness always has some content: there is no empty pure consciousness. We cannot see God with either ordinary or yogic perception. God dwells in the selves but is unknown until one is liberated (*mukta*). Rebirth is ended through the knowledge that Brahman is the inner controller of individuals and matter; this knowledge is attained by God's grace when he is pleased with the performance of one's duties done only for the Lord (BSR 1.1.1).

Grace is not earned, but a devotee's devote actions are a prerequisite. However, God has an all-consuming, protective, and forgiving love (*ashrita-vatsalya-vivasha*), and out of his great compassion, God freely chooses to become available to those who acknowledge their dependence upon him. As Ramanuja put it, one who has totally surrendered has nothing to do with their salvation but leaves it in the hands of God. With liberation, the effects of past karmic actions are ended. One's life becomes a matter of studying or helping others. After death, the liberated self does not become one with God or lose its individuality but is united to God in an eternal, loving relationship.

There is tension in the idea of somehow having to put oneself in a position to earn unearnable grace. At first, Ramanuja's followers held that even *bhakti* devotion is not necessary. Only one sincere act of surrender to God is needed; only once in a lifetime is this act of submission needed. One who has truly surrendered relies totally upon God. One does not even call for God's aid when alone in a jungle on a dark night with wild animals all around and lightning flashing since devotees are not concerned with their own benefit at all. God's grace is available to anyone regardless of caste or gender if they are truly fully devoted to the Lord. (Although, Ramanuja limited *bhakti* to only the twice-born classes.) However, even surrender does not *earn* grace; no act can force it. Two schools later arose over the need for human action to receive God's grace. According to the Vadakalai of northern India, we must act in ways prescribed by scripture to receive God's grace. The Tenkalai counter that all we need to do is submit totally to God: liberation is only possible through "other-power," not any type of "self-power."

Ramanuja also added a new secret: God needs devotees' love. God is unable to bear not having it. Thus, there is a mutual dependence between God and the single-minded devotee (BGR 7.18). But Ramanuja did add "as it were" here.

Dualistic and Non-Dualistic Bhaktism

Nondualist Bhaktas assert that we are God or can become God in some sense, but dualist Bhaktas deny that. The most famous dualist (*dvaita*) is a Vaishnava from southwest India, Madhva (ca. 1199–1278). According to him, there is one independent reality—God (Vishnu/Krishna), or Brahman with attributes—and two types of realities that are dependent on him, yet genuinely distinct. These are the multiple real selves and inanimate matter, which are each distinct from each other. All are eternal. The phenomenal realm (*maya*) is the creation of a distinct reality, but it still depends upon God, as in mainstream Abrahamic theism. However, as with Ramanuja, God pervades all phenomena and is the inner controller of each self. Thus, all phenomena depend on God for their being, but, unlike for Ramanuja, they are nevertheless also distinct from him and remain so after liberation. In this pluralistic metaphysics, each phenomenon is unique, and each self is a reflection of God. (Madha interpreted *advaita* to mean "free from impurities and imperfections," not non-duality.[37]) In a type of occasionalism, God is also the underlying cause of all causes. There is no universal cosmic nescience causing an illusion as Shankara had asserted. Each individual has their own personal *avidya*. Some selves will have their nescience removed by God's grace, but some are doomed to an eternal cycle of rebirths, and some—including Shankara—are condemned to eternal damnation. Knowledge of the relation of the self to God alone is not enough to expect God's grace; *bhakti* devotion or an act of total surrender arising from that knowledge is needed. One may gain a conviction from studying and analyzing the differences between God, selves, and matter, or one may meditate (*dhyana*) continuously on the Lord based on that knowledge, but only devotion or total surrender can be the means of salvation. Liberation is a state of continually serving God, and after death, God and each self are like lovers, but each self retains its identity.

By the tenth century, Kashmiri Shaivas reacted against Buddhism by adopting Tantric practices and a nondualism of Shiva as a pure consciousness that grounds individuals, who each remain distinct. They produced their own texts (*agamas*). The Muslim Ibn Arabi influenced the Pratijna (affirmation) school, but it died out in the twelfth century when Muslims gained control of Kashmir. Unlike for Advaitins, their nondualism involves an active consciousness that creates, maintains, and destroys the universe through acts of will free (*iccha*). This creative consciousness has an inherent power (*shakti*) and self-transforms (*parinama*) to create the world. The world is real, not an illusion in any sense. In a return to Gaudapada, the universe is seen as a vibration (*spandita*) or waves of the transcendent consciousness arising spontaneously from Shiva. This also figures in Tantrism. Their goal is recognizing (*pratyabhijna*) that the self is ontologically identical to Shiva (*samarasya*). The result of this recognition is a tranquil extrovertive mystical experience of the world as a manifestation of God.

For most Bhaktas, mystical experiences involve becoming aware that one is a part of God. However, some Vaishnava and Shaiva Bhaktas also came to espouse both pure nondualism (*shudda-advaita*) and dualism while maintaining that the selves and matter are dependent upon God. Brahman both transforms into the world and, paradoxically, remains unchanged (*avikrita*). This nondualism is considered purer than Shankara's because Bhaktas see Shankara as making *maya* a force independent of Brahman. For the nondualist Vallabha (1479–1531) from northern India, *maya* is the power of Brahman that emanates real fragments of the absolute. Thus, the phenomenal world is a fragment of Brahman. Each self is a spark of Brahman and attains release through devotion but is not absorbed into God. Instead, they share the joy of his company (*nitya-lila*). The blessed perceive God in all things. Brahman without attributes (*nirguna*) is only a relatively minor aspect of Lord Krishna. For the Kashmiri Shaiva non-dualist Abhinavagupta (fl. ca. 1000 CE), we must directly experience our identity to the consciousness of Shiva. The enlightened then become equal to Shiva in powers (*shaktis*). (He also helped to develop right-handed Tantrism.) He believed that phenomenal objects exist within consciousness, so if consciousness were constantly changing, as Buddhists assert, there could be no stable continuity of objects since they are constituted by Brahman who is consciousness; memory also requires both a stable object and a stable subject.

North Indian Vaishnava Bhaktas and some lower class and outcaste Sants in the Punjab also adopted a purer nondualism with the goal of achieving a distinctionless nonduality in which the finite self disappears in God without attributes. They rejected ritual and emphasized devotional experiences, seeking a return to God by the repetition of his name. Some Sants accepted the Lord as incarnated in images in temples. The most famous Sant was Kabir (1398–1448), for whom there is one ineffable god having many names. Unlike most Bhaktas, he espoused a *nirguna*-type *bhakti*: God is free of all qualities and, thus, formless.

Sikhism arose in the Punjab region and was influenced by the Sants, especially Kabir. It combined elements of Islamic and Hindu mysticism, including Islam's condemnation of idolatry and Indian beliefs in *karman* and rebirth. Its founder Guru Nanak (1469–1539) had mystical experiences and adopted the Sufi meditation of the remembrance of God's name (*dhikr*) and Islamic anti-idolatry. His goal was to be one with God. He also practiced yoga to integrate the self with God. Hindus, Muslims, and Sikhs all claim him, but he ridiculed both Muslims and Hindus as well as any other group that excludes anyone. He exclaimed: "The Hindu says Ram is the beloved, the Turk says it's Rahim. Then they kill each other." However, this attempt at an interreligious reconciliation generated hostility from Muslims and even some Hindus.[38]

The charismatic Bengali Vaishanava Chaitanya (1486–1534) deserves mention, not least for the fact that the International Society for Krishna Consciousness (the Hare Krishnas) arose from his tradition. Initially, he had a disdain for the emotional devotion of *bhakti* worship, but he had a dramatic conversion experience when a South Indian renouncer from Madhva's tradition introduced him to a deep love for Krishna. After this, he had many ecstatic experiences and later took ascetic vows while remaining a Bhakta. He was "God-intoxicated"—dancing, singing, laughing, and weeping—with moments of ecstatic joy mixed with moments of the agony of separation (*viraha*). He accepted the possibility of liberation in this life.

Chaitanya left few writings, but his disciples characterized his doctrine as espousing a difference and non-difference between a devotee and God that cannot be understood (*achintya-bheda-abheda*). God is the source of all reality; the world and the selves are real but dependent on him for their existence. Attributeless Brahman is only the peripheral brilliance of Lord Krishna. Each self is a fragment of Lord Krishna, and our true nature is to be servants and lovers of Krishna. Chanting the names of God (*nama-japa*) revealed the power of speech: each syllable is enough to generate the power of God within a devotee. He distinguished different types of love of Krishna, with the highest being that of a woman for her lover (modeled on Krishna, his wife Radha, and the milkmaids). There is a strong erotic element here as devotees saw themselves as Krishna's female lovers while singing and dancing. In ecstasy, they forget that they are separate realities. Chaitanya also taught that God needs and enjoys this communion.

Tantrism

The last form of Indian mysticism to surface was Tantrism. Hinduism, Buddhism, and Jainism all had Tantric traditions. Left-handed Tantrism (*vama-marga*) is especially interesting in the history of mysticism for its inversion of orthodox values and rules of conduct. Desire (*kama*) and antinomian practices abhorrent to the orthodox become the means to enlightenment in overcoming all the dualities the unenlightened mind sets up. The rules of social and religious duties (*dharma*), caste, and purity were intentionally violated. But right-handed Tantrism, such as the Dalai Lama's Tibetan tradition, gives innocuous symbolic interpretations to all the extreme teachings—for example, substituting milk for alcohol and flowers for sex—and right-handed Tantrikas only practice the forbidden rituals internally in the mind.

While many Tantrikas are ascetics, this tradition's evaluation of the world is the opposite of classical ascetics' evaluation; ending rebirths is still the ultimate goal, but Tantrikas do not renounce the world, instead embracing it and cultivating the forbidden as a direct means to achieving enlightenment. Paranormal powers also become an end. Magic is cultivated to gain worldly ends. What is most distinctive about the Tantric practices is the utilization of sex for a religious end. Like Bhaktism, the Tantric path is considered the quick path to enlightenment—possibly in this lifetime, not only after eons of rebirths. (t is sometimes hard to distinguish Bhaktism from Tantrism since a person may worship a deity in multiple ways at different times, but there is less emphasis on love in Tantrism and more emphasis on worldly ends. Also, like Bhaktism, many consider it the only means to enlightenment possible in our spiritually dark age (the *kali-yuga*). It is deemed more effective than traditional forms of Indian mysticism because it works on both the mind and the body as a unit, not just on the mind, and utilizes both desire and thinking, not just thought. Everything in life is employed to gain enlightenment. This is also considered easier than the arduous work of traditional forms of yogic discipline.

Tantrism's origins are obscure, but it is hard to see it arising from Vedic sources since it is a reaction against all forms of orthodoxy—although magic does figure prominently in the Atharva Veda. It appears that early indigenous religious practices resurfaced. Goddess worship in the Indus Valley, the cult of fearsome howling female yoginis in southern India, shamanism, sorcery, and early renouncers who lived outside of society may all have contributed.

Tantrikas claim that their texts are, like the Vedas, revealed; they are revealed by Shiva, Vishnu, or the goddess (Devi, Uma, Kali, or Parvati) and are superior to the Vedas. The oldest existing Tantric texts are Buddhist, but Tantrism probably first arose as a Hindu phenomenon. Its texts appear to have been composed first in northern India in the seventh century CE; it spread to all of India and later to Southeast Asia and, through Buddhism, to Central and East Asia, where it still exists today. (Tantrikas built the temples at Angor Wat in Cambodia and Borobudur in Java.) Tantrism declined in India after the establishment of Islam in the twelfth century. By then, Tantrism had permanently shaped mainstream Hindu and Buddhist traditions, especially in the area of worship (*puja*), and had jettisoned its antinomian practices. Nevertheless, Hindu Tantrism lost its acceptability in popular and intellectual circles in the modern era as reformers tried to "purify" Hinduism. Buddhist Tantrism thrived in Tibet until the Chinese occupation, but it survives in Nepal.

Within Hinduism, there are different Vaishnava, Shaiva, and Shakta Tantric traditions. Tantrism was especially prominent among Shaivas. A goddess may stand alone without a male consort, but most Shaivas and Shaktas regard a god and goddess as inseparable, with the goddess providing the cosmic energy (*shakti*) for an otherwise lifeless male deity. The body is a microcosm of the universe's energy, and a Trantrika taps into that latent energy through the body's *kundalini* physiology. Through that energy, one attains progressively higher states of consciousness. When the energy reaches the highest *chakra*, the female energy is united with the male god.

Early Shaiva Tantric metaphysics is pluralistic: Shiva, selves, and the world are all considered separate. Nondualism later became the norm in Hindu and Buddhist Tantric traditions; the metaphysics grounding this belief for most schools is a nondualism based on a union of the male and female principles. The basic principles are personified into active gods and goddesses that unite all forces. Sexual intercourse with a consort is seen as the bodily union of the male and female principles at work in the universe. The universe works through passive and active principles coming together. So, Tantrikas conclude, we should duplicate this cosmic process in ourselves, free of any social conventions since those conventions are not part of the forces. In Hindu Tantrism, the male (Shiva) is considered passive and the female power (Shakti) active. In Buddhism, the roles are reversed: the male is active (*upaya*, means) and the female inactive (*prajna*, insight). With sexual intercourse, the cosmic duality is overcome. All sense of duality is lost. The basic union of the forces of the universe is thereby recreated in the body. However, these deities are seen as merely projections of the powerful positive and negative forces within our minds; but, then again, all objectness is only a mental creation, and deities are as real as tables and chairs. (Many also take the *kundalini* "subtle body" physiology to be imaginary as merely a mental device for focusing the mind.)

The basis of this metaphysics is that the universe is the concrete manifestation of a divine energy (*shakti*), usually personified as female, that creates and sustains the universe; the universe is seen as not an illusion but a transformation (*parinama*) of Brahman; the world emanates from this energy by vibration or by sound (*vac*); through rituals, Tantrikas seek to appropriate and channel that energy within the human body for worldly and liberating ends (Padoux 2017, 15–16). The Nathas of the Deccan region believed that the doctrine of the unity of Shiva and Shakti transcends both dualism and nondualism, but the emphasis in Tantrism is on practice and experiences, not doctrines. In dualist traditions, the means to liberation is ascetic practice (*sadhana*), while in nondualist traditions, the means is knowledge (*jnana*).

Tantric teachings were kept secret from the general population. The highest Tantric texts are encoded in a twilight language (*sandhya-bhasha*) that is made deliberately unintelligible to the uninitiated. Many of the codes are now lost. This is done both to protect the ordinary person, who may be harmed by mishandling the powerful and dangerous knowledge, and to transport the initiated into a new world of knowledge. One needs the oral teachings of a master (*guru*) to understand them. Thus, this tradition is properly labeled *esoteric*. However, the texts—including Tantric Upanishads—enabled Tantric ideas to spread from renouncers to householders, who are now its main practitioners (Padoux 2017, 59–60).

The enlightened are free from all pairs of opposites and are no longer bound by *karman*. The Tantric liberated state (*jivan-mukti*) differs from that in other Indian traditions in being much more worldly; magical powers (*siddhis*) and worldly desires (*bhuktis*) figure much more prominently. Tantric ritual practices embrace the body and sexuality. (The Bhakta Abhinavagupta claimed that he was conceived in a Tantric ritual.) Many are ascetic practitioners, while others emphasize keeping the body strong. Tantrikas may share the metaphysics of the world as a dream with Advaitins, but as noted previously, they value the world differently. We are part of the dream, so the body is not considered foul and disgusting. Instead, God is within the body, and all the pleasures of the world are to be enjoyed. Tantrikas do not differentiate manipulating the energies of the universe through magical means for worldly ends from the religious end of enlightenment. The cosmic energy of the universe is neutral—energy is energy however we choose to use it. Thus, Tantrikas have many magical formulas (*mantras*) for eliciting paranormal powers for this-worldly matters of wealth, pleasure, and power over others as well as for escaping rebirths.[39] Offerings are made to a ferocious god or goddess, but the objective for Tantrikas is to achieve a theurgic control of the deity through magic to make the god or goddess do their bidding. Mantras and rituals also transform Tantrikas into deities and concentrate the universe's energy or a god's power in their body. One may become omnipotent and omniscient like Shiva even while still in this world.

The inversion of values is not merely the common antinomian claim that the enlightened are beyond the restriction of rules and so can do anything: "to the pure everything is pure." Rather, it insists that unenlightened Tantrikas on the path to enlightenment should also practice the opposite of orthodox practices to advance their spiritual career. Thus, offerings of blood, sexual fluids, and alcohol are made to the god or goddess. What is repulsive to the orthodox becomes, to those who know how, a way to release from rebirth. It is a case of transmuting poison into medicine that can produce a healthy state.

Thus, this is a matter of utilizing the world to access the transcendent. The world itself is pure (*shuchi*, radiant); since everything is divine energy, everything is pure. Hence, there should be no restrictions or discriminations. It is only our discriminations that make things seem impure. The objective is to return to the pure mind prior to such discriminations. For this, all sense of duality must be abolished. All rules and evaluations are based on polarities and discriminations; thus, all must be broken to see the meaninglessness of our conceptualizations and to reveal what is real.

The role of gurus in initiation (*diksha*, consecration) and teaching is central to all Tantric groups. They also are said to transfer energy mentally to their students. Some Tantrikas are initiated into the mysteries by sex with special women (*dakinis*), who are said to have paranormal powers and to pass their powers to the initiated through sexual intercourse. In fact, in Hindu Tantrism, women in general are deemed more powerful than men because they are filled with power (*shakti*). There also are female Tantric renouncers.

Like Vedism, rituals are more important than renunciation, but the development of Tantric antinomian practices utilizing forbidden substances and outcaste women was a direct reaction to orthodox rituals and values. Tantrikas intentionally do everything the orthodox condemn; the more polluting, the better. They also sometimes utilize psychedelic drugs such as cannabis and datura as well as an intoxicating nectar called *amrita* (deathless). However, Tantrikas only yield to desires while devoting sustained attention to each act of desire, its causes, and its consequences; the object of desire must also be transformed into a deity. Otherwise, one is only an animal (*pashu*). Nevertheless, there is no need to destroy sexual impulses, which would be unnatural and impossible in any case. Instead, Tantrikas engage in sex only in a highly ritualized manner and not for pleasure. Indeed, Tantrikas are hyper-ritualists; although, after the classical period, *bhakti* devotion lessened the importance of rituals (Padoux 2017, 13, 53).

The central ritual, set in cremation grounds and other places considered extremely unclean by the orthodox, begins with the guru and his consort—representing Shakti—seated in the center of a circle of initiated students—representing in Buddhism a deity's *mandala*). They all then drink wine from the same cup and eat meat—preferably beef—and fish from the same plate. To make matters more disgusting, excrement, urine, blood, or vomit is mixed in with the food and wine, since these are as pure as the food. The women present may be of low class or outcastes or young girls. Adultery and incest are also suggested. If the women are menstruating, so much the better since the orthodox consider this impure. The females are then made into vehicles of the divine energy (*devis*) by means of mantras. All then take aphrodisiacs, such as parched grain, and have sexual intercourse in a ritualized way, such as mentally reciting verses during intercourse. Outside this ritual, Tantrikas have other rituals. Some may involve drugs, sex with corpses, or cannibalism. Worshipping the female sexual organ (*yoni*) is a common practice.

Tantrikas may flaunt the laws of pollution by living in graveyards or using human skulls as cups or begging bowls. Most traditions are open to all castes and genders. Most significantly, the rules of proper conduct (*dharma*), such as those against stealing and murder, are broken in a highly ritualized fashion with close attention. What is evil becomes good—that is, useful for enlightenment. Thus, the dichotomy of proper conduct and improper conduct (*adharma*) is completely broken down. *Adharma* becomes the path to enlightenment. If one is attached to a value—like labeling something as good or evil—then one has not transcended the conceptualizing mind. One must perform acts—including rape and murder—to see the emptiness of human dichotomies. A Tantrika finds enlightenment in the embrace of a young girl or with her murdered body.

As the Buddhist *Hevajra Tantra* puts it: "The world is bound by passion (*raga*), and by passion it may also be released." The Buddhist *Guhyasamaja Tantra* adds: "No one succeeds in gaining perfection by means of difficult and wearying exercise, but perfection can be easily won by satisfying all of one's desires." The universe runs on desire, and the Tantrikas are mastering desire. However, Tantrikas are not indulging a desire to burn it out by overdosing on it and, thus, becoming weary of it or revolted by it. Rather, they are harnessing and transmuting desire for a religious end. The point is to do what is prohibited precisely because it is prohibited since to abhor something is as much an attachment as valuing it. All shame, disgust, and fear must be overcome. One can then observe the desires at work and see that everything is pure in itself, free of socially defined evaluations. The very energies of the universe are at work in us, not anything evil. Thus, Tantrikas gain mastery over desires by seeing that no phenomena are more desirable than others. Hence, when they internalize the enlightening knowledge, their inner dispositions are not altered the way that most mystics' dispositions are—that is, by eliminating all desires. The enlightened no longer have the disposition of an ordinary person (*pashu*, an animal), or even a hero (*vira*), but a deity (*divya*).

Their doctrines and highly ritualized lives keep this mysticism from being an unstructured life of pure lust. Moreover, Tantrism in Hinduism and Buddhism became incorporated into mainstream mystical traditions, but one only got to the Tantric rituals after a long period of training in traditional forms of yoga, study of orthodox texts, and following the standard ethics and practices of the tradition. Once on the Tantric path, there are strict vows governing all aspects of one's life. One's daily life is a long stream of mantras, visualization meditations, and rituals. Sex is restricted to rituals and, there, strictly governed by rules. The ritual is an elaborately and carefully choreographed event. Far from being an orgy, the Tantrika soberly observes the actions going on in order to see the energies at work in reality. They must remain thoroughly detached. If they do not recognize the deity during the ritual or otherwise lose focus on observing the energies at work and become attached to the act, they have not converted the poison into medicine. Without that control, they are no more than an animal committing an impure act that will hurt them karmically. Buddhist Tantrikas bring this point home by insisting that no ejaculation of sperm may occur during the sex.

Likewise, Tantric mysticism is not a matter of fulfilling desires. Rather, Tantrikas merely expose desires for what they are. They see their abstention from the Indian codes of conduct of not killing, not eating meat, and so forth as discriminations in themselves; the codes are attachments and, thus, obstacles to enlightenment. Theirs is a matter of overcoming nescience and attachment, not desires. Suffering is caused by the nescience of seeing dualities in the phenomenal world as reflecting something real. Evaluations are not real; only the energies of the world are. Nothing real, in fact, is "unclean" or "impure," and Tantrikas see this directly through the experiences occurring within their own bodies. In short, they act on the principle of how things really are, showing no attachments or revulsions. Ritualization keeps desires from becoming new objects of attachment. Any precepts designed to lessen attachments become themselves objects of attachment.[40] Nothing distinguishes such precepts from any other objects of attachment that must be broken. Thus, a moral concern for others would tend to absolutize the realm of nescience by making persons "real." For what is wrong with stealing or killing if all phenomena are ultimately illusions?

In sum, Tantrism was a new means for the unenlightened to overcome the conceptualizing mind and its resulting attachments. Indian mysticism started by attacking attachments, but its practices—meditation, austerities, judgments of pure and impure, renouncing the world—eventually became seen new sources of attachment and deception themselves. Rules of unenlightened conduct were seen as no more than idols of the mind—more obstacles to be overcome. Desire was transformed into the means to break the hold of these attachments. Seen in this light, Tantrism is not, as is often claimed, a degeneration of the Indian traditions but simply a mystical response to absolutist understandings of a world that is without any real substance. As a reaction to earlier traditions, the Tantric approach only extends or stretches the schools—one possible meaning of the word *tantra*. In fact, this is logically the last possible position in this form of mysticism: Tantrikas do not advance a new set of evaluations but reacting with mystical detachment to there being any set of valuations at all.[41]

Modern Hinduism

A number of prominent mystics arose in India during the Hindu Renaissance of the nineteenth century that occurred in response to Western influences, pro and con. Ramakrishna (1836–1886) from Bengal is especially important. He was initially an ascetic who had a vision of the Absolute as a luminous triangle giving birth to an infinite number of worlds. He then had visions of Kali, and the Virgin Mary, and became a Vaishnava Bhakta. He adopted an Advaita framework but continued to have visions of the mother of the universe. He attained a state of objectless concentration (*nirvikalpa samadhi*) that lasted six months, during which he had to be taken care of. After that, he took up Tantric practices. The Shakta tradition and the goddess Kali were central. However, in 1866 he began practicing Islamic mysticism and chanting the name *Allah*. He had a vision of a radiant figure whom he took to be Muhammad. He next worshipped his young wife as the embodiment of the divine Mother. In 1874 he became interested in Christianity and had experiences in which he identified himself with Jesus. He took Kali, Krishna, Radha, Rama, Hanuman, Muhammad, and Jesus all as expressions of Brahman, the primal energy (*shakti*). He distinguished his visions of God (*ishvara-dharshana*) from his inner experiences of seizing God (*ishvara-labhda*). The erotic—which sometimes contained homosexual overtones—also played a major role in apparently celibate life.

Overall, both *bhakti* devotion and knowledge (*jnana*) mysticism played roles in Ramakrishna's life. He provided first-hand accounts of his own mystical experiences. Prior to him, most Indian mystical works were primarily on doctrines and yogic techniques. Commentaries on the scriptures and devotional texts were the most common types. Any available mystical experiences came from the various hagiographies of saints, where actual experiences may be hard to identify. He also taught the harmony of all religions, claiming religions are merely different rivers all flowing into the same ocean, with the ocean being best depicted in terms of a theistic God and the world as a physical emanation of God. According to him, all religions err, but it is possible to get to God through any religion, so all of them are true in the sense of being effective vehicles for experiencing God. No one path is necessary, so, despite his own history, he recommended everyone remain within their own tradition. This may have been the first Hindu cross-cultural religious pluralism, although he also criticized religions, especially Vaishnava and Christianity on sin.[42]

Ramakrishna's disciple Swami Vivekananda (1863–1902) devised Neo-Vedanta as the truth underlying all religions despite their surface differences. This he brought to the West, and it has deeply influenced Westerners' view of Hinduism. He envisioned Hinduism as a world religion rather than one tied to Indian cultural norms. For him, Hinduism is a "scientific" religion that is the "mother of all religions," and Advaita is its central philosophy and the only basis for a universal religion. Hinduism's eternal *dharma* (*santana-dharma*) also became a matter of more abstract values and virtues. All religions are lower forms of truth that are helpful for the ignorant, but all are inferior to the higher truth of Advaita's *nirguna* Brahman. The Absolute cannot be known, but its incarnations—including the Buddha and Jesus—can be. He believed all paths lead to God, but he rejected the emotionalism of Bhaktism. The Divine Mother unites the nonpersonal and personal Brahman as the immanent ground of the universe. She has two natures: as conditioned, she is God, nature, and our soul; as unconditioned, she is unknown and unknowable. His Neo-Vedanta philosophy is popular in India today among English-speaking Hindus. Unlike Ramakrishna, Vivekananda remained an Advaitin all his life, but he was influenced by modern Western secularism and individualism. He attempted to forge a modern, socially minded mysticism, unlike Ramakrishna who adhered to the traditional world-denying form of mystical Hinduism and attached little importance to reforming this world. However, late in life, Vivekananda too returned to the traditional Hindu world-rejecting mystical stance.

Mohandas Gandhi (1869–1948)—the Great Soul (*maha-atma*)—was also influenced by Western values. He combined mysticism and social action, particularly in peaceful noncooperation against the British Raj for its oppression. But his involvement in politics led to his death. He was assassinated by conservative Hindus for his acceptance of the division of the Indian subcontinent into separate Hindu and Muslim countries. Nevertheless, he is an example of a mystical way of life that valued social change. For him, God alone is real and all else is ultimately unreal. His practice of "holding fast to reality" (*satya-graha*) led to maintaining the celibate life of an ascetic. He believed that renunciation produced great spiritual power, but most aspects of Hinduism—including its rituals—did not interest him, and his concerns included trying to free the untouchables from their status in the Hindu social system. He was drawn to the teachings of Jesus (especially the Sermon on the Mount) but not Christianity after seeing how Christians treated persons of color in South Africa, where he lived for twenty-one years as a young lawyer.

Shri Aurobindo Ghose (1872–1950) too was influenced by the West, especially by the science of evolution. He had mystical experiences, including a samadhic experience while in prison for his activities to free India from British rule. This experience led him to abandon his political activities and adopt a complete life of renunciation. His doctrine of integral yoga was based in the Upanishads, the Yoga school, and Tantrism. For him, the world is fully real, and there is a cosmic mind between it and the unmanifested Brahman. Realizing this nonpersonal god "within and without" leads to the extinction of a sense of a separate phenomenal self and to knowledge of the true cosmic self. He attempted to synthesize evolution and mysticism through an emanationism: Spirit "in-volves" in the universe as the material world "evolves" as a gradual manifestation of the eternal Absolute. Through evolving levels of consciousness, the world is brought back to the Absolute. After he moved into seclusion in 1926, his collaborator Mirra Alfassa (1878–1973), known as the Mother, became the spiritual leader of his ashram in Pondicherry.

Beginning with the Theosophical Society in the nineteenth century, forms of Hinduism have influenced the West. Jiddhu Krishnamurti (1895–1986) was born in India but raised in the West to be the enlightened one of the Theosophical Society. However, he rejected this after having a series of experiences in 1922, one of which he described as a mystical union leading to immense peace. He continued to have such experiences, though he generally avoided the word *mystic* because of its negative connotations. He spoke of breaking the religious, political, and personal "images" that divide us. For him, Truth was not tied to any particular religion, meditative technique, or path. Instead, we should not seek the truth and should stop having views; then, the Truth/Reality will appear. He taught a form of mindfulness that he called *choiceless awareness* or *objectless awareness* while rejecting interest in metaphysics. Freedom consisted of a pure observation not shaped by past beliefs, intent, motives, or fear of punishment or hope of reward.

The Tamil mystic Ramana Maharishi (1879–1950) taught a pure Advaita nondualism. By meditating on the question "Who am I?" one strips away the masks of roles and personae to see that the true self is pure consciousness. For him, there is no greater mystery than the fact that we keep seeking reality when in fact we already *are* that reality. His teachings influenced New Age gurus such as Andrew Z. Cohen. Another Advaita-inspired guru, Maharishi Mahesh Yogi (1918–2008), influenced Western pop culture with a simple concentrative meditative technique called Transcendental Meditation involving short, silent mantras.

Today, Hinduism is no longer limited to India and its traditional sphere of influence but has become a world religion, and Westernized forms of Hinduism are now influencing Indian thought. Mysticism has been part of the resurgence of conservative Hindu nationalism that rejects India being a secular state. This nationalism, however, has led to bloody conflicts between Hindus, Muslims, and Christians.

Key Themes

• *Hinduism* is an umbrella term for a variety of related traditions sharing some common beliefs and practices that are given at least nominal allegiance: belief in rebirth, *karman*, and permanently escaping suffering by ending rebirths in this world (*moksha*); a general acceptance of the revealed nature of the Vedas; the authority of a guru; and practicing certain rituals.[43] (The Indian government also includes Buddhism and Jainism as "Hindu" since they arose in India.) Meditation, in one form or another, is a pan-Indian phenomenon. Mystics and mystical theorists in all the classical orthodox and heterodox traditions constantly interacted on common issues. Thus, sometimes it is hard to treat yogic mysticism separately from Buddhist mysticism, and so on within Indian mysticisms. Tantrikas reacted against central Hindu valuations.

• Sages in India in the Axial Age turned inward, not in search for one creator god as in the Abrahamic traditions but for one unifying nonpersonal reality underlying both the phenomenal realm and human mental life—something underlying all objective and subjective phenomena. In the Upanishads, that abstract principle was identified as Brahman. To be that reality, the *One* must be something that all things constituting the *many* have in common; thus, it cannot have any phenomenal features (which would be limited to only some items and not encompass everything). Brahman transcends the world, but it is also the ontic essence (*atman*) of all things, including human beings. What is real must be eternal and must also remain the same throughout all changes, both internal and external to a person. This principle cannot be directly experienced externally through mediated sense experiences, but it can be directly experienced inwardly since it also constitutes true reality.

• Appearance is distinguished from reality. What is real is eternal and unchanging, and thus whatever changes is unreal. The phenomenal world is a problem: even if we treat its being as eternal and unchanging—and thus real—it is in constant change—and thus the changing forms are not real). Treating the world as a magical trick (*maya*) only means that the phenomenal world lacks independent existence and is outwardly deceptive in character. The world still exists, but it is dependent upon, or is part of, something that is permanent and eternal (Brahman or God). Even for Shankara, there is something real (Brahman/Atman), and the world is not totally unreal (*asat*), although Advaitins claim its status is indefinable. For theists, *maya* only indicates God's power in creating the world. That Brahman underlies the world is not a pantheism—Brahman is still more than the world.

• Mysticism is at the very foundation of Hinduism. The earlier Vedism was a matter of external forms and rituals, but mysticism shifted attention to inner states of consciousness. The idea of an introvertive mysticism is central to Hindu mysticism; it entails a metaphysics of a transcendent ground that connects to either the phenomenal world or a transcendent person with an extrovertive mystical enlightened state (*purusha*). Hindu mysticism encompasses non-dualisms, dualisms of consciousness and non-sentient matter with multiple persons, personal ultimate realities, and nonpersonal ultimate realities. The world and the phenomenal individual have been seen as real creations, emanations, and less than fully real illusions.[44] Bhakti theists accommodate the world more than nondualists. This variety of introvertive mystical metaphysics—perhaps all the viable options there are—along with the vigorous debates between schools and the quantity of texts disputing other texts have led to India being called the laboratory for mysticism.[45] Such debates led to much rational analysis and argument concerning different understandings and valuations of mystical experiences and how those understandings are to be defended.

• The student/teacher relationship is central to all forms of Indian mysticism. A qualified guru is needed to explain the meaning of the texts—some of which are only summary aids or esoteric—teach meditative techniques, and show how to live.

• The mainstream position is that there is no literal union in mystical experiences. A person's ontic essence (*atman*) is already Brahman or there is a separate individual center of consciousness (*purusha*), and through these experiences, mystics become aware of that. In Samkhya Yoga, the objective is to isolate one's true essence from matter, not to unite them. In Advaita, there is only one ontic essence to everything so no second reality to unite. The most common position in the theistic traditions is that God supplies being, and there is an intimate communion with God in enlightenment, but devotees remain distinct in some sense.

• Knowledge (*vidya*), not any temporary experience (*anubhava*), is central in most traditions to attaining enlightenment. Metaphysical knowledge always has a soteriological purpose in India: casting off the basic illusion that the phenomenal world exists independently of a transcendent source and consists of multiple real objects to discover its true nature. Our nescience (*avidya*) is a misperception that veils reality; thus, enlightening knowledge is not merely an intellectual matter of adopting new factual claims but actually seeing reality as it truly is. Doing this requires yogic practices that alter one's state of consciousness.

• The goal common to these mystical traditions is securing liberation (*moksha, mukti, nirvana*) from the exhausting chain of rebirths in the phenomenal realm. Liberation is achieved through mystical knowledge or the grace of God. Social and religious dharmic requirements may be superseded. This is most commonly achieved by stilling all desires to correct one's knowledge of what is real, not aligning one's will with a god's. However, not all Hindu mysticism is dispassionate in nature, as Bhaktism and Tantrism show. Enlightenment does not ontologically change anything in one's being; but after death, the enlightened either do not reemerge from Brahman, become isolated as with Samkhya Yoga and Jainism, or—in most theistic systems—remain distinct but have some communion with God.

• Detachment and even-mindedness toward changes in the world are the central attitudes in most enlightened ways of living. These can be adapted to any way of life, including fighting a war, as in the *Bhagavad Gita*.

• A theistic god is central to Bhaktism and Tantrism, but a god does not play a role in all forms of Hindu mysticism. Rather, a nonpersonal reality—Brahman—is deemed more fundamental in Advaita, and a theistic creator god is not essential to the Yoga and Samkhya schools. In the theistic and Tantric schools, the role of female cosmic power (*shakti*) as equal or superior to male power is noteworthy.

• As in the Abrahamic traditions, mystics rely on the basic scriptural texts of their traditions to provide the correct knowledge. The standard for knowledge is certainty, and only revealed texts provide that. Mystics do not see themselves as innovators but, rather, as commentators on the basic scriptures or as supplying supplemental treatises. However, mystics interpret the texts to fit their metaphysics and have different ideas of what constitutes liberating knowledge. The Vedantins Shankara, Ramanuja, and Madhva are examples of mystics who sometimes had to twist the plain meaning of some Upanishadic passages to make the texts say what they wanted them to say. Since the doctrines in the Upanishads are not all consistent with each other, Vedantins picked passages they felt were key and explained away the conflicting passages. This shows how a text taken by all as divine and absolute can still lead to different understandings and competing traditions.

Chapter 8

Indian and Tibetan Buddhist Mysticism

Hinduism presents a variety of depth mysticisms that focus on introvertive mystical experiences and different theories of transcendental realities, but in this environment of depth mysticisms, a mystical tradition arose that shifted the focus to an extrovertive mysticism of the nature of the phenomenal world and persons: Buddhism.[1] This tradition did not turn away from the phenomenal world but emphasized one type of extrovertive mystical experience—mindfulness—although introvertive mystical experiences came to hold an important place in Buddhist history. Buddhism started as a mystical path, and meditation and mystical experiences have informed Buddhism throughout its history, but like all religions, it also developed non-mystical practices and forms of religiosity.

The Buddha

The Buddha—the one who has awakened (*budh*)—was born Siddhartha Gautama to one of the ruling families of the Shakya clan in Northeast or Central India.[2] (His traditional dates are 563–483 BCE, but scholars believe that he lived about a hundred years closer to the present.) After witnessing sickness, old age, and death, he left his comfortable life in a quest to avoid the suffering (*duhkha*) inherent in simply being alive. He thought within the Indian framework of *karman* and a cycle of births and deaths (*samsara*), and his quest was to escape that cycle. He became a wandering renouncer and trained with two teachers, under whom he attained certain states of introvertive concentration (*dhyanas*) to still his perceptions and feelings.

However, he realized that these states of consciousness are only temporary and that he would return to the same problems once he returned to ordinary consciousness. Thus, these experiences were not a permanent answer to the problem of suffering. He practiced extreme asceticism for years but found that it only weakened his body and made it hard to concentrate (MN I.160–75, I.237–51).[3]

Finally, after six years of searching, Siddhartha sat down under a tree near Bodhgaya in modern Bihar and resolved not to leave until he had a solution. That night, he entered different introvertive states of concentration (the first four *dhyana* states). The knowledge (*jnana*) he attained in concentrative absorption (*dhyana*) was not the enlightening gnosis (*prajna*, insight), but concentrative meditation was necessary to prepare the Buddha's mind for insight into the nature of things. With his mind calmed and focused by this inward turn, he had visions of thousands of his past lives. He saw the world as clearly as though reflected in a spotless mirror and saw that it was free of selves. He also saw that rebirths arose through causes and conditions (nescience and desire) and were connected and determined by karmic deeds. By dawn, he had become tranquil, free of the taints (*asravas*) of desire, craving for existence, and nescience. He had realized the answer he sought: all existential suffering results from desires that arise from misperceiving the nature of the world and ourselves as permanent and inherently pleasurable, and this can be corrected only by being mindful of the events and states of mind occurring in the present. In short, by seeing the world properly, desire ends and, thereby, *karman* and rebirth also end. He was hesitant to teach because he felt that no one would understand his message, but after a god convinced him to do so for the benefit of those who would understand, he spent the next forty-five years teaching his doctrine of the path to "further shore" of peacefulness. He taught throughout the Ganges region to anyone regardless of class, rank, or gender. His final words were: "All constructed things are open to decay—strive with mindfulness!" (DN II.156).

The suffering (*duhkha*) that concerned the Buddha does not mean that all experiences are painful—there are indeed pleasures and joys in this life—but even pleasurable experiences are transitory. Since we are reborn indefinitely, even the happiest of lives are only transient and are ultimately frustrating and disappointing. Such dissatisfaction is ingrained in the very fabric of any life. It is this inherent, existential dis-ease in our lives that needs a cure. The only way to end it completely is to get out of the chain of rebirth that keeps us in the realm of suffering, and the Buddha offered the way out.

The Buddha analyzed the problem into four noble truths, formulated in parallel to ancient Indian medical practices: (1) The disease is diagnosed: the existential suffering entailed by merely being alive (illness and other physical pains, aging, dying); (2) Its cause is identified: desire (*trishna*, thirst) driven by misperceptions of reality drives karmic actions and, thereby, rebirth; (3) The cure is indicated: ending desire; and (4) A treatment is prescribed: the noble eightfold path that ends desires.

The path is divided into three areas: insight (*prajna*), or right understanding and resolve; right conduct (*shila*), or right speech, action, and livelihood; and right mental discipline (*samadhi*), or right effort to eliminate unwholesome states of mind and cultivate wholesome (*kushala*) ones, mindfulness, and concentration (*dhyana*) (MN I.301).[4] *Right* (*samyag-*) means more than "correct"; it means "complete," "pure," or "perfect." The path contains both a factual component and an evaluative component, thus prescribing an analysis of reality and a course of conduct to achieve the goal. All the components are to be developed concurrently in an encompassing way of life. Right conduct alters the unproductive dispositions driving one's actions, while meditation works on the deeper levels of the mind, and insight works on the cognitive structures that inform the other two. Thus, there is an interplay between philosophy and practices; the doctrines present a picture of reality that makes desirelessness plausible, and action implements them.[5]

Internalizing these teachings through meditation and conduct results in a state of consciousness in which nescience and desires have ended: *nirvana*.[6] With the desires that drive rebirth ended, rebirth is terminated, and the quest to end suffering is completed. One may become enlightened in this life. Persons in such a state are able to live out this life free of existential suffering.[7] They act without producing any new karmic effects and will have their final release (*parinirvana*) upon death, when all of their pre-enlightened *karman* has finally worked itself out.

Because the Buddha's concern is only with ending suffering, many philosophical questions are dismissed unanswered (MN I.140, II.122, IV.431; SN IV.419), just as when a person is shot with a poisoned arrow they want an antidote and not answers about who made the arrow, its composition, and so forth (MN I.426). Thus, the Buddha did not discuss whether a transcendent source or other reality exists, both because it did not matter for his existential concerns and because any answer would create a new mental image to which we could become attached and, thus, would be a hindrance to the quest. He responded to the assertions of various competing views simply, "I do not hold that view." Likewise, any term referring to phenomena does not apply (*na upeti*) to what occurs to the enlightened after death (MN I.486) since after death the enlightened do not have any of the fundamental elements (*dharmas*) constituting the phenomenal world, and the terms *exist* and *do not exist* apply only to phenomena with those elements.

Early Buddhist Beliefs

The Buddha set forth an analysis of the phenomenal world in terms of impermanence.[8] According to this analysis, our suffering results from misperceiving the nature of the world: we cut the world up into distinct entities that we treat as permanent and able to satisfy us, and we attempt to manipulate the rest of the world for the advantage of what we take to be a separate, fixed, and eternal self (*atman*). But since reality is not so constituted, we inevitably suffer. In the Nikaya texts, the no-self doctrine (*anatman*) was not extended beyond persons to other phenomena.[9] Entities constructed of parts were simply considered impermanent (*anitya*). Everything is transitory and conditioned by other things; only *nirvana* and space (*akasha*) are not constructed (*asamskrita*) by any other event and, hence, permanent. Everything arises through this conditionality called *dependent co-arising* (*pratitya-samutpada*). The general formula follows: "Dependent upon *x*, *y* arises; without *x*, *y* does not arise" (SN II.28). There is also a twelve-step scheme related specifically to persons that shows how our nescience is the base condition upon which desire (craving and clutching) depends and how desire leads to future rebirths.[10] Thus, if we uproot this error, the entire process of rebirth collapses. No further effort is needed since it is the nature of things (*dharmata*) that a person who knows and sees reality as it truly is becomes free of craving (AN V.313).

Root nescience (*avidya*) is mistaking what is intrinsically impermanent as permanent, what can only bring suffering as pleasurable, what is repulsive as fair, and what is without a self as having a self (AN IV.52). Nescience is not merely a lack of knowledge but an active error that distorts how we see things and how we think. Of greatest importance is the absence of any experienced essence to a person; no permanent self (*atman*) underlying our transient experiences is ever experienced. We have a deep-seated prejudice in favor a self, but when we examine our experiences, we observe the constantly changing material form, feelings, perceptions, dispositions, and consciousness (the five *skandhas*) that we associate with a person; we never experience a permanent, unchanging observer.[11] Thus, Buddhists see no reason to posit a permanent and unaffectable core, or a self. Rather than a self, there is a connected stream of transitory and conditioned elements (*dharmas*) in the continuous cycling of rebirths. If we think of the person's life as a string of beads, the person is the beads—the momentary mental and physical events—but there is no string. When the person is reborn, there is no soul that passes to a new body but only a karmic residue from the present and past lives that conditions what comes later. Each person is a stable, functioning whole made of changing parts like a chariot: the parts are real but impermanent, and there is no "chariot" in addition to the parts (*Questions of King Milinda* 27–28).[12] In sum, denial of a self does not mean that the person does not exist but only that there is no permanent subject or other entity that exists in addition to the rest of the flux of elements that has experiences: the mental events occur, just without a central monitor or actor.

Thus, if we ask "Who is enlightened?" or "Who has insight?" we are already off on the wrong track. There is only a subjectless, constantly changing consciousness.[13] A person becomes no longer a *who* but a *what*—a collection of impermanent physical and mental elements. Thus, terms such as *self* and *rebirth* do not refer to any entity. Nevertheless, this is not nihilism. There is an impermanent whirl of reality behind conventional concepts; and, in principle, occurrences can be restated in terms that more accurately reflect what is real—a stream of conditioned elements. For example, conventionally saying that "an enlightened person is not reborn" is better stated as "a stream of selfless elements ends." We can still accept selves and chariots as conventionally real—a convenient shorthand like treating the world as flat for road maps—but in the ultimately correct ontology, they do not exist, and their parts are impermanent.[14]

In basic Buddhist ontology, the interconnection of things is not between distinct entities. Such entities are only abstractions from the flow of interdependent phenomena; there are no external relationships of distinct entities, only the conditioned flow. However, this ontology is realist in the commonsense meaning of the term. Buddhists deny that there are independent entities separated off from a subject and from each other, but they affirm that there is a "reality as it truly is" (*yathabhutam*) independent of these false discriminations: the fundamental components of our experienced world (the impermanent *dharmas*). Right views are based on seeing things as impermanent, selfless, and leading inevitably to suffering (DN II.311). This understanding is a direct reaction against the three characteristics of the world set forth in the Upanishads, though Buddhism remains silent on whether there is any unexperienced transcendent reality such as a creator god or Brahman. The world is impermanent, not permanent (*sat*, real); it is suffering, not blissful; there is no permanent essence (*atman*) in each person's makeup other than a transcendent ontic essence.[15]

By experiencing the world and ourselves in the prescribed manner, we see persons and objects as no more than the flux of rising and falling impermanent elements conditioned by other impermanent elements, and we overcome the egocentric attitude that gives rise to the craving that generates a new rebirth. Thus, our fundamental misalignment with reality is a matter of cognition, not will. *Nirvana* results from liberating insight (*prajna*) based on experiencing the impermanent nature of the phenomenal world. No accumulation of merit, no meditative experience, no action, no ritual, and no discursive knowledge (*jnana*) can force the transformation of one's cognitive state needed to end suffering. The conceit "I am" is uprooted only by insight (SN III.83–84).

Thus, in early Buddhism, *nirvana* is not a thing, place, or transcendent reality that can be attained or gone to. There is no destruction of the self since there is no self to destroy. Rather, *nirvana* is simply the state of a person in which the fires of hatred, greed, and delusion are extinguished (AN I.38, SN III.251). The alleged self does not go anywhere since it is not real—it vanishes just as a flame vanishes when a fire is extinguished. With nescience ended, desire and karmic actions end. Thereby, the process of rebirth ends, and "the stopping of becoming is *nirvana*" (SN II.117). *Nirvana* is described in negative terms to contrast with the normal state of consciousness, but it is a positive extrovertive mystical state of consciousness. Nirvanized persons (Pali, *nibbuto*) have internalized a way of seeing that is informed by the Buddhist doctrines about reality; they understand that there is nothing real—nothing permanent and nothing independent of other things—to crave, and there is no self-enclosed "person" around which to orient their lives. The enlightened still have sense experiences and can still use language and reasoning, but—in their enduring state of mindfulness free of a sense of self—they see the factors of the experienced world (the *dharmas*) as they really are: free of any permanence or self-existence. To prepare the mind for enlightenment, the Buddhist cultivates the introvertive states of concentrative meditation (*dhyana*) that destroy all mental taints. The mind then becomes quiet and focused. However, the actual enlightening insight occurs outside the introvertive states in an extrovertive state of consciousness that is free of taints and reflects reality as it truly is.

Thus, as with the Upanishads, enlightenment is not a matter of simply hearing and understanding a doctrine. Merely understanding the three marks of reality—that everything is impermanent, that there is no eternal self, and that everything is ultimately unsatisfying—is not difficult; these claims are reasonable enough. Rather, to achieve enlightenment, it is necessary to change one's way of experiencing the world. The persistent sense of permanence among inner and outer phenomena must be eliminated from one's consciousness. Mindfulness alone is not enlightenment; one must be completely free of a sense of self, and the metaphysics of impermanence must be internalized. With this perspective fully internalized, one directly experiences all things—including oneself—as impermanent and conditioned by other things. In the Buddhist analogy, this is the difference between intellectually accepting the idea that water quenches thirst and actually drinking water (SN II.115). It is no longer a matter of dualistic understanding but immediate knowledge. Additionally, the mystical awakening that occurs when one sees reality without a sense of self or self-contained parts alters the consciousness from its normal ego-driven state. Conversely, enlightenment can be lost: not by forgetting a claim about reality but by losing a state of consciousness.[16] If no ASC were involved, one could simply be reminded of the Buddhist doctrine, and one would again be enlightened.

Early Buddhist Meditative Practices

To gain enlightenment, the Buddha presented a middle path between ascetic austerity and indulgence. Meditation is central, especially mindfulness (*smriti*): a practice free of goals, desires, or aversions in which one observes whatever occurs in one's mind without controlling or judging.[17] This results in bare awareness: a direct perception (*pratyaksha*) of whatever is presented to the senses, free of conceptualizations (*kalpanas*).[18] Buddhists characterize this as "emptying the mind" or switching from a conceptualizing mind to a non-conceptualizing "shining consciousness" that mirrors what is presented to it (AN I.8–10). Later manuals such as Buddhaghosa's *Path of Purification* (*Visuddhimagga*) from the fifth century CE—but based on earlier oral traditions—standardized the various meditative techniques for ending mental taints and inducing mindfulness and various introvertive states.

There are two types of meditative cultivation (*bhavana*, causing to become): introvertive cultivation of concentration that is achieved by calming and stabilizing the mind (*shamatha*), leading to one-pointedness (*ekagrata*) in concentrated awareness (*samadhi*); and cultivation of mindfulness (*smriti*, *vipashyana*) that is tied directly to the insight (*prajna*) constituting enlightenment. A certain level of concentration and mental stability are necessary to gain the enlightening insight, but it is this insight meditation that applies the Buddhist analysis to reality. This is what eradicates the latent mental taints (*asravas*, *kleshes*) and the mental impressions (*samskaras*) produced by root-nescience that are embedded in the mind.

The four domains of mindfulness are the body, sensations and feelings, the mind, and the categories of the Buddhist teachings (MN I.10). Mindfulness exercises include observing one's breath—rather than trying to control it, as in the Yoga school—which is described as the "complete method for attaining *nirvana*" (SN V.326). However, mindfulness is applied to all of one's activities, including sitting, standing, lying down, walking, eating, and working. The enlightened person is receptive to what occurs in both their mind and the sensed world, and they see that there is nothing real—permanent—in the world to desire or fear. Likewise, there is nothing real in the individual to enhance. They rest content with the present moment and do not grieve the past or plan for the future (SN I.10). Yet, the enlightened mind still has concepts since the enlightened speak and have memories; their awareness is not free of all structure, and they can employ language to help guide others to enlightenment.[19] However, in their mindful state, the enlightened have no sense of discrete, self-enclosed realities corresponding to those concepts. The enlightened mind does not project concepts onto what is experienced as reified, distinct objects.

The nine stages of meditative concentration (*dhyana*) are divided into three groups according the three realms (*dhatus*) of the cosmos: the world of desire (*kama*), the realm of form (*rupa*), and the formless (*arupa*) realm. Concentrative meditation begins with discursive thought, but all conceptualizations cease with the second stage of *dhyana*. Tranquility replaces joy in the third and fourth stages. The lower stages are supported by an inner image, while the higher ones are without such support. The higher stages—those without form (*arupa*)—are not necessary to stabilize and calm the mind for the liberating insight. Once the mind is cleansed of all latent mental taints, the higher levels result from various degrees of the cessation of thought brought about by samadhic concentration. These lead to depth-mystical experiences devoid of conceptual content. Paranormal powers can also be gained in the higher stages—for example, creating multiple apparitional bodies, hearing things at a great distance, reading the minds of others, and remembering past lives.

Different realms are accessed through different stages of consciousness. On the night of his enlightenment, the Buddha through meditation accessed the highest heaven in the realm of form through meditation. Higher meditations on boundless space, boundless consciousness, nothingness, and the idea of "neither perception nor nonperception" relate to introvertive mystical cognition. The highest form of concentrative meditation results in a state where perceptions, feelings, and dualistic consciousness cease. It predates Buddhism and was practiced by the Buddha in his ascetic stage. The specific stages probably are pre-Buddhist and later fell out of favor in Buddhism, but concentrative meditation remained a complement to insight meditation.

Thus, Buddhism has roles for both extrovertive mystical experiences and introvertive ones in its soteriological scheme, but the extrovertive insight is valued over introvertive experiences for insight into reality. However, the focus of insight meditation is paying attention to what is presented to the mind. The pure awareness of depth-mystical experiences plays, at best, a limited role in temporarily breaking mental habits or otherwise preparing the mind, but Nikaya schools do not draw any metaphysical conclusions from the experiences.

One begins the quest to end suffering with an analytic meditation (*vichaya*), which requires studying and reflecting on what one has heard to clear up doubts and focus the mind. There are practices, such as focusing on the foulness of the human body, and visualization exercises, such as visualizing cemeteries or the world filled with skeletons or decaying corpses, to ingrain the fact that all people are destined to die. Four introvertive divine abodes (*brahma-viharas*) are practiced: loving kindness or friendliness (*maitri*), compassion (*karuna*), sympathetic joy (*mudita*), and even-mindedness (*upeksha*). The development of each attitude ends with each being radiated outward in all directions to all sentient beings. They are not part of the eightfold path but are auxiliary meditative exercises.[20] They are also practiced in the enlightened state. Their focus is not on moral actions but on a meditator's own state of consciousness. The express objective of these exercises is counteracting the practitioner's negative emotional states: friendliness is to be practiced by the ill-willed, compassion by those with evil thoughts, sympathetic joy by those who are jealous of others, and even-mindedness by those who lust. That is, their purpose is to conquer a meditator's unwholesome (*akushala*) states of mind and to replace them with ones that lead the meditator toward *nirvana*. Bliss is associated more with the introvertive absorptions than mindfulness, and the bliss of the *dhyanas* is replaced with a calm equanimity in the enlightened extrovertive state.

The Theravadins list seven factors of awakening (*bodhyangas*): basic mindfulness; the intellectual investigation (*vichaya*) of the mental states presented in the mindful state; energy or effort in cultivating those mental states; an ecstasy (*priti*) pervading one's being; a more subtle happiness (*prashabdhi*) as the ecstasy fades; continuous inner concentration (*samadhi*) resulting in introvertive, lucid absorptions (*dhyanas*); and the resulting state of tranquility and even-mindedness (*upekasha*). The enlightened state, like reality as it truly is, is depicted as indescribable. Enlightening knowledge may be depicted as a clear light or luminous.

Nikaya Schools and Abhidharma

Sometime after the Buddha's death, a council was held to standardize his teachings. The discourses (*sutras*) recorded in the Theravada canon resulted, and they are the closest we have to the Buddha's actual teachings. Buddhism developed monasteries before Hinduism did, and the rules governing the monastic life are also recorded, but different schools have variations since the rules were not set at the time of the Buddha's death. The early schools can be called *Nikaya* because they accepted only three "baskets" (*nikayas*) of scrolls: the Buddha's addresses (*sutras*), the monastic order rules (the Vinaya), and the Abhidharma commentaries. The first major split developed over differences in the Vinaya, not doctrines; the Mahasanghikas wanted to ignore minor rules and accused the Elders (*theras*) of adding more.

Four Nikaya schools deserve mention for their doctrines: the Mahasangha, Theravada (Sanskrit, Sthaviravada), Sarvastivada, and Pudgalavada. The Mahasanghikas arose out of a later council. They claimed to be the larger community of monks—the "great *sangha*," in contrast to the Elders—and to represent the majority of the laity. Their texts were mostly destroyed later by invading Muslims, but one of their doctrines, which claimed the Buddha was an eternal transcendent being (*lokottara*, beyond the world), became important for the Mahayanists. The other Nikaya schools treated the Buddha as only a human being, but probably most of the laity from the beginning saw him as supernatural. The Mahasanghikas also discussed the Buddha's prior career as a Bodhisattva, as related in the *Jataka Tales*. The Elders split into various schools, of which only the Theravada of South India survives, existing today in Sri Lanka and Southeast Asia. They emphasize analyzing the irreducible factors of the experienced world (the *dharmas*) and meditating upon them. They maintain that there is only one Bodhisattva today: Maitreya. Another branch of the Elders, the Sarvastivada, existed in Northwest India and spread into China. Its defining doctrine was that while the *dharmas* are impermanent, they are not momentary but exist both before and after the present. Hence, "all exist" (*sarva-asti*).[21] This, they believed, explained memories and the continuity of past karmic actions with their effects. Sarvastivadins also argued that the Buddha continued to exist after death: How else could Buddhists continue to go to him as a refuge? This influenced the Mahayana. Their doctrine of the six perfections was adopted in the Perfection of Insight texts. The Pudgalavadins maintained that there is a subject or person (*pudgala*) that exists as a reality perceptible only to the Buddha. This person is not an eternal self that is separate from the factors of an individual. Rather, it underlies those factors and is neither identical to nor distinct from them, like fire is to its fuel. This being provides the connection of rebirths, enables past karmic actions to bear fruit in the future, and is the vehicle for entering *nirvana*.

Theorists in the Nikaya traditions produced texts embodying a systematic reflection on the doctrines contained in the discourses: the Abhidharma literature.[22] Abhidharmists analyzed experiences to reveal the real ultimate elements of the experienced world (the *dharmas*) and sorted them into numerous categories—the Theravadins had eighty-two, the Sarvastivadins seventy-five—most dealing with different mental factors.[23] They believed that the ultimate reality of the experienced world, the *dharmas* revealed by clear analytical thinking, can be directly experienced in higher meditative states. The *dharmas* each have a unique defining characteristic: a self-nature (*svabhava*).[24] Constructed entities (*samskritas*) are not ultimately real; they are composed of *dharmas* but are not themselves *dharmas*. However, we erroneously treat impermanent, constructed things as abiding realities, and this leads to attachment and suffering. Abhidharmists also introduced the distinction between truths about reality as it truly is (*paramartha-satyas*) and conventional truths about constructed entities and appearances (*samvriti-satyas*). This analysis, they believed, leads to insight about the absence of any personal abiding self (*atman*) and, thus, leads to the end of nescience and desire.

The Abhidharmists' approach led to two reactions. First, one branch of the Sarvastivadins—the Sautrantikas—reacted by rejecting all later commentaries and treatises on the Buddha's discourses (its name means "ending with the *sutras*"). Sautrantikas also rejected the general Sarvastivadins' doctrine of *dharmas* lasting both before and after the present. For them, *dharmas* are only momentary, but karmic actions plant seeds (*bijas*) that sprout later. Second, in the Perfection of Insight texts, the budding Mahayana tradition emphasized that the *dharmas* are empty (*shunya*) of any self-existence (*svabhava*); this was a direct reaction to Abhidharmists analyzing numerous categories of the ultimate elements of reality. To them, the Abhidharmists' obsession seemed to plant conceptions more firmly in the mind.

Mahayana

A few hundred years after the death of the Buddha, a different form of mysticism rose to the surface in Buddhism. Older meditative practices remained employed, with a few new ones added—such as visualization of deities—but a different ethos and different beliefs informed the new mysticism. Some monks began to criticize the Nikaya schools, claiming their concern for only the individual's own spiritual advancement was Hinayana (the Small Way). They advocated instead a Great Way—the Mahayana—that embraced the ideal of the Bodhisattva. Enlightened Bodhisattvas remain in the cycle of rebirths to help others, unlike enlightened Nikaya disciples (the Arhats).[25] The earliest literature are the Perfection of Insight (*Prajna-paramita*) texts and the *Lotus Sutra*, both circa 100 BCE to 100 CE.[26]

For Mahayanists, the objective was still to end one's own suffering by attaining *nirvana*, but two new concerns supplemented this: to end others' suffering by helping them attain release from rebirth and to attain the full wisdom (*bodhi*) of a Buddha. Thus, they made the great vow of a Bodhisattva (one whose being is wisdom), swearing that they will help others attain enlightenment through many lives. The standard fourfold version is:

However innumerable sentient beings are, I vow to save them;
However inexhaustible the binding passions are, I vow to
  extinguish them;

However immeasurable the Buddha's *Dharma* is, I vow to
    master it;
However unsurpassable the Buddha-way is, I vow to attain it.

Bodhisattvas commence their careers with the sincere determination to attain Buddha-wisdom during meditation for the sake of all sentient beings (the *bodhichitta*). "Saving beings" means that a Bodhisattva sets beings on a path to the end of rebirths. Bodhisattvas realize that even though in the correct ontological analysis there are no unenlightened beings, nor any enlightened ones, there are realities who can be helped—streams of selfless, conditioned elements.

The six basic Mahayana virtues to be perfected are: giving (*dana*), proper conduct (*shila*), patience (*kshanti*), vigor (*virya*), concentrative meditation (*dhyana*), and insight (*prajna*).[27] Giving includes material gifts, such as food to the poor and medicine to the sick, as well as teaching and giving guidance to individuals or groups. Giving and proper conduct are the main sources of the laity's merit (*punya*) for better rebirths. Patience is the forbearance of one's own suffering, forgiveness of others for the harm they do us, tolerance of others' actions, and confidence (*shradda*) in the efficacy of the Buddhist teachings and one's teacher. One accepts harm done by others without anger or resentment, knowing that we are only suffering the karmic consequences of our own past deeds and that there is no reality being harmed or harming us. Patience produces merit, while its opposites—impatience, resentment, and anger—destroy merit. Vigor is energy and courage, sustaining the quest to benefit others and attain a Buddha's wisdom. Meditation involves both focusing attention and mastering mindfulness. Thus, both practices designed for stabilizing and calming the mind (*shamatha*) and practices designed for insight meditation (*vipashyana*) are involved. Compassion (*karuna*) is notable by its absence from the list of virtues, but it is the master value affecting each virtue.[28]

Bodhisattvas initially have the desire (*chanda*) for a Buddha's full wisdom (*bodhi*) and the salvation of all sentient beings, but when their insight is perfected, they are free of all desires. Now free of any sense of self, their practice of the other virtues is also perfected. All sense of self and other are gone, yet they carry on, even-mindedly helping all. Having perfected *dhyana*, they are permanently in a tranquil, concentrative meditative state, even while teaching or otherwise helping others. Thus, by practicing the virtues, Bodhisattvas both help others and advance themselves.

Different schools delineate different stages (*bhumis*) that Bodhisattvas advance through. They first become enlightened—attain *nirvana*—but they forgo their own private postmortem release (*parinirvana*) so that they may be reborn again and again in the realm of suffering to save other beings and attain the complete and perfect wisdom (*bodhi*) of a full Buddha that transcends all dualities. Bodhisattvas who have attained *nirvana* do not have the mental taints caused by hatred, greed, and delusions. They have attained the tranquility, concentration, and even-mindedness of a nirvanized state of mind.[29] Bodhisattvas see that their insight is to a fully enlightened Buddha's what a grain of sand is to the earth, but they elect to persevere (APP 304). Moreover, while they could remain delighting in the bliss of the blessed rest free from rebirths, as Arhats do, they would still bear in mind all suffering beings. This reaction is totally at variance with the value system of the Nikaya schools; for those schools, practitioners should not forgo their own escape from rebirths to help others.

Freed from existential suffering themselves, Bodhisattvas remain in the realm of suffering for countless eons, focused on helping others. In the earliest strata of the Perfection of Insight texts, they help by setting beings on one of three paths to the end of suffering—that of a Buddha, a solitary Buddha who does not teach others (*pratyeka-buddha*), or an Arhat—and mature them by means of positive acts, such as examples of selfless action, once they are on the paths. The *Lotus Sutra* claims there is only one path, the Bodhisattva's, and teaching the other paths was only an instance of the Buddha's skillful means (*upaya-kaushalya*) for leading his disciples to the true path. As part of their skillful means, enlightened Bodhisattvas could even violate various precepts when compassion requires it. Such violations are alien to Nikayas, where the codes of ethic serve only one's own self-development. Since the violations are only in order to help others, they do not make the Mahayanists immoral; such violations may be called *antinomian*, but they are done only for moral purposes.

The Mahayana movement may have begun as a way for monks and nuns living outside of monasteries to justify their practices, but the results were practices that helped the laity and not just themselves. A person did not need to be a monastic to become enlightened. The enlightened layman Vimalakirti is considered an exemplar of the Bodhisattva way of life. Like some Bodhisattvas in the Perfection of Insight texts, he is portrayed as rich and powerful, living in luxury, well-educated, and eloquent. He was a householder with a wife, son, and concubines, but he was considered to be free of passions and followed the full monastic discipline; he was in the married state as only an expedient means (*upaya*) for aiding others. He ate and drank lavishly but only to create opportunities to convert others; he himself remained pure and dispassionate throughout these experiences. He mixed with all classes of people and participated in government. He wore ornate clothes and attended sports and gambling houses to help mature those attending. He frequented brothels, but only to convert the prostitutes and patrons. He was a landlord and engaged in business endeavors, yet he had no interest in profit or possessions and spent his wealth to help the poor. He met with teachers of other religions. He talked to people on the street while always maintaining a concentrative state of mind. He feigned illness in order to lure monks and others to come inquiring about his health, thereby giving him the opportunity to teach for their benefit. He was said to be second only to the Buddha in the depth of his understanding of the Buddhist teachings.

Mahayanists also expanded the number and nature of the Buddhas. In some schools, Buddhas vicariously take the suffering of other beings upon themselves, or the pantheon of cosmic Buddhas and Bodhisattvas create heavens (Pure Lands) through their vast stores of merit, which provide ideal conditions for the unenlightened to proceed toward release from rebirth. This reveals an evolving shift in beliefs away from attaining one's own release (self-help) toward helping others (other power). Other power was justified as a way of letting go of the last vestiges of one's sense of self—giving up even the idea that one could become enlightened by one's own power. Eventually, these schools ended up in quite theistic terms. Some schools made the Buddha, other Buddhas such as Amitabha, and Bodhisattvas into virtually savior gods and objects of worship (*puja*) with corresponding visions. The *Lotus Sutra* (298–99) states that anyone who hears the name of the Bodhisattva Avalokiteshvara and single-mindedly calls his name immediately gains deliverance. These schools also expanded the ritual and devotional elements present in earlier traditions, such as veneration of relics.

Some Mahayana traditions introduced monistic transcendent absolutes to explain how the Buddhist path works. They were probably advanced to win over Hindus since the devotional theism of the Bhakti movement was developing at the time. These transcendent realities were personified as deities and were worshiped and appealed to for aid. In these traditions, the emphasis shifted to introvertive experiences and transcendent mysticism, but the mixing of Buddhist beliefs with monistic mysticism did not produce a simple transcendent metaphysics. For example, one doctrine tells of the Buddha's multiple bodies (*kayas*). In the standard Mahayana version, there are three bodies: the historical Buddha's physical body (*nirmanakaya*) is a manifestation of the body of bliss (*sambhogakaya*), which also creates various Buddha-lands to help people become enlightened; the *dharmakaya* is the body of the teachings, or the pure components of the Buddha or any enlightened mind, and it is the source of the other two bodies.[30] The *dharmakaya* is unmanifested and transcendent (*lokottara*). It has its own existence or true nature (*svabhavakaya*) and is absolute reality: the *Dharma*-realm (*dharma-dhatu*). Another such doctrine is of the embryo of Buddhahood (*tathagata-garbha*), which serves as the basis for an innate Buddha-nature that exists in each person and each phenomenon and is the ultimate eternal reality of all things. Some take the "storehouse consciousness" that is discussed later to be identical to that embryo.

The *Mahaparinirvana Sutra* (ca. 200–400) completed the return to an Indian nondual transcendent reality by claiming that the Buddha's denial of eternal realities and a permanent self only exemplified his skillful means for adapting the teachings in ways that help listeners break mental idols and have experiences of the ultimate reality. In fact, there is an eternal, permanent great self (*maha-atman*) underlying all phenomenal reality. The transcendent reality and the existence of the enlightened after death are unknowable only to the unenlightened, dualistic mind. All Buddhist teachings, even those of direct meaning and ultimate truth, are only the Buddha's skillful means for leading the unenlightened to *nirvana*. The teachings are effective in leading the unenlightened to enlightenment, but they are not true in the final analysis. In the parable found in the *Lotus Sutra*, it is like a father who cannot get his children to leave a burning house, so he tells them something untrue by calling out that he will give them carts, and this untruth lures them out. The children did not get what he claimed but received something much better.

Compassion and Insight

Mahayanists elevated compassion (*karuna*) to equal status with insight (*prajna*) itself. This infused a moral concern into their way of life. The shift in ethos from the Nikaya Buddhists' self-interest to the Mahayanists' compassion is epitomized in a revision to *Dharmapada* verse 183. The Theravada version states that the essence of the Buddha's teaching is to avoid demerit (*papa*), to cultivate the wholesome (*kushala*), and to purify the mind. Mahayanists replaced the last phrase with "to save many beings." Mahayanists also group the Nikaya Solitary Buddhas and Arhats together as selfish; they focus only on getting themselves out of the realm of suffering while the whole world suffers.[31] Early Mahayanists accepted that Solitary Buddhas and Arhats were enlightened and out of the cycle of rebirth although they did not possess the full wisdom of a Buddha since they harbored a vestige of a sense of self by distinguishing between their own salvation and the salvation of others. Later, the doctrine developed such that all sentient beings would eventually become full Buddhas; thus, Solitary Buddhas and Arhats were not, in fact, out of their chain of rebirths but only in a temporary repose.[32]

Besides the shift in ethos, an innovation in factual beliefs permitted a revolutionary new way to implement concern for others. After *nirvana*, the enlightened can opt to remain in the realm of suffering even though they do not perform karmic actions. They are beyond the sanction of *karman* and so can control their destiny to choose new rebirths that will help others the most. Under the standard law of *karman*, this is not possible. One's karmic actions dictate where one is reborn, and those who end *karman* achieve *nirvana* and are not reborn; there is nothing they can do about it. For the Nikaya Buddhists, even the Buddha was gone after his final death, but Mahayanists modified the *karman* doctrine.

Compassion and insight became the two bases supporting the Bodhisattva's quest for a Buddha's full wisdom.[33] They are interlocked in the Bodhisattva's development: insight internalizes a worldview that reinforces the disposition of compassion, and compassion gives expression to the worldview through action. Compassion is, in short, insight in action. The Bodhisattvas' meditations expanded their concerns beyond themselves—first to their loved ones, then to neutral people, to enemies, and finally to all beings—identifying each as having once been their mother in a previous life. But compassion is not merely a meditative exercise for self-cultivation as with Nikaya Buddhists: it manifests itself in actions that help others. This compassion is free of attachments and, thus, is combined with impartiality and even-mindedness. The result is non-discriminating compassionate action for all. When formulating reasons to be compassionate, some later Mahayana texts dropped all references to oneself, and thus to any self-regarding motives (*svartha*). Another's welfare (*parartha*) is the only concern.

(This does set up the dualism of oneself and others that Mahayanists accuse Arhats of having, but it reverses the Arhats' priority.)

Insight is the other base of a Buddha's full wisdom. As with Nikaya Buddhists, insight involves seeing the three characteristics of reality: constructed things are impermanent, there is no separately existing self, and everything inevitably involves suffering. Nikaya Buddhists emphasized the impermanence of constructed things, but Mahayanists shifted the focus to the parts. Just as a person has no self but is only a collection of ever-changing parts—a body, feelings, and so on—a person's real parts (*dharmas*) also are all void of anything that would give them an independent permanent existence. That is, even the parts are empty (*shunya*) of any type of essence, nature, power, or substance that could give things their own self-subsisting existence (*svabhava*, self-becoming).[34] In short, no part of the experienced world is self-enclosed and existing independently of other things. Everything is impermanent and conditioned by other things.

In this way, Mahayanists expanded the Nikaya *anatman* doctrine from applying only to a person to applying to all phenomena. Abhidharmists treated *dharmas* as the fundamental components of reality, but Mahayanists argued that these too are empty of any essence that would make them real—in the sense of being permanent, unchanging, and independent of other things. Thus, the phenomena of the world do exist, but nothing exists by reason of itself. Nothing is real. Everything arises and falls based on causes and conditions; thus, there is no multiplicity of self-enclosed entities. Things have no mark or sign that sets them apart from the rest of reality as distinct entities. There is nothing real to attach a name to. Words—*is, is not, a being, a dharma, nirvana*—do not denote any independently existing entity (APP 5–6, 39, 47).[35] As the Perfection of Insight texts put it, one who sees reality correctly does not "cling" to concepts or "course in signs" (*nimitta-carati*) but "courses in the signless." Thus, a Bodhisattva realizes that thinking, "I am a Bodhisattva" is still coursing in signs. No entity is denoted by the word *Bodhisattva*, only a stream of selfless, conditioned elements (APP 11–18).

One consequence of the emptiness of things is that nothing is separate from the rest of the world. Only real entities have the capacity to be the same or different from anything else, but all things arise dependently and, thus, are without self-existence and are not real. Nothing can be ontologically identical to or different from another thing (MK 18.10). All phenomena are empty of any essence (*svabhava*) that only real entities can have, so nothing ontologically distinguishes one thing from another. This leads to other odd sounding claims. For example, *nirvana* is not different from samsara (the cycle of rebirths) since neither *nirvana* nor samsara are real entities. That is, neither are real, so neither can be the same as or different from the other. Thus, in this ontology, they are non-different. For this reason, the Perfection of Insight texts used *nondual* to depict the thus-ness (*tathata*) of things, but phenomenal items are not the same either. The ontology was never described as monistic. It was not necessary to point out that *nirvana* and samsara are not the same—only the fact that both are not real, and thus not ontologically different, was news. Nagarjuna never said that *nirvana* and samsara are the same, only that they are not different (MK 25.19). To claim that they are the same, as scholars routinely do today, is to miss the point of the Mahayana ontology of emptiness completely.[36]

Insight is simply seeing the flux of reality as it truly is without the illusion that there is a plurality of distinct and independent entities; it is seeing the rising and falling of conditioned things. It involves a state of mindfulness in which sense experience is freed from the normal confines of conceptualization. It is directly experiencing reality free of the mental discriminations (*vikalpa*, *samjna*) that arise when the unenlightened reify mental images and concepts into distinct entities by projecting their concepts onto reality. The mind then functions as a mirror of what is really there without adding to, distorting, or judging. In this state, one does not value any person—including oneself—more than any other. With insight perfected, the enlightened see that reality does not consist of a set of objects that they can attach themselves to or that can fully satisfy their desires. With no fixed points for attachment, the mind becomes calm and the body pliant. Thus, sense experiences still occur, but the enlightened react only to what is truly there. Emptiness ends all the mental processes that give rise to *karman*. In sum, the enlightened still think, feel, speak, and act but without discriminating separate self-contained entities.[37] They act with compassion, free of the false idea of independent realities.

Prajnaparamita and Madhyamaka Philosophy

Mahayanists are realists in the ordinary sense: they do not deny that there is a reality independent of conceptions—the *dharmas* as they truly are (*yathabhutam*, *dharmata*)—even if that reality cannot be reflected in any language since all languages operate by making distinctions. No idea, name, concept, or conventional expression connects to what is there (APP 177). However, Mahayanists only deny that there is a set of ontologically distinct, self-existing (*svabhava*) entities that can be apprehended, "settled down" in, or desired. Neither the phenomenal world nor the individual is constituted of a collection of distinct parts existing independently of each other. Reality is tranquil since there are no distinct parts banging into each other. Likewise, reality is nondual, non-produced, inexpressible, and free of any fixed abodes since there are no self-enclosed parts to it. But what is real still functions. The configuration of things called a *chair* still supports the person who sits in it even though there is no such real entity and its parts are empty of any permanent core. It exists, just not in the manner unenlightened folk think. Most importantly, this is also true of persons.

Thus, those who have perfected insight see that there is no basis for treating the elements of experienced reality (the *dharmas*) as real entities. That things are empty of anything giving them self-existence does not mean that they are in fact unreal (*asat*). Emptiness stands in the middle between permanence and nonexistence. There is no thingness to reality—no separate, self-contained entities—but there is also no nothingness—total lack of existence. Reality is just as it is (*tathata*, thus-ness or such-ness), void of differentiating substances. There is no thing for the mind to grasp. What is real is likened, as in Advaita Vedanta, to a dream, a magician's illusion, a mirage, clouds constantly forming and reforming, foam, or an echo. That is, something is there, but we mistake it for something it is not—an entity existing in its own right, independent of the rest of reality (APP 38–39, 512–13). Reality is nondual (for example, APP 265) because of the lack of substances that could differentiate one thing from another. Thus, we need nondual awareness and knowledge to see reality as it truly is, free of illusions we impose.

The first important Mahayana thinker was Nagarjuna (fl. ca. 200 CE). The school that followed him is the Madhyamaka: the "middle way" between *it is* (*asti*) and *it is not* (*na asti*) or eternalism (*shashvata*) and extinction (*uccheda*), between the eternal and permanent (the real) and the totally non-existent (the unreal). According to Nagarjuna, we see genuine phenomena in the world, so we must reject that they are totally nonexistent; but we also see them arise, change, and perish, so we must reject that they are fixed and unchanging. In his *Fundamental Verses on the Middle Way* (*Mula-madhyamaka-karikas*), he emphasized dependent co-arising and impermanence. According to him, anything existing by its own power cannot change in any way, so the Buddhist path, and everything else, could not work if anything were self-enclosed. Thus, if people were—in fact—real, the unenlightened could not change and would be permanently unenlightened. Additionally, nothing real could arise or cease. But since we see change, everything must be empty (*shunya*) of self-existence (*svabhava*). Therefore, dependent co-arising must be correct by default; no positive defense of emptiness has to be advanced. Likewise, words too are not real, and the Buddha did not teach any real doctrine (MK 25.24).

Nagarjuna's *Overturning the Objections* (*Vigrahavyavartani*) shows how difficult it must have been for him to convince his opponents that something could work or even exist if it was not real. His opponents—at least as he saw them—could not accept that anything exists unless it exists in its own right; thus, claiming that something exists but is not self-contained was nonsense. To them, if something is empty of self-existence, it is totally nonexistent (*asat*) and powerless to achieve anything. They believed that, in order to make any arguments at all, Nagarjuna must have been committed to real entities that existed in themselves. Otherwise, he was espousing nihilism (*na-astika*). Something must either exist in its own right (*svabhava*) or not exist at all, so his denial of *svabhava* meant that nothing exists. Some Western scholars today also claim this idea and see Nagarjuna as a nihilist or anti-metaphysician. However, Nagarjuna did not deny there are phenomena; only their mode of existence is not what his opponents believed (see Jones 2020b). Things exist, but they do so impermanently, conditionally, and dependently. Ontology does not depend on endorsing *svabhava*. Following the Buddha, Nagarjuna rejected the applicability of the ideas "exists," "does not exist," "both exists and not exists," and "neither exists nor does not exist." That is, if we are thinking in terms of something "existing" or "not existing," we are on the wrong track since we are still tacitly thinking in terms of discrete, self-contained entities (see Jones 2022b, 160–63). According to the Tibetan traditions, those who think that emptiness is nihilism end up being reborn as demons because of the damage they do.

However, Nagarjuna did not deny that conventional objects and *dharmas* are in the world; they simply are not self-contained entities existing unconditionally and independently of other things. *Emptiness* is simply a name for dependent co-arising (MK 24.18). Under the unenlightened view of language, words can refer only to things that are discrete, so no words apply to reality as it truly is—a mere that-ness (*tattva*) of impermanent things. As long as we believe that words require isolated referents to be meaningful, we will continue to mistakenly project words onto what is, in fact, real and to reify independent objects. But reality as it truly is (*yathabhutam, dharmata*) is undisturbed by our projection of concepts and is thus pacified (*shanta*). We should abandon the fabrications of *is* and *is not* (MK 9.12). Peace is the stilling of all conceptual supports and projections of concepts onto reality (MK 25.24). The enlightened, mindful mind sees only what is really there without grasping or distortion.

The Madhyamaka school emphasized dialectic arguments and refutations of opponents as the way to clear the mind of mental idols—in particular, by applying the *reductio ad absurdum* method to their arguments. Tibetans saw the school as split in two: following Buddhapalita (ca. 470–540), the Prasangikas—such as Chandrakirti (ca. 600–650) and Shantideva (ca. 650–750)—only made arguments against others' positions, while the Svatantrikas—such as Bhavaviveka (ca. 490–570)—advanced and defended positive arguments for the Madhyamaka positions. But the Madhyamaka had relatively little influence on subsequent Indian Buddhism: the Abhidharma schools continued to flourish and did not bother to respond to the Madhyamka critique, and Buddhist epistemologists also ignored this school.

The Yogachara School

The other major Indian Mahayana school, the Yogachara (Vijnanavada, Chittamatra), emphasized meditation over arguments as a way to free the mind of conceptualized perceptions; practitioners cleanse their minds of taints, thus making the mind calm and composed. Earlier Mahayana texts such as the *Lankavatara Sutra* and the *Sandhinirmochana* suggest that some of this school's teachings were developed earlier, but the school was founded by two brothers: Asanga (ca. 310–390), who is said to have received his teachings from the Bodhisattva Maitreya, and Vasubandu (ca. 320–400). Yogacharins treated the Perfection of Insight texts and the Nikaya discourses as texts of indirect meaning in need of interpretation. As set forth in Vasubandu's *Twenty Verses on Establishing Consciousness Only* (*Vimshatika-vijnaptimatrata-siddhi*), Yogacharins focus on perception and cognition. One branch—exemplified by Dignaga (fl. ca. 500) and Dharmakirti (sixth or seventh century)—focused on logic and epistemology. The other presented a phenomenological analysis of sense perception. Both focused on perceptual cognition. In their doctrine of consciousness (*vijnana*), the alleged objects of perception are only internal mental images, not something existing outside of consciousness. Names and concepts are modifications (*parinamas*) of consciousness and have no referents in the extra-mental world. Thus, there are no things outside the mind in the external world to apprehend and also no distinct entity (self) to apprehend them. All we know is the ever-changing flow of our own internal perceptions.

However, the common claim that Yogacharins are idealists who deny external reality is wrong. There is a reality that is independent of our conceptualized perceptions: the realm of *dharmas* (the *dharma-dhatu*). Thus, they do not deny an extra-mental world of *dharmas* or treat it as only a creation of the mind. Only the ideas of independent external objects (*bahyarthas*) and selves, which are projected by the mind onto reality, are denied. That is, Yogacharins did not claim that the world is mind-only; the only error is dividing *dharma-dhatu* up into allegedly discrete objects. There are objects of cognition and intention (*artha*), but these "objects" are in the mind and only seem to be external and real. What is actually real in the external world is not within the mind.

In short, only object-ness is denied, not the *dharma-dhatu*. Thus, the common criticism of this school—if there is no external world, how did we initially get the idea of, say, a cow?—does not apply. The external world exists, but our ideas are mistakenly projected onto it, creating the illusion of distinct real entities. What is real is beyond language; our conceptions only falsify the picture. We never experience the *dharma-dhatu* in ordinary perceptions (*pratyaksha*)—in ordinary consciousness, we only know the content of our unenlightened minds[38]—but the inexpressible *dharmas* can be experienced directly in a conceptless state of concentration (*nirvikalpa-samadhi*). With the obstacles in ordinary perception removed, we see the thus-ness (*tathata*) of the inexpressible *dharma-dhatu* with correct cognition. However, according to Yogacharins, an ontological analysis of the *dharma-dhatu* is irrelevant to solving suffering. To end accruing *karman*, we need to end our desires by correcting our perception.

Thus, only the mental divisions that separate what is real into distinct objects are consciousness only (*chitta-matra*), not the reality that exists apart from conceptualizations (the *dharma-dhatu*). Likewise, early Yogacharins did not, as is often alleged, deem consciousness to be the ultimate reality or the source of the world. We mistakenly attribute independent subjective and objective existence (*svabhava*) to what is, in fact, only the flow of mental content. We project entities into the pure givenness of our experiences (*vastu-matra*), but the content of ordinary awareness is entirely mental: the objects that we apparently see are nothing but our own mental creations. The objects of ordinary sense experience are like dream events or the visions in visualization exercises; they are entirely mental representations (*vijnapti-matra*) with no corresponding external objects. External objects are no more real than the hair-like forms seen by someone with an eye disease and have no more reality or causal power than what appears in dreams. Thus, we have no evidence to believe that objects in the mind exist externally any more than dream objects and characters. The form (*akara*, shape) that we impose on the *dharma-dhatu* consists only of mental fabrications, and since no external objects exist, there is no perception by a knowing consciousness, and so there is no self. The idea of a self-existing internal entity that grasps objects is also only a fabrication (*kalpitatmana*). In sum, all that ever exists in the ordinary mind are things created by the mind, but this is not to deny that an extra-mental world exists.

For Yogacharins, the mind is real, has its own nature (*svabhava*), and is empty (*shunya*) of the duality of subject and object. But the mind as an entity, a self, that grasps objects is an illusion; it is no more real than any other object. There are, in fact, three different natures (*svabhavas*) revealed from different points of view. Asanga gave the analogy of seeing a mirage: that the water is only imagined to be real is its fabricated nature (*parikalpita*); that the mirage itself is a state of consciousness arising from causes and conditions is its dependent nature (*paratantra*); and the enlightened realize the highest nature (*parinishpanna*) in seeing that the mirage is a state of consciousness, devoid of any subject/object duality and completely lacking any real content. The highest nature is the cessation of false construction and, hence, is a pure state of mind. It is a nondual awareness of the mind of the real *dharma-dhatu*, and it is empty of objectified content. However, the nature of the apparent content of the mirage is ineffable (*anabhilapya*). The basis of the cycle of rebirth is the flow of perceptions that we erroneously conceptualize into objects—accepting conventional objects as real—and the basis of *nirvana* is realizing the true nature of things.

As the sixth-century monk Sthiramati pointed out, if in "self-awareness" the mind appears as an object of awareness, one is not aware of it as it truly is since one has made subjective awareness into an object of consciousness. Vasubandhu had earlier said that even the thought "all of this is appearance only" involves a mental object, and anything that places something in front of consciousness is not consciousness alone; there is still duality. Once enlightened, no illusory posited objects are present in the mind, so it is not possible to grasp a subject either. There is only an objectless and subjectless consciousness. After this analysis is understood, yoga is required to achieve this supramundane (*lokottara*) awareness, allowing the practitioner to gain nonconceptual knowledge (*nirvikalpa-jnana*). Reality (*dharma-dhatu*) can then be directly perceived, free from all projected dualistic characterizations. Thus, enlightenment is a mirror knowledge (*adarsha-jnana*) that reflects only what is really there.

For Yogacharins, nondual consciousness devoid of any subject or object is real, but all conscious events are momentary and arise dependently upon conditions. They did advance the idea of an underlying storehouse consciousness (*alaya-vijnana*) that contains seeds from past actions and constitutes the medium for future karmic effects and rebirths, but it and the seeds are also impermanent and without self-existence. As with other early Buddhist schools, each individual has a separate mind (*manas*); there is no one common universal consciousness or mind. The storehouse consciousness of the enlightened has been freed of all taints—the unwholesome seeds—through the path of seeing (*darshana-marga*) and the path of meditative cultivation (*bhavana-marga*). Later, one branch of the Yogacharins considered the storehouse consciousness to be the pure mind of the enlightened; for the other branch, the storehouse consciousness of the enlightened is replaced by a pure consciousness that is the basis (*ashraya*) of all reality.

In the final stages of Indian Buddhism, the Madhyamaka and Yogachara schools fused within a Svatantrika Madhyamaka framework, combining the idea that the phenomenal world is empty of self-existence with the idea that objects are consciousness only. Shantirakshita (ca. 725–788), a Tantric who was the last important abbot of the Nalanda teaching center, was its most prominent proponent.

The Status of the Phenomenal Realm

As noted, many Buddhists accuse Madhyamakas of being nihilistic. Their charge is that without something being real (*sat*), phenomena are supported by nothing but other unsupported phenomena. Thus, there is ultimately no substance, no ground, no nothing. For Yogacharins, *emptiness* (*shunyata*) means that reality as it truly is (the *dharma-dhatu*) is empty only of subject/

object duality.[39] However, Nagarjuna argued that empty entities are neither real (self-existent) nor totally without existence (*asat*). Rather, entities do exist but are dependent on other empty things. As the Dalai Lama puts it: "The *existence* of things and events is not in dispute; it is the *manner in which* they exist that must be clarified" (2005a, 113). *Emptiness* simply denotes the state of the phenomenal world: free of self-existent realities. It is not a transcendent void, a ground, or a substance out of which objects arise.[40] No transcendent source or other alleged reality is part of Nagarjuna's philosophy, and, he added, anyone who thinks that emptiness is itself a self-existent reality is "incurable" (MK 13.8). Rather, emptiness, like everything else, is empty of any power of self-existence. It, too, is a concept with no real referent (MK 22.11).[41]

Madhyamikas and Advaitins both accept the same criterion for reality: what is real (*sat*) is eternal, permanent, and unchanging. Thus, *real* is a term of art for these Buddhists; it does not mean "to exist." What is real cannot arise, or cease to exist, or change its nature. Something can exist through dependent co-arising but cannot be real in that restricted sense. Both traditions also reach the same conclusion about the insubstantiality of phenomena within the world of sense experience, but Nagarjuna deals only with the phenomenal world. The objective of his work is to get us to see the impermanence of everything in the phenomenal world and, thus, end our attachments. This is an extrovertive mysticism. Nagarjuna did not posit any transcendent reality or focus on introvertive mystical experiences. On the other hand, Advaitins focused on Brahman as the transcendent source of the phenomenal world as a whole. Gaudapada asserted that the phenomenal world is a projection of the inactive, contentless consciousness. For Shankara, the world is not real or unreal but an illusion with an indefinite ontological status.

In fact, Gaudapada adopted some of Madhyamaka's terminology and argumentation to support the existence of Brahman. For example, the analogy of the firebrand is employed both by Gaudapada and in the Perfection of Insight and Madhyamaka texts, but the Buddhists focus on the unreality of the wheel of fire caused by spinning a firebrand, while Gaudapada focuses on the unchanging and singular reality of the fire, whose vibration (*spandita*) generates the false images. *Chitta* is a word Buddhists use for consciousness or awareness; but, for them, consciousness is a series of momentary events. For Advaitins, it is a constant and unchanging light. Likewise, Gaudapada went from accepting the Buddhist idea, "There is no real birth or change" to the Advaita idea, "There is the unborn and changeless reality transcending phenomena." The Sanskrit words for "there is no birth" and "there is the unborn" can be the same, but these statements are very different. By bringing in the transcendent reality of Brahman, Advaita's mysticism revamps Buddhist ideas and terminology for a transcendent metaphysics with introvertive depth-mystical experiences, while Perfection of Insight and Madhyamaka Buddhism remains a matter of extrovertive experiences and this-worldly metaphysics alone. Both agree that the objects in the human field of experience are illusory rather than real, but Advaitins added the argument that illusions are possible only if there is something real (*sat*) to ground them—as Nagarjuna's Buddhist critics also argued—and that that reality transcends the phenomenal world. To Advaitins, transient phenomena are unimaginable without such a permanent, transcendent, fundamental reality to ground them, but Buddhism stopped with the phenomenal world and its nature; any possible transcendent reality does not play a role in Perfection of Insight or Madhyamaka thought.

Thus, both Madhyamikas and Advaitins speak of nondualism but in different senses. The nondualism in Advaita is vertical, existing between the phenomenal realm and a transcendent reality (Brahman), and experienceable in depth-mystical experiences. In Buddhism, the nondualism is horizontal, existing between the "empty" parts within the phenomenal realm, and experienceable in extrovertive mindfulness. For Advaita, nondualism is that there is only one essence (*atman*) to reality: Brahman. For Nagarjuna, all phenomena are non-different because the nature of everything is the same; that is, they are all empty of any essence or power that would generate multiple independent objects. Thus, from the Advaita point of view, extrovertive Buddhism is about what is happening within the dream, while introvertive Advaita is about the transcendent dreamer waking up to the fact that their sense of having an individual self in a real phenomenal world is only an illusory dream.

Buddhism and Social Action

The virtues cultivated in Buddhism are individual in nature, not social. *Human rights* and *injustice* are concepts that have no role in the ethos of either Nikaya or classical Mahayana Buddhism. The history of Mahayana Buddhism supports the conclusion that it has no political values and can be accommodated to differing sociopolitical settings. From the Buddhist point of view, no political system is intrinsically better than another, nor is there a need to abolish them all. Political concerns, as with Nikaya Buddhists, were irrelevant to the goal of ending the existential suffering of individuals. Inner liberation, not transformation of the society, is what matters.

This does not mean, however, that Mahayana Buddhists are totally bereft of all social activity. Unenlightened Bodhisattvas are urged to provide this-worldly help—caring for the sick, feeding the poor, guiding the blind, and educating the young. This work is usually done in face-to-face interactions, but there are instances of Buddhists collectively helping on a society-wide scale. Nagarjuna commended rulers for engaging in social projects related to health and clean water supply and feeding the poor and animals, among others. The Zen master Hakuin wrote to the ruling class on behalf of the oppressed farmers and peasants in Japan. In the 1960s, some Vietnamese Zen monks set themselves on fire during the Diem regime to bring the world's attention to Vietnam's plight and to move the hearts of those involved in the war through their intense suffering.[42] Some examples of skillful means also involve political acts such as killing oppressive kings or taking ill-gotten wealth from rulers à la Robin Hood.[43] Buddhist monasteries in China had hospitals, orphanages, and homes for the elderly. They did everything from feeding the poor to building roads and digging wells.

However, most Buddhist masters see danger in this-worldly acts. There is a spiritual danger both to the worker and to the recipient. The Tibetan master Milarepa (ca. 1052–1135), when asked if monks may perform worldly works that were in a small way beneficial to others, answered: "If there be not the least self-interest attached to such duties, it is permissible. But such detachment is indeed rare; and works performed for the good of others seldom succeed, if not wholly freed from self-interest. . . . It is as if a man hopelessly drowning were to try to save another man in the same predicament" (Evans-Wentz 1958, 271). He recommended instead resolving to attain Buddhahood for the good of all sentient beings. Before enlightenment, monks do not know the true nature of reality and, thus, may inadvertently hurt both themselves and those they are trying to help even with their teaching. Thus, in the long run, becoming enlightened first is the best way to help others as well as oneself. Once enlightened, Bodhisattvas focus on ending others' suffering completely by ending others' rebirths, not worldly works. This involves teaching the path, being an exemplar for the unenlightened to emulate, and establishing beings in one of the ways to the end of rebirths (for example, APP 300, 322, 325, 333). But Bodhisattvas should focus on teaching Buddhist doctrines only after enlightenment. Once enlightened, Bodhisattvas can even-mindedly educate an infinite number of beings, expounding both the letter and meaning of the doctrine (APP 105).

Thus, enlightened Bodhisattvas focus exclusively on providing direct soteriological help, not reorganizing society. Ending all poverty, war, and illness would not end the fundamental existential suffering of decay, death, and rebirth, so they are not concerns for an enlightened Bodhisattva. When faced with an epidemic, an enlightened Bodhisattva thinks only, "There is no element of reality (*dharma*) that sickness could oppress, nor is that which is called 'sickness' an element of reality" and then thinks about creating a Pure Land with the best conditions for realizing that sickness is not an element of reality (APP 364–65). Indeed, not intervening at all in a social problem might be more positive—indicating the ultimate unimportance of all worldly comfort—although this may seem cold to the unenlightened.[44] Doing anything that establishes the unenlightened on a path to *nirvana* helps more in the long run of future rebirths. In sum, helping to free people completely from suffering by demonstrating the Buddha's teachings is the greatest aid possible and the only form of aid the enlightened focus on.

In this way, the doctrines of *karman* and existential suffering in Buddhism lead to an individualist and other-worldly orientation; society is merely a collection of individuals, and moral concern for others is best directed toward aiding individuals in ending their rebirths. The enlightened can accept the status quo and focus on the inner transformation of individuals in helping people toward the soteriological goal. They would be critical of a person's attachment to any political system, and they would not favor one political system over another since they do not value worldly distinctions.

Tantric Buddhism

As discussed in the last chapter, Tantrism emerged in India by the seventh century CE, probably first in Shaiva Hinduism. Earlier, a Mantrayana (way of mantras) arose within Buddhism in the second century CE, where magical formulas (*mantras* and *dharanis*) were considered deities. The most famous mantra is *Om Mani-Padme Hum*, which invokes Avalokiteshvara as the bearer of the jewel and lotus. Tantrism continued the Indian interest in magic present since Vedic times, but historians have not found a good reason for why it appeared when it did. Perhaps Mahayana practices had become ossified, and a revitalization movement was needed within Buddhism. In any case, Tantrism began outside of monasteries, but it wasn't long before Tantric monks were studying in the same monasteries and Buddhist centers of teaching in northern India as Mahayanists. It became the final form of Buddhism in India, with multiple schools. In China and Japan, the sexual rituals were downplayed, but there is even a Theravada form of Tantrism in Cambodia.

Tantrikas see Tantrism as a "third turning of the wheel of *Dharma*." (The first turning was the Nikaya teachings and the second the Mahayana. Yogacharins also claim to be the third turning.) It was open only to advanced monks who had strong minds and great compassion. Tantric monks also first took the Mahayana Bodhisattva vow and training. Lamas in the right-handed Tantric Geluk tradition of Tibet study other Buddhist texts for twenty years before being initiated. It is considered the Vajrayana, the way of the diamond or thunderbolt, for its swift smashing of mental idols.[45] A highly ritualized daily life was the way to detachment. By working on the mind and body and utilizing desires and passions as well as thought, Tantrism made it possible to become enlightened in this life rather than working through three eons of rebirths.

The highest of the four classes of Tantric texts concern working on the body in a *kundalini*-like system, leading to a mind of clear light and nonconceptual knowledge that is not fabricated by the mind. In Tantric yogic rituals, one utilizes the body, speech, and mind: visualizing oneself as a particular deity (and cultivating the accompanying emotions), magical formulas, hand gestures (*mudras*), bodily movements and positions, and *mandalas* (two-dimensional diagrams of a deity's palace).[46] Gurus give their students guardian deities to visualize; these may include the wrathful female Dakinis and male Herukus, but they are considered compassionate, helping to break delusions and redirect energies in the body toward enlightenment. Tantrikas have also utilized psychedelic drugs such as cannabis and datura. Achieving worldly paranormal powers (*siddhis*) was prominent. There were antinomian left-handed traditions, but these were probably practiced only by a minority. Only the socially acceptable, tame, right-handed traditions that follow a conservative Vinaya code have survived to the present. For example, the *Hevajra Tantra* explains "killing living beings" symbolically as meaning only having a "singleness of thought," and sexual contact is practiced only in the mind.

Tantrism replaced the Mahayana in India, but Buddhist Tantrism took over many of the Mahayana doctrines as its philosophical framework, especially those of the synthesized Yogachara-Madhyamaka school. It accepted a nondualist transcendent metaphysics. The ritualized sexual union was seen as uniting insight (the inactive female) and skillful means (the active male) in the mind. In addition to overcoming dualism in this manner, in visualization meditation, the practitioner becomes the deity and the deity becomes the practitioner, although both are illusory beings. In the end, the illusory world becomes a manifestation of the transcendent Buddha. These Tantric teachings remained esoteric until its texts were published in the last hundred years.

Tibetan Buddhism

Buddhism all but disappeared from the Indian subcontinent by the thirteenth century. Today, there are relatively few Buddhists in India. External factors contributed to its demise: the Muslim Turks' invasion of the Ganges valley and their destruction of Buddhism's two principal learning centers, Nalanda and Vikramashila; the rise of Vaishnava and Shaiva theism; and the absorption of key Buddhist ideas and practices into Hinduism. But internal factors were also involved; Buddhism had become disconnected from the general communities around it, transforming into an elitist religion of monastics that relied on the unstable patronage of rulers who came and went.

The Tantric Shantarakshita (fl. eighth century) brought the Madhyamaka-Yogachara school to Tibet from northern India. His disciple Kamalashila (ca. 740–795) wrote important treatises on meditation and the Bodhisattva path. Another Tantric, Padmasambhava, arrived earlier, in 747. At first, Indian and Chinese Buddhist schools mixed—especially Chan. Padmasambhava founded a monastery, but Buddhism did not take hold until Atisha (982–1054) arrived from India in 1042, establishing an Indian form of right-handed Tantric Buddhism and teaching the doctrines of multiple Buddhist schools. He also reestablished the importance of teachers. Since then, gurus have remained central in personally transmitting secret Tantric teachings.

New schools thereafter arose but with very few doctrinal innovations. Visualization exercises became more important as Buddhism absorbed many fierce gods and demons as well as other religious customs from indigenous

Himalayan and Central Asian religions. Right-handed Tantrism became the standard practice in all the schools. Following Atisha's program, monks first studied Nikaya and Mahayana doctrines before being initiated into the Tantric practices. Monasteries became the principal institution in Tibetan society by being the greatest source of merit-making for the laity. Since the eleventh century, education in these centers has intellectually approached Buddhist doctrines based on the seventh-century Dharmakirti's works on logic, Abhidharma theories, the Perfection of Insight texts, and Madhyamaka's middle way—all within a Tantric framework.

Four schools have survived: Nyingma, founded by Padmasambhava; Kagyu, which emphasizes meditation; Sakya, which is more text-oriented; and Geluk (meaning adherents of virtue), who emphasize Madhyamaka dialectics as preparation for meditation on emptiness. The schools have basically the same doctrines and differ mainly only in their lineages from different lamas, although they did develop a rivalry for political power. The Geluk became the most prominent and has remained so despite the other schools adopting a nonsectarian approach in the mid-nineteenth century. Their major doctrinal dispute is over whether to accept a transcendent explanatory reality that exists by its own nature (*svabhava*), such as the Buddha-embryo, or to accept the Madhyamaka approach that forgoes such realities. All rank the teachings of four Indian schools: two Svatantrika branches (the Vaibhashika and Sautrantika) and two Mahayana schools (the Yogachara and Madhyamaka), with the Madhayamaka deemed the highest. The first pilgrims from India favored Svatantrika Madhyamaka, but the Prasangika branch prevailed. The only major innovation of the surviving schools was the ability for advanced meditators to direct their next rebirth to a person who could be identified in childhood as their reincarnation (*yang sird*)—although this, too, may have come from India.

The most important early Kagyu was the poet and yogin Milarepa (ca. 1052–1135). He was a disciple of the translator Marpa (ca. 1012–1097), who studied under Naropa (ca. 956–1041) and founded the Kagyu school. He first studied indigenous sorcery but turned to Buddhist gurus out of guilt when his act of vengeance killed dozens. He became well-known for his devotion to meditation, which included spending many years meditating in a cave. After his enlightenment, he became an exemplar of the Bodhisattvas.

Tsongkhapa (1357–1419) of the Geluk school wrote important works on Prasangika Madhyamaka and the practice of Bodhisattvas. One of his disciples is considered the first Dalai Lama and another the first Panchen Lama.[47] He emphasized learning and reinstated a rule of celibacy for monks. He also tried to reconcile Buddhism with Tibetan shamanism; magic played an important part in Indian religiosity, and Tibetan Buddhist monks took over the shamanic functions of exorcizing demons and healing from local practitioners. Shakyans believed that the Geluk school spent too much time on debates and not enough on meditation. Shakya Chokden (1428–1507) reconciled the conceptual Madhyamaka approach for reaching reality as it truly is through negations with Gorampa's (1429–1489) approach that even the negations must be negated by treating them as merely two different routes to breaking the grip that conceptualizations have on our mind; both led to the same unmediated experience of the transcendent ground—the nondual "primordial mind" that transcends conceptualizations and the sub-ject/object division and is, in fact, the only reality.

Buddhism Today

As the Buddha was dying, he commissioned his disciples to spread the teachings; over the centuries, that has occurred. Buddhism was the first world religion. The Theravada tradition expanded into Greco-Bactria in Afghanistan as well as into Sri Lanka and Southeast Asia, where it thrives today. Mahayana traditions spread to Central Asia, China, Korea, and Japan. Tantric traditions were exported to Tibet and East Asia. In Tibet, the last Indian Buddhist teachings—those of the eighth century—have been pre-served virtually untouched. Today, Tibetan Buddhism is the dominant form of Buddhism in Central Asia and has spread to Siberia, Northeast China, far eastern Russia, parts of India, and—more recently—the West.

In the 1800s, Buddhism was introduced to the Western world. At first, Westerners were interested in Buddhist doctrines but not its practices and experiences. Later, its meditation practices and analyses of the mind became the focus, but Buddhism was Westernized in Europe and America. Western notions of *Emptiness* usually understand it as a dynamic, self-emptying Void rather than a phenomenal reality empty of anything giving things their own existence as it was understood in the Perfection of Insight and Madhyamaka texts. The Dalai Lama and Neo-Buddhists have become interested in modern science, especially for any bearing it may have on Buddhist doctrines of the mind and consciousness.[48] Recently, a socially engaged form of Buddhism derived from Western values of human rights and the environment that is not related directly to attaining enlightenment has also arisen in the United States and Europe.

Key Themes

• According to the Buddha, his teaching has only one flavor: how to permanently end the suffering (*duhkha*) that is inherent in simply being alive (MN I.22). This soteriological quest permeates Buddhist mysticism. The goal, as in Hinduism, is to escape suffering by ending rebirths, but Buddhists approach the matter with a very different type of metaphysics: a person can never experience any unchanging essence, nor do they have an unchanging consciousness. The objective is not to realize that reality is Brahman or a transcendent self but to realize that nothing within one's experience indicates that anything is permanent. There is nothing within a person to protect or augment, and nothing within the phenomenal world is enduring or capable of satisfying desires. In short, there is nothing to become attached to. Buddhist meditation, doctrines, and action-guides remove mental incrustation and contrary perspectives of reality.

• A root metaphor for early Buddhism is the impermanence of a chariot; the parts are real, but the aggregate object is impermanent. Mahayanists expanded the doctrine of no essence in a person (*anatman*) to the parts of the chariot and to all other phenomena (*nihsvabhava*), including the basic components of the experienced world (the *dharmas*). Reality, as it is independent of conceptualizations (*yathabhutam*), is impermanent and interconnected. That is the basic Buddhist ontology of the phenomenal realm. The Buddha held the Axial Age concern that led to world-renunciation in India, but, unlike for Hindu mystics, introvertive mystical experiences had no direct soteriological value. The phenomenal world was a dream in Advaita, so Advaitins focused on the transcendent dreamer, but Buddhists focused only on the content of the dream. The question of the ontological status of the world *in toto* was left unanswered. Buddhists accepted transcendent deities and various heavens, but their objective was ending rebirth by focusing on the lack of permanence in the phenomenal world and the phenomenal person.

• Thus, Buddhist mysticism is extrovertive at its core. Introvertive mystical experiences were originally only seen as aids for focusing and calming the mind on the path to enlightenment, not cognitions of alleged transcendent realities. Rather, enlightenment is an insight into the nature of phenomenal reality and oneself. The resulting state of *nirvana* is an extrovertive mystical state of consciousness in which enlightened individuals experience the world and themselves as free of any real parts—not independently existing, self-enclosed entities—and respond only to what is actually there. Likewise, the enlightened think free of the ideas of discrete enduring entities even if experiences in the enlightened state remain conceptually structured. Unenlightened emotions associated with a sense of self, such as greed and hatred, end.

• Even though Buddhism is an extrovertive mysticism, its goal is transcendent: to escape the suffering in the phenomenal world by ending the cycle of rebirths. In its Indian and Tibetan forms, its metaphysics is a matter of analyzing experiences into their components (*dharmas*) because it is necessary for escaping attachments and ending suffering, not out of interest for this world per se. The soteriological goal remains central.

• Mahayanists switched the earlier focus on saving only oneself from rebirths to include saving others. They advanced a new understanding of *karman* to do so; one ends *karman*'s control by becoming enlightened, but the enlightened can choose to remain in the cycle of rebirths to help others. Becoming an enlightened Bodhisattva then became the initial goal, and becoming a full Buddha was the ultimate goal. A moral concern for others was at least as central as ending one's own suffering. Compassion (*karuna*) was not merely a meditative exercise for self-cultivation, as with the Theravadins; it manifested itself in actions that helped others. It became the central Mahayana value, like love in Christianity.

• Early Buddhism is unique among the world religions in discouraging any search for a transcendent source to the phenomenal world or a person. There are deities and demons in Buddhism, but no creator, sustainer, or loving theistic sovereign lord of the phenomenal world. It is atheistic or agnostic in this regard. But the Axial Age desire in India for a transcendent, unifying, cosmic principle did return in the Mahayana with such doctrines as an innate Buddha-nature. In later Mahayana traditions, transcendent realities entered the picture, and introvertive mystical experiences took on greater cognitive importance. Buddhas and Bodhisattvas who could provide help toward enlightenment became deities in some Mahayana and Tantric traditions. In Tantric traditions, one could become a deity through visualizations, but no mystical union was involved since Buddhahood is already innate in each individual. However, the goal was not to become a deity; such visualization exercises were only an aid.

• Left-handed Tantrikas use immoral means to break attachments in order to attain enlightenment. It appeared in one of the branches of Indian Buddhism in which Buddhas and Bodhisattvas were treated more theistically. (Theism, or at least belief in deities, appears more conducive to antinomianism than mysticisms involving only nonpersonal realities.) Right-handed Tantrism prevailed.

• Buddhism thrives around the world today in diverse forms. Its core metaphysics of the phenomenal world has proved to be adaptable to different cultural settings, and there has been no central authority to impose orthodoxy.

Chapter 9

Chinese Mysticism

The atmosphere of mysticism in classical China is very different from that of classical India and the West. Its mysticisms are more this-worldly, with a focus on conforming to a natural principle underlying the world: the *Dao*. There is no supreme transcendent deity or unconnected principle. There is a focus on the phenomenal world and social reality that is absent in Abrahamic and Indian mysticisms. Happiness is to be found in living in conformity with the natural *Dao*. But unlike the rest of the natural realm, human beings do not automatically conform to the flow of the *Dao*; we need a form of inner cultivation in order to return to it.

The Early Chinese Worldview

By the Axial Age, the Chinese saw nature as being in constant motion and transformation. Cosmic energy (*qi*, literally breath or vapor) constitutes the natural realm and generates growth and changes. Nature exhibits patterns of the waxing and waning of the energy's in interlocking positive and negative phases—the *yang* and the *yin*. These two terms originally referred to the bright and shady sides of a mountain that change as the day wears on. The balance in the universe that is achieve by all things operating harmoniously in conformity with the *Dao* is central. *Dao* originally meant a path or road, but it took on an ontological and cosmological dimension in addition to meaning "a way to be followed." It is also a verb. There is no major division between the natural and social orders; the *Dao* orders both.[1] The distinction of appearance and underlying reality also was not prominent in classical Chinese thought until Buddhism showed up.

In Daoism's ontological hierarchy, the unnameable *Dao* generates the One (being) that, in turn, generates the two (*yin* and *yang*), then the three (*yin*, *yang*, and *yin*-and-*yang* in harmony), and finally everything (*wan-wu*, the ten thousand things) (D 42).[2] Unlike the unchanging absolutes of classical Greek and Indian thought, what is real here is constantly in flux and perpetually new—a metaphysics of becoming rather than being—although the aspect of the *Dao* as the transcendent source of phenomena is uncreated, eternal, permanent, and unchanging. Hinduism emphasized transcendent realities, but early Chinese culture did not emphasize the *Dao* as the source of the world; rather, it emphasized the *Dao*'s dynamic function of regulating order within nature.

In an emanationist cosmology that took shape by the second century BCE, everything emerges from the *Dao* and returns to it at its end. It is the womb of nonbeing (*wu-ji*), the reality from which the being of the natural universe arises. Thus, the *Dao* is both a transcendent and immanent reality—the transcendent source and ground of the natural realm, whose order permeates and guides *qi* in this realm. *Qi* energy is the material aspect of the *Dao*, but the *Dao* also regulates it. Thus, *qi* is manifested in the forms of *yang* (assertion, strength, masculinity, light, the sun, and so forth) and *yin* (yielding, weakness, femininity, darkness, the moon, and so forth). From the *Dao*, the three forces of the sky and earth (*tian-di*) and humanity (*ren*) arise. So do the five phases (*wuxing*) that, in different combinations, constitute all that exists: wood is the lesser *yang*, fire the greater *yang*, soil a balance of *yin* and *yang*, metal the lesser *yin*, and water the greater *yin*. These are not static material elements. Each phase generates the next, and the pattern repeats; wood produces fire, fire soil, soil metal, metal water, and water produces wood again. In destructive action, this is reversed. Summer is the greater *yang*, winter the greater *yin*. Anger is the lesser *yang*, joy the greater *yang*, worry both *yin* and *yang*, sadness the lesser *yin*, and fear the greater *yin*.

Yang and *yin* are not opposing or competing forces that are fighting each other but merely different phases of *qi*. Neither is better than the other, nor is one good and one evil. Every event is a combination of both complementing phases, and both are in a constant ebb and flow, one increasing as the other is decreasing. When one extreme is reached, the *Dao* reverses toward the other extreme. The things of the world are in a self-balancing rhythm: when one phase increases, the other decreases; hence, there is a zero-sum to changes in the world. Likewise, there is stability to the changes. This is visualized in the classic *yin-yang* symbol of a circle with an S-shaped line in the middle dividing *yang* and *yin* into equal portions. When one is at its zenith, the other begins to grow. Each half also contains a dot of the other, representing that nothing is purely one or the other. The *Book of Changes (Yijing)* describes the cycles of the movement of *yang* and *yin*.

The world is considered purely natural and not in need of an external explanation; it is "a continuous whole consisting of natural processes that are interconnected through paths and cycles of mutual productiveness," with humans being an integral part of the world (Coutinho 2014, 148). The immanent order of the *Dao* is at the heart of things. Classical Chinese thought did not emphasize the interwoven whole but the interaction of the parts. The harmony (*he*) of the interconnected parts is central, but it also emphasized the individuality of things operating with the *Dao*. Indeed, the Daoist Zhuangzi emphasized the variety and particularity over the interconnections—the uniqueness of each person and their destiny.

We have a certain amount of *qi* from birth, and it is dispersed at death, but it can be maintained and replenished during our lives through everything from breathing clean air to positive social interactions. The more *qi* that we expend striving against the currents of the *Dao*, the less life-energy we have to use for extending our life. Thus, by reducing this friction we conserve and nourish our *qi*, and this leads to keeping the body supple and to the longest life we can have in the world. (Throughout Chinese history, an early death has been regarded as one of the greatest disasters possible [Kohn 1992, 85].) By cultivating the energies of the body, we can also transform the *qi* into the spirit (*shen*) that connects us to heaven.[3]

In classical Chinese thought, deceased ancestors played a role in religious life, but there was relatively little concern for one's own destiny after death. Each person is a microcosm, containing the same forces that operate in parallel on other scales—on the family, society, natural world, and heavens. As with many other mystical traditions, Daoists made correspondences and hidden connections between different phenomena—for instance, correlating fire with summer, the planet Mars, and the heart. Such correlations are not matters of causation but resonances. Because of the hidden connections of things, an individual person can affect other people and events in the natural world by affecting the flow of the *Dao*. For example, the ruler's actions can affect the weather. Thus, we are as much a part of the natural world as nonhuman phenomena, and the person in the natural world and the body are emphasized more in China than in the other classical cultures. In

292 | A History of Mysticism

addition, people were seen as innately social, so mystics typically remained in society. (However, Daoism has hermits, and Buddhism introduced monasteries.) There is also a political dimension to much Chinese mysticism. The ruler carries out the mandate of heaven (*tian-ming*) for a society, and unrest among the people shows that the ruler is failing. The *Dao* manifests itself in each thing as an inner power (*de*), enabling that thing to fulfill the destiny in this world that heaven has mandated for it.

The social psychologist Richard Nisbett (2003) points to differences in worldviews and the resulting ways of thinking to explain differences between the cultures of East Asia and the West. (India can be grouped with the West on these points). He does not say that everyone in a given culture thinks the same way but only that there are general cultural patterns of thinking. He argues that Westerners typically detach an object from its context and categorize objects by their attributes—he calls this *analytical thinking*—while East Asians are typically oriented toward an object's context and environment as a whole—*holistic thinking*. Analytical thinkers explain and predict in terms of rules governing an object's attributes; holistic thinkers explain and predict in terms of an object's relation to its context and other objects. The former utilize chronological and historical relationships; the latter, causal patterns. The former are drawn to objects; the latter, to a perceptual field as a whole. The former decontextualize an object and manipulate its environment; the latter adjust things to their environment. The former try to understand the whole by how the parts work; the latter understand the parts by starting with the whole. The former see a logical contradiction between true and false; the latter see some merit on both sides and look for a middle way between them. The former naturally see distinct objects; the latter see a common substance. The former look for causes and agents; the latter, relationships. The former come up with models that simplify how things work by removing objects from their environments; the latter accept the complexity of the world. Western thinking fed Greek curiosity about how the world works and led naturally to the type of empirical science that developed in the West. However, note that nothing Nisbett says ties the East Asian approach to mystical experiences or altered states of consciousness. He does say that Daoism and later Buddhism shaped the Chinese orientation to life (2003, 12–17), but he does not refer to mystical experiences for this. Despite this, the East Asian worldview may help to explain why the Chinese adopted the mysticisms that they did—why Daoism arose there and not in India—and why it transformed Buddhism.

The Confucian Backdrop

In the Axial Age, thinkers began to reflect within this worldview of the *Dao*. Confucius (Kong Fuzi, 551–479 BCE) was concerned with human affairs and with the *Dao* as it manifests in a harmonious society (*ren dao*). Harmony in the world was a matter of one's proper place in the social scheme. The rules of appropriate ritual and social behavior (*li*) set forth in the Confucian classics outlined one's roles and relationships within the hierarchy of society. In order to know how to act in situations not covered in these rules, thinkers needed a sense of reciprocity (*shu*), summarized in a negatively stated Golden Rule: "Never do to others what you would not like them to do to you" (*Analects* V.11, XII.2, XV.23). This reflects an inner, underlying sense of what is appropriate (*yi*). Once we can carry out the appropriate behavior without having to think of what is right, we act with sincerity (*cheng*) and our actions spontaneously manifest the *Dao* of humaneness (*ren*).

Thus, in the Confucian project, self-cultivation (*xiushen*) is a matter of learning and internalizing social conventions and becoming educated in social status, obligations, and etiquette rather than a mystical cultivation, although some scholars do see some mysticism in the works of Mencius (Mengzi, ca. 380–290 BCE). The social sphere is where we develop fully into human beings, and we become fully realized human beings only by an inner transformation (*xin*). *Humaneness*, or benevolence, is defined relationally rather than individualistically: the symbol for *ren* combines the symbols for *human being* and *two*. It is only through developing five virtues that we become fully human: integrity (*xin*), propriety (*li*), knowledge (*zhi*), humaneness (*ren*), and righteousness/justice (*yi*). Humaneness is the master value governing the application of the other virtues. Until we have internalized a sense of what behavior is called for in each situation, we need external rules (*li*) to follow. However, Confucians disagreed with Legalists (*fa-jia*) over the need for laws; regulations can force changes in behavior by means of reward and punishment, but they cannot cause the inner transformation of character needed for one to become a fully realized human being.

Confucius's own life reflects the difficulty of attaining this state: at fifteen, he set his heart on learning the classics; at thirty, he established himself in that pursuit; at forty, he no longer had any perplexities; at fifty, he knew the will of heaven; at sixty, his ear was attuned to heaven's will; but only at age seventy could he follow his heart's desire without transgressing the boundaries of appropriate conduct (*Analects* II.4). His heart and mind were then aligned with the *Dao* of humanity, and he could do whatever he wished. Only at that age was he truly an exemplary gentleman (*junzi*).

Individual self-cultivation is the basis for reforming society into a more harmonious whole. For Confucius, there is a hierarchy of social roles, with the family being the foundation. His rival Mozi focused on human nature and rejected the Confucian emphasis on ritual rules in favor of an all-embracing love (*ai*) free of any hierarchical relations, but Confucians dismissed such universal and egalitarian love as utopian; it does not reflect the reality that we live in a hierarchy of social relationships and that we are rightly partial toward family and friends. It is inhuman to think of oneself as independent of familial and social relations or to refuse serving in government, let alone to withdraw from society entirely. Once we align our inner dispositions with humaneness, our families will be transformed; with each family transformed, the society as a whole will be well run; and finally, with each country well run, there will be peace in the world. This is bottom-up social reform. The government is reordered by the "rectification of names" (*zhengming*) so that each government official fulfills his duties properly. That is, a government action can only be effectively fulfilled when a government official speaks of what is proper for him to carry out and accurately expresses what he means (*Analects* XIII.3). Actions then tally with words, and language encodes the important social distinctions, properly guiding action.

The Daoist Reaction

Daoism was a reaction to this dominant Confucian culture. It is a collection of related movements, not one unified school. Their earliest text is the Book of the *Dao* and Its Power (*Dao De Jing*), attributed to Laozi (the Old Master). Zhuangzi calls him "Old Long Ears." He is said to have been a reclusive government archivist who lived around 500 BCE. Legends have him both instructing Confucius and traveling West to become the Buddha. The *Dao De Jing* contains both mystical and non-mystical passages written in stylized verse addressed principally to a sage ruler (*shengren*).[4] In its present form, it is a conglomeration of different ideas of the time, with passages on governing and military defense. We cannot tell which ideas existed before it and which were new. (Daoist-like hermits occasionally appear in the *Analects* confronting Confucius.) Versions of it from the fourth century BCE contain some of its lines in different places; its final form is from the Han period (206 BCE–220 CE).

The other early text, the *Zhuangzi*, is also from this period.[5] The narrative stories in its Inner Chapters (1–7) were probably the product of Master Zhuang Zhou himself (Zhuangzi, d. ca. 286 BCE), but the book is an anthology containing chapters of later miscellaneous material from different schools with different points of view. The Inner Chapters make no mention of the *Dao De Jing* or Laozi. Angus Graham (1981) labels the other strands as *primitivists*, who made the personal cultivation of rulers central (see D 80); *syncretists*, who combined Daoist ideas of the *Dao* with Chinese cosmology; and *hedonists*, who followed the ideas of Yang Zhu (ca. fourth century BCE) of showing disregard for others and having personal longevity as the goal. The *Zhuangzi* is about how private persons should live, not how to govern.

Only one pre-Han work, the *Guanzi*, has material articulating Daoist introvertive meditation practices—sections entitled "Inner Training" (*Neiye*) from around 350 BCE and "Techniques of the Mind" (*Xinshu Shang*) from around 250 BCE that describe practices for removing desires, emotions, knowledge, and thoughts; aligning the body with the *Dao*; controlling the breath (*qi*); unifying awareness; stilling the mind; "holding fast to the One"; and performing Buddhist-like concentrative and insight meditations. The *Huainanzi* (ca. 150 BCE) synthesizes the earlier ideas within a framework centering on the patterns or principles (*li*) of the *Dao* and introvertive meditation practices for the sage ruler.[6]

Confucians place human beings at the center of the scheme of things, while Daoists treat them as only one of the "ten thousand things." Increased learning of distinctions and rules is the central task of Confucian cultivation. Confucius begins the *Analects* by praising the pleasure of learning. However, Confucian self-cultivation is not mystical; nothing in the *Analects* suggests any altered states of consciousness, and enlightenment is only a matter of following the myriad of social rules effortlessly once they have been thoroughly internalized. Thus, names and rules that are devised by the mind are central and are ingrained in the enlightened Confucian way of life. But, to Daoists, such social embellishments are precisely what we must unlearn to allow the *Dao* to operate in us unimpeded by human artificiality. That is, to Daoists, what Confucians value most is exactly what interferes with the natural flow of the *Dao* and, thus, must be removed. Zhuangzi's parable of enforcing uniformity by drilling seven holes into the primordial unformed Chaos (*hundun*), thereby killing it, to make it like us illustrates

Daoists' attitude to all things cultural (Z 7). It imposes a human order on the naturalness of reality.

In short, Daoism is a matter of uncultivation in order to attune oneself with the *Dao*. We must return to what we really are prior to culture. Any names, rules, or rituals are imposed on us externally and only impede the flow of the *Dao* in us. Thus, we must eliminate the layers of artificiality added to us from the outside in order to let the *Dao*'s power manifest itself in us. How nature acts free of the artificial inventions of culture is the model for how we should act (D 25) since the various parts of nature follow the *Dao* spontaneously and effortlessly.[7] This means that Daoism does not complement Confucianism—it is not the *yin* to Confucius's *yang*—and Daoist knowledge is not a matter of internalizing Confucian learning in a different manner. Rather, Daoists offer an alternative approach to society and individuals that eliminates what Confucians value. Zhuangzi's reaction to his wife's death was a complete rejection of Confucian ritual requirements; once he reconciled with her transformation, he sang and banged on a tub (Z 18).

In sum, the entire thrust of Daoism is toward less social cultivation in order to allow the *Dao* to flow spontaneously through us. The Daoist approach involves a lack of coercion and a yielding in all actions. This leads to naturalness and spontaneity. Its objective is to live as long a life as possible (e.g., D 50, 52, 55; Z 28–31), and not being in accord with the *Dao* leads to an early demise (D 30). Being content and knowing when to stop striving leads to a long life (D 33, 44, 46). Violent and fierce people do not come to a natural end (D 42), but all cultural enterprises involve some type of assertive striving. Daoists value the twisted, gnarly tree more than artificially cultivated trees since the latter end up being cut down for lumber while the former is ignored and lives longer (Z 1). (Daoist gardens are deliberately asymmetrical to contrast with the rigid symmetries of Confucian courtyards and to represent spontaneous nature unstructured by human beings.) Likewise, Zhuangzi values people with mutilations (Z 5).

This view is very much an ethos of being at home in the world, not renouncing it. Daoists disparage nothing about this world except the cultural accretions that we impose on it, and early Daoist texts do not suggest a goal outside this life. Zhuangzi made death a major topic—although not suffering, as with the Buddhists—but had no great fear of it. He was light-hearted even about death since it is merely part of the transformation (*hua*) of things—a return to the forces at work in nature. He was even-minded; from the point of view of the "equality of all things" (Z 2), whether he was alive or dead made no difference. There is no individual independent of the *Dao* to consider. Moreover, Daoists ask: How do we know that love of life is not a delusion and that those who fear death are not like a child who is lost and cannot find their way home (Z 2)?

Strategies for attaining a long life differed for Laozi and Zhuangzi. As discussed later in this chapter, Laozi emphasized an introvertive depth-mysticism, discovering the *Dao* by stilling the mind and emptying it of all content. Zhuangzi emphasized an extrovertive awareness that involved stilling the mind (*jing*) of conceptual clutter. He also added philosophical points to try to crack the rigidity of thinking that one's own point of view is somehow grounded in reality in a way that others' points of view are not: How do we know that we know (Z 2)? His most famous parable is of a dream in which he was a butterfly and had no idea he had ever been anything else; when he awoke, he asked himself, "Did Zhuangzi dream he was a butterfly, or is the butterfly now dreaming he is Zhuangzi?" (Z 2, 6).[8] The point of the parable is that we are unable to know what the correct point of view is or to transcend our own limited point of view to reflect the point of view of the *Dao*. What one animal considers beautiful, another considers ugly. There is no one standard for all, nor is there a fixed or universal human point of view. From the "point of view of heaven," all our limited points of view reduce what is real to only what is valuable for us. They do not let reality be as it truly is. Believing one's own point of view is superior is like a frog in a well that sees only a small sliver of the sky and thinks it sees the whole (Z 17).

The Daoists' *Dao*

For early Daoists, the *Dao* is twofold: the inexhaustible underlying source and ground of everything in the world that transcends phenomena and also a principle operating within the world that structures order and thereby guides the transformation (*hua*) of phenomena.[9] All things emerge from this great mysterious root source (*ben-yuan*) or womb and ultimately return to it (D 6, 16, 40; Z 18). We can dip from it, but it never empties (Z 2). The unnameable, constant *Dao* is the empty hub of a wheel where all the spokes meet (D 6), and the nameable *Dao* is the rim consisting of all things. The *Dao* is the origin of all things, yet it still flows through them; it both creates and sustains everything (D 51). The nameable *Dao* is the organizing structure that gives order to the flux of change in the world. The unnameable and the named *Dao* are the same reality, but after things arose, it had different aspects (D 1). That the source and the phenomenal realm are one and the same is "the mystery of mysteries" (*xuan*, deep and profound) and "the gateway to all wonder" (D 1). It is formless and, thus, not experienceable by the senses (D 14; Z 6). Although it is deep and obscure, in it are forms, things, and the essence of phenomena (*jing*, or their *qi*) (D 21). It is not dependent on anything but is formless, unchanging, all-pervading, never-failing, and soundless.

From this, the *Dao De Jing* sets forth a cosmogony: the unnameable constant *Dao* (*heng-dao*) is the unchanging ground of heaven and earth; the nameable *Dao* is the mother (D 1, 20, 25) or the father (D 21) or the inexhaustible ancestor (D 4, 51) of all things in the world and is eternally present, nourishing everything.[10] The transcendent, unnameable, and constant aspect of the *Dao* creates heaven and earth. The nameable, transforming *Dao* is immanent (D 1). The unnameable *Dao* is the nonbeing (*wu*)—the reality that is the source of being (*you*) (D 1, 40; Z 12)—out of which everything arises and into which everything returns. The nameable *Dao* emerges from this abyss of nonbeing and is called the "One" (D 10, 22, 39), the "Great One" (Z 24), or the raw "uncarved block" (*pu*) (D 28, Z 9). From this undifferentiated oneness, *yin* and *yang* emerged; from this, *yin* and *yang* in balance emerged; and from that, the multiplicity of all things emerges (D 42). The unnameable *Dao* cannot be followed, but the nameable *Dao* is embedded in all things and can be followed (D 1, 14, 21, 24). The *Zhuangzi* often avoids naming it directly, calling it, for example, the "Great Forge" or the "Great Smelter" (Z 6), the "original ground" (*gu*) (Z 19), or the "celestial potter's wheel" of the transformations (Z 27).

The *Dao* is not caused by an external agent and, thus, is its own cause (*ziran*, self-so) (D 4, 11, 25, 40; Z 6, 12). It is eternal and unchanging (*chang*) (D 1, 41), but there is an infinite regress only of temporal beginnings and of being emerging from and returning to nonbeing (Z 2). The *Dao* "pervades and unifies" (Z 2). Zhuangzi emphasized the perpetual transformation of things and never elevated the permanence of the source over that dynamic change, while Laozi emphasized things' inevitable return to the inexhaustible root source (*fan-dao*). Sages set aside what is beyond the world without discussion and stop at what they do not know (Z 2). However, even as all phenomena are perpetually transforming, the *Dao* is unchanging (Z 1, 6, 7; D 1) and operates impartially in all things (Z 2, 6, 18). Daoists make no suggestion of a theistic god or entity intervening in nature. Rather, the *Dao* is a nonpersonal natural reality—a self-giving source that benefits all equally. The *Dao* is like gravity in Einstein's theory: natural objects moving under the "force" of gravity are actually guided by the curvature of space-time. Here, nature and the enlightened sage, in effect, float on the waves of the *Dao*.

The *Dao* is the source of effective action (Z 12). The *Dao* is manifested in a particular thing as that thing's inner potency or power (*de*). This is the concrete power of the *Dao* operating in each thing, human or nonhuman (D 21, 51). Although the unnameable *Dao* is constant in its action, *de* varies from thing to thing, reflecting the capacity that each individual thing has received from the *Dao*. Those correctly aligned with the *Dao* are filled with *de* and express their inner power in their actions. *De* is usually translated "virtue" in the sense of capacity—as in, "The virtue of this pen is that it writes smoothly." The symbols making up *de* are *step*, *straight* or *correct*, and *heart/mind* (*xin*). In the Inner Chapters of the *Zhuangzi*, *de* also refers to virtue in an ethical sense (Z 4, 5; see also D 63), but in the *Dao De Jing*, *de* usually refers to a potency in all things in reality as it does the Outer and Miscellaneous Chapters of the *Zhuangzi* (Z 8, 9, 16, 20).

While the *Dao* can be thought of in the singular as the all-embracing organizing principle, it manifests differently in different things. The *Dao* that can be walked—"*dao*-ed"—is not the constant, nameless *Dao* (D 1). We can follow the nameable *Dao*, but there are multiple manifestations of the nameable *Dao* and, hence, many ways—"*dao*'s"—to nature, each determining what something's natural activity is. The "equality" all things have as products of the *Dao* does not mean all things have one master pattern to which all the various patterns that plants, animals, and human beings follow can be reduced. It is these ways that can be followed to manifest a phenomenon's *de*. All of nature automatically follows the *dao* of its particular type, thereby producing a harmonious order, but most human beings are out of step with the human *dao*.[11]

Thus, despite its profundity (*xuan*), the *Dao* has a natural order for each thing, and we can discern and follow the natural human *dao*. Laozi held up infants as exemplars (D 10, 49) because they naturally follow the *Dao* due to their total lack of enculturation. But this does not mean that he thought that adults should be infants or animals. Only if we fulfill the particular human *dao* can we return to our proper niche in the natural order of things. It is a matter of finding the natural human way, not reducing us to something we are not.

Language and the *Dao*

Enlightened Daoists are totally free of fixed conceptualizations, having "forgotten" all distinctions, Confucian and otherwise. Thus, in perceptions, the enlightened see a continuum of colors without cutting it up into five distinct categories (one possible reading of D 12). However, being literally free of all concepts is hard to reconcile with the fact that Laozi and Zhuangzi could talk and write. That Daoists wrote and held particular ideas means that there is some role for language and beliefs in their view of the human *dao*. Guo Xiang (d. 312 CE) in his commentary on the *Zhuangzi* was the first Daoist to point out that words and human knowledge are as much a part of the universe as natural objects and, thus, are part of the human way. The consciousness necessary to use language may be foreign to the depth-mystical experience, but it is not foreign to the extrovertive enlightened state in which a sage's consciousness is aligned with the *Dao*.

Thus, the enlightened can speak about the *Dao* without falling out of sync with it. Most human beings, however, have fallen out of step with our way; the discriminating mind cuts the uncarved world up into distinct parts, thereby alienating us from the *Dao*. We do not spontaneously move with the *Dao*. The culprit, according to Laozi, is our habit of living according to conceptual distinctions that we ourselves devise. We reason what is right or wrong, and we accept our concepts as reflecting the nature of reality, but concepts only reflect our preferences and needs. Nevertheless, our own creations fix our attention, and we respond to our concepts rather than to reality. All languages carve the "uncarved block" of nature into differentiated entities based on our artificial distinctions (D 19, 28). Concepts arise by differentiating; we call something beautiful only when we see something ugly to contrast with it (D 2, 38). If everything were beautiful, we would have nothing to contrast beauty with, so we would have no term *ugly* and, hence, no term *beautiful*. Thus, like other contrasts, the concepts *being* and *nonbeing* produce each other (D 2). To use a Daoist image, fish have no concept of water because it is a constant in their experience; thus, they never have anything with which to contrast with it and are not even aware of it unless they are removed from the water. The same occurs with values. Concepts of humaneness and righteousness/justice arose only when the great *Dao* declined and only reflect a particular culture and era (D 5, 18; Z 9). Thus, what Confucians value and endeavor to maintain do not put us in sync with the *Dao*; their rules and paths are hopelessly snarled and jumbled (Z 2).

When the world conformed automatically to the *Dao*, there were no standards to state because we were not aware of another condition. The man of superior power (*de*) is not conscious of his power because he has nothing to contrast with it (D 38). That is, we are only aware of power when we are not one with the *Dao* and, thus, are aware of a distinction between it and something else. When we are aware of discriminations, we live in a world of those discriminations, not in accord with the *Dao*. Our actions are artificial (*wei*) rather than a natural response to the situation (*wei wuwei*). We need to return to the oneness of the "uncarved block" that is prior to differentiations arising from names, not a Confucian rectification of names (D 32, 37). This frees us from personal desire (*yu*), we attune ourselves to the *Dao*, and the world becomes peaceful of its own accord (D 37). In a society at one with the *Dao*, there would be no terms concerning the *Dao* or *de* because we would unaware of the *Dao* or its power in us.

Zhuangzi, too, noted how language generates discriminations. The concept of *this* produces the concept of *that* and vice versa (Z 4). The very concept of division means there is something to divide—something undivided prior to division—that is missed after the fact. Thus, to discriminate between alternatives is to fail to see something real (Z 5). The world does not come precut for our distinctions. Adopting a set of names means adopting a point of view, but only the point of view of the *Dao* is absolute. Any other perspective makes something the center of the phenomenal world, but there is no such center; all things are related to other things and are perpetually transforming. All our words draw boundaries between things, but these boundaries are constantly shifting as our interests and preferences change while reality remains the same. The enlightened would use language pragmatically to navigate the world but would be willing to abandon any linguistic distinctions and adopt others as the situation requires.

The parable of the monkeys and the nuts illustrates Zhuangzi's point. The monkeys complained about getting only three nuts to eat in the morning but four in the evening, so their keeper placated them by giving them four in the morning and three in the evening. The substance of what they got was exactly the same as the day before, yet the monkeys were happy because they were caught up in the labels (Z 5). If we realize that the substance remains the same, our minds do not become fixed by whatever set of words or point of view we adopt; we can utilize them and still wander freely. However, people who are still within the borders of "knowing" and "not knowing" cannot see through Zhuangzi's words (Z 17). Once we catch a fish, we forget about the trap. Likewise, words exist because of their meaning. Once we have gotten the meaning, we can forget the words and not be trapped. Where, Zhuangzi asked, could he find someone who has forgotten words so that he could have a word with them (Z 26)?

Laozi had more trouble reconciling a theory of language with the fact that he used language to describe the profound *Dao* (D 2, 23, 25, 43, 70, 73, 78). The enlightened reflect the *Dao*, but the *Dao* is silent, so one who knows does not speak, and one who speaks does not know (D 56, Z 22). The *Dao De Jing* begins with the problem that the eternal and constant *Dao* (*chang-dao*) cannot be *dao*'ed (walked or spoken) and that there is the nameless (D 1; see also 14, 20, 25, 32, 37, 41). However, Laozi also names the unseen, unheard, and ungrasped as such (D 14), thereby making it an object to be a referent for the name. He distinguished a "private name" (*ming*) from a "public name" (*zi*), and he said that the term *Dao* is used only in the first sense since there is no public name for it (D 25). However, this does not get around the fundamental problem: private names as much as public ones mark off one object from all other objects. If all names distinguish, how can we name the undifferentiated reality from which all else emerges? What can we contrast it with? Thus, the constant *Dao* cannot be named since names set limits and the constant *Dao* is limitless. It is nameless and cannot even be spoken of at all since it is dark and mysterious (*xuan*). All Laozi can do is style it as "the Way" (D 25, 34).

Nevertheless, Laozi (or others) did write, even if he claimed a "doctrine with no words" (D 2, 43; see also Z 5) and ascribed attributes to the *Dao*—such as source of the world's order and impartiality. The *Scripture of Western Ascension* offers an explanation of this paradox of speaking the unspeakable by comparing knowledge of the *Dao* to hearing music. One can hear music and know the appropriate sounds, but the mouth is unable to formulate it; similarly, one can know the deep and subtle *Dao* and not be able to speak of it (Kohn 2011, 132–33). Yet, Laozi still spoke of the *Dao*. In fact, he said his words were easy to understand and to practice (D 70). This means that, for him, not all language is foreign to the human *dao*: the nameable *Dao* can be discerned or conformed to in some manner and thereby followed (D 1), and language at least leads us to following the *Dao* properly.

However, to Daoists, Confucius's way is language-guided while the Daoists' is reality-guided and free of the artifices of culture embodied in a language's distinctions. We need to turn from the cultivated self and allow our natural capacity (*de*) to flow forth. That is how we become properly human, not by dwelling in learned discriminations. To Daoists, Confucians paint by numbers, while Daoists spontaneously create landscape paintings based on the inner reality of the scene.

The *Dao* and Mystical Experiences

The point that these Daoists made about the relation of language to reality can be seen as a logical one: language cannot mirror reality because language divides while reality is undivided and because words are static while phenomena are impermanent and constantly changing. This is so too with the point about different limited human perspectives: languages do not reflect reality but our interests. However, the impetus for their theory may also be mystical experiences. This claim is open to dispute since there is no extensive treatment of meditative practices or methods but only hints of them in either the *Dao De Jing* or the *Zhuangzi*. Mystical states are likewise only hinted at.[12] Daoists do not see any need for an ontological "union" with the *Dao* since we are already products of the unnameable *Dao* and as substantively at one with it as we are ever going to be. We need a union (*he-dao*) merely in the sense of aligning our inner lives with the human *dao*. There is also less in these texts on the loss of a sense of an individual self than in most mystical traditions. Becoming free of self-assertion and personal desires is necessary to conform to the *Dao* for Laozi and Zhuangzi, but the person is part of the natural realm and life after death.[13]

Despite these disclaimers, there are many passages in both texts whose least-forced interpretation is that mystical cultivation and inner transformation are the means for realigning ourselves with the *Dao* away from self-interests. That is, it is by decultivating Confucian standards and cultivating an inner clarity and stillness (*qing-jing*) that the *Dao* manifests itself in us; and, thereby, we are able to follow the natural human way in a state of consciousness devoid of a sense of self. This would mean that there is a mystical dimension to all the activities discussed in the texts and that mystical experiences seen within the context of the ancient Chinese worldview may have been the source of the Daoist doctrines.

Laozi's mysticism appears to be an introvertive depth mysticism. He refers to concentrating the breath and sweeping clean the profound mirror (*xuan-jian*) of the mind (D 10). Other passages are more cryptic but suggestive. For example, the "profound merging" (*xuan-tong*): we should close our mouths (become silent) and shut our doors (the senses), blunt the sharpness (of the dualizing mind), untangle the knots (of conceptualizations and attachments), soften the light, and become one with the dusty world (D 4, 52, 56). We can know (*zhi*) the world without stepping out of the door and see the *Dao* of heaven without looking out windows; the farther we go outside, the less we know (D 47). This may refer simply to not getting caught up in worldly matters, or it may be a symbolic statement for stopping sense experience during concentrative meditation (D 56). Other passages suggest a mystical quest: attaining complete emptiness (*wu*) and maintaining complete tranquility (*jing*) (D 16); decreasing desires and abolishing learning (D 3, 19, 37, 46, 64); always being without desires (D 1, 19, 37, 57; Z 9, 12, 18, 20, 23, 25); embracing simplicity (D 19); and not overindulging the senses (D 12). We increase daily by learning, but we decrease daily by practicing the *Dao*, indicating the total end of conceptual discrimination as a goal (D 48). We should embrace the undifferentiated One (D 10, 22). Thus, the sage has learned to "unlearn" (D 64), has no extensive knowledge (D 81), and is ignorant (D 20). In the resulting enlightened state, one conforms fully with the *Dao* (D 55).

Laozi is not against mystical knowledge of the root (the *Dao*) but only against the learning (*xue*) that is an obstruction to realizing the *Dao* (D 52, 57). To know the mother (the *Dao*) is to know the sons (all things, D 52) since everything has the same ontic source. The *Dao* is accessible but not as an object of knowledge; we need to unlearn the content of the mind to realize it. The central practice, thus, is embracing the One and attaining the complete emptiness (*xu*) and stillness (*jing*) of realizing the eternal (D 15, 16, 39). We need to reduce selfishness and desires because the *Dao* is without desires (D 1, 3, 7, 19, 37, 46, 57, 64). We need to return to the simplicity of the "uncarved block" (D 28) and the root (D 1, 16). The *Dao* is invisible, inaudible, and without form (D 14, 25, 35), and only by the inward illumination (*ming*) do we know the everlasting (D 10, 16, 22, 24, 41, 52, 55).

Zhuangzi also emphasized emptying the mind of sensory and conceptual content through the practices of "sitting and forgetting" (*zuo-wang*) in oblivion and "fasting of the heart/mind" (*xin-zhai*)—not listening with the ears or the mind but with the spirit (*qi*) and unifying one's attention (Z 4, 6, 22). The heart is like withered wood and the mind like dead ashes (Z 2, 19–24). The *Dao* flows without resistance (Z 11). Zhuangzi lists seven stages, beginning with practicing concentration for three days, that lead to freedom beyond life and death (Z 6). There are also passages that suggest controlled breathing—the *Dao* gathers in this emptiness (e.g., Z 4). The *Zhuangzi* includes names such as "Bear Stride" and "Bird Stretches" that may refer to yogic positions (Z 15). From holding fast to the One, the resulting cultivated states include tranquility (*jing, an*), equanimity (*qi*), silence (*mo*), serenity (*tian*), and detachment (*dan*). Resulting traits include non-assertive action (*wei wuwei*), selflessness (*wusi*), simplicity (*su*), and spontaneity (*ziran*).

The doctrines that scholars meticulously learn and memorize cramp their vision as much as the limited point of view of a frog in a well (Z 17) and, thus, must be forgotten. Zhuangzi's philosophical points fit naturally here. There can never be any fixed knowledge of reality because reality is constantly changing; there is nothing constant for our words to correspond to, and reality will never remain contained in the conceptual boxes we create. "Forgetting" or "fasting the mind" is to lose all the conventions and distinctions associated with a Confucian sense of self.[14] It is totally forgetting oneself. "I drop away my limbs and body, drive out perception and intellect, cast off the body and do away with knowledge, and merge with the Great Thoroughfare" (Z 6). Such cultivation involves discarding little and great knowledge—"casting off the fetters of the mind" (Z 23) to become clear (Z 26)—and wandering outside the realm of forms and bodies (Z 5). Only by unknowing what others take to be knowledge can we hope to know the *Dao* (Z 24) since non-mystical knowledge obscures the *Dao*. Emptiness (*xu*) is the knowledge that does not know (for example, Z 4, 13, 15). The *Dao* settles in such emptiness (Z 4).[15]

Zhuangzi saw Laozi as going for a stroll at the origin of things, but he himself remained firmly within the myriad of the "ten thousand things." Thus, while Laozi saw the depth-mystical experience as the route to the *Dao*, Zhuangzi remained with an extrovertive illumination (*ming*) of the everyday realm that opens things up to the "lucid light of heaven" (Z 2) that operates in everything. As Lee Yearley (1983) calls it, it is an "intraworldly mysticism." The *Zhuangzi* does have passages suggesting that introvertive depth-mystical experiences empty of all objects are the means to align oneself with the *Dao*, but Zhuangzi valued more the mystical extrovertive state that expresses this alignment once one returns to the everyday world (see Roth 2000).

Zhuangzi spoke of seeing things as equal (*qiwu*): "The sage leans on the sun and moon, tucks the cosmos under his arm, merges himself with things, leaves the confusion and muddle as it is, and looks on slaves as exalted. Ordinary men strain and struggle; the sage is stupid and blockish. He takes part in the ten thousand things and achieves simplicity in oneness" (Z 2; Watson 1968, 42). If we perceive things with attention to differentiating factors, then our own liver and gallbladder are as different as different countries; yet, from the point of view of their commonality, all natural phenomena are one since they are all equally products of the *Dao* (Z 5, 17). The unmoving "axis of the *Dao*" (*dao-shu*) on which all phenomena move and change indicates that what is high from one creature's point of view is low from another's. What is death from one point of view is a return to the process of change—a birth of sorts—from another. From the point of view of the *Dao*, there is nothing greater in all the world than the smallest item (Z 2, 17). All things are equal from the perspective of their source. Freed from the confines of the conflicting human points of view, one can "embrace the ten thousand things and roll them into one" (Z 1). This flattens any emotions based on personal preferences and attachments such as joy and sadness (Z 2).

This evenness comes from all things sharing the same nature as equal products of the *Dao*, but achieving it requires an experiential shift rather than merely adopting a philosophical point about the thatness of reality that exists apart from our division of reality into things. The enlightened way of seeing levels out the "this" and "that" (*qiwu*) produced by our limited human perspectives (Z 2); and, thus, the enlightened are not attached to any particular feature. This includes themselves. With their death, nothing real is lost; whatever is real returns to the root for another transformation. More generally, all passion and desire, all likes and dislikes, are foreign to the *Dao* (Z 2, 6). The ultimate objective is to remove the blocks interrupting the flow of the *Dao* in order to revert to the original harmony of heaven, earth, society, and the physical body. Things then succeed by themselves through their own power (*de*). Using the constant *Dao* is using the clarity or illumination of the still mind (*ming*). This does not blur out differences in perception—indeed, variety and individuality are celebrated—but all particular things are seen as products of the *Dao*. Only then do we reach the impartiality of the Great Understanding (Z 26). We have leaped into the Boundless (Z 2), free of emotions and of attachment generated by our conceptual differentiations.

Zhuangzi on the Enlightened State

Through inner cultivation, we remove the encrustation of culture. We cannot see the *Dao*, but we can realize it internally since it is always present, sustaining us (Z 6). For Zhuangzi, the perfected "untrammeled man" (*zhen-*

ren) is completely in harmony with the natural flow of the *Dao*.[16] The *Dao* is represented as sound (Z 2), and the enlightened are in tune with it. In the contemplative mode (*guan*) of the enlightened state, one is receptive, calm, free of attachments, even-minded (*ping*), and emotionally unaffected by either disasters or ordinary everyday concerns. The untrammeled are without feelings and free from dreams and worries as they wander through the world (Z 5, 6).

The enlightened embody the human way fully—their potency (*de*) is fully active—and they mesh seamlessly with the daos of the rest of nature. They are one with the rhythm of nature's changes. Thereby, they move frictionlessly through life. They are at ease (*shi*) in all situations. The enlightened thrive in the *Dao* like fish do in water. This knowledge is not intellectual but mystical; one does not merely understand the *Dao* as one would an object of study, but one participates in it. Knowing how the *Dao* works is the "inner lucidity" (Z 2). By guarding the root (the One), the myriad affairs are done (Z 12), but the enlightened are mindful of what occurs.

Any conceptual elements from culture that remain in the mind of the enlightened do not fix the mind; but, instead, the mind's focus goes with the flow of experience. Nothing attracts attention more than anything else. Free of desires, the mind (*xin*, located in the heart) makes no interpretations or judgments. The mind is empty and still, letting reality fill it. In an image utilized in Chan Buddhism, the mind, like still water, becomes an unclouded mirror, fully attentive but merely reflecting what is really there—seeking nothing, welcoming nothing, responding but storing nothing as one wanders in a world without a beginning (Z 7, 33). Small things mean as much as great things; thus, one remains dispassionate and quiet at the sight of magnificent scenes (D 26).

The enlightened sage is still, and nothing disturbs them, but they are not inactive. They move from moment to moment, letting events come and go. They forget what happened before and respond immediately to what is before them. Enlightened actions can be called simple, natural, and spontaneous since no artificiality from cultural conventions or personal desires interferes with the flow of the *Dao*. The enlightened are free of both personal concerns and deliberations; thus, their actions are spontaneously self-generated (*ziran*). Mindful knowledge mirrors only what is there, and enlightened actions mirror that knowledge by responding only to what is there.

The *Zhuangzi* refers to this as "wandering free and easy, tending to nothing" (Z 1, 19), but enlightened action is not purposeless or mindless—there are objectives to attain. Zhuangzi's examples of skilled individuals who had a mirror-like mind from following the *Dao* all had goals (Z 3, 19). The point is that the enlightened stay centered, focused on what is really there before them, and respond immediately—free of deliberation but not literally mindless. Zhuangzi's exemplars of enlightened action come mainly from lower-class artisans—cooks, wood-carvers, wheelwrights, cicada catchers—whom Confucians looked down upon. In each case, the artisan's attention is totally absorbed in the object they deal with. They spread their attention over the whole situation, let their mind's focus roam freely, and forget themselves in this total absorption; then, the artisan's hand reacts spontaneously with a confidence and precision that is impossible for anyone who applies rules and thinks out their moves.

Consider some of Zhuangzi's examples. Before picking a piece of wood to carve into a bell stand, Qing the wood-carver fasted for seven days in order to forget everything—his rewards and salary, any praise or blame, his skill or clumsiness, even his body and limbs (Z 19). He then went into the forest with his skill concentrated, and all outside distractions faded away. He remained open and flexible. If he did not find a superlative piece of wood, he left. If he did, he saw a bell stand, and his hand then spontaneously followed the natural patterns and carved it. He was simply matching his heavenly nature with that of the wood. Similarly, Ding the cook carving up an ox: early in his career, he saw the whole carcass; after three years, he saw no more whole animals; finally, he worked only with his spirit, not with his eyes and understanding. Thereupon, when carving an ox, his hand moved his cleaver smoothly through the hollows and openings of the animal, missing all ligaments, tendons, and joints. Thus, his blade was never dull again (Z 3; see also D 28). All perception and all understanding of the ox had ceased; only then could his spirit move where it wanted since it no longer needed the control of his senses. His final skill did not involve scientific knowledge of the anatomy of an ox. Instead, he followed the structure immediately before him without applying any external knowledge of the nature and location of the ox's parts. He responded with a still mind to whatever was there, not imposing a preconceived notion of what he would find or what he would do. Only by unknowing all discursive knowledge did he achieve his spontaneous skill. Any intellectual knowledge would go against the grain; it is "underbrush" filling the mind, cluttering up the person, and interfering with what they are doing (Z 1). Freed of such clutter, the enlightened become one with their activity. This was also the case with Zhuangzi's example of the swimmer: he stayed afloat not by fighting the currents but by forgetting everything, including himself, and moving with the flow of the swirls and eddies in the whirlpool; thereby, he did not drown in a river even fish could not swim in (Z 19).

More generally, the enlightened apply such mystical skills to life. In harmony with the *Dao* and free of fixed human perspectives, they move effortlessly through the empty spaces of the world and do not perish.[17] Free of the interference of the self-assertive mind, people with skillful spontaneity are like drunks who fall from a carriage without being hurt (Z 19) since the *Dao* flows freely through them as they flow along in it (Kohn 2016, 202).

Scholars typically see Zhuangzi's artisans in terms of acquired skill and use examples of skills acquired through practice—playing tennis, typing—to make the point that we respond automatically when a skill is finally perfected. Enlightened action is, indeed, a type of skill and takes time to develop, but Zhuangzi mentioned nothing about repeated practice for acquiring each skill. Ding the cook did not become an expert carver just through years of practice but by emptying his mind of preconceptions. With the calculating conceptual mind inactive, he automatically followed the spaces in the joints without resistance. This is not a skill acquired by repeating certain strokes thousands of times but an ability to follow the natural guidance of the *Dao* achieved through inner cultivation. His real skill is in following the *Dao*, not in practicing a human activity. In short, it is a mystical knowledge gained by participating in the *Dao*, not a conventional know-how acquired by repeated practice. The enlightened share with supremely skilled athletes or musicians being lost in the moment and responding automatically (and also the ineffability involved in trying to articulate clearly any type of expertise), but the point of Zhuangzi's stories is about conforming to the *Dao*. Scholars miss all this by imposing something familiar, their distinctions, on the unfamiliar—no doubt, something Zhuangzi would have found amusing.

Wei Wuwei

In any situation, Laozi emphasized taking the yielding tack more than Zhuangzi. He employed a number of images to describe the *Dao*: the weak over the strong (D 30, 36, 76); softness over hardness (D 43, 78); the soft, flexible, supple, and yielding as the principle of life (D 76, 78); water conforming to the space available but wearing down even the hardest rock (D 78); water nourishing all and not competing (D 8); children and infants rather than adults (D 10, 20, 28, 49, 55); the feminine rather than the aggressive masculine (D 6, 25, 28); the mother of heaven and earth rather than the father (D 1, 3, 20, 25, 34, 52, 59); the womb that pours out and receives back all beings (D 6); the root rather than the trunk and branches (D 16); the empty vessel (D 4); the vacuous bellows that produce without fail (D 5); the valley that receives the rivers (D 6, 15, 28, 32, 39, 41); the empty hub of the wheel where the spokes meet (D 11); silence and emptiness (D 4, 25, 33); the dark and mysterious rather than the bright and known (D 1, 4). The *Dao*—the vague and elusive receptive source of everything—operates by weakness (D 40), non-contention (D 8), and receiving beings back (D 40). When its work is done, it withdraws (D 9). The virtues that we are to cultivate reflect the *Dao*: passivity, humility, stillness, and simplicity free of self-assertion. One becomes more like a child, with their genuineness and spontaneity free of enculturation, than a learned scholar of high social standing. In short, one knows the *yang* but adheres to the *yin* (D 28, Z 33). By cultivating the negative, the sage operates in conformity with the *Dao*, and their potency (*de*) is maximized.

Enlightened action is *wei wuwei*, literally "action without action" (D 63; Z 11, 22). The phrase has led to many misleading translations: "inaction," "no action," "not doing," "doing nothing," "taking no action," "nonaction," "directionless action," "unintentional action," "purposeless action," "passivity." Most of these leave the initial *wei*—action—out of the full expression. Some of these phrases capture the contradiction in the Chinese phrase, but the concept of *wei wuwei* in the context of the full *Dao De Jing* and *Zhuangzi* in no way suggests inaction or lack of purpose: only action free of personal desires or perspectives. The enlightened act, but without any self-assertion. They take no acts of personal self-will, and the *Dao* acts through them. They do not take any personal initiative or lead (D 3, 7, 22, 37, 57, 67). Thus, "nonassertive action," "action free from personal striving," or "yielding action" would all be better translations. That is to say, if we remove all artifices of the Confucian cultivation of humaneness, all personal desires, and all other self-assertions from our actions, the *Dao* will act spontaneously in us; and, thereby, what is needed to be done will occur naturally (*ziran*). It is like gravity: instead of fighting to defy it and losing, we should use it to accomplish a goal and live easily within it, without sticking personal desires in the way.

Thus, the actions of the enlightened are non-self-assertive actions automatically following the *Dao*, not assertions of personal purposes or interests. Being free of self-assertion does not mean that we cannot have objectives in our actions but only that we do not value ourselves more than others or otherwise assert our personal interests. Zhuangzi's artisans are good examples of *wei wuwei*, although he rarely employed the term. For Laozi, the term is most often associated with the sage ruler, whose purpose is to govern. The enlightened sage cannot be totally discounted—they are, after all, part of reality too and must eat and so forth to survive. To deny their own existence would be as out of step with reality for a sage as over-asserting themselves, but the sage does not assert themselves over others. With *wei wuwei*, the sage does not try to bend a situation, either for their personal profit or in reaction to preconceived expectations or judgments of good or bad. It is the way to bring about objectives most in keeping with actual reality. In sum, we should stop planning and pushing and just let the *Dao* operate through us.

For Laozi, *wei wuwei* is simply *yin*-action: taking the yielding position to accomplish an objective. The *yin* is always to be emphasized over the assertive *yang* as the way to restore balance within our *yang*-dominated human world. Holding to the *yin* may seem as one-sided as always advancing *yang*-actions, but other than *yang*-actions needed for self-survival that are a natural part of the world and the human *dao*, *yang*-actions reflect only unenlightened human norms. Thus, advancing the *yin* is needed to counter the *yang* and establish a balance of the two. Holding to the inexhaustible source of *yin* in all actions counterbalances people's normal assertive *yang*-action. It reflects the *Dao* as the source of everything and conserves *qi*. The enlightened do not exhaust themselves by asserting personal goals that would interfere with the flow of the *Dao*. They do not resist but let the flow of the *Dao* work through them to accomplish actions.[18] *Yin*-actions are noncontentious, noninterfering, free of deliberation, and conform to the path of least resistance. The enlightened have no partiality-laden personal motives, so they do not impose themselves on the world. Even conceptualizations create obstacles to the *Dao* and, thus, friction if we hold them rigidly rather than treat them as changeable cultural conventions. All self-assertions, personal motivations, and attachments—including the emotions of joy, anger, delight, worry, and sadness (Z 2, 4, 5)—go against the grain of the *Dao*. The *Dao* takes no assertive action; and yet, nothing is left undone by a sage's power (*de*) flowing from the *Dao* (D 37, Z 18). Sages, too, "do nothing [through self-assertion] and everything will be done [naturally by the *Dao*]" (D 48, Z 18).

For Laozi, war is an evil to be avoided, never a tactic to be used to gain any type of power. All aggression is the epitome of the assertive *yang*-action that goes against the *Dao*.[19] However, the *Dao De Jing* contains passages on defensive war (D 30, 31, 68, 69). Laozi indicated that the *Dao*-inspired response is to try to avoid an impending war in the first place (D 68), to fight only when compelled to (D 69), to retreat whenever possible (D 69), and to mourn even in victory (D 31). By taking the yielding *yin*-action of the *Dao*, the sage ruler wins because they never compete—they take no *yang*-action (D 3, 8, 66, 68, 81)—just as the *Dao* does not compete and yet achieves victory (D 73). But despite taking defensive *yin*-actions, Daoists will strike if necessary and use sharp weapons (D 30, 31).

Wuwei is part of a family of *wu* forms in the *Dao De Jing*, all indicating the absence of something: *wu-ji* (nonbeing), *wu-si* (no-self), *wu-yu* (absence of personal desire), *wu-xing* (absence of form), and *wu-zhi* (absence of knowledge). But just as nonbeing is the positive source of being (D 40), so too, each absence is filled by something positive: absence of self-assertion with the power of the *Dao*; absence of desire with enjoyment without attachments; absence of form with true reality; absence of learned knowledge with direct, nonconceptual knowledge of the *Dao*; and absence of assertive action with the activity of the *Dao*. By yielding, we tap into an inexhaustible reserve of the *Dao*'s power (*de*), and all is accomplished. Events occur naturally of their own accord (*ziran*, self-so). Through the uncultivation of Confucian or other standards, we become empty of all self-assertion and consequently harmonize with the natural course of the *Dao*. With our entire inner character aligned with the *Dao*, its power shines forth. With our being firmly rooted in the *Dao*, our actions express a state of being where attention and action flow effortlessly and naturally rather than struggling to implement our plans or desires. In short, Daoist action is the self-expression of the *Dao*. Acting in this manner, the enlightened live a long life free from strife.

Governing by *Wuwei*

Laozi's sage has tasks that he wants to accomplish (D 2, 3, 9, 17, 30, 34, 37); he does not simply let things happen without human action. Rather, through *wei wuwei*, he utilizes the *Dao*'s power as the means to achieve his goals most effectively and efficiently (D 47).[20] For Laozi, chief among these goals is governing society. Zhuangzi, on the other hand, was thoroughly uninterested in governing and looked only to restore the balance within each individual through inner self-cultivation. He did not abandon society, but he was indifferent to political affairs and social reforms. He did not want his mind disturbed with talk of governing the world, but he did say that if an untrammeled man could not avoid governing, he should do it through *wuwei*: letting the sage's mind wander in simplicity, blending his spirit with the vastness, following along with things the way they are, and making no room for personal views. This is the way of "inner sagehood and external kingship" (Z 33). But Zhuangzi himself preferred simply to drag his tail in the mud (Z 7, 17). For him, trying to govern the world is like trying to walk across the ocean, drill a hole through a river, or have a mosquito shoulder a mountain (Z 7).

However, much of the *Dao De Jing* is about actualizing the *Dao* in political affairs. This is not surprising since the book was compiled during a period of political instability in China, so people were looking for ways to reestablish harmony and order. To Laozi, anyone who acts assertively will harm others and will fail (D 29, 48, 64). The more a ruler acts assertively, the more difficult the people are to govern (D 75). Thus, the sage ruler keeps actions to a minimum, as with cooking a small, delicate fish (D 60). To be qualified to rule, one must be tranquil (D 45, 58).

Using *wuwei* is the ideal (D 63). Then, the sage ruler acts but takes no personal assertive actions (D 2, 10, 51, 77, 81). They have no mind of their own but consider the minds of the common people to be their mind (D 49). To lead, the sage ruler must put themselves below and behind the people (D 66). The sage ruler is to their people what the *Dao* is to all of reality. Like the *Dao*, they lead but do not master (D 10, 30)—this is their dark power (*de*) (D 51). They never strive to do what is great and, thus, achieve great things (D 63). They do not rely upon themselves but take only yielding actions (D 61). Their achievements do not appear to be their own (Z 7). Thereby, they are no longer part of the picture—perfectly following the *Dao* leaves no trace (D 27; see also Z 2)—yet, their goal is achieved. We praise loyal ministers only when the country is in disorder: when the *Dao* has declined (D 18). The problem of the awareness of distinctions returns. As soon as there were regulations and institutions, there were names; and once there are names, we have drifted from the *Dao*, and it is time to stop (D 32). When, instead, the *Dao* acts effortlessly through the ruler (D 2, 29, 30, 32, 34), all things return to their natural state (D 2, 64). All happens of its own accord (*ziran*) (D 17).

Through *wuwei*, all is duly administered (D 3). By never striving for self-assertion, the sage ruler's task is accomplished. The *Dao* takes no action, but all is accomplished (D 37, 48); its natural pattern of governing takes over. The people are clothed and fed (D 2, 34). The sage does not dominate with force or oppression (D 30, 72) and does not attempt to be the people's master (D 2, 10). There is no need for capital punishment (D 74) or heavy taxation (D 75). The ruler need not impose order on things since the people transform themselves under the influence of the *Dao*. Conversely, the more laws there are, the more robbers there are (D 57). Thus, without laws or compulsion, the people dwell in harmony (D 32). When the people are not contending, the spontaneity of the *Dao* prevails in the society (D 46).

In sum, when the ruler achieves a noncoercive and nonauthoritarian government through *wei wuwei* in this top-down reform, the people are free of desires and spontaneously transform themselves (D 37, 50, 57), all things return to their original state of harmony (D 48, 54, 65), and the country is at peace (D 37). The ruler only needs to transform themselves through cultivating an inner stillness and practicing *wuwei* to bring about the transformation of all. Unlike exemplars of conduct who inspire people to change by their example—as with Confucius (*Analects* XII.19, II.1)—the ruler is not self-assertive, and when the country is being run properly, they will be barely known (D 15, 17, 22, 24). The ruler's most active duty is keeping the people uneducated and lessening their desires (D 2, 3, 19, 20, 65). The process may be an inversion of the process of discrimination; by doing away with laws, people will automatically revert to the state prior to these distinctions (D 19).

One passage suggests that the sage's sitting and meditating is enough to accomplish this (D 62). Some scholars suggest that the ruler's inner power (*de*) is magical (for example, Waley 1958). There are passages that strongly suggest a magical dimension to *de*: one who possesses *de* in abundance will not be stung by poisonous insects, mauled by beasts, or attacked by predatory birds (D 55) and has no place for death to enter (D 50). Similarly, the *Zhuangzi* states that when a person has perfect *de*, fire cannot burn them, water cannot drown them, cold and heat cannot afflict them, and birds and beasts cannot injure them (Z 17). These passages may indicate some paranormal power gained by aligning with the *Dao*, or they may refer simply to fitting smoothly into nature and, thus, avoiding dangers, enabling a person to live a long life (D 16, 44, 52).[21] It may be that through fasting their mind and *wuwei*, the ruler cultivates a force of the *Dao*'s power that can radiate outwardly and transform other people, causing them to conform to the natural patterns of the *Dao* (D 32, 35). However, the hidden connections specified in the classical Chinese correspondences may be enough; the effect of meditating on the body may affect the correlates in other scales of the cosmos without requiring anything else.

According to Laozi, however the transformation of society occurs, the society that will automatically arise under the sway of the *Dao* is one of small agrarian groups (D 80). In the *Dao's* natural society, utensils, boats, carriages, and weapons would not be used; records would be kept by knotted cords, not writing; and people would not have the urge to travel or even visit nearby settlements (D 53, 80). It would be a land of uncultivated fields. All machines and other contrivances of industrial society would fall into disuse. All social hierarchy and status would disappear. Nothing that could increase the people's learning or personal desires would be present. Freed from artificiality, we would then be what we are truly meant to be by being in tune with the human *dao*. People would be content, living together peacefully, free of coercion or any other self-assertions that impede the *Dao*, and the *Dao* would feed and clothe them (D 34, 58). This envisions a very simple form of society, but it does not abolish society, nor does it see people as something other than human beings. This may be a return almost to the Stone Age, but according to the *Dao De Jing*, being free of the artificiality of Confucian culture and technology is our natural state.

Some passages in the *Zhuangzi* also suggest opposition to technology and a return to the natural (Z 10). For Zhuangzi, any artificial means is torture. What is natural for an ox is having four feet, and what is of man is being yoked and having a rope through its nose (Z 17). A hermit chided a ruler who wanted to use the *Dao* to make more grain grow for feeding the people and to direct *yang* and *yin* to secure the comfort of all. The hermit felt the ruler was concerned only with the material and that the ruler's only desire was to control scattered fragments of things, not to return people to their natural state (Z 11). Likewise, a farmer refused to employ a device to irrigate his field in less time and with less energy than he was currently using because it would introduce him to a competitive way of life, disrupting the purity of his nature; in the disquieted state, the *Dao* would not dwell in him (Z 1).

For Laozi, the sage ruler is given an essential role in reforming society. Here is an example of a mysticism in which the state of mystical enlightenment is valued for its social impact. Thus, mysticism and politics can be related even though mystical experience is personal, private, and involves the vertical dimension of the depth of being, while politics is a matter of the horizontal dimension of relationships among people.

Daoist Values

Daoists accept the same basic values of humaneness (*ren*) and righteousness/ justice (*yi*) as Confucians, but Laozi claimed that evaluative concepts, like our factual concepts, introduce artificiality into the situation. Evaluations, which are always based on interests and desires, impede the *Dao*. Thus, we should do away with all evaluations (D 20). However, Laozi's point is about doing away with artificiality; it is not a claim about the moral status of the *Dao*. That is, we become aware of "goodness" only when there is something to contrast with it—such as "evil"—but this does not necessarily mean that the *Dao* is not good. It simply means that once we see the contrast of good and bad, the *Dao* no longer prevails in the world. Whether the *Dao* is moral, immoral, or nonmoral is another question.

The issue arises with Laozi's remark that the *Dao* is not humane (*ren*) (D 5). Scholars translate this negation of *ren* as "ruthless," "inhumane," "unkind," or "nonbenevolent" and, thus, conclude that the *Dao* is not moral. However, all Laozi is saying is that the *Dao* does not follow the artificiality of Confucian evaluations; the *Dao* is not "humane" only in that it does not follow human standards. Our moral categories do not govern the *Dao*, but this says nothing about its own moral status. The doctrines of humaneness and righteousness/justice only arose when the *Dao* declined (D 18). Only with the decline of the *Dao* in society do we have evaluations in general (D 18, 38). Striving to "do good" is forcing the *Dao* and only leads to harm caused by imposing our values on things. Instead, we should act without self-assertion, and the *Dao* will prevail on its own. When the *Dao* prevails, we have no other situations to contrast with it, so we have no evaluative terms like *humane* and *inhumane*. Laozi, in fact, suggests more: if we simply stop seeing things in terms of humaneness and righteousness/justice, people will automatically return to filial piety and compassion (D 19).

Laozi was not neutral on values. He adopted what he saw as the natural values of the *Dao*, and he condemned actions that were contrary to the *Dao* (D 53). His was a realist theory that values are grounded in the *Dao*. Thus, we should model ourselves on the *Dao* (D 25). Anything leading to that end is valued: stillness, lessening desires, decreasing learning, and so forth. In all situations, the yielding position of holding to the *yin* is to be valued over the *yang* (D 28). For example, we should repay injury with kindness (D 63). Water reveals the highest value; it benefits all and does not compete but takes the lower places that people treat with disdain (D 8, 81; see also Z 33). The underlying principle that should guide actions is acting non-self-assertively; if we do not act selfishly, we will not impede the *Dao*, the *Dao* will act through us, and our resulting *wuwei yin*-actions will benefit all.

The *Dao*'s two central values are impartiality and compassion (*ci*).[22] It is not a consciously chosen compassion; it flows automatically from the *Dao*'s nature, impartially benefitting all. The *Dao* is alike to the good and the bad and has no favorites but benefits all (D 5, 8, 16, 34, 79). It supports and benefits both good and bad people (D 62). It does not despise the greedy or the low (Z 17)—the *Dao* operates as well in a robber as in anyone (Z 29).[23] Being impartial and disinterested, the sage too has no desires and makes no personal judgments. Emotions revealing partiality—love and hate, joy and sadness—are contrary to the *Dao*, so the sage is free of them. Likes and dislikes do not enter the sage and burden their body by sapping *qi* (Z 5). The sage treats good people with goodness and bad people with goodness (contra *Analects* XIV.36), so their actions produce goodness (D 49). The sage reflects the *Dao*'s beneficial compassion, promoting the good of everyone without selecting some for favor over others. So, too, if the sage discards learning and desires, the people naturally return to filial piety and compassion (D 19).

What exactly Laozi meant by compassion is not clear, but he considered it basic (D 8, 31, 67). The standard edition of the *Dao De Jing* ends by saying that the *Dao* of heaven benefits others and does not harm, and the *Dao* of the sage is to act for others and to not compete (D 81). The *Dao* is self-emptying and so is the sage, although the sage benefits too since the more they bestow on others the more they have (of *qi*), and having given away everything, they are richer still (D 81). The *Dao* is long-lasting because it does not live for itself (D 7) and likewise for the sage. Thus, Daoist compassion results in positive sympathetic actions toward others, like a parent's love for their child (D 18, 19). Of course, the concepts of *filial piety* and *parental kindness* only arose when familial relations no longer held their natural harmony (D 18). Filial piety and love for children conflict with impartiality, but these reveal the type of concern that the sage extends impartially to all according to their individual needs and regardless of their social status.

Enlightened sages act spontaneously, free of any conceptions of good and bad, but all of their actions reflect these values of impartiality and compassion (D 2). If they are aware of doing "good" or avoiding "bad," they are not completely in phase with the *Dao* and, thus, not enlightened. But even though the enlightened do not intentionally do "good" in response to human labels, they also do not operate free of all values. The sage has thoroughly internalized what Laozi took to be the *Dao's* values of applying compassion impartially.

Zhuangzi agreed with Laozi that the concepts of *good* and *bad* produce each other. Just as the recognition of *this* requires recognition of *that*, where there is recognition of *right* there must be recognition of *wrong* (Z 2); we cannot have one without the other. It was only when the *Dao* declined that the distinction of right and wrong appeared that individual bias was formed (Z 2). Zhuangzi, however, concentrated more on the fact that there are no fixed universal standards of rightness and wrongness; what is right from one point of view is wrong from another's (Z 2). No line can be drawn between right and wrong (Z 17). However, with the axis of the *Dao*, we see that each *this* is a *that*, each *right* is a *wrong* (Z 2). Just as there are no fixed standards of beauty for all beings, the rules of humaneness and righteousness/justice—the paths of right and wrong for Confucian culture—are likewise hopelessly snarled and jumbled (Z 2). All are learned cultural distinctions. There are no natural distinctions of right and wrong grounded in reality that fix our varying aesthetic and ethical evaluations as universally applicable.

From the point of view of the *Dao*, all things are the same; all are equal in worth (Z 2). Any cultural point of view will make value distinctions, which then are internalized as personal interests and desires, but from the point of view of the *Dao*, there is no reason to prefer one's own interests over another's or to make any value judgments at all. Judging "right" and "wrong" are human activities, not activities of the *Dao*. Moreover, what seems "good" for us now may, in fact, turn out to be "bad" later and vice versa. Only the impartiality of the *Dao* that is independent of personal interests reflects how things really are (Z 2, 6, 18). Thus, we should forget all human conventions and partial perspectives. These are merely forms of self-assertion and inhibit the *Dao*. We should forget humaneness, righteousness/justice, and rules of proper behavior (*li*) as part of our "fasting of the mind" (Z 6). If *right* were truly right, it would differ so clearly from what is not right that there would be no need for argument, but since that is not so, we should forget all distinctions and simply leap into the Boundless (Z 2). In short, all our valuations warp the *Dao* and, thus, must be forgotten.

The idea of forgetting right and wrong has led many scholars to conclude that Zhuangzi was totally free of any values or a radical moral relativist. However, the text does not support such conclusions; Zhuangzi was not a radical skeptic about the *Dao's* basic values or his beliefs about the *Dao*.[24] The *Zhuangzi* provides a framework that transcends human points of view that are relative to cultures. Being free of rules, ethical reflections, and judgments is one thing; having no values is another. To use his analogy: when our shoes are comfortable, our feet forget about them, and when our mind is comfortable, our understanding forgets about right and wrong (Z 19), but merely because we have forgotten all evaluative categories does not mean no values are operating when we act. We are still wearing the "shoes" even if we are unaware of them. Just as Ding the cook had an objective implicitly operating in him when he effortlessly carved the ox without consciously following any plan, untrammeled persons likewise have implicit beliefs and values operating when they "respond with awareness" and "wander free and easy." Without such beliefs, their actions would be totally random and directionless, and the enlightened Daoists' actions are not that. Thus, forgetting our own biased conventions permits the *Dao*'s impartial perspective and values to prevail. It does not mean valuelessness.

Zhuangzi agreed with Laozi on the *Dao*'s value of impartiality. He also endorsed another of the *Dao*'s values: humaneness (*ren*). This is not a rule-driven behavior since the category of "humaneness" is to be forgotten (Z 6), but the Great Humaneness that exists prior to our conceptualized humaneness will shine forth when we get beyond the category (Z 2, 12). For Zhuangzi, discard "goodness," and goodness will come of itself (Z 26). Likewise, we cannot have "peace" without "war"; if we lived in a world that had never had war, we would not have the concept *peace*, but a Great Peace (*taiping*) nevertheless would prevail, even though we would have no concept of it (Z 2). Thus, the enlightened forget all recognition of "right" and "wrong" and illuminate everything in the light of heaven (Z 2). Their actions then mirror the Great Humaneness of the *Dao*.

Zhuangzi's position, too, is a form of moral realism. The *Dao*'s values are part of the objective order of reality and, thus, independent of human judgments. The *Dao* is real and can be relied upon (Z 6). There is the fixed axis of the *Dao* above our relativized points of view; the fundamental impartiality and humaneness of the *Dao* are above any relativism or skepticism concerning socially generated values and rules. More generally, all virtues that conform to the *Dao* are affirmed. Central ones suggest mystical cultivation: emptying the mind of fixed conceptualizations, tranquility (*jing*), even-mindedness, and acting without asserting one's personal interests over others' (*wuwei*) (Z 6, 13). The sage has the impartiality of the *Dao*; they have no delight in bringing success, no affection for particular people, can withstand profit and loss, do not calculate the right time to act, and do not think of fame (Z 6). They are lofty; dignified in their correctness but not insistent; vast in their emptiness, having a mind free of fixed conceptualizations, but not ostentatious; mild and cheerful; reluctant but acting; relaxed in their potency (*de*); tolerant; towering alone; withdrawn unto themselves; and bemused. They appear to lack but accept nothing, and when annoyed, they let it show in their face (Z 6). Their mind is still and mirrors what is there, free of desires and preconceptions. Thus, their actions, imbued with the *Dao*, respond in the most beneficial way to what is before them. Undistracted by the myriad of things, the sage's actions succeed because they are the *Dao*'s actions (Z 13).

The Outer and Miscellaneous Chapters of the *Zhuangzi* suggest that one can adopt the norms of any culture and be a Daoist. The difference is in how the enlightened fulfill them: spontaneously and effortlessly (Z 10). The sage's actions may conform to a society's standards but only in a way that aligns with the *Dao*. The enlightened accords with humaneness but does not set great store by it; they draw close to appropriate behavior (*yi*) but do not labor over it; they respond to the demands of the rules of proper conduct (*li*) and do not shun them; they dispose of affairs and make no excuses (Z 10). Zhuangzi accepted two conventions without reservation: service to one's parents—which is rooted in a love that "cannot be dispelled from the heart" and, thus, accords fully with the *Dao*—and the service of a minister to their ruler—which we must accept as inevitable, but we still must learn to "roam free inside the cage" (Graham 1981, 13). However, Zhuangzi's intentional flaunting of the Confucian rules of conduct in response to his wife's death expresses the Daoist spirit toward rituals (Z 18). The *Dao De Jing* has no such condemnation.

According to Daoists, the *Dao* is not a propertyless reality like Advaita's Brahman, nor is it a personal creator god with intentions and commands. The *Dao* does not have emotions such as love and hate. Instead, it guides worldly phenomena with an impartial compassion. The values and actions that Laozi and Zhuangzi set forth counter Angus Graham's (1981) claim that the *Dao*'s impartiality is only compatible with moral quietism and indifference. Its impartiality is not indifference but an evenness that is beneficial to all. Nonassertive *yin*-actions are, according to both Laozi and Zhuangzi, always the correct course of action. Sages abandon concepts of right, wrong, and humaneness and let the *Dao* flow through them, impartially benefitting all—although, the untrammeled man will not make a show of his humaneness or charity (Z 17). The enlightened are naturally compassionate or humane, free of the confines of concepts or the need to follow rules. They assist in the natural self-becoming (*ziran*) of all beings through non-self-assertive *yin*-actions. Far from renouncing the world or withdrawing from society, they are skillfully engaged at all times in helping others and do not abandon any of them (D 27). They use all they have in helping others (D 81). In that way, the sage achieves great deeds (D 23, 27, 63). Embracing the One, the sage is a model to all under heaven; they are not self-absorbed and shine forth (D 22). They engage in beneficial activities at all levels of society (D 54). None of this suggests indifference or inaction.

Thus, the enlightened sage, mirroring the selfless giving of the *Dao*, does not live for themselves but benefits all beings (D 7, 8). They are at one with an inner self-giving potency (*de*) (D 38). The sage ruler's *yin*-actions transform society in a way that Daoists believe is beneficial to all. The enlightened's inner clarity (*ming*) or "light of heaven" guides their non-assertive actions (Z 2). The sage no longer looks to do "good" and avoid "evil." Dwelling beyond any categories of right and wrong, freed from the mental constraints of evaluations and rule-following, the sage engages in an outpouring of beneficial actions (D 19). In short, the natural expression of their character toward others is the supportiveness of the *Dao*.

Daoist Religion

The different parts of the *Dao De Jing* and the *Zhuangzi* do not form one unified school but are parts of a collective Daoist alternative to Confucianism. Western scholars used to exaggerate the contrast between the earlier philosophical Daoism (*dao-jia*, the family of the *Dao*) and the later religious Daoism (*dao-jiao*, teachings of the *Dao*)—seeing them as separate schools—in order to make the *Dao De Jing* and the *Zhuangzi* more palatable to Westerners. But there is more continuity and influence of the *Dao De Jing*—and, to a lesser extent, the *Zhuangzi*—in the history of later Daoism than such a contrast suggests. However, in the late Han and post-Han period from 200 to 900 CE, Daoism was transformed, especially by Buddhism. The movement became more institutionalized, but it was not distinct from earlier Daoism, especially when it comes to mysticism. In the third and fourth centuries CE, Daoism was the leading tradition in China. Late in the Tang dynasty (618–906), Daoism was briefly the official religion of the imperial court. During the Qing dynasty (1644–1911), Daoist ideas and practices became an established part of the general culture. Today, forms of Daoism remain widespread throughout China.

Different Daoist schools proposed specific celestial realms to be attained, ethical codes to follow, rituals for inducing visions, and a variety of mystical and magical practices to master, ranging from physical refinements of *qi* to advanced forms of meditation. (Daoists devising codes of precepts that reflect these values did go directly against the spirit of early Daoism's assault on the conceptualizing mind and its dualisms, but such guides were aids to the unenlightened.) The ethical texts espoused humaneness and righteousness/justice and condemned greed and desire. Their ethics were egalitarian and universal, not hierarchical as in Confucianism. Outer alchemy was a matter of brewing elixirs for extending the life of the body, and inner alchemy (*neidan*) was a matter of gaining immortality (*xian*) in this life in a perfected bodily form or in heaven by preserving one's inner essence (*jing*), *qi*, and spirit (*shen*) through meditation. Sometimes, the schools employed psychoactive drugs such as cannabis, resulting in a variety of altered states of consciousness. They worshipped numerous gods and immortals (*xianren*) who had completed the inner alchemical process of transformation to achieve divinization in the next life. Indigenous shamanic divination, exorcism, mediumship, communication with the gods, and healing practices from the second millennium BCE Shang and early Zhou periods reemerged.[25] There are also accounts of sages' shaman-like ecstatic journeys to the heavens, flying wingless and roaming beyond the clouds in chariots drawn by dragons and celebrating in celestial palaces. Symbols of ascension are common (Kohn 2016, 176–78). Living immortals show little patience for social restrictions and are portrayed as eccentric, happy-go-lucky bums, drinking, laughing, and playing games with no social commitments or cares (179, 202). The unmoving center of the constant *Dao* was emphasized more than in earlier Daoism. On the microcosmic scale of a person, this was the unmoving mind.

The *Dao De Jing*'s emphasis on the sage ruler subsided, but later Daoist sects participated in social works. Their monasteries in the mountains, modeled on Buddhist ones, fed orphans and the poor, cared for the sick, helped with public projects like building roads, and were retreats for public officials. These Daoists also were not all recluses but often participated at court. Some were political reformers. Some led revolts such as the peasant Yellow Turban Rebellion of 184 CE. Books such as the *Book of Great Peace* (*Taipingjing*) also set forth how to bring about a millenarian golden age of great peace and equality through the *Dao*—a celestial kingdom on earth—but no social reform was seen as important as the inner transformation of people, which could not be accomplished through external laws or force.

Buddhists in northern China introduced not only monasticism but also various meditative practices and the ideas of rebirth, karmic retribution, personal saviors, and new views on the nature of a person. Their influence was significant enough that scholars refer to a Buddho-Daoism strand of Daoism. Daoism became more heaven-oriented. Now, its quest was no longer to attain the longest natural life possible in this world through harmony with the *Dao* but to transform one's body into unalloyed *qi* and become immortal upon death—either in the celestial realm or on earth in caves on distant mountains to the west or distant islands to the east. Daoists attempted to manipulate the *Dao* in a quest for immortality that is the opposite of *wei wuwei*; inner practices were advanced to transform one's nature into pure *yang*. In this cosmology, the *Dao* became more of an active agent with a will and human emotions than a nonpersonal natural principle, and Laozi became deified as a divine being who personified the *Dao* and helped people on earth. The *Dao* gave rise to the One, which in turn unfolded as three *qi* energies that coalesced into the first god, Laozi; then the nine heavens; other gods; the sacred Daoist texts; and, finally, this world. The idea of universal immortality—since we all participate in the *Dao*—also became prevalent.

A Daoist yoga of withdrawing the senses and focusing on the flow of the *Dao* within the body also developed (Kohn 2016, 131–40). It was a practice of inner observation (*neiguan*). Overall, it implemented both the stillness practice (*jing-gong*) of meditation for cultivating one's innate nature and consciousness and a movement practice (*dong-gong*) for health and longevity (Komjathy 2014, 132–33). In the fifth century, the *Scripture of the Western Ascension* (*Xishengjing*) recorded the Daoist doctrines and practices that Laozi supposedly taught a gatekeeper before he departed for India. They practiced controlled breathing, rhythmic chanting to balance the *yang* and *yin* forces in the body, meditating on "guarding the One" within oneself (constant awareness of the *Dao*) and on the One as a god within oneself, and visualizing *qi* as deities both within the body and without. (Early Daoists appear more ascetic than later Daoists.) One technique involved slow, deliberate, and mindful body movements and deep breathing, leading to the Qigong practices of today. One could align oneself with the *Dao* by working on the *qi* in one's body. A kundalini-type inner physiology was advanced with the objective of opening up the *qi* energy channels and activating its centers in the body to let *qi* flow easily. Its focus was on balancing the cosmic powers on the microcosmic level in the body—which then would radiate throughout the cosmos—in order to grow the spirit (*shen*) that can leave the body in flights through the heavens and becomes a celestial immortal in this life or upon death. By the seventh century, contemplation (*guan*) shaped by Buddhism and the *Book of Inner Neiye Training* (*Neiguanjing*) to overcome passions and attachments dominated. The *Book of Clarity and Stillness* (*Qinglingjing*) shows how the innately clear and calm mind is defiled by passions and how the One can be realized only by seeing that things are empty of any individuating substance.

Neo-Daoism

From the third to the sixth centuries, Confucian and Daoist scholars of the "black learning" (*xuan-xue*, learning of the Profound) movement—the study of the dark, mysterious, and profound *Dao* and its political implications—gave rise to a Neo-Daoism. Its focus was first on the nonbeing or nothingness (*wu*) of the unnameable *Dao* from which all beings emerge (D 11, 40). *Wu* is not the absence of reality but a fecundity that produces all things through their self-becoming (*ziran*). This movement was influenced by Buddhism and influenced Chinese Buddhism.

Two scholars in particular were important. Wang Bi (226–249) edited the *Dao De Jing* and wrote an important commentary on it, treating the *Dao* as an original, natural nonbeing (*benwu*) with no definable characteristics and phenomenal being as the branches (*mo*) emerging from this root (*ben*). All things emerge from this fecund nothingness, and the nonbeing of the source pervades all things. Thus, the *Dao* is twofold; the universe has a dark, silent, inactive *yin* (nonbeing) that supports an active *yang* (being) that we should align with. (In contrast to this philosophy, the slightly earlier *Heshang Gong* commentary on the *Dao De Jing* treated the One as *qi* rather than nonbeing.) It is *one* not as a number but as the reality making numbers possible. It is formless and, thus, can have no name or description, so words cannot apply. "One honors the root and calms the branches." Nonassertive action (*wuwei*) is simply letting things happen of their own accord (*ziran*). From such naturalness, the Great Peace can be restored.

Guo Xiang (d. 312) edited the *Zhuangzi*, removing many chapters as inauthentic and thereby reducing it to its present size, but he also integrated Confucian hierarchies into Daoism. Wang made nonbeing at least border on a transcendent reality, while Guo emphasized being (*you*) and *qi*, not *wu*. Nonbeing (*wu*) cannot produce being but is simply nothing and thus does not exist. Being—and hence, the universe—has no cause outside of itself but is eternal and self-generated. There is only self-production (*zisheng*) and self-transformation (*zihua*).

Like Laozi, Wang emphasized the oneness of things. For him, the unnameable *Dao* is a nondual source that transcends binary categories and unfolds through transformation into the ten thousand things. In this sense, all things are one. A person (*si*) is not a distinct ontological entity but an element in the dynamic flow of the *Dao*. But like Zhuangzi, Guo emphasized the diversity of things and change.

Chinese Buddhism

Buddhism arrived from India in the first century through Central Asia via the Silk Road. At first, the Chinese looked down upon Buddhists since anything from outside China was considered inferior. Certainly, these celibate and ascetic "barbarians" from the West with their other-worldly concerns, who did not speak or dress properly and who did not know the proper Confucian social and familial duties, were to be shunned. Withdrawing into monasteries in remote mountains was also objected to as not contributing to society, although Daoists and even some Neo-Confucians later adopted the practice. The doctrines of *karman* and rebirth were also hard to reconcile with ancestor veneration.[26] (The idea of a chain of rebirths played a less prominent role in East Asian Buddhism.) Buddhism was first appreciated not for its doctrines but for its meditative practices. This was, perhaps, seen as a way of gaining magical powers. By 220 CE, some Nikaya meditation manuals from Kashmir and northwest India were translated by substituting Daoist terms for Buddhist terms (the *geyi* method)—for example, *wu* for *shunyata*—but the inadequacy of this method soon became apparent because of the differences of the concepts. Kumarajiva (344–413 CE) arrived from India around 400 and brought with him Perfection of Insight and Madhyamaka texts, along with the *Lotus Sutra* and the *Vimalakirtinirdesha Sutra*. He was the first translator fluent in both Sanskrit and Chinese, and he established a new standard for translations.

The Buddhist ontology of impermanence and interdependence fit well with part of the Chinese ontology of the *Dao* guiding the course of events. By the late fifth or early sixth century, Buddhism was firmly rooted in northern China—which was then controlled by non-Chinese—and had made inroads into the Confucian south where it was seen as a form of Daoism, prompting attacks by the Confucians. With their individualistic orientations, all the Nikaya schools except one failed—the Dharmagup-takas—whose monastic rules spread to all Chinese Buddhism. By the mid-eighth century, Buddhism was repressed by both Confucians and Daoists; but in a case of skillful means, Buddhism adapted to the Chinese worldview, and three distinctly Chinese schools of Buddhism arose: Tiantai (Jpn., Tendai), Huayan (Kegon), and Chan (Zen). The theistic-like worship of Amitabha Buddha (Amida) and reliance on "other-power" for salvation through the recitation of his name also became popular.[27] Later, the Qingtu school arose around such devotion; its goal is being reborn in Amitabha's Pure Land with its ideal conditions for becoming enlightened. Pure Land remains the major form of Buddhism practiced in East Asia today.

The Yogachara-influenced Tiantai school was founded by Zhiyi (538–597). It accepts the *Lotus Sutra* as the highest teaching of the Buddha, along with the *Mahaparinirvana Sutra* and its doctrine of the embryo of Buddhahood (*tathata-garbha*). According to this school, all sense phenomena arise from the One Mind in its defiled state, and Buddhahood arises from its pure state. The idea of a Buddha-nature (*fo-xing, li*) also became important in this and the other Chinese Buddhist schools: all phenomena have a common reality immanent in their core that enables them to become enlightened. The *Mahaparinirvana Sutra* denied that material objects have Buddha-nature, but Chan and the other schools disputed that idea. *The Awakening of Faith in the Mahayana Sutra* (*Dasheng quixinlun*) asserts that the pure luminous One Mind has two aspects: the worldly mind and the absolute suchness (*tathata*) that grounds all phenomenal reality and all sentient beings. The Tiantai also embraced the doctrine of the interpenetration of all phenomena based on the *Avatamsaka Sutra*, an immense collection of texts famous for using Indra's net of jewels to illustrate this point. In this net, all the jewels are arranged in such a manner that each one reflects all the others. (This image is popular in New Age circles today.) This represents how the empty factors of the phenomenal world (the *dharmas*) each enter into one another. Thus, by knowing any one phenomenon, we know them all.

The innovative Huayan school founded by Dushun (557–640) is also built around the *Avatamsaka Sutra*. Its doctrines influenced Chan. Like the Yogachara, this school's position is that the world of multiple objects lacks self-existence (*svabhava*) but is mind-made; through meditation and visualization exercises, one can enter into all objects and move unimpededly in the world. In his *Essay on the Golden Lion* (*Jin shizi zhang*), Fazang (643–712) explained that the gold of the statue of a lion was the Buddha-nature, and the shape was only form. The Buddha-nature is empty of self-existence and takes different forms under different causes and conditions.[28] All things are empty of self-existence, and their interdependence is not an external relation between separate entities but actually constitutes all phenomena. Likewise, there is no obstruction between the form and the underlying principle. As with Indra's net, in each hair of the lion, there is a golden lion. All the lions in the hairs simultaneously and instantaneously enter into each single hair; thus, in each hair, there are an infinite number of lions. All forms are perfect expressions of the Buddha-nature, and all forms are both distinct (qua forms) and identical (qua the one Buddha-nature); therefore, each form (qua Buddha-nature) reflects every other form. We achieve a direct perception of reality—the *dharma-dhatu*—with our non-obstructed mind when we let go of the ego and all conceptualizations. Phenomenal reality is structured by the principles (*li*) with the *Dao*.

With the unification of northern and southern China during the Tang dynasty (618–907), Buddhism gained widespread popularity, but the Daoist emperor prosecuted Buddhist monastics from 841 to 845 for tax evasion and for undermining families, thereby leading to the decline of China's prosperity. This all but wiped out the Tiantai and Huayan schools. The Chan and Qingtu schools remained accepted, but after the beginnings of Neo-Confucianism early in the Song dynasty (960–1279), these schools began to merge, combining meditation with the Pure Land practice of the recitation of the Buddha's name and combining the Buddha-nature within with Amitabha Buddha without. However, the other-power of chanting the Buddha's name became a self-power exercise by the meditations on the *koan*, "Who recites the name of the Buddha?" Distinctly Chan teachings disappeared during the early Ming dynasty (1368–1644). Despite syncretic attempts to combine Buddhism with Daoism (and local shamanic cults), and despite each tradition borrowing from the other (or perhaps because of it), there was a strong tension and animosity between the two traditions. Buddhists won a series of debates in 1281 that led to many Daoist texts being burned.

Tibetan Buddhism was introduced around 720 and was the official religion of northern China under the Mongol rulers of the Yuan dynasty (1279–1368), but its lamas were expelled during the Ming dynasty. Tantrism was never very popular in China; its sexual images, let alone practices, were seen as violating Confucian values. However, Tantrism flourished in Japan in the esoteric Mantra School (Shingon) founded by Kukai (774–835). Teachings were transmitted from master to pupil and not written down. The Tibetan Geluk school was accepted during the Qing dynasty (1644–1911), and a small esoteric sect survives through a secret lineage today. Buddhism was all but wiped out in China by the mid-1800s and had to be reintroduced from Japan. Buddhism arrived in Korea in the fourth century, and thinkers tried to reconcile the differences in Chinese Buddhist schools. In Japan, Buddhism was marked by a simplicity of doctrine and practice, reflecting both a reaction against the confusing and corrupt diversity of non-Japanese forms of Buddhism and the belief that we are now living in a degenerate age (*mappo*) that requires the development of simple and fail-safe religious practices.[29]

The Chan/Zen Meditation Schools

Chan (Zen) became the most popular Chinese Buddhist school and was so named for valuing concentrative meditation (Skt., *dhyana*) over reading and chanting texts or relying on a transcendent other-power. It was a reaction to the perceived over-intellectualized forms of Buddhism that emphasized studying the scriptures. Here was a transmission of insight (*prajna*) outside of the texts—after all, the Buddha himself did not rely on any texts. Bodhidharma (d. ca. 530) is said to have introduced Chan from India. He spent nine years wall-gazing (*biguan*) in a cave, although his exact practice is not known.

The direct path to enlightenment is not based on texts but on the transmission of insight from a master to a disciple and is summarized in Bodhidharma's poem:

A special tradition outside the scriptures,
Not depending on words or letters,
Directly pointing to the human heart/mind,
Seeing into one's own nature and gaining Buddhahood.

The Buddha's disciple Kashyapa is said to have received insight through a direct, silent, mind-to-mind transmission from the Buddha when the Buddha held up a flower and said nothing. Kashyapa passed the insight down through a line of teachers to Bodhidharma. A direct transmission of the enlightening knowledge between master and disciple was necessary because the insight into nature and becoming a Buddha is ineffable and thus does not rely on words. Words are only of indirect value, like fingers pointing at the reflection of the moon (*Lankavatara Sutra* 196–97, 224); we should not get caught up in the sign and miss the reality it is pointing toward. Only a master could tell if a disciple was enlightened or not. Chan was seen as an experience-based form of Buddhism that did not depend upon doctrines or rituals, but Chan masters frowned on extreme asceticism. Under the influence of Daoism, Chan masters adapted mindfulness practices to ordinary activities in everyday life as well as the arts—especially painting and calligraphy—and the martial arts. It eventually spread to Japan, Korea, and Vietnam.

However, even if a master could not communicate the true nature of things in words, there still were Mahayana doctrines to study in order for the disciple to understand the silent insight properly. Bodhidharma brought with him the *Lankavatara Sutra*, a text connected to the Yogachara school about purifying the mind, the doctrines of storehouse consciousness, and the innate Buddha-nature or Buddhahood-embryo in each of us. Chan soon embraced the Perfection of Insight and Madhyamaka texts on phenomena being empty (*shunya/kong*) of self-existence, although purifying the mind was still deemed necessary before one could gain the enlightening knowledge. This shifted the focus from introvertive *dhyana* concentration to extrovertive mindfulness exercises. Like Daoists, Chan Buddhists want to be free of the conceptualizing mind, but this state of no mind (*wuzin*) and no thought has not kept the enlightened from speaking and writing; the mind is only free of seeing words as reflecting separate entities. Indeed, Chan Buddhists, ironically, began developing their own texts reflecting the Chinese worldview and values, as did Huayan and Tiantai Buddhists. The school also stressed the importance of the master/disciple relationship and the importance of physical work in daily monastic life. Monasticism was also introduced into the Chan school in the 600s.

During the Tang dynasty, the Chan tradition broke into five lineages, of which two survived: the Linji (Rinzai) and the Caodong (Soto). A central dispute was whether enlightenment came *in toto* all at once as a sudden flash, as Daoists accepted, or was a gradual growth in insight.[30] However, both schools emphasized activities occurring in the enlightened state in one's everyday life over any isolated enlightenment experience. Additionally, meditation did not end with enlightenment for either school. Having experiences that were unmediated by concepts was the objective, but both schools also emphasized the study of Buddhist texts, with the Perfection of Insight texts and the *Vimalakirtinirdesha Sutra* becoming more central than the *Lankavatara*. In Chan's most famous text, the *Platform Sutra of the Sixth Patriarch*, Huineng (638–713) tried to mediate the disputes between the two Chan schools.[31] He argued for the doctrine of sudden enlightenment (*dunwu*) over gradual enlightenment, stating that the mind is pure by nature since nothing real (self-existent) exists to stain it, that meditation and insight are not different but are essentially the same, and that the fundamental pure thus-ness (*tathata*) of things is covered by our falsifying mind. He espoused *no mind*—the elimination of falsifying conceptual projections—and letting shine forth the insight of the nonduality of phenomena since there are no isolated, self-existing realities. In China, the distinction between sudden and gradual enlightenment decreased, and the two schools merged during the Ming dynasty, but they remained distinct in Japan.

Rinzai's most famous technique is an active type of meditation involving a "public case" (*gong-an/koan*) given by a master to a disciple in a private interview. This practice began in the eleventh century, and the Soto school also occasionally employed them; Dogen assembled two long anthologies of public cases and commentaries on them. Each case is a mental puzzle that is designed to force the disciple to see how concepts control their mental life, thereby producing a sudden breakthrough to the true, selfless Buddha-nature. It uses the conceptual mind to break free of the grip of the conceptual mind. An example is Hakuin's (1685–1768) famous question "What is the sound of one hand clapping?" Any conceptualization of this situation must fail, and the disciple is supposed to see that the same applies to all conceptualizations of reality. Disciples may be given more than one koan in the course of their training. The problem with such tactics in mystical training is that they themselves can become expected and thus lose their effectiveness as enlightenment techniques. Koans became standardized, and books containing answers that could be memorized were produced, but the answer that the disciple gave was not as important as how they gave it, thereby revealing their attitude toward concepts. A disciple must demonstrate to the master that they have gained insight or transformed, not merely parrot back some expected answer.

The Soto school places less emphasis on any breakthrough experiences (Jpn. *kensho*) or more lasting experiences of *satori* occurring upon the "death of the self" than on applying the ever-deepening enlightened state of mind to everyday events.[32] The silent sitting of *zazen* breathing meditation is central, but meditation is not limited to that setting. Likewise, introvertive one-pointed concentration is not central, but the power of concentration (*samadhi/joriki*) must be maintained in all situations. It is equally important to execute concrete actions in a mindful state of consciousness, free of emotions and mental images intervening between the individual and what is really there. With the mind free of fixations on artificial distinctions and focused instead by concentrative meditation, one sees the world clearly and can let the mind and body take their course in the immediacy of the present moment. In this state of no mind, or no thinking, or no thing—where the inner turmoil of the dualizing "monkey mind" has been quieted—one responds without reflection and thus spontaneously and without hesitation to what is present. This state leads to very practical conduct: "When hungry, I eat; when tired, I sleep." This differs from the ordinary way of performing activities in that the mystic is totally focused on the present activity, not thinking about something else as we normally do. No more thought is involved than when a child plays with a toy. There is no longer a duality between the actor and the act. Even the conceptual duality of *duality* and *nonduality* no longer governs mental life. In this positionless position, things are neither dual—since there are no distinct entities but, rather, everything is of one nature and interconnected—nor nondual—since there is diversity to phenomena. The tea ceremony and archery are famous exercises in focusing on the task at hand with the concept-driven mind turned off. This approach is applied to work, art, and all other activities. The issue becomes *how* we do something, not *what* we do. It is said, "If you can serve a cup of tea properly, you can do anything." Thereby, all of life becomes a meditative exercise.

Contrary to popular belief, Chan is not merely a matter of meditation. Classical Chan was a way of life that adopted mainstream Mahayana doctrines from the Perfection of Insight and other texts. Teachers may have burned Buddhist texts, but this was only a teaching technique used to make the point that insight is independent of words; in monasteries, the study of Buddhist texts (including Chan texts) was stressed. We need words to get to a state beyond words where the self-contained entities designated by them are no longer imagined. Chan doctrines also deemphasize words: the direct mind-to-mind transmission of enlightenment from teacher to disciple without words or seeing denotative language as merely a finger pointing at the reflection of the moon and not a mirror of what is real. However, these doctrines do not negate the ultimate need to use words in order to reveal a purity of mind in which wordless enlightenment can occur and to understand the nature of things from the enlightened point of view after the insight.

The same applies to values. The great Japanese Soto teacher Dogen (1200–1253) held a very conventional view of Buddhist values while emphasizing the silent "just sitting" (*shikan-taza*) practice of *zazen*. For him, the fact that the Buddha continued to meditate after his enlightenment showed that meditation is itself enlightenment—the realization of our Buddha-nature. (This does not mean that everyone who sits in the lotus position is enlightened but only that, once enlightened, there is no more to enlightenment than the experiences occurring in meditation.) He took "just sitting" in the lotus position as returning to the practice of the historical Buddha and as the way of expressing our innate Buddha-nature. For him, the impermanence of things is the Buddha-nature. All things are the self-expression of this emptiness and the Buddha-nature. Thus, he stated in *The Universal Recommendation for Zazen* (*Fukan Zazengi*) that "the total experience of a single thing is the same as the experience of the totality of all things" since all things have the same ontic nature (being empty of self-existence). The process of "forgetting the self" has to progress throughout one's life since there is always more to our sense of self to forget. His school was criticized for accepting quietness rather than the insight that broke the chain of rebirths, but meditation is not, as his critics claimed, trying to make a mirror by rubbing a tile—an analogy going back to Mazu Daoyi (709–788)—but necessary for realizing that the mind is already clear. For this, practice is still necessary.

Additionally, the need for the transmission of insight to occur outside the scriptures did not mean that Dogen permitted disciples to ignore the scriptures; rather, Zen and the scriptures are one (*kyozen itchi*). With meditation, one realizes the full presence of things as they really are by "dropping the body" (*shinjin datsuraku*) and "non-thinking" (*hi-shiryo*). The empty mind is like a mirror, free of all deliberation, free of judgments of "right" and "wrong" or "good" and "bad." Non-thinking is "beyond thinking and not thinking." All dualisms, including "enlightenment" and "practice," are denied. In *The Treasury of the Eye of True Dharma* (*Shobogenzo*), he insisted that the Buddhist code of conduct be rigorously followed by all, including advanced monks. He also advocated a set of monastic rules to regulate the monks' behavior.

Chan and "Beyond Good and Evil"

Dogen rejected as Abhidharmist any discrimination distinct categories. Thus, he rejected thinking in terms of good or evil or judging right and wrong while still insisting on following Buddhist rules (Masunaga 1971, 29–30, 37). But even though he was free from discriminations, he could still state that it is a grave error for Zen monks to prefer evil acts, say there is no need to practice what is good, or accumulate merit (55) and that once we have thoroughly realized the nature of reality, we know that evil is always evil and good is always good (56). Following the precepts may be a matter of self-cultivation, but by following the Buddha's way, we see our own nature—the Buddha-nature or original mind—and become naturally compassionate.[33] That is, if we get beyond our "thinking" mind that discriminates different values, we will spontaneously be compassionate.[34]

This means that the phrase "beyond good and evil," common in D. T. Suzuki's works, can be easily misunderstood when applied to Chan. Dogen made clear that *good* may be a term without a self-existent referent, but not all acts are acceptable. Most importantly, he still valued compassion. Only discriminating the concepts of good and evil as fixed principles is attacked as interfering with a more spontaneously compassionate mind. It does not mean that Chan Buddhists ultimately devalue compassion. The unenlightened mind gets fixated on dualisms of values: we set a goal of trying to do good rather than emptying our mind of unenlightened ideas and letting our natural compassion flow as the situation requires. When we think in terms of a dualism of good and evil, we impose values and do not see what is really there, but the enlightened see the reality behind the concepts. Just as there is a reality behind the concept of a person to lead to enlightenment but no self-existent entity, there are also no independent entities called *good* and *evil*, but reality nevertheless involves compassion. Dogen, thus, could still speak in terms of good and evil without "coursing in signs."

Chan meditation gives a sense of selflessness, enabling the enlightened to express compassion more spontaneously. Rather than relying only on sitting meditation, Rinzai masters often use shock tactics. For example, masters shout at and strike meditators who are falling asleep rather than gently admonishing them. Or, Rinzai's call to commit the cardinal sins of Buddhism: "If you meet the Buddha on the road, kill him! If you meet the Patriarchs, kill them; if you meet enlightened Nikaya disciples, kill them; if you meet your parents, kill them. Then for the first time you will see clearly." Texts were burned, icons smashed. In one story, a cat was killed to make a point. But these teachings are meant to help students by startling them; they are not meant to guide their actions. The objective is to "kill" all mental idols or attachments to texts that we might have, thereby breaking the hold of ordinary conceptualized consciousness on our mind. Chan had its own rigorous code of conduct for monastics to follow attributed to Baizhang (749–814), with no such ethical anomalies.

Nevertheless, Chan is often considered antinomian. The Rinzai tactics are said to show that enlightenment has nothing to do with morality, and the Soto school's emphasis on sitting meditation is said to lead to moral quietism. The state of mind resulting from these practices is said to be such that the discriminations necessary for morality are impossible. However, these conclusions badly misrepresent classical Chan. The compassion of a Bodhisattva was supremely valued in Chan from its founder Bodhidharma on. The state of *no mind* does not mean "mindless": the enlightened have internalized a moral point of view, and they have the agency needed to be moral. A fitting image of the role of moral action in Chan is the classic version of the ox-herding pictures. They present an allegory of the quest, beginning with a man seeking a lost ox (enlightenment) and ending with him entering the marketplace riding the ox with helping hands. That is, the quest ends with the now-enlightened seeker ready to help others.

However, Chan throughout its history has been readily adaptable to whatever political setting it happens to find itself in. For all their iconoclasm, Chan masters—with a few exceptions—have supported the status quo and aligned themselves with the conservative elements in whatever society they were in. Chan is a matter of mystical inner development that can be adopted by anyone, regardless of one's walk of life or political views. In Japan, Zen and other Buddhist temples had armies of warring monks. With its emphasis on living in the present and its indifference to death, Zen was adopted as the way of the warrior (*bushido*) by the medieval samurai; its naturalness became a skill for war. That Chan has strict discipline and is extremely authoritarian, requiring the student's complete submission to the will of the master, warrants notice here. This unquestioning of one's Buddhist teacher also fed loyalty to the Shogun or a lesser feudal lord. Moreover, in the twentieth century, Zen Buddhists adopted a nationalist and imperialistic stance in Japan. In fact, Zen temples prepared soldiers for World War II.[35] That the German author of the popular *Zen in the Art of Archery* became a Nazi after his Zen training in Japan has to be at least disquieting for a tradition based in Mahayana compassion. All of this does give some credence to the idea that Zen has the potential to ignore compassion and go "beyond good and evil" in an antinomian manner.

Neo-Confucianism

Chan reached the apex of its influence in China during the Song dynasty (960–1260). During the late Tang dynasty (618–907), Confucianism was revived in reaction to the corrupt practices of government officials of the day and, especially, in reaction to the prominence of Daoism and Buddhism among both the elite and the uneducated over the previous millennium. Later in the Song dynasty, Confucianism returned to its former dominance. Buddhism lost its political power but remained popular among the uneducated classes. Daoism, by that time, was basically a form of inner alchemy for attaining immortality and was also popular, mainly among the uneducated. However, Neo-Confucianism was not primarily a socio-political movement but an intellectual renaissance that attempted to synthesize the metaphysics of classical Confucianism with the religious mysticism of Chan Buddhism (Huang 1999, 11). Neo-Confucianism became the official religion of China from the Song period until 1911 and spread to Korea, Japan, and Vietnam.

The new Confucian scholars saw themselves as returning to the thought of Confucius and Mencius. In reaction mainly to Buddhism, these scholars saw themselves as merely giving original Confucianism a new metaphysical framework, but what they produced was transformed by Buddhism and Daoism into a more mystical form of Confucianism. They presented a cosmology in terms of *qi* and a natural universal ordering principle, *li*—a term from the *Book of Changes* (*Yijing*)—to counter the Buddhist emphasis on the emptiness of things and the Daoist emphasis on a creative nonbeing (the nameless *Dao*).

Neo-Confucianism absorbed many of Chan's doctrines and the organization of its monasteries, but its goal was to become an exemplary Confucian gentleman (*junzi*), now re-envisioned as something like a Daoist sage. Such a person realizes a "bright virtue" that aligns the person with heaven and earth and brings about a Great Peace in the world by means of their virtue's natural radiation. Through meditation, the innate knowledge needed for this transformation is revealed. Sagehood is a natural property that, like Buddhahood, is innate in everyone. Thus, quiet sitting (*jing-zuo*) was the way for the Confucian elite to grasp the original nature (*benxing*) within each person from birth. However, Confucian scholars feared that meditation alone might lead to valuing the experiences, being indifferent to social and political activities, and valuing Daoism and Buddhism over Confucianism. Thus, they insisted that studying the Confucian classics and social concerns was also necessary. Meditation became the way to internalize the classical Confucian perspective. Selfishness in social interactions was replaced by impartiality. The ideal person had empathy for all people and gave selflessly to all. Anger and happiness were both accepted as natural.

The most important Neo-Confucian thinker was Zhu Xi (1130–1200). He was dismissed from the government for his Neo-Confucian views; but after his death, his writings became required reading for the civil service exam. He believed that there had been no true Confucians after Confucius and Mencius and that he rehabilitated their teachings. The natural ordering principle (*li*) is never separate from the material force (*qi*) and is different from its many manifestations. Following the early Daoist distinction of an unnameable and a nameable *Dao*, *li* is the non-ultimate from which arose the Great Ultimate (*taiji*): the originating root-substance (*benti*) of all things. *Li* is the state of the universe before the generation of the ordered realm. It is the nonbeing (*wu*) that existed before heaven and earth existed, from which all phenomena come. (There was less emphasis on the *Dao* in order to contrast Confucianism and Daoism.) Through movement, the natural principle generated *yang* and through tranquility, *yin*. All things are one in that they all participate in the same natural ordering principle.

The school formed from Zhu's ideas (the Cheng-Zhu) is deemed rational in its rejection of any transcendent world or creator, chain of rebirths, idea of karmic reward and punishment, and many other Daoist and Buddhist ideas as superstitions. It is only about a natural, inner, ordering principle. Human nature is innately good, and through training based on the five virtues—integrity, propriety, knowledge, humaneness, and righteousness/justice—all selfishness is overcome, and the mind becomes identical with the impartiality of heaven; the enlightened have the "mind of heaven." Its exemplary gentleman is a highly learned Confucian scholar. The learning results in radiating humaneness. There are eight steps of self-cultivation leading to social change: investigating the natural principle (*li*) in all things (*gewu*), extending that knowledge (*zhizhi*), making one's intention sincere, rectifying the mind, cultivating the person by maintaining sincere intentions and mental control, regulating the family, ordering the state, and bringing peace to all.

Zhu emphasized self-cultivation, but it was less a matter of mystical experiences and more a matter of Confucian learning and intellectually investigating external things: an extension of that knowledge through external study of the natural principle of heaven and earth that underlies the world. This led not to science but to the study of ethical qualities and social relationships (Huang 1999, 216). Zhu practiced meditation—quiet sitting in a kneeling position—based on Chan's *zazen*. However, this was not to empty his mind but to focus his mind on *li*. Nothing suggests that he experienced an enlightened ASC mystical state free of a sense of self. Instead, his meditation was more a matter of self-examination that aided in absorbing Confucian beliefs, resulting in reverence for both quiet sitting and action. (He said that Laozi at least wanted to do something, while Zhuangzi did not.) His motto was "quiet sitting for half a day and reading for half a day."

A more mystical school based on the study of mind became dominant: the Lu-Wang. It was based on the teachings of Wang Yangming (1472–1529), who gave up the extrovertive contemplation of nature for an inner quest to gain knowledge of all reality (Smart 1967, 423). He practiced Buddhist and Daoist meditation when he was young and had a mystical experience while he was banished to a remote government outpost; under the poor and menial conditions, he experienced his doctrine (423). Central to his thinking was the idea that the person is a natural part of the world. He believed that since the underlying natural principle is in all things, it is also in each person as the heart/mind (*xin*); thus, *li* should be discovered primarily there through introspective practices such as quiet meditative sitting, not investigating external things as Zhu had favored. The mind becomes the still "mind of heaven," free from attachments to external things—a clear mirror reflecting what is really there without adding anything or acting. Under the influence of Buddhism, pure consciousness and *li* are considered identical. The inner nature of all of nature is thereby understood by understanding one's own mind.

By the late Ming dynasty, Confucian quiet sitting changed. Confucian scholars were producing meditation manuals in reaction to Buddhist and Daoist works of the time. Wang Ji (1489–1583) valued quiet sitting over studying. He adopted Daoist terminology of inner alchemy (*neidan*) in utilizing regulated breathing to find our original nature. He believed that this nature is "beyond good and evil" and that it could only be attained inwardly by getting beyond all moral efforts. Xue Hui (1489–1541) represents another trend that more orthodox Confucians rejected: he devalued the Confucian classics. Critics again objected that attempts to attain the "original nature" drew meditators away from the traditional teachings and social engagement. Xue believed that Daoism and Buddhism explored deeper levels of the mind than Confucianism—which focused only on the surface and everyday affairs—but all three traditions needed to be transcended to attain the deepest level of the mind. Thus, discussing the differences between the traditions, he believed, was a waste of time. But he thought that our original nature was the source of more universal ethical norms. Yuan Huang (1533–1606) criticized earlier Confucian ideas of quiet sitting as superficial, comparable only to the introductory level of Chan Buddhism, and claimed that his masters offered a deeper and more authentic type of meditation.

By the eighteenth century, quiet sitting was no longer generally practiced by Confucian scholars. Dai Zhen (1723–1777) reacted against the inward turn, metaphysical speculation on the immanent natural principle (*li*), and speculation on *qi* as the source or substance of reality. He believed instead that knowledge of *li* was to be gained through social learning and investigation of the external world. He accepted that when the mind is not clouded by selfishness, it is in a pure and clear state of supreme illumination. When it is still and unmoving, the mind is pure and attains the perfection of heavenly virtue. However, the *Dao* reflected classical Confucian virtues. Humaneness was once again placed centrally among the virtues. Sincerity (*cheng*) and earnestness (*jing*) were added to the earlier Confucian virtues. For example, we know the phenomenal world is real because the *Dao* is sincere, so we too should be sincere. Earnestness in self-cultivation was always important to Neo-Confucianism, and as Daoism and Buddhism subsided as threats, Neo-Confucians adapted more of their doctrines and meditative practices.

In classical China, a person may follow Confucian rituals as a public official, go to a Daoist priest for medical services, and have a Buddhist funeral, but such a compartmentalization of life does not mean—as many Neo-Confucians claimed—that the doctrines of the three traditions are all the same. Likewise, that these traditions, along with Chinese folk religion, share many beliefs does not mean that they all really teach the same thing in the end. The Neo-Confucian Zhu Xi attacked both Daoism and Buddhism as harmful to inculcating the *Dao*. Similarly, the Zen master Dogen said that those who think the three teachings are the same do not understand Buddhism. The three were different but interrelated mysticisms, and to the extent that any of their beliefs structure mystical experiences, different mystical experiences occurred even when the meditative practices were similar or the same.

Key Themes

• The *Dao* informs all Chinese mysticisms. The *Dao* transcends all phenomena as their source, but unlike other nonpersonal Axial Age ontological grounds, it is still an immanent element of the natural universe that guides all of nature. Only human beings have fallen out of step with it due to our dualizing minds. Pre-Axial ideas of ancestors, deities, and spirits were retained in the culture, but there is otherwise little interest in realities that transcend the natural realm, unlike in other Axial Age cultures. There is no creator god or principle completely beyond the natural realm. The *Dao* is not personal in nature, has no will, and is not loving, but it can be characterized in Daoism as benevolent and compassionate to all. Thus, there is a difference from Abrahamic and Indian mysticism: we are to attune ourselves to an embedded principle that orders the natural world from within. In this world-affirming worldview and ethos, the focus remains on the phenomenal realm. This realm is not considered an illusion, nor is the body considered negatively as a prison to be escaped but another vessel of the *Dao*. Each person is a replica in miniature of the entire cosmos; thus, we can directly find the *Dao* within and thereby resonate with the underlying power creating and ordering the full universe.

• The *Dao* transcends particular phenomena, but whether it transcends the entire natural universe (and thus also exists apart from natural phenomena) or is a part of the natural universe as phenomena's ground is not clear. If the phenomenal world were to go out of existence, the Neoplatonist One, a theistic god, and Brahman would still exist. In that way, they transcend the world. The situation is not so clear with the *Dao*. The *Dao* is tied more closely to the workings of nature than the sources in other traditions. Nonbeing (*wuji*, the limitless) early on was a natural cosmic *yin* to the manifest *yang*. The *Dao De Jing*'s addition of an unnameable aspect of the *Dao* only complicates the picture. It is a "womb of nonbeing," but does it transcend the natural universe? The *Liezi*, a Daoist text from the late third century CE, does suggest a transcendent reality based on philosophical considerations rather than mystical experiences (Coutinho 2014, 148). It asks whether there is an origin distinct from the source of all things and concludes that there must be something unproduced (*busheng*) and untransformed (*buhua*) in addition to the enduring produced things (*sheng*) (150–51). In Neo-Confucianism, the ordering principle (*li*) was never separate from the material *qi*, and transcendent realities are denied.

• Daoism shows that a mystical strand of Chinese culture existed from early classical times. Since this world is the only reality of immediate concern, extrovertive mystical experiences are valued over introvertive ones for how we lead our lives, but introvertive experiences help cleanse the mind and harmonize it with the *Dao*. Harmony with the natural *Dao*, the immanent principle (*li*) guiding the world, or the ultimate mind (*xin*) is the objective. Buddhism was a second source of mysticism affecting East Asian culture, but Buddhism has a clearly transcendent goal, and becoming an immortal became the goal in Daoism.

• There is an interlocking positive (*yang*) and negative (*yin*) flow of the world's vital energy (*qi*) that needs to be balanced in us. Chinese mystics may speak of uniting the mind to the *Dao* when a person harmonizes with it, but there is no ontological union with the *Dao* to be attained since the *Dao* already flows in us. For Daoists, we merely have to clear away the cultural clutter in our mind blocking its operation. When the mind is cleared, the *Dao* that is always in us is unblocked and can flow naturally. With an illuminated mind, the *Dao* will be manifested in our non-self-assertive actions and in refraining from interventions. This requires mystical cultivation—emptying the mind of cultural encrustation—not the increase in cultural learning of Confucianism, although Neo-Confucians adapted such cultivation to their learning. With the final removal of the cultural blocks, our actions automatically follow the natural ordering principle appropriate to human beings—we, in effect, will float on the *Dao*. The extrovertive enlightened state of mind is emphasized, not any special enlightenment experiences. With their dualizing minds out of the way, the enlightened move properly and spontaneously without self-assertion in a new state of consciousness. Language and cultural conceptions are still present in the enlightened mind, but the enlightened are no longer confined by them. Impartiality is emphasized over emotions such as joy.

• People are taken to be as much a part of the natural realm as anything else. Being fully integrated parts of the natural world, the natural and social contexts of our existence are both important. Eliminating self-assertion and purifying the mind of dualisms to reveal the illuminating mind are major themes, but they are not framed within a metaphysics questioning the existence of a self. Thus, denial of the self is not a major theme in Daoism or Neo-Confucianism. Even in Chinese forms of Buddhism, having "no mind" is more central than having no sense of "self." As Huangbo Yixun (d. 850) put it, attaining "no mind" is not becoming mindless but restoring one's original whole mind (*yixin*). One must give up self-based thoughts and actions to resonate with the *Dao*, but there is no denial of the reality of the person. The objective is a to perfect the person within the world or attain immortality of the spirit (*shen*) after death. A person is not bifurcated into "mind" and "body"; one has to transform the whole person. Consciousness became more of a focus of attention after Buddhism arrived.

• Harmony among people and between humanity and nature is also important. Part of the this-worldly ethos is a political dimension that is central to parts of Daoism and Neo-Confucianism. This was never central in Indian and Abrahamic mysticisms. In fact, it usually is totally absent. Sagehood in Daoism is about a long life in this world or immortality after death, but the sage ruler is central to the *Dao De Jing*. Confucians may seem more society-oriented and some Daoists more individualistic, but being in harmony with other people through the *Dao* is part of being in harmony with all of the natural realm for all Daoists. Thus, mysticism and a political dimension to social life were fused in much Chinese mysticism in a way that is not present in the major traditions of other world cultures.

• Buddhism took on a distinctly Chinese character in China—Chan most of all. Chan was influenced by the *Zhuangzi*, the *Dao De Jing*, and Daoist meditation techniques. In turn, Buddhism influenced Neo-Daoism and Neo-Confucianism. The doctrines of no self and *nirvana* played a lesser role. All the schools took on a depth-mystical interest in realities that at least approached transcending the natural realm through the *Dao* and Buddha-nature (Buddha-embryo, the immutable One Mind) that is present in all phenomena and persons. Such a monistic foundationalism has drawn criticism from some East Asian Buddhists today.

Chapter 10

Mysticism in the West Today

The previous chapters bring this history nearly up to today. The Age of Enlightenment that began in the seventeenth century severely damaged interest in mysticism in the West; mysticism seemed the antithesis of then-popular rationality and medieval rather than modern. The general atmosphere was more hostile toward interests in transcendent realities or altered states of consciousness than in any culture had been previously. Mysticism was seen as conflicting with science and as fundamentally irrational. Yet, in the early twentieth century, mysticism regained some respectability through studies done by William James, William Ralph Inge, Rufus Jones, and Friedrich Baron von Hugel and was popularized by Evelyn Underhill and Richard M. Bucke. In the twentieth century, there were also some prominent mystics—in particular, Thomas Merton and Mohandas Gandhi. Histories of mysticism—primarily of the Christian tradition—began to appear. Teilhard de Chardin and Shri Aurobindo responded to modern science by trying to combine mysticism with evolution. By the 1950s, books about mystical traditions outside of Christianity by such scholars and advocates of mysticism as Aldous Huxley, D. T. Suzuki, Christmas Humphries, Christopher Isherwood, Reynold Nicholson, A. J. Arberry, and Gershom Scholem reached audiences in a way that had not occurred anywhere in the past. Indeed, every tradition became known worldwide. Mystical literature was no longer the preserve of small groups that remained isolated from the general public.

The works of Allen Ginsburg and Gary Snyder as well as Jack Kerouac's more superficial *The Dharma Bums* reveal an interest in Asian mysticism among the Beats. In the 1960s and 1970s, the public's interest in mysticism and drug-enabled altered states of consciousness grew. In the second half of the twentieth century, Asian teachers began to settle in the West, and some sociologists believe that there is more mystical exploration today in the West than in Asia. Assorted gurus and communities attracted young people in Europe and the United States. These included teachers such as Shri Chinmoy (1931–2007)—who combined meditation with athletic activity—Thich Nhat Hanh (1926–2022), and groups such as the Hare Krishna devotees. Maharishi Mahesh Yogi's (1918–2008) Transcendental Meditation (TM) program, which involves concentrative meditation and a watered-down Hinduism, has remained popular in the United States and Europe.

The cultural interest in mysticism that resurged in the 1960s faded by the 1980s. However, Buddhism, especially Zen Buddhism, has retained popularity. The Dalai Lama (b. 1935) has also generated interest in Buddhism.[1] Today, some religious groups, such as the Santo Daime tradition in Brazil and the Native American Church in North America, have made psychedelics a sacrament. Some forms of "spirituality" among the churched and unchurched also involve mysticism. Some Christians—like William Johnston (2000)—think a new Western mysticism informed by Asian meditation is emerging in the West: a mysticism that embraces spirit and matter, is free of the dualisms inspired by the Greek philosophies of God versus creation and mind versus matter, and that does not involve the "flight of the alone to the Alone." Interest in altered states of consciousness has also led practitioners of Neo-Shamanism to adopt shamanic practices for altering consciousness such as sweat lodges and drum circles (Harner 1980). Even tours to the Amazon basin to sample the psychedelic ayahuasca brew have become popular.

The New Age movement from the twentieth century has also retained popularity, but many of its groups quickly ossified into institutions mainly concerned with ritual and recruiting new members. Some groups devolved into dangerously controlling and destructive cults. In Japan, Asahara Shoko claimed that a mystical experience inspired him to found the Aum Shinrikyo (Aum Supreme Truth Sect) that unleashed a sarin gas attack on the Tokyo subway in 1995, killing twelve people and injuring hundreds. They also sought nuclear weapons. He claimed that the spiritual power necessary to survive the impending destruction of civilization could be attained only through meditative and ascetic practices. There have also been sex and money scandals involving gurus such as the Buddhist Chogyam Trungpa

Rinpoche (1939–1987), who was an open alcoholic and economically and sexually exploited his followers, and Bhagwan Shree Rajneesh (1931–1990) and his ashram; devotees defended the latter by comparing his actions to that of Krishna and his milkmaids. Many teachers claiming to be enlightened, such as Da Free John (1939–2008), were shown to be egotistical and manipulative (Feuerstein 1991; Storr 1996; O'Brien-Kop and Newcombe 2021, 8–9).

On the other hand, secular interest in meditation has grown. Billions of dollars are spent each year in the United States on yoga classes, yoga gear, smart phone apps, and books on meditation. Surveys show that more than 10 percent of Americans practice some form of yoga or meditation; however, much of it is only stretching exercises for physical fitness.[2] Periodicals tout a "mindfulness revolution." Jon Kabat-Zinn speaks of mindfulness as having the potential to ignite a "global renaissance." The new field of "contemplative studies" is developing in universities (Roth 2006, Gunnlaugson 2014, Komjathy 2018).[3] Interest in the effects of psychedelic drugs is also growing in the fields of psychology and neuroscience, but this interest is largely related to how meditation and psychedelics affect human psychological and physiological health rather than for any deeper mystical goal.

The traditional goal of meditation was to achieve a deep exploration of the mind, altering one's very being, but meditation today is more often only used as a pragmatic application for treating depression and so forth (Goleman and Davidson 2018, 2–3). Transcendental Meditation was initially presented as mainly for spiritual development, but it is now promoted more for health benefits (Woods, Windts, and Carter 2022, 3). Traditional meditative techniques have been adopted in the West to calm the mind or focus attention in order to increase happiness, not to live in accordance with reality in the deepest way human beings are capable of. Some public schools, corporations, and MBA programs now offer classes to aid in focusing attention, increasing mental flexibility and efficiency, and decreasing absenteeism. Even the military now offers meditation classes, with meditation being "weaponized" as part of a program to produce "super soldiers" (Komjathy 2018, 194). Some medical schools are beginning to train physicians in meditation for clinical work, but their aim is to relieve patients' stress, anxiety, and depression; treat substance abuse; and manage pain. These are all certainly valuable goals, but they are not the traditional core mystical goals. The closest any programs come to the goals of traditional mysticism are in offering specific compassion meditations that allow students, through practice, to become kinder to other students.

The Climate against Traditional Mysticism Today

Many factors in Western culture work against taking mysticism seriously today. Within academia, those who bother to take any metaphysical position usually adopt one of naturalism—that all that exists is only what is open, in principle, to scientific examination—often without examining the issues. Naturalists reject all transcendent realities or explanations since, by definition, these are untestable by scientists. Thereby, all transcendent realities—with the possible exception of mathematical entities—are rejected in favor of the natural world. Charles Taylor speaks of an "immanent frame" of a self-sufficient, impersonal, and natural order covering cosmic, social, and moral matters (2007, 539). Naturalists seek meaning within the natural world.[4] As noted in chapter 1, naturalists can accept that genuine introvertive mystical experiences do, in fact, occur; they simply deny that they are cognitive of transcendent realities. They can also accept any verified physiological or psychological benefits of meditative practices or psychedelic therapies as more than merely a placebo effect.[5] However, naturalism rules out classical introvertive forms of mysticism by denying transcendent realities.

Nevertheless, naturalists themselves, including a number of prominent atheists, have had mystical experiences. Usually, the experiences are of the nature-mystical variety; the experiencer's sense of self dissolves while contemplating the night sky and the vastness of things. Friedrich Nietzsche wrote of experiencing ecstasy in which the reality of everything was affirmed in its eternal return; everything is of value, and the eternal return of everything counters its deterioration in value through time. However, these experiences may have only had the effect that a near death experience had on the atheist A. J. Ayer; it slightly weakened his conviction that death would be his end, but it did not cause him to give up his beliefs. The impacts of these experiences may have been great, but they were still seen as only a matter of emotion and did not upset the naturalists' basic beliefs. Bertrand Russell had a mystical experience in 1901, induced by seeing the suffering of cancer patients, that transformed him into a more loving person who opposed war; it affected his values and emotions but not his agnostic beliefs. The physicist

Alan Lightman also had a mystical experience while looking up at the night sky from his boat, in which he dissolved and merged into the infinity of the universe. The experience did not cause him to give up his materialism, but he then saw the structures of nature as sacred. In fact, these experiences may have had a negative effect on religious beliefs, as with the philosopher Pierre Hadot. No doubt, most experiencers today see religious significance in these events, but naturalist explanations have become a viable cultural option, and they amplify the philosophical issue of how much one really learns in a mystical experience.

Naturalists explain these experiences in terms of the workings of the brain, although some become less certain of their metaphysical assumptions. Their explanations keep all introvertive and extrovertive mystical experiences within the natural universe. People are seen as having no transcendent dimension. Naturalists may deny that "empty" depth-mystical experiences occur, arguing that all experiences are intentional; thus, the conscious mind is never truly empty of all diverse content. Or, if they admit such an experience, they will insist that it is the result of the brain malfunctioning; only a feedback effect of the natural mind's monitoring activity, which continues even in the absence of content to process; or, at most, an awareness of a purely natural consciousness in its bare state. They insist that consciousness arose and evolved through natural forces or is programmed into nature-like physical forces, and a depth-mystical experience is the experience of that natural consciousness. Thus, they conclude these experiences, at most, show that the purely natural mind has greater depth and more accessibility than normally accepted; there is no transcendent consciousness or self separate from the body that survives death, and there is no consciousness underlying the natural universe. Likewise, the experienced sense of bliss results only from the purposeless spinning of mental gears that occurs when one is aware but has no mental content to work on. That mystics take this bliss as love or as otherwise indicating an experience of something transcendent only shows that they misinterpret the experience. Theists erroneously attach more significance to any experiences of light or warmth as experiences of God only because of the strangeness of these states of consciousness; their prior beliefs in a supreme transcendent reality; and their belief that others had mystical experiences of God, so these experiences must be the same. The religious expect to experience God, so they naturally interpret mystical experiences that way, even though the experiences are only natural brain events.

To naturalists, introvertive mystical experiences with content are merely cases where the mind's subconscious content wells up into the conscious mind. Mindfulness is only an act of paying extraordinarily close attention to one's experience of the world. It merely switches one's mental focus from differentiations to that-ness and, thus, reveals nothing new about what is or is not real. Experiences of beingness are no more cognitive than ordinary, structured perceptions of differentiated parts; pieces remain real and distinct, even if when one focuses on beingness, the boundaries between the person and other phenomena disappear. With this switch in focus to the sheer beingness of the natural realm, the area of the brain responsible for sensing a boundary between the self and the rest of the universe has less blood flow, while the area that attaches importance to events is more active; so mystics naturally feel more connected to the universe. In naturalistic metaphysics we, in fact, are connected to the universe.[6] This switch in focus does not, as advocates of traditional mysticism would argue, inhibit the mechanisms that prevent us from experiencing transcendent realities. The self-transcendence valued in spirituality can thereby be achieved, even though this transcendence does not exceed the natural realm. Cosmic consciousness and nature-mystical experiences just add a subjective dimension to other extrovertive mystical experiences. Likewise, simply because meditative manipulations of the mind and drugs produce the same experiences in people regardless of culture does not mean that these experiences are cognitive; it only means that we all share a common neurology.

Thus, to naturalists, mystical experiences are no more insightful than the interesting but cognitively empty effects of psychedelic drugs such as LSD, which distort a person's perceptions and consciousness. An experienced sense of selflessness can be explained away as merely being momentarily unaware of the self in an overwhelming experience. Or, selflessness can be treated as empirical support for naturalistic theories such as Daniel Dennett's theory that a person's sense of "I" is an illusion; a person possesses only various brain monitoring activities without any one unified center, let alone a distinct reality called the sense of the "self." The self is only a useful construct that the brain spins out of these monitoring activities. Living totally concentrated on the now without a sense of self and without concerns for the future would bring a sense of calm and peacefulness, but it does not negate anything about the complexity of the world or life. Such an escape greatly eases stress, but it does not tell anything new about the way things really are. Everything that makes a person human is tied to their sense of the reality of a phenomenal self, even if they deny the existence of a discrete reality called the self. Overall, traditional mysticism is not seen as a means to align oneself with what is actually real but only to evade it.

Many scholars in religious studies today would not go even that far toward accepting mystical experiences. There is a pervasive lack of interest in religious experiences in religious studies in favor of observable sociological and historical data.[7] According to June McDaniel during the 2017 American Academy of Religion meeting, a "visceral hatred of religious experience" is shown (2018, 1). There is now a "hostility" toward the idea of mystical and ecstatic experiences "that used to be found in theologians talking about heresies" (3). Thus, the surge of academic interest in meditation and entheogens is mainly in other departments, as is interest in the neurology of how we experience and know. Apparently, scant attention is also being paid to more general spirituality (Mosurinjohn and Watts 2021). Harold Roth (2006), an advocate of the budding field of contemplative studies in higher education, proposes to revitalize religious studies by studying subjective religious experiences, but he remains very pessimistic about the prospects for change. The dominance of constructivism and attribution theory in religious studies plays down the significance of mystical experiences. Under the latter approach, mystical experiences become nothing but a mystical overlay given to ordinary emotional experiences. Under the former approach, mystical experiences are accepted as possibly genuine and unique, but they are seen as having no independent cognitive content—cultural beliefs determine their alleged cognitive import—so they play no role in developing any tradition's mystical or other doctrines (Jones 2020a). These approaches enable scholars to focus exclusively on mystical texts or observable cultural phenomena and to ignore experiences. Religious experiences have become more commonly reduced to nonreligious phenomena. As Kimberley Patton notes: "The unreality of the divine object, once only a premise of anthropology and sociology, is now taken so much for granted in the study of religion as to go virtually unchallenged" (Patton 2000, 154). The role of scholars in religious studies now is to explain away the field's subject matter by denying anything unique to it, reducing religion to other phenomena. As Jeffrey Kripal says, by reducing religious experiences to material claims, the field has, in effect, denied its own subject matter (2010, 26). It is "as if taking the sacred seriously is equivalent to surrendering one's intellect and critical faculties to the faith claims" of a religious tradition (26).

Postmodernists in academia may tend to deny that there are any genuine mystical experiences and ignore neuroscientific studies suggesting that unique mystical experiences occur. Their emphasis on the Other and cultural difference is not congenial to focusing on experiences or ideas that may be common across cultures. Under postmodernism, mysticism is reduced to only a form of writing (Cupitt 1998, 137; Harmless 2008, 235). There is nothing to study in the field outside of each tradition's texts. More generally, any mention of mysticism in the study of specific religious traditions is becoming rare. Indeed, in the humanities, mysticism has become "unfashionable" and now has a "bad name" (Cupitt 1998, 56, 45). Mystical experiences, if they are accepted at all, have been pushed aside as, at most, a curiosity of interest to neuroscientists studying the brain.

Within Christian theology, the situation is similar. A generation ago, the Jesuit William Johnston lamented that "from the time of Thomas à Kempis better men than I have been attempting to convert the theologians [to the need for theologians who are also mystics]—and they have been conspicuously unsuccessful. The theologians remain unregenerate" (1978, 58). Thomas Merton thought the separation of theology and spirituality was a "disaster" (2017, 1). According to the Benedictine monk Willigis Jager, there has been no place for mysticism in Christian theology for two hundred years (2006, xix). Nelson Pike (1994) appears to be the last mainstream theologian to take mystical experiences seriously. With a few exceptions, Christian philosophers, theological historians, and comparative theologians have not contributed to the discussion of such experiences today (Spencer 2021, 3).

One "highly distinguished Christian theologian" once suggested to Daniel Spencer that "the proper response to such [mystical] claims [as Aldous Huxley's] is to shrug the shoulders, say 'Some people believe crazy things,' and move on" (Spencer 2021, 4). For postmodern theologians, to view God through the lens of experience is hopelessly naive (Hart and Wall 2005). The questions that mystical experiences raise for theology visibly embarrass many academic theologians (McIntosh 1998, 14), although perhaps not as much as visions. In theology today, any experientialist approach to mysticism that focuses on private, inner experiences and affirms genuine mystical experiences is "thoroughly dated" (Nicholson 2011, 194). All experiences are only reflections of objective culture. The *via negativa* is discussed without mention of mystical experiences. "Mystical theology" downplays mystical experiences and any experiences of God as much as possible (Howells and McIntosh 2020). Some scholars question whether classical mysticism was actually informed by mystical experiences (Turner 1995, Sharf 2000). Scholars who speak of spirituality rather than religion typically focus more on an individual's experiences, personal development, sense of well-being, sense of connectedness to the rest of reality, and sense of purpose or meaning that makes life seem worth living rather than institutions of religion or traditional religious doctrines. However, spirituality is not always connected to mysticism. Indeed, some in the field believe that past focuses on interiority in spirituality were a mistake (for example, Thomas 2000). Any "privatization" of spirituality leaves it without doctrinal content or social focus (Carrette and King 2005, 68–69).

Outside of academia, interest in adopting a mystical way of life remains in general decline in the Abrahamic religions. In mainline Christian churches, the split between spirituality and theology that occurred in the early modern period has led to a decrease in interest in anything mystical. There still are monks and nuns, but there is no longer much institutional or social support for mysticism, nor are there strong living mystical traditions for most Christians to draw upon. Willigis Jager could not find mystical guides within the Catholic church and had to ask his superiors for permission to study Zen in Japan (2006, xix). According to Michael Buckley, the divorce of spirituality from fundamental theology in Catholicism has led to bracketing the witness of spiritual experiences as having no cogency (quoted in McIntosh 1998, 14). Many Christians see mystical experiences as impossible since God must remain separate; God might hear prayers and respond, but a creator god, by definition, is wholly other and thus unexperienceable. They also see mysticism as leading people away from Christianity since there is nothing distinctly Christian about having mystical experiences; rather, mystical experiences are common in all religions and outside religion altogether. Any focus on inner development, radical self-transcendence, or transforming one's character through mystical ways of life has been discouraged by liberal churches as unnecessary, if it is possible at all. Such self-centered activity does not make someone a better Christian than others. Liberal theists may be happy with theistic mystics' message that the universe is animated by love, but claims that someone actually experienced God only make them uncomfortable since God is seen as withdrawn from his creation. Conservative churches emphasize other types of experiences related to personal salvation, and the idea of any direct mystical awareness of God is seen as blasphemous.

Fears of antinomianism have limited mystical influences in most Jewish traditions today. Few people believe that traditional Jewish mysticism can be revived. Likewise, Islam today has witnessed a steep decline of Sufism. In monasteries, East and West, there is little emphasis on serious meditative development. A generation ago, the Trappist monk Thomas Merton complained that there were few or no real contemplatives, even in many Catholic contemplative monasteries, because rigid conformity to rules prevented it (2003, 78, 123–30). The same complaint was voiced outside the West when Agehananda Bharati noted that few monks in Thailand under age fifty meditated (1976, 233).[8] And, if reports are correct, the same holds in most Asian Buddhist monasteries today. *Nirvana* is seen as only a long-term goal to be achieved over many life-times; only about 10 percent of Japanese Zen temples have meditation halls, and although there has been a small increase in meditation today, rituals and customs take up more of a monk's activity (Miller 2003, 8–9). (But more monastics in the past may well have been more like this than we might suppose.) The authoritarian nature of monastic training also runs counter to the spirit of our age.

Psychotherapy today only strengthens one's ego and self-esteem. In the modern West, individualism is prized, and the mystical denial of a phenomenal self makes mystics appear irrational and their passivity seem immoral. Instead, the sense of self should be reaffirmed. The use of psychedelic drugs and meditation in psychotherapy—applied mysticism—in the end only strengthens one's sense of self. The self-aggrandizement of self-realization is the goal. Transpersonal psychology includes states of consciousness that are not self-centered, but few people want to give up their sense of individual existence when assertions of self-will dominate current culture. Purposefully inducing selflessness is precisely what most people do not want to do. Humanistic psychology's goal of self-actualization is more common. Its focus on the self is a matter of self-enhancement, not self-transcendence. Buddhist teachings on selflessness have been transformed into a way to solidify one's sense of self. Psychotherapy may help remove some attachments rooted in the subconscious, but one advocate of Buddhism dismissed psychotherapists as "pimps for the cycle of rebirths."

More generally, our era can be defined by its "loss of faith in transcendence, in a reality that encompasses and surpasses our quotidian affairs" (quoted in Smith 2000, 655; Smith 2001, 41). It is not that all people have lost such faith, but the public cultural norm is that there is only one ontological plane to reality. Only the ordinary state of consciousness is taken to be cognitive, and the only interests in altered states of consciousness are for scientific research or recreation. We no longer live, as premodern people did, in a sacred universe in which all aspects of life are permeated with transcendent significance. Even if one intellectually accepts transcendent realities, they are cut off from everything in this world; thus, they do not engage us or otherwise affect our ways of living. God becomes a deistic transcendent reality who created and set up the natural universe but is now not active in it, not a full-blooded, theistic god. Religious naturalists have abandoned transcendent realities and have given a religious veneer to naturalism, seeing all of the natural world as sacred and reinterpreting biblical passages in terms of naturalism; God is now merely the laws of nature (Goodenough 1998). Such naturalists highlight awe and wonder at the majesty of nature, even if mystical and psychedelic experiences do not play a major role in this religiosity (see Crosby 2008). Many people who are scientifically minded have lost any comprehensive myth to make this world understandable and the travails of life bearable. Many scientists lack so little interest in religious matters that they do not even bother to consider themselves atheists. In such an atmosphere, naturalism will prevail as the intellectual norm for the foreseeable future, not because naturalists have stronger arguments but simply because fewer and fewer people are interested in the alternative or even realize that there is an issue.

New Age Mysticism

Despite decreasing interest in mysticism, surveys suggest that mystical and other spiritual experiences remain common in the United States and the United Kingdom today (Hardy 1983, Hood 2005).[9] Not all of the religiously unaffiliated (the nones) are uninterested in traditional religious matters or searching for a meaning to life within a transcendent framework. However, mysticism must be distinguished from general spirituality. Even among those who consider themselves spiritual or seekers, most today do not exhibit serious commitment to a mystical way of life in their quest for meaning. Spirituality has slowly severed its ties to mysticism from the 1950s and is replacing mysticism, its ties to ancient cultures, and otherworldliness in the cultural marketplace with non-mystical alternatives (Carrette and King 2005). However, with traditional religious institutions weakening in fulfilling the religious needs of many, meditation has become an experiential form of religiosity for some. It adds an inner dimension to social life and contemporary religion, which are otherwise seen as only matters of ritual and external actions. These experiences need not be encumbered by the authority of ancient scriptures or medieval dogmas when it comes to trying to understand their nature and significance. It also gives people personal control over their religious life. Being individualistic and experiential in nature, cultivating mystical experiences may become one form of spirituality for today's world.

Indeed, in one segment of society today, interest in mysticism has increased. New Age enthusiasts say that we are living at the dawning of a Second Axial Age with a globalized culture or that we are moving toward an Age of Spirit. In contrast to the Enlightenment's relegation of God to the sidelines, religion in the Age of Spirit will be experience-based rather than word-based, and everyone will become a mystic. A new form of humanity—*Homo mysticus*—is dawning, and its culture will be based on a higher consciousness, love, and wisdom. Other New Age enthusiasts claim we are entering a transpersonal age in which human consciousness is evolving from being individualized in societies seen as collections of distinct atoms into a new, connected network of global consciousness. Earlier mystics are seen as forerunners of this new age. Bede Griffiths saw the violence of our age as resulting from the out-of-control unconscious and, through this violence, God is leading us to a new era (Johnston 2000, 5). In some New Age–type thinking, the Christian theologian Teilhard de Chardin (1881–1955) views Christ as the "Omega point" of the universe that draws all matter forward toward him, culminating in a final cosmic celebration of unity.[10] Some New Age theologians today believe that the Holy Spirit is the dynamic power that drives the evolution of the cosmos toward its final goal of conscious union with its source: the Supreme Good. Some believe that even meditating only for secular effects aids in generating this new consciousness.

New Age mysticism evolved out of Western esoteric traditions such as Theosophy and Rosicrucianism and through contact with Asian mystical traditions, especially Zen Buddhism and yoga (Haegraaff 1999). It arose most directly out of the remnants of the spiritual branch of the 1960s Age of Aquarius counterculture and the human potential movement that arose from personal growth institutes such as Esalen in Big Sur. Communes such as Stephen Gaskin's farm in Tennessee appeared, though most failed or have been transformed.

New Agers tend to privilege Asian mysticism over Western mysticism, but compared to classical mysticisms, New Age treatments of any tradition are superficial. Traditional religions are replaced by references to a vague perennial philosophy or a water-downed Buddhism or Vedanta.[11] The result is a diluted and eclectic mashing together of conflicting teachings—a weakened spirituality that some label "Buddhism Lite." Of course, most people in established religious traditions may also be eclectic, but eclecticism across the world's religious traditions is built into New Age spirituality.[12] New Agers tend to accept no authority other than themselves. They may be interested in Buddhist meditative techniques but not in why traditional Buddhists meditate. Such spiritual consumerism reflects the current Western pluralistic and individualistic culture and is an effect of our having all the world's mystical traditions readily available. Many New Agers follow their own inner light to a rootless universalism and believe that their own doctrines represent the true meaning of the conflicting doctrines of the world's mystical traditions.[13] Their own mystical experiences are the source of authority for their cobbled-together doctrines, not—as in traditional mysticisms—revealed texts and traditional authorities that provide proper understanding.

The most common New Age position is not that there is a wholly transcendent source to the world. The general this-worldly view is that God is the universe, the self is divine, so the individual is part of God. Often, the doctrines are pantheistic, unlike traditional mysticisms, espousing a nonpersonal, non-transcendent god as a universal force in the world and focusing on the natural realm and the individual. When a transcendent source is embraced, it is a cosmic mind or consciousness that is also immanent to the physical universe, energizing it with love. Nature is seen holistically as a divine and interconnected living entity that is in an eternal process of evolving into a new consciousness. Interest in healing is common, as is interest in the paranormal. New Agers see science as finally coming around to how all ancient mystics allegedly saw reality and anticipate that it will become more holistic (see Capra 2000, Zukav 2001; for criticism, see Jones 2014, Jones 2019b).[14] To them, each individual contains a divine essence within, a higher self, whether that self is on a transcendent plane or part of the naturalistic god. Although this self is deathless, belief in reincarnation and *karman* as a law that enforces a *yin-yang* type balance—but is not a source of any eternal punishment—is also popular. New Agers believe humans are actually spiritual beings that descended into this material world, and they need to undergo radical transformation to return to higher levels of being and recover their true state. They commonly accept ideas of visitors from other planets and channeling ancient spirits. Humans may need the help of divine intervention provided by angels, or they may tap into the universe's spiritual energy through meditation and physical yoga since such energy is present in the body.

Alan Watts advanced an alternative but equally New Age view: since we are already Brahman, we are already enlightened, and there is nothing to do (1966). It is not necessary to achieve any altered state of consciousness or experience to see reality correctly. We are already Brahman, and the state caused by root ignorance (*avidya*) is as much a state of Brahman as anything we might try to achieve through strenuous meditative efforts, so don't bother. There is nothing to change or gain, nor is there any need to become selfless. Everything is perfect as it is, so just accept that you are Brahman. However you choose to live is fine. Antinomianism is fine. Watts himself became an alcoholic.

Overall, depth mysticisms are dying as New Age spirituality blossoms. On the internet, people claiming to be mystics and spiritual masters flourish. There are serious students of mysticism and mystical teachers, such as Father Thomas Keating, but there are also Western "spiritual masters" and "gurus" who have had an introvertive or extrovertive mystical experience of one type or another and have concluded from that experience that they are enlightened—they know what all mystics know. There is no need to attain an enduring ASC state to be enlightened. They believe that they have had the same experience as all the great mystics of the past—even though, say, an extrovertive connectedness to nature is not the same as an empty introvertive experience—so they now must know what all mystics throughout history have known. They cite mystics' writings out of context and with no understanding of the mystic's actual teachings. New gurus quote Meister Eckhart and Zen Buddhists together because they know that these mystics were really talking about the same thing, which they themselves have also experienced. Their experience is all they need to understand the true meaning of any mystic's teachings.

Consider some prominent New Age thinkers:

• Eckhart Tolle was born Ulrich Tolle; but, as an adult, he took the name *Eckhart* to honor Meister Eckhart. When he was thirteen, he had the insight that the subjective *I* is not the object that the mind creates out of self-consciousness. The true *I* is always a subject and can never be a perceptible object of consciousness (1999, 1–3). The objective I is an illusion, and only the subjective I exists. His insight was accompanied by intense joy, and he took the insight to be a mystical enlightenment. (Kant and Wittgenstein made the same point about subjectivity and accepted the reality of the subjective I without any hint of an ASC mystical experience.) Tolle claims we fabricate an image of an entity that exists independently of the subjective I: a separate reality to defend and build up. He claims the next step in human evolution will be a transformation that would transcend the self-based state of consciousness.

• At age sixteen, Andrew Z. Cohen had a transformative mystical experience: an overwhelming sense of the beingness of the world, sense that the whole universe became conscious in him, and sense that, at some deeper level, everything will be all right no matter what happens to one's body and individual person. That is the basis of his claim to mystical enlightenment—although, at age thirty-three, he did spend two weeks with an Indian Advaita guru. Some of his former students, including his mother, have accused him of psychological and physical abuse (Yenner 2009). His disciples excused his abuse by pointing out Zen masters' shock tactics and Buddhists' skill in means or by pointing to claims of absolute authority among classical mystical masters. They also separated the message from the messenger. In 2013 he admitted that he had been arrogant, lacking in compassion, and cruel: a "guru with a big ego." He began a sabbatical "to become a better man." Since then, he has fallen from his former prominence.

• Ken Wilbur's writings on consciousness and an integral "theory of everything" (2006, 2007) were initially respected, but once criticism of his ideas began to appear on the internet, he lashed out in a bizarre, obscenity-laced, cowboy-themed entry to his blog in 2006 and lost much of his influence.

• For Deepak Chopra, consciousness generates reality: "The quantum field is just another label for the field of pure consciousness and potentiality." Thus, to create a better reality, we need to correct our consciousnesses. We now have Chopra's quantum yoga and quantum healing at the interface of matter and energy. Through these activities, we can become "metahuman." He once claimed mindfulness and visualization could cure cancer and end aging.

• There are also New Age thinkers within Christianity, such as Wayne Teasdale—a disciple of Bede Griffiths—who emphasizes the idea of global spirituality and the Second Axial Age, which has mysticism as its ground (1997). For him, Christian Eastern Orthodox deification is only another name for awakening to our Buddha-nature.

• In Matthew Fox's panentheistic "creation spirituality," God is in nature, and nature is in God (1991). He advocates a holy relationship between humanity and nature, tying Christianity to a deep ecological concern and Western liberal values including compassion and justice. Jesus is revamped into a Cosmic Christ that connects all the phenomenal world and all religions. He believes that, deep down, we are all mystics, and he expects a great outpouring of the Holy Spirit on the whole human race. He was a Dominican priest but was expelled from the order for such claims as replacing the personal savior with the Cosmic Christ, referring to God as *Mother*, replacing original sin with original blessing, and his lack of interest in the institutional church. Whether he has had mystical experiences is not clear, but he illustrates his concern for nature with accounts of others' extrovertive mystical experiences. He has been accused by some Christian theologians of not being mystical enough, in effect making all Christian mystical experiences nature-mystical experiences.

Ten points should be noted about such New Age thinkers:

• The lives of many gurus highlight the difference between merely having a mystical experience and attaining an enlightened state of selfless consciousness. In the New Age, enlightenment is reduced to a transient experience occurring with little or no training. One may have a taste of a transcendent reality, but becoming truly selfless is more than having any isolated experience. No matter how powerful a mystical experience is, one may still return to a normal, self-centered state of consciousness. No mystical experience, whether occasioned by meditation or drugs or occurring spontaneously, can guarantee the ASC transformation that constitutes a state of enlightenment. Mystics who retain a sense of self are not enlightened in the traditional sense, and that appears to be the case with many New Age gurus. Mystical experiences can alter how one lives and one's beliefs and values without transforming one's consciousness into a selfless state, but changing one's beliefs without changing one's state of consciousness is not the same as becoming enlightened. Permanently overcoming a sense of self is not easy; humans have evolved a sense of self for survival. Additionally, a mystical experience may not change one's character. One may think that with a pill one can gain in twenty minutes what it takes Tibetan monks twenty years to gain, but that is wrong. Once the experience wears off, you are the same person you were, just with different beliefs.

• A mystical experience may change one's perspective and cause one to be more moral, but it may not. Having a mystical experience also does not entail any one value such as compassion. Indeed, the resulting conduct of some teachers can be very harmful to others. History shows that a basic moral concern for others is not an automatic product of these experiences. Mystical experiences may affect the scope and application of one's own values, but basic ethical values come from elements of a tradition that include more than only these experiences.

• The third point is a consequence of feeling "enlightened" after a mystical experience. These supposed feelings can inflate one's ego rather than making one more selfless and other-regarding. Thinking of oneself as enlightened can easily build up a sense of self-importance since one is now privileged with a special knowledge; one is among the chosen few. The Japanese Buddhist Hakuin said that his pride soared after his first ego-shattering *satori*. Spontaneous mystical experiences may be the most dangerous in this regard since the experiencer gains "knowledge" totally unexpectedly. The experience comes upon the experiencer without doing any work, so they feel specifically selected. Even repeated experiences, if not incorporated into a mystical tradition, may only increase one's sense of importance. Meditation, too, can reinforce the ego rather than end it. This can easily lead to a grandiose narcissism and megalomania. In sum, mystical experiences, ironically, can easily reinforce a sense of self once one returns to ordinary states of consciousness.

• The indispensable role of teachers and meditation masters can also lead these masters to hold inflated opinions of themselves. Their authority gives them power, and the principle that "power corrupts" applies in the guru business as much as in any enterprise. Self-obsessed people can exhibit their ego by exercising power through such tactics as abuse, exploitation, and humiliation. Charismatic gurus may become self-indulgent and concerned with maintaining their own status. Some claim that disciples can become enlightened simply by sitting and worshiping them or fulfilling their personal needs. Some may start out as sincere teachers and succumb to the addictive allure of power. Such self-aggrandizement shows that one can have a mystical experience and even participate in a mystical way of life and still retain an undiminished sense of self-importance.

- Having one type of mystical experience does not mean that all the mystics of history had that same experience. There are a variety of both extrovertive and introvertive experiences, and deeper experiences of each type may occur later.

- Having a mystical experience also does not entitle one to claim that one's own beliefs are the true essence of the teachings of all mystics across the globe and throughout history. Traditional doctrines genuinely differ.

- Having a mystical experience does not give one license to claim that one understands the doctrines of all mystics from different eras and cultures, no matter what degree of certainty one may attach to one's own beliefs or how God-intoxicated one may feel. A mystical experience does not entitle one to claim that, without studying, one knows the doctrines and values of one mystical tradition, let alone those of all traditions. It also does not entitle one to claim one knows what all mystics actually meant, regardless of what they wrote. Having a mystical experience may give one a sense of transcending the self, and this may help to understand mystical texts in a general way, but it may also cause one to distort texts by imposing one's understanding of the significance of these experiences or assuming that all mystical doctrines are really the same. Mystical experiences do not entail only one doctrine, and merely having a mystical experience does not permit an experiencer to downplay the differences in mystical beliefs and ways of life.

- Most New Age gurus advance what Arthur Versluis calls "immediatism" (2014). Americans want instant gratification; and, here, it means instant *nirvana*: attaining direct, spontaneous spiritual knowledge or illumination without much effort. Immediatism is often coupled with the assertion that traditional practices do not lead to immediate illumination (248). As part of a consumer society, Americans want the experiences of and a claim to enlightenment now, not to spend years on guided meditative practices within a mystical tradition. Commitment to a stringent mystical way of life is out. One can go on a retreat for a week or two and be certified as "enlightened" by a self-proclaimed spiritual master. There is also no need to develop enlightenment further once one is instantly enlightened.

- New Age enlightenment is mostly individualistic, focusing only on oneself, with no resulting communities (Versluis 2014, 243). Many of the communities that do arise quickly fail or end up corrupt.

- Lastly, mysticism in the New Age tends to be reduced to a matter of only having mystical experiences, not a transformed life. One is supposedly enlightened just by having any type of mystical experience or belief. The experiences are everything, not the alleged knowledge gained or training to align one's life to reality with that knowledge. This makes having mystical experiences an end in themselves, and any understanding of their nature or what is experienced is extraneous and unnecessary. Even when New Agers do mention an enlightened way of life, their focus quickly shifts almost exclusively to mystical experiences.[15] Even within Christianity, Willigis Jager makes having a mystical experience the be-all and end-all of "genuine mysticism" and of a "transconfessional mystical spirituality" that is beyond all religions (2006). The purpose of all religions is to experience the divine; all beliefs are dismissed as only part of religion, not mysticism, and something that must be transcended. However, traditional mysticism is about aligning one's life with reality—for Christians, aligning one's life with God's will—not attaining unusual experiences. Even if these experiences give one a taste of a reality that transcends normal experiences, alignment with such a reality depends on one's beliefs about what is real.[16] But, in the New Age, the superstructure of mystical traditions can be jettisoned as ultimately valueless once a mystical experience occurs.

Meditation, too, is treated superficially in the New Age. Adapting meditation techniques from one tradition to another tradition need not be problematic, but decoupling meditation from any total mystical way of life changes the purpose of meditation. Its adaptation to deal with limited psychological problems was noted previously. Meditation with a secular motivation and intent may also produce different experiences, even if traditional techniques are employed (Schmidt 2011). Meditation with a spiritual component may produce different effects on the mind than meditation with a secular approach and may produce experiences with more mystical characteristics (Wachholtz and Pargament 2005). Whether meditating in secular contexts to cope with the stress of modern life has no more than a placebo effect is also a matter of debate.

However, meditation has been domesticated. It has been removed from its original religious setting and is practiced for only its purported limited psychological and physiological benefits. Ronald Purser labeled the new meditation "McMindfulness" (2019).[17] Today, yoga in America is more often about exercise than mysticism. Interest in yoga and meditation has led to a revival of interest in the religious aspects of mysticism only for relatively few practitioners. Likewise, many psychedelic drug advocates consider drugs superior to contemplation for inducing experiences, and since the experiences are all that matter, contemplation and a total mystical way of life can be ignored when a pill will do. Even ignoring asceticism, the rigors of the disciplined meditative practices of traditional mystical ways of life, along with the world-rejection of mystics in many cultures, seem totally out of place in New Age spirituality, as does any enduring loss of a sense of self.

We cannot tell whether meditation will be a fad or a lasting part of the cultural scene; but, as Louis Komjathy notes, we need to confront the possibility that, at least in the United States, "meditation may be a form of largely white, middle-class escapism" (2015, 719). To date, the New Age has done a disservice to mysticism by trivializing traditional meditation, limiting its attention to only some aspects of one's life. A selfless ASC is not a prerequisite for New Age metaphysical knowledge; just thinking that one is part of something infinite is enough to be deemed enlightened. For many, reading mystics' works does not lead to changing their lives. Jiddu Krishnamurti's complaint in the 1930s that thousands flocked to his lectures but no one tried to transform their life is applicable to most New Age mysticism today. New Age spirituality is more about validating how one currently leads one's life than about making any serious change in direction, let alone developing a state of consciousness free of any sense of self. It is a sign of our culture's spiritual decline that such New Age spirituality is considered a religious advance.

The New Age guru movement has declined in recent years, and with no sense of a common community, the movement has had little effect on general society. New Age optimism also contrasts with the suspicion of all things religious arising from religious violence since 9/11, the rise of fundamentalism in religions across the globe, and disclosures of clerical sex abuse. Nevertheless, interests in mysticism today may spike among those who consider themselves spiritual as people search for senses of certainty, foundation, and rightness in a time of uncertainty. People are searching for a way to feel experientially grounded in the cosmos and for deeper connection to others. However, there is little interest in committing to the rigors of a traditional mysticism with the depth it has developed in different religions. Interests in mysticism reflect contemporary individualism and concerns about being trendy more than the values and goals of traditional mystics. It is not surprising that few people stick to serious meditation long-term.

Scientific Studies of Mysticism

Both secular and religious interest in mysticism has been reinforced by the resurgence in the last twenty-five years of a scientific focus on the possible effects of mystical experiences on the brain and other parts of the body. That scientists take meditation and psychedelics seriously gives them credence and a positive cultural image. Early in the last century, William James was interested in conversion experiences and how nitrous oxide could act as a trigger for mystical experiences (1958). Scientific interest lapsed until John Lilly developed sensory deprivation isolation tanks in the 1950s and Aldous Huxley, Alan Watts, Timothy Leary, Richard Alpert (Ram Dass), and Ralph Metzner made psychedelic drugs popular in the 1960s. In turn, scientific interest faded in the cultural reaction against hippie culture; even members of the political counterculture objected to the drugs and the apolitical stance of "turn on, tune in, drop out." Interest in the neurophysiological effects of meditation and other forms of mystical and religious practices on the body lagged for a few decades, but trying to identify the neural bases of different mystical experiences and states is now a major research topic, part of a renewed interest in studying consciousness and the brain through cognitive science that was popularized in the 1990s (the Decade of the Brain).[18] Refinements in neuroimaging technology also make experiments more exact and noninvasive.[19] In particular, the number of scientific papers on mindfulness meditation has mushroomed in this century.[20] Scientists are now finding that the dissolution of a sense of self correlates with an increase in the connectivity of neural activity and an overall global integration of the brain.[21]

Academic interest in certain psychedelic drugs used recreationally in the 1960s and 1970s has also been revived greatly in the past two decades, focusing now on their potential as triggers for mystical experiences and their possible psychological benefits in therapy. Contemplating nature, music, dancing, illness, stress, despair, silence or chanting, sex or celibacy, sensory deprivation or sensory overload can all sometimes trigger extrovertive or introvertive mystical experiences, especially if the experiencer's mental set—their beliefs, expectations, mood, and so forth—and the physical and social setting are supportive for inducing mystical experiences.[22] Thus, the drugs alone do not mechanically produce a mystical experience but only open the mind to the possibility of visions, mystical experiences, or other ASCs that depend on various factors in the experiencer's mental make-up.[23] On the other hand, many meditate daily for decades without any mystical experiences occurring. Likewise, many have taken psychedelic drugs repeatedly and never come close to experiencing profound states of consciousness, spiritual or otherwise (Ellens 2015, 2:22–23; Richards 2016, 15). However, certain drugs administered to subjects cause a percentage of them—sometimes 70 percent or more—to have some type of mystical experience. This interest has been primarily in neuroscience, not religious studies. However, more books in the anthropology of religion and outside mainstream theology are being published on entheogenic plants that have historically played a vital part in religious rituals. These plants include peyote, which has been integral to the American Plains Indians—including the Native American Church, in which it is a sacrament—and the ayahuasca vine, brews of which contain DMT and have been used by various Amazon River basin tribes. New entheogenic drugs are also being synthesized.

Psychedelic drugs helped to establish Buddhism and Hinduism in Western culture in the 1950s and 60s. Drug experiences led some Westerners to adopt a mystical way of life. However, this does not usually happen. When drug-enabled experiences are not grounded in seeking a religious way of life, one may dismiss any sense of oneness or interconnectedness the next day as nothing more than a delusion produced by the chemical reaction in the brain. Those who seriously pursue a Buddhist or Hindu tradition usually give up the drugs since they do not initiate a continuous state of mystical consciousness but only transient experiences; one must study and practice a full way of life to alter the mind permanently. Drug experiences have not proven to be efficient in producing mystical lives, let alone ushering in a selfless enlightened state. Hence, there is a mystical objection to drugs. Mysticism is about aligning one's life with reality, not any momentary experience—even if the experience awakens one to the possibility of enlightenment.

Some theists have found their drug-enabled mystical experiences to be more intense than "natural ones" (Doblin 1991, 14), but drug-enabled experiences, especially those occurring outside of mystical training, apparently are not as full in content as cultivated mystical experiences. Nevertheless, many among the religious are enthusiastic about these scientific results, claiming that drugs enable the same experiences enabled by other means such as fasting and meditation by producing the same chemical conditions in the brain as those activities do and that this proves mystical experiences are veridical. On the other hand, others object on theological grounds that these are not genuine mystical experiences, only superficial copies with no spiritual component. True mystical experiences are different in nature and content and come only from God. Theists are inclined to dismiss drug experiences as delusions, as with LSD distortions of perception and one's sense of time. They are not the mystical intoxication with God that is achieved through direct encounter with a personal transcendent reality given by God's grace. No set of natural conditions created by meditating or ingesting a drug can compel God to act. To some, drug-enabled mystical experiences seem unearned and undeserved—a cheap grace. If genuine mystical experiences could occur without Christian faith, then grace would not be restricted to Christians. That comparatively few theistic experiences occur through drugs also upsets theists; most drug-enabled introvertive mystical experiences do not involve any sense of experiencing a personal reality. However, others argue that there is no reason to suspect that the base conditions in the brain are different when a drug or other artificial trigger is applied as opposed to meditative preparations or spontaneous mystical experiences, so there is no reason to think that the ASCs are different. The same trigger—for example, psilocybin—may enable different mystical or non-mystical experiences; thus, it appears that different triggers do not produce different mystical experiences.[24] Drug experiences are not in a separate class but simply involve a different trigger to disrupt baseline brain conditions. If so, genuine mystical experiences may be triggered artificially. This means that the nature of the phenomenological content in these experiences does not differ from those enabled by other means or that occur spontaneously.[25]

According to scientific reports, drugs enable visions of realities distinct from the experiencer more often than mystical experiences. They also do not enable introvertive mystical experiences without differentiated content as readily as they enable extrovertive ones and introvertive experiences with such content. Moreover, the mystical experiences that drugs enable do not transform subjects into an enduring, selfless, enlightened state of consciousness as often as those cultivated in mystical ways of life through meditation. Roger Walsh notes that Westerners trained in shamanic practices may report unitive experiences, but they are experiences of union with the universe rather than with a transcendent deity (1990, 240). Any sense of a transcendent reality is typically nonpersonal, although theists may reinterpret their conception of God as nonpersonal in order to fit the experience of something without personal traits—such as a deistic reality, nonpersonal transcendent consciousness, or ground of being. However, introvertive theistic experiences that give the experiencer a sense of communing with a divinity that is personal in nature do occur.

Secular Mysticism

Western society today is not so much secularized as pluralistic. A common religious legitimation to society has been lost, so people now have a pluralism of options regarding religion—including adopting none—to choose from (Berger 2014). This trend is also spreading to other parts of the world. It is not surprising that in this open atmosphere, a new phenomenon has entered the cultural mix: the total separation of mystical experiences and meditation from any spiritual interest, a secular or naturalized mysticism.[26] New scientific interest in meditation, cultural interest in meditating for help with limited psychological or physiological problems, and the adoption of psychedelics in some psychotherapies have given rise to a naturalistic understanding of the nature of mystical experiences and, consequently, a secular mysticism. Science now gives credence to mystical experiences as distinct events and validates their possible psychological effects for human well-being. Mystical experiences break the sense of a narrow self and make one feel connected to others and the rest of the world; secularists see this in terms of the natural world alone. This natural spirituality appears more tied to mystical experiences than other types of psychedelic experiences (Letheby 2021, 200).

The connection between mystical experiences and religion is natural since religions present pictures of the ultimate nature of reality and human beings, and mystical experiences seem—to most experiencers—to involve realizing an ultimate reality. In the past, anything powerful was assumed to have religious significance, including mystical experiences. But mystical experiences need not be connected to religion, transcendent realities, or a quest for meaning. In fact, while mystical experiences normally have a positive effect on one's religiosity, these experiences can have a negative impact and lead to becoming convinced that no god or life after death exists, causing one to abandon religion entirely (Newberg and Waldman 2016, 60, 67–81). Indeed, an emphasis on gaining mystical experiences alone can lead away from pursuing religion as a means to foster these experiences or provide a framework for understanding them. Even if many people do not explicitly endorse the metaphysics of naturalism, they implicitly assume that there is no knowledge of transcendent realities involved in these experiences. The alleged noetic quality of mystical experiences is downplayed or rejected.

Thus, the understanding of mystical experiences and the means for facilitating them—in particular, psychedelics, mindfulness, and simple concentrative meditation focusing attention on an object—has become secularized for many people. Even among those who endorse mystical experiences for our well-being (e.g., Kornfield 2001, Forman 2011, Harris 2014), the value of mystical experiences is cut off from traditional mysticism. Nevertheless, experientially transcending the mundane world and the baseline state of consciousness that is centered on a sense of a self still attracts many, even when the resulting experiences are not deemed cognitive of a transcendent reality. A sense of selflessness may lessen desires and fears and increase a sense of being connected to others and nature, but it may not be taken as indicating a reality transcending the natural world or having any further ontic significance. Susan Blackmore and Sam Harris advocate jettisoning traditional Buddhist beliefs in an afterlife, rebirth, and transcendent realities while still retaining Buddhist meditative practices (see also Batchelor 2015). Secular forms of meditation for limited psychological and physiological benefits rather than transforming one's character, such as Herbert Benson's concentrative *relaxation response* and the Acem Meditation program from Norway, are growing. Jon Kabat-Zinn's eight-week, mindfulness-based stress reduction program (MBSR) is particularly popular. Meditation helps with psychological and physiological problems whether one's understanding of it is secular or religious.

Meditating for overall well-being today means well-being only within a naturalist framework: improved moods, higher self-esteem, and overall satisfaction with one's life. A total inner transformation is not the goal. Secularists may accept religious texts as useful for outlining practices and delineating states of consciousness; but eventually these texts will be discarded as no more helpful here than in astronomy. For secularists, traditional religious metaphysics and postmortem goals will become ignored as anachronisms even when the experiences have a profound emotional impact. Meditation guides are still necessary, but teachers of metaphysical doctrines are no longer needed, nor is adherence to difficult monastic codes.

In this way, mystical experiences and their cultivation have been absorbed into modern culture without any interest in understanding what has been experienced. Any claims that mystical experiences provide possible cognitive insights into aspects of the phenomenal world or reveal a transcendent reality are not so much denied as simply not of interest. Naturalists may remain agnostic on such issues. All that matters is the physiological or psychological well-being that mystical experiences or meditation may foster. One need not adopt a transcendent or other worldview to provide an explanation; neurological theories of the brain explain all that is of value. Only the practical, worldly effects of mystical experiences are valued. William Richards tells of a successful business leader who had a spontaneous experience that met all the criteria of mystical consciousness. The man's reaction was "That was nice. What is it good for?" (2016, 124; see also Bharati 1976, 226–27).

Scientific studies enhance the public's view of mysticism by giving scientific backing to the claims that mystical experiences are unique and that meditation can promote well-being. However, to date, these studies have reinforced the view that the only value in mystical experiences is their effect on the body. The experiences are "real" neurologically, and that is all that matters. To naturalists, the significance and value of mystical experiences is exhaustively explained by scientific accounts. The possibility that the changes in brain states that scientists observe may merely be setting up the base conditions that permit transcendent input may not even be seen as an issue. If mystical cognitive claims are considered at all, they are dismissed on naturalistic grounds. Only the effect on the brain matters. If drugs could be devised that had the beneficial psycho-physiological effects without producing any mystical experiences, secularists would be content since the experiences are only epiphenomenal byproducts. Mystical experiences are merely subjective events produced by the brain, even if they have positive effects on health and well-being. As noted previously, the only positive interpretation that naturalists can give to mystical experiences is that they reveal something about the nature of the natural mind or the natural world (Angel 2002, Letheby 2021).

But since only the natural world is deemed real for naturalists, mystical experiences can still be seen as aligning experiencers with how things really are if they enable experiencers to have greater personal well-being and function better in the world. Indeed, mystical experiences can be taken as making us more at home here; with no transcendent realities to worry about, such experiences make us feel more connected to reality (as defined by naturalists) and, thus, help us overcome any emotional alienation from the natural world generated by the social self. There is no need to practice arduous mystical ways of life. To secularists, they are not deluded by the material world: it is the traditional enlightened mystics who are and need their beliefs corrected.

Yet, if mystical experiences are incorporated into one's way of life to bring one more in line with reality as they understand it, then secular mysticism is, indeed, a mysticism. No doubt, most people who have mystical experiences today see them in terms of transcendent realities and religious interests, but such a secular mysticism may increasingly become the option of choice for many. Perhaps in an era where participation in religious institutions is declining, the immediate future of mysticism lies in a secular form. The value of mystical experiences will be seen only for its demonstrable this-worldly benefits and sense of meaning, not in any alleged cognition fostered by classical mystical ways of life. However, naturalists can accept those benefits and also accept that mystical experiences may help us overcome any sense of isolation from the rest of reality by helping us realize that we are thoroughly embedded in the world and connected to each other.

A Mystical Revolution?

Despite the position of naturalism today, a transcendent framework for understanding mystical experiences and the possibility of traditional mystical ways of life have not disappeared from more pluralistic contemporary Western societies. Mainstream religion in the West today has not satisfied the spiritual needs of many, and there has been a crisis of meaning, leading to a spiritual malaise. Many desire to know their place in the cosmos. As noted earlier in this chapter, some people seek solid foundations in our era of uncertainty and instability through direct experience of something they deem an unchanging and ultimate reality. Some have turned to religious traditions outside Western culture. However, the option of understanding one's mystical experiences naturalistically is real today in a way it was not in the past. Advocates of mysticism now have to argue, even to the religious, that traditional mysticism matters.

Without regular injection of intense, personal, spiritual experiences—for theists, encounters with a living god—religion becomes no more than a social club with a bloodless metaphysics. Some religious advocates argue that something visceral, like a reinvigorated mysticism, may be needed to revitalize religion—not more intellectual ideas or social work. Religion should not be reduced to a matter of belief and cultural identity. The philosopher Louis Dupré believes that all religions "retain their vitality only as long as their members continue to believe in a transcendent reality with which they can in some way communicate by direct experience" (2005, 6342). Professor of world religions Robert Ellwood suggests that it is hard to conceive of religion persisting without the continual input of mystical experiences on the part of some religious people. Experiences of ultimacy are the only guarantor of any future for religion since only they point to the one undeniable fact: that now, as much as ever, people report having experiences of mystical intimacy (1999, 190). If religions ignore this, mystical experiences will continue without them. Karl Rahner, the most prominent Catholic theologian in the second half of the twentieth century, predicted that "the Christian of the future will be a mystic [i.e., one who has experienced God] or not be a Christian at all." In Western society today, institutional support for Christianity has lessened, so Christianity will have to be grounded in individuals who have had immediate experiences of God (1984, 22).[27] Likewise, many in Asia since World War II have argued that the future of religion in general—or even the future of civilization itself—depends on a strong continuing presence of mystics.

There have been religious reawakenings in the past when societies were in crisis. Nevertheless, even if Western culture continues to maintain religions as social institutions, current cultural conditions are not ripe for a mystical revolution within religion. Adopting a worldview shaped by science does not require denying that mystical experiences are cognitive of a transcendent element to reality or that aspects of the phenomenal world are outside the scope of scientific examination, so mysticism today may contribute to the world's current religious situation even for the scientifically minded.[28]

However, factors mitigate against mysticism's ability to have a widespread influence on culture, at least in the near future. First, as discussed previously, the spirit of the age remains anti-mystical, and as long as higher education and mainstream media remain predominately secularized, the prospects for mysticism being a major cultural force are limited. This is so despite growing secular interest in the effects of meditation and psychedelic drugs. It is not that science or philosophy have refuted mystical claims to knowledge but rather that we have lost interest in mystical matters, or we see mysticism as counterproductive.

Second, being "poor" and "humble" in spirit is out of place in societies where individuals seek fortune and fame. Indeed, Western culture has become too affluent and comfortable for people to want to escape it and too materialistic for many to give the vertical dimension of beingness any importance. From any classical mystical point of view, we have lost sight of the ontic source of this realm: we do not even consider the possibility that we are in Plato's cave. In addition, our awareness of alternative systems of belief makes it harder for us to commit fully to any one system. We end up being less committed, and our beliefs end up more general and superficial. In addition, technology has produced so many distractions that it is difficult to still the mind or commit fully to the moment, even during meditation, in the barrage of so many options confronting us and so much information at our fingertips. Ours, indeed, can be called the "Age of Distraction" (Loy 2008).

Third, even with New Age spirituality, it is hard to maintain that there are dramatically more mystical experiences occurring in toto today than in the past. Of course, there are more *accounts* of mystical experiences today since more people today can write than a thousand years ago, and the Internet makes communication much easier and more anonymous. But if mystical experiences are, in fact, a normal product of a healthy brain and common among the population at large, then it is likely that mystical experiences were at least as prevalent in the past as they are now. Yet, mystical experiences did not transform past societies, even when they did not have to contend with a secular environment. Psychedelic drugs have also been employed throughout history. We may be more alienated from each other and the natural world now than in the past, but mysticisms were more common in premodern societies in which family and community were central, and mysticism still did not become dominant in any very large cultures or stop modern alienation. There is little reason to suppose that mystical experiences could have a wider cultural impact on our modern societies.

Many New Age advocates think that we are on the verge of a new stage in human evolution. But why should we think that mystical experiences would change society today—in a culture that so values self-assertion—if they did not produce mystical societies in the past, when circumstances were more congenial and uninfluenced by modern individualism and materialism? This is especially so when many experiencers today do not accept their experiences as cognitive. It may be overly optimistic to believe that we are seeing not only the twilight of older religions but also the birth of some new, general spiritual revolution. The "New Age" may remain only a fringe movement among a small segment of the affluent in our pluralistic society and, thus, unable to bring about any large-scale evolution of human consciousness.

Fourth, mystics typically are more interested in transcending the world than in transforming it. They focus on the development of the individual, not changes in social-level structures. Mysticism is a matter of inner change in one's character that cannot be brought about by changing political structures. It is an individualistic form of religiosity even in social settings. While there are some exceptions—including political Daoism; some Christians, such as Catherine of Siena; and Gandhi—the idea of reforming society or advocating social justice is a relatively recent development in mysticism (see Johnston 1995, 254–68; Jones 2004, 347–77). If mystics themselves did not produce social reforms in the past when they had more influence, why would they be harbingers of change today, when interest in mystical experiences is only in its psycho-physiological effects rather than insights about the relationship between attained states of consciousness and reality? Without a cognitive dimension, the scope of mystical experiences' impact is limited.

Fifth, throughout history, mystics' lack of interest in social matters has tended to make them conservative on such matters—except when they are coupled with a radical movement arising for non-mystical reasons; thus, mysticism can easily become counterproductive to social change (Ellwood 1999, 190).[29] Mystical experiences may not energize or validate changes. Rather, if mystical experiences are seen as self-validating, they will make mystics as dogmatic as before their experiences or even more so concerning their former ideas (189). This may apply to mystics' social beliefs; they may simply support maintaining the status quo. Moreover, mysticism inevitably focuses energies on inward experience—energies that otherwise might be used to effect outward change (190). In the 1960s, drug-enabled experiences did not have a political effect. Hippies had no institutional support system, and the only lasting cultural effect of this time period was an increase in the individualism and general hedonism of the "Me Generation." The consciousness raising movements that did have roots in 1960s—which had concerns for social justice, feminism, environmentalism, and opposition to war and nuclear weapons—proceeded without connections to any alteration in our state of consciousness. There is no reason to think that the conditions for a mystical revolution are any more conducive today.

Sixth, it should not be forgotten that a world of mystics is not necessarily one of compassion and a sense of interconnectedness. Mysticism is not all peace and love; mystics have supported inquisitions, crusades, wars, and religious fanaticism, often in the name of love. And, as noted previously, some spiritual masters become narcissistic egomaniacs who exploit their followers. Having had a mystical experience or being a skilled meditation instructor may not change a person's character. Likewise, drugs and meditation can aggravate negative psychological conditions. It must be remembered that the basic beliefs and values of a mystic come from outside mystical experiences, so any positive social vision must also come from outside the mystical experiences. Mysticism may provide energy for enacting the adopted vision or sap energy from making any social changes, but rootless mystical experiences may only open people up to dangerous psychological events or reinforce their unenlightened beliefs and sense of self. If many New Age gurus are any example, a society dominated by untutored mystics may be very unpleasant and dangerous, if it is viable at all. In sum, adding some mystical practices may counterbalance a life devoted solely to the external, but looking upon mysticism as a simple remedy for our social ills is certainly misguided.

What Are the Prospects for Traditional Mysticism Today?

In sum, Western interest in meditation and, to a lesser extent, psychedelic drugs has gone from a Bohemian phenomenon to more mainstream. There is now growing interest in secular mysticism, and traditional mysticism has been sidelined, but might classical mysticism be resurrected in reshaping religion—at least in a limited role? Late in his life, the Christian theologian Paul Tillich said that the question for his time was this: "Is it possible to regain the lost dimension, the encounter with the Holy, the dimension that cuts through the world of subjectivity and objectivity and goes down to that which is not world but is the mystery of the Ground of Being?" (quoted in Smith 2000, 32). From what was discussed previously, the prospects for more fully incorporating parts of traditional mysticism as one component of a reinvigorated general religious life look bleak for the near future. Mysticism does not mesh with all forms of religiosity. Most theists still staunchly resist claims that there is any presence of God within the natural universe through panentheism or emanationism, and Matthew

Fox's and Willigis Jager's modern forms of Christian mysticism got them in trouble with Catholic authorities. Equally important, how can mystical ASCs be incorporated into a modern worldview as anything but subjective products of brain states?

As Robert Ellwood notes, any "universal mysticism" is not likely to become "the tangible religion of the future for more than a few pure spirits" since most people are content with the specific religious tradition they grew up in, even if they apply perennial philosophy or another such theoretical framework to understand the tradition's doctrines (1999, 189). Mysticism may be important to some Christian theologians for its ecumenical dialogue between religions, but there is no suggestion today that mystical theorists are converging on one doctrine or religious tradition or advancing a mystical basis for a synthesis of one "world faith." That religions in general are not coming together to form one unified tradition should also be pointed out. Instead, the number of religious subtraditions is proliferating. As Ellwood also notes, the actual dynamics of religious history strongly militate against the takeover of any syncretism made up of any combination of the present world religions (189). Further, not all advocates of mysticism see need for a synthesis. Most perennial philosophers see no need for a new religion since each established religion is already a vehicle to the same truth.

But perhaps our species is *Homo religiosus*, as Mircea Eliade along with many others in religious studies and some in anthropology have asserted. Perhaps there is a natural human need to seek meaning in terms of transcendent realities, to bring coherence to our lives; so, perhaps we will always have a thirst for transcending the natural realm. Believing that contact with more of reality occurs in mystical experiences can lead a person to experience a fuller life and utilize more of their mental capacities. Mystical selflessness also may widen the circle of application for whatever values one adopts. Even if mystical experiences are not cognitive, they may open us to the possibility that there is more to reality than the natural world or more than what ordinary states of mind can begin to comprehend. They may help us overcome a sense of alienation from the natural world—that we are separate realities set off against it—by giving us a deeply felt sense of being connected to the world and to each other. This would affect how we see ourselves and how we treat others. Today, we can see ourselves as the heirs of all the major mystical traditions of the world. Individuals who believe that mystical experiences are cognitive of a normally hidden dimension of reality or are otherwise important for our views of both ourselves and the world are in a position to utilize those contemplative traditions to develop new mystical doctrines or ways of life in association with science and modern cultural interests.[30]

Perhaps the different world religions will each develop a new mysticism by reflecting on the history of their respective traditions and their encounters with other traditions' mysticisms. However, for any classical mysticism that takes introvertive mystical experiences as cognitive to be acceptable in Western culture today, it must embrace the full reality of the natural world. The problem is how to take the world seriously within a transcendent framework without being estranged from the world. We may reject the secularization of values along with the metaphysics of naturalism that accepts only the world open to science as real, but the reality of the world revealed by science—along with its natural suffering—is simply irreducible and cannot be denied. The vast cosmos of billions of galaxies, perhaps located in a multiverse and in an infinite time-frame, exhibits an incredibly intricate structure that begins on a truly minuscule scale and leads to complexities on the everyday level that include life and conscious beings. To dismiss this world as unreal in any sense—Advaita being the paradigm of this—may be logically possible, and doing so would certainly relieve stress by making everything unimportant, but it is simply no longer credible. Gaining an overwhelming sense that one has experienced what is ultimately real in a mystical experience need not lead to denying the reality of the natural realm. One can remain tentative about one's beliefs about what is ultimately real or agnostic about the nature of what one appears to experience, but this world is still part of that reality. The waves are as real as the still depth of the ocean.

Likewise, any acceptable mysticism today must take people and society seriously. Human beings are integrated into the natural world. Making our natural state something transcendent or making our goal rejecting life in this world and escaping from it does not treat this world and human existence as fully real. Detachment and even-mindedness may lead to seeing something more of reality, but having passions and attachments are part of being a human being and, thus, part of reality too. History has also shown that mystics need not treat the body as impure, a hindrance, or illusory, and any mysticism that could work in the modern world would have to treat the body as important. Likewise, treating people as characters in a dream or otherwise less than fully real denies their social reality, and that may well lead to immoral actions since one cannot rationally care about what happens to the unreal characters in a dream. Moreover, totally denying our own reality (or the reality of the body or personality), denying responsibility for our actions, or selflessly giving everything to others regardless of the consequences to ourselves also conflicts with reality since we are as real as any other node in the flux of phenomena. However, the nonduality in mystical states of consciousness, regardless of any particular religious or nonreligious understanding of those states, may lead a person to be less egocentric, more open, more tolerant of others, and less anxious or depressed and may generally lead to greater psychological well-being that carries over once the experiences have passed—although the psychological dangers of these experiences cannot be dismissed.

Whether we accept any mysticism as valuable today ultimately depends upon our basic philosophical judgments. The acceptance of mysticism may not necessarily be religious in nature—the impact mystical experiences have on a person's life will be controlled by the person's frame of reference and wider worldview. However, the secular appropriation of meditation and psychedelic drugs for limited physiological and psychotherapeutic ends may cut off any appeal a more encompassing mysticism may have for the foreseeable future.

Appendix

Correcting Some Misunderstandings about Mysticism

The history presented in this book reveals that mystical experiences and classical mysticism are often misunderstood today by both the general public and scholars. Some misunderstandings are philosophical in nature and thus lie beyond the scope of this book, including whether mystical experiences are self-justifying, whether mystics are rational in their thought and arguments, and problems raised by the diversity of mystical doctrines (see Jones 2016). Different definitions of the terms *mystical* and *mysticism* lead to different points, but some general misunderstandings about the experiences and phenomena deemed mystical in this book should be addressed.

Mystical Experiences and Mystical Enlightenment

Enough was presented to show that there is not only one type of experience that all mystics have, even within the restricted range of experiences within altered states of consciousness and other states deemed "mystical" here. Some experiences are oriented toward transcendent realities and some toward the natural world. Some introvertive experiences appear to be empty of any differentiated content and some do not. Extrovertive mindfulness is different from cosmic consciousness. It is not as if all introvertive and extrovertive experiences are the same in nature and that what can be said about the nature the empty depth-mystical experience is true of extrovertive mindfulness. The Samkhya-Yoga realization of the true self (*purusha*) is significantly different from a nature mystical experience. So, too, an Advaitin experience of Brahman (*anubhava*) is different from a theistic introvertive experience. Thus, mystical experiences should not be referred to as "*the* mystical experience" in the singular. Typologies such as the one set forth in chapter 1 are useful in that regard. Likewise, not all mystics are ascetics, practice the same meditative techniques, or have the same encompassing ways of life. Their individual trainings and their resulting experiences must be looked at more closely.

Equally important, mystics do not all have the same enlightened state. Those states are structured by the beliefs and values provided by a given mystic's religious and cultural traditions. The transformed state of enlightenment is both a noetic and emotional change that can only occur only outside of any introvertive mystical experiences—when a state of consciousness with differentiated content is involved—in order to see the applicability of the insight to reality. Some traditions emphasize a change in knowledge; some emphasize losing personal desires. The resulting enlightened ways of life are not necessarily other-worldly; they may be quite mundane and not require withdrawing from the world for a life of perpetual meditation. Enlightenment may be expressed in quiet serenity or joyful laughter, in compassionate actions toward others or withdrawal from involvement with society.

Mystics and Knowledge Claims

One major misunderstanding is the idea that mystics are not interested in doctrines but only in having mystical experiences—that doctrines are merely tools to lead to nondual experiences and are otherwise valueless and can be ignored once the experiences occur. However, mystics are interested in living in accord with how reality truly is, and this makes doctrines about the true nature of reality central to mysticism. Mystical experiences are not ends in themselves. It is gaining knowledge that mystics emphasize. Mystics may need to hold all doctrines in abeyance to gain the necessary experiential knowledge, but some account of reality is necessary for providing a framework of understanding that incorporates the experiences into their way of living. That is, the implosion of reality in a mystical experience may shatter the mystic's sense of a phenomenal self, but the full significance of the experience and what is taken to be the experiential insight is a matter of beliefs held outside of the experience. Classical mystics may decry the inadequacy of doctrinal accounts, but they do endorse some truth claims as less inadequate than others.

In sum, classical mystics do endorse truth claims.[1] This leads to another misunderstanding: there is not one generic set of mystical truth claims. Realizing that one is not their thoughts or other mental contents does not lead to only a single metaphysical idea. However, it should be noted that a pantheism that equates a transcendent reality with the natural world—such as God with creation, the One with its emanations, or Brahman with the projected world of *maya*—does not reflect any classical mystical tradition. Nature mystics to not need to be pantheists. The newer concept of an encompassing *panentheism* can accommodate emanationism as long as it entails that the transcendent also indwells within the world. The transcendent source is other than the impermanent effects of the phenomenal world, yet it is immanent in the world as its sustainer and, perhaps, its inner controller.

Thus, it should be reiterated that these experiences do not carry their own interpretations. Different types of mystical experiences do not entail one obvious or natural understanding, either for all mystical experiences or for each category of mystical experiences. Even if mystics could be certain that what was experienced in any mystical experience is infinitely more real than what is revealed by any ordinary experience, this certainty cannot be transferred to any of the conflicting accounts of that reality's nature (see Jones 2016, chap. 3). Likewise, even if meditative techniques, trainings, or drugs produce the same experiences in all human beings regardless of their culture, it does not follow that all mystics' understandings of what is involved in mystical experiences is the same despite divergences in the terminology employed by different traditions—contra perennial philosophy, as discussed in the preface. Seeing an experience as cognitive; seeing an experience as only an interesting, subjective, brain-generated, and cognitively empty event; seeing what is experienced as a foundation of love for the natural world; or seeing the world as inconsequential all depend on factors outside the experiences themselves. That is, the knowledge that is allegedly gained in a mystical experience will always involve some elements of the mystic's belief system that are external to the experience itself. This leads to a diversity of mystical knowledge claims made within diverse ways of life. And, it should be added, classical mystics have disputed and rejected mystical doctrines that conflict with their beliefs—even those within their own traditions.

Moreover, mysticism is not even inherently religious, either in the sense of involving transcendent ontologies or being tied to a meaning of life. As discussed in the last chapter, people today may see the significance and value of mystical experiences only in natural terms related to physical or psychological well-being with no cognition of transcendent realities. One can engage in meditation only for physical and psychological health benefits and not for transforming one's character. The experiences remain secular by being understood in terms that are independent of religious ways of life and transcendent worldviews. If introvertive mystical experiences do, in fact, involve transcendent realities, an experiencer may still misinterpret the experience after it is over and give it a naturalistic interpretation. If so, it may not have a transformative effect on the experiencer or be seen as meaning-bearing. Extrovertive experiences of nature mysticism or cosmic consciousness—and even the sheer that-ness of things in mindfulness—are usually seen as having religious significance, but they need not be. What seems like a visceral experience of God or Jesus Christ to a Christian may seem to the nonreligious to be an unusual but purely natural, brain-generated occurrence.

A sense of a oneness, unity, or nonduality to one's consciousness is a feature of mystical experiences, but how the content of that nondual ASC is understood varies; for example, it may be seen as only unifying one's consciousness. Classical mystical metaphysics reflect two types of nonduality. In introvertive mysticism, there is a vertical nonduality of the transcendent source of a person's being or the entire phenomenal world's being and the world or person. In extrovertive mysticism, the nonduality is the horizontal absence of a plurality of independently existing entities within the phenomenal world. Introvertive metaphysics stresses the timeless and changeless dimension of being, while extrovertive metaphysics—such as in early Buddhism—stresses only the constantly changing world of becoming. One's essence may be a transcendent reality or lack of any substance at all if one is only connected horizontally to other phenomenal realities. Likewise, there are different corresponding vertical and horizontal senses of unity and oneness: realizing the one simple, undivided reality of a transcendent source that supplies one beingness to everything versus realizing that everything in the diverse phenomenal realm is connected or of the same nature in sharing the one natural beingness common to all things. This is also the case with nothingness; nothingness is the introvertive sense of a transcendent source of phenomena that is the opposite in nature from all phenomenal things and properties, not a literal lack of existence. In extrovertive mysticisms, *nothingness* refers to the lack of distinct objects within the phenomenal world and, thus, the lack of real referents to which words could apply, not the denial of the reality of the phenomenal world. Our conceptions are mistakenly projected onto the world, thereby creating the illusion of a multiplicity of distinct objects, but the phenomenal world does exist.

This is also the case with realizing the unity of the transcendent self versus realizing that we are not isolated entities within the phenomenal world but phenomena of the one horizontally connected, impermanent whole of the natural realm. Likewise, the idea of *illusion*—contrary to the popular understanding of mysticism—is not used to dismiss the phenomenal world as totally illusory. The world also does not disappear with enlightenment. Even in classical Advaita nondualism, the phenomenal realm is not treated as nonexistent even though only Brahman is real. In depth-mysticism generally, the illusion is that the natural universe is real independently of the transcendent source of being and populated with distinct, independently real entities. In extrovertive mysticism, the illusion results from conceptualizing discrete, self-enclosed entities—in particular, a self—from the perpetual connected flow of impermanent phenomena, but it affirms a reality beneath the concept-generated illusions. Only the object-ness generated by the mind in reifying concepts is the illusion.

It is also a misconception that ultimate reality is a reality that is not dependent upon anything else for its existence. There need not be one single ultimate reality. In depth mysticisms, there may be one transcendent reality (God, Brahman) or a plurality (the multiple transcendent selves in Samkhya-Yoga and Jainism), while extrovertive mysticisms—including secular ones—may take the phenomenal world to be all that is real. Thus, defining *mystical experience* as the "direct experience of ultimate reality" must be qualified; such a definition eliminates traditions with multiple transcendent realities as well as any extrovertive experiences in which the experiencer does not take the phenomenal realm to be ultimate reality but the creation of God or an emanation from a transcendent source. Theists may take a depth-mystical experience to be only an experience of the ground of the soul or may dismiss the experience as simply a noncognitive, brain-generated event.

As noted in chapter 1, all mystics do not value their experiences in the same way. Theistic mystics may value introvertive theistic experiences over empty depth-mystical experiences as conveying the most important ontological insight. For example, Martin Buber valued the mysticisms of the Abrahamic traditions over those of South and East Asia because the former had an I-Thou relation with the ultimate reality, while he believed that, in the latter, one only seeks oneself or attempts to make oneself God.

The medieval Christian Richard Rolle valued the "rapture without abstention of the senses," in which the senses and affections are purified, over the "rapture involving abstention from the bodily senses" since even sinners can have the latter but the former is a rapture of love coming from God (McGinn 2006a, 344–46). For theists, a personal reality remains fundamental; there is a self-emptying source of the world's being, although some theists also see a nonpersonal, silent, inactive ground like the Godhead of Meister Eckhart's Neoplatonist-influenced system. Theists may also contend that revelations offer deeper insights into the nature of what is experienced in depth-mystical experiences and may value the process of emptying the mind in mystical training only for making it easier for visions and theistic introvertive experiences to occur.

Of course, nontheists dispute theists' position. Advaitins invert the order and place all differentiated experiences, including theistic introvertive mystical ones, on a lower level. All differentiated experiences involve an incomplete emptying of the mind of dualistic content, and only emptying the mind completely leads to the final insight of seeing the nondual nature of reality. They can treat positive and negative differentiated experiences as projections of the unenlightened mind, including subconscious mental forces. For them, only the nonpersonal Brahman is real. But if depth-mystical experiences are devoid of differentiable content, nothing within them can support either a nontheistic or a theistic metaphysics over other interpretations.

In sum, there is no consensus among the world's mystics on fundamental mystical knowledge. Mystical experiences may give one a sense of confidence in the meaningfulness of reality or confidence that reality is greater than ordinary consciousness suggests, but they do not dictate a specific understanding. Mystical knowledge is a product of both experiences and a mystic's cultural framework. This is the case even if all introvertive mystics experience the same transcendent reality. It is not true that all mystics make the same knowledge claims and simply present them in different cultural idioms; mystics' understandings of their experiences genuinely diverge in different traditions. All mystics do not share one abstract mystical knowledge that is present within but independent of all religious traditions—as perennial philosophers assert (see Jones 2021a). Rather, divergence in understandings of the nature of mystical experiences is a prominent feature of the history of mysticism. There is no overall convergence. A variety of mystical claims, even within the same tradition, is the more prominent feature of the history of mysticism. In short, these experiences may confirm to mystics that something real exists, but understanding what that reality is requires philosophical consideration.

William James spoke of an "eternal unanimity" to all mystical utterances (1958, 321), but he admitted that if we take religious history as seriously as "religious mysticism has taken itself, we find that the supposed unanimity largely disappears" (325). Philosophers may achieve convergence on a set of doctrines endorsed by all the world's mystics by artificially abstracting mystics' actual doctrines—for example, by seeing God, Brahman, and a transcendent self all as types of transcendent realities—but the actual concrete claims that mystics live by in their ways of life diverge. Divergence holds not only for belief claims but also for values and ethics, as discussed later. Thus, there are genuinely diverse mysticisms.

The Problem of Language

However, mystics have trouble expressing their beliefs. Mystics use language in different ways, but their attempts to describe what they experience present an issue that is not replicated in attempts to explain phenomenal experiences. They have the task of describing color to those who are totally blind. Mystics often claim that what they experience is indescribable, inexpressible, and even unnameable, and then they proceed to name, express, and describe it. Thus, records of mystical experiences can be confusing; mystics can write copiously and impressively about what they have experienced and then immediately turn around and claim that nothing can be said on that topic or that language cannot convey the truth. How can Eckhart say "God is above all names" (2009, 139, 153) when he just identified the reality by name? How can the author(s) of the *Dao De Jing* say "those who know do not speak, and those who speak do not know" while writing a book on the *Dao* (D 56)? Both the experiences and what is experienced seem totally other than normal experiences and conventional realities. Thus, mystics are rightfully concerned that speaking about what they experienced appears to reduce the experience to one of ordinary objects and to miss its true nature.

Language seems to necessarily distort the nature of both the experiences and what is experienced in a way that ordinary language does not distort ordinary things. To speak, a mystic must leave the states of consciousness of introvertive mystical experiences. Therefore, how can language express those ASCs? Likewise, how can the unity that mystics experience be expressible in any language since all languages must make distinctions and, hence, are inherently dualistic? And doesn't language make any reality into an object for the conceptualizing consciousness—a referent for a word or name—and thereby alter the basic nature of a mystical experience? For Plotinus, at the moment of touching the One, there is no power whatsoever to make affirmations; however, after the experience, the individual can again reason about the One, and the individual knows that they had a sudden vision of the light from the Supreme (Enn. V.3.17). However, after the separation, what the individual sees is not the One but an object of the analytic mind (V.3.17). But even then, how can a transcendent reality that is utterly unlike any phenomenal object be described in terms that designate phenomenal properties? On the extrovertive side, language necessarily consists of static terms that set up divisions. How can any language express a phenomenal reality that is dynamic and without discrete parts? Giving new meanings to old terms or inventing new terms to designate what is experienced does not help: the nature of language itself is the problem. There is a basic conundrum of naming the nameless. Don't we at least need to identify the reality with a word in order to know what we are talking about? Or even to be able to say that the reality is ineffable? In short, don't mystics have to name the nameless? However, the unenlightened would interpret any designation as indicating only a phenomenal object among other phenomenal objects.

The primary way that introvertive mystics counter any positive characterizations is not by remaining silent but by negating any possible characteristic of transcendent realities since such realities are totally unlike anything phenomenal. Thus, mystics are major advocates of the *via negativa*—the denial of any possible positive description of the transcendent—which was introduced to Western theistic traditions through Neoplatonism. Images of darkness, emptiness, a desert, an abyss, nothingness, and nakedness are common, though even metaphors are dangerous since they must be drawn from the unenlightened dualistic point of view, and the unenlightened may inadvertently reduce the transcendent to just another finite phenomenal object. Art and symbolism are other ways that mystics express what they experience, but they too can ingrain dualism.[2]

However, for mystics, there is always a fundamental positive affirmation beyond the negations: a *reality* is experienced. Thus, although the *via negativa* is a movement beyond any linguistic affirmations, it is never a complete denial. There is a negation of negation. That is, this approach does not deny that there is some positive reality that mystics claim is open to experience; it only emphasizes the reality's otherness from all worldly phenomena and their properties. Thereby, the *via negativa* directs our attention away from the phenomenal realm. However, it is dangerous to use the process of negation to merely separate one object from other objects in the mind. The unenlightened still think in terms of a phenomenal entity; it is only one without certain attributes. Even attributing nonbeing to a transcendent reality or saying that it does not exist still produces an image in the mind of a phenomenal object. Perhaps this is why the Pseudo-Dionysius said that neither affirmation nor negation applies to God (*Mystical Theology* 1000b). But the negative approach has never been the predominant trend in the Abrahamic religions for more than short periods—since it seems unorthodox in light of the positive claims about God in the scriptures and from theologians—except in Eastern Orthodox Christianity, where it has remained dominant. Even Muslims, who stress the unknowability of God to all but prophets and mystics, do not emphasize this approach. Theists always attribute positive features to God from their scriptures. In Christianity, in the beginning was the word (*logos*, John 1:1), not silence.

This leads to the issue of mystical ineffability. All experiences are ineffable—try to describe the taste of a banana to someone who has not tasted one. At least with the banana, we can try to compare it to other tastes, but this is not possible with something wholly other than anything phenomenal. No description can completely capture the uniqueness of anything since descriptive terms necessarily involve generalities. What is particular to mystical ineffability is its total otherness from the conventional in both the reality that is experienced and the ASC experiences themselves. No phenomenal attributes apply even analogously to what is transcendent. Thus, God or Brahman cannot even be said to exist. The knowing is alien to any intentional knowledge of an object since there is no sense of an experiencing subject and the content is free of all differentiations.

Ineffability, in the sense of complete inexpressibility, is a modern philosophical obsession. Classical mystics usually state that what they experience is more than can be expressed rather than literally inexpressible. That is, something about what they experience can be stated even if aspects of it surpass expression. The term *inexpressibility* merely highlights both the reality's greatness and its otherness from natural phenomena. For example, Eckhart said—even while expounding a metaphysics of the ground involving emanation from the Godhead—that everything that is in the Godhead is one and, of that, nothing can be said (2009, 294). Mystics also often assert that mystical experiences do not exhaust the reality that they experienced; thus, mystery remains beyond their experience. Likewise, their experience may be "bright and dazzling," not obscure, though it still baffles the conceptualizing mind. Again, the unenlightened, dualizing consciousness will distort whatever it hears by setting off what is expressed into a distinct entity.

Thus, calling what is experienced *ineffable* accentuates its otherness, fullness, and value. Nevertheless, some conceptualizations must be advanced for even mystics to understand what they experienced and incorporate it into their lives. This is true even though all conceptualizations introduce dualisms and so must also be jettisoned from the mind for a mystical experience to occur. Hence, there is a paradox: all conceptions must be both advanced and abandoned. This is reflected, for example, in Plotinus's One, which is both everything and not anything since it supplies the existence of everything but is not any phenomenal object (Enn. V.2.1). These claims stress the otherness of mystical knowledge and transcendent realities, but combining different aspects of a transcendent source—which is how the unenlightened see things dualistically—can lead to paradox. Some examples are the stillness of the Godhead, the Neoplatonist One, and the unnameable *Dao*, which juxtapose the overflowing activity of the creator god or nameable *Dao* that produces the dynamic phenomenal realm.[3] Some mystics even go so far as to declare what is logically impossible—that neither the term *one* nor *many*, neither *is* nor *is not*, can apply—in order to show that none of our categories for phenomenal reality fit a transcendent reality. To Plotinus, only the "sheer dread of holding to nothingness" forces mystics back to the everyday realm of language (IV.7.38; see also VI.9.3).

The states of consciousness in which introvertive and some extrovertive mystical experiences occur are also different from the mindful and ordinary states of consciousness in which language can operate. Thus, attempting to express what is experienced in such mystical experiences removes the mystic from these mystical states of consciousness, unlike in ordinary experience.[4]

The Question of Mystical Union

Since most people in the West are theists or ex-theists of one stripe or another, the idea of a union with God is probably the most common interpretation of any mystical experience, and it makes sense from a dualistic point of view. However, using that characterization for any extrovertive or introvertive mystical experience, even a theistic one, is misleading. First, it can mean different things—from feeling a sense of continuity with nature, to communing with God, to identifying with a transcendent nonpersonal reality. Second, classical mystics do not speak in terms of merging or uniting two substances into one substance. There is no fusion of the experiencer and another reality into one, creating one reality where there had previously been two. The unenlightened are as much "united" to their transcendent source as the enlightened; mystical experiences change nothing in this regard, only revealing to the experiencer what was always true. The change to an enlightened state of consciousness is cognitive or affective, but it is not an ontological change in one's nature. One's state may change—for example, ending rebirths—but one's nature remains what it always was.

In extrovertive experiences, one's sense of self and the conceptual barriers by which one differentiates phenomena are broken down, and one perceives oneness or a unity of phenomena. One realizes that everything shares the same substance or being—and, therefore, are the same as everything else in that regard—or that one is connected to everything else.[5] With the loss of a sense of self, the experiencer may for the first time sense the connection that all people have always had to the rest of reality, but the true ontological situation has not changed. For mystical metaphysics that accept the existence of a soul or self, there is no ontological loss of the self. However, when one loses their sense of a distinct, self-enclosed, experiencing entity that is separate from other phenomena and when one loses the conceptual boundaries that they habitually impose on their sense experiences, they may feel that they are merging with the rest of the cosmos, that their being is the same as the being of everything else in nature, or that their consciousness has expanded to embrace all things. They gain a new experiential sense of connectedness, but they were always ontologically connected with everything else in the universe. Thus, one experiences a sense of uniting or a sense of one's individuality melting away, but there is no ontological change in one's nature from what was always true. No new ontological state is acquired. There is no absorption into the beingness of the cosmos. One only gains knowledge by participating in an ASC.

With the conceptual barriers dissolved, the individual feels one with any objects they observe, but they are not unified or identical with everything on the level of differentiated objects. Phenomena remain diverse: a transcendent reality may be without parts, but the phenomenal world is made of various connected parts even though those parts are impermanent. Classical mystics do not believe that all phenomena are one, except that all phenomena share a common source of being or being connected. Even Advaitins accept a diversity of phenomena within the dream realm. This is also true for classical extrovertive mysticism; the imposed boundaries fall away, but the phenomenal realm remains diffuse. The spatially diverse phenomenal realm remains intact even if there are no perceived fixed conceptual boundaries to reflect mystics' cultural distinctions. Identity or union is limited to everything sharing the same being or being connected to the rest of the phenomenal world in an interconnected whole, but there are no self-contained things that can be identical to in the diverse phenomena of the world.

Robert Forman gives an instance of "becoming" what he saw. Once, while driving, he had an extrovertive mystical experience in which he felt that he *was* the mile-marker he saw (2010, 164–65). However, he did not physically become the mile-marker; he was still driving his car, and he did so without getting into an accident. Thus, he still could see distinctions in his field of vision, and the experience did not have debilitating effect on his ability to think or use language. But he lost his sense of a separate observer witnessing an object that exists in its own right. There was no conceptualized boundary dividing the marker and himself—no "something other" set off against him as a distinct object (2010, 165; see also Newberg and Waldman 2016, 44–45). Nevertheless, Forman did not unite with another reality that had previously been ontologically distinct, nor did he experience any other ontological change.

This follows for depth-mystical experiences. A sense of oneness in a state of undifferentiated consciousness is characteristic of these experiences, but in the mainstream of all major mystical traditions, oneness is not understood as two previously distinct substances becoming unified into one reality. The experiencer gains participatory knowledge of a transcendent reality. In an altered state of consciousness, their mind is filled with God, Brahman, the *Dao*, or the true transcendent self, so the experiencer may feel like they are united in a way they were not before. However, after the experience, the sense of unity is not interpreted that way. There is no ontological transformation, transmutation, or transubstantiation of the experiencer's nature that converts them into a transcendent reality. Again, they simply realize what has always been the case.

The standard position in the Abrahamic mystical traditions is that the idea of creaturehood must be maintained; they insist that we cannot be united to God. An individual may temporarily lose awareness of their soul during the blinding light of an experience of God, but their nature does not change into God's, and they remain a discrete reality. God is always present in the individual as the ground of their being. Mystics do not bring him to them or go to him. They only experience the divine being that has always been immanent in them and in all of creation; the soul is not destroyed. Common images in medieval Christianity are of fire heating an iron rod and the air being pervaded by the warmth of the sun. There is no literal merging or absorption of one reality into another resulting in only one entity (Jantzen 1989). The term *unio mystica* was devised in the thirteenth century, but few Christian mystics used that term before the modern era (McGinn 2001, 132; Harmless 2008, 252–54), and only in the modern study of mysticism has *unio mystica* received a central place (McGinn 2006a, 427). When mystics did use the language of union—for example, Teresa of Avila likening the soul that absorbs and is saturated with God to a sponge and water—the idea was more of communion with God than union.

Overall, Christian mystics struggled over what becoming one with God meant, but they usually meant it in terms of a loving union of their will with God's or even a fusion of their mind with God's (McGinn 2006a, 427–29). However, this is an alignment of spirits, not an ontological union of different substances that were once distinct: one has received the Holy Spirit or waves of God's love, but one has not become God. For Eckhart, there is a loving union of two spirits, one created and one uncreated (McGinn 2001, 46). In becoming a "begotten son of God," one does lose one's form, but one is born in God and transformed (Eckhart 2009, 526). One does not lose one's distinction from God or one's created nature. The individual is nothing without the being of the Godhead, but individual existence is not lost in the nothingness of the Godhead even though the Godhead supplies the same one being to everything. There is a oneness of the individual's will with God's will (522). Additionally, love mysticism is inherently dualistic: there is a connection of a lover and the beloved, not a literal union. In often erotic imagery based on the biblical Song of Songs, Christian mystics spoke metaphorically of a kiss and an enduring state of marriage with the personal God or Christ as the bridegroom and the soul as the bride. There is already a permanent substantive union with God since he supplies being, but there can also be a transitory or permanent, transformative union of one's will and one's other mental faculties—a "union of likeness" of love, although one's nature remains distinct from God's (*Ascent of Mount Carmel* 2.5.2–7).

This is also true for the deification (*theosis*) of Eastern Orthodoxy. God transforms the person, stripping away all that is creaturely, but the person is not absorbed into God. The transformation means only becoming as God-like as humanly possible. God's will and the mystic's will are simply in "unison," becoming one in spirit (1 Cor. 6:17). This is how most Christian mystics understand the biblical passage from Paul, "It is no longer I who live, but Christ who lives in me" (Gal. 2:20). The person is transformed to the state before the fall of Adam and Eve, but one's identity is not lost.

Some Jewish and Islamic mystics believe the sense of an individual self is an illusion, but mainstream mystics in both traditions do not agree. Cleaving to God (*devekut*) in Kabbalah does not negate the two realities. According to the Hasidic Baal Shem Tov, the devout and God are glued together but remain distinct even though God supplies the being of the person. In Sufism, the annihilation of the self (*fana*) and its replacement by the continuing presence of God, or abiding in God (*baqa*), is taken to mean only that what is exclusively human passes away. The divine presence remains, but the gift of individual existence is not destroyed.

In Plotinus's Neoplatonism, the One supplies the being of the emanated realities, but the One is not identical to those realities. A person's lower soul may fall away, but their higher soul is never obliterated, nor does the higher soul ever get past its place in the Nous. Plotinus did use language of union (*henosis*, oneness), being one'd (*henothenai*, to be brought into unity, Enn. VI.7.3, VI.8.18), and being filled with the light of the One (VI.7.36, VI.9.4), but for him individuals remain distinct drops in the ocean of the Nous's being. Union is a matter of contemplating the One from the Nous. The individual is united with the Nous's being, not the One (V.8.10). The One has always supplied being, so no new union is accomplished. The individual retains nothing of their lower soul, and from their dualistic point of view, it may seem as if they cease to exist, but this is only "as it were" (*hoion*) (VI.9.10). The higher soul's individuality remains. For the One, nothing ever changes (VI.9.1, VI.9.9). The centers of the One and the individual soul may converge in a mystical experience, but they remain distinct (VI.9.10), and anything said of the One must be qualified using "as it were." Theists who adopt a Neoplatonist emanationism may endorse a panentheism in which people and other phenomena are nothing apart from God, but there is no union then either. The radiated selves remain distinct items within God's being.

The situation is the same for South and East Asian traditions: enlightenment is merely coming to realize what one already is. For the Upanishads, realizing that "you are that" (CU 6.8.7) is realizing what has always been the case, even if language of union may be used (e.g., BU 4.3.21). One's ontic essence (*atman*) is exactly the same as that of any other phenomenon: Brahman. In its emanationism, one is automatically reabsorbed into Brahman in sleep and at death, but one does not lose their individuality, and the same individual reemerges afterwards. In the Samkhya and Yoga schools, the sense of unity in the depth-mystical state of consciousness is understood to be the separation of the true individual self (the *purusha*) from matter (*prakriti*) and the realization of the simplicity of that self, not the union of something with anything. Indian Bhakti traditions do speak of an ultimate state of union of the devotee and God, but when expounding the doctrines, nondualist Bhaktas typically speak of a communion in which the individual is not totally lost. Tantrism accepts transcendent monism and sexual union as ways to express this state, but enlightenment is, again, a matter of realizing what has always been the case. In Tantric visualization exercises, one may temporarily become a deity, but no permanent change occurs.[6]

Even in Advaita Vedanta, there is no union, although its nonduality (*a-dvaita*) is usually mischaracterized in the West as the union of Brahman and the self (*atman*) within a person. Advaitin nonduality means only that there is no second reality after Brahman. It is not about a person's essence becoming or uniting with a transcendent reality. There is no reality but Brahman; thus, there is nothing else to unite with it. It is not the ground of reality but the only reality. Union is an inherently dualistic concept: two realities becoming one. For Shankara, there is no absorption of an independent self into the Absolute and no merging of an individual consciousness or essence (*atman*) with a cosmic consciousness. Even thinking in terms of an individual self or essence as real sets up a dualism that is foreign to Advaita's nondual metaphysics. In the depth-mystical experience (*anubhava*) one is aware of nothing but Brahman, and in the enlightened state one switches to Brahman's point of view.

Shankara did speak of "merging" and "union" with Brahman because the texts he was commenting on did (BSS 1.1.9), but he made it clear in his final analysis that this is a faulty, dualistic way of looking at the situation produced by root-nescience (*avidya*). The essence (*atman*) within the individual is already identical to the highest Brahman (BSS 4.3.9). If the self and Brahman were different, they could not be made one by meditation (BUB 1.4.7). The popular image of a drop of water merging into the ocean and losing its identity does not fit Shankara's metaphysics. He explicitly rejected that image (BSS 3.2.9; see also 1.4.22) and, in fact, employed an exactly opposite image. He claimed that all of reality (Brahman) is entirely contained in each part of the phenomenal world just as the sun is reflected in its entirety in each ripple of a pond (for example, BSS 3.2.18–20).[7] It is like dreams. The dreamer's total consciousness is present in each portion of the dream; consciousness is not a reality that can be parceled out in segments to different parts of the dream. Likewise, in this metaphysics, phenomenal objects within the dream remain distinct (BSS 2.1.13, 4.1.4). One object is not in another—the sun and the moon are not in the dreamer or united to the dreamer—but the same one being (*sat*) is everything. Similarly, all reality that is present at any time is present in all times in an eternal now that transcends the temporal continuum.

The Asian mystical traditions also treat extrovertive mystical experiences as central. In Buddhism, *nirvana* is not an entity in any sense, although many Westerners treat it as such. It is not a reality that can be united with or attained. Rather, it is the state in which a person's fires of hatred, greed, and delusion have been exhausted (AN I.38, SN III.251). Meditative absorptions (*dhyanas*) are a matter of concentrating one's mind, not a matter of one reality being absorbed into another. Mindfulness is not a union of anything with anything else: there are neither selves nor self-enclosed entities. Thus, there are no realities to unite. Any sense of union is a misunderstanding of the Buddha-nature that is already inherent in each person. In Chinese traditions, the *Dao* is always flowing in us; we merely have to unblock that flow by ending self-centered desires. Thus, the *Dao* is not a reality that one has to become connected to. One only has to align their mind with what is already there by stepping out of its way.

In sum, framing mystical experiences in terms of a mystical union seems natural from a dualistic point of view, but it misrepresents classical mysticisms. Even mystics who use the term do not refer to a synthesis of two distinct entities. Mystical experiences do involve a felt sense of nonduality and freedom from conceptual differentiations, but Western commentators have inherited a theological framework of duality between God and creatures for understanding these experiences and states. Thus, they mistakenly make the idea of mystical union central. Mystics too may feel the need to resort to the language of union to contrast mystical experiences with ordinary ones since there is no language specially designed for mystical experiences, but it is not meant literally. The unitive state of consciousness must be distinguished from the metaphysics of what is experienced. That is, mystics must distinguish the felt sense of nonduality and absorption, since the individual's boundaries are broken, from the later understanding that a mystic endorses. In a mystical experience, mystics are not united to God or another transcendent reality in any ontic way that did not previously already occur. In enlightenment, only a mystic's knowledge, will, and emotions change. These become aligned with the correct understanding of reality as it is defined by the mystic's particular tradition. One may feel their true ontic status for the first time, but there is no ontic change. The experiencer does not obtain or become anything ontologically new, nor do two realities become unified into one.

Mysticism and Morality

Some scholars argue that mysticism is the source of the human sense of morality, that mystics are necessarily moral, or even that only mystics are truly moral or compassionate since only they have eliminated all self-centeredness. Others argue the opposite. The belief that only Brahman or the One is real means that there is no other reality or other real beings to have moral concern toward. A mystic cannot treat people morally if they are deemed unreal any more than a person can rationally be concerned with characters that exist only in a dream. At most, unreal "people" become mere props to be used in a mystic's quest. Thus, mysticism and morality are incompatible. Still, others argue that mystical experiences are themselves morally neutral and that the mystical path and enlightened state are filled by beliefs and values from a given mystic's particular religious tradition. If so, mysticism is neither inherently moral nor immoral (Jones 2004; 2016, chap. 9).

Usually, however, scholars argue that if mystics follow a code of conduct, that they must be moral or that anything connected to a religious *summum bonum* is, by definition, moral. Scholars routinely present the codes and ideals of religious ways of life, but few discuss the issue of why these norms are observed—in particular, whether codes are followed out of genuine concern for the welfare of the people with whom mystics interact, and thus the mystics are being moral, or only for mystics' own interests, and thus the mystics are not being moral. We cannot simply assume that because we value morality, all codes and ideals are always being followed out of genuine moral concern for other people rather than selfish motivation for a mystic's own mystical development, even if their actions have side effects that benefit others. Mysticism involves certain experiences related to the beingness of reality, while morality involves relationships between people. One who has had an experience of selflessness need not incorporate a concern for others into either their path or their enlightened way of life. On the other hand, possessing a central concern for enlightenment does not mean that mystics cannot also incorporate a genuine moral concern for others if morality or compassion is built into the ultimate reality of the mystic's metaphysics.

Thus, rather than beginning with a philosophical or theological position on what the relationship of mysticism and morality must be, we have to examine various traditions. When mystical traditions are examined (see Jones 2004, part II), we can see that there is no one simple relation of all of mysticism to morality. There are three options for the path and the selflessness of an enlightened state:

- *Moral*: Having other-regarding values shape one's motivations (i.e., genuinely valuing other people's interests)

- *Immoral*: Letting selfishness prevail in circumstances where a moral concern should prevail

- *Nonmoral*: Having values prevail that are neither other-regarding nor selfish (as with a nonmoral transcendent reality)

A mystical experience need not make one indifferent or uncaring about the welfare of those upon whom one's actions impinge, but it can—as evidenced by some antinomians in the past and some New Age gurus today. Moral concern may be expressed and central, as with the Buddha and the Mahayana Bodhisattvas, or it may be more implicit in a way of life, as with the Abrahamic traditions.[8] However, mystics may be immoral, as left-handed Tantrikas potentially are. Likewise, mystics can be selfish even without believing in a permanent entity called a self; one can still act immorally by trying to enhance the well-being of one's impermanent and conditioned node in the web of the cosmos by exploiting other nodes. One can also be nonmoral. Immorality requires devaluing others or actually harming them, while nonmorality involves adopting values other than moral or immoral ones but being indifferent to the welfare of others. That is, mystics are necessarily less self-oriented, but they need not be other-oriented either. One can be nonmoral in valuing one's own quest for enlightenment above all else and ignoring the effects of one's actions on others but still not intentionally or knowingly harming others with one's actions. Theravada monks on the path in the first generation of Buddhism offer an example of this indifference; these monks literally stepped over sick monks to get to the Buddha to obtain a teaching that benefitted them until the Buddha instituted a Vinaya rule against that practice. Buddhism also shows how the same basic worldview can ground a nonmoral ethos, a moral ethos, and an immoral ethos.[9] A conflict with morality may be a matter of values, as with Nikaya Buddhism and Advaita, or a matter of the factual presupposition of morality, as with Advaita, that requires that there is a reality to be morally concerned about: that is, other real persons or sentient beings.

Adopting a nondual metaphysics makes reconciling mysticism and morality difficult. There is no other reality for a mystic to be morally concerned about. In Advaita, there is only one reality (Brahman), and no real individuals (*jivas*) to help or hurt. What is real in a person (Brahman) is unaffectable and, therefore, cannot be helped or hurt by others' actions. Mystics' beliefs can lead to inaction—as in the case of the enlightened ideal in Jainism and one option under Advaita—but not all mystics embrace passivity or a moral quietism of holy indifference toward others. Stilling the mind and self-will and becoming resigned to whatever God does need not lead to moral indifference; these two senses of quietism should not be conflated. A mystic can see their activity as reflecting the will of God, and if the mystic sees God as moral, God's intentions will be reflected in their moral actions. Indeed, many Christian mystics were very active in society or in administering their religious orders.

However, mystics' actions need not be compassionate. Nor need they be nonviolent but may in fact appear to the unenlightened to be harmful, as with Arjuna's actions in the *Bhagavad Gita*'s war.[10] Christian love (*agape*) did not prevent Christian mystics from supporting the Spanish Inquisition, the Crusades, and persecuting heretics. Zen Buddhists trained Japanese soldiers for World War II (Victoria 2006). Even Buddhists have a just war doctrine: a greater good may be achieved by killing non-Buddhists if the Buddhist teaching is thereby preserved (Jones 2004, 156–57). Yet, mystics can be indifferent to the entire natural realm—as with Advaita—or concerned with society—political Daoism and Gandhi. Moral mystics may aim to aid others in terms of this-worldly, material well-being—as epitomized by the Christian Meister Eckhart, who valued giving a cup of soup to the sick over remaining in the highest mystical experience (2009, 496). Moral mystics may also aim to provide other-worldly aid by helping others escape this realm entirely, as with the enlightened Bodhisattvas' teachings to others.

Mystical experiences do not make one moral. Isolated mystical experiences will not change an immoral, self-indulgent, or antisocial person into a moral one. As Agehananda Bharati notes concerning the depth "zero-experience," it is a mode of consciousness that has no moral value or implication (1976, 74–75) and need not change one's character (53). An isolated mystical experience may shatter one's old views, and one may elect to be moral, but an isolated experience of selflessness may not change a person's negative psychological characteristics. In fact, the experiences may inflate their pride and ego. The sense that one has been graced by God may increase one's sense importance and lead to immoral, selfish acts. After cracking the sense of self, Charles Manson followed a murderous path based on the belief, "If God is one, what is bad?" Remember again that there are some morally questionable, "perfect" masters in the West today.

All of this points to the reality that a mystic's ethical values come from sources other than mystical experiences. Mysticism has less logical relevance for morality, either positively or negatively, than is usually supposed: mysticism is not tied to morality but to selflessness, however that is expressed in one's actions toward others. In transforming their lives, mystics focus on their inner life, and their resulting inner selflessness may be compatible with nonmoral values. Thus, moral values and mystical values are not identical, and one set does not entail the other. Mystical values are reality-centered, not necessarily other-regarding. How the enlightened fill their new sense of selflessness and freedom and, thus, how they act depends on factors outside mystical experiences themselves. The enlightened may ceaselessly help others or they may walk away from society altogether. We cannot argue that because someone is indifferent to others, they never had a mystical experience or are not enlightened.[11]

We may like to think that all mystics are exemplars of morality with only a few aberrations that can be ignored, but the presence of antinomianism in all religious traditions has to be accounted for. If mystical experiences did, in fact, compel a mystic to radiant compassion or love, we would have to explain why, for example, the Buddha did not mention compassion at all in his inaugural address to his disciples or in his final words as codified in the Theravada canon. We would also have to explain why the Upanishads and Shankara do not claim that Brahman is moral, compassionate, or loving; other features applicable to a theistic god are stressed—omniscience and omnipotence—but benevolent qualities are not mentioned. In Advaita, even when Brahman is misinterpreted as the creator Ishvara, he is depicted as omniscient, omnipotent, and omniscient but not as benevolent, loving, or caring (e.g., BSS 2.2.3). There simply is no second reality to care about.

Women in Mysticism

Classical mysticism in all the world's traditions was male-dominated, but it was not exclusively the domain of men.[12] In Greece, women were among the initiates in the Eleusinian Mystery cult, and women were students of

Pythagoras and Plotinus. Women mystics have been important in all traditions except Judaism—where, in the classical period, women were almost totally absent. However, Kabbalists did give the divine world a female side: God's dwelling place or presence (*shekhinah*).[13]

In Christianity, women mystics have existed since the days of the early desert monastics. Indeed, women have made important contributions to this religion, and Christian mysticism may be more accommodating to women than other strands of religiosity. However, women also presented a challenge to the power and authority of church leaders and to accepted roles in society; the burning of Marguerite Porete at the stake is an extreme instance of control by church authorities. But women have also been leaders and innovators within the Christian community (Hollywood 2002, 6), and women mystics have been made saints. The four women doctors of the Roman Catholic Church—Teresa of Avila, Therese of Lisieux, Catherine of Siena, and Hildegard of Bingen—were all mystics or visionaries. Even though many women were visionaries rather than mystics, the significance of women in Western Christian spirituality grew in the thirteenth and fourteenth centuries, when love mysticism came into prominence and withdrawal from the world into monasteries and convents was no longer deemed necessary for cultivating mystical experiences.

Within Islam, Sufism has a strong history of women mystics, with the first important Sufi being the ascetic Rabiah al-Adawiyyah. Ibn al-Arabi's first two Sufi teachers were women. According to the major historian of Islam's mystical traditions, Annemarie Schimmel, "Sufism was more favorable to the development of feminine activities than were other branches of Islam" (2011, 426).

In Hinduism, it was mainly in the Bhakti and Tantric traditions that women gained significance. There were also women renouncers. Two women are mentioned in the Upanishads expressing views in philosophical debates (BU 2.4.14, 4.5.15, 3.6.1). However, Indian mysticism overall has not been equalitarian; and, in mystical traditions generally, women have held a secondary place. Buddhism in India carried on the inequality: the Buddha said women could attain *nirvana*, but tradition maintained that women must switch their sex just before that attainment. There were Buddhist orders of nuns, but tradition recalls that even the most senior nun was ranked behind the most junior monk. Theravada orders of nuns expired in many South and Southeast Asian countries in the early second millennium, but they started to become reestablished in the twentieth century. Among the Chinese traditions, women were more prominent in shamanic Neo-Daoism.

Women recluses and immortals were recognized. Some women are also esteemed in Chan/Zen.

The study of mysticism was also male-dominated until the late twentieth century (Jones 2021b, 105–108). Women scholars have pointed out the male-dominated language and symbolism of Christianity—starting with God the Father and Eve being created from Adam—and Christianity's patriarchal organization.[14] Belittling and suppressing women's visionary and mystical experiences was an effect of the general subordination of women by the church. Most mystics are, no doubt, absent from the historical record, but women mystics may have been disproportionally underreported. Medieval Christian ecclesiastical and cultural authorities thought women were more susceptible to being possessed by the devil. Such beliefs led to marginalizing women and their experiences. The belief expressed by Julian of Norwich that "as truly as God is our Father, so truly is God our Mother" was ignored. Indeed, in the Middle Ages the church prohibited women from interpreting the Bible and engaging in formal philosophical discussions.

There is a difference of emphasis—in particular, joy over knowledge—and stylistic expression in Christian women mystics' writings that often reflects the individual mystic's social and educational background (Wawrytko 1992, 199–200). There is evidence that women have a proclivity for certain types of mystical experiences: connecting or uniting in body-oriented love and bridal mysticisms rather than the oneness and emptiness of the depth-mystical and knowledge mystical experiences (Jacobs 1992, 277). But does this mean that the actual experiences were different? Do women's introvertive differentiated experiences differ in content from men's? Are there some mystical experiences that are unique to women? Or do women simply more typically take the path of love rather than the path of knowledge? Or, do women only exhibit a preference for the model of interpersonal relationships (God the lover/spouse) to explain and express the experiences over a model of a relationship to a father (God the father) (Wawrytko 1992, 219)? Janet Jacobs (1992) suggests that men and women may have different mystical experiences, but further research is still needed to establish whether women contemplatives experience God differently than their male counterparts and whether experiences that are uniquely women's exist (Lanzetta 2005, 42). Feminists agree that women in the West have a disproportionally greater percentage of mystical experiences than men, perhaps because women are brought up to be more receptive and to value relationships with others, while masculinity is identified with autonomy and separateness and, thus, is a barrier to mystical experiences. Feminists also agree that, after having mystical experiences, women construe them differently than men (Jacobs 1992, Mercer and Durham 1999).

How gender figures outside of mystical experiences in total mystical ways of life also requires study. Further study on the role of women in Sufism, Tantrism, and other mystical traditions and study on the nature of the cosmic female principle (*shakti*) in Bhakti and Tantrism may change our understanding of women mystics further.

Conclusion

Evelyn Underhill's classic definition of mysticism as "the art of union with Reality" (1961, 23) shows how mysticism has been misconstrued over the years. Mysticism is more than cultivating mystical experiences. The experiences do not involve an actual union of two realities, and what is deemed "Reality" differs in different mystical traditions. Ultimate reality is not necessarily God, and this does not fit traditions that involve realizing one's ultimately real but independent self in introvertive mystical experiences. Likewise, today there are naturalistic options for understanding the significance of mystical experiences. Moreover, while certain ASCs are necessary to classify a person as a mystic, classical mysticism is about transforming one's entire inner life in accordance with reality as it truly is—as defined by one's metaphysics—free from a sense of a separate phenomenal self. It is not about cultivating mystical experiences for their own sake. Not all mystics fit the caricature of world-hating ascetics or indifferent, other-worldly escapists sitting blissed out on a mountain top in a trance. In fact, most mystical belief systems grant both the temporal world and human beings sufficient reality such that actions for others' welfare is possible, and mystical experiences and the activities of mystical ways of life may well generate an abundance of helpful actions. Generalizations that all mystics must accept certain beliefs or behave in certain ways do not reflect what the history of mysticism actually reveals.

Notes

Preface

1. For the record, I have had some experiences that I would classify as mystical as stipulated here. One was a spontaneous, brief, and mild nature-mystical experience. Some have been from drugs (I have not had any psychologically negative experiences), but none of them were overwhelming, to put it mildly. This is also the case with my meditative experiences in general. My chattering "monkey mind" apparently really does not want to be stilled. The experiences did give me a sense of something beyond what is given in ordinary states of mind, but most importantly for the issues at hand, I do not think that these experiences have been significant for understanding the specific doctrines of mystics from around the world.

2. Mystics can likewise *assess* whether their experiences are genuine, *determine* the role their own mystical experiences should play in their lives, and *articulate* doctrines only outside introvertive mystical experiences in a state of consciousness with differentiations.

3. The problem is aggravated by the variety of mystical literature—hagiography, prayers, poetry, letters, meditation instruction manuals, commentaries on basic religious texts, treatises, and so forth (see Keller 1978)—and we should not make the mistake of assuming that mystics are only interested in mystical experiences or that all mystical texts are really just psychology texts about mystical experiences. To mystics, understanding the nature of reality is more important than mystical experiences. In fact, premodern mystics seldom wrote about their own experiences. What was important is what was experienced, not one's personal experience of it; what is experienced is the source of our well-being, not the experiences themselves.

4. For problems similar to the term *mysticism* with the umbrella terms *yoga* and *meditation*, see O'Brien-Kop and Newcombe 2021, 5–8.

5. For a history of God, see Armstrong 1993.

6. The term *Hinduism* was introduced by invading Muslims in the eleventh century, and many scholars today think it is inappropriate: grouping the various

Indian traditions together because they share some religious practices or other features is no more warranted than treating the three Western theistic traditions as merely three branches of one religion called *Abrahamism*. However, both of these umbrella terms will be employed when they seem useful, but this does not paper over differences.

7. Membership in a mystical tradition or religion does not disqualify a person from studying mysticism in all traditions, but it would require the historian to examine their biases more thoroughly. Indeed, all historians should carefully examine their biases since all topics are approached with assumptions. However, identifying one's own biases is difficult. Often, it is only other people who expose a scholar's prejudgments.

8. There also can be mystical and non-mystical readings of a text. For example, Luke 17:21 means something social—"the Kingdom of God is *among* [Gk., *entos*] you"—but many people take it to mean something more mystical: "the Kingdom of God is *within* you." However, the question here for any scriptural passage is not what it may have originally meant but what a given mystic *understood it to mean*. A similar problem applies to translations of mystical texts: a translation may reflect the translator's beliefs more than the author's.

9. Extreme constructivists in the philosophy of mysticism believe that the construction of experiences renders all alleged commonalities or typologies of mystical experiences groundless. The unique configuration of cultural concepts in each mystic's mental set makes each mystical experience absolutely unique in kind (see Jones 2020a).

10. Focusing on beliefs does not mean that all mystics of a given tradition necessarily accept all of that tradition's "official" or "normative" doctrines. Many mystics, like most people, may not care much about doctrines and be more interested in the practices of their way of life. Religious faith is not a matter of commitment to doctrines. The views of some mystics are, in fact, at variance with the mainstream views of their traditions. Nor are mystics always consistent. John Rist points out that Plotinus was "not a stickler for exact terminology" (1967, 95), and the same can be said of many other well-known mystics, including those with a philosophical bent (such as Meister Eckhart and Shankara). Mystics' general reliance on metaphors and images also complicates their presentation and reasoning.

11. Many traditional cultures reject the very idea of a history of a tradition's doctrines altogether, claiming that there are no new truths discovered over time but only the recovery of the timeless truths that are to be found in the basic religious texts of their tradition. Mystics are merely commentators, not innovators. The only history is hagiography—accounts of mystics as exemplars of the tradition's timeless truths often written many years after they lived. Even in the West, where history is seen as the arena in which God works out his plan, mystics attach little significance to history.

Chapter 1

1. Some scholars prefer to avoid the word *experience* because the term connotes a dualism of an experiencer witnessing an object distinct from them. A depth-mystical experience free of all content but consciousness would not be an experience of any object but is still an awareness or realization of a reality. Bernard McGinn prefers *consciousness* (1994, xviii) or *awareness* (2006, xv–xvi), but most philosophers today argue that *consciousness* and *awareness* are also inherently intentional—a subject's consciousness *of* something—and thus necessarily dualistic. He believes that this awareness, like all of awareness, belongs to the experiencer and that there is always a sense of ownership in any experience; thus, there is no transpersonal, nonpersonal, or selfless awareness or consciousness. There may be a dissolution of the "narrative self" but not of the core "subject self"—the "self of ownership" is present in any state of consciousness. McGinn also uses "presence of God" (1994, xvii), a phrase common in theistic discourse, but it too suggests a dualism: the presence of something that is distinct from the experiencer (as in a vision), enabling an encounter of two things. One can have a sense of presence in an ordinary state of consciousness. It also would not apply to experiences of things like Brahman, Plotinus's One, or the Godhead that are always present in us. Robert Forman prefers the term *event* (1990, 8) for its awareness of pure consciousness, but that term does not capture the felt nature of the occurrence. We, unfortunately, do not have any experiential terms that do not connote a separation of subject and object since that is how the terms arose; even *realization* is realization of something. So, too, with *apprehension*. Thus, mystics have to use terminology from ordinary experiences but then assert that the terms do not apply since no separation of subject and object is present in a mystical experience or state.

2. Altered states of consciousness involve, in Charles Tart's definition, a qualitative shift in one's stabilized pattern of mental functioning—from the baseline state of consciousness to a new, unique configuration, despite changes in input and subsystems (1969, 1). Unlike giving up a sense of self, not all ASCs are unusual or require a major shift in consciousness. Some are easy to attain and are familiar (like dreaming or being drunk). Both meditation and psychedelics can disrupt this baseline state centered around the sense of a self, thereby permitting other states of consciousness to emerge, but for most people in Western culture, the alert, sober state of ordinary awareness is taken to be the state of consciousness for deciding all cognitive matters.

3. This raises a question of terminology. Is anyone who has had a mystical experience a mystic even if the experience did not affect their life? Or must one continuously be in an altered state of consciousness? Can a mystic be anyone who engages in a mystical way of life, even if they have not had a mystical experience?

4. Psychedelics do not necessarily make an atheist into a theist, but there may be "significant decreases in identification as atheist and agnostic and significant

increases in belief in ultimate reality, higher power, God, or universal divinity" (Davis 2020, 1018). Psychedelic-enabled experiences tend to cause a shift in the experiencer's metaphysics away from "hard" materialism to accepting transcendent realities or accepting consciousness as a fundamental property of nature (Timmermann et al. 2021).

5. Visions may be internal occurrences generated by the brain, but they still seem, to the experiencer, to involve seeing something external—the felt phenomenological content seems like a perception.

6. That a mystical text does not mention the author's own mystical experiences does not mean that it could not be informed by the author's own experiences, but this does make it harder to determine if a text was written by a mystic or instead by a *mystical theorist*—one who has had no mystical experiences nor practiced a mystical way of life but is influenced in their works by mystics. Moreover, most texts handed down to us today have gone through one or more redactions, and biographies are often idealized accounts, exacerbating the problem. Thus, we must try to determine if mystical experiences informed edited passages that seem to discuss experiences only opaquely. That is, does a personal mystical experience seem to shine through someone's body of work?

7. There are exceptions, such as the Pali Theragatha and Therigatha texts, but even in the Tibetan Buddhist *namtar* autobiographical texts it is uncommon for someone to claim that they achieved the direct realization of ultimate reality (Komarovski 2015, 243).

8. We are not aware of an experiencing self during the vast majority of our everyday experiences—we sense things, not sense that we are aware of things—but during or after an everyday experience, we can become aware of the sensing and that we "own" it: it is I who had the experience. This awareness does not alter our state of consciousness. This is not so with most types of mystical experiences.

9. Intercessory prayers and prayers of gratitude and submission do not fall into this characterization of meditation (Eifring 2016, 18), but chanted prayers such as *dhikr* in Sufism, *japa* in Hinduism, and the Jesus prayer of Eastern Orthodox Christianity do.

10. All religions have some "esoteric" traditions in which the final knowledge is reserved for only the elite. Some texts are written in code to keep the teachings from the public. Mystical knowledge in some traditions is kept secret from all but the initiated—a *gnosis* passed along orally from teacher to student with nothing written down or through secret texts. This is partly because of the alleged danger of the knowledge to aspirants when it is not understood properly. However, most classical mystical traditions did not close off all mystical teachings from the public, although advanced teachings may be reserved only for advanced students. All mystical traditions stress the need for training with qualified teachers and meditation masters who have established lineages to earlier figures. Teachers not only explain the doctrines and aid a pupil's meditation but also guide and evaluate those on the path, and demonstrate how a mystic should live.

11. While such mystics as Eckhart and Shankara invoke the foundational scriptures of their traditions for the authority of their claims, they interpret the scriptures to fit their ideas. Thus, their mystical ideas determine their understandings of scriptures (including how they translate passages). This means that scripture has less control over their understandings of their experiences than scholars usually suppose; mystics' own theories, in the end, determine their understandings of both scripture and their experiences.

12. What exactly is meant by a "loss of a sense of self" in psychedelic and meditative experiences is a matter of debate in neuroscience (see Milliere 2018). In mysticism, it is not merely not being aware of a subject sensing something (most experiences are like that) but that during the experience, or looking back after the experience, the experience seemed to lack ownership or to not be attached to the person. But it is not a loss of subjectivity. In Theravada Buddhism, the no-self doctrine does not deny subjectivity or a subjective point of view but, rather, denies that there is a substantive experiencer in our experiences that exists independently of the components of the mind and body. That is, there is no discrete entity in the phenomenal realm. However, it still recognizes that there is an impermanent and conditioned configuration of sensing, feeling, and thinking even though no separate self is ever found in any of our phenomenal experiences. Similarly, for advanced mindfulness in general, there is no subject that acts as a separate reality or dualism of subject and object, but a subjective element need not be denied.

13. Wainwright points out that any typology must be taken with a grain of salt; there may be borderline cases that cannot be subsumed neatly under a typology's categories (1981, 38). Typologies based on theological reasons rather than study of the history of mysticism end up being a Procrustean bed that distorts mystical claims. For example, to make Buddhism fit his typology, R. C. Zaehner (1958, 99) had to tell Buddhists what they really experienced—an eternal self (*atman*)—even though they explicitly rejected that notion. He later admitted that Zen experiences do not fit his typology.

14. Most commentators agree that the understanding of what is experienced is mediated by the experiencer's beliefs, but are the mystical experiences themselves affected by the experiencer's cultural beliefs? This brings up the philosophical issue of constructivism (see Jones 2020a; 2016, 37–70).

15. Experiences of light and light as a metaphor are both prominent in various mystical traditions throughout the world. It has not gained much attention in the scientific study of meditators and psychedelic subjects.

16. Pantheism is a concept devised by John Toland in the eighteenth century within a theistic framework to contrast the idea of such an identity of the world and God with classical theism. It is popular today with New Agers.

17. *Timelessness* in mysticism typically means existing outside of the temporal sequencing of time, not the eternity of all times. That is, temporal categories do not apply to the reality experienced or to the content of the experiences themselves, but the unenlightened may well understand talk of timelessness as phenomenal eternity.

18. The *Chandogya's* clay/pot example is from the metaphysics of an introvertive mystical tradition: what is real (Brahman) is not a phenomenal reality open to the senses but a transcendent reality that can be experienced only inwardly by stilling the mind. However, the analogy is drawn from the phenomenal world and works as well for extrovertive mysticism.

19. Something is retained from the depth-mystical experience, but the experience may still be a pure consciousness event. If, during an experience, a meditator is aware of silence and thinks "There is no sound here," then that experience is not empty: there is that thought and, therefore, something conceptual in nature is present in the experience. However, realizing that "I had a silent experience" after the experience does not mean that the thought was present during the experience itself; the experience may still have been empty of anything conceptual, and the meditator is conceptualizing it only after the experience is over. This is also the case with realizing later that there was no sense of self or ownership in the experience. In sum, just because the experiencer has a thought after the experience does not mean that they were aware of the fact at the time.

20. *Pure consciousness* can refer to an extrovertive, dynamic, pure mindfulness (a core, unstructured awareness reflecting only what is received by the senses) or to a changeless, introvertive depth-experience (the core awareness devoid of all content but itself). Scientists often focus only on the former and ignore or deny the latter, treating the consciousness as the same in both. A further question that scientists usually do not address is whether pure consciousness is merely another state of consciousness that may inform scientists about the general nature of consciousness or is the substrate underlying all states of consciousness.

21. The term *enlightenment* entered the lexicon of mysticism as the translation of the term *bodhi* by the Pali scholar T. W. Rhys Davids (1843–1922), who intentionally linked it to the idea of knowledge in the European Enlightenment. *Bodhi* comes from the same root as the word *Buddha* (*budh*). It can be better translated as *awakening*, as in the Buddha is one who has awakened from the sleep of root-ignorance.

22. How does one remain centered in a transcendent reality while maintaining everyday activities? How can two levels of consciousness operate at once? Think of carrying on a conversation while driving a car: the driver's focus is always on the road, but they can still talk to the passenger. Meister Eckhart gave the analogy of a thirsty man who can do other things besides drink and can turn his mind to other thoughts, but he never loses the thought that he needs something to quench his thirst (2009, 491–92). However, one's attention is split, so one does not seem totally engaged in the worldly activity.

23. Mental dispositions and their roots are all to be eradicated. It should not be overlooked that there also are subconscious processes operating in the everyday state of mind—the *samskaras* of Buddhism and the *Yoga Sutra*. Part of the enlightening process is sweeping the mind clean of these negative forces, but they may seem

frightening as they emerge into consciousness (Johnston 2000, 103–104). According to Indian mystical schools, by letting subconscious emotions enter our consciousness, we can release them, and all subconscious processes are ended in enlightenment.

24. That classical mystics did not discuss their own experiences complicates the matter of the development of mystical doctrines. Did, for example, Shankara develop his doctrines after having a depth-mystical *anubhava* experience? Or did he develop them without any mystical experiences? The development of doctrines may be continued by non-mystics.

25. Calling a transcendent source *infinite* means that it is totally apart from finite phenomenal realities and not limited by anything finite. The term *infinite* only conveys the transcendent's otherness from anything *finite*—a transcendent reality is non-finite. It is not an infinite amount of the stuff of the natural realm or an all-embracing phenomenal whole.

26. Devotional "love" mystics are more positive in their characterization of what is experienced (and utilize more sexual imagery). "Wisdom" or "knowledge" mystics are more prone to the *via negativa*. Wisdom traditions usually began first in a religious tradition. However, devotional mysticism became more dominant around the world early in the second millennium CE, even in Buddhism.

Chapter 2

1. That mystical experiences can occur before a sense of self is developed in a culture will be noted in the next chapter (note 1). Frits Staal claimed that "the altered states of mystical consciousness constitute a return to a state of the human mind that existed before the emergence or origination of language" (1988, xxiii). This suggests that all prelinguistic cavemen were mystics and our now ordinary state of consciousness developed later, but that is unlikely since early hominids would have needed to be able to make distinctions to survive—food from poison, dangerous animals from non-dangerous ones, and so forth—even without a language to express those distinctions. Language codifies the distinctions that we consider important and enables us to pass along knowledge, but it is only a product of the ordinary state of consciousness, not its cause. Thus, it is unlikely that consciousness before language arose was perpetually mystical. For similar reasons, it is questionable that mystical selflessness can be equated with a universal state of consciousness that existed before the emergence of an awareness of a self.

2. Some scholars restrict the term *shamanism* to Siberian societies. Many others restrict the term to only those societies in which all the shamanic roles are found only in a single practitioner and refer to different shamanistic practices and techniques that are dispersed among other functionaries in stratified societies. (For a history of different scholarly uses of the term *shamanism*, see Tomášková 2013.) Shamans did not perform all the same functions in all societies. Likewise, different

cultures had variations in the general Neolithic worldview. Thus, there is no one universal *shamanism* but different *shamanisms*. But like the term *mysticism, shamanism* can be used as an umbrella term with cross-cultural applications regardless of the term's cultural origin. It is not a distortion to label some practices that later specialists share with shamans *shamanic* as long as the limited range of the religious specialists is made clear. However, not all "techniques of ecstasy" should be labeled *shamanic* since that term carries connotations that may not apply.

3. The term *shaman* comes from the language of a Siberian Tungus tribe for a word probably meaning "one who is excited, moved, raised" or "one who shakes." How old the term is is a matter of dispute. Some linguists note the similarity between it and a Sanskrit term for wandering ascetics (*shamanas*) or a term for song (*sama*) and suggest that these may be the source of the term. But while Indic ascetic and yogic practices did influence peoples as far away as Siberia, that etymology is doubtful.

4. Whether all people share a common set of visual signs and symbols for images in myths in a Jungian-type collective unconsciousness is debated in shamanic studies (e.g., Sayin 2014).

5. Sickness is seen as resulting from the soul of the sick leaving the body, not from physical causes. Shamans must become "sick" to retrieve the souls from the spirit realm.

6. That such paintings are not found near the entrance to the caves but deep inside shows that more than simply shielding them from the weather was involved. As noted in the following chapters, caves (along with windowless rooms and other dark places) were utilized to dampen sensory input in early mysticism.

7. Sounds and repetitive vibrations, especially in places deemed sacred, are a way to induce ASCs. There is evidence that hominids acquired their ability to sing through vocalizing prior to the development of language, and some mimetic rituals (drumming and communal vocalizations) appear to exist among primates such as chimpanzees as a means of social communication (see Winkelman 2013). Chanting is common in Abrahamic and South Asian religious traditions. Chanting does not depend upon the intellectual content of what is chanted: it is a different mental process than thinking about the content, and the rhythmic repetition of the sounds has different effects upon the brain. Overtone-based music (e.g., with bells or Tibetan singing bowls) or singing has proven more conducive to inducing mystical experiences than Western classical music, let alone rock and roll.

8. Shamans are said to see the skeleton and organs of animals and people. Shamanic art often attempts to portray the inner reality or vital forces of objects—e.g., showing the bones or organs of animals in X-ray style paintings (Hayden 2003, 53).

9. For possible neurological bases for these experiences, see Winkelman 2010. A hardwired biological basis for the effects of, for example, the rhythm of drumming or chanting on our brain suggests that the use of rhythm in rituals goes far back into the prehistory of religion and may have played an important adap-

tive role in early human evolution (Hayden 2003, 65–66). If the neurology of all people has been basically the same since the Paleolithic era, and if drumming and other techniques for altering consciousness are universal, then there is no need to advance cultural borrowing or diffusion as an explanation for why shamanism is so widespread. This is likewise with mysticism and a common human neurology: common types of experiences and explanations do occur in different cultures, but there is no need to claim mystical experiences and mystical doctrines arose in one culture and spread throughout the world.

10. Calling drugs *triggers* is somewhat misleading since nothing can force a mystical experience to occur 100 percent of the time. For example, a substantial number of people have ingested psychoactive drugs on many occasions without experiencing any profound ASCs (Richards 2014, 657). Neither meditation nor any other action can guarantee a mystical experience will occur. It is also important to note that different triggers do not appear to produce different types of mystical experiences; based on the phenomenological accounts of mystics and experimental subjects, psychedelics, meditation, and other natural (and perhaps nonnatural) triggers produce some experiences that are experienceably indistinguishable. Mystical experiences that occur spontaneously (i.e., with no preparation or intent and without a chemical or a trigger) complicate questions about whether brain events alone are the cause and how one can initiate the event.

11. There is no good name for such drugs. They can be called *psychoactive*, but not all psychoactive drugs are relevant. *Hallucinogenic* and *entheogenic* are both question-begging concerning the issue of cognitivity, the first con (i.e., generating hallucinations) and the second pro (i.e., generating God within). The term *psychedelic*—literally, "mind-opening" or "soul-revealing"—is better. It had fallen into disrepute over recreational use but has regained its use in scientific research.

12. Shamans in cultures that utilize ayahuasca train for years to understand their experiences and to distinguish veridical visions from false ones. Such training was likely part of shamans' training in most cultures.

13. Psychedelic substances may have evolved as a defense mechanism for plants since they are toxic to most animals, but hominids evolved in a way to utilize them (Winkelman 2014, 343–44). It may be that the resulting experiences were a byproduct of an advantageous adaptation (a *spandrel*) that nevertheless led to evolutionary advantages both on the individual level (leading the experiencer to be more open and trusting of others within the group) and the social level (through the related rituals leading to more social cohesion).

14. A barley ergot has become a popular explanation of the ecstatic states of the witches of Salem in 1692. A salve made from psychedelic herbs—mandrake, belladonna, and henbane—has been suggested as causing the visions of flight in medieval European witches.

15. R. Gordon Wasson made a strong case for *soma* being the fly-agaric mushroom, perhaps mixed with other psychedelic plants, but more recently it has

been argued that *soma* was Syrian rue (*harmala*), which contains alkaloids such as harmaline (Flattery and Schwartz 1989).

16. Some phenomena in the Bible are common to shamanism—symbolism of ladders and trees connecting this realm and heaven, spiritual journeys of ascent, descending into hell to visit or retrieve the dead, spirit guides, and the importance of visions—but this does not necessarily mean that their historical origins are in an earlier shamanism.

Chapter 3

1. Julian Jaynes (1976) argues that the sense of self—a sense of "me" separate from the rest of the world—appeared about the time of the Homeric epics. In the *Iliad* individuals have no conscious mind or will, with the gods directing the action, but in the *Odyssey* individual consciousness and will come to the fore. Prior to that, people were more like different parts of a social machine than discrete individuals: they were merely their social role. (The full modern sense of the individual and individualism of autonomous agency and human rights may not have begun to arise until the twelfth century in the West [see Flood 2013, 37–42, 202–208].) And in ASCs, what the nondominant brain hemisphere furnishes to the conscious mind was taken to be voices of gods. Mystical experiences were needed to contact profound realities only after the breakdown of this bicameral mind (Jayne 1976, 440; see also McGilchrist 2019). However, a sense of self is not needed for a mystical experience: emptying the mind of all conceptual divisions, for extrovertive experiences, or all diverse phenomena, for introvertive ones, is still possible, although without a sense of self, the effects of the experiences may be alarming or worse. Nevertheless, it was only after a sense of self developed that overcoming it became the central obstacle. The idea of a way of life devoted to the mystical inward quest may also have arisen only then.

2. McTaggart had mystical experiences of the world as fundamentally unified by love. His mystical experiences may have led to his belief about the unreality of time, but his argument against the reality of time is not based on mystical experiences even indirectly.

3. Some scholars overstate the situation and label all early Greek philosophers *shamans*. Indeed, some claim that Socrates was "the last of the shamans." Shamanism may be the historical root of some ideas that were espoused by Greek philosophers (e.g., a soul existing independently of the body and a flight to the realm of the gods), and some shamanic practices may be attributed to early philosophers (e.g., healing the sick), but Pierre Hadot (2001) easily shows that none of the philosophers were full-blown shamans and that there is no trace of any shamanic rituals being practiced for the community's welfare.

4. That the author of the book of Revelation in the New Testament received his revelation in a cave points to the importance of caves for such matters in the Greek world.

5. All seven of the Seven Sages—the poet Orpheus, Epimenides, Pythagoras, Aristeas, Abaris the Hyperborean, Hermotimus, and Empedocles—are portrayed as having shamanic features, as was the god Apollo. Aristeas made a journey to southern Russia and the steppes of Asia where there were shamans. Peter Kingsley (2010) argues that Abaris the Hyperborean was a traveling shaman from Mongolia who met Pythagoras.

6. The name *Pythagoras* is, apparently, odd in Greek. Some scholars believe that it is a title and not the name of one individual. If it is cognate with Sanskrit, it would mean "the father (*pitri*) of the teachers (*gurus*)."

7. Plotinus also endorsed the idea of a cosmic harmony. He saw the "heavenly circuit" of the stars as an order that arranged things collectively (perhaps referring to the *logos*), a single ballet being performed in a rich variety of dance movements (Enn. IV.4.33). That the harmonious vibration of music can induce ASCs should also not be overlooked (see Richards 2016, 155–57).

8. Early references to philosophical exercises (*askesis*) may refer to gaining a healthy body and mind rather than asceticism in the modern sense.

9. Scholars debate whether there was Indian influence on Greek philosophical thought (e.g., Harris 1982). Going east to investigate Persians and Indian ideas first-hand appears to have been "a perpetual longing of the Greeks" (Rist 1967, 5). By the beginning of the Common Era, Greeks (and Philo of Alexandria) were referring to *gymnosophists* (naked sages) from India. The possibility that Plotinus knew of the Upanishads cannot be ruled out, but there were cultural contacts between Greece and India from an early time, so ideas that were foreign to Greek thought (e.g., rebirth) may have come from Indian thought. Pyrrho of Elis (ca. 360–270 BCE) traveled in Alexander the Great's train to India and may have gotten the idea for skepticism from Jaina or Buddhist monks. He also believed that a neutral, skeptical state of mind leads to peace. However, the basic idea that mystical experiences may be cognitive needs no cultural borrowing, nor do most elements of Greek mysticism. Some meditative techniques may involve cultural borrowing, but some common practices may arise independently in different places. Likewise, some ideas (e.g., to be real is to be eternal and permanent) may arise in different cultures without any diffusion from a common cultural source. The absence of relevant historical texts makes the issue of whether there was cultural borrowing, independent development, or a common source impossible to answer.

10. The Mystery cults of Dionysus from Trace and of Demeter in Eleusius introduced the idea of salvation in the afterlife. Before then, the afterlife was only a shadowy existence.

11. An example of the problems caused by the sparseness of the pre-Socratic record is that some references to *thought* come from the word *diaphragm* (*prapides*) as the seat of thought—just as we refer to the heart for emotions. Thus, we cannot determine if the reference means controlling the breath or just reflection.

12. A case can be made that Heraclitus had some familiarity with the doctrines of the Upanishads (McEvilley 2002, 39–44), but due to the closeness of the

dates involved, this is speculative. This is also the case with Parmenides's illusionism concerning change and differentiation. The ideas apparently occurred at about the same time in India and Greece before there was exchange of philosophical influences between the cultures; there is no evidence of diffusion from some now unknown common source.

13. *Divine madness* (*theia mania*) meant any high state of emotion, enthusiasm, transport, or inspiration (Bussanich 2013, 282). The *Phaedrus* (244a–245c) refers to four types of divine madness, all gifts from the gods: prophetic (inspired by Apollo), ritualistic (inspired by Dionysus), poetic (inspired by the Muses), and erotic (aroused by Eros and Aphrodite) (see Dodds 2004, 64–101, 270–282). The role of *eros* in Plato's and Plotinus's thoughts will also be noted. *Eros* in Greek thought was the "desire for completion" (Bussanich 1987, 176), not *eroticism* in the modern sense. According to D. C. A. Hillman (2008, 179), by the fifth century BCE, intoxication from any source (including psychedelics) and mental inspiration were nearly indistinguishable concepts in Greece.

14. Socrates's final words—"We owe a cock to Asclepius. Pay the debt, and do not be careless."—should be understood in light of his way of life. That is, he is thanking the god of healing for making him and his followers philosophers; he tells his followers to pay that debt and not to ignore the gift they have been given but to be careful with their lives, vigilant in their examinations of themselves and in taking care of their souls. Being vigilant in one's philosophical examination of themselves is also how his motto from the temple at Delphi should be understood: "Know thyself."

15. The *daimonion* was never identified as a person but only as a *something* or *sign*. In Plato's works, it only told Socrates not to do something; in Xenophon's, it also gave him positive directions.

16. Socrates's method of teaching also should not be modernized: he was trying to awaken knowledge of the eternal Forms and so forth that his listeners had forgotten, not engaging merely in a rational discussion of ideas.

17. The Eleusinian Mysteries arose around 1500 BCE in Eleusis, near Athens, around the Goddess of agriculture Demeter and her daughter Persephone. They gained importance and spread throughout the Hellenistic world by the time of the Roman Empire. The idea that an experience is the culmination of philosophical contemplation may have come from the cults. The initiations used the drink *kykeon*. Its contents are no longer known, but it is said to have a psychedelic effect. By drinking *kykeon*, one traveled underground to the plains of Elysion. There were two levels of mystery: the mysteries known to the public and the mysteries known only by the initiated (*mystai*). Both men and women were initiates.

18. Aristotle's metaphysics was adapted by mystics in the Middle Ages. His principal impact on the Abrahamic mystical traditions was for those mystics who saw God as the supreme mind.

19. Whether any parallels in Plotinus's thought to Indian thought are the result of cultural influence is a matter of dispute among historians (see Harris 1982). His only work, the *Enneads*, is occupied only with Greek philosophy, but Porphyry's *Life of Plotinus* shows some interest in Indian mysticism.

20. Neoplatonists did write that mystical experiences "came upon them" while they were passive. Christians who try to make Plotinus into a theist call this *grace*, but the One is not conscious, is not concerned with people, and does not act. Thus, the One could not act in giving a mystical experience or initiating one.

21. The Nous and souls are not parts of the One that were ejected in the Big Bang: the One remains transcendent and is not the substance of the universe (which has no Being). In its overflowing (*proodos*), the One is not transformed into what "flows out of it." The emanations are of a different nature than the One and, thus, not a material flowing out of the One itself. The emanations are self-giving one of the One, and they flow forth from a single root that does not itself emerge or become manifested. Like everything connected to the One, to speak of *emanation* or *overflowing* is metaphoric. The One remains totally other in nature from Being or Beingless matter; it is not infinite Being but "beyond Being" and lacks any qualities attributable to anything having Being (Enn. VI.9.3, V.1.10, VI.6.1; see also *Republic* 509b). Nor is the One an artisan who creates or fashions a world or the Forms. The world is eternal, so there was no initial act of creation at all; what was there was fashioned by the demiurge. Every act of the Nous is timeless (Enn. IV.4.1). Time emerges out of eternity in the movement between the Nous and World Soul (III.7.11).

22. Why the Nous has multiplicity is not explained. The One is simple and without parts or any diversity, but somehow the Nous has structures and the World Soul has souls; therefore, the world has multiplicity.

23. *Nous* is often translated as "mind" or "intellect." This omits its ontological dimension as Being. Moreover, its activity (*noesis*) is translated as "thought" or "intellection," but the activity of the Nous is something other than rational thought. It is a contemplative activity of a reality encompassing more than an individual mind. It is not the activity of an individual or the collective activities of beings, nor is it a "cosmic mind" thinking thoughts or creating the world. We should not think of the Nous in dualistic terms as a subject knowing an object since the Nous encompasses the contemplation, the act of contemplation, and what is contemplated. For classical Greeks, the Nous is more about what is contemplated than what is contemplating, but it is both.

24. Plotinus used the word *Being* in a technical sense but not *exist*. To be, for Plotinus as for Plato, is to be eternal and changeless (Enn. VI.5.2). The One is "above" the changing material world or even the Being of the Nous. Thus, the words *exist* and *Being* must be distinguished here: something can exist but have no Being. A perceived tree is not unreal; it is the same in nature as the image of a tree in a

mirror or a dream in that it is a reflection and not identical to the Platonic Form of trees. More generally, the world is non-Being and yet still exists. The world is a reflection (of the Platonic Forms), but it is not an illusion. It exists independently of our sensing even though it has no Being.

25. An analogy for how a nondimensional transcendent reality (the One) can be totally present in each part of the three-dimensional natural world is that of a dreamer and a dream. The whole of the dreamer's consciousness is present in each character and each part of the dream; consciousness cannot be divided up into parts. It is not as if in a dream of a flying airplane part of the dreamer's consciousness makes the airplane and part makes the sky, or different parts of the consciousness are active in different parts of the dream. Consciousness does not have parts. Thus, when one becomes the Nous, one becomes all (Enn. VI.5.12) just as the dreamer is the being of the entire dream. But all emanations of the One are also real for Plotinus while reflections, such as matter and lower selves, are without Being. In fact, the totality of the world is a living organism with one soul encircling all living beings within it (IV.4.30, IV.4.32).

26. Plotinus has no word for a *total self*: there is a higher soul, a lower soul, and a body. The total inner self can change as the higher soul ascends to the Nous.

27. Plotinus's notions of the nature of the mind and body do not mesh neatly with a Cartesian mind/body dualism: the entire Being is in each higher soul.

28. According to Plato, those who have purified themselves have no body in their rebirth in more beautiful places (*Phaedo* 114c).

29. The word *mystical* (*mystikos*) occurs only once in the *Enneads* (III.6.19), where it is used in the sense developed by the Neopythagoreans from the secret language, hidden knowledge (*gnosis*), and rituals of the Mystery cults, not experiences. To Neoplatonists, a philosopher is an expounder of the mysteries (*hierophanten*).

30. Plotinus also allegedly had great paranormal powers (*Life of Plotinus* 10–11), including telepathy that aided him in teaching different individuals.

31. As John Dillon says, Plotinus would gladly help a little old lady across the street *if* he notices her at all, but he would remain unmoved if she were squashed by a passing wagon (1996, 324). Dillon asks whether Plotinus can be said to have a moral theory since it is "uncompromisingly self-centered" and not other-regarding (331–32).

32. For Plotinus, the unenlightened only react to the desires of the body. Only beings fully in the realm of the Nous have freedom of choice, but they do not need it since all actions will be dictated by their virtue (Enn. VI.8.1–7); the nousified soul will act for the Good (III.8.6). Whether he denies free will for the embodied souls or only randomness is not clear. He believed in a rational order to things and a karma-like providence (*pronoia*) (IV.3.16, III.3.1–3), but a rational causal order to actions should be distinguished from a determinism of events (see Jones 2018a, chap. 13). A true determinism for the unenlightened cannot be reconciled with the ability to choose a quest for enlightenment.

33. J. M. Rist is correct in asserting that Plotinus's doctrine of the One cannot be equated with Brahman (1967, 224–26), at least in Shankara's Advaita. On the one hand, for Shankara there is no emanationism or levels or degrees of reality; there is only one reality (Brahman/*atman*). On the other hand, for Plotinus there are multiple souls that never lose their individuality or are the One, even while losing the personality of the lower soul. Self-knowledge is perfected in the Nous (Enn. V.3, V.5). In addition, Plotinus claims that the One cannot be conscious since it is beyond all worldly attributes, while Brahman is consciousness only.

34. To use another analogy, consider the One and the Being it emanates as red and each soul as purple, a mixture of the red of Being that it always has and the blue produced by the lower soul's individuality. In contemplating the One, the One never takes on the blueness to become purple. When the soul in the Nous and the One are one'd through contemplation of the One, the soul loses its lower self (the blue) and so is only red. The soul overlays the One but remains distinguishable and never loses its individuality even though both are red. When the soul leaves the Nous and returns to the body, it becomes purple again. Before realizing the Nous and the One, we are unaware of our redness (Being), but after we return to the body, we are aware of both our blueness and our redness.

35. The Chaldean Oracles from the late second century CE are attributed to Julianus the Theurgist or his father. They speak of the *Intelligible* or *Father* beyond the reach of the intellect. To know him by the "flower of the intellect," the soul must become concentrated, avoid conceiving the Intelligible as an object, and "stretch out an intellect devoid of content." The Oracles were presented in the form of an inspired poem given by the gods to Julianus or his father in a trance. The poem is now lost. It supposedly contained the wisdom of Chaldea (Babylonia), although *Chaldean* at that time meant any magician. By the time of Iamblichus and Proclus, the Oracles' theurgy was a major part of Neoplatonism. Iamblichus supposedly wrote at least twenty-eight volumes of commentary on them.

36. Neoplatonism also returned with the seventeenth-century Cambridge Platonists. But with the possible exception of Henry More and John Smith, they remained unmystical philosophers. More and Smith offered a mystically inspired alternative theory to both scientific naturalism and conventional Protestantism (Versluis 2017, 21–23).

37. William Inge put the point: "The vision of the One is no part of his philosophy, but is a mischievous accretion" (1899, 98). But as John Bussanich states (1997a, 341), few readers of *Enneads* VI.7 and VI.9 would deny that ecstatic states play an essential role in Plotinus's philosophy. Many Christians see the One as God and hence unexperienceable.

38. Eviatar Shulman (2014) makes a similar point about meditation and philosophy in early Buddhism. For mysticism in general, there is no practice without some theory that explains it and no theory that is not implemented directly or indirectly in practice.

39. According to Porphyry, Plotinus preferred to keep his teachings oral. However, he consented to having some of his teachings written down after notebooks of his students began to circulate beginning in 253 CE. Porphyry wrote that Plotinus composed each treatise in one sitting in a state of inspiration, refusing to move until it was completed and then refusing to go back and revise or edit it. Porphyry grouped the treatises into six groups of nine treatises each—hence, the title *The Nines* (*Enneads*).

40. The Corybantes employed drums and pipes to induce frenzy. According to John Bussanich (1999, 44), the Corybantic theme is widespread in Plato, and the state of consciousness associated with possession by the Corybantes is a transrational state of mind that Socrates put in tune with the celestial laws in his *Crito*.

41. Mateusz Stróżyński gives an instance of this effect occurring today to someone reading out loud a fragment of Plato's *Symposium*: he experienced a transformation of consciousness in which he suddenly felt that he was a spirit that was ever-present, eternal, immaterial, immortal, indestructible, and separate from his body (2008, 148). The text did not speak of such an eternal self and spoke of an experience contrary to his (149).

42. Visualization exercises are also mentioned (Enn. V.8.9; see also Stróżyński 2008, chap. 2).

43. Since his objective is to lead students to see the One and become nousified, not to present a metaphysical system, consistency in his doctrines was not the top value. As Rist said, Plotinus was not a "stickler for exact terminology" (1967, 95). He sometimes applies language to the One that strictly applies to the Nous, and his thought on the One and the soul varied, leaving Plotinus open to different interpretations. Having to rely upon the language of dualistic experiences also does not help.

44. Plotinus is a good example of the dangers of imposing typologies in comparative mystical studies. J. M. Rist (1989) follows R. C. Zaehner's dichotomy of introvertive mystical experiences being either *monistic* or *theistic* and, thus, concludes that the experience of the soul being one'd with the One is not monistic (the soul and the One are not identical, nor is there a union or identity of two distinct realities). Therefore, it must be theistic. For Rist, there are no other options; if the experience is not monistic, it must be theistic. That there may be introvertive experiences that do not fit either category is not a possibility (e.g., Samkhya-Yoga's pluralism). However, Plotinus's mysticism is also clearly not theistic: the One is transcendent but is not personal in nature or concerned with the natural realm (Enn. V.5.12), nor is it conscious, nor does it love people, nor do mystics experience it by a grace or any work of the One. But this does not stop Rist and others from creating a unique "Hellenistic monotheism" since the experiences must be deemed *theistic* somehow. John Kenney imports the concept of *henotheism* into the Greco-Roman world to try to make Plotinus into a "Greco-Roman monotheist" (1997, 324–25).

These categories simply do not fit. Emanationist metaphysics in general does not fit either monistic or dualistic, transcendent or immanent dichotomies. Theists who think God is wholly transcendent find the idea of emanation from a transcendent reality and any resulting immanence paradoxical or nonsensical. Typologies such as Zaehner's should not be forced on cases that were not carefully studied before the typologies were set up.

Chapter 4

1. As asceticism developed in Judaism, it was limited. It was practiced within the framework of a married life since there was a religious injunction to have children. There were also no monasteries. Judaism rejected living apart from the general Jewish community. The Essenes and Qumran were exceptions.

2. When Moses asked to see God's "glory," God said that no human could see his face and live, but he did show Moses his "back" (Exodus 33:12–23). Moses approached God, who was in a thick cloud of darkness (20:21). Later on, some visionaries and mystics saw the throne of God but not God himself, and Christians adapted a "cloud of darkness" and a "cloud of unknowing" to mystical experiences.

3. On the surface, traditional Jewish prayer and mystical cultivation are markedly far apart and even antagonistic. Mysticism requires cultivating a unique individual experiential relationship with God, while prayer is a public social ritual involving repeating the same words and phrases, representing a communal relationship with God (Dan 2002, 27). However, such praying/chanting could also be utilized to attain ASCs, including mystical states.

4. Numerical modes of interpretating scripture are also present in Christian, Muslim, Hindu, Buddhist, Daoist, and Confucian commentary traditions.

5. The idea of life after death entered from Greek thought, leading to the idea of an embodied afterlife in heaven. In Judaism, mystical experiences were not seen as a foretaste of such a life after death. The idea of reincarnation apparently entered Judaism in Babylonia from Persian or Indian sources.

6. Kabbalists do not equate the Infinite with a transcendent consciousness, nor do they reduce a person to consciousness. Overall, there is less on consciousness in Jewish mysticism than in the mysticisms of other world religions.

7. Not all Jewish mysticism is messianic, nor is messianism necessarily mystical, but a mystical awareness of a sense of contact with God and a sense that an individual has been selected by God can lead to feelings of self-importance and even to seeing oneself as the Messiah.

8. A later claimant to messiahship, Jacob Frank (1726–1791), was more extreme in his sexual license and claimed redemption through sinfulness (Scholem 1941, 292–99).

9. After cosmic perfection is attained and the world restored, whether Jews could backslide (as with the golden calf) is an issue. Even in the restored realm, Jews might have to follow the commandments.

10. There were also esoteric Christian Kabbalists who incorporated Jesus into the process of emanation and argued that Kabbalah proved his divinity. The sefirotic emanation system was also adapted to the trinity. Such Christians lived mainly in the Renaissance, but their works were read by thinkers including Leibniz, Locke, and Newton.

11. Loew is better known for being the inventor of the legendary Golem, a human-like creature made from mud and animated through Kabbalist magic going back to Adam to protect the Jews of Prague from Christian persecution. Tradition said that only one who has mastered the *Sefer Yetzirah* can create such a creature.

12. Originally, the prohibition against images of God was not because he was considered incorporeal—it was assumed he had a body or could assume one—but because of our inability to depict it.

13. Some scholars follow Moshe Idel and distinguish speculative *theosophic Kabbalah*, which is more theoretical, from *ecstatic Kabbalah*, which focuses more on practices and techniques. For example, the *Zohar* is considered more theosophic/ theurgic, but this does not mean that the former involved only mystical theorists rather than actual mystics.

14. Some scholars argue that God did not tell Moses his name on Mount Sinai (Exod. 3:14) in order that Moses would not have any magical/theugric power over him.

15. Reconciling this with the claim by many Kabbalists and Hasidim that nothing happens by chance—everything is under God's control and providential action—is an issue.

16. Buber wrote a German translation and commentary on the Daoist *Zhuangzi* about ten years before he wrote *I and Thou*.

Chapter 5

1. After a period of dispute over whether Judaism or a distinct new tradition called *Christianity* fulfilled the Old Testament, early Christians tried to separate themselves from Judaism, and this limited Judaism's influence on early Christian mysticism. It was replaced by Greek influence.

2. Whether Jesus himself was a mystic is impossible to determine since all we have are faith accounts of his life. In the Gospel of John (and in the more gnostic Gospel of Thomas), Jesus appears mystical in nature but not in the other Gospels. Faith accounts of pivotal figures in other religions (e.g., the Buddha) are usually more uniform.

3. The word *mysticism* (*mystikos*) does not occur in the New Testament, but *mystery* (*mysterion*) figures prominently in Paul's letters in referring to God's plan

for salvation that was previously hidden but revealed in the death and resurrection of the Christ.

4. Guy Stroumsa (1996) makes a strong case that early Christian mysticism involved an "interiorization of esotericism." The esotericism owed more to Jewish visionary esotericism, which was a matter of secret doctrines, than to Greek Mystery cults, which were primarily a matter of secret rituals. Secrets and mysteries are mentioned in the New Testament (e.g., Matt. 13:11, 1 Cor. 4:1, Col. 1:26–27), including mentions of Christ as the "secret wisdom" (1 Cor. 2:7) and the Holy Spirit as revealing secrets (1 Cor. 2:9–10). There is some evidence that early Christianity involved initiation rituals and reserved the Eucharist only for the initiated. Esoteric language and doctrines were the building blocks of very early Christian mystical language. Unlike in Judaism, esotericism and special initiates did not last long in Christianity (although the Neoplatonist Pseudo-Dionysius still espoused it) because Christians took all their knowledge to be revealed by God in the Bible and in the person of Jesus. God's "secret wisdom" was transformed through Christ from a secret not to be revealed to the uninitiated into an openly proclaimed message (1 Cor. 2:6–7). However, mystics believed this secret wisdom could not be understood without a spiritual experience. Thus, mysticism established another connection to mysteries. Esotericism came to an end in Christianity when *mysterion* came to imply "ineffable things" rather than "hidden things" (Stroumsa 1996, 8).

5. Christian mystics make much of this verse. If Paul's consciousness was truly transformed and free of any sense of self, he should then be classified as a mystic.

6. Like the rest of the New Testament, the Gospel of John presumed that the end-times were at hand, but this leads to less concern for the present and to more focus on the future: the opposite of living in the present moment, as in mysticism.

7. This use of *logos* may have come from the Stoic philosophers' idea of a single principle underlying all of reality, including persons, and could have easily led to the idea that a person can unite with this cosmic principle in a mystical experience. Philo picked up the idea of the *logos*. For Christians, the *logos* became an aspect of God. Christ was the *logos* and was the "first born" existing before everything visible and invisible in heaven and earth; the entire universe was created through him and for him, and all things are held together in him (Col. 1:15–17). The three principles of Plotinus became God the Father (the One), the Son (the *logos* within the Nous and eventually replacing it), and the Holy Spirit (World Soul).

8. Søren Kierkegaard in *Works of Love* presents the argument—not based in any way on mystical experiences—that being a Christian demands such absolute impartiality. No preference should be given even for one's own family or friends, let alone oneself.

9. The term *gnosis* was commonly used by early Christians, but it did not always mean the esoteric knowledge of the elite in the ascetic Gnostic tradition: an immediate knowledge of divine being. In the New Testament, it refers to the hidden mysteries of God that the risen Christ revealed (McGinn 1994, 72). John does not use the word. For Paul, the love of Christ is beyond all knowledge (Eph.

3:16–19). But a Gnostic religiosity was prevalent in early Egyptian Christianity, including a full gnostic path to realization within Christianity. Gnostic religiosity was based on specific beliefs. First, is assumed dualities of good and evil realities and dualities of body and soul (perhaps derived from Zoroastrian teachings). Second, the world was not created by an all-powerful god but by a weak and perhaps evil demiurge. Third, the higher part of the soul is divine by nature, and fourth, an esoteric transcendent knowledge (*gnosis*) is the goal of human life. Such salvific knowledge involved obtaining a "higher sense" than sense-experience or reason in a series of ASC experiences meant only for the elite (Hanegraaff 2008). An early Christian Gnostic, Basilides, who taught in Alexandria around 125 CE, appears to have been a mystic in his practices and teachings and was the first to refer to *unknowing*: the supreme revelation that requires silence for God is "nothing." However, he accepted Christianity and had no secret doctrines for the initiates that conflicted with church teachings. Christians also rejected the Gnostic belief that the world was evil; creation is good (Gen. 1:31), and the incarnation of God validates the world. They also rejected the idea that the human body is unreal or evil. Gnosticism's principal effect on Christianity was to make any esotericism suspect (McGinn 1994, 99). Christian mysticism, even with its interpretations of the hidden meaning of the Bible, remained exoteric.

10. Some Christians condemned the desert ascetics' physical suffering as not truly *imitatio Christi*, or at least not imitating the full life of Jesus. However, they also saw withdrawal from the world as foreshadowing of what was to come after death. Journeying into the desert became a symbol of emptying the mind of all content. The Israelites forty years of wandering in the desert and John the Baptist's sojourn in the desert were also used as allegories.

11. An early heresy was that of the Messalians or Euchites (Syriac and Greek for "those who pray"). They claimed that only prayer mattered; fasting, asceticism, morality, rituals such as baptism and the eucharist, and the institutions of the church were all beside the point (Louth 1981, 114–25). They remained a point of tension for Eastern Orthodoxy (124–25). They also claimed to have experienced bodily visions of God (McGinn 2006a, 487–88).

12. *Deification* did not have an exact meaning until the Pseudo-Dionysius explained it as "attaining the likeness of God and a union with him as far as is possible" (Russell 2006, 1). Being called *gods* in Psalms 82:6 went from an honorary title to a realistic understanding of being transformed by participating in God (Russell 2006, 1–2; see also Eckhart 2009, 105, 180). Through the Pseudo-Dionysius and Maximus the Confessor, deification—becoming as God-like as is humanly possible—became established in the Byzantine monastic tradition as the experiential goal of the spiritual life (15).

13. In Christianity, as in other religions, not all ascetics have mystical experiences and not all mystics are extreme ascetics. In Christianity and Islam, ascetics in the border areas of Syria and Central Asia were sometimes warriors for their

armies, not proto-mystics (Green 2012, 23). There were also Hindu warrior ascetics (Pinch 2006).

14. In his sermons, Meister Eckhart portrayed the active Martha as spiritually more mature (2009, 77–90); her life integrated contemplation with action, while contemplative Mary was still on the path. Under this interpretation, Mary may have chosen the "better part" in choosing the contemplative life, but Martha had the best life: one that bore the fruit of the spirit in moral actions toward others.

15. Does stripping ourselves of self-will mean that God's will replaces the human will, so we have no free will? Is one's final act of free will to let God take over? The Third Council of Constantinople in 680 held that Jesus had a real human will. However, reconciling the two wills is not easy.

16. Origen agreed with Plato (and Plotinus) that *eros* is a divine force that leads the soul from earth to heaven (McGinn 1994, 119). Protestant theologian Anders Nygen drew a stark contrast between the passionate drive of *eros* and *apage/ caritas* in that *eros* does not reflect love in Christian mysticism since the former can inform the latter.

17. See MacGregor 1978 on belief in rebirths in the history of Christianity.

18. When theists refer to God as *non-being* or *nothing* they are not saying that God is nonexistent but that he is wholly other than the being of the phenomenal world.

19. Studying Plotinus and Porphyry's Neoplatonism played an important role in Augustine's gradual conversion to Christianity from Manicheanism with its dualism of good and evil competing in the physical world. According to his biographer, the words of Plotinus consoled him late in his life. From Neoplatonism, he came to accept a higher level beyond the physical world: God is immanent in the world but also transcendent. Likewise, there is an inner soul, although unlike for Neoplatonists, it does not have the transcendent One at its core but is a contingent and fallen creation that is powerless to reach God without grace. Thus, the "eye of the soul" sees a reality distinct from itself, not something in its own depths.

20. By *intellectual vision* Christian mystics do not mean ideas formed by the rational mind but an experience of the suprarational intellect (*nous*). As Teresa of Avila put it, the vision is without external or internal image; it is not seen with the eyes of the body or soul and may last for years (*Interior Castle* 6.8.2). It formed part of her everyday life. Likewise, John of the Cross used the language of visions to represent the internal knowledge of God's secrets, which were given not to the senses but to the "passive intellect" that penetrates the substance of the soul (*Spiritual Canticle* 14–15.15).

21. At that time, mirrors mainly consisted of polished brass, not glass, so the reflections were less than perfect and usually fuzzy.

22. The Pseudo-Dionysius may have been a convert from Neoplatonism. Whether he himself had mystical experiences is far from obvious (see Vanneste 1963). He appears to have been a theologian applying Neoplatonism to Christianity:

a mystical theorist. And Neoplatonism by his time was no longer strongly mystical. Religious conventions and magical rituals played a larger part. He did speak of divine inspiration, which occurred not simply through study (*mathon*) but through experience (*pathon*) (*Divine Names* 29). This is an opposition that goes back to Aristotle's discussion of the Eleusinian mysteries. *Experience* here may not refer to mystical experiences, despite later Christians treating it as such.

23. Here, the Pseudo-Dionysius followed the Neoplatonist Proclus in his commentary on *Parmenides* (142A) and on the denial of all assertions and negations about the One.

24. There is less literature on meditative techniques in Western mysticism than in Asian mysticism, but there is more than many scholars realize, perhaps because mystical experiences are seen as gifts from God and not something in which human effort is important. However, stilling the mind, emptying it of personal desires, and then simply waiting is part of all traditions, even if they do not perceived God's grace to be involved.

25. In the Middle Ages, prayer (*oratio*), reading (*lectio*), meditation (*meditatio*), and contemplation (*contemplatio*) were distinguished. Prayers were oral. Meditation involved both thinking about a scriptural passage, painting, or holy relic and introspection that lead to self-knowledge. Contemplation could involve inner exercises such as breathing, focusing the mind, or repeating biblical verses; it could also refer to receiving an insight by the intellect. Only contemplation had an exclusively mystical goal.

26. The distinction between a creator god and an unknowable primary god came from Hellenistic Hermetic writings from the first to third centuries CE, which also contain the idea of the soul descending into this world from heaven and ascending back from the earthly realm (McGinn 1994, 42–43).

27. Since the soul is considered female, there is often imagery in bridal mysticism that can be taken to be homoerotic. This also occurs in other traditions: in Hindu Bhakti, men have written songs where the man longs for Krishna as a wife longs for her husband (modeled on Krishna's wife Radha) or as the Gopi milkmaids longed for him.

28. Nicholas of Cusa is said to be the original source of this saying made famous by Voltaire. Nicholas wrote "God, who is everywhere and nowhere, is the [universe's] circumference and center" (*On Learned Ignorance* II.12).

29. In the Middle Ages, few Christian, ascetic, male saints engaged in mystical practices and vice versa. In fact, there was a negative correlation between mysticism and extreme asceticism (Kroll and Bachrach 2005, 217–18). In the late period, the rate of extreme asceticism among women saints was much greater than among men saints, and there was a modest correlation between mysticism and extreme asceticism (215, 217).

30. The danger of damaging one's health in devoting oneself solely to a life of contemplation also has not been overlooked (e.g., *Interior Castle* 83–84).

31. Aquinas had a profound experience while saying mass in 1273 that may well have been mystical in nature. He declared: "All that I have written seem to me like straw compared to what has been revealed to me." He never clarified what he meant or, indeed, wrote again (he died three months later). He may have meant either that his theological writings were wrong or that all his theological writings from the analytic mind were worthless compared to what he experienced.

32. Vision (*visio*), rapture (*raptus*), and mystical union (*unio mystica*) were distinguished in the Middle Ages. Some Medieval male mystics (Walter Hilton being notable) decried the putative direct communications from God given in visions (Jantzen 1995, 325).

33. This may sound reminiscent of Buddhism, but the point is different. Eckhart's focus is on the transcendent source not on the lack of independent substances in the phenomenal realm. Elsewhere, Eckhart stated that during the quest for God, "all things must be as nothing" (2009, 418). That is, they are not literally nothing but are to be ignored, as are all images and differentiations, during exercises in the mystical quest.

34. In the twentieth century, Thomas Merton made a similar point: "At the center of our being is a point of nothingness which is untouched by sin and by illusion, a point of pure truth, a point or spark which belongs entirely to God, which is never at our disposal, from which God disposes of our lives, which is inaccessible to the fantasies of our own mind or the brutalities of our own will. This little point of nothingness and of absolute poverty is the pure glory of God in us" (1968, 158).

35. A similarity is often drawn to Advaita Vedanta's distinction between *saguna* and *nirguna brahman*, but the ideas are different. To Shankara, *saguna* and *nirguna brahman* are two forms of the same reality—Brahman, the only reality—while Eckhart's Neoplatonic emanationist metaphysics distinguishes the Godhead from God and does not deny the reality of creatures. Eckhart also used terms to describe the Godhead that are reminiscent of the transcendent *Dao*: the abyss, the river, the soil out of which all things emanate. He is also mistaken for a pantheist, but in his system, the Godhead remains beyond the natural universe. God and his creatures share a common being emanated from the Godhead but remain distinct.

36. God is *pure nothing* in three senses. (1) God, like everything else, is a pure nothing in himself since he does not exist without the being supplied by the Godhead. (2) He is a creator only in relation to what is created; if it were not for us, a creator would not exist. Thus, we are the cause of God being God (2009, 424). (3) God has no phenomenal attributes.

37. Eckhart adopted from Neoplatonism the idea that the intellect (*nous*) is a power of the mind distinct from reason (intelligence) and sense experience (2009, 349). It is the power by which we see the ground of the soul. Only it can reach God because God is beyond our power to reason and beyond our senses. For Neoplatonists, the intellect only has being (*esse*) as its object. In sum, the intellect

permits the mystical experience of being. The soul's "inner eye" sees into being (336, 570–71). Since the intellect is one, the intellect with which we contemplate God is the same intellect with which God contemplates us; the eye with which God sees the being in us is the same inner eye with which we see being in God (298). Thus, for Eckhart there is a mutual knowing in mystical experiences between God and the experiencer.

38. Part of this involves freeing our consciousness from images, but part also involves a Neoplatonism-influenced emanationism in which reality pours itself out into its "image" or Platonic Form. Thus, an image has some reality, even though it is filled by the reality that it reflects and is nothing else. The mystic's objective is to get beyond the image and back to the reality reflected.

39. It should be noted that Eckhart's "pathless path" is a second way into God—the first is to see God in all creatures—and is not the goal. Being "at home is the goal, i.e., seeing God without means in His own being" (2009, 87).

40. Before the modern period, most Christian theologians treated nature (as well as the Bible) as constructed of allegories and symbols for our salvation that we must decipher.

41. John also enjoyed physical labor and designed monasteries and an aqueduct.

42. Negative episodes in which joy is replaced by pain and progress seems blocked, of course, occurred early on in both Christian mysticisms and other theistic mysticisms. The sense of being abandoned by God also occurs in the writings of mystics. For example, the Franciscan Angela of Foligno (1248–1309) gave up great wealth to serve the poor without giving up an ever-deepening inner life. Negative episodes occur to mystics in all traditions, although they are not always interpreted theistically.

43. Bonaventure referred to "a shaft of light flashing out of the divine, mysterious darkness." Mystics often refer to experiences of *light*, but some Christians such as Gregory of Nyssa, the Pseudo-Dionysius, the author of the *Cloud of Unknowing*, and John of the Cross also refer to *darkness*. However, they approach *darkness* in different ways and the ways should not be confused (see Louth 1981, 181–90). Some make references to experiences, while some reference a theology of God. Images of light and darkness converge on the transcendent source.

44. Writings in vernacular languages addressed to the laity got both Eckhart and Teresa in trouble with the church. In 1559, the Index of Prohibited Books forbade the circulation of any mystical text not written in Latin or Greek. That some teachings were condemned is not unusual—even Thomas Aquinas had some of his doctrines condemned before he was declared a saint and the church's *doctor angelicus* and *doctor communis*.

45. Anne Fremantle (1964) employed a very broad definition of *mysticism* to counter Walter Stace's alleged claim that Protestantism had no mystics. She ended up including many artists, poets, and scholars who may have been influenced by mystics but who may well not have had mystical experiences. No doubt some art-

ists and poets (e.g., Tennyson) have had mystical experiences, but not every artist working on a religious theme can be classified a *mystic*.

Chapter 6

1. Within Islam, the term *Sufi* refers to mystics and others in the majority Sunni tradition. In the minority Shi'a tradition in Iran, mystics were called proponents of *irfan* (*gnosis*). There are also mystics among the Druze and Nizari Ismailis of North Africa descending from the esoteric Fatimid caliphate of the tenth to twelfth centuries CE. However, today's convention of calling all mystics within Islam *Sufis* is followed in this chapter.

2. In the past, Western scholars routinely saw Sufism (and indeed Islam as a whole) as derivative of other religions: monasticism came from Buddhism or Christianity; Neoplatonism from Greek philosophy; ladder and night journey symbolism from shamanism; and the practices of *dhikr*, singing, and other yogic practices from India. The Islamic world was indeed a crossroads for cultural influences in the Middle Ages, but while there were identifiable interreligious interactions and influences, there is little reason to believe that similar mystical practices and ideas would not have arisen on their own independently of other mystical traditions, so there is little reason to ascribe everything mystical to other cultures. Ideas and practices can result from universal human capacities and require no common cultural origin. Unique features can be attributed to the cultures in which Islam flourished. There certainly is no reason to suggest that mystical experiences and other ASCs would not have occurred in any culture without influence from outside.

3. Carl Ernest points out that the key term for religious identity among Muslims is not *islam* (submission of the will) but *iman* (faith). *Iman* occurs hundreds of times in the Quran since faith was a major topic while *islam* occurs only eight times (2011, xvi).

4. In the calendar used in this book, CE is the abbreviation for Common Era. It is more neutral for the Western calendar than AD (in the year of the Lord), but it is common only to Christians and Jews. The dating excludes Muslims, who did not come along for another six centuries. The Islamic calendar begins in 622 CE with the establishment of the first Muslim community in Medina. Thus, CE still shows bias. It also shows the problem of coming up with anything truly neutral in comparative studies.

5. Translations of the Quran are usually qualified in the title—for example, *The Quran Interpreted*. This is because Muslims consider the Quran literally the words of God, so only the Arabic in which it is expressed is the Quran itself. The Quran was originally an oral text, and recitation of it is central to most Islamic rituals. The sound of the text chanted in Arabic may also have the capacity to alter one's state of consciousness.

6. The word *Allah* is technically not a proper name but means "the god." However, Muslims treat it as a name. Christians in Arabic-speaking countries use *Allah* as the name of the Christian God, although at least one Muslim country has outlawed that practice. Conservative Christians in the United States also do not equate the Christian God and Muslim God. A professor at Wheaton College had to leave for making the simple claim that Christians and Muslims worship the same creator.

7. To be a Muslim is to attempt to align oneself with God's will. The words *Islam* and *Muslim* come from Arabic root *slm*, meaning "submitting." Hence, the difficulty Arabic-speaking Christians and Jews have when trying to say that they, too, are trying to submit their will to God's but are not Muslims—in effect saying, "I am muslim but not a Muslim."

8. This is not to suggest that most Sufis (or most mystics around the pre-modern world) were literate or philosophically minded. Masters were needed not just for guidance in meditative practices but for providing oral teachings, giving explanations of written texts, and acting as exemplars of how to live the Sufi life.

9. Not only is God unseen, the Quran also distinguishes the invisible realm (*ghayb*) from the visible realm (*shahada*) (e.g., Q 39:46). It also distinguishes the real from appearance.

10. Sufis renounce worldliness (attaching significance to anything temporal) but not the reality of the world. There is less celibacy in Sufism than in the other mystical traditions, as most Sufis have not "abandoned the world." Dry and uninspiring "world renouncers" were regularly mocked in Sufi poetry (Knysh 2000, 170).

11. In a hadith, Muhammad stated that the greater jihad is the inner battle against evil in one's own heart, not against external enemies.

12. Ghazali did not take truthfulness to be absolute. For example, a lie to save the life of a Muslim may be deemed a meritorious act in the eyes of God (Knysh 2000, 308).

13. The link between the spiritual and the sensual permeates Sufism in a way that is foreign to Christianity. Within the Sufi tradition, there is a well-established strain that attempts to integrate sensuality and the higher states of mystical union (Awn 1995, 370).

14. In the Middle Ages there also were Jews and Christians practicing in Sufi groups in Egypt. Sufis may also have been influenced by Hindu Bhaktas on love and vice versa.

15. God's reciprocal love for those who love him or the mutuality of love is not expressed as often in Islamic works as Christian ones.

16. Many later Sufis denied the claim that suffering in Hell would be eternal. Ibn Arabi repeatedly argued that God is all-merciful and would make such suffering only temporary.

17. In Sufi manuals, mystical knowledge is described by various terms besides *kashf* (unveiling), including direct vision (*mushahada*), flashes (*lawaqih*), gnosis (*marifa*), illumination (*ishraq*), direct tasting (*dhawq*), and verification (*tahqiq*) (Knysh

2000, 311). *Kashf* is a lightning flash in which rational arguments for God are replaced with the evidential proof (*bayan*) provided by experience (312).

18. In Judaism, Philo earlier used the phrase *sober intoxication* to describe how the mind is taken out of itself in the upward way (McGinn 1994, 39–40).

19. *Kalam* attempted to understand Quranic teachings in rational terms with the help of Greek philosophy. When faced with verses in the Quran asserting God's immanence and presence, theologians resort to interpretations (*tawil*), many forced, to explain the verses away (Chittick 2000, 29).

20. In asserting the supremacy of God, some medieval Islamic (and Christian) thinkers, including Ghazali, defended occasionalism, claiming there is no natural causation or any fixed laws of nature in the universe. Instead, God is the only real cause at work in any event, and the apparent causal order of things is not a matter of necessary connections but is only God's habit (*sunna*), which God will not change (Q 33:62, 48:23). Miracles were planned by God's foreknowledge at the beginning of creation and are not breaks in God's habit. Thus, all events are determined by God, and we have no free will (yet, we are responsible for our actions). Alternatively, Ghazali also argued that God establishes order in the universe through secondary causes (*asbab*) that he can change at any time. This occasionalism was seen as a consequence of God being the only true reality.

21. "Seeing God" in the phenomenal world fits better in an ontology in which God is the only reality rather than the source and sustainer of the world. However, Ghazali, like most Sufis, espoused an emanationism in which the emanations are not literal parts of God.

22. From the early days of the ascetics on, Sufi poets utilized local languages in India and Turkey and, indeed, throughout the Islamic world. Ibn al-Farid (d. 1234) of Egypt is considered the greatest mystical poet in Arabic, writing on the Sufi path and the wine of divine bliss.

23. Actually, *Rumi* is a title. Turkey was the major Roman province in the Islamic world and was known as *Rum*. Thus, famous Jalal al-Din was known as *the Roman*.

24. Whether he would have expanded this view to include religions such as nontheistic branches of Hinduism and Buddhism is subject to debate. Early on, Sufis championed orthodoxy and rejected any ideas suggesting polytheism or unbelief, but over the centuries, Sufis came to accept that "the ways to God are as many as the breaths of men" and that one who enters the flaming ocean of love is no longer capable of discerning Islam from unbelief (Schimmel 2011, 286). The Quran (16:36) affirms that a messenger is sent to every nation, even suggesting 124,000 have been sent (26:407). Of course, Sufis accepted that the same God was worshiped in every case.

25. In Africa, many orders are militant. Also, the Tijaniyya do not trace their teachings to early companions of the Prophet but claim a new revelation from the order's founder.

26. There are fundamentalists who are mystical, such as the Sunni Naqsh-bandi order that began in the fourteenth century and has spread from what is now Uzbekistan through the Islamic world today from Egypt to China.

27. The charge that Sufism had lost its heart is not new. In the eleventh century, Ali al-Hujwiri of Lahore said, "Formerly Sufism was a reality without a name, now it is a name without reality. The pretense is known and the practice is unknown." Sufi literature is full of criticisms of teachers who preserved the trappings of Sufism but lacked the requisite transformation (Chittick 2016, 92). Falsely claiming to be a Sufi miracle-worker was common.

28. Contemporary perennial philosophy arose out of a mixture of Sufism, Advaita Vedanta, and esotericism. René Guénon and Frithjof Schuon had early Sufi ties, as did George Gurdjieff, but perennialism dropped all connections to Islamic law and rituals.

29. More literally, the Arabic reads, "There is no god *if* not God."

Chapter 7

1. The word *brahman* may derive from a root meaning "to grow," suggesting the meaning "great-making power." It is a neuter noun, not the masculine *Brahma* that designates a god.

2. That the power behind ritual speech (*brahman*) became seen as the power behind all of reality should not be too surprising in the Indian context. Sanskrit was not understood as having been created but as a divine reflection of reality. Likewise, thinkers created theories—for example—in which the reality constituting the pots existed in the clay prior to the pots being created; this meant that nothing was truly created, and the word *pot* had a referent prior to the work of the potter. Thus, when Upanishadic thinkers and Buddhists claimed that phenomenal objects such as pots and persons were not real but only impermanent "names and forms," this was a revolutionary stance.

3. Earlier Indo-Europeans in Central Asia had shamans. Whether the Indian branch had them is not clear, although some scholars see shamanism expressed in the Vedic texts.

4. There were women renouncers, and two women are mentioned in the early Upanishads (BU 3.6.1, 4.5.15), but Indian mysticism overall is not equalitarian. Outside Bhakti and Tantrism, mystical traditions generally gave women a secondary place and also adopted the caste system.

5. Starting with Greek philosophy, ontology in the West usually takes priority over epistemology; what is real determines the means of knowledge and what can be known. But in India, this is reversed; the limits of ontological claims are set first by establishing what are the correct means of knowledge (*pramanas*). Likewise, debates must first establish a common ground upon which to argue (Lusthaus 2014, 7).

6. The importance of sound established by identifying the power of ritual chant with the reality underlying all of reality (Brahman) continues in the Upanishads by identifying the sound *Om* (Aum) with Brahman (CU 1.1.1–10; TU 1.8; ManU 1, 8, 12). Om is a meditative object or the "sounded Brahman" (MaiU 6.21–23).

7. Terms such as *dhyana* and *samadhi* in Sanskrit can refer either to the practices of meditation and concentration or their resulting ASCs.

8. Non-injury (*ahimsa*) has so many qualifications in Hindu texts that it actually seems out of place in classical Hinduism. Gandhi said he got the idea from Jainism and Buddhism.

9. This criterion for what is *real*—being eternal and unchanging—is shared by both Greeks and Indians. This includes Buddhists. Buddhists emphasize that there is nothing real in that sense within either the phenomenal world or ourselves. Note that this criterion is only about the substance of reality; possible permanent and unchanging structures such as *karman* that guide changes in the phenomenal world are not considered. Since we see change, we usually reject the premise that reality is eternally one and unchanging. Experiences conflict with the premise, so we reject it. But Advaitins (and the Greek Parmenides) go the other way and instead reject observed changes as no more real than changes in dreams. History is about changes in the impermanent phenomenal realm and, thus, is not a major topic for classical Indians. Tales of history such as the *Mahabharata* retain a secondary status.

10. The term *atman* was originally a reflexive pronoun for referring to oneself. It meant simply "myself" without any metaphysical implications—not "my Self." In the early Upanishads, the essence of a person (*atman*) is conceived concretely in terms of the life breath (*prana*). The self or person is identified as a dwarf, as small as a barley corn, or the size of a thumb and hidden in the human body within a space within the heart (BU 5.6.1; CU 3.14.5; KaU 5.12–13).

11. It is worth noting that the *Samkhya-karikas* never refers to the transcendent centers of consciousness (the *purushas*) as *atmans*. *Samkhya-karikas* 19 lists names and attributes of the *purushas* but does not include *atman*.

12. There are suggestions of Samkhya's metaphysics of evolutes of matter in the later Upanishads. Whether this is the beginning of Samkhya or shows that the school already existed for some time is not clear. The *Yoga Sutra* is older than the *Samkhya-karikas*, but the Samkhya school may nevertheless be older than the Yoga school, and the two are not always congruent.

13. This has not kept all yogins from developing paranormal powers for more worldly matters. By modern times, the higher classes considered many yogins to be frauds and criminals (White 2009; 2012, 11–12).

14. The classical Indian theory of perception is not that light rays bounce off objects and impinge the eye but that rays from the mind (*manas, antahkarana*) go out through the eye to an object, conform to it, and bring an image back. The mind is thereby modified (*vritti*) and communicates the perception to the self or consciousness. Once one's mind is pure, one sees the object directly without

attributes (*nirvikalpa-pratyaksha*). When one's mind is still impure, the mind distorts the perception. Yoga is a matter of purifying the consciousness of all conditioning modifications (*vrittis*) so that we see objects as they truly are and also see their ontic essence (*atman*).

15. Emanationism presents a problem for a school that advocates that what is real does not change. Are the rays of the sun real or unreal? They get their substance from the sun (and so are real), but they involve change (and so are unreal). Thus, the emanated effect is both different and not different from the cause, as in the relation of milk and cream: substantively they are the same, but each also has some different properties. The being is one but the forms are many, introducing the perennial problem of reality in Indian philosophy.

16. Advaitins did not use a word for *monism*—such as *ekatvavad*—possibly because that would suggest that Brahman has the phenomenal attribute of oneness or that the phenomenal realm is fully real.

17. For Plotinus, the transcendent source (the One) is not conscious, but for Gaudapada and Shankara, it is. Indeed, for the Advaitins, the only reality is consciousness.

18. The term *maya* occurs only rarely before Advaita (e.g., SU 4.10, BG VII.14). In those instances, it just means God's or Brahman's creative power to produce the phenomenal realm, with no connotations of illusion. It can also mean simply *magic* (e.g., RV 10.177).

19. Some later Advaitins interpreted Brahman in terms of only one phenomenal self (*eka-jiva*); only a single universal self exists in the phenomenal realm, not a plurality of *jivas*. This universal self was the foundation of nescience, and the rest of the phenomenal realm is only appearance (*abhasa*). However, this was never the majority view.

20. According to Shankara, the *karman* that has begun to bear fruit before enlightenment must run its course after enlightenment until it is exhausted (*prarabdha-karma*) before the enlightened can die, just as a potter's wheel keeps spinning after the potter stops spinning it (BSS 4.1.15). That is, once *karman* begins to produce effects, nothing can stop it. Enlightening knowledge uproots old karmic seeds that have not yet begun to bear fruit and prevents future actions from having karmic fruit, but it cannot stop the fruit that has begun to sprout. However, this means that *karman* has some reality with power over even the enlightening knowledge of Brahman. Shankara admits that such *karman* is stronger than knowledge (BUB 1.4.7) even though the Upanishads hold that participatory knowledge (*vidya*) is itself Brahman.

21. Some Indian traditions (especially theistic ones) deny that liberation in this life (*jivan-mukti*) is possible. Being tied to a body and a mind with subconscious functions keeps us from ever becoming truly selfless. However, most Advaitins affirm liberation while in the world since enlightenment is solely a matter of one's knowledge, regardless of one's bodily state or experiences. *Avidya* no longer

operates in one who knows. Thus, being in the dream realm with all its suffering does not present a problem for them as long as one can maintain the enlightened state of consciousness and thereby know that this is only a dream. The enlightened state for Gaudapada and Shankara might be seen as a normal dualistic state, not an ASC. That is, after an ASC experience of Brahman, the practitioner returns to a dualistic consciousness simply free of belief in a real ego despite the experience. Later, Advaitins made the enlightened state more clearly a matter of an ASC.

22. All analogies and metaphors (e.g., the dream/dreamer or the rope/snake) are of necessity drawn from dualistic experience—from within the dream—so are limited and problematic for Advaita. Indeed, so is its metaphysics since it, too, is drawn from a dualistic point of view.

23. Shankara adopted Gaudapada's idea of superimposing the subject on the object and vice versa, but it does not really fit a metaphysics of only one reality since there is nothing to superimpose except our ideas and no distinct reality to superimpose them on—a separate ground or substratum (*adhara*, *adhikarana*, *adhisthana*). There are no layers or levels of reality, just Brahman. The concept lost its importance after Shankara. *Avidya* also became a cosmic principle and material with power.

24. There is a danger in seeing this as an instance of linguistic philosophy: for Shankara, transcending "speech" is shorthand for transcending all the bodily organs and their functions (*pranas*). Thus, this includes hearing, touching, and so forth.

25. "Brahman without attributes" and "Brahman with attributes" may be taken as simply two ways of experiencing the same reality through different ASCs. Ishvara is experienced when one object fills the mind (*savikalpa-samadhi*), and Brahman without attributes (*nirvikalpa-samadhi*) is experienced when there is no object (the depth-mystical experience). However, Advaitins take the ASC without differentiated content to be epistemologically more fundamental. Seeing Brahman "with attributes" (Ishvara) is only a product of nescience—Brahman connected with limiting adjuncts (*upadhis*)—and does not lead to liberation from rebirths (BSS 1.1.11). Then again, the idea of "Brahman without attributes" and the very distinction of two Brahmans are made only from within the dream.

26. *Anubhava* is normally translated "experience"; but more literally, *anu + bhava* means "coming to be" or "coming after." This suggests a new, enduring state of consciousness rather than a transient experience. However, by this term, Shankara as well as later Advaitins appear to only mean the transient introvertive mystical experience of Brahman that occurs with the rise of knowledge of Brahman.

27. Why the Upanishads should conflict on nondualism if they are eternal and revealed accurately to the seers is not clear.

28. In fact, Shankara could accept that there is no real self in the phenomenal world, just as Buddhists do with their *anatman* theory. This claim only sounds startling to modern readers because we are so accustomed to the term *atman* being translated as "the Self" that the translation controls our way of looking at

the matter. But Shankara, too, accepted that the phenomenal self (*jiva-atman*) is only a constantly changing illusion devoid of reality (*sat*). There are no realities in the dream. The essence (*atman*) in us is not a phenomenal self but something that transcends the phenomenal realm entirely.

29. Who is reborn or *transmigrates*? It cannot be Brahman because it does not change, nor can it be the individual (*jiva*) because it is unreal. Shankara ultimately has to say of its Atman, "as it were" (*Upadeshasahasri* 1.18.45). Hinduism is often contrasted with Buddhism on rebirth, but for both, there is no entity that passes from one life to the next. Rather, some karmic residue without an independent entity passes on.

30. Scholars suggest that the Gita originally ended with the grand theophany of chapter 11: the first six chapters discuss different paths, chapters 7 to 11 discuss the nature of God, and chapters 12 to 18 are miscellaneous add-ons added later.

31. The medieval Puranas took Vedantic teachings and practices from the elite and popularized them for the masses. Theism was important in these texts. The grace of God could be attained through simple acts of devotion such as uttering the god's name or worshiping the god's image. Ramanuja appeals to these texts as almost scripture.

32. Unlike in Abrahamic theism, statues and images in Hindu traditions are seen as physical manifestations of God. In this image incarnation (*archavatara*), God is present in the statues and images in a way that he is not present in all of the phenomenal world as its sustainer. Devotees see God in the images even if they do not completely see his fullness.

33. *Beloved* (*bhagavad*) is also a Buddhist title for the Buddha.

34. Shiva (the auspicious one) may have been non-Aryan in origin. He is identified with the minor Vedic god Rudra, a fierce god of the untamed aspects of nature such as storms and disease (e.g., RV 1.114). By the time of the Shvetash-vatara Upanishad, Shiva is a theistic god. Shiva is often represented holding the psychedelic plant datura.

35. The compound *vishishta advaita* is usually translated as "qualified non-dualism," but it can be translated "nondualism of the differentiated or modified [i.e., God, selves, and matter]." It is not the absoluteness of the fundamental nondualism of Brahman but accepts the realities of the modifications. Thus, the selves and matter are differentiated (the primary meaning of *vishishta*) within the nondual beingness of Brahman or God. Even when enlightened, selves are still real and distinguishable in some sense.

36. For Ramanuja, evil actions and pains occur by the will of God, but they do not affect his divine substance or his enjoyment of his purposeless, spontaneous activity (*lila*).

37. Madhva's writings show one problem of translation: the Sanskrit line "*sa -tm- tat tvam asi*" is usually translated "That is the atman. You are that." But in Sanskrit, *-tm-* ends in a long *-*; when *a* or *-* ends a word and the next word begins

with *a*, they run together and are combined to form a long *~*. Thus, "*atm~tat*" here may be "*~tm~-tat*" or "*~tm~-atat*," with *atat* meaning "not that." The dualist Madva treated it as the latter and gave the line a dualistic reading: "You are not that [*atat*]." But this goes against the meaning of the complete passage. In effect, he amended the text to get it to say what he wanted. However, even few dualists follow that reading. Some try to get around the identity by adding words that keep a duality: "You are [like] that" or "You are [accompanied by] that."

38. The Bahai religion arose out of Shiite Islam in Persia in the nineteenth century. It was also an attempt at universalism and condemned by Muslims.

39. The mantras' effectiveness lies in their sound (see note 6). Thus, the sounds may be without meaning, but proper pronunciation when repeating them is important. The power of sound for bringing about altered states of consciousness was noted in earlier chapters.

40. One can object that left-handed Tantrikas, by deliberately breaking the rules of conduct just because they are norms, have made *adharma* itself rather than *dharma* the object of attachment: simply inverting the values would lead as much to attachments as before. Shouldn't the next logical would be to do away with all restrictions—abolishing rules of conduct altogether? However, this value inversion is part of Tantrikas' attempt to break the hold of artificial valuations and rules on the mind. Simply indulging the desires themselves would entirely abolish the quest to end a false worldview. One would be an animal (*pashu*). In the West, Neo-Tantrism—such as Bhagawan Shree Rajneesh's group—often merely gives a religious veneer to exercising materialistic and hedonistic desires.

41. One might ask why Tantrikas attack values and not the basic nondualist and dualist metaphysical doctrines. Arguably, they see our evaluations as not reflecting reality, and they see their beliefs—whether pluralistic or non-dualistic—as reflecting reality as it truly is and, thus, as providing the ground legitimizing their actions and exercises within the body. But those beliefs are still conceptualizations made from within the dream.

42. There is more exclusivism and intolerance in Indian history than Westerners accustomed to Neo-Vedanta think. For example, there is a story that the theist Madhva advised a king to have thousands of Jainas impaled on stakes. More typically, groups teach that one must ultimately convert to that group in some life to become enlightened. Other traditions are incorporated in a hierarchy of traditions only as lower rungs. Some exclude opponents' teachings; Ramanuja thought Shankara was the son of a devil. So, too, there are stories of teachers—including Shankara—being killed by rival students.

43. Westerners artificially made Hinduism a polytheism with conflicting doctrines by grouping different traditions under the umbrella term *Hinduism*. There are Vaishnavas, Shaivas, and so on, but most traditions accept one god with different manifestations. They are no more polytheistic than are Christians who see one god as three persons.

44. Treating the world as less than fully real need not be labeled *pessimistic* as long as a mystical tradition offers a positive way out of suffering. It denies something unreal—a phenomenal world or self—while affirming a true reality behind it—Brahman.

45. Some positions have been winnowed out. The *Brahma Sutra* mentions positions that no longer exist (1.4.21, 3.4.45, 4.4.6). To give two examples: one school of Vedanta combined ritual action (*karman*) and knowledge (*jnana*) as the means to liberation (3.4.27, 4.1.18), and a teacher named Audulomi held that the individual atman is totally different from Brahman up to the point of release, at which point it merges with Brahman.

Chapter 8

1. Jainism also arose in this environment. This introvertive mysticism is probably older than Buddhism and was more ascetic. The most recent exemplar of crossing the river of rebirths (*tirthankara*) is Vardhamana (Mahavira, meaning Great Hero), an older contemporary of the Buddha. Its emphasis on not harming any creature (*ahimsa*) influenced Hinduism. It has an older view of *karman*; all acts have a subtle karmic matter that clings to a person, regardless of motive or detachment, and all actions continue to produce that matter even after enlightenment. Thus, nonviolence and austerity became especially important. This also means that the ideal for the enlightened was to stop acting altogether and, consequently, to starve to death. The postmortem enlightened state is like that in the *Yoga Sutra*: an isolation (*kaivalya*) of each soul (*jiva*).

2. A few scholars suggest that the name *Sakya* derives from *Scythia* and indicates the presence of Iranians in the Upper and Central Ganges Valley beginning in the ninth century BCE. If so, there may have been Iranian influences on the *shramana* movement—for example, the Zoroastrian idea of a post-mortem judgment for one's actions in body, speech, and mind in this life, thereby ethicizing actions (*karman*) (unlike in the Vedas). If so, Buddhism and Jainism may not have been the beginning of a new movement but may have drawn on ideas from other cultures.

3. The *Visuddhimagga* distinguishes strict, medium, and mild asceticism. The Buddha's condemnation of extreme asceticism and his middle path between austerity and indulgence did not prevent asceticism from flourishing in later Buddhism, especially in Tantrism.

4. As part of the inner turn of mysticism, Buddhism defines action (*karman*) in terms of one's inner intention (*chetana*) (AN III.207, III.415) rather than the external action alone.

5. As with other mysticisms, extreme perspectives that present Buddhism as interested only in philosophy or only in meditation are both wrong (see Shulman 2014, 8–13). Both are part of seeing and experiencing reality correctly to end

rebirths. Enlightenment is a matter of aligning oneself with how reality truly is, and that requires beliefs about the nature of reality. Additionally, we should not see Buddhist doctrines as arising directly out of meditative experiences but as arising from a mixture of introvertive and extrovertive experiences and practices within the crucible of the contemporary Indian framework of beliefs.

6. This includes eliminating the desire (*trishna*) to not exist, which is as deluded as any other ego-centered desire. Even the desire for enlightenment (*chanda*) must be overcome. Otherwise, it is simply substituting one desire for another.

7. Physical pains still occur in the lives of the enlightened (SN II.82)—the Buddha himself experienced pain (AN I.27, SN I.174)—but neuroscientists have found that meditation can lessen reactions to pain (Goleman and Davidson 2018, 147–150, 238–41). For the enlightened, pain no longer generates craving and other emotional reactions because of the change in their state of consciousness. In sum, the enlightened feel physical pain but without its normal accompanying mental pain; the emotional connection is lessened or completely severed. More extremely, yoga masters may not feel pain at all (Kakigi 2005).

8. The Buddha can be seen as teaching only a prescribed point of view to end suffering, not a metaphysical ontology of what is real. That is, his teachings are a prescription to end suffering rather than a description of how the world really exists apart from the point of view needed to end suffering. In effect, he says, "I don't care what the world is like in itself, but if you look at the things in the world, including yourself, as impermanent and conditioned, this will lead to ending your desires and attachments, and this will end your existential suffering." Only later did philosophers such as the Abhidharmists and Nagarjuna work out ontologies to ground the prescribed perspective (see also the appendix in this book, note 1).

9. There are a few instances of the Nikaya texts claiming all *dharmas* are without a self or are not-self (*anatta*)—such as *Dharmapada* 279—but they are made in the context of the impermanence of the bodily *dharmas* (the *skandhas*), not all things (Shulman 2014, 78).

10. The twelve-step scheme is probably a later development in Nikaya Buddhism. There are versions with fewer steps and versions with more steps (Shulman 2014, 89). Early on, dependent co-arising concerned just the person; only later was it expanded to include all phenomena. Originally, the steps were presented in reverse order: dependent-cessation (100).

11. If you are feeling sad and you know that you are feeling sad, the knowing is not the same as the feeling. Those who accept the existence of a self take that knowing as evidence of a permanent observer that exists independent of acts of knowing, but Buddhists see it as only another impermanent mental act.

12. The Buddha did not address whether chariots or persons as whole entities have distinct causal powers and, thus, did not address whether a reality emerges from the parts that did not exist before. The idea of a person as an agent is particularly problematic for Buddhism. Buddhist metaphysics seems to require rejecting such

an idea, the Pudglavadins notwithstanding. Assemblages of causes and conditions are not causes themselves (MK 20.23). This metaphysics is reductive in that sense. The person is reduced to an impermanent aggregate of material and mental dharmic components (the *skandhas*), but this metaphysics does not reduce consciousness to something material.

13. Consciousness (*vijnana*) was an early suggestion of what survives the final death of the enlightened, but in early Buddhist ontology, consciousness was just another conditioned *dharma* constituting a person. It would not survive. Each event of consciousness is a single conditioned event; there is no overarching consciousness. Indeed, each sense is deemed a different type of consciousness.

14. Abhidharmists and Nagarjuna later employed the distinction between conventional truth (*samvriti-satya*) and ultimate, or ontologically correct, truth (*paramartha-satya*) for understanding the Buddha's teachings (MK 24.8–10). Other traditions such as the Yogachara distinguished passages of final meaning (*nitartha*) from those that needed interpretation (*neyartha*).

15. *Udana* VIII.3 does state that there is an "unborn, unarisen, uncreated, and unformed" reality since otherwise there could be no escape from the realm of the impermanent. Most scholars believe that this is a later insertion since it conflicts with the rest of the Pali canon. In any case, *nirvana* did not take on the cosmic functions of Brahman in Hinduism or the great self in later Indian Buddhism.

16. Teresa of Avila makes a similar claim in Christianity: one may lose enlightenment for a day or two and fall back into their "natural state" (*Interior Castle* 7.4.1–2). There are instances of sick Buddhist monks who committed suicide when they were in a state of enlightenment because they could not maintain the stable enlightened ASC (see Jones 2004, 173–74). The Buddha did not condemn them for taking their lives since the enlightened do not desire a new rebirth or to escape pain. As acts not driven by selfish desires, their actions were beyond the sanction of *karman*.

17. Mindfulness meditation may have been the Buddha's innovation. The term for mindfulness, *smriti*, literally means "remembrance." It requires keeping in mind the impermanence of things—along with the rest of Buddhist metaphysics—as one experiences the world and one's inner life in the present. There was no better word for this type of mindfulness at the time. Later, *vipashyana* replaced *smriti*.

18. The Buddhist logician Dignaga's (ca. 480–540) theory of perception posed that ordinary sense perception (*pratyaksha*) is actually immediate and not structured by concepts (*kalpanas*); each instance of a perception has its own unique mark (*svalakshana*), but the unenlightened misconstrue reality by later applying universals (*samanyalakashanas*) to what they perceived. The more common Buddhist position is that the unenlightened misconstrue reality in their sense perceptions due to mental processing. Only through analysis and meditation can one attain a nonconceptual (*nirvakalpa*), direct awareness of reality as it truly is (*yathabhutam*). Chandrakirti made this explicit for the Prasangikas.

19. The Buddha was called *Shakyamuni*, the "silent one of the Shakya clan." This is usually interpreted as referring to his meditation, but the Madhyamaka Chandrakirti had an alternative explanation of the Buddha's silence: the enlightened have no conceptuality and so are free of thoughts, knowledge, and any cognitive activity at all—their mind and mental processes completely cease—so the human Buddha could not speak. In effect, the Buddha literally had no mind. Rather, the transcendent reality (*dharma-kaya*) caused sounds to be emitted from his body that answered the disciples' questions or otherwise helped (see Dunne 1996).

20. These practices also appear in *Yoga Sutras* 1.33—again, only as meditative aids. In the introvertive state of *samadhi* that is the goal of the Yoga school, the positive feelings generated must be transcended along with all negative tendencies.

21. The doctrines of impermanence and momentariness are usually treated as the same, but they are not. Something that lasts ten years and then decays is impermanent but not momentary.

22. The Abhidharmists were the first Indians to create a systematic treatment for their beliefs. This first arose in Northwest India, and Abhidharmists may have gotten the idea of creating a systematic treatment from interactions with Greeks who occupied the region, although Greek philosophical ideas did not influence the content of their treatments. The idea of public debates may have also come from the Greeks.

23. The analysis is not proto-scientific. Buddhism's focus is on experiencing the world for ending suffering rather than for the world in itself. The *dharmas* are elements of these experiences of the world. The only Buddhist interest in matter is its form (*rupa*)—how things appear to us—not what is behind appearances or what things may be like independent of experience. To Buddhists, we give what is actually real a form through naming; hence, the common phrase for the physical world, "name and form" (*nama-rupa*). Abhidharmists include the experienced form among their lists of *dharmas*, not matter. (*Dravya* in Sanskrit can mean "matter," but the Sarvastivada Abhidharmists use the phrase *sat-dravya* to mean any real substance.) Likewise, *loka* (world) relates to the experienced world, not the objective world per se. The phenomenal world is *kama-loka*, the "realm of desire." Psychological analysis was limited to only states of consciousness and mental factors pertinent to ending suffering; it was not an objective search for all mental states.

24. *Svabhava* is not an "essence" in the Western philosophical sense of a universal. For Buddhists, trees do not exist by some universal essence of tree-ness. Rather, *essence* here means that there is something in each individual thing that makes it self-contained and not conditioned by or dependent upon anything else.

25. Both Nikaya and Mahayana Buddhists lived in the same monasteries and attended the same teaching centers in India. All used the same meditative practices and typically followed the same monastic code (Vinaya) but differed in their beliefs. Tantrikas also joined them. These monasteries also taught Hindu doctrines and sciences such as medicine, astronomy, and astrology.

26. The Theravada canon records the Buddha as saying that he held no teachings back (DN I.16) and that the authentic doctrines would disappear (AN I.72–73, SN II.267), but Mahayanists claimed that their texts were the actual words of the Buddha and thus had to explain why they had not been heard earlier. Their explanation for the Perfection of Insight texts was that the Buddha knew people of his time would not understand them, so he stored them with the Nagas—human-headed, snake-like beings who lived under the water—until someone was born who could understand them. That person was Nagarjuna, whose name means "the conqueror of the Nagas." The earlier texts were only provisional. Tantrikas claimed that their esoteric texts were passed down secretly from the Buddha by lineages of masters to disciples or hidden by female Dakinis. Chan/Zen Buddhists claimed that their teachings arose from the Buddha beginning with a wordless gesture—holding up a flower—that only his disciple Kashyapa understood, and it was then carried forward by a chain of teachers and disciples. What comes from specific authors such as Nagarjuna are considered treatises.

27. These five basic precepts of Nikaya codes of conduct commend abstaining from (1) directly or indirectly taking the life of any human or other sentient being, including abortions; (2) directly or indirectly taking what is not freely given or taking anything by deception; (3) adultery, homosexuality, and certain other sexual practices—for monks and nuns, all sexual activity; (4) false, malicious, harsh, frivolous, or misleading speech; and (5) consuming any alcohol or drugs that would disturb the mind's calm or mindful state. Its focus is on how the actions affect the actor; actions that violate these restraints disturb the actor's mind. The longer lists of eight or ten precepts utilized in addition to the initial five—including not eating after midday and so forth—do not contain anything concerning actions impinging others. In sum, proper conduct (*shila*) is cultivated within a way of life that develops a practitioner's state of mind, leading to *nirvana*. The basic concern is for the practitioner, not for their possible impact on others in one's conduct.

28. Compassion can also turn the entire nature of an apparently self-serving virtue upside down. Patience becomes a type of other-regarding action. Enemies, by providing an opportunity for one to practice patience, become an instrument for one's own enlightenment; thus, the enemies themselves also gain merit (*Bodhicharyavatara* V.107). Shantideva also pointed out a strange consequence: the enemies go to hell for harming us, so we injure them while they help us to practice patience (V.47–49). Hence, there is a bizarre circumstance of thanking the people beating us up while we feel sorry for them.

29. Bodhisattvas continue to deepen their insight after enlightenment. Nikaya Buddhists reject that idea, as illustrated in the example in the *Lotus Sutra* in which the Arhats walked out angry and puzzled by the Buddha's claim that Buddhas had a deeper insight than they did.

30. The Nikaya texts refer to two bodies: the Buddha's body of form (*rupa*) and the *dharma-kaya*. One of the paranormal powers listed in the Nikaya texts for

advanced meditators is the ability to generate a mind-made body (DN I.77). The *nirmana-kaya* doctrine builds on this for Buddhas. The *dharma-kaya* doctrine may have arisen from the ideas that the Buddha had the teachings (the *Dharma*) as his body (*kaya*) (DN III.84) and that one who sees the Buddha sees the *Dharma* and vice versa (MN I.191, SN III.120).

31. How can one be selfish in a worldview with no selves? *Selfish* is merely another conventional term. A more ontologically correct statement would be that a stream of conditioned elements is directed toward its termination without concern for the other streams, but even *stream* is not an ultimately correct designation since it is a constructed entity. However, ultimate truths cannot be stated without resort to conventional terms (MK 24.10).

32. Not all Buddhist schools accept that all beings will eventually escape rebirth. One Yogachara branch asserts that some beings do not that have the seeds of enlightenment in their storehouse consciousness. Sections were added to the *Mahaparinirvana Sutra* expressly to counter this; even the very wicked will eventually become Buddhas.

33. In Tantrism, a deity holds a bell in the left hand to symbolize insight or emptiness and a scepter in the right to symbolize skill in the means for helping others. In East Asia, insight became personified as the Bodhisattva Manjurshri and compassion as the Bodhisattva Avalokiteshvara, who became the most popular among the laity as the goddess Guanyin.

34. Emptiness is occasionally mentioned in the Nikaya texts to refer to the absence of a self or anything belonging to the self in the experienced world (*loka*) (SN IV.54). The five bodily elements (*dharmas*) are likened to a ball of foam, a bubble, a mirage, a (coreless) banana tree, and an illusion (SN III.140).

35. Some texts such as the *Diamond Sutra* state this in a paradoxical manner when they say there is neither a self nor a not-self. They mean that reality as it truly is has nothing in it with the nature of a self; there is no self, nor any absence of a self, nor anything related to a self. That is, since there are no real selves, the absence of one is not possible either. This is also true for anything even indirectly related to a self. Thus, when one thinks of the unreality of the self, one is still erroneously thinking in terms of a self. In sum, any thinking about reality in terms generated by the notion of a self proves that one is unenlightened (see Nagarjuna on the four alternatives in Jones 2022b, 160–63).

36. The Sanskrit version of the *Heart Sutra* does state: "Form [*rupa*] *is* emptiness, emptiness *is* form," and this is also the case for the other *skhandas* constituting a person. This is problematic. It should read: "What has form is empty, what is empty has form." That is how the line is rendered in the classical Tibetan texts (see Jones 2012b, 224–26). The Sanskrit text may be a poor translation of a sutra originally written in Chinese.

37. The enlightened do make normal discriminations—they eat food, not rocks and drink water, not gasoline even while acknowledging that all is of the

same nature. They simply do not discriminate distinct entities from the flow of the experienced world.

38. As noted in the last chapter, the Indian theory of perception is that consciousness emits rays from the mind that conform to things that are external to the mind. For Yogacharins, nescience causes the illusion that consciousness conforms to discrete extra-mental objects. One's past karmic actions also play a role in determining what objects they see. The Nikaya Sautranikas asserted that only images (*akaras*) of external objects are given in perceptions, but we can make accurate inferences from the images to external objects.

39. Other Mahayana traditions also use *shunyata* in senses other than the emptiness of self-existence. Advocates of the storehouse consciousness use it to mean the absence of any defilements in consciousness. The *Lion's Roar of Queen Shrimala* (ca. 200–250) equates it with the pure and changeless "embryo of Buddhahood" (*tathagata-garbha*).

40. Modern Westerners often interpret *emptiness* in light of quantum physics' understanding of a lack of solid, gapless matter, but Buddhists never spoke of solid matter (see Jones 2019b). Rather, the idea was that there is no ontological power of any kind that can give something its own existence and independence from other objects.

41. It should be noted that Nagarjuna infrequently used the noun *emptiness* (*shunyata*). He more often used the adjective *shunya* in describing phenomena and *dharmas*.

42. At the time, most Vietnamese Buddhists frowned upon these acts. (The motives of the unenlightened, by definition, are never only other-regarding but are mixed.) These acts are distinguished from suicide since they, like the Buddha-to-be's acts in the *Jataka Tales*, were done for the benefit of others and not for any self-serving purpose—although it was expected that merit would accrue to acts of self-sacrifice. The objective was to show others their suffering. They were giving their lives for others, not taking their own. Any resulting merit was dedicated to the welfare of the others in the worldly form of bringing peace to the world.

43. For example, in the 840s the Tibetan king Langdarma, who persecuted Buddhists, was assassinated by a Buddhist monk for the king's own good. This act was deemed necessary to prevent the king from committing more anti-Buddhist acts that would damage himself karmically in his future rebirths. Of course, in the Buddhist view, no real person was killed or did the killing, nor was there a real killing. But the monk who did the killing was karmically rewarded for his selfless act (see Jones 2004, 195–98).

44. Another reason not to intervene under the Indian worldview is that a person's illness is seen as the karmic fruit of their past actions working itself out. If someone interferes, the *karman* will still have to work itself out later.

45. The *vajra* is a common Indian symbol for enlightenment. In Nikaya Buddhism, the mind of an enlightened disciple is said to be like a *vajra* (AN I.124).

46. Hindus utilize abstract diagrams (*yantras*) in some meditations that represent manifestations of a deity—paintings of deities and other visual aids (*kashinas*)—but mandalas are specifically Buddhist. Mandalas display the energies of the universe, with a deity at the center and other entities at lower levels. Whether projecting oneself into an image or internalizing an image, one becomes the deity upon whom one meditates. Thus, with mandala meditations, one can participate in the flow of the energy through the various levels and harmonize one's consciousness with the deity at the center.

47. *Dalai* comes from a Mongolian word meaning "ocean." *Panchen* comes from the Sanskrit word for "scholar." *Lama* means "guru." Beginning with the fifth Dalai Lama, the Dalai Lama has been the temporal head of the Geluk tradition, and the Ganden Tripa its spiritual head. Tibet remained a Buddhist theocracy from 1642 to 1950.

48. The Dali Lama asserts that science must be given a free hand and that Buddhism should conform to demonstrated scientific findings (Gyatso 2005b, 3). However, he will not give up core Buddhist beliefs on such matters as causal order throughout the natural world—even in the quantum realm—or consciousness as not being an evolved natural product (see Jones 2021b, 141–43).

Chapter 9

1. In early Chinese, there was no term for *nature*. Nature was not placed in a separate category; the body, family, state, planet, and cosmos are only different levels of what was ordered by the *Dao*.

2. This interpretation comes from later Chinese thought. The *yin-yang* theory was not fully developed at the time of the composition of the *Dao De Jing*.

3. There is no mind/body dualism; *qi* constitutes both. The person has both a soul of celestial origin (*hun*) and a material soul (*po*) that remains with the body.

4. More so than any other texts discussed in this book, the translation of the *Dao De Jing* is very much an interpretation based on what a translator thinks early Daoist thought entails. (After the Bible, it is the most translated book in the world.) But there are limits to the variations (see Robinet 1996). The translations of the *Dao De Jing* consulted here are Waley 1954, Chan 1963, Lau 1963, Mair 1990, and Ames and Hall 2003. Watson 1968, Graham 1981, and Mair 1994 are the sources for the *Zhuangzi*. Citations are to chapters.

5. The *Liezi*, assembled in the third century CE, has similarities to the *Zhuangzi* and may contain some passages edited out by Guo Xiang. It was influenced by Buddhism, as perhaps was the *Zhuangzi*. It became important in Neo-Daoism.

6. On Daoist meditative techniques, see Kohn 1989; 1993; 2010; 2016, 131–40; Wong 1997, 199–211; and Komjathy 2014, chap. 6.

7. There is a focus on nature in Daoism that is absent in Confucianism, but to see the *Dao De Jing* or the *Zhuangzi* as scientific or even proto-scientific is

to misread Daoists' approach to nature (see Jones 1993). Nor was there a Daoist interest in environmentalism; their interest was in how to live in the world, not how to understand it scientifically or how to change nature, improve, or even preserve it. Daoists work on themselves, not nature, and do not value nature for its own sake but for its use to them and their communities (J. Miller 2003, 171–72).

8. It is worth reading Socrates's comments in *Theaetetus* 158a–e in this regard.

9. An analogy in Western theism is Meister Eckhart's distinction between the Godhead and the creator God, but the *Dao* is nontheistic and is embedded in the world guiding it.

10. This is very much an interpretation of the first four lines of the *Dao De Jing*: the *Dao* that can be "*dao*'d" (i.e., followed) is not the unnameable and constant *Dao* that is the source of heaven and earth but the named *Dao* that creates diverse phenomena within the universe—the "mother of the ten thousand things" (D 25). The second part could mean simply that names carve the "uncarved block" (*pu*), but there is a *dao* that human beings can follow, and this line may indicate that. However, there may not be only one cosmogony in the text.

11. Early Chinese philosophy did not address how and why human beings, unlike the rest of reality, could fall out of step with the *Dao* by imposing their "defiled mind" and self-interest. Where does our defiled, dualizing consciousness come from? Conceptualizing and thinking are part of the human *dao*, as Guo Xiang acknowledged, but why do we also have the ability to misperceive these processes and construct a false world of conceptual constructions according to our selfish interests, thereby diverging from our *dao*? The issue of free will also does not come up, nor how it would relate to the enlightened giving up self-interest and being aligned with the *Dao*, thus engaging in no self-assertion.

12. Many commentators on Daoism reject the idea that it is mystical. Instead, the *Dao De Jing* is about governing or military strategy, and the *Zhuangzi* is about linguistic philosophy, relativism, or skepticism. But this ignores the fact that mysticism has more dimensions than just cultivating mystical experiences. Mysticism involves full ways of life that may include political, social, and other dimensions, and one can be a mystic and a philosopher, or politician, and so forth at the same time. It also ignores the fact that the two texts are compilations with different themes.

13. The *Dao De Jing* states that the sage is free of personal desires (D 27) but also that being without desires is the way to *gain* the things that one desires (D 7, 28, 48, 66, 67), such as a long life or immortality. So, the more a sage does for others, the more they gain for themselves (D 81). This suggests that both ends—the sage's own and others'—are accomplished by the same acts and, thus, that the sage makes no real sacrifice by yielding their actions.

14. Another problem is translating the Chinese. For example, does D 19 refer to reducing a sense of self (*si*) or to reducing selfishness? Translating "forgetting yourself" as "forgetting the self" is too metaphysical a reading of this idea; it brings in the issue of whether there is an entity called the self. One can lose awareness of

a self in an experience without denying later that there was a self involved. We are simply unaware of it in some experiences and states. Zhuangzi and Laozi make the lack of self-assertion the central feature in mystical cultivation but only in the sense of not imposing one's personal desires or conceptualizations upon reality. People, including the enlightened, are considered part of the world. There is no need to give up a sense of self if selves are part of the human *dao*.

15. Daoist Emptiness (*xu*) should not be confused with emptiness (*shunyata*) in the Perfection of Insight and Madhyamaka Buddhism—that is, the lack of any reality that would give a phenomenon its own existence (*svabhava*). Here, emptiness may be either the ontic source—a cosmic Void—that both gives and receives phenomenal beings or the mind free of any conceptual content.

16. Daoism also recognized women recluses (e.g., Z 6). Women played a major role in the Daoist religion, and there were women immortals.

17. Interestingly, there is an analogy from Plotinus that Zhuangzi could have used: in a great company of dancers, a tortoise is trampled on the floor because it was unable to get out of the way of the dancers' ordered movement; if it had ranged itself with the dancers' movements, it would not have been harmed (Enn. II.9.7).

18. Trying to follow the *Dao*, as the unenlightened may do, rather than letting things be involves as much self-assertion as any other *yang*-action. The enlightened are free of self-assertion and, thus, follow the *Dao* automatically and effortlessly without trying.

19. Animals, as part of their natural self-assertion, can be aggressive and do kill to survive, but according to Laozi, such aggressive action is not part of the human *dao*.

20. The Daoists were not the only theorists to utilize the concept of *wuwei* in connection with governing. (The word *Wuwei* was inscribed above the emperor's throne.) Other schools in different ways also saw an orderly society as a manifestation of the *Dao*, and all schools thought that what they advocated was natural action reflecting reality, not anything artificial. Even the *Analects* refer to the idea when discussing an emperor's inaction (XV.4), although that chapter may be a later addition. Hanfeizi and the Legalists also invoked *wuwei*. They saw the ruler, like the *Dao*, as the still, empty center of the state, but the state was to be run by active ministers, an extreme number of laws, and with generous rewards and severe punishments. In principle, the country would be ruled effortlessly under an impersonal system of law. The isolated ruler could be inactive because the state would run automatically, like a machine under the tight control of an elaborate administrative system. But such an order-dominated regime is the extreme opposite of Laozi's view of ruling through the innate *yin*-action of the *Dao*.

21. On Daoist paranormal abilities, see Wong 1997, 99–118; and Komjathy 2014, 176–80.

22. *Dao De Jing* 67 lists two virtues other than compassion: frugality, which leads to generosity, and daring not to be ahead in the world, which leads to becoming a leader.

23. Zhuangzi puts a Daoist teaching in the mouth of a vicious robber leading an army of nine thousand men (Z 29). This does not mean that all actions are in conformity with the *Dao* (D 53) but only that the *Dao* does not judge and can flow in all, even if it is impeded by self-interest. Much of the rest of this Outer Chapter is an attack against fame, greed, and power.

24. Zhuangzi was not irrational or anti-intellectual in using reasoning to show that reasoning cannot establish one human point of view as absolute or otherwise uniquely grounded in reality. One can use reason to expose the limits of reasoning.

25. See Wong 1997, 11–18 for the shamanic roots of Daoism. The emperors employed magical practitioners (*fangshi*). Shamanic techniques for inducing ASC experiences and interacting with the spirits influenced Daoism. It also influenced Buddhism in Tibet, Mongolia, and Korea. In Japan, indigenous shamanic beliefs and practices heavily shaped what became Shinto and also influenced its Buddhism.

26. It was finally accepted that one could help one's ancestors by transferring the merit that one has earned to whatever rebirth an ancestor currently happens to be in.

27. Chanting a mantra or the Buddha's name is easier than most forms of meditation, and repetitious chanting can lead to ASCs. However, in a survey, more Chan Buddhists reported introvertive mystical experiences featuring a loss of a sense of self and a sense of space-time and also spoke more of introvertive unity than did the chanting Pure Land Buddhists (Chen et al. 2011).

28. The gold/lion image is reminiscent of the clay/pot image from the Upanishads (CU 7.1). The latter is used for a depth mysticism. The Hindu grammarian Bhartrihari (ca. 570–651 CE) also used the gold/ornament analogy for Brahman's relation to phenomena. The Christian Nicholas of Cusa made a similar claim about each thing being in each thing in his account of how God is present in how he unfolds his creation. Buddhism in China also came to take a reality transcending phenomena as central. In China, the ground may have an unchanging character, but it is not a static, eternally unchanging reality. Instead, it is a dynamic part of the natural world with no fixed form.

29. For an overview of Japanese mysticism, see D. Miller 2003.

30. "Sudden enlightenment" does not mean that the path to enlightenment was seen as quicker or easier than that of "gradual enlightenment" or that no meditative preparation was needed. Rather, for a sudden enlightenment tradition, enlightenment involves a single, complete uncovering of the enlightening knowledge. It is like climbing a mountain covered with trees; the enlightening knowledge is obscured until we reach the very top, and then we get the entire view all at once. For gradual enlightenment, the mind is like a mirror that slowly reveals more and more as it is cleaned. It is like climbing a mountain with no trees; with each step we see a little more of the view, but it is only when we reach the top that the view is complete. Both paths require the work of climbing a mountain, and both end with the same view. The gradual enlightenment position prevailed in Tibet.

31. The Fifth Patriarch had groomed his star disciple to succeed him. The disciple produced a four-line summary of the doctrine: "The body is the Bodhi-tree / The mind is a clear mirror / Take care to keep it always clean / Allow not a speck of dust on it!" But the nearly illiterate Huineng spontaneously spoke out: "No Bodhi-tree ever arose / Nor is there a stand with a clear mirror / From the beginning not a single thing ever exists. / What then is a speck of dust to cling to?" Huineng was appointed the next patriarch.

32. Part of the reason Chan masters advise against dwelling on exotic experiences is that students may take a temporary ASC clearing of the mind in a *satori* as achieving the goal instead of attaining a permanent ASC state of enlightenment. There is also the danger that, as the mind is being cleared of ordinary consciousness, demonic images (Jpn., *makyo*) may arise from the subconscious, and students may take them to be objectively real.

33. Whether we are innately good or not was an issue of dispute in classical China. Daoists, early Neo-Confucians, and most Buddhists adopted the belief that we are naturally good or compassionate. To use the illustration from the Confucian Mencius, if we see a child about to fall into a well and are not naturally moved to help, we are not human.

34. Dogen held the typical Chan view that mind and body cannot be separated and often referred to them together (*shin-jin*). He criticized the *koan* technique as one-sided since it involved only the mind.

35. See Victoria 2006. The Mount Shaolin monastery in southern China became a famous center for training Buddhists in the martial arts, but Mahayana Buddhism has a larger history of militant monks. Some texts (e.g., the *Mahaparinirvana Sutra*) state that monks can kill to protect the Buddhist doctrine. This has led to monasteries of monks warring with each over which school has the correct understanding of the doctrine. They also aided their governments in wars. Korean Buddhist schools resisted Japanese invasions.

Chapter 10

1. Tibetan Buddhism is currently the flavor of the month. The word *Tibetan* is now added to common Buddhist claims making them seem uniquely Tibetan.

2. Hatha yoga was a physical meditation; but, for most people today, it has been reduced to a stretching exercise. There is now also "doga" for practicing yoga together with one's dog.

3. *Contemplation* in contemplative studies is defined as how human beings across different cultures and eras have found ways to concentrate, broaden, and deepen conscious awareness as a gateway to cultivating their full potential and leading more meaningful and fulfilling lives (Roth 2006, 1788).

4. Without a religious interpretative framework, some mystical experiences may not have positive effects but lead instead to less well-being (Byrd, Lear, and Schwenka 2000). Thus, naturalists may have to work out a naturalistic framework in which mystical experiences, including different types of introvertive ones, are treated positively as cognitive of natural realities if mystical experiences are not to have a negative effect on their sense of well-being. It is possible for naturalists to work out a framework for a meaning of life (Jones 2018, 167–70).

5. The reported benefits of meditation have, to date, been moderate but measurable. If these results can be shown to be achievable by means other than hours of meditation, interest in meditation may fade quickly.

6. Some advocates today of more traditional mysticism see mystical experiences and psychedelics as decreasing the blocking or filtering functions of the brain, thereby letting in more of a transpersonal or transcendent consciousness into the conscious mind. F. W. H. Myers, William James, Henri Bergson, C. D. Broad, and Aldous Huxley advanced a "reducing valve" theory of the brain; the brain normally limits the input it receives to what we need to survive, but mystical experiences loosen the valve.

7. Today, the distinction between mystical experiences and dualistic, numinous experiences—such as visions and voices—is falling out of favor in religious studies. Both types of experiences are subsumed under the category *religious experiences* as if all religious experiences are the same in nature and whatever is said about any one of them applies equally to all. Lumping significantly different experiences together reflects a growing lack of interest in subjective experiences in religious studies in favor of observable phenomena.

8. Thailand, often considered the world's most Buddhist country, exhibits the problem of modernity. As its prosperity grows today, there is less religious activity, and there has been over a 50 percent drop in the number of monks. There are also sex and money scandals among the monks in addition to the violent ethnic cleansing of Muslims by the Buddhist majority.

9. Surveys may be worded in a way that makes it hard to see if genuinely mystical experiences are involved; the details needed to discern the type of experience are missing. For example, a survey respondent may construe being "lifted out of yourself" to mean any spiritually uplifting experience. Any emotional state in a religious setting may be taken as "union with God." Some Christians may feel "one with God" or have their "hearts filled with the Holy Spirit" every Sunday morning in a church service. One may feel "bathed in God's love" even if no personal elements were present in the experience simply because *God* is the go-to word for anything that feels profound; most people would not know any other way to express the magnitude of the experience. One survey initially found that 65 percent of respondents were aware of or influenced by a "presence or power," but the number dropped to 29.4 percent in follow-up interviews; 20.2 percent had numinous experiences, and 9.2 percent had a sense of union (Hardy 1983). That there are different types of mystical experiences may be overlooked.

10. De Chardin had experiences of a "glowing universe" and a vision of Christ shining with an "indescribable shimmer or iridescence."

11. Asian religions are entering a new phase as they become adapted in the West. New Age Kabbalah, Neo-Sufism, and Transcendental Meditation ostensibly have deep roots in a mystical tradition, but they have more in common with various New Age syncretic beliefs and practices than any of the traditional teachings.

12. New Agers are usually light on doctrines, but whether they are members of a formal religion or not, they still must have some beliefs for understanding their own mystical experiences. They may have less theological detail, but they need some beliefs and values to integrate mystical experiences into their lives. However, their beliefs and values are often a disjoined, eclectic blend of only what the person likes in different religious and nonreligious traditions, without any highly ramified doctrines of a specific tradition's theology. In Western consumer society, people tend to pick the parts of traditional mystical practices and doctrines they like a la carte and ignore the difficult or unpleasant aspects or beliefs of traditional mysticisms. Seekers come up with their own individual sense of meaningfulness. *Sheilaism* is the term that a young nurse applied when attempting to explicate her religious beliefs to the sociologist Robert Bellah. It has since become a term among researchers for "a fiercely individualistic, narcissistic spirituality that is independent of, if not in outright opposition to, religion" (Hood 2004, 40).

13. New Agers tend to treat all mystical experiences as being of one type and grouped with visions: a "common experiential core." However, the history of mysticism demonstrates a variety of types of mystical experiences. New Agers also tend to treat understanding mystical experiences as independent of any one religious tradition, claiming that mystics have a "perennial philosophy" that transcends any one religious tradition. Classical mystics, however, believe that their own religious tradition supplies the correct or at least best understanding and do not reject that understanding in favor of a cross-cultural perennialist understanding (Jones 2021b).

14. The metaphysics of some mystical traditions may provide a framework for integrating science as a way of knowing and its current theories and findings into a larger mystical worldview, but this does not make mystics into scientists or vice versa. What Wilhelm Halbfass says of Buddhism can be applied more broadly to mysticism: "Following the experiential path of the Buddha does not mean to continue a process of open-ended experimentation and inquiry. There is no 'empiricist' openness for future additions or corrections; there is nothing to be added to the discoveries of the Buddha and other 'omniscient' founders of soteriological traditions. . . . There is no programmatic and systematic accumulation of 'psychological' data or observations, no pursuit of fact-finding in the realm of consciousness. . . . [T]here is no more 'inner experimentation' in these traditions than there is experimentation related to the 'outer' sphere of nature" (1988, 393–94).

15. This also happens with psychedelic drug advocates. For example, according to Thomas Roberts, religion should only be about experiences; rituals and beliefs are no more than ways to induce mystical experiences (2013). They are not ways

to incorporate mystical experiences into one's life. "Word-based" religion is only recipes, while mystical experiences are actually tasting the food.

16. New forms of historical mystical traditions devised today—such as "socially engaged" Buddhism—may break from or radically distort classical mystical approaches.

17. Many sociologists have criticized the growing role of mindfulness in society. They see it as "the quintessential neoliberal and capitalist technology of the self," offering allegedly simplified long-term solutions to personal and social problems that have not been fulfilled (Sauerborn, Sökefeld, and Neckel 2022, 1).

18. Scientific findings concerning meditators often conflict today. Part of the problem is that there are no standardized definitions in the scientific community for the term *meditation*; many disparate practices and states of consciousness are grouped together under it (Nash and Newberg 2013).

19. Such research may also lead to refinements in meditative techniques or new forms of meditation (for example, Newberg and Waldman 2016, 198–211).

20. The scientific study of meditators and drug patients leads to interesting philosophical questions (Jones 2016, chap. 4), but studying experiences from the outside limits the relevance of neuroscience for understanding the inner world of the felt phenomena of mystical experiences (Jones 2018b, Jones 2019a).

21. In principle, neuroscience can give as complete an account of what occurs in the brain during mystical experiences and states as it can for any conscious events, but identifying the place of consciousness as a phenomenon or a possible cause still remains problematic. Merely identifying brain activity does not explain consciousness unless a reductionism or eliminationism is adopted, and even then, why a new level of phenomena such as consciousness should arises from brain activity is not explained.

22. It should also be noted that participants of the famous 1962 Good Friday experiment were theological students (Pahnke 1966, Doblin 1991). This would predispose the participants toward religious understandings and lasting religious impacts. Likewise, if volunteers in drug experiments today are usually self-selected and are people already looking for a religious experience, the findings may skew toward the religious and may not reflect the population as a whole.

23. A person's beliefs need not be tied to a particular religious tradition. Any religious or nonreligious beliefs will do as long as they open the experiencer to the possibility of having mystical experiences. Likewise, the content of the experiences may surprise any person.

24. It appears that the trigger does not affect the content of the experiences or that different triggers enable unique types of experiences. Thus, the triggers do not appear to be part of the experience, but theists still argue that God triggers substantively different experiences—despite similarities in phenomenology—and that experiences enabled by other means are not real or genuine mystical experiences.

25. Among the secular, mystical experiences will be different to the extent that cultural concepts are components of the experiences themselves, but this does not

affect the general nature of the experiences. Secularists in their mystical experiences and beliefs are as much shaped by personal and cultural beliefs as the religious.

26. In the history of Christianity, *secular* was often used to describe anything worldly, in contrast to *religious*. Today, some Christians use secular mysticism as a way to experience God through worldly means: nature mysticism becoming cosmic consciousness. But, here, *secular mysticism* refers to a mysticism that denies a creator god, other transcendent realities, life after death, and related traditional religious claims.

27. Rahner also believed that mystics are the paradigms of being truly human. The rest of us fall short by blocking our latent mystical potential latent.

28. Introvertive and extrovertive mysticisms can be reconciled with science's focus on the structures of the natural realm by treating mysticism in terms of a focus on beingness, although stumbling blocks prevent an overly facile reconciliation (Jones 2010, chap. 16).

29. An interest in mysticism need not lead to liberal values. Many early perennial philosophers were conservative and even fascist (see Sedgwick 2004). The man who began the political party in Munich that became the Nazi party came from a perennialist circle.

30. Is there a continuous need for new revolutions in mysticism to keep beliefs from being hindrances? Mysticism is more than the means to mystical experiences, and mysticisms have to adapt to new knowledge of the world to be viable. But do institutions and doctrines naturally ossify and stand in the way of experiences even in mystical traditions? On the other hand, an indefinite number of revolutions highlights a problem: Are all mystical doctrines by their very nature inadequate and ultimately wrong? Is there no convergence on truth? In the end, do beliefs about what is real not matter in the selflessness embedded in enlightenment as long as one has the subjective sense of having aligned one's life with the way reality truly is? Even if some understanding of what is experienced is needed to incorporate the experiences into one's way of life, will virtually any understanding suffice?

Appendix

1. Those who argue that doctrines about the nature of the phenomenal world and any purported transcendent realities ultimately do not matter to classical mystics cite the Buddhist analogy of the raft: the Buddha's doctrine (*Dharma*) is only a means to the other shore (i.e., the escape from rebirths), and once one has reached that shore, the raft should not be clung to but abandoned (MN I.22). One should get rid of views (*drishtis*) (DN 1.1). However, the Buddha's address to his disciples—in which the raft analogy is set—has nothing in it to suggest that the Buddhist doctrines are incorrect or do not inform the Buddhist enlightened way of life. It only emphasizes that improper understandings of the doctrine—grasping the doctrine improperly—should be let go on the path to enlightenment. Likewise,

views are tied to a sense of self and permanence and so should be abandoned. The Buddha also employed a graduated method of teaching different things to different listeners according to their capacity to understand (AN I.10)—he may have even taught the idea that "there is a self" to beginners—but this does not mean that what he taught to his advanced disciples was not the final truth. Mystical experiences may be beyond words, but a mystic's doctrines show how reality is constructed so that their enlightened mystical way of life is possible.

2. According to Kieran Kavanaugh, John of the Cross considered his poetry "closer to his mystical experiences than his commentaries" because it "represented an overflow in figures and similes from the abundance of God's spiritual communication" (1958, 27). In his poetry, "John felt himself pouring out secrets and mysteries rather than rational explanations" (27). But the problem of how the unenlightened understood his language remains.

3. On paradox in mystical discourse, see Jones 2016, 238–52.

4. For a way out of mystics' problems with language, see Jones 2016, chap. 6.

5. Paul Marshall (2005, 60–64) delineates four types of unity in extrovertive mysticism: being an integral part of the whole, immersion within the whole, identity with the whole, and incorporation into the whole.

6. In Tantrism, deities are for meditative purposes and are as much groundless projections as tables and chairs. They are not the source of the power of the universe.

7. In England in the thirteenth century, the Christian Richard Fishacre made a similar claim to explain how God could be omnipresent without being spatial: since God transcends the universe, he is eternal in the sense of transcending any sense of time; similarly, he transcends spatiality; thus, being spaceless, God can exist *in toto* in every segment of space. That is, what is nondimensional can be present in each portion of the three-dimensional world, just as a timeless god is present in all times. However, the idea of a transcendent god located entirely in every part of space never gained support within the Western theisms.

8. Bodhisattvas may go to the extreme of totally denying their own reality in selflessly helping others regardless of the consequences to themselves, but this actually conflicts with reality. All things are impermanent and conditioned, but a person's node in the web of phenomena is as real as any other, and to devalue it completely in favor of others is as much a value attachment and distortion of reality based on dualizing distinctions as valuing it more than the other nodes. Bodhisattvas are as much a part of reality as those they want to help.

9. Buddhist "no self" metaphysics can ground morality as well as moral indifference: there are no real persons, but there are still "streams of impermanent and conditioned entities" that can be directed toward enlightenment. Thus, there is a reality toward which a Bodhisattva can exhibit a moral concern. Likewise, there are no enlightened beings, but streams of rebirth can be ended (see Jones 2004, 189–92).

10. The Madhyamika Buddhist Aryadeva (third century CE) is said to have died when he was stabbed by the student of a teacher whom he had just defeated;

he taught the student the Buddhist middle way as he lay dying. One legend concerning Shankara claims that he died from being cursed by a teacher whom he had just defeated, and one of Shankara's prominent students transferred the curse back against that teacher, who also died.

11. Mystical detachment should be seen in light of this selflessness. It is a lack of interest in the repercussions of one's actions for oneself, not a lack of concern for the effects of those actions on others; *disinterested* does not mean *uninterested*. Such detachment need not lead to passive withdrawal from the world. Eckhart's "living without a why," the *Bhagavad Gita*'s *karma-yoga*, and Daoist *wei wuwei* are examples of reconciling action with disinterested detachment.

12. In early and more recent shamanic societies, most shamans have been men, but some are women. Women also figure prominently in other entheogenic traditions in religious traditions (Winkelman 2017, 52–53).

13. There is also a long tradition in Christianity of treating the soul and wisdom (*sophia*) as female. This finds expression especially in bridal mysticism. Such expressions also occur in other traditions. For example, in Hindu Bhakti, men have written songs with the man longing for Krishna as a wife longs for her husband—modeled on Krishna's wife Radha—or as the Gopi milkmaids longed for him.

14. Theistic symbolism is often erotic. For an argument that the role of the body in Christian meditation and prayer may indicate that the erotic symbolism that mystics employ is more than merely symbolic, see Mallory 1977.

References and Further Reading

Preface

Abhyananda, Swami. 2012. *History of Mysticism: The Unchanging Testament.* Fallsburg, NY: Atma Books.

Armstrong, Karen. 1993. *History of God: The 4000-Year Quest of Judaism, Christianity, and Islam.* New York: Ballantine.

Bouyer, Louis. 1980. "Mysticism: An Essay on the History of the Word." In *Understanding Mysticism*, edited by Richard Woods, 42–55. Garden City, NY: Image Books.

Certeau, Michel de. 1992a. *The Mystic Fable: The Sixteenth and Seventeenth Centuries.* Translated by Michael B. Smith. Chicago: University of Chicago Press.

———. 1992b. "Mysticism." *Diacritics* 22 (2): 11–25.

Dupré, Louis. (1987) 2005. "Mysticism." In *Encyclopedia of Religion* Vol. 9, edited by Lindsay Jones, 6341–59. Detroit: Macmillan Reference USA.

Ernst, Carl W. (1997) 2011. *Sufism: An Introduction to the Mystical Tradition of Islam.* Boston: Shambala.

Jones, Richard H. 1993a. "Concerning Carl Jung on Asian Religious Traditions." In *Mysticism Examined: Philosophical Inquires into Mysticism*, 169–83. Albany: State University of New York Press.

———. 1993b. "Concerning Joseph Needham on Taoism." In *Mysticism Examined: Philosophical Inquires into Mysticism*, 127–46. Albany: State University of New York Press.

———. 2004. *Mysticism and Morality: A New Look at Old Questions.* Lanham, MD: Lexington Books.

———. 2021a. *Introduction to the Study of Mysticism.* Albany: State University of New York Press.

———. 2021b. "Perennial Philosophy and the History of Mysticism." *Sophia* 60 (2): 1–20.

Keller, Carl A. 1978. "Mystical Literature." In *Mysticism and Philosophical Analysis*, edited by Steven T. Katz, 75–100. New York: Oxford University Press.

McGinn, Bernard. 1994. *The Presence of God: A History of Western Christian Mysticism*. New York: Crossroad.

Miller, James. 2003. *Daoism: A Beginner's Guide*. Oxford: Oneworld Publications.

Newberg, Andrew B., and Mark R. Waldman. 2016. *How Enlightenment Changes Your Brain: The New Science of Transformation*. New York: Penguin Random House.

O'Brien-Kop, Karen, and Suzanne Newcombe. 2021. "Reframing Yoga and Meditation Studies." In *Routledge Handbook of Yoga and Meditation Studies*, edited by Karen O'Brien-Kop and Suzanne Newcombe, 3–11. New York: Routledge.

Potter, Karl. 1963. *Presuppositions of India's Philosophies*. Englewood Cliffs, NJ: Prentice-Hall.

Rist, J. M. 1967. *Plotinus: The Road to Reality*. New York: Cambridge University Press.

Schmidt, Leigh Eric. 2003. "The Making of Modern 'Mysticism.'" *Journal of the American Academy of Religion* 71 (June): 273–302.

Stoeber, Michael. 2017. "The Comparative Study of Mysticism." *Oxford Research Encyclopedia of Religion* (online). Last modified January 25, 2017.

1. Mysticism and Mystical Experiences

Bharati, Agehananda. 1976. *The Light at the Center: Context and Pretext of Modern Mysticism*. Santa Barbara, CA: Ross-Erickson.

Bucke, Richard Maurice 1901. *Cosmic Consciousness: A Study in the Evolution of the Human Mind*. New York: Dutton.

Byrd, Kevin R., Delbert Lear, and Stacy Schwenka. 2000. "Mysticism as a Predictor of Subjective Well-Being." *The International Journal for the Psychology of Religion* 10 (4): 259–69.

Cattoi, Thomas and June McDaniel, eds. 2011. *Perceiving the Divine Through the Human Body*. New York: Palgrave Macmillan.

Dunn, Bruce R., Judith A. Hartigan, and William L. Mikulas. 1999. "Concentration and Mindfulness: Unique Forms of Consciousness." *Applied Psychophysiology and Biofeedback* 24 (3): 147–65.

Eifring, Halvor, ed. 2013. *Meditation in Judaism, Christianity and Islam: Cultural Histories*. New York: Bloomsbury.

———. 2014. *Hindu, Buddhist and Daoist Meditation: Cultural Histories*. Keysville, VA: Hermes Publishing.

———. 2016. *Asian Traditions of Meditation*. Honolulu: University of Hawai'i Press.

Ellwood, Robert S., Jr. (1999) 2012. *Mysticism and Religion*. 2nd ed. San Francisco: Seven Bridges Press.

Frieberger, Oliver, ed. 2006. *Asceticism and Its Critics: Historical Accounts and Comparative Perspectives*. New York: Oxford University Press.

Forman, Robert K. C. 2011. *Enlightenment Ain't What It's Cracked Up to Be*. Washington, DC: O-Books.

————, ed. 1990. *The Problem of Pure Consciousness: Mysticism and Philosophy*. New York: Oxford University Press.

Griffiths, Roland R., Matthew W. Johnson, William A. Richards, Brian D. Richards, Una McCann, and Robert Jesse. 2011. "Psilocybin Occasioned Mystical-Type Experiences: Immediate and Persisting Dose-Related Effects." *Psychopharmacology* 218 (December): 649–65.

Happold, F. C. 1970. *Mysticism: A Study and Anthology*. New York: Penguin Books.

Harmless, William. 2008. *Mystics*. New York: Oxford University Press.

Hollenback, Jess Byron. 1996. *Mysticism: Experience, Response, and Empowerment*. University Park: Pennsylvania State University Press.

Idel, Moshe, and Bernard McGinn, eds. 1996. *Mystical Union in Judaism, Christianity, and Islam: An Ecumenical Dialogue*. New York: Continuum.

James, William. (1902) 1958. *The Varieties of Religious Experience: A Study of Human Nature*. New York: New American Library.

Jantzen, Grace M. 1995. *Power, Gender and Christian Mysticism*. Cambridge: Cambridge University Press.

Johnston, William. 1978. *The Inner Eye of Love: Mysticism and Religion*. New York: Harper and Row.

Jones, Richard H. 2004. *Mysticism and Morality: A New Look at Old Questions*. Lanham, MD: Lexington Books.

————. 2016. *Philosophy of Mysticism: Raids on the Ineffable*. Albany: State University of New York Press.

————. 2020a. "On Constructivism in the Philosophy of Mysticism." *Journal of Religion* 100 (1): 1–41.

Katz, Steven T. 2013. *Comparative Mysticism: An Anthology of Original Sources*. New York: Oxford University Press.

Kohn, Livia. 2008. *Meditation Works: In the Daoist, Buddhist and Hindu Traditions*. Magdalena, NM: Three Pines Press.

Komjathy, Louis, ed. 2015. *Contemplative Literature: A Comparative Sourcebook on Meditation and Contemplative Prayer*. Albany: State University of New York Press.

Kripal, Jeffrey J. 2001. *Roads of Excess, Palaces of Wisdom: Eroticism and Reflexivity in the Study of Mysticism*. Chicago: University of Chicago Press.

Kroll, Jerome, and Bernard Bachrach. 2005. *The Mystic Mind: The Psychology of Medieval Mystics and Ascetics*. New York: Routledge.

Lindahl, Jared R., Nathan E. Fisher, David J. Cooper, Rochelle K. Rosen, and Willowby B. Britton. 2017. "The Varieties of Contemplative Experience: A Mixed-Methods Study of Meditation-Related Challenges in Western Buddhists." *PLOS ONE* 12 (5). https://doi.org/10.1371/journal.pone.0176239.

Marshall, Paul. 2005. *Mystical Encounters with the Natural World: Experiences and Explanations*. New York: Oxford University Press.

McGinn, Bernard. 1994. *The Foundations of Mysticism: Origins to the Fifth Century*. New York: Crossroad.

———, ed. 1978. *Classics of Western Spirituality*. New York: Paulist Press.

———. 2006b. "How Augustine Shaped Medieval Mysticism." *Augustinian Studies* 37 (1): 1–26.

Newberg, Andrew, Eugene d'Aquili, and Vince Rause. 2002. *Why God Won't Go Away: Brain Science and the Biology of Belief*. New York: Ballantine Books.

Obeyesekere, Gananath. 2012. *The Awakened Ones: Phenomenology of Visionary Experience*. New York: Columbia University Press.

Parsons, William B., ed. 2011. *Teaching Mysticism*. New York: Oxford University Press.

Perovich, Anthony N. 2011. "Taking Nature Mysticism Seriously: Marshall and the Metaphysics of the Self." *Religious Studies* 47 (2): 165–83.

Revel, Jean-François, and Matthieu Ricard. 1999. *The Monk and the Philosopher*. New York: Schocken Books.

Shear, Jonathan, ed. 2006. *The Experience of Meditation: Experts Introduce Major Traditions*. New York: Paragon House.

Smart, Ninian. 1967. "History of Mysticism." In *Encyclopedia of Philosophy* Vol. 5, edited by Paul Edwards, 419–29. New York: MacMillan.

Smith, Huston. 2001. *Why Religion Matters: The Fate of the Human Spirit in an Age of Disbelief*. New York: HarperCollins.

Soltes, Ori Z. 2008. *Mysticism in Judaism, Christianity, and Islam: Searching for Oneness*. Lanham, MD: Rowan and Littlefield.

Staal, Frits. 1975. *Exploring Mysticism: A Methodological Essay*. Berkeley: University of California Press.

Stace, Walter Terrence. 1960a. *Mysticism and Philosophy*. New York: Macmillan.

———. 1960b. *The Teachings of the Mystics*. New York: New American Library.

Tart, Charles T. 1969. *Altered States of Consciousness: A Book of Readings*. New York: Wiley.

Taylor, Steve. 2012. "Spontaneous Awakening Experiences: Beyond Religion and Spiritual Practice." *Journal of Transpersonal Psychology* 44 (1): 73–91.

Wainwright, William J. 1981. *Mysticism: A Study of Its Nature, Cognitive Value, and Moral Implications*. Madison: University of Wisconsin Press.

Wimbush, Vincent L., and Richard Valantasis, eds. 1998. *Asceticism*. New York: Oxford University Press.

Woods, Richard, ed. 1980. *Understanding Mysticism*. Garden City, NY: Doubleday.

Woods, Toby J., Jennifer M. Windt, and Olivia Carter. 2022. "Evidence Synthesis Indicates Contentless Experiences in Meditation Are Neither Truly Contentless nor Identical." *Phenomenology and the Cognitive Science*. https://doi.org/10.1007/s11097-022-09811-z.

Yaden, David B. and Andrew B. Newberg. 2022. *The Varieties of Spiritual Experience: 21st Century Research and Perspectives*. New York: Oxford University Press.

Zaehner, Robert Charles. 1958. *At Sundry Times: An Essay in the Comparative Study of Religions*. London: Faber and Faber.

Zagano, Phyllis. 2013. *Mysticism and the Spiritual Quest: A Crosscultural Anthology.* Mahwah, NJ: Paulist Press.

2. The Prehistory of Mysticism

A. SHAMANISM

Brown, Joseph Epes. 1971. *The Sacred Pipe: Black Elk's Account of the Seven Rites of the Oglala Sioux.* New York: Penguin Books.

Clottes, Jean, and David Lewis-Williams. 1998. *The Shamans of Prehistory: Trance and Magic in the Painted Caves.* Translated by Sophie Hawkes. New York: Harry Abrams.

Dubois, Thomas. 2009. *An Introduction to Shamanism.* New York: Cambridge University Press.

Eliade, Mircea. (1951) 1972. *Shamanism: Archaic Techniques of Ecstasy.* Princeton, NJ: Princeton University Press.

Harner, Michael J. 1980. *The Way of the Shaman: A Guide to Power and Healing.* New York: Bantam Books.

———. 2013. *Caves and Cosmos: Shamanic Encounters with Another Reality.* Berkeley: North Atlantic Books.

Hayden, Brian. 2003. *Shamans, Sorcerers, and Saints: A Prehistory of Religion.* Washington: Smithsonian Books.

Lewis, I. M. 1989. *Ecstatic Religion: An Anthropological Study of Spirit Possession and Shamanism.* 2nd ed. London: Routledge.

Lewis-Williams, David, and David Pearce. 2005. *Inside the Neolithic Mind: Consciousness, Cosmos and the Realm of the Gods.* London: Thames and Hudson.

Neihardt, John G. 2014. *Black Elk Speaks: The Complete Edition.* Lincoln: University of Nebraska Press.

Pharo, Lars K. 2011. "A Methodology for the Deconstruction and Reconstruction of the Concepts 'Shaman' and 'Shamanism.'" *Numen* 58 (1): 6–70.

Rossano, Matt J. 2007. "Did Meditation Makes Us Human?" *Cambridge Archeological Journal* 17 (1): 47–58.

———. 2009. "Ritual Behavior and the Origins of Modern Cognition." *Cambridge Archeological Journal* 19 (3): 243–56.

Rudgley, Richard. 1999. *The Lost Civilizations of the Stone Age.* New York: Simon and Schuster.

Sayin, H. Ümit. 2014. "Does the Nervous System Have an Intrinsic Archaic Language? Entoptic Images and Phospenes." *NeuroQuantology* 12 (September): 427–55.

Tomášková, Silvia. 2013 *Wayward Shamans.* Berkeley: University of California Press.

Walsh, Roger N. 1990. *The Spirit of Shamanism*. Los Angeles: Jeremy P. Tarcher.

Winkelman, Michael. 2010. *Shamanism: A Biological Paradigm of Consciousness and Healing*. 2nd ed. Santa Barbara, CA: Praeger.

———. 2013. "Shamanism in Cross-Cultural Perspective." *International Journal of Transpersonal Studies* 31 (2): 47–62.

B. Psychedelic Drugs

Allegro, John M. (1970) 2009. *The Sacred Mushroom and the Cross: A Study of the Nature and Origins of Christianity within the Fertility Cults of the Ancient Near East: 40th Anniversary Edition*. London: Gnostic Media Research and Publishing.

Beckstead, Robert, Bryce Blankenagel, Cody Noconi, and Michael James Winkelman. 2017. "The Entheogenic Origins of Mormonism: A Working Hypothesis." *Journal of Psychedelic Studies* 3 (2): 212–60.

Brown, Jerry B., and Julie M. Brown. 2016. *The Psychedelic Gospels: The Secret History of Hallucinogens in Christianity*. Rochester, VT: Park Street Press.

Davis, Alan, John M Clifton, Eric G. Weaver, Ethan S. Hurwitz, Matthew W. Johnson, Roland R. Griffiths. 2020. "Survey of Entity Encounter Experiences Occasioned by Inhaled N,N-dimethyltryptamine: Phenomenology, Interpretation, and Enduring Effects." *Journal of Psychopharmacology* 34 (9):1008–1020.

Devereux, Paul. 1997. *The Long Trip: A Prehistory of Psychedelia*. New York: Penguin Books.

Ellens, J. Harold, ed. 2014. *Seeking the Sacred with Psychoactive Substances: Chemical Paths to Spirituality and to God*. 2 vols. Santa Barbara, CA: Praeger.

Flattery, David Stophlet, and Martin Schwartz. 1989. *Haoma and Harmaline: The Botanical Identity of the Indo-Iranian Sacred Hallucinogen "Soma" and Its Legacy in Religion, Language, and Middle Eastern Folklore*. Berkeley: University of California Press.

Forte, Robert. 1997. *Entheogens and the Future of Religion*. San Francisco: Council on Spiritual Practices.

Harner, Michael J., ed. 1973. *Hallucinogens and Shamanism*. New York: Oxford University Press.

Hillman, D. C. A. 2008. *The Chemical Muse: Drug Use and the Roots of Western Civilization*. New York: St. Martin's Press.

Huxley, Aldous. 1954. *The Doors of Perception*. New York: Harper and Row.

———. 1955. *Heaven and Hell*. New York: Harper and Row.

———. 1962. *Island*. New York: Harper and Row.

McKenna, Terence. 1992. *Food of the Gods: The Search for the Original Tree of Knowledge*. New York: Bantam Books.

Merkur, Dan. 2001. *The Psychedelic Sacrament*. Rochester, VT: Park Street Press.

Milliere, Raphael, Robin L. Carhart-Harris, Leor Roseman, Fynn-Mathis Trautwein, and Aviva Berkovich-Ohana. 2018. "Psychedelics, Meditation, and Self-Consciousness." *Frontiers in Psychology* 9 (September): 1–29.

Muraresku, Brian C. 2020. *The Immortality Key: The Secret History of the Religion with No Name.* New York: St. Martin's Press.

Richards, William A. 2016. *Sacred Knowledge: Psychedelics and Religious Experiences.* New York: Columbia University Press.

Roberts, Thomas, ed. 2001. *Psychoactive Sacramentals: Essays on Entheogens and Religion.* San Francisco: Council on Spiritual Practices.

———. 2012. *Spiritual Growth with Entheogens: Psychoactive Sacramentals and Human Transformation.* Rochester, VT: Park Street Press.

Ruck, Carl A. P. 2006. *Sacred Mushrooms of the Goddess and Secrets of Eleusis.* Oakland, CA: Ronin Publishing.

———. 2017. *Dionysus in Thrace: Ancient Entheogenic Themes in the Mythology and Archaeology of Northern Greece, Bulgaria, and Turkey.* San Francisco: Regent Press.

Rudgley, Richard. 1993. *Essential Substances: A Cultural History of Intoxicants in Society.* New York: Kodansha International.

Shanon, Benny. 2003. *The Antipodes of the Mind: Charting the Phenomenology of the Ayahuasca Experience.* New York: Oxford University Press.

———. 2008. "Biblical Entheogens: A Speculative Hypothesis." *Time and Mind: The Journal of Archeology, Consciousness, and Culture* 1, no. 1 (March): 51–74.

Shipley, Morgan. 2015. *Psychedelic Mysticism: Transforming Consciousness, Religious Experiences, and Voluntary Peasants in Postwar America.* Lanham, MD: Lexington Books.

Smith, Huston. 2000. *Cleansing the Doors of Perception: The Religious Significance of Entheogenic Plants and Chemicals.* New York: Penguin Putnam.

———. 2005. "Do Drugs Have Religious Import? A Forty Year Follow-Up." In *Higher Wisdom: Eminent Elders Explore the Continuing Impact of Psychedelics,* edited by Roger Walsh and Charles S. Grob, 223–39. Albany: State University of New York Press.

Strassman, Rick. 2001. *DMT—The Spirit Molecule: A Doctor's Revolutionary Research into the Biology of Near-Death and Mystical Experiences.* Rochester, VT: Park Street Press.

Timmermann, Christopher, Hannes Kettner, Chris Letheby, Leor Roseman, Fernando E. Rosas, and Robin L. Carhart-Harris. 2021. "Psychedelics Alter Metaphysical Beliefs." *Scientific Reports* 11, no. 22166 (November): 1–13.

Wasson, R. Gordon, Stella Kramrisch, Jonathan Ott, and Carl Ruck. 1986. *Persephone's Quest: Entheogens and the Origins of Religion.* New Haven, CT: Yale University Press.

Watts, Alan. 1962. *The Joyous Cosmology: Adventures in the Chemistry of Consciousness.* New York: Pantheon Books.

Weil, Andrew. 1986. *The Natural Mind: An Investigation of Drugs and the Higher Consciousness.* Boston: Houghton Mifflin.

Winkelman, Michael. 1999. "Altered States of Consciousness and Religious Behavior." In *Anthropology of Religion: A Handbook,* edited by Stephen D. Glazier, 393–428. Westport, CT: Greenwood Press.

———. 2013. "Shamanism and Psychedelics: A Biogenetic Structuralist Paradigm of Ecopsychology." *European Journal of Ecopsychology* 4:90–115.

———. 2014. "Evolutionary Views of Entheogenic Consciousness." In *Seeking the Sacred with Psychoactive Substances: Chemical Paths to Spirituality and to God* Vol. 1, edited by J. Harold Ellens, 341–64. Santa Barbara, CA: Praeger.

———. 2016. "Shamanism and the Brain." In *Religion: Mental Religion,* edited by Niki Kasumi Clements, 355–72. New York: Macmillan Reference USA.

———. 2017. "The Mechanisms of Psychedelic Visionary Experiences: Hypotheses from Evolutionary Psychology." *Frontiers in Neuroscience* 11:1–17.

———. 2019. "Introduction: Evidence for Entheogen Use in Prehistory and World Religions." *Journal of Psychedelic Studies* 3 (2): 43–62.

———. 2021. "Anthropology, Shamanism, and Hallucinogens." In *Handbook of Medical Hallucinogens,* edited by Charles S. Grob and Jim Grigsby, 46–67. New York: Guilford Press.

3. Mysticism in Classical Greek Philosophy

A. Axial Age

Armstrong, Karen. 2006. *The Great Transformation: The Beginning of our Religious Traditions.* New York: Knopf.

Bellah, Robert N., and Hans Joas, eds. 2012. *The Axial Age and Its Consequences.* Cambridge, MA: Harvard University Press.

Jaynes, Julian. 1976. *The Origin of Consciousness in the Breakdown of the Bicameral Mind.* Boston: Houghton Mifflin.

McGilchrist, Iain. 2019. *The Master and His Emissary: The Divided Brain and the Making of the Western World.* Expanded ed. New Haven, CT: Yale University Press.

B. Early Philosophers

Bussanich, John. 1999. "Socrates the Mystic." In *Traditions of Platonism: Essays in Honor of John Dillon,* edited by John J. Cleary, 29–51. Burlington, VT: Ashgate.

————. 2013. "Socrates' Religious Experiences." In *The Bloomsbury Companion to Socrates*, edited by John Bussanich and Nicholas D. Smith, 276–300. New York: Bloomsbury.

————. 2016. "Plato and Yoga." In *Universe and Inner Self in Early Indian and Early Greek Thought*, edited by Richard Seaford, 87–103. Edinburgh: Edinburgh University Press.

Decker, Jessica Elbert, and Matthew Mayock. 2016. "Parmenides and Empedocles." In *The Cambridge Handbook of Western Mysticism and Esotericism*, edited by Glenn A. Magee, 26–37. New York: Cambridge University Press.

Dodds, Eric Robertson. (1951) 2004. *The Greeks and the Irrational*. Berkeley: University of California Press.

Guthrie, W. K. C. 1966. *Orpheus and Greek Religion: A Study of the Orphic Movement*. New York: W. W. Norton.

Hadot, Pierre. 1995. *Philosophy as a Way of Life: Spiritual Exercises from Socrates to Foucault*. Translated by Michael Chase. Oxford: Wiley-Blackwell.

————. 2001. "Shamanism and Greek Philosophy." In *The Concept of Shamanism: Uses and Abuses*, edited by Henri-Paul Francfort and Roberte N. Hamayon, 389–401. Budapest: Akadémiai Kiadó.

Kingsley, Peter. 1995. *Ancient Philosophy, Mystery, and Magic: Empedocles and Pythagorean Tradition*. New York: Oxford University Press.

————. 1999. *In the Dark Places of Wisdom*. Inverness: Golden Sufi Center.

————. 2010. *A Story Waiting to Pierce You: Mongolia, Tibet, and the Destiny of the Western World*. Point Reyes, CA: Golden Sufi Center.

McEvilley, Thomas. 2002. *The Shape of Ancient Thought: Comparative Studies in Greek and Indian Philosophies*. New York: Allworth Press.

Ustinova, Yulia. 2009. *Caves and the Ancient Greek Mind: Descending Underground in the Search for Ultimate Truth*. Oxford: Oxford University Press.

Vlastos, Gregory. 1981. *Platonic Studies*. Princeton, NJ: Princeton University Press.

Yount, David J. 2017. *Plato and Plotinus on Mysticism, Epistemology, and Ethics*. New York: Bloomsbury.

C. Plotinus and Neoplatonism

Armstrong, A. H. 2000. *Plotinus*. 7 vols. Cambridge, MA: Harvard University Press.

Brisson, Luc. 2017. "Can One Speak of Mysticism in Plotinus?" In *Defining Platonism: Essays in Honor of the 75th Birthday of John M. Dillon*, edited by John F. Finamore and Sarah Klitenic Wear, 96–116. Steubenville, OH: Franciscan University Press.

Bussanich, John. 1987. "Plotinus on the Inner Life of the One." *Ancient Philosophy* 7:163–89.

————. 1994. "Mystical Elements in the Thought of Plotinus." *Aufstieg und Niedergang der Römischen Welt* 2 (36): 5300–5330.

————. 1997a. "Non-Discursive Thought in Plotinus and Proclus." *Documenti e Studi Sulla Tradizione Filosofica Medievale* 8:191–210.

————. 1997b. "Plotonian Mysticism in Theoretical and Comparative Perspective." *American Catholic Philosophical Quarterly* 71 (3): 339–65.

Dillon, John M. 1996. "An Ethic for the Late Antique Sage." In *The Cambridge Companion to Plotinus*, edited by Lloyd P. Gerson, 315–35. New York: Cambridge University Press.

Gerson, Lloyd. 1994. *Plotinus*. New York: Routledge.

Hadot, Pierre. 1986. "Neoplationist Spirituality: Plotinus and Porphyry." In *Classical Mediterranean Spirituality: Egyptian, Greek, Roman*, edited by A. H. Armstrong, 230–49. New York: Crossroad.

————. 1993. *Plotinus or The Simplicity of Vision*. Translated by Michael Chase. Chicago: University of Chicago.

Harris, R. Baine, ed. 1982. *Neoplatonism and Indian Thought*. Norfolk: International Society for Neoplatonic Studies.

Kenney, John Peter. 1997. "Mysticism and Contemplation in the *Enneads*." *American Catholic Philosophical Quarterly* 71 (3): 315–37.

MacKenna, Stephen, trans. 1991. *Plotinus: The Enneads*. Abridged ed. New York: Penguin Books.

Majercik, Ruth. 1995. "Plotinus and Greek Mysticism." In *Mysticism and the Mystical Experience East and West*, edited by Donald H. Bishop, 38–61. Selinsgrove, PA: Susquehanna University Press.

O'Meara, Dominic J. 1995. *Plotinus: An Introduction to the Enneads*. Oxford: Clarendon Press.

Rappe, Sara. 2000. *Reading Neoplatonism: Non-Discursive Thinking in the Texts of Plotinus, Proclus, and Damascius*. New York: Cambridge University Press.

Rist, J. M. 1967. *Plotinus: The Road to Reality*. New York: Cambridge University Press.

————. 1976. "Plotinus and Moral Obligation." In *The Significance of Neoplatonism*, edited by R. Baine Harris, 217–33. Norfolk, VA: International Society for Neoplatonic Studies.

————. 1989. "Back to the Mysticism of Plotinus: Some More Specifics." *Journal of the History of Philosophy* 27 (2): 183–197.

Strożyński, Mateusz. 2008. *Mystical Experience and Philosophical Discourse in Plotinus*. Poznan, PL: Poznań Society for the Advancement of the Arts and Sciences.

Versluis, Arthur. 2017. *Platonic Mysticism: Contemplative Science, Philosophy, Literature, and Art*. Albany: State University of New York Press.

Wallis, R. T. 1986. "The Spiritual Importance of Not Knowing." In *Classical Mediterranean Spirituality: Egyptian, Greek, Roman*, edited by A. H. Armstrong, 460–80. New York: Crossroad.

————. 1995. *Neoplatonism*. 2nd ed. London: Hackett Publishing.

4. Jewish Mysticism

Afterman, Adam. 2016. *"And They Shall Be One Flesh": On the Language of Mystical Union in Judaism*. Boston: Brill.

Arbel, Daphna. 2016. "Early Jewish Mysticism." In *The Cambridge Handbook of Western Mysticism and Esotericism*, edited by Glenn A. Magee, 59–68. New York: Cambridge University Press.

Ariel, David. 2006. *Kabbalah: The Mystic Quest in Judaism*. Lanham, MD: Rowman and Littlefield.

Besserman, Perle. 1997. *The Shambhala Guide to Kabbalah and Jewish Mysticism*. Boston: Shambhala.

Buber, Martin. 1947. *Between Man and Man*. Translated by Maurice Friedman. New York: Routledge and Kegan.

———. 1970. *I and Thou*. Translated by Walter Kaufmann. New York: Charles Scribner's Sons.

Dan, Joseph. 1998–99. *Jewish Mysticism*. 4 vols. Northvale, NJ: Jason Aronson.

———, ed. 2002. *The Heart and the Fountain: An Anthology of Jewish Mystical Experiences*. New York: Oxford University Press

———. 2007. *Kabbalah: A Very Short Introduction*. New York: Oxford University Press.

Elior, Rachel. 2006. *The Mystical Origins of Hasidism*. Portland, OR: Littman Library of Jewish Civilization.

Greenspahn, Frederick E., ed. 2011. *Jewish Mysticism and Kabbalah: New Insights and Scholarship*. New York: New York University Press.

Hoffman, Edward, 2010. *The Kabbalah Reader: A Sourcebook of Visionary Judaism*. Boston: Trumpeter.

Horwitz, Daniel M. 2016. *A Kabbalah and Jewish Mysticism Reader*. Philadelphia: The Jewish Publication Society.

Idel, Moshe. 1988a. *Kabbalah: New Perspectives*. New Haven, CT: Yale University Press.

———. 1988b. *The Mystical Experience in Abraham Abulafia*. Translated by Jonathan Chipman. Albany: State University of New York Press.

———. 1995. *Hasidism: Between Ecstasy and Magic*. Albany: State University of New York Press.

———. 1998. *Messianic Mystics*. New Haven, CT: Yale University Press.

———. 2013. "Jewish Mysticism." In *Comparative Mysticism: An Anthology of Original Sources*, edited by Steven T. Katz, 25–154. New York: Oxford University Press.

Kohav, Alex. 2013. *The Sôd Hypothesis: Phenomenological, Semiotic, Cognitive, and Noetic-Literary Recovery of the Pentateuch's Embedded Inner-Core Mystical Initiation Tradition of Ancient Israelite Cultic Religion*. Denver, CO: MaKoM Publications.

Laenen, J. H. 2001. *Jewish Mysticism: An Introduction*. Translated by David E. Orton. Louisville, KY: Westminster John Knox Press.

Lancaster, Brian L. 2005. *The Essence of Kabbalah*. Edison, NJ: Chartwell Books.

Matt, Daniel C. 1988. *Zohar: The Book of Enlightenment*. New York: Paulist Press.
————. 1995. *The Essential Kabbalah: The Heart of Jewish Mysticism*. San Francisco: Harper.
Mayse, Ariel Evan, ed. 2014. *From the Depth of the Well: An Anthology of Jewish Mysticism*. New York: Paulist Press.
Schäfer, Peter. 1992. *The Hidden and Manifest God: Some Major Themes in Early Jewish Mysticism*. Translated by Aubrey Pomerance. Albany: State University of New York Press.
Scholem, Gershom G. 1961. *Major Trends in Jewish Mysticism*. New York: Schocken Books.
Sherwin, Byron L. 2006. *Kabbalah: An Introduction to Jewish Mysticism*. Lanham, MD: Rowman and Littlefield.
Winston, David. 1996. "Philo's Mysticism." *Studia Philonica Annual* 8:74–82.
————. 2001. "Was Philo a Mystic?" In *The Ancestral Philosophy: Hellenistic Philosophy in the Second Temple Period: Essays of David Winston*, edited by Gregory E. Sterling, 151–70. Providence, RI: Brown Judaic Studies.
Wolfson, Elliot R. 1994. *Through A Speculum that Shines: Vision and Imagination in Medieval Jewish Mysticism*. Princeton, NJ: Princeton University Press.
————. 1995. "Varieties of Jewish Mysticism: A Typological Analysis." In *Mysticism and the Mystical Experience: East and West*, edited by Donald H. Bishop, 133–69. Selinsgrove, PA: Susquehanna University Press.
————. 2005. *Language Eros Being: Kabbalistic Hermeneutics and Poetic Imagination*. New York: Fordham University Press.
————. 2006. *Venturing Beyond: Law and Morality in Kabbalistic Mysticism*. New York: Oxford University Press.

5. Christian Mysticism

Bernard of Clairvaux. 1987. *Selected Works*. Translated by G. R. Evans. New York: Paulist Press.
Bonaventure. 1978. *The Soul's Journey into God, The Tree of Life, The Life of St. Francis*. Translated by Ewert Cousins. Mahwah, NJ: Paulist Press.
Dupré, Louis. 1981. *The Deeper Life: An Introduction to Christian Mysticism*. New York: Crossroad.
Dupré, Louis, and James A. Wiseman, eds. 2001. *Light from Light: An Anthology of Christian Mysticism*. 2nd ed. New York: Paulist Press.
Egan, Harvey, ed. 1991. *An Anthology of Christian Mysticism*. Collegeville, MN: Liturgical Press.
Fanning, Steven. 2001. *Mystics of the Christian Tradition*. New York: Routledge.
Fremantle, Anne, ed. 1964. *The Protestant Mystics*. Boston: Little, Brown and Co.

Green, Deirdre. 1989. *Gold in the Crucible: Teresa of Avila and the Western Mystical Tradition*. Rockport, ME: Element Books.

Hanegraaff, Wouter J. 2008. "Altered States of Knowledge: The Attainment of Gnōsis in the Hermetica." *International Journal of the Platonic Tradition* 2 (1): 128–63.

Harmless, William. 2004. *Desert Christians: An Introduction to the Literature of Early Monasticism*. New York: Oxford University Press.

Hoffman, Bengt, trans. 1980. *The Theologia Germanica of Martin Luther*. Mahwah, NJ: Paulist Press.

Hollywood, Amy, and Patricia Z. Beckman, eds. 2012. *The Cambridge Companion to Christian Mysticism*. New York: Cambridge University Press.

Ignatius of Loyola. 1991. *Spiritual Exercises and Selected Works*. Translated by George E. Ganns. New York: Paulist Press.

John of the Cross. 1958. *Ascent of Mount Carmel*. 3rd ed. Translated by E. Allison Peers. Garden City, NY: Image Books.

———. 1987. *Selected Writings*. Translated and edited by Kieran Kavanaugh. New York: Crossroad.

Johnston, William, ed. 1973. *The Cloud of Unknowing and the Book of Privy Counseling*. Garden City, NY: Image Books.

———. 1995. *Mystical Theology: A Science of Love*. Maryknoll, NY: Orbis Books.

———. 2000. *The Mysticism of the Cloud of Unknowing*. 2nd ed. New York: Fordham University Press.

Julian of Norwich. 1978. *Showings*. Translated by Edmund Colledge and James Walsh. Mahwah, NJ: Paulist Press.

Law, William. 1978. *A Serious Call to a Devout and Holy Life, the Spirit of Love*. Mahwah, NJ: Paulist Press.

Lerner, Robert E. 1972. *The Heresy of the Free Spirits in the Late Middle Ages*. Berkeley: University of California Press.

Lossky, Vladimir. 1957. *The Mystical Theology of the Eastern Church*. London: Clark.

Louth, Andrew. 1981. *The Origins of the Christian Mystical Tradition: From Plato to Denys*. New York: Oxford University Press.

Luibheid, Colm, trans. 1987. *Pseudo-Dionysius: The Complete Works*. New York: Paulist Press.

MacGregor, Geddes. 1978. *Reincarnation in Christianity: A New Vision of the Role of Rebirth in Christian Thought*. Wheaton, IL: Theosophical Publishing House.

Mallory, Marilyn May. 1977. *Christian Mysticism: Transcending Techniques—A Theological Reflection on the Empirical Testing of the Teaching of St. John of the Cross*. Amsterdam: Van Gorcum Assen.

McGinn, Bernard. 1994. *The Foundations of Mysticism: Origins to the Fifth Century*. New York: Crossroad.

———. 1996. *The Growth of Mysticism: Gregory the Great Through the 12th Century*. New York: Crossroad.

———. 1998. *The Flowering of Mysticism: Men and Women in the New Mysticism (1200–1350)*. New York: Crossroad.

———. 2001. *The Mystical Thought of Meister Eckhart: The Man from Whom God Hid Nothing*. New York: Crossroad.

———. 2005. *The Harvest of Mysticism in Medieval Germany*. New York: Crossroad.

———, ed. 2006a. *The Essential Writings of Christian Mysticism*. New York: Random House.

———. 2006b. "How Augustine Shaped Medieval Mysticism." *Augustinian Studies* 37 (1): 1–26.

———. 2008. "Mystical Consciousness: A Modest Proposal." *Spiritus* 8 (Spring): 44–63.

———. 2012. *The Varieties of Vernacular Mysticism (1350–1550)*. New York: Crossroad.

———. 2013. "Christian Mysticism." In *Comparative Mysticism: An Anthology of Original Sources*, edited by Steven T. Katz, 157–246. New York: Oxford University Press.

———. 2017a. *Mysticism in the Golden Age of Spain (1500–1650)*. New York: Crossroad.

———. 2017b. *Mysticism in the Reformation (1500–1650)—Part 1*. New York: Crossroads.

———. 2020. *The Persistence of Mysticism in Catholic Europe: France, Italy, and Germany 1500–1675*. New York: Crossroad.

———. 2021. *The Crisis of Mysticism: Quietism in Seventeenth-Century Spain, Italy, and France*. New York: Crossroad.

McLaughlin, Eleanor. 1972. "The Heresy of the Free Spirit and Late Medieval Mysticism." In *Medieval and Renaissance Spirituality*, edited by Paul M. Clogan, 37–54. Denton, TX: North Texas State University Press.

Meister Eckhart. 2009. *The Complete Mystical Works of Meister Eckhart*. Translated and edited by Maurice O'C Walshe. Revised by Bernard McGinn. New York: Crossroad.

Merton, Thomas. 1968. *Conjectures of a Guilty Bystander*. Garden City, NY: Image Books.

———. 2003. *The Inner Experience: Notes on Contemplation*. Edited by William H. Shannon. New York: HarperOne.

———. 2007. *New Seeds of Contemplation*. New York: New Directions.

———. 2017. *A Course in Christian Mysticism*. Collegeville, MN: Liturgical Press.

Moltmann, Jürgen. 1980. *Experiences of God*. Minneapolis: Fortress Press.

Nicholas of Cusa. 1997. *Selected Spiritual Writings*. Translated by H. Lawrence Bond. New York: Paulist Press.

Payne, Steven. 1990. *John of the Cross and the Cognitive Value of Mysticism: An Analysis of Sanjuanist Teaching and Its Philosophical Implications for Contemporary Discussions of Mystical Experience*. Boston: Kluwer Academic Publishers.

Porete, Marguerite. 1993. *The Mirror of Simple Souls*. Translated by Ellen L. Babinsky. New York: Paulist Press.

Russell, Norman. 2006. *The Doctrine of Deification in the Greek Patristic Tradition*. New York: Oxford University Press.

Ruusbroec, John. 1985. *The Spiritual Espousals and Other Works*. Translated by James A. Wiseman. New York: Paulist Press.

Steere, Douglas V. 1983. *Quaker Spirituality: Selected Writings*. Mahwah, NJ: Paulist Press.

Stoumsa, Guy G. 1996. *Hidden Wisdom: Esoteric Traditions and the Roots of Christian Mysticism*. Leiden: Brill.

Suso, Henry. 1989. *The Exemplar, with Two German Sermons*. Translated by Frank Tobin. New York: Paulist Press.

Tamburello, Dennis E. 2013. "The Protestant Reformers on Mysticism." In *The Wiley-Blackwell Companion to Christian Mysticism*, edited by Julia A. Lamm, 412–21. New York: Wiley-Blackwell.

Tauler, John. 1985. *Sermons*. Translated by Maria Shrady. Mahwah, NJ: Paulist Press.

Teresa of Avila. 1979. *The Interior Castle*. Translated by Kieran Kavanaugh and Otilio Rodiguez. Mahwah, NJ: Paulist Press.

Van Dyke, Christiana. 2023. *A Hidden Wisdom: Medieval Contemplatives on Self-Knowledge, Reason, Love, Persons, and Immortality*. New York: Oxford University Press.

Vanneste, Jan. 1963. "Is the Mysticism of Pseudo-Dionysius Genuine?" *International Philosophical Quarterly* 3 (3): 286–306.

Walsh, James, trans. and ed. 1981. *The Cloud of Unknowing*. Mahwah, NJ: Paulist Press.

———. 1988. *The Pursuit of Wisdom and Other Works by the Author of the Cloud of Unknowing*. New York: Paulist Press.

Wear, Sarah K., and John Dillon. 2007. *Dionysius the Areopagite and the Neoplatonist Tradition: Despoiling the Hellenes*. Burlington, VT: Ashgate.

Windeatt, Barry, ed. 1994. *English Mystics of the Middle Ages*. New York: Cambridge University Press.

6. Islamic Mysticism

Abrahamov, Binyamin. 2003. *Divine Love in Islamic Mysticism: The Teachings of al-Ghazâlî and al-Dabbâgh*. New York: Routledge Curzon.

Algar, Hamid. 2001. *Imam Abu Hamid Ghazali: An Exponent of Islam in Its Totality*. Oneonta, NY: Islamic Publications.

Aminrazavi, Mehdi. 1995. "Antinomian Tradition in Islamic Mysticism." *Bulletin of the Henry Martyn Institute of Islamic Studies* 14 (January–June): 17–24.

Andrae, Tor. 1987. *In the Garden of Myrtles: Studies in Early Islamic Mysticism*. Albany: State University of New York Press.

Arberry, A. J. 1966. *Muslim Saints and Mystics*. Chicago: University of Chicago Press.

Attar, Farid Ud-Din. 1984. *The Conference of the Birds*. Translated by Afkham Darbandi and Dick Davis. London: Penguin.

Awn, Peter J. 1995. "Sensuality and Mysticism—The Islamic Tradition." In *Asceticism*, edited by Vincent L. Wimbush and Richard Valantasis, 369–72. New York: Oxford University Press.

———. 2013. "Sufism." In *Comparative Mysticism: An Anthology of Original Sources*, edited by Steven T. Katz, 247–319. New York: Oxford University Press.

Baldrick, Julian. 1989. *Mystical Islam: An Introduction to Sufism*. Albany: State University of New York Press.

Chittick, William C. 1983. *The Sufi Path of Love: The Spiritual Teachings of Rumi*. Albany: State University of New York Press.

———. 1989. *The Sufi Path of Knowledge: Ibn al-'Arabī's Metaphysic of Imagination*. Albany: State University of New York Press.

———. 2000. *Sufism: A Beginners' Guide*. London: Oneworld Publications.

———. 2016. "Sufism." In *The Cambridge Handbook of Western Mysticism and Esotericism*, edited by Glenn A. Magee, 83–94. New York: Cambridge University Press.

Chodkiewicz, Michel. 1993. *An Ocean without Shore: Ibn Arabi, the Book, and the Law*. Albany: State University of New York Press.

Corbin, Henry. 1998. *Alone with the Alone: Creative Imagination in the Sufism of Ibn 'Arabi*. Princeton, NJ: Princeton University Press.

Ernst, Carl W. (1997) 2011. *Sufism: An Introduction to the Mystical Tradition of Islam*. Boston: Shambala.

Fakhry, Majid. 1997. *A Short Introduction to Islamic Philosophy, Theology and Mysticism*. Oxford: Oneworld Publications.

Ghazali, Abu Hamid. 1976. *On the Duties of Brotherhood*. Translated by Muhtar Holland. Woodstock, NY: Overlook Press.

———. 1998. *The Niche of Lights*. Translated by David Buchman. Provo: Brigham Young University Press.

Green, Nile. 2012. *Sufism: A Global History*. Malden, MA: Wiley-Blackwell.

Ibn Al'Arabi. 1980. *The Bezels of Wisdom*. Translated by R. W. J. Austin. Mahwah, NJ: Paulist Press.

Karamustafa, Ahmet T. 2007. *Sufism: The Formative Period*. Berkeley: University of California Press.

Knysh, Alexander. 2000. *Islamic Mysticism: A Short History*. Boston: E. J. Brill.

Lewis, Franklin D. 2008. *Rumi Past and Present, East and West: The Life, Teachings, and Poetry of Jalal al-Din Rumi*. London: Oneworld Publications.

Lewisohn, Leonard, ed. 1999. *The Heritage of Islam*. 3 vols. Oxford: Oneworld Publications.

Lings, Martin. 1975. *What Is Sufism?* Berkeley: University of California Press.

Milson, Menahem. 1975. *A Sufi Rule for Novices: Katāb Ādāb al-Murīdīn*. Cambridge, MA: Harvard University Press.

Morewedge, Parviz. 1992. *Neoplatonism and Islamic Thought*. Albany: State University of New York Press.

Nasr, Seyyed Hossein, ed. 1987. *Islamic Spirituality*. New York: Crossroad.

———. 1999. *Sufi Essays*. 3rd ed. Chicago: KAZI.

———. 2008. *The Garden of Truth: The Vision and Promise of Sufism, Islam's Mystical Tradition*. New York: HarperCollins.

Renard. John. 1996. *Seven Doors to Islamic Spirituality and the Religious Life of Muslims*. Berkeley: University of California Press.

———, trans. 2004. *Knowledge of God in Classical Sufism: Foundations of Islamic Mystical Theology*. New York: Paulist Press.

Rumi, Jalal al-din. 1926–1934. *The Mathnawī*. 3 vols. Translated by R. A. Nicholson. London: Luzac.

———. 1961. *Discourses*. Translated by A. J. Arberry. London: John Murray.

———. 1968. *Mystical Poems of Rūmī*. Translated by A. J. Arberry. Chicago: University of Chicago Press.

Schimmel, Annemarie. 1993. *The Triumphal Sun: A Study of the work of Jalāloddin Rumi*. Albany: State University of New York Press.

———. 2011. *Mystical Dimensions of Islam*. 2nd ed. Chapel Hill: University of North Carolina Press.

Sells, Michael A. 1995. *Early Islamic Mysticism: Sufi, Qur'an, Mi'raj, Poetic and Theological Writings*. New York: Paulist Press.

7. Hindu Mysticism

Bader, Jonathan. 1990. *Meditation in Sankara's Vedanta*. New Delhi: Aditya Prakashan.

Bryant, Edwin, trans. 2009. *The Yoga Sutras of Patanjali: A New Edition, Translation, and Commentary*. New York: North Point Press.

Carman, John B. 1974. *The Theology of Rāmānuja: An Essay in Interreligious Understanding*. New Haven, CT: Yale University Press.

Dasgupta, S. N. (1927) 1971. *Hindu Mysticism*. New York: Frederick Ungar Publishing.

Deutsch, Eliot. 1969. *Advaita Vedānta: A Philosophical Reconstruction*. Honolulu: University Press of Hawai'i.

Deutsch, Eliot, and Rohit Dalvi, eds. 2004. *The Essential Vedānta: A New Source Book of Advaita Vedānta*. Bloomington, IN: World Wisdom.

Dyczkowski, Mark S. G. 1987. *The Doctrine of Vibration: An Analysis of the Doctrines and Practices of Kashmir Shaivism*. Albany: State University of New York Press.

Eliade, Mircea. 1970. *Yoga: Immortality and Freedom*. Princeton, NJ: Princeton University Press.

Feuerstein, Georg. 1996. *The Philosophy of Classical Yoga*. Rochester, VT: Inner Traditions.

———. 1998. *Tantra: The Path of Ecstasy*. Boston: Shambhala.

Flood, Gavin. 1996. *An Introduction to Hinduism*. New York: Cambridge University Press.

———. 2004. *The Ascetic Self: Subjectivity, Memory and Tradition*. New York: Cambridge University Press.

———. 2006. *The Tantric Body: The Secret Tradition of Hindu Religion*. New York: Palgrave Macmillan.

———. 2013. *The Truth Within: A History of Inwardness in Christianity, Hinduism, and Buddhism*. New York: Oxford University Press.

Forsthoefel, Thomas A. 2002. *Knowing beyond Knowledge: Epistemologies of Religious Experience in Classical and Modern Advaita*. Burlington, VT: Ashgate.

Fort, Andrew O., and Patricia Y. Mumme, eds. 1996. *Living Liberation in Hindu Thought*. Albany: State University of New York Press.

Halbfass, Wilhelm. 1988. "The Concept of Experience in the Encounter Between India and the West." In *India and Europe: An Essay in Understanding*, edited by Wilhelm Halbfass, 378–402. Albany: State University of New York Press.

Harper, Anne, and Robert L. Brown. 2002. *The Roots of Tantrism*. Albany: State University of New York Press.

Jones, Richard H., trans. 2014a. *Early Advaita Vedanta Philosophy* Vol. 1. New York: Jackson Square Books, Createspace.

———, trans. 2014b. *Early Indian Philosophy*. New York: Jackson Square Books, Createspace.

———, trans. 2022a. *Early Advaita Vedanta Philosophy* Vol. 2. New York: Jackson Square Books, Createspace.

Klostermaier, Klaus K. 2007. *A Survey of Hinduism*. 3rd ed. Albany: State University of New York Press.

Kripal, Jeffrey J. 1995. *Kali's Child: The Mystical and the Erotic in the Life and Teachings of Ramakrishna*. 2nd ed. Chicago: University of Chicago Press.

Lipner, Julius. 1986. *The Face of Truth: A Study of Meaning and Metaphysics in the Vedantic Theology of Rāmānuja*. New York: Macmillan.

Lutyens, Mary. 1991. *Krishnamurti: His Life and Death*. New York: St. Martin's Press.

Matilal, Bimal Krishna. 1977. *The Logical Illumination of Indian Mysticism*. New York: Oxford University Press.

Miller, Barbara Stoler, trans. 1986. *The Bhagavad-Gita: Krishna's Counsel in Time of War*. New York: Columbia University Press.

———. 1998. *Yoga: Discipline of Freedom*. New York: Bantam Books.

Nicholson, Andrew. n.d. "Bhedābheda Vedanta." In *Internet Encyclopedia of Philosophy*.

Olivelle, Patrick, trans. 2008. *Upanisads*. New York: Oxford University Press.

Padoux, André. 2017. *The Hindu Tantric World: An Overview*. Chicago: University of Chicago Press.

Phillips, Stephen H. 1986. *Aurobindo's Philosophy of Brahman*. Boston: Brill.

Pinch, William. 2006. *Warrior Ascetics and Indian Empires*. Cambridge: Cambridge University Press.

Potter, Karl. 1963. *Presuppositions of India's Philosophies*. Englewood Cliffs, NJ: Prentice-Hall.

———, ed. 1983. *Encyclopedia of Indian Philosophies*. Delhi: Motilal Banarsidass.

Radhakrishnan, Sarvepalli. 1948. *Indian Philosophy*. 2 vols. London: George Allen and Unwin.

Ramanujan, A. K. 1973. *Speaking of Siva*. Baltimore: Penguin.

Samuel, Geoffrey. 2008. *The Origins of Yoga and Tantra: Indic Religions to the Thirteenth Century*. New York: Cambridge University Press.

Sarbacker, Stuart Ray. 2005. *Sāmadhi: The Numionous and Cessative in Indo-Tibetan Yoga*. Albany: State University of New York Press.

Shackle, Christopher, and Arvind Mandair, eds. *Teachings of the Sikh Gurus: Selections from the Sikh Scriptures*. New York: Routledge.

Veliath, Cyril. 1993. *The Mysticism of Ramanuja*. New Delhi: Munshiram Manoharlal Publishers.

Werner, Karel. 1989. "The Longhaired Sage of RV 10.136: A Shaman, a Mystic or a Yogi?" In *The Yogi and the Mystic: Studies in Indian and Comparative Mysticism*, edited by Karel Werner, 33–53. London: Curzon Press.

White, David Gordon, ed. 2000. *Tantra in Practice*. Princeton, NJ: Princeton University Press.

———. 2003. *Kiss of the Yoginī: Tantric Sex in Its South Asian Context*. Chicago: University of Chicago Press.

———. 2009. *Sinister Yogis*. Chicago: University of Chicago Press.

———, ed. 2012. *Yoga in Practice*. Princeton, NJ: Princeton University Press.

Witz, Klaus G. 1998. *The Supreme Wisdom of the Upanisads*. Delhi: Motilal Banarsidass.

8. Indian and Tibetan Buddhist Mysticism

Bronkhorst, Johannes. 1993. *Two Traditions of Meditation in Ancient India*. 2nd ed. Delhi: Motilal Banarsidass.

Carter, John Ross, and Mahinda Palihawdana, trans. 2000. *The Dhammapada*. New York: Oxford University Press.

Coleman, Graham, and Thupten Jinpa, eds. 2006. *The Tibetan Book of the Dead: The First Complete Translation*. Translated by Gyurme Dorje. New York: Viking Penguin.

Conze, Edward. 1956. *Buddhist Meditation*. New York: Harper and Row.

———. 1978. *The Prajñāpāramitā Literature*. 2nd ed. Tokyo: Reiyukai.

———. 2001. *Buddhist Wisdom: The Diamond Sutra and the Heart Sutra*. New York: Vintage Spiritual Classics.

Dunne, John D. 1996. "Thoughtless Buddha, Passionate Buddha." *Journal of the American Academy of Religion* 64 (3): 525–56.

Evans-Wentz, W. Y. 1958. *Tibet's Great Yogi, Milarepa.* New York: Oxford University Press.

Garfield, Jay. 1995. *The Fundamental Wisdom of the Middle Way: Nāgārjuna's Mūlamadhyamakakārikā.* New York: Oxford University Press.

Gyatso, Tenzin (14th Dalai Lama). 2005a. *Essence of the Heart Sutra.* Somerville, MA: Wisdom Publications.

———. 2005b. *The Universe in a Single Atom: The Convergence of Science and Spirituality.* New York: Morgan Road Books.

Harvey, Peter. 2013. *An Introduction to Buddhism: Teachings, History and Practices.* 2nd ed. Cambridge: Cambridge University Press.

Hopkins, Jeffrey. 1983. *Meditation on Emptiness.* Boston: Wisdom Publications.

Jones, Richard H., trans. 2011–2012. *Indian Madhyamaka Buddhist Philosophy After Nagarjuna.* 2 vols. New York: Jackson Square Books, Createspace.

———, trans. 2012. *The Heart of Buddhist Wisdom: Plain English Translations of the Heart Sutra, the Diamond-Cutter Sutra, and Other Perfection of Wisdom Texts.* New York: Jackson Square Books, Createspace.

———. 2020b. "On What is Real in Nagarjuna's 'Middle Way.'" *Comparative Philosophy* 11, no. 1 (January): 3–31.

———, trans. 2022b. *Nagarjuna: Buddhism's Most Important Philosopher.* Revised and expanded ed. New York: Jackson Square Books, Createspace.

King, Richard. 1994. "Early Yogacara and its Relation to the Madhyamaka School." *Philosophy East and West* 44:659–86.

King, Winston L. 1980. *Theravada Meditation: The Buddhist Transformation of Yoga.* University Park: Pennsylvania State University Press.

Klein, Anne C. 1988. *Knowledge and Liberation: Tibetan Buddhist Epistemology in Support of Transformative Religious Experience.* Ithaca, NY: Snow Lion Publications.

Komarovski, Yaroslav. 2015. *Tibetan Buddhism and Mystical Experience.* New York: Oxford University Press.

Long, Jeffrey D. 2009. *Jainism: An Introduction.* New York: I. B. Tauris.

Lopez, Donald S. 2001. *The Story of Buddhism: A Concise Guide to Its History and Teachings.* San Francisco: HarperSanFrancisco.

Lusthaus, Dan. 2006. "Yogacara." *Encyclopedia of Philosophy* (online).

———. 2014. "What Is and Isn't Yogacara." Yogacara Buddhism Research Association. http://www.acmuller.net/yogacara/articles/intro.html.

McMahan, David L. 2008. *The Making of Buddhist Modernism.* New York: Oxford University Press.

Nanamoli, Bhikkhu. 1991. *The Path of Purification (Visuddhimagga): The Classic Manual of Buddhist Doctrine and Meditation.* 5th ed. Kandy, LK: Buddhist Publication Society.

References and Further Reading | 471

Nhat Hanh, Thich. 1988. *The Heart of Understanding: Commentaries on the Prajñāpāramitā Heart Sutra.* Berkeley, CA: Parallax Press.
———. 2010. *The Diamond That Cuts through Illusion: Commentaries on the Prajñāpāramitā Diamond Sutra.* Berkeley, CA: Parallax Press.
Powers, John. 2007. *Introduction to Tibetan Buddhism.* Ithaca, NY: Snow Lion Publications.
Queen, Christopher S., and Sallie B. King, eds. 1996. *Engaged Buddhism: Buddhist Liberation Movements in Asia.* Albany: State University of New York Press.
Rahula, Walpola. 1974. *What the Buddha Taught.* Revised and expanded ed. New York: Grove Press.
Samuel, Geoffrey. 1995. *Civilized Shamans: Buddhism in Tibetan Societies.* Washington, DC: Smithsonian Institute Press.
Shaw, Sarah, ed. 2009. *Introduction to Buddhist Meditation.* New York: Routledge.
———. 2014. *Spirit of Buddhist Meditation.* New Haven, CT: Yale University Press.
Shulman, Eviatar. 2014. *Rethinking the Buddha: Early Buddhist Philosophy as Meditative Perception.* New York: Cambridge University Press.
Siderits, Mark, and Shōryū Katsura. 2013. *Nāgārjuna's Middle Way: The Mūlamadhyamakakārikā.* Boston: Wisdom.
Skilton, Andrew. 1997. *A Concise History of Buddhism.* Cambridge: Windhorse Publications.
Thurman, Robert A. F. 1977. *The Holy Teaching of Vimalakirti.* University Park: Pennsylvania State University Press.
———. 1991. *The Central Philosophy of Tibet: A Study and Translation of Jey Tsong Khapa's Essence of True Eloquence.* Princeton, NJ: Princeton University Press.
———. 1995. *Essential Tibetan Buddhism.* New York: HarperCollins.
Trivedi, Saam. 2005. "Idealism and Yogacara Buddhism." *Asian Philosophy* 15 (3): 231–46.
Wayman, Alex, trans. 1978. *Calming the Mind and Discerning the Real: Buddhist Meditation and the Middle View from the Lam rim chen mo of Tson-kha-pa.* New York: Columbia University Press.
———. 1996. "A Defense of Yogacara Buddhism." *Philosophy East and West* 46:447–76.
Wayman, Alex, and Hideko Wayman, trans. 1974. *The Lion's Roar of Queen Śrīmālā: A Buddhist Scripture on the Tathāgatagarbha Theory.* New York: Columbia University Press.
Westerhoff, Jan, trans. 2010. *Nāgārjuna's Vigrahavyāvartanī: The Dispeller of Disputes.* New York: Oxford University Press.
Williams, Paul. 2009. *Mahāyāna Buddhism: The Doctrinal Foundations.* 2nd ed. New York: Routledge.
Williams, Paul, Anthony Tribe, and Alexander Wynne. 2012. *Buddhist Thought: A Complete Introduction to the Indian Tradition.* 2nd ed. New York: Routledge.

9. Chinese Mysticism

A. GENERAL

Ames, Roger T. 1983. *The Art of Rulership: A Study in Ancient Chinese Political Thought*. Honolulu: University of Hawai'i Press.

Chan, Wing-tsit. 1963. *A Source Book in Chinese Philosophy*. Princeton, NJ: Princeton University Press.

Chen, Zhuo, Ralph W. Hood, Jr., Wen Qi, and P. J. Watson. 2011. "Common Core Thesis and Qualitative and Quantitative Analysis of Mysticism in Chinese Buddhist Monks and Nuns." *Journal for the Scientific Study of Religion* 50, no. 4 (December): 654–70.

Hansen, Chad. 1983. *Language and Logic in Ancient China*. Ann Arbor: University of Michigan Press.

Nisbett, Richard E. 2003. *The Geography of Thought: How Asians and Westerners Think Differently . . . and Why*. New York: Free Press.

Schwartz, Benjamin. 1985. *The World of Thought in Ancient China*. Cambridge, MA: Harvard University Press.

B. DAOISM

Ames, Roger T., ed. 1998. *Wandering at Ease in the Zhuangzi*. Albany: State University of New York Press.

Ames, Roger T., and David Hall, trans. 2003. *Dao De Jing: A Philosophical Translation*. New York: Random House.

Chan, Alan. 1991. *Two Visions of the Way: A Study of Wang Pi and Ho-shang-kung Commentaries on the Laozi*. Albany: State University of New York Press.

Ching, Julia. 1997. *Mysticism and Kingship: The Heart of Chinese Wisdom*. New York: Cambridge University Press.

Cleary, Thomas. 1999. *The Taoist Classics*. 4 vols. Boston: Shambhala.

Coutinho, Steve. 2014. *An Introduction to Daoist Philosophies*. New York: Columbia University Press.

Csikzentmihalyi, Marc, and Philip J. Ivanhoe, eds. 1999. *Religious and Philosophical Aspects of the Laozi*. Albany: State University of New York Press.

Eno, Robert. 1996. "Cook Ding's *Dao* and the Limits of Philosophy." In *Essays on Skepticism, Relativism, and Ethics in the* Zhuangzi, edited by Paul Kjellberg and Philip J. Ivanhoe, 127–51. Albany: State University of New York Press.

Eskidsen, Stephen. 1998. *Early Taoist Asceticism*. Albany: State University of New York Press.

Graham, Angus C., trans. 1981. *Chuang-tzŭ: The Seven Inner Chapters and Other Writings from the Book of Chuang-tzŭ*. London: George Allen and Unwin.

————. 1989. *Disputers of the Tao: Philosophical Argument in Ancient China.* La Salle, IL: Open Court Publishing Company.

————, trans. 1990. *The Book of Lieh-tzŭ: A Classic of the Tao.* New York: Columbia University Press.

Henricks, Robert. 2000. *Lao Tzu's Tao Te Ching: A Translation of the Startling New Documents Found at Guodian.* New York: Columbia University Press.

Jones, Richard H. 1993. "Concerning Joseph Needham on Taoism." In *Mysticism Examined: Philosophical Inquiries into Mysticism,* edited by Richard H. Jones, 127–46. Albany: State University of New York Press.

Kohn, Livia, ed. 1989. *Taoist Meditation and Longevity Techniques.* Ann Arbor: University of Michigan, Center for Chinese Studies Publications.

————. 1991. *Taoist Mystical Philosophy: The Scripture of Western Ascension.* Albany: State University of New York Press.

————. 1992. *Early Chinese Mysticism: Philosophy and Soteriology in the Taoist Tradition.* Princeton, NJ: Princeton University Press.

————. 1993. *The Taoist Experience: An Anthology.* Albany: State University of New York Press.

————. 2001. *Daoism and Chinese Culture.* Cambridge, MA: Three Pines Press.

————. 2004. *Cosmos and Community: The Ethical Dimension of Daoism.* Cambridge, MA: Three Pines Press.

————. 2008. *Introducing Daoism.* London: Routledge.

————. 2009. *Readings in Daoist Mysticism.* Dunedin, FL: Three Pines Press.

————. 2010. *Sitting in Oblivion: The Heart of Daoist Meditation.* Dunedin, FL: Three Pines Press.

Kohn, Livia, and Michael LaFargue, eds. 1998. *Lao-tzu and the Tao-te-ching,* Albany: State University of New York Press.

Komjathy, Louis. 2014. *Daoism: A Guide for the Perplexed.* New York: Bloomsbury.

LaFargue, Michael. 1992. *The Tao of the Tao-te-ching.* Albany: State University of New York Press.

Lau, D. C., trans. 1963. *The Tao Te Ching.* New York: Penguin Books.

Mair, Victor H., trans. 1990. *Tao Te Jing: The Classic Book of Integrity and the Way.* New York: Bantam Books.

————. 1994. *Wandering on the Way: Early Taoist Tales and Parables of Chuang Tzu.* New York: Bantam Books.

————, ed. 2010. *Experimental Essays on Chuang-tzu.* Dunedin, FL: Three Pines.

Miller, James. 2003. *Daoism: A Beginner's Guide.* Oxford: Oneworld Publications.

Robinet, Isabelle. 1993. *Taoist Meditation: The Mao-shan Tradition of Great Purity.* Translated by Norman Girardot and Julian Pas. Albany: State University of New York Press.

————. 1996. "The Diverse Interpretations of the *Laozi.*" In *Essays on Skepticism, Relativism, and Ethics in the* Zhuangzi, edited by Paul Kjellberg and Philip J. Ivanhoe, 127–51. Albany: State University of New York Press.

———. 1997. *Taoism: Growth of a Religion*. Translated by Phyllis Brooks. Stanford, CA: Stanford University Press.

Roth, Harold D. 1999. *Original Tao: Inward Training (Nei-Yeh) and the Foundations of Taoist Mysticism*. New York: Columbia University Press

———. 2000. "Bimodal Mystical Experience in the Qiwulun Chapter of *Chuang Tzu*." *Journal of Chinese Religions* 28 (1): 1–20.

———. 2022. *The Contemplative Foundations of Classical Daoism*. Albany: State University of New York Press.

Slingerland, Edward G. 2004. *Effortless Action: Wu-wei As Conceptual Metaphor and Spiritual Ideal in Early China*. New York: Oxford University Press.

Waley, Authur. 1958. *The Way and Its Power: A Study of the Tao Tĕ Ching and Its Place in Chinese Thought*. New York: Grove Press.

Watson, Burton. 1968. *The Complete Works of Chuang-tzu*. New York: Columbia University Press.

Wong, Eva. 1997. *The Shambhala Guide to Taoism*. Boston: Shambhala.

———. 2001. *Lieh-Tzu: A Taoist Guide to Practical Living*. Boston: Shambhala.

Yearley, Lee. 1983. "The Perfected Person in the Radical Chuang Tzu." In *Experimental Essays on the Chuang Tzu*, edited by Victor Mair, 125–39. Honolulu: University of Hawai'i Press.

C. Buddhism

Cleary, Thomas. 2005. *Classics of Buddhism and Zen*. 5 vols. Boston: Shambhala.

Cook, Francis H. 1977. *Hua-yen Buddhism: The Jewel Net of Indra*. University Park: Pennsylvania State University Press.

Dumoulin, Heinrich. 2005. *Zen: A History*. 2 vols. Revised and expanded ed. Translated by James W. Heisig and Paul Kittner. Bloomington, IN: World Wisdom.

Heine, Steven, and Dale Wright, ed. 2000. *The Kōan: Texts and Contexts in the History of Zen Buddhism*. New York: Oxford University Press.

———. 2004. *The Zen Canon: Understanding the Classic Texts*. New York: Oxford University Press.

Kapleau, Philip. 1989. *The Three Pillars of Zen: Teaching, Practice, and Enlightenment*. Revised ed. New York: Doubleday Anchor.

King, Winston Lee. 1993. *Zen and the Way of the Sword: Arming the Samurai Psyche*. New York: Oxford University Press.

Masunaga, Reihō, trans. 1971. *A Primer of Sōtō Zen: A Translation of Dōgen's Shōbōgenzō Zuimonki*. Honolulu: East-West Center Press.

Miller, David. 2003. "It's More than a Zen Thing: The Mystical Dimension in Japanese Religion." In *Mysticism East and West: Studies in Mystical Experience*, edited by Christopher Partridge and Theodore Gabriel, 3–18. Carlisle, UK: Paternoster.

Victoria, Brian. 2003. *Zen War Stories*. New York: Routledge.

————. 2006. *Zen at War*. 2nd ed. New York: Rowman and Littlefield.
Waddell, Norman. 2002. *Wild Ivy: The Spiritual Biography of Zen Master Hakuin*. Boston: Shambhala Publications.
Yampolsky, Philip B. 1967. *The Platform of the Sixth Patriarch*. New York: Columbia University Press.
Yokoi, Yuho, with Daizen Victoria. 1976. *Zen Master Dogen: An Introduction with Selected Writings*. New York: Weatherhill.
Zücher, Erik. 1972. *The Buddhist Conquest of China: The Spread and Adaptation of Buddhism in Early Medieval China*. 2 vols. Leiden: E. J. Brill.

D. Neo-Confucianism

Chan, Wing-tsit. 1963. *Instructions for Practical Living and Other Neo-Confucian Writings by Wang Yang-ming*. New York: Columbia University Press.
————. 1989. *Chu Hsi: New Studies*. Honolulu: University of Hawai'i Press.
Ching, Julia. 1976. *To Accumulate Wisdom: The Way of Wang Yang-ming*. New York: Columbia University Press.
de Bary, Wm. Theodore. 1989. *The Message of the Mind in Neo-Confucianism*. New York: Columbia University Press.
Huang, Xiuji. 1999. *Essentials of Neo-Confucianism: Eight Major Philosophers of the Song and Ming Periods*. Westport, CT: Greenwood Press.
Keenan, Barry C. 2011. *Neo-Confucian Self-Cultivation*. Honolulu: University of Hawai'i Press.

10. Mysticism in the West Today

A. General

Angel, Leonard. 2002. "Mystical Naturalism." *Religious Studies* 38 (September): 317–38.
Barry, William A., and William J. Connolly. 1982. *The Practice of Spiritual Direction*. New York: Seabury Press.
Batchelor, Stephen. 2015. *After Buddhism: Rethinking the Dharma for a Secular Age*. New Haven, CT: Yale University Press.
Berger, Peter L. 2014. *The Many Altars of Modernity: Toward a Paradigm for Religion in a Pluralistic Age*. Boston: De Gruyter.
Carrette, Jeremy, and Richard King. 2005. *Selling Spirituality: The Silent Takeover of Religion*. New York: Routledge.
Crosby, Donald A. 2008. *The Thou of Nature: Religious Naturalism and Reverence for Sentient Life*. Albany: State University of New York Press.
Csikszentmihalyi, Mihaly. 1990. *Flow: The Psychology of Optimal Experience*. New York: Harper Perennial.

Cupitt, Don. 1998. *Mysticism after Modernity*. Oxford: Blackwell.

Goodenough, Ursula. 1998. *The Sacred Depths of Nature*. New York: Oxford University Press.

Gunnlaugson, Olen, E. W. Sarath, C. Scott, and Heesoon Bai, eds. 2014. *Contemplative Learning and Inquiry across Disciplines*. Albany: State University of New York Press.

Harris, Sam. 2014. *Waking Up: A Guide to Spirituality without Religion*. New York: Simon and Schuster.

Hart, Kevin, and Barbara Wall, eds. 2005. *The Experience of God: A Postmodern Reader*. New York: Fordham University Press.

Horgan, John. 2003. *Rational Mysticism: Dispatches from the Border between Science and Spirituality*. Boston: Houghton Mifflin.

Howells, Edward, and Mark McIntosh, eds. 2020. *The Oxford Handbook of Mystical Theology*. New York: Oxford University Press.

Jäger, Willigis. 2006. *Mysticism for Modern Times: Conversations with Willigis Jäger*. Edited by Christoph Quarch. Translated by Paul Shepherd. Liguori, MO: Liguori/Triumph.

Johnston, William. 1978. *The Inner Eye of Love: Mysticism and Religion*. New York: Harper and Row.

———. 2000. *"Arise, My Love . . ." Mysticism for a New Era*. Maryknoll: Orbis.

Jones, Richard H. 2018a. *Mystery 101: The Big Questions and the Limits of Human Knowledge*. Albany: State University of New York Press.

———. 2020a. "On Constructivism in the Philosophy of Mysticism." *Journal of Religion* 100 (1): 1–41.

———. 2022. "Secular Mysticism." *Religions* 13, no. 7 (July): 650–77.

Juergensmeyer, Mark. 2000. *Terror in the Mind of God: The Global Rise of Religious Violence*. Berkeley: University of California Press.

Keating, Thomas. 2006. *Open Mind, Open Heart*. New York: Continuum.

King, Ursula. 1980. *Towards a New Mysticism: Teilhard de Chardin and Eastern Religions*. London: Collins.

Komjathy, Louis. 2018. *Introducing Contemplative Studies*. New York: Wiley-Blackwell.

Kornfield, Jack. 2001. *After the Ecstasy the Laundry: How the Heart Grows Wise on the Spiritual Path*. New York: Bantam.

Kripal, Jeffrey J. 2010. *Authors of the Impossible: The Paranormal and the Sacred*. Chicago: University of Chicago Press.

Loy, David R. 2008. "Awareness Bound and Unbound: Realizing the Nature of Attention." *Philosophy East and West* 58 (April): 223–43.

McDaniel, June. 2018. *Lost Ecstasy: Its Decline and Transformation in Religion*. New York: Palgrave MacMillan.

McIntosh, Mark. 1998. *Mystical Theology: The Integrity of Spirituality and Theology, Challenges in Contemporary Theology*. Cambridge: Blackwell.

Newberg, Andrew B., and Mark R. Waldman. 2016. *How Enlightenment Changes Your Brain: The New Science of Transformation*. New York: Penguin Random House.

Nicholson, Hugh R. 2011. *Comparative Theology and the Problem of Religious Rivalry*. New York: Oxford University Press.

Osto, Douglas. 2016. *Altered States: Buddhism and Psychedelic Spirituality in America*. New York: Columbia University Press.

Partridge, Christopher. 2018. *High Culture: Drugs, Mysticism, and the Pursuit of Transcendence in the Modern World*. New York: Oxford University Press.

Patton, Kimberley C. 2000. "Juggling Torches." In *A Magic Still Dwells*, edited by Kimberley C. Patton and Benjamin C. Ray, 153–71. Berkeley: University of California Press.

Pike, Nelson. 1994. *Mystic Union: An Essay in the Phenomenology of Mysticism*. Ithaca, NY: Cornell University Press.

Rahner, Karl. 1984. *The Practice of Faith: A Handbook of Contemporary Spirituality*. New York: Crossroad.

Reed, Angela. 2019. "Rediscovering Mysticism: Theological Foundations for the Contemporary Practice of Spiritual Direction." In *Mysticism and Contemporary Life: Essays in Honor of Bernard McGinn*, edited by John J. Markey and J. August Higgins, 111–25. New York: Crossroad.

Robert, Bernadette. 1993. *The Experience of No-Self: A Contemplative Journey*. Revised ed. Albany: State University of New York Press.

Roth, Harold D. 2006. "Contemplative Studies: Prospects for a New Field." *Teachers College Record* 108, no. 9 (September): 1187–1215.

———. 2014. "A Pedagogy for the New Field of Contemplative Studies." In *Contemplative Learning and Inquiry Across Disciplines*, edited by Olen Gunnlaugson, E. W. Sarath, C. Scott, and Heesoon Bai, 97–118. Albany: State University of New York Press.

Schmidt, Stefan. 2011. "Mindfulness in East and West—Is It the Same?" In *Neuroscience, Consciousness and Spirituality*, edited by Harald Walach, Stefan Schmidt, and Wayne B. Jonas, 23–38. New York: Springer.

Sharf, Robert H. 2000. "The Rhetoric of Experience and the Study of Experience." *Journal of Consciousness Studies* 7:267–87.

Sheldrake, Philip. 2014. *Spirituality: A Guide for the Perplexed*. New York: Bloomsbury.

Spencer, Daniel. 2021. "The Challenge of Mysticism: A Primer from a Christian Perspective." *Sophia* 50 (January): 1–18.

Taylor, Charles. 2007. *A Secular Age*. Cambridge, MA: Harvard University Press.

Thomas, Owen C. 2000. "Interiority and Christian Spirituality." *Journal of Religion* 80 (1): 41–60.

Turner, Denys. 1995. *The Darkness of God: Negativity in Christian Mysticism*. New York: Cambridge University Press.

Volker, Fabian. 2022. "Methodology and Mysticism: For an Integral Study of Religion." *Religions* 13 (1): 1–19.

B. Meditation

Goleman, Daniel. 1988. *The Meditative Mind: The Varieties of Meditative Experience.* New York: Tarcher/Putnam.

Heller, Rick. 2015. *Secular Meditation: 32 Practices for Cultivating Inner Peace, Compassion, and Joy.* Novato, CA: New World Library.

Kabat-Zinn, Jon. 2005. *Wherever You Go, There You Are: Mindfulness Meditation in Everyday Life.* New York: Hachette Books.

Laird, Martin. 2006. *Into the Silent Land: A Guide to the Christian Practice of Contemplation.* New York: Oxford University Press.

Tart, Charles. T. 1994. *Living the Mindful Life: A Handbook for Living in the Present Moment.* Boston: Shambhala.

C. Scientific Study of Meditators and Mysticism

Austin, James H. 1998. *Zen and the Brain: Toward an Understanding of Meditation and Consciousness.* Cambridge, MA: MIT Press.

Benson, Herbert, and Miriam Z. Klipper. 2000. *The Relaxation Response.* New York: HarperCollins.

Bruya, Brian J. 2010. *Effortless Attention: A New Perspective in the Cognitive Science of Attention and Action.* Cambridge, MA: MIT Press.

Byrd, Kevin R., Delbert Lear, and Stacy Schwenka. 2000. "Mysticism as a Predictor of Subjective Well-Being." *The International Journal for the Psychology of Religion* 10 (4): 259–69.

Doblin, Rick. 1991. "Pahnke's 'Good Friday Experiment': A Long-Term Follow-Up and Methodological Critique." *Journal of Transpersonal Psychology* 23 (1): 1–28.

Dunn, Bruce R., Judith A. Hartigan, and William L. Mikulas. 1999. "Concentration and Mindfulness: Unique Forms of Consciousness." *Applied Psychophysiology and Biofeedback* 24 (3): 147–65.

Eisner, Bruce. 1989. *Ecstasy: The MDMA Story.* Berkeley, CA: Ronin Publishing.

Goleman, Daniel, and Richard J. Davidson. 2018. *Altered Traits: Science Reveals How Mediation Changes Your Mind, Brain, and Body.* New York: Avery.

Goodman, Neil. 2002. "The Serotonergic System and Mysticism: Could LSD and the Nondrug-Induced Mystical Experiences Share Common Neural Mechanisms?" *Journal of Psychoactive Drugs* 34 (July–September): 263–72.

Griffiths, Roland R., Matthew W. Johnson, William A. Richards, Brian D. Richards, Una McCann, and Robert Jesse. 2018. "Psilocybin-Occasioned Mystical-Type Experience in Combination with Meditation and Other Spiritual Practices Produces Enduring Positive Changes in Psychological Functioning and in Trait

Measures of Prosocial Attitudes and Behaviors." *Journal of Psychopharmacology* 32 (1): 49–69.

Halberstadt, Adam, and Mark Geyer. 2012. "Do Psychedelics Expand the Mind by Reducing Brain Activity?" *Scientific American Global*, May 15, 2012. https://www.scientificamerican.com/article/do-psychedelics-expand-mind-reducing-brain-activity/.

Hardy, Alister. 1979. *The Spiritual Nature of Man: A Study of Contemporary Religious Experience*. Oxford: Clarendon Press.

———. 1983. *The Spiritual Nature of Man*. Oxford: Clarendon Press.

Harrington, Anne, and Arthur Zajonc, eds. 2006. *The Dalai Lama at MIT*. Cambridge, MA: Harvard University Press.

Hood, Ralph W., Jr. 1995. "The Facilitation of Religious Experience." In *The Handbook of Religious Experience*, edited by Ralph W. Hood, Jr., 568–97. Birmingham, AL: Religious Education Press.

———. 1997. "The Empirical Study of Mysticism." In *The Psychology of Religion: Theoretical Approaches*, edited by Bernard Spilka and Daniel N. McIntosh, 222–32. Boulder, CO: Westview Press.

———. 2001. *Dimensions of Mystical Experiences: Empirical Studies and Psychological Links*. Amsterdam: Rodopi.

———. 2002. "The Mystical Self: Lost and Found." *The International Journal for the Psychology of Religion* 12 (1): 1–14.

Hood, Ralph W., Jr., R. J. Morris, and P. J. Watson. 1993. "Further Factor Analysis of Hood's Mysticism Scale." *Psychological Reports* 73:1176–78.

Hood, Ralph W., Jr., Nima Ghorbani, P. J. Watson, Ahad Framarz Ghramaleki, Mark N. Bing, H. Kristl Davison, Ronald J. Morris, and W. Paul Williamson. 2001. "Dimensions of the Mysticism Scale: Confirming the Three-Factor Structure in the United States and Iran." *Journal for the Scientific Study of Religion* 40:691–705.

Jones, Richard H. 2016. *Philosophy of Mysticism: Raids on the Ineffable*. Albany: State University of New York Press.

———. 2018b. "Limitations on the Neuroscientific Study of Mystical Experiences." *Zygon: Journal of Science and Religion* 53 (4): 992–1017.

———. 2019a. "Limitations on the Scientific Study of Drug-Enabled Mystical Experiences." *Zygon: Journal of Science and Religion* 54 (3): 756–92.

Josipovic, Zoran, and Vladimir Miskovic. 2020. "Nondual Awareness and Minimal Phenomenal Experience." *Frontiers in Psychology* 11, no. 1 (August): 2087–2096.

Kakigi, Ryusuke, Hiroki Nakata, Koji Inui, Nobuo Hiroe, Osamu Nagata, Manabu Honda, Satoshi Tanaka, Norihiro Sadato, and Mitsumasa Kawakami. 2005. "Intracerebral Pain Processing in a Yoga Master Who Claims Not to Feel during Meditation." *European Journal of Pain* 9:581–89.

Laughlin, Charles D., and Adam J. Rock. 2020. "A Neuroepistemology of Mystical Experience." *Transpersonal Psychology Review* 22 (2): 37–57.

Letheby, Chris. 2021. *Philosophy of Psychedelics*. New York: Oxford University Press.

Lutz, Antoine, John D. Dunne, and Richard J. Davidson. 2007. "Meditation and the Neuroscience of Consciousness: An Introduction." In *The Cambridge Handbook of Consciousness*, edited by Philip David Zelazo, Morris Moscovitch, and Evan Thompson, 499–552. New York: Cambridge University Press.

Nash, Jonathan D., Andrew Newberg, and Bhuvanesh Awasthi. 2013. "Toward a Unifying Taxonomy and Definition of Meditation." *Frontiers in Psychology* 4 (November): article 806. https://doi.org/10.3389/fpsyg.2013.00806.

Newberg, Andrew B., and Eugene G. d'Aquili. 1999. *The Mystical Mind: Probing the Biology of Religious Experience*. Minneapolis: Fortress Press.

Newberg, Andrew, Eugene d'Aquili, and Vince Rause. 2002. *Why God Won't Go Away: Brain Science and the Biology of Belief*. New York: Ballantine Books.

Ospina, Maria B., Kenneth Bond, Mohammad Karkhaneh, Lisa Tjosvold, Ben Vandermeer, Yuanyuan Liang, Liza Bialy, Nicola Hooton, Nina Buscemi, Donna M Dryden, and Terry P. Klassen. 2007. "Meditation Practices for Health: State of the Research." *Evid Rep Technol Assess* 155 (June): 1–263.

Pahnke, Walter N. 1966. "Drugs and Mysticism." *International Journal of Parapsychology* 8 (Spring): 295–414.

Pahnke, Walter N., and William A. Richards. 1966. "Implications of LSD and Experimental Mysticism." *Journal of Religion and Health* 5 (July): 175–208.

Persinger, Michael A. 1987. *Neuropsychological Bases of God Beliefs*. New York: Praeger.

Richards, William A. 2016. *Sacred Knowledge: Psychedelics and Religious Experiences*. New York: Columbia University Press.

Roberts, Thomas B. 2013. *The Psychedelic Future of the Mind: How Entheogens Are Enhancing Cognition, Boosting Intelligence, and Raising Values*. Rochester, VT: Part Street.

Sauerborn, Elgen, Nina Sökefeld, and Sighard Neckel. 2022. "Paradoxes of Mindfulness: The Specious Promises of a Contemporary Practice." *Sociological Review* 70 (5): 1–18.

Schmidt, Stefan, and Harald Walach, eds. 2014. *Meditation—Neuroscientific Approaches and Philosophical Implications*. New York: Springer.

Sedlmeier, Peter, Juliane Eberth, Marcus Schwarz, Doreen Zimmermann, Frederik Haarig, Sonia Jaeger, and Sonja Kunze. 2012. "The Psychological Effects of Meditation: A Meta-Analysis." *Psychological Bulletin* 138 (November): 1139–71.

Smith, Allan L., and Charles T. Tart. 1998. "Cosmic Consciousness Experience and Psychedelic Experiences: A First-Person Comparison." *Journal of Consciousness Studies* 5 (1): 97–107.

Valentine, Elizabeth R., and Philip G. Sweet. 1999. "Meditation and Attention: A Comparison of the Effects of Concentrative and Mindfulness Meditation on Sustained Attention." *Mental Health, Religion and Culture* 2 (1): 59–70.

Wachholtz, Amy B., and Kenneth I. Pargament. 2005. "Is Spirituality a Critical Ingredient of Meditation? Comparing the Effects of Spiritual Meditation,

Secular Meditation, and Relaxation on Spiritual, Psychological, Cardiac, and Pain Outcomes." *Journal of Behavioral Medicine* 28 (4): 369–84.

Yaden, David B., Khoa D. Le Nguyen, Margaret L. Kern, Nancy A. Wintering, Johannes C. Eichstaedt, H. Andrew Schwartz, Anneke E. K. Buffone, Laura K. Smith, Mark R. Waldman, Ralph W. Hood Jr., and Andrew B. Newberg. 2017. "The Noetic Quality: A Multimethod Exploratory Study." *Psychology of Consciousness: Theory, Research, and Practice* 4 (1): 54–62.

Yaden, David B., Khoa D. Le Nguyen, Margaret L. Kern, Alexander B. Belser, Johannes C. Eichstaedt, Jonathan Iwry, Mary E. Smith, Nancy A. Wintering, Mark R. Waldman, Ralph W. Hood Jr., and Andrew B. Newberg. 2017. "Of Roots and Fruits: A Comparison of Psychedelic and Nonpsychedelic Mystical Experiences." *Journal of Humanistic Psychology* 57 (4): 338–53.

D. New Age

Capra, Fritjof. (1975) 2000. *The Tao of Physics: An Exploration of the Parallels between Modern Physics and Eastern Mysticism.* 4th ed. Boston: Shambhala Press.

Chardin, Teilhard de. 1965. *Hymn of the Universe.* Translated by Simon Bartholomew. New York: Harper and Row.

Chopra, Deepak. 1989. *Quantum Healing.* New York: Bantam Books.

Chopra, Deepak, and Menas Kafatos, 2017. *You Are the Universe.* New York: Harmony Books.

Cohen, Andrew Z. 2011. *Evolutionary Enlightenment: A New Path to Spiritual Awakening.* New York: Select Books.

Feuerstein, Georg. 1991. *Holy Madness: The Shock Tactics and Radical Teachings of Crazy-Wise Adepts, Holy Fools, and Rascal Gurus.* New York: Penguin Arkana.

Forman, Robert K. C. 2011. *Enlightenment Ain't What It's Cracked Up to Be.* Washington, DC: O-Books.

Fox, Matthew. 1991. *Creation Spirituality: Liberating Gifts for the Peoples of the Earth.* San Francisco: HarperOne.

Halbfass, Wilhelm. 1988. *India and Europe: An Essay in Understanding.* Albany: State University of New York Press.

Hanegraaff, Wouter J. 1998. *New Age Religion and Western Culture: Esotericism in the Mirror of Secular Thought.* Albany: State University of New York Press.

Jones, Richard H. 1986. *Science and Mysticism: A Comparative Study of Western Natural Science, Theravāda Buddhism, and Advaita Vedānta.* Lewisburg, PA: Bucknell University Press.

———. 2014. *Piercing the Veil: Comparing Science and Mysticism as Ways of Knowing Reality.* New York: Jackson Square Books, Createspace.

———. 2019b. "Mysticism in the New Age: Are Mysticism and Science Converging?" In *Mysticism and Meaning: Multidisciplinary and Perspectives*, edited by Alex S. Kohav, 247–77. St. Petersburg, FL: Tree Pines Press.

Kohn, Livia. 2016. *Science and the Dao: From the Big Bang to Lived Perfection*. St. Petersburg, FL: Three Pines Press.

Mosurinjohn, Sharday, and Galen Watts. 2021. "Religious Studies and the Spiritual Turn." *Method and Theory in the Study of Religion* 33 (5): 482–504.

Purser, Richard E. 2019. *McMindfulness: How Mindfulness Became the New Capitalist Spirituality*. London: Repeater Books.

Sauerborn, Elgen, Nina Sökefeld, and Sighard Neckel. 2022. "Paradoxes of Mindfulness: The Specious Promises of a Contemporary Practice." *The Sociological Review* 70 (5): 1044–1061.

Storr, Anthony. 1996. *Feet of Clay—Saints, Sinners, and Madmen: A Study of Gurus*. New York: Free Press.

Teasdale, Wayne. 1997. "The Inter-Spiritual Age: Practical Mysticism for the Third Millenium." *Journal of Ecumenical Studies* 34 (1): 74–91.

———. 2001. *The Mystic Heart: Discovering a Universal Spirituality in the World's Religions*. Novato, CA: New World Library,

Tolle, Eckhart. 1999. *The Power of Now: A Guide to Spiritual Enlightenment*. Novato, CA: New World Library,

Versluis, Arthur. 2014. *American Gurus: From Transcendentalism to New Age Religion*. New York: Oxford University Press.

Watts, Alan. 1966. *The Book: On the Taboo Against Knowing Who You Are*. New York: Vintage Books.

Wilbur, Ken. 2006. *Integral Spirituality: A Startling New Role for Religion in the Modern and Postmodern World*. Boston: Integral Books.

———. 2007. *The Integral Vision: A Very Short Introduction to the Revolutionary Integral Approach to Life, God, the Universe, and Everything*. Boston: Shambhala Press.

Wilson, Colin. 2000. *Rogue Messiahs: Tales of Self-Proclaimed Saviors*. Charlottesville, VA: Hampton Roads.

Wilson, Peter. 1997. "The Strange Fate of Sufism in the New Age." In *New Trends and Developments in the World of Islam*, edited by Peter B. Clarke, 179–209. London: Luzac Oriental Press.

Yenner, William. 2009. *American Guru: A Story of Love, Betrayal and Healing—Former Students of Andrew Cohen Speak Out*. Rhinebeck, NY: Epigraph Books.

Zukav, Gary. (1977) 2001. *The Dancing Wu Li Masters: An Overview of the New Physics*. New York: HarperCollins.

E. Gender Studies

Bynum, Caroline Walker. 1982. "Women Mystics in the Thirteenth Century: The Case of the Nuns of Helfta." In *Jesus as Mother: Studies in the Spirituality of the High Middle Ages*, edited by Caroline Walker Bynum, 170–261. Berkeley: University of California Press.

Furlong, Monica. 2013. *Visions and Longings: Medieval Women Mystics*. Boston: Shambhala Publications.

Hollywood, Amy. 2002. *Sensible Ecstasy: Mysticism, Sexual Difference and the Demands of History*. Chicago: University of Chicago Press.

Jacobs, Janet L. 1992. "Religious Experiences among Women and Men: A Gender Perspective on Mystical Phenomena." *Research in the Social Scientific Study of Religion* 4 (2): 261–79.

Jantzen, Grace M. 1994. "Feminists, Philosophers, and Mystics." *Hypatia* 9 (4): 186–206.

———. 1995. *Power, Gender and Christian Mysticism*. Cambridge: Cambridge University Press.

Lanzetta, Beverly. 2005. *Radical Wisdom: A Feminist Mystical Theology*. Minneapolis: Fortress Press.

Mercer, Calvin, and Thomas W. Durham. 1999. "Religious Mysticism and Gender Orientation." *Journal for the Scientific Study of Religion* 38 (1): 175–82.

Soelle, Dorothee. 2001. *The Silent Cry: Mysticism and Resistance*. Translated by Barbara Rumscheidt and Martin Rumscheidt. Minneapolis: Fortress Press.

Wawrytko, Sandra A. 1995. "The 'Feminine' Mode of Mysticism." In *Mysticism and Mystical Experience: East and West*, edited by Donald H. Bishop, 195–229. London: Associated University Press.

F. Perennial Philosophy

Abhyananda, Swami. 2012. *History of Mysticism: The Unchanging Testament*. Fallsburg, NY: Atma Books.

Ferrer, Jorge N. 2000. "The Perennial Philosophy Revisited." *Journal of Transpersonal Psychology* 32 (1): 7–30.

Huxley, Aldous. 1945. *The Perennial Philosophy*. New York: Harper and Row.

Jones, Richard H. 2021a. "Perennial Philosophy and the History of Mysticism." *Sophia* 60 (2): 1–20.

Lings, Martin, and Clinton Minnaar, eds. 2007. *The Underlying Religion: An Introduction to Perennial Philosophy*. Bloomington, IN: World Wisdom.

Nasr, Seyyed Hossein. 1981. *Knowledge and the Sacred*. New York: Crossroad.

———. 1993. "The *Philosophia Perennis* and the Study of Religion." In *The Need for a Sacred Science*, edited by Seyyed Hossein Nasr, 53–68. Albany: State University of New York Press.

Schuon, Frithjof. 1975. *The Transcendent Unity of Religions*. Translated by Peter Townsend. New York: Harper and Row.

Sedgwick, Mark J. 2004. *Against the Modern World: Traditionalism and the Secret Intellectual History of the Twentieth Century*. New York: Oxford University Press.

484 | References and Further Reading

Shear, Jonathan. 1994. "On Mystical Experiences as Support for the Perennial Philosophy." *Journal of the American Academy of Religion* 62 (2): 319–42.

Smith, Huston. 1976. *Forgotten Truth: The Primordial Tradition*. New York: Harper and Row.

———. 1987. "Is There a Perennial Philosophy?" *Journal of the American Academy of Religion* 55 (3): 553–66.

Smith, Huston, and Henry Rosemont, Jr. 2008. *Is There a Universal Grammar of Religion?* Chicago: Open Court.

Stoddart, William. 2005. "Mysticism." In *Ye Shall Know the Truth: Christianity and the Perennial Philosophy*, edited by Mateus Soares de Azevedo, 57–69. Bloomington, IN: World Wisdom.

Appendix.
Correcting Some Misunderstandings About Mysticism

Barnard, G. William, and Jeffrey J. Kripal, eds. 2002. *Crossing Boundaries: Essays on the Ethical Status of Mysticism*. New York: Seven Bridges Press.

Hardy, Alister. 1983. *The Spiritual Nature of Man: A Study of Contemporary Religious Experience*. Oxford: Clarendon Press.

Harmless, William. 2008. *Mystics*. New York: Oxford University Press.

Hood, Ralph W., Jr. 2005. "Mystical, Spiritual, and Religious Experiences." In *Handbook of the Psychology of Religion and Spirituality*, edited by Raymond F. Paloutzian and Crystal L. Park, 348–64. New York: Guilford Press.

Jantzen, Grace M. 1989. "'Where Two Are to Become One': Mysticism and Monism." In *The Philosophy in Christianity*, edited by Geoffrey Vesey, 147–66. Cambridge: Cambridge University Press.

Jones, Richard H. 2004. *Mysticism and Morality: A New Look at Old Questions*. Lanham, MD: Lexington Books.

———. 2016. *Philosophy of Mysticism: Raids on the Ineffable*. Albany: State University of New York Press.

McGinn, Bernard. 2001. *The Mystical Thought of Meister Eckhart: The Man from Whom God Hid Nothing*. New York: Crossroad Publishing.

———. 2006b. "How Augustine Shaped Medieval Mysticism." *Augustinian Studies* 37 (1): 1–26.

Underhill, Evelyn. (1915) 1961. *Practical Mysticism*. New York: E. P. Dutton.

Index